Measures for Clinical Practice

A SOURCEBOOK

Second Edition

Volume 2. Adults

JOEL FISCHER
KEVIN CORCORAN

THE FREE PRESS

New York   London   Toronto   Sydney   Tokyo   Singapore

The Free Press
A Division of Simon & Schuster Inc.
1230 Avenue of the Americas
New York, N.Y. 10020

Printed in the United States of America

printing number
    4 5 6 7 8 9 10

Library of Congress Cataloging-in-Publication Data

Fischer, Joel.
    Measures for clinical practice: a sourcebook / Joel Fischer,
Kevin Corcoran, — 2nd ed.
        p. cm.
    Corcoran's name appears first on earlier ed.
    Includes bibliographical references and index.
    Contents: vol. 1. Couples, families, and children — vol. 2. Adults.
    ISBN 0-02-906685-9 (vol. 1). — ISBN 0-02-906686-7 (vol. 2)
    1. Psychological tests.   I. Corcoran, Kevin (Kevin J.)
II. Title.
    [DNLM: 1. Psychological Tests.   WM 145 F529m 1994]
BF176.C66 1994
150'.28'7—dc20
DNLM/DLC
for Library of Congress   93-32384
                                                              CIP

To Renee H. Furuyama, with love and appreciation,
and to Dr. Olivetti and
"The Boys" at Siegerson Olivetti Moriarty and Wilson

CONTENTS

VOLUME 2

INSTRUMENTS FOR PRACTICE

VOLUME 1

PART
I   MEASUREMENT AND PRACTICE

PART
II   INSTRUMENTS FOR PRACTICE

INSTRUMENTS FOR ADULTS
(Volume 2)

INSTRUMENTS FOR COUPLES
(Volume 1)

INSTRUMENTS FOR FAMILIES
(Volume 1)

INSTRUMENTS FOR CHILDREN
(Volume 1)

INSTRUMENTS CROSS-INDEXED BY PROBLEM AREA

(Instruments in **boldface** are in Volume 1 and those in standard type are in Volume 2.)

PROBLEM AREA	INSTRUMENT

Contents

PROBLEM AREA

INSTRUMENT

PROBLEM AREA   INSTRUMENT

PROBLEM AREA   INSTRUMENT

PROBLEM AREA	INSTRUMENT

FOREWORD

In the year 2000 historians will inevitably review the progress of the human race in the twentieth century. Historians of behavioral science reviewing progress in the provision of human services will have to confront a curious issue. They will note that the twentieth century witnessed the development of a science of human behavior. They will also note that from mid-century on, clinicians treating behavioral and emotional disorders began relying more heavily on the systematic application of theories and facts emanating from this science to emotional and behavioral problems. They will make observations on various false starts in the development of our therapeutic techniques, and offer reasons for the initial acceptance of these "false starts" in which clinicians or practitioners would apply exactly the same intervention or style of intervention to every problem that came before them. But in the last analysis historians will applaud the slow but systematic development of ever more powerful specific procedures and techniques devised to deal successfully with the variety of specific emotional and behavioral problems. This will be one of the success stories of the twentieth century.

Historians will also note a curious paradox which they will be hard pressed to explain. They will write that well into the 1980s few practitioners or clinicians evaluated the effects of their new treatments in any systematic way. Rather, whatever the behavioral or emotional problem, they would simply ask clients from time to time how they were feeling or how they were doing. Sometimes this would be followed by reports in an official chart or record duly noting clients' replies. If families or married couples were involved, a report from only one member of the interpersonal system would often suffice. Occasionally, these attempts at "evaluation" would reach peaks of quantifiable objectivity by presenting the questions in somewhat different ways such as "how are you feeling or doing compared to a year ago when you first came to see me?"

Historians will point out wryly that this practice would be analogous to physicians periodically asking patients with blood infections or fractures "how are you feeling" without bothering to analyze blood samples or take X rays. "How could this have been?" they will ask. In searching for answers they will examine records of clinical practice in the late twentieth century and find that the most usual response from clinicians was that they were simply too busy to evaluate what they were doing. But the real reason, astute historians will note, is that they never learned how.

Our government regulatory agencies, and other institutions, have anticipated these turn-of-the-century historians with the implementation of procedures requiring practitioners to evaluate what they do. This practice, most often subsumed under the rubric of "accountability," will very soon have a broad and deep hold on the practice of countless human service providers. But more important than the rise of new regulations in an era of deregulation will be the full realization on the part of all practitioners of the ultimate logic and wisdom of evaluating what they do. In response to this need, a number of books have appeared of late dealing with methods to help practitioners evaluate what they do. Some books even suggest that this will enable clinicians to make direct contributions to our science. Using strategies of repeated measurement of emotional and behavioral problems combined with sophisticated case study procedures and single case experimental designs, the teaching of these methods is increasing rapidly in our graduate and professional schools. But at the heart of this process is measurement, and the *sine qua non* of successful measurement is the availability of realistic and practical measures of change. Only through wide dissemination of realistic, practical, and accurate measures of change will practitioners be able to fulfill the requirements of accountability as well as their own growing sense of personal obligation to their clients to evaluate their intervention. Up until now this has been our weakness, not because satisfactory measures did not exist, but because so many widely scattered measurement tools existed that it was impossible for any one practitioner to keep track of these developments, let alone make a wise choice of which measures might be useful.

Now Fischer and Corcoran have accomplished this task and the result is this excellent book that not only describes the essentials of measurement but also presents the most up-to-date and satisfactory measures of change for almost any problem a practitioner might encounter. Concentrating on what they call rapid assessment instruments (RAIs), they present a series of brief questionnaires most of which fulfill the criterion of being under 50 items, thereby requiring no more than several minutes to fill out. By cross-referencing these RAIs by problem areas, no practitioner need take more than a few minutes to choose the proper questionnaire for any problem or combination of problems with which he or she might be confronted. With its well-written and easy-to-read chapters on what makes a brief questionnaire measure satisfactory or unsatisfactory, this book should be on the shelf of every practitioner working in a human service setting. Through the use of this book practitioners will not only be able to meet growing demands for accountability, but also satisfy their own desires for objective, quantifiable indications of progress in a manner that can be accomplished in no more than several minutes. As this activity becomes an integral part of the delivery of human services, the value of this book will increase.

David H. Barlow, Ph.D.
Center for Stress and Anxiety Disorders
Department of Psychology
State University of New York at Albany

PREFACE TO THE SECOND EDITION

The purpose of this book, like the first edition, is to provide practitioners and students with a number of instruments that they can use to help them monitor and evaluate their practice. These instruments were specifically selected because they measure most of the common problems seen in clinical practice, they are relatively short, easy to score and administer, and because we believe they really will help you, the reader, in your practice. Unlike the first edition, however, this edition comes in two volumes. Volume 1 contains measures for couples, families, and children. Volume 2 contains measures for adults with problems outside the context of the family.

We know through our own practice, and the practice of our students and colleagues, how difficult it sometimes is to be clear about where you are going with a client and whether or not you actually get there. We also realize the frustrations of trying to help a client be specific about a particular problem rather than leaving the problem defined in some global, vague—and therefore, unworkable—way.

These essentially are problems in *measurement*: being able to be as clear as possible about what you and the client are working on. Without a clear handle on the problem, the typical frustrations of practice are multiplied many times. We believe the instruments we present in this book will help relieve some of the frustrations you may have experienced in attempting to be precise about clients' problems. We also hope that we will be able to overcome the old myth of clinical practice that "most of our clients' problems really aren't measurable." We plan to show you that they are, and just how to go about doing it.

Practitioners in all the human services—psychology, social work, counseling, psychiatry, and nursing—increasingly are being held accountable for monitoring and evaluating their practice. One of the simplest yet most productive ways of doing this is to have available a package of instruments that measure the wide range of problems that practitioners typically face. Then you simply would select the instruments most appropriate for the problem of the client (individual, couple, or family) and use those to monitor practice with that client or system.

There are a number of such instruments available. Unfortunately, they are widely scattered throughout the literature. With this book, we hope to save you the time and energy required to go into the literature to find and select the appropriate instrument. We not only provide information about those instruments, we include copies of them so that you can immediately assess their utility for your practice. We also provide information as to where you can obtain copies of the instruments if you want to use them.

This book is addressed to members of all the helping professions who are engaged in clinical or therapeutic work with individuals, couples, or families. Further, we believe the instruments contained in this book will be useful to practitioners from all theoretical orientations who are interested in monitoring or evaluating their practice. Indeed, one of the great appeals of these instruments is that they are not limited to use by adherents of only one or even a few clinical schools of thought or theoretical orientations. If you believe that it is useful to be able to keep track of changes in your client's problem as your intervention proceeds, then we think this book is for you.

Although we don't mean to oversimplify the task, we believe this book can be useful to students and practitioners with very little experience in using measures such as we have included here. Of course, we will provide information on how to use these instruments, including relevant data on their reliability and validity and other characteristics. Indeed, we believe this book also will be useful to researchers who will be able to use these instruments to help them conduct their studies in a wide range of problem areas.

We hope this book will prove useful to you. Most of all, we hope it will help you enhance the efficiency and effectiveness of your practice.

ORGANIZATION OF THE BOOK

Unlike the first edition of this book, this edition is divided into two volumes. Volume 1 includes an introduction to the basic principles of measurement, an overview of different types of measures, and an introduction to the rapid assessment inventories included in this book: how we selected them, how to administer and score them, and how to avoid errors in their use. Volume 1 also contains copies of actual instruments for use with couples, families, and children. Volume 2 contains instruments to be used with adults when the problem of concern is not focused on the family or couple relationship.

In both volumes, the measures are listed alphabetically. However, for more help in finding an instrument that is specially designed for a particular problem area, consult the third part of the Table of Contents. We have presented a list of instruments cross-indexed by problem area. Thus, if you need an instrument for evaluating your client's anxiety, you could look under Anxiety in the Table of Contents and see which instruments are designed for measurement of anxiety. We hope this will facilitate the selection process.

ACKNOWLEDGMENTS

We are very grateful to several people who have helped us complete this book. Hisae Tachi, Daphne Asato, Carolyn Brooks, and Al Mann have provided a tremendous amount of help and support. We are also grateful to our deans for providing the environment that stimulated and supported this work: Dr. Patricia Ewalt of the University of Hawaii, Dr. James Ward at Portland State University, and Dr. Karen Haynes at the University of Houston. And we'd also like to note that the order of our names in this book has nothing to do with how much either of us contributed to its completion, despite the fact that each of us is convinced that he did most of the work.

INTRODUCTION TO VOLUME 2

Volume 2 of this book, unlike Volume 1, consists exclusively of measures you can use in your practice. However, in the first part of Volume 1, we reviewed the role of measurement to help in monitoring your client's progress and in evaluating your effectiveness. Our discussion included an overview of the basic principles of reliable and valid measures, the principles related to using measures in practice, and issues regarding interpreting scores. We also discussed some of the different types of measures, including the advantages and disadvantages of rapid assessment instruments (RAI) which are the focus of this book. While we believe this type of measure is particularly valuable, we *know* that there may be times when you will want other measurement tools as well as additional rapid assessment instruments. To this end we presented information on determining what to measure within the context of practice, how to locate measures, and pertinent questions you might ask when evaluating which measure to use. Finally, we presented some guidelines for you to consider when administering instruments.

We now turn to the rationale and procedures we used to locate and select the instruments presented in both volumes. We have not included all rapid assessment instruments in existence, but we believe that the measures that are included cover most of the client problem areas commonly encountered in practice.

The primary rationale for including an instrument in these volumes was that it measures some specific client problem or treatment goal relevant to clinical practice. Thus, we excluded certain instruments that we believed just were not relevant to treatment. For example, a measure of one's personal epistemology was not included because this is not a frequently seen clinical problem.

We also excluded instruments that measure *practitioner* behaviors that might occur during your interventions. While there is indeed a growing concern for measuring what you do as a clinician, we believe you are more likely to want to measure particular *client* problems or treatment goals. This, after all, is one of the best ways to monitor practice.

We also decided to include mainly self-report instruments that can be used for rapid assessment. While numerous other types of measurement are available, as we discussed in Chapter 3 of Volume 1, we believe you are more likely to monitor your practice with those on which your client directly reports his or her perceptions, feelings, or experiences. Not only are clients often the best source of this information, but RAIs can be used in conjunction with your own clinical assessment.

In the same vein, we have included only those instruments that are relatively short. While there is no concrete agreement on how short an instrument should be in order to be used for rapid completion and scoring, we have included mainly those that are 50 items or less. There are a few, however, that are somewhat longer than 50 items; we included these because shorter measures were not available for that particular problem, because the instrument has subscales that can be used for rapid assessment, or because the instrument can be completed quickly despite its length.

Finally, most of the instruments we include have some evidence of reliability and/or validity. All have some practice utility, providing information that will help you monitor your client's progress and evaluate your effectiveness. In order to facilitate your use of these instruments to monitor practice, we have used a standardized format to critique each instrument to help you make judgments about which instruments would be best for your particular purposes. Like many measures in the behavioral and social sciences, some of those included here lack convincing reliability, validity, or other important data. This is not to imply that no data were available, just that more is needed to be thoroughly convincing. When you use one of these instruments, even one with sufficient reliability and validity data for that matter, we hope you will approach it with a judicious degree of caution and your own critique.

LOCATING THE INSTRUMENT

In order to locate measurement tools, we began with a computer literature search. Additionally, we identified key volumes and journals that pertained to measurement in practice and reviewed them for appropriate instruments. (See Volume 1, Chapter 5, Tables 5.2 and 5.3.) For the journals we identified, all volumes were reviewed from 1974, except the *Journal of Clinical Psychology* and the *Journal of Personality Assessment*, which were reviewed from 1964 through 1992. For journals that first appeared later than 1974, all volumes were reviewed.

THE FINAL SELECTION

Whenever possible, we have tried to include more than one instrument to measure a problem, not only to provide a choice, but because different instruments tap different aspects of a problem. For example, you will notice there are several measures of anxiety. One of these may be more appropriate for use with a given client than others. Finally, there are obviously more instruments available to measure certain types of problems than other types. For example, relatively few measures are available to assess children, because children tend to have more difficulty in filling out self-report instruments than adults. Thus, while we included as many self-report RAIs as we could, we also included some rating scales for children. In this and a few other areas as well, where the nature of the people or problem suggests that self-report measures may be difficult to administer, observer rating scales may be an appropriate substitute.

In this volume, we have focused solely on measures for adults where the problem does not seem primarily concerned with other family members. We recognize that categorizing measures this way—adult measures in this volume and measures for couples, families, and children in Volume 1—leaves something to be desired. There is obvious overlap among many of the categories for several problems. Nevertheless, we hope this organization of the two volumes will make selection of measures for your practice as smooth as possible.

In sum, we have not included all available self-report rapid assessment instruments. For example, a few that we would have chosen to include, such as the Beck Depression Inventory (Beck et al., 1961), were not available for reproduction. However, we believe the instruments we have chosen cover most of the client problem areas commonly encountered in practice. Nevertheless, we must stress that other measures are available, and you should consider using them in conjunction with the RAIs included here. We hope the instruments presented in these two volumes will get you started, and help you develop more measurement tools for use in monitoring clients and evaluating your practice effectiveness.

INSTRUMENTS FOR ADULTS

ACHIEVEMENT ANXIETY TEST (AAT)

AUTHORS: Richard Alpert and Ralph N. Haber

PURPOSE: To measure anxiety about academic achievement.

DESCRIPTION: The AAT is a 19-item instrument designed to measure anxiety about academic achievement. The AAT consists of two separate scales, a "facilitating scale" (items 2, 6, 8, 9, 10, 12, 15, 16, 18) which assesses anxiety as a motivator, and a "debilitating scale" (remainder of items) which assesses the degree to which anxiety interferes with performance. The two scales are administered on one questionnaire but scored separately. The value of these scales is in their specificity, both in defining the two aspects of anxiety, and in measuring anxiety specifically related to academic achievement. The AAT predicts academic performance, particularly verbal aptitude, more accurately than do the general anxiety scales.

NORMS: The AAT was developed with several samples of undergraduate introductory psychology students. The total number of subjects was 323, with no other demographic data reported, although it appeared that respondents were male. The mean score on the facilitating scale was 27.28, and on the debilitating scale, 26.33.

SCORING: The two subscales are scored separately with scores on each of the items summed to produce the overall score. Each item has a different response category, although all are on 5-point scales indicating the degree to which the statement applies to the respondent. Items 8, 10, and 12 from the facilitating scale are reverse-scored as are items 3, 4, 13, 17, and 19 from the debilitating scale.

RELIABILITY: The AAT has excellent stability: ten-week test-retest correlations of .83 for the facilitating and .87 for the debilitating scale, and eight-month test-retest correlations of .75 for the facilitating scale and .76 for the debilitating scale. No internal consistency information was reported.

VALIDITY: The AAT has good criterion-related validity, correlating significantly with several measures of academic performance. Both subscales also are correlated with verbal aptitude. The AAT also has good predictive validity, significantly predicting grade point averages.

PRIMARY REFERENCE: Alpert, R. and Haber, R. N. (1960). Anxiety in academic achievement situations, *Journal of Abnormal and Social Psychology*, 61, 207–215. Instrument reproduced with permission of the American Psychological Association.

AVAILABILITY: Journal article.

AAT

Please circle the number for each item that comes closest to describing you on a sliding scale from "1" to "5."

1. Nervousness while taking an exam or test hinders me from doing well.
    Always   Never
       1   2   3   4   5

2. I work most effectively under pressure, as when the task is very important.

    Always   Never
       1   2   3   4   5

3. In a course where I have been doing poorly, my fear of a bad grade cuts down my efficiency.

    Never   Always
       1   2   3   4   5

4. When I am poorly prepared for an exam or test, I get upset, and do less well than even my restricted knowledge should allow.

    This never   This practic-
    happens   ally always
    to me   happens to me
       1   2   3   4   5

5. The more important the examination, the less well I seem to do.

    Always   Never
       1   2   3   4   5

6. While I may (or may not) be nervous before taking an exam, once I start, I seem to forget to be nervous.

    I always   I am always
    forget   nervous
       1   2   3   4   5

7. During exams or tests, I block on questions to which I know the answers, even though I remember them as soon as the exam is over.

                                       I never block
    This always   on questions to
    happens to   which I know
    me   the answers
       1   2   3   4   5

8. Nervousness while taking a test helps me do better.

It never helps				It often helps
1	2	3	4	5

9. When I start a test, nothing is able to distract me.

This is always true of me				This is never true of me
1	2	3	4	5

10. In courses in which the total grade is based mainly on one exam, I seem to do better than other people.

Never				Always
1	2	3	4	5

11. I find that my mind goes blank at the beginning of an exam, and it takes me a few minutes before I can function.

I almost always blank out at first				I never blank out at first
1	2	3	4	5

12. I look forward to exams.

Never				Always
1	2	3	4	5

13. I am so tired from worrying about an exam, that I find I almost don't care how well I do by the time I start the test.

I never feel this way				I almost always feel this way
1	2	3	4	5

14. Time pressure on an exam causes me to do worse than the rest of the group under similar conditions.

Time pressure always seems to make me do worse than others on an exam				Time pressure never seems to make me do worse than others on an exam
1	2	3	4	5

15. Although "cramming" under preexamination tension is not effective for most people, I find that if the need arises, I can learn material immediately before an exam, even under considerable pressure, and successfully retain it to use on the exam.

I am always   I am never
able to use   able to use
the "crammed"   the "crammed"
material   material
successfully   successfully

1	2	3	4	5

16. I enjoy taking a difficult exam more than an easy one.

Always   Never

1	2	3	4	5

17. I find myself reading exam questions without understanding them and I must go back over them so that they will make sense.

Never   Always

1	2	3	4	5

18. The more important the exam or test, the better I seem to do.

This is true   This is not
of me   true of me

1	2	3	4	5

19. When I don't do well on a difficult item at the beginning of an exam, it tends to upset me so that I block on every easy question later on.

This never   This almost
happens to   always
me   happens to me

1	2	3	4	5

ACTIVITY-FEELING SCALE II (AFS-II)

AUTHOR: Johnmarshall Reeve

PURPOSE: To measure organismic needs and motivation.

DESCRIPTION: This 16-item instrument measures organismic needs which
    theoretically give rise to intrinsic motivation. There are four organismic
    needs: competence, self-determination, relatedness, and curiosity. Tension
    is antithetical to motivation. Competence refers to one's perceived capability
    for achievement. Self-determination refers to one's internal locus of causal-
    ity. Relatedness concerns the emotional bonds and attachments between
    persons. Curiosity concerns seeking information and dispels moments of
    uncertainty. Tension, in contrast, diminishes motivation. In completing the
    scales, clients are asked to rate their affective reactions to a target activity,
    such as work or recreational activity. This allows one to use the AFS-II for
    specific problems when a client may lack motivation, such as problems
    related to procrastination. Clinicians may also find the AFS-II useful in
    evaluating a client's motivation in treatment or their response to various
    homework assignments. The AFS-II consists of four subscales for each of
    the intrinsic needs and for tension.

NORMS: Specific norms are difficult to report because scores vary according
    to the activity being evaluated. A sample of 50 college students exposed to
    an intrinsically motivating activity reported means (and standard deviations)
    for competence, self-determination, relatedness, curiosity, and tension of
    4.45 (1.45), 5.52 (.99), 2.12 (1.26), 3.85 (.79), and 3.80 (1.73), respectively.

SCORING: Respondents indicate their degree of agreement to any particular
    stimulus recorded on the scale. Scores are the sum of each item score
    averaged by the number of items. Competence is composed of "capable" +
    "competent" + "achieving." Self-determination is composed of "offered
    choices what to do" + "that my participation is voluntary" + "my decision
    to continue is voluntary" + "forced to participate" (which is reverse-scored).
    Relatedness is composed of "involved with friends" + "part of a team" +
    "brotherly/sisterly." Curiosity is composed of "curious" + "want to know
    more about it" + "stimulated." Tension is composed of "pressured" +
    "stressed" + "uptight." Scale scores range from 1 to 7 with higher scores
    reflecting stronger intrinsic needs.

RELIABILITY: Reliability has been estimated with Cronbach's alpha from
    seven studies. The average internal consistency for each subscale was:
    competence, .85; self-determination, .70; relatedness, .79; curiosity, .72; and
    tension .92. Test-retest reliability over a one-hour period was estimated in
    two studies as follows: competence, .52 and .68; self-determination, .64 and
    .62; relatedness, .65 and .59; curiosity, .66 and .62; tension, .61 and .63.
    Additional and similar coefficients of stability over five consecutive weeks

are reported from a sample of students in an introductory psychology class. The moderate test-retest coefficients suggest that intrinsic needs are "states" as opposed to enduring aspects of the individual ("traits").

VALIDITY: Validity has been tested with factorial validity with the subscales showing modest intercorrelations, ranging from .09 to .34. Predictive validity was estimated by correlating AFS-II scales with self-report and behavioral measures of intrinsic motivation in three separate studies. There were strong correlations between AFS-II scales and the self-report measures, ranging from .22 to .77, but only moderate correlations with the behavioral measures, ranging from .12 to .36. Construct validity has been shown by differences in competence scores for subjects in an experiment that manipulated success and failure where subjects receiving an objective source of competence information reported significantly greater perceived competence than those receiving information suggesting incompetence. Similar construct validity results are reported for the self-determination, relatedness, and curiosity scales. Validity also has been estimated by determining the emotional correlates of each scale. Competence is correlated with positive emotions and enjoyment and inversely with negative emotions. These results suggest the emotional consequence of competence is enjoyment, while the emotional experience of incompetence is distress. Fairly similar associations are reported for the other scales, although there were some complex relationships between the needs and emotionality.

PRIMARY REFERENCES: Reeve, J. and Robinson, D. T. (1987). Toward a reconceptualization of intrinsic motivation: Correlates and factor structure of the activity-feeling scale, *Journal of Social Behavior and Personality*, 2, 23–36. Chang-way, L. and Reeve, J. (1989). *Manual for the Activity-Feeling Scale II* (submitted for publication).

AVAILABILITY: Johnmarshall Reeve, Department of Psychology, University of Rochester—River Campus, Rochester, NY 14627.

AFS-II

The items listed below ask how puzzle-solving makes you feel at the present time. For each item, circle a number near 7 if you strongly agree that puzzle-solving makes you feel that way. Circle a number near 1 if you strongly disagree that puzzle-solving makes you feel that way. If you agree and disagree equally that puzzle-solving makes you feel that way, then circle a number near 4.

(TARGET ACTIVITY) MAKES ME FEEL:

	Strongly disagree		Agree and disagree equally			Strongly agree	
Capable	1	2	3	4	5	6	7
Offered choices what to do	1	2	3	4	5	6	7
Curious	1	2	3	4	5	6	7
Part of a team	1	2	3	4	5	6	7
Stressed	1	2	3	4	5	6	7
Involved with friends	1	2	3	4	5	6	7
Stimulated	1	2	3	4	5	6	7
Pressured	1	2	3	4	5	6	7
Competent	1	2	3	4	5	6	7
Want to know more about It	1	2	3	4	5	6	7
That my participation is voluntary	1	2	3	4	5	6	7
My decision to continue is voluntary	1	2	3	4	5	6	7
Uptight	1	2	3	4	5	6	7
Achieving	1	2	3	4	5	6	7
Brotherly/sisterly	1	2	3	4	5	6	7
Forced to participate	1	2	3	4	5	6	7

ADULT HEALTH CONCERNS QUESTIONNAIRE (HCQ)

AUTHORS: Richard L. Spoth and David M. Dush

PURPOSE: To measure psychiatric symptoms.

DESCRIPTION: The HCQ is a 55-item psychiatric symptom checklist. The items on the HCQ were derived from the DSM III-R. Its brief format and simplicity of structure make it very easy to use. Factor analysis reveals 10 factors, described in the original article. The HCQ has a two-level response format: respondents first underline any concern that applies to them and then rate the underlined items on a 5-point Likert-type scale regarding severity. Use of the HCQ without the distress ratings is not recommended. The HCQ is designed as a tool for clinical use especially for diagnosis and assessment. Subsequent research may reveal the HCQ to be equally useful as a tool to evaluate therapeutic outcomes.

NORMS: The HCQ was studied initially with two samples, the first involving 167 in- and outpatients referred to a psychology service in a private, nonprofit general hospital (with a mean age of 38 and 64% female), and the second, another 82 patients referred to the psychology service plus 32 patients attending a headache pain clinic and 15 college students. Actual norms are not presented, although means for the 10 most frequently (.95 to 1.90) and 10 least frequently (.09 to .35) checked items were reported.

SCORING: Two scores can be obtained from the HCQ. The first is a simple total of all items underlined. The second is a total distress score, a simple sum of distress ratings for all items underlined.

RELIABILITY: No actual data other than the results of the factor analysis were provided.

VALIDITY: The HCQ has fair concurrent validity, with several scales of the MMPI being correlated with both number of items completed on the HCQ and the total distress score. Only one scale on the Psychological Screening Inventory (Neuroticism) was correlated with the total distress score on the HCQ.

PRIMARY REFERENCE: Spoth, R. L. and Dush, D. M. (1988). The Adult Health Concerns Questionnaire: A psychiatric symptoms checklist, *Innovations in Clinical Practice: A Sourcebook*, 7, 289–297.

AVAILABILITY: Journal article.

HCQ

Part One: Please *underline* any of the following concerns that apply to you.

____ Marital stress	____ Too many drugs
____ Other family problems	____ Too much alcohol
____ Other relationship problems	____ Feel negative about the future
____ Problems at work/school	____ Hard to make friends
____ Health problems	____ Feeling lonely
____ Financial problems	____ Sexual problems
____ Legal problems	____ Less energy than usual
____ Sad/depressed	____ More energy than usual
____ Loss of appetite	____ Very talkative
____ Loss of weight	____ Restless/can't sit still
____ Gain of weight	____ Nervous/tense
____ Difficulty sleeping	____ Panicky
____ Difficulty concentrating	____ Shaky/trembling
____ Quick change of moods	____ Hard to trust anyone
____ Dwelling on problems	____ Problems controlling my thoughts
____ Problems with breathing	____ Upset stomach
____ Hot or cold spells	____ Sweating
____ Problems controlling anger or urges	____ Light headed/dizzy
____ Feeling suicidal	____ Too much worry
____ Feeling worthless	____ Too many fears
____ Drawing away from people	____ Feeling guilty

_____ Lack of interest/enjoyment   _____ Feeling angry/frustrated

_____ Nightmares   _____ Memory problems

_____ Feel ignored/abandoned   _____ See/hear strange things

_____ Too much pain   _____ Feel used by people

_____ Confused   _____ Feel others are out to get me

_____ Laugh without reason   _____ Watched/talked about by others

                                          _____ Other

Part Two: In front of each concern underlined, please rate its *severity* as:

1 = Mildly distressing
2 = Moderate
3 = Serious
4 = Severe
5 = Very severely distressing

ADULT SELF-EXPRESSION SCALE (ASES)

AUTHORS: Melvin L. Gay, James G. Hollandsworth, Jr., and John P. Galassi

PURPOSE: To measure assertiveness in adults.

DESCRIPTION: This 48-item assertiveness instrument was developed from the College Self-Expression Scale (an assertiveness measure for college students) along with a pool of 106 additional items. Items were selected according to rigorous psychometric standards, including item-total correlations and item discrimination. The instrument contains 25 positively worded items and 23 negatively worded items. The content of the ASES items reflects specific verbal assertive behavior in particular interpersonal situations where assertion may be problematic. Consequently, in addition to the rapid assessment of assertion, the ASES is useful in isolating situations where a client has difficulty asserting him/herself.

NORMS: Means and standard deviation are reported for a sample of 464 community college students, ranging in ages from 18 to 60 years of age (mean = 25.38). For males (n = 192), the mean was 118.56 and the standard deviation was 18.57. For females (n = 268), the mean was 114.78 and the standard deviation was 21.22. Married respondents had a mean of 118.47 with a standard deviation of 19.62, while singles had a mean of 114.26 and a standard deviation of 20.60. A sample of 32 people seeking counseling services had a mean of 101.81 and a standard deviation of 26.99.

SCORING: Items 7, 8, 9, 10, 11, 12, 13, 15, 16, 17, 19, 20, 22, 25, 28, 29, 32, 35, 36, 43, 44, 47, and 48 are reverse-scored. All item scores are then summed for a total score. Scores range from zero to 192 with higher scores reflecting higher levels of assertiveness.

RELIABILITY: Test-retest reliability was determined for a two-week period (r = .88) and for a five-week period (r = .91), which suggests the ASES is a stable measure of assertiveness. Data on internal consistency were not available.

VALIDITY: Concurrent validity is evidenced with correlations between the ASES and measures of defensiveness, self-consciousness, lability, achievement, dominance, affiliation, heterosexuality, exhibition, autonomy, and aggression. Scores on the ASES were also associated with anxiety and locus of control. A sample of persons seeking counseling services had significantly lower scores than the sample of community college students.

PRIMARY REFERENCE: Gay, M. L., Hollandsworth, J. G., and Galassi, J. P. (1975). An assertiveness inventory for adults, *Journal of Counseling Psychology*, 22, 340–344. Instrument reproduced with permission of John Galassi.

AVAILABILITY: The Free Press.

ASES

The following inventory is designed to provide information about the way in which you express yourself. Please answer the questions by writing a number from 0 to 4 in the space to the left of each item. Your answer should indicate how you generally express yourself in a variety of situations. If a particular situation does not apply to you, answer as you think you would respond in that situation. Your answer should *not* reflect how you feel you ought to act or how you would like to act. Do not deliberate over any individual question. Please work quickly. Your first response to the question is probably your most accurate one.

0 = Almost always or always
1 = Usually
2 = Sometimes
3 = Seldom
4 = Never or rarely

____ 1. Do you ignore it when someone pushes in front of you in line?
____ 2. Do you find it difficult to ask a friend to do a favor for you?
____ 3. If your boss or supervisor makes what you consider to be an unreasonable request, do you have difficulty saying no?
____ 4. Are you reluctant to speak to an attractive acquaintance of the opposite sex?
____ 5. Is it difficult for you to refuse unreasonable requests from your parents?
____ 6. Do you find it difficult to accept compliments from your boss or supervisor?
____ 7. Do you express your negative feelings to others when it is appropriate?
____ 8. Do you freely volunteer information or opinions in discussions with people whom you do not know very well?
____ 9. If there was a public figure whom you greatly admired and respected at a large social gathering, would you make an effort to introduce yourself?
____ 10. How often do you openly express justified feelings of anger to your parents?
____ 11. If you have a friend of whom your parents do not approve, do you make an effort to help them get to know one another better?
____ 12. If you were watching a TV program in which you were very interested and a close relative was disturbing you, would you ask them to be quiet?
____ 13. Do you play an important part in deciding how you and your close friends spend your leisure time together?
____ 14. If you are angry at your spouse/boyfriend/girlfriend, is it difficult for you to tell him/her?
____ 15. If a friend who is supposed to pick you up for an important engagement calls fifteen minutes before he/she is supposed to be there and says that he/she cannot make it, do you express your annoyance?

_____ 16. If you approve of something your parents do, do you express your approval?

_____ 17. If in a rush you stop by a supermarket to pick up a few items, would you ask to go before someone in the check-out line?

_____ 18. Do you find it difficult to refuse the requests of others?

_____ 19. If your boss or supervisor expresses opinions with which you strongly disagree, do you venture to state your own point of view?

_____ 20. If you have a close friend whom your spouse/boyfriend/girlfriend dislikes and constantly criticizes, would you inform him/her that you disagree and tell him/her of your friend's assets?

_____ 21. Do you find it difficult to ask favors of others?

_____ 22. If food which is not to your satisfaction was served in a good restaurant, would you bring it to the waiter's attention?

_____ 23. Do you tend to drag out your apologies?

_____ 24. When necessary, do you find it difficult to ask favors of your parents?

_____ 25. Do you insist that others do their fair share of the work?

_____ 26. Do you have difficulty saying no to salesmen?

_____ 27. Are you reluctant to speak up in a discussion with a small group of friends?

_____ 28. Do you express anger or annoyance to your boss or supervisor when it is justified?

_____ 29. Do you compliment and praise others?

_____ 30. Do you have difficulty asking a close friend to do an important favor even though it will cause him/her some inconvenience?

_____ 31. If a close relative makes what you consider to be an unreasonable request, do you have difficulty saying no?

_____ 32. If your boss or supervisor makes a statement that you consider untrue, do you question it aloud?

_____ 33. If you find yourself becoming fond of a friend, do you have difficulty expressing these feelings to that person?

_____ 34. Do you have difficulty exchanging a purchase with which you are dissatisfied?

_____ 35. If someone in authority interrupts you in the middle of an important conversation, do you request that the person wait until you have finished?

_____ 36. If a person of the opposite sex whom you have been wanting to meet directs attention to you at a party, do you take the initiative in beginning the conversation?

_____ 37. Do you hesitate to express resentment to a friend who has unjustifiably criticized you?

_____ 38. If your parents wanted you to come home for a weekend visit and you had made important plans, would you change your plans?

_____ 39. Are you reluctant to speak up in a discussion or debate?

_____ 40. If a friend who has borrowed $5.00 from you seems to have forgotten about it, is it difficult for you to remind this person?

_____ 41. If your boss or supervisor teases you to the point that it is no longer fun, do you have difficulty expressing your displeasure?

_____ 42. If your spouse/boyfriend/girlfriend is blatantly unfair, do you find it difficult to say something about it to him/her?

_____ 43. If a clerk in a store waits on someone who has come in after you when you are in a rush, do you call his attention to the matter?

_____ 44. If you lived in an apartment and the landlord failed to make certain repairs after it had been brought to his attention, would you insist on it?

_____ 45. Do you find it difficult to ask your boss or supervisor to let you off early?

_____ 46. Do you have difficulty verbally expressing love and affection to your spouse/boyfriend/girlfriend?

_____ 47. Do you readily express your opinions to others?

_____ 48. If a friend makes what you consider to be an unreasonable request, are you able to refuse?

AFFECT BALANCE SCALE (ABS)

AUTHORS: Norman Bradburn and E. Noll

PURPOSE: To measure psychological well-being.

DESCRIPTION: The ABS is a 10-item instrument designed to measure psychological well-being, especially mood state or happiness. The current version was modified from the original. The ABS is an extensively studied scale with excellent data on its applicability in a broad range of situations and cultures. The current version yields scores on two distinct conceptual dimensions, positive affect (items 1, 3, 5, 7, and 9) and negative affect (items 2, 4, 6, 8, and 10). The ABS is highly recommended as a brief, easy to score and administer measure of psychological well-being in a variety of populations.

NORMS: Data are not available.

SCORING: The ABS is easily scored by summing item responses for the two subscales and the total scale score; numbers on the scale are assigned to each score as indicated on the instrument (e.g., a "yes" on item 1 is assigned a score of 3).

RELIABILITY: The ABS has shown good to excellent internal consistency in a number of studies with alphas that consistently exceed .80.

VALIDITY: The ABS has extensive data on concurrent, predictive, and construct validity. It is correlated in predicted directions with numerous measures including the Depression Adjective Checklist, reports of levels of activities and response to illness among the elderly, life satisfaction, and social interaction.

PRIMARY REFERENCE: Bradburn, N. M. and Noll, E. (1969). *The Structure of Psychological Well-Being*. Chicago: Aldine.

AVAILABILITY: Primary reference.

ABS

We are interested in the way people are feeling these days. Please circle "yes" or "no" for each item.

During the past few weeks, did you ever feel:

Yes No   1.   Particularly excited or interested in something?
(3)   (2)

Yes No   2.   So restless that you couldn't sit long in a chair?
(6)   (5)

Yes No   3.   Proud because someone complimented you on something you
(9)   (8)   had done?

Yes No   4.   Very lonely or remote from other people?
(3)   (2)

Yes No   5.   Pleased about having accomplished something?
(6)   (5)

Yes No   6.   Bored?
(9)   (8)

Yes No   7.   On top of the world?
(3)   (2)

Yes No   8.   Depressed or very unhappy?
(6)   (5)

Yes No   9.   That things were going your way?
(9)   (8)

Yes No   10.   Upset because someone criticized you?
(3)   (2)

AGGRESSION INVENTORY (AI)

AUTHOR: Brian A. Gladue

PURPOSE: To measure aggressive behavioral characteristics or traits.

DESCRIPTION: This 30-item instrument is designed to measure different aggressive traits. Respondents rate the items on a five-point scale, ranging from "does not apply at all to me" to "applies exactly to me." The AI consists of four subscales: physical aggression (PA = 9 + 11 + 12 + 13); verbal aggression (VA = 3 + 4 + 6 + 7 + 8 + 16 + 21); impulsive/impatient (II = 15 + 18 + 20 + 24 + 25 + 28 + 30); and avoidance (Avoid = 17 + 22). Because of possible gender differences in many aspects of aggression, scores on the AI must be considered separately for women and men. For example, factor analyses provide differences in terms of the explained variance of the construct of aggression for the assembly of subscales. For men the pattern of explained variance was PA (32.6%); VA (12.7%); II (8.4%); and Avoid (4.9%). For women the pattern was VA (33.9%); II (15.2%); PA (5.6%); and Avoid (5.3%).

NORMS: The AI was studied with 960 undergraduates enrolled in introductory psychology classes. This population was primarily Caucasian (96%) and consisted of 517 male and 443 female young adults (mean age = 20.4 years, ranging from 18 to 34). For males the mean subscale scores were PA = 2.34; VA = 3.04; II = 2.80; Avoid = 2.85. For females the subscale mean scores were PA = 1.82; VA = 2.58; II = 2.68; and Avoid = 3.06.

SCORING: The subscales are scored by summing the item responses and then dividing by the number of items for the particular subscale. Scores range from 1 to 5 with higher scores reflecting more aggression.

RELIABILITY: The AI has fair to good internal consistency. For men the alpha coefficients were PA = .82; VA = .81; II = .80 and .65 for Avoid. For women the alpha coefficients were PA = .70; VA = .76; II = .76; and .70 for Avoid. Data on stability were not reported.

VALIDITY: The validity of the AI subscale has been supported by factor analysis and differences between men and women. The latter serves to suggest the AI has fair known-groups validity where men and women significantly differed on each subscale and on all but six of the individual items.

PRIMARY REFERENCE: Gladue, B. A. (1991). Qualitative and quantitative sex differences in self-reported aggressive behavior characteristics, *Psychological Reports*, 68, 675–684. Instrument reproduced with permission of Brian A. Gladue and *Psychological Reports*.

AVAILABILITY: Dr. Brian A. Gladue, Department of Psychology, 115 Minard Hall, North Dakota State University, P.O. Box 5975, Fargo, ND 58105-5075.

AI

Each statement in this questionnaire asks about you, how you interact with other people or how you typically respond in a variety of situations. For each statement please select the response which applies BEST to YOU. Please record the applicable response for each item on the space next to it. Using the following rating scale select the response which applies BEST to YOU, and record it in the space next to each item.

1 = Does NOT apply AT ALL to me
2 = Applies SOMEWHAT to me
3 = Applies FAIRLY WELL to me
4 = Applies WELL to me
5 = Applies EXACTLY to me

____ 1.   I enjoy working with my hands doing repetitive tasks.
____ 2.   I admire people who can walk away from a fight or argument.
____ 3.   When a person is unfair to me I get angry and protest.
____ 4.   When a person tries to "cut ahead" of me in a line, I firmly tell him not to do so.
____ 5.   Whenever I have trouble understanding a problem, I ask others for advice.
____ 6.   When a person criticizes me, I tend to answer back and protest.
____ 7.   When a person tries to boss me around, I resist strongly.
____ 8.   I think it is OK to make trouble for an annoying person.
____ 9.   I get into fights with other people.
____ 10. When a person criticizes or negatively comments on my clothing or hair, I tell him/her it is none of their business.
____ 11. I really admire persons who know how to fight with their fists or body (not using any weapons).
____ 12. When another person hassles or shoves me, I try to give him/her a good shove or punch.
____ 13. When another person picks a fight with me, I fight back.
____ 14. I prefer to listen to rock-and-roll instead of classical music.
____ 15. I become easily impatient and irritable if I have to wait.
____ 16. When another person is mean or nasty to me, I try to get even with him/her.
____ 17. Whenever someone is being unpleasant, I think it is better to be quiet than to make a fuss.
____ 18. Others say that I lose patience easily.
____ 19. I consider myself to be an authority figure for some people.
____ 20. More often than others, I seem to do things that I regret later.
____ 21. If a person insults me, I insult him/her back.
____ 22. I prefer to get out of the way and stay out of trouble whenever somebody is hassling me.
____ 23. When I am on bad terms with a person, it usually ends up in a fight.
____ 24. I become easily impatient if I have to keep doing the same thing for a long time.
____ 25. It often happens that I act too hastily.

____ 26. Whenever I build something new, I read the instruction booklet
          before doing anything.
____ 27. I really admire persons who know how to fight with weapons.
____ 28. I often act before I have had the time to think.
____ 29. When I am very angry with someone, I yell at them.
____ 30. When I have to make up my mind, I usually do it quickly.

AGGRESSION QUESTIONNAIRE (AQ)

AUTHORS: Arnold H. Buss and Mark Perry

PURPOSE: To measure four aspects of aggression.

DESCRIPTION: This 29-item instrument measures four aspects of aggression: physical aggression (PA: items 1, 5, 9, 13, 17, 21, 24, 26, 28), verbal aggression (VA: items 2, 6, 10, 14, 18), anger (A: items 3, 7, 11, 15, 19, 22, 29), and hostility (H: items 4, 8, 12, 16, 20, 23, 25, 27). The AQ is a refinement of the Hostility Inventory. a widely used instrument developed by the first author over thirty years ago. The AQ was developed from a pool of 52 items, many of which were from the original Hostility Inventory, by means of principal component factor analysis and confirmatory factor analysis. The instrument allows one to assess not only how aggressive one is by using total scores, but also how that aggression is manifested, which is determined by the subscale scores.

NORMS: For a sample of 612 undergraduate males, the AQ subscale had the following means (and standard deviations): PA = 24.3 (7.7), VA = 15.2 (3.9), A = 17.0 (5.6), H = 21.2 (5.5); the mean for the total score for this sample was 77.8 with a standard deviation of 16.5. From a sample of 641 female college students the means (and standard deviations) for the subscales were PA = 17.9 (6.6), VA = 13.5 (3.9), A = 16.7 (5.8), and H = 20.2 (6.3); total scores had a mean of 68.2 and a standard deviation of 17.0.

SCORING: Items 24 and 29 are first reverse-scored. Subscale scores are the sum of the item scores for those items in the subscale. A total score is the sum of all item scores and ranges from 29 to 145. Higher scores reflect more aggression.

RELIABILITY: The internal consistency of the AQ is very good. Alpha coefficients were .85, .72, .83, and .77 for the PA, VA, A, and H subscales. Total scores had an alpha of .89. The AQ is a stable instrument with good test-retest reliability; over a nine-week period the test-retest correlations were .80, .76, .72, and .72 for the PA, VA, A, and H subscales and .80 for total scores.

VALIDITY: Scores on the AQ were moderately correlated with each other. However, when the variance in the correlations due to the anger score was partialed out, correlations were not significant; this supports the theoretical validity of the AQ in that the associations between physical aggression, verbal aggression, and hostility are due to their connection with anger. Scores also have good concurrent validity, with no significant association between the PA and VA and emotionality, but strong correlations between emotionality and the A and H subscales. Scores on all four subscales correlated with impulsiveness, competition, and assertiveness, although noticeably lower correlations were found between assertiveness and PA and

H subscales. Construct validity was evidenced with correlations between the AQ and peer observations of aggression, sociability, and shyness.

PRIMARY REFERENCE: Buss, A. H. and Perry, M. (1992). The Aggression Questionnaire, *Journal of Personality and Social Psychology*, 63, 452–459. Instrument reproduced with permission of Arnold Buss and the American Psychological Association.

AVAILABILITY: Journal article.

AQ

For the following items please rate how characteristic each is of you. Using the following rating scale record your answer in the space to the left of each item.

1 = Extremely uncharacteristic of me
2 = Somewhat uncharacteristic of me
3 = Only slightly characteristic of me
4 = Somewhat characteristic of me
5 = Extremely characteristic of me

____ 1. Once in a while I can't control the urge to strike another person.
____ 2. I tell my friends openly when I disagree with them.
____ 3. I flare up quickly but get over it quickly.
____ 4. I am sometimes eaten up with jealousy.
____ 5. Given enough provocation, I may hit another person.
____ 6. I often find myself disagreeing with people.
____ 7. When frustrated, I let my irritation show.
____ 8. At times I feel I have gotten a raw deal out of life.
____ 9. If somebody hits me, I hit back.
____ 10. When people annoy me, I may tell them what I think of them.
____ 11. I sometimes feel like a powder keg ready to explode.
____ 12. Other people always seem to get the breaks.
____ 13. I get into fights a little more than the average person.
____ 14. I can't help getting into arguments when people disagree with me.
____ 15. Some of my friends think I'm a hothead.
____ 16. I wonder why sometimes I feel so bitter about things.
____ 17. If I have to resort to violence to protect my rights, I will.
____ 18. My friends say that I'm somewhat argumentative.
____ 19. Sometimes I fly off the handle for no good reason.
____ 20. I know that "friends" talk about me behind my back.
____ 21. There are people who pushed me so far that we came to blows.
____ 22. I have trouble controlling my temper.
____ 23. I am suspicious of overly friendly strangers.
____ 24. I can think of no good reason for ever hitting a person.
____ 25. I sometimes feel that people are laughing at me behind my back.
____ 26. I have threatened people I know.
____ 27. When people are especially nice, I wonder what they want.
____ 28. I have become so mad that I have broken things.
____ 29. I am an even-tempered person.

AGORAPHOBIC COGNITIONS QUESTIONNAIRE (ACQ)

AUTHORS: Dianne L. Chambless, G. Craig Caputo, Priscilla Bright, and Richard Gallagher

PURPOSE: To measure catastrophic thinking in agoraphobia.

DESCRIPTION: The ACQ is a 14-item instrument (with an optional fifteenth item) designed to measure thoughts concerning negative consequences of experiencing anxiety. The ACQ was developed on the basis of interviews with clients being treated for agoraphobia. The ACQ comprises two factors: physical consequences and social/behavioral consequences. However, the total score can be used as an overall measure. The ACQ actually measures "fear of fear" and, as such, is a very important tool for use in evaluating treatment programs for agoraphobia.

NORMS: The ACQ was studied initially with 173 clients applying for treatment at the Agoraphobia and Anxiety Programs at Temple University. The sample had been agoraphobic for a median of eight years; 80% were female. The mean ACQ score was 2.32 (SD = .66).

SCORING: The ACQ is easily scored by averaging responses across the individual items.

RELIABILITY: The ACQ has good internal consistency, with an alpha of .80. It also has good stability, with a one-month test-retest correlation of .75.

VALIDITY: The ACQ has good concurrent validity, correlating with the Beck Depression Inventory, the neuroticism score of the Eysenck Personality Questionnaire, and the State-Trait Anxiety Inventory. The ACQ also has good known-groups validity, distinguishing among agoraphobics, "normals," and clients with other depression and anxiety disorders. The ACQ also is sensitive to changes due to treatment.

PRIMARY REFERENCE: Chambless, D. L., Caputo, G. C., Bright, P., and Gallagher, R. (1984). Assessment of fear in agoraphobics: The Body Sensations Questionnaire and the Agoraphobics Questionnaire, *Journal of Consulting and Clinical Psychology*, 52, 1090–1097.

AVAILABILITY: Dr. Dianne Chambless, Department of Psychology, American University, Washington, DC 20016.

ACQ

Below are some thoughts or ideas that may pass through your mind when you are nervous or frightened. Please indicate how often each thought occurs when you are nervous. Rate from 1–5 using the scale below.

1 = Thought never occurs
2 = Thought rarely occurs
3 = Thought occurs during half of the times I am nervous
4 = Thought usually occurs
5 = Thought always occurs when I am nervous

_____ 1. I am going to throw up.
_____ 2. I am going to pass out.
_____ 3. I must have a brain tumor.
_____ 4. I will have a heart attack.
_____ 5. I will choke to death.
_____ 6. I am going to act foolish.
_____ 7. I am going blind.
_____ 8. I will not be able to control myself.
_____ 9. I will hurt someone.
_____ 10. I am going to have a stroke.
_____ 11. I am going to go crazy.
_____ 12. I am going to scream.
_____ 13. I am going to babble or talk funny.
_____ 14. I will be paralyzed by fear.
_____ 15. Other ideas not listed (Please describe and rate them)

ALCOHOL BELIEFS SCALE (ABS)

AUTHOR: Gerard J. Connors and Stephen A. Maisto

PURPOSE: To measure beliefs and expectations about alcohol's effect.

DESCRIPTION: This 29-item instrument assesses one's beliefs about the effects of alcohol and its usefulness. The ABS is composed of two parts. Part A contains 17 items assessing the impact of different amounts of alcohol on behaviors and affect. This portion of the instrument assesses four domains of alcohol's effect: control issues (CI; items 1, 8, 11, 15); sensations (SEN; items 5, 7, 9, 13); capability issues (CAP; items 2, 6, 10, 12, 14, 17); and social issues (SI; items 3, 4, 16). Part B consists of 12 items where a respondent indicates how useful the consumption of different doses of alcohol would be, such as in self-medication or in order to forget worries. Part B has three factors or subscales: useful for feeling better (FB: items 4, 8, 9, 10); useful for feeling in charge (FC; items 1, 5, 6, 12); useful for relieving emotional distress (RED; items 3, 7, 11). These subscales may be useful in monitoring change, in treatment planning, or when the goals of treatment include cognitive restructuring.

NORMS: From a sample of 420 male drinkers including 250 inpatient alcoholics, 79 problem drinkers, and 81 non-problem drinkers, the means (and standard deviations) for CI were .03 (2.11), −.49 (1.91), −.55 (1.32), respectively. The mean CAP scores were −.43 (1.78), −.66 (1.72), and −1.03 (1.31) for alcoholics, problem drinkers, and non-problem drinkers, respectively. Norms for the other subscales are not reported.

SCORING: Part A is scored on an eleven-point rating scale from "strong decrease in the behavior or feeling" (−5) to "strong increase in the behavior or feeling" (+5). This rating is made for three different quantities of alcohol consumption. Part B instructs a respondent to note the usefulness of the three levels of alcohol consumption over a four-hour period. Again, an eleven-point scale is used ranging from "not at all useful" (0) to "very useful" (10). Scale scores are the total of item scores divided by the number of subscale items. Scores range from −5 to +5 for the subscales in Part A, and 0 to 11 for those in Part B.

RELIABILITY: Data on reliability were not available for the ABS.

VALIDITY: The ABS has demonstrated known-groups validity, distinguishing among groups of alcoholic addicts, problem drinkers, and drinkers with no problems. There were also differences on the responses due to different doses of alcohol. Non-problem drinkers expected greater impairment on control issues and capability issues subscales than problem drinkers; in turn, addicts reported less impairment than the problem drinkers. Usefulness (Part B) also differed based on amount of alcohol consumed.

PRIMARY REFERENCE: Connors, G. J. and Maisto, S. A. (1988). Alcohol Beliefs Scale. In M. Hersen and A. S. Bellack (eds.), *Dictionary of Behavioral Assessment Techniques*, pp. 24–26. New York: Pergamon Press. Instrument reproduced with permission of Gerard J. Connors.

AVAILABILITY: Dr. Gerard J. Connors, Research Institute on Alcoholism, 1021 Main Street, Buffalo, NY 14203.

ABS

Please answer the questions in Parts A and B below using the following definition of 1 standard drink. One (1) standard drink contains either 1 oz. spirits (hard liquor), or 12 oz. of beer, or 4 oz. table wine (12%).
We want you to answer every question on this form using three different levels of drinking. Those levels are (1) after consuming 1–3 standard drinks, (2) after 4–6 standard drinks, and (3) when "drunk."

Before starting, please indicate here how many standard drinks it takes to make you feel "drunk": _____ standard drinks.

Part A

Please rate the extent to which 1–3 standard drinks, 4–6 standard drinks, and "drunkenness" will cause, for you, a decrease or increase in the following behaviors and feelings over a four-hour period (including time spent drinking). Use the following scale to indicate your ratings, which are to be written in the appropriate spaces for each question.

−5	−4	−3	−2	−1	0	1	2	3	4	5

Strong decrease in the behavior or feeling	No change in the behavior or feeling	Strong increase in the behavior or feeling

Behavior or Feeling	1–3 Standard drinks	4–6 Standard drinks	When "drunk"
1. Feeling in control of a situation	____	____	____
2. Stress	____	____	____
3. Elation	____	____	____
4. Interacting in groups	____	____	____
5. Depression	____	____	____
6. Making decisions	____	____	____
7. Nonsocial anxiety (e.g., caused by wild animals or sickness)	____	____	____

Behavior or Feeling	1–3 Standard drinks	4–6 Standard drinks	When "drunk"
8. Feeling powerful	_____	_____	_____
9. Light-headed	_____	_____	_____
10. Speed at which you react to something	_____	_____	_____
11. Problem solving	_____	_____	_____
12. Thinking clearly	_____	_____	_____
13. Head spinning	_____	_____	_____
14. Ability to drive a car	_____	_____	_____
15. Judgment	_____	_____	_____
16. Feelings of courage	_____	_____	_____
17. Estimation of the passage of time	_____	_____	_____

Part B

Rate the extent to which *you* feel 1–3 standard drinks, 4–6 standard drinks, and "drunkenness" are useful for the following reasons over a four-hour period (including drinking time). Use the following scale to make your ratings:

0	1	2	3	4	5	6	7	8	9	10

Not at all — Moderately useful — Very useful

"Reason" to Drink	1–3 Standard drinks	4–6 Standard drinks	When "drunk"
1. Increase the effects of other drugs	___	___	___
2. Be more sociable	___	___	___
3. Relieve depression	___	___	___
4. Get in a better mood	___	___	___
5. Increase courage	___	___	___
6. Be aggressive	___	___	___
7. Escape stress	___	___	___
8. Feel happy	___	___	___
9. Become disinhibited	___	___	___
10. Feel you have more control over what's happening	___	___	___
11. Forget worries	___	___	___
12. Attract attention to yourself	___	___	___

ARGUMENTATIVENESS SCALE (ARG)

AUTHORS: Dominic A. Infante and Andrew S. Rancer

PURPOSE: To measure argumentativeness.

DESCRIPTION: The ARG is a 20-item scale designed to measure the tendency to argue about controversial issues (or argumentativeness). Argumentativeness is viewed as a generally stable trait which predisposes the individual in communication situations to advocate positions on controversial issues and to attack verbally the positions other people take on those issues. Ten of the items indicate a tendency to approach argumentative situations and ten involve the tendency to avoid argumentative situations. The ARG is considered useful for examining communication and social conflict and dysfunctional communication. Both areas have implications for clinical practice in that high scores on the ARG may identify the incessant arguer whose behavior impairs interpersonal relations while very low scores may identify people who almost never dispute an issue and are compliant and/or easily manipulated. Thus, the ARG may prove useful particularly in couple and family counseling.

NORMS: A series of studies largely involving over 800 students in undergraduate communication courses formed the basis for much of the research on the ARG. No demographic data are reported nor are actual norms.

SCORING: Scores for each item ranging from 1 to 5 are totaled separately for the two dimensions. The total score for the tendency to avoid argumentative situations (items 1, 3, 5, 6, 8, 10, 12, 14, 16, 19) is subtracted from the total score for the tendency to approach argumentative situations (2, 4, 7, 9, 11, 13, 15, 17, 18, 20) to provide an overall score for the argumentativeness trait.

RELIABILITY: The ARG has good to excellent internal consistency, with the approach dimension (ARG ap) having a coefficient alpha of .91 and the avoidance dimension (ARG av) having an alpha of .86. The ARG also is a stable instrument with an overall ARG test-retest reliability (one week) of .91 and test-retest reliabilities of .87 for ARG ap and .86 for ARG av.

VALIDITY: The ARG has fairly good concurrent validity, correlating significantly and in the expected direction with three other measures of communication predispositions. In addition, the ARG significantly correlates with friends' ratings of argumentativeness. Further, the ARG has some degree of construct validity in accurately predicting a series of behavioral choices which should and should not correlate with argumentativeness.

PRIMARY REFERENCE: Infante, D. A. and Rancer, A. S. (1982). A conceptualization and measure of argumentativeness, *Journal of Personality Assessment*, 46, 72–80. Instrument reproduced with permission of Dominic A. Infante and the *Journal of Personality Assessment*.

AVAILABILITY: Journal article.

ARG

This questionnaire contains statements about arguing controversial issues. Indicate how often each statement is true for you personally by placing the appropriate number in the blank to the left of the statement. If the statement is *almost never true* for you, place a "1" in the blank. If the statement is *rarely true* for you, place a "2" in the blank. If the statement is *occasionally true* for you, place a "3" in the blank. If the statement is *often true* for you, place a "4" in the blank. If the statement is *almost always true* for you, place a "5" in the blank.

_____   1.   While in an argument, I worry that the person I am arguing with will form a negative impression of me.

_____   2.   Arguing over controversial issues improves my intelligence.

_____   3.   I enjoy avoiding arguments.

_____   4.   I am energetic and enthusiastic when I argue.

_____   5.   Once I finish an argument I promise myself that I will not get into another.

_____   6.   Arguing with a person creates more problems for me than it solves.

_____   7.   I have a pleasant, good feeling when I win a point in an argument.

_____   8.   When I finish arguing with someone I feel nervous and upset.

_____   9.   I enjoy a good argument over a controversial issue.

_____ 10.   I get an unpleasant feeling when I realize I am about to get into an argument.

_____ 11.   I enjoy defending my point of view on an issue.

_____ 12.   I am happy when I keep an argument from happening.

_____ 13.   I do not like to miss the opportunity to argue a controversial issue.

_____ 14.   I prefer being with people who rarely disagree with me.

_____ 15.   I consider an argument an exciting intellectual challenge.

_____ 16.   I find myself unable to think of effective points during an argument.

_____ 17.   I feel refreshed and satisfied after an argument on a controversial issue.

_____ 18.   I have the ability to do well in an argument.

_____ 19.   I try to avoid getting into arguments.

_____ 20.   I feel excitement when I expect that a conversation I am in is leading to an argument.

ASCRIPTION OF RESPONSIBILITY QUESTIONNAIRE (ARQ)

AUTHORS: A. Ralph Hakstian and Peter Suedfeld

PURPOSE: To measure willingness to ascribe specific responsibility.

DESCRIPTION: The ARQ is a 40-item instrument designed to measure one's ascription of responsibility. Conceptually, ascription of responsibility is similar to locus of responsibility and locus of control. The ARQ is composed of four subscales: traditional focused (TF: items 1, 5, 14, 18, 22, 26, 29, 31, 33, 39) reflects ascription of responsibility to traditional authority such as parents and schools and is closely related to conservatism; diffused responsibility (DR: items = 2, 6, 8, 11, 15, 19, 23, 27, 30, 34, 36, 38) is the tendency to see social groups as the locus of authority; exercised responsibility (ER: items = 3, 9, 12, 16, 20, 24, 40) assesses how much a person has exercised authority; and individual focused responsibility (IFR: items 4, 7, 10, 13, 17, 21, 25, 28, 32, 35, 37) reflects belief in more inner-directed individualistic ethics.

NORMS: Normative data are available from a sample of 654 university undergraduates. There are no normative differences between women and men. The TF had a mean of 46.65 and a standard deviation of 10.53. For the DF the mean was 56.13 and standard deviation was 9.03. For ER the figures are 36.67 and 6.76, and for IFR the mean and standard deviations were 56.91 and 7.93.

SCORING: After reverse-scoring item 12, scores for each subscale are simply the sums of the scores on designated items. In order to maintain a common score range, the summed score may be divided by the number of subscale items. This will produce a score range from 1 to 7, with higher scores reflecting more ascription of responsibility.

RELIABILITY: The subscales have modest internal consistency. From two studies of college students, alpha coefficients ranged from .56 to .76 and averaged .68. The test-retest coefficient of stability for a one-week period ranged from .74 to .90, and averaged .84.

VALIDITY: Concurrent validity was evidenced by correlations with scores on conceptually related scales. The ARQ scores did not correlate with Rotter's Locus of Control Scale. Some evidence of known-groups validity is available as seen in differences in TF scores for Catholics and Protestants compared to respondents with no religious affiliation.

PRIMARY REFERENCE: Hakstian, A. R., Suedfeld, P., Ballard, E. J., and Rank, D. S. (1986). The Ascription of Responsibility Questionnaire: Development and empirical extensions, *Journal of Personality Assessment*, 50, 229–247. Instrument reproduced with permission of A. Ralph Hakstian.

AVAILABILITY: The Free Press.

ARQ

Indicate the extent to which you are in agreement with each item by putting one number next to the item.

7 = Agree strongly
6 = Agree somewhat
5 = Agree slightly
4 = Neither agree nor disagree
3 = Disagree slightly
2 = Disagree somewhat
1 = Disagree strongly

_____ 1. I have always respected my parents highly.
_____ 2. Fate plays an important role in our lives.
_____ 3. I have a lot of responsibility in my present job and extracurricular activities.
_____ 4. Most people on welfare are lazy.
_____ 5. I attended church often as a child.
_____ 6. All old people should get a pension.
_____ 7. Ability should be rewarded.
_____ 8. The state is responsible for the well-being of its citizens.
_____ 9. I enjoy taking charge of things.
_____ 10. Good behavior should be rewarded, bad behavior punished.
_____ 11. As a student, I would feel students should have a say in which professors receive tenure.
_____ 12. I prefer following rather than leading.
_____ 13. Every sane individual is responsible for his every action.
_____ 14. My family and I are very close.
_____ 15. Our country should take the first step toward world disarmament.
_____ 16. I often make suggestions.
_____ 17. Robbery with violence should be severely punished.
_____ 18. My parents were always willing to give me advice on things that were important to me.
_____ 19. Students should decide how they want their teachers to evaluate their knowledge of the course.
_____ 20. I was given a lot of responsibility as a child.
_____ 21. Your personality is what you make it.
_____ 22. Pornography should be censored to protect the innocent.
_____ 23. As a student, I would feel that what I study should be completely up to me.
_____ 24. I have often been a group leader.
_____ 25. Society should reward only merit.
_____ 26. Human destiny is ordained by a Supreme Being.
_____ 27. When a country has done its utmost, but does not have the resources to maintain itself, it is the responsibility of other countries to come to its aid.
_____ 28. Justice is better than mercy.
_____ 29. People can be controlled by supernatural forces.

_____ 30. As a teacher, I would feel it is my job to make sure none of my students fails my course.

_____ 31. I enjoyed going to church.

_____ 32. If a child insists on having a pet, he should be responsible for its care.

_____ 33. Heaven is the reward for those who have followed the precepts of their belief.

_____ 34. All decisions should be made by groups.

_____ 35. Parents should not financially support offspring who could make a living for themselves.

_____ 36. Students should have equal representation at all levels of school administration concerning any policy.

_____ 37. Society does not owe you a living.

_____ 38. Students should be responsible for the evaluation and firing of teachers.

_____ 39. My parents attended church often when I was a child.

_____ 40. I have held many positions of responsibility in the past in my job(s) and extracurricular activities.

ASSERTION INVENTORY (AI)

AUTHORS: Eileen Gambrill and Cheryl Richey

PURPOSE: To measure three aspects of assertiveness.

DESCRIPTION: This versatile 40-item instrument measures three aspects of assertion: discomfort with assertion (DAI), response probability (RP) of engaging in assertive behavior, and identification of situations (IS) where assertion needs improvement. In order to calculate scores on all three scales, each item must be answered three times. However, any one of the three scores can be used. The measure can also be used to characterize a client as "assertive," "unassertive," "anxious performer," and "doesn't care." This typology is helpful in selecting an intervention which best fits the type of assertion problem of the client. Finally, in terms of known gender differences on assertion, the AI compares favorably with other assertion instruments by having a balance between negative and positive assertive behaviors.

NORMS: Normative data are available on samples of college students in Berkeley and Seattle ($N = 608$). The mean DAI, RP, and IS scores were 93.9,103.8, and 10.1, respectively.

SCORING: DAI scores and RP scores are the sums of the ratings on each item in the respective columns. The IS score is the total number of items circled. Client profiles are determined by categorizing scores from the DAI and RP scores as follows:

RP Scores

		≥ 105	≤ 104
DAI Score	≥ 96	Unassertive	Anxious performer
	≤ 95	Doesn't care	Assertive

For example, if a client's DAI score is greater than or equal to 96 and the RP score is greater than or equal to 105, the client's problem would be considered unassertive. The AI can also be scored as eleven factors reflecting specific situations of discomfort (see primary reference.)

RELIABILITY: The AI has very good stability, with test-retest correlations of .87 and .81 for DAI scores and RP scores respectively. Data on internal consistency were not available.

VALIDITY: The validity support of the AI is very strong. Tests of known-groups validity illustrate that scores discriminate between clinical and "normal" samples. The instrument also is sensitive to change, as demonstrated by differences between pre- and posttherapy scores.

PRIMARY REFERENCE: Gambrill, E. D. and Richey, C. A. (1975). An assertion inventory for use in assessment and research, *Behavior Therapy*, 6, 550–561. Instrument reproduced with permission of Cheryl A. Richey.

AVAILABILITY: Dr. Cheryl A. Richey, School of Social Work (JH-30), 4101 15th Avenue N.E., University of Washington, Seattle, WA 98195.

AI

Many people experience difficulty in handling interpersonal situations requiring them to assert themselves in some way, for example, turning down a request or asking a favor. Please indicate your degree of discomfort or anxiety in the space provided before each situation listed below. Use the following scale to indicate degree of discomfort.

1 = None
2 = A little
3 = A fair amount
4 = Much
5 = Very much

Then, go over the list a second time and indicate after each item the probability or likelihood of responding as described if actually presented with the situation.* For example, if you rarely apologize when you are at fault, you would mark "4"after that item. Use the following scale to indicate response probability:

1 = Always do it
2 = Usually do it
3 = Do it about half the time
4 = Rarely do it
S = Never do it

Please indicate the situations you would like to handle more assertively by placing a circle around the item number.

*Note: It is important to assess your discomfort ratings apart from your response probability. Otherwise, one may influence the other. To prevent this, place a piece of paper over your discomfort ratings while responding to the situation a second time for response probability.

Degree of Discomfort		Situation	Response Probability
____	1.	Turn down a request to borrow your car	____
____	2.	Compliment a friend	____
____	3.	Ask a favor of someone	____
____	4.	Resist sales pressure	____
____	5.	Apologize when you are at fault	____
____	6.	Turn down a request for a meeting or date	____
____	7.	Admit fear and request consideration	____
____	8.	Tell a person with whom you are intimately involved when he or she says or does something that bothers you	____
____	9.	Ask for a raise	____
____	10.	Admit ignorance in some area	____

Degree of Discomfort		Situation	Response Probability
____	11.	Turn down a request to borrow money	____
____	12.	Ask personal questions	____
____	13.	Turn off a talkative friend	____
____	14.	Ask for constructive criticism	____
____	15.	Initiate a conversation with a stranger	____
____	16.	Compliment a person you are romantically involved with or interested in	____
____	17.	Request a meeting or a date with a person	____
____	18.	Your initial request for a meeting is turned down and you ask the person again at a later time	____
____	19.	Admit confusion about a point under discussion and ask for clarification	____
____	20.	Apply for a job	____
____	21.	Ask whether you have offended someone	____
____	22.	Tell someone that you like him or her	____
____	23.	Request expected service when such is not forthcoming, for example, in a restaurant	____
____	24.	Discuss openly with a person his or her criticism of your behavior	____
____	25.	Return defective items in a store or restaurant	____
____	26.	Express an opinion that differs from that of the person with whom you are talking	____
____	27.	Resist sexual overtures when you are not interested	____
____	28.	Tell a person when you feel that he or she has done something that is unfair to you	____
____	29.	Accept a date	____
____	30.	Tell someone good news about yourself	____
____	31.	Resist pressure to drink	____
____	32.	Resist a significant person's unfair demand	____
____	33.	Quit a job	____
____	34.	Resist pressure to use drugs	____
____	35.	Discuss openly with a person his or her criticism of your work	____
____	36.	Request the return of a borrowed item	____
____	37.	Receive compliments	____
____	38.	Continue to converse with someone who disagrees with you	____
____	39.	Tell a friend or co-worker when he or she says or does something that bothers you	____
____	40.	Ask a person who is annoying you in a public situation to stop	____

ASSERTION QUESTIONNAIRE IN DRUG USE (AQ-D)

AUTHORS: Dale A. Callner and Steven M. Ross

PURPOSE: To measure assertion in drug users.

DESCRIPTION: The AQ-D is a 40-item instrument designed to measure assertion in heavy drug users, particularly males. Six assertion content areas were
selected as most relevant to drug users: positive feedback (+F: items 1, 7,
13, 19, 26, 32), negative feedback (−F: items 2, 8, 14, 20, 27, 33), drug (D:
items 3, 9, 15, 21, 28, 37), authority (A: items 4, 10, 16, 22, 29, 38),
heterosexual (H: items 5, 11, 17, 23, 30, 35), and general assertiveness (Gen.:
items 6, 12, 18, 24, 25, 31, 34, 36, 39, 40). This measure is seen as particularly
useful in work with substance abusers where assertion or social skills
training is a major intervention.

NORMS: The AQ-D was studied initially with 16 male veterans who were
inpatients in a drug abuse program (age range from 18 to 25), and 16
age-matched veterans who were not drug users and were solicited from the
community. The drug use group had a mean of 8.5 years of education and
the nondrug-use group had a mean of 9.4 years. All subjects were either
divorced or married. No actual norms were presented.

SCORING: Respondents rate each item on the AQ-D on a 4-point scale with
items summed for scores on the content area scales or total scales. The total
score can range from −80 to +80, the Gen subscale (10 items) from −20 to
+20, and the remaining content areas (six items each) from −12 to +12. High
positive scores represent extreme assertive ratings and high negative scores
represent extreme nonassertive ratings.

RELIABILITY: The AQ-D has very good stability, with a seven-day test-retest
correlation of .86. No data on internal consistency were presented.

VALIDITY: The AQ-D has excellent concurrent validity, with correlations
ranging from .71 to .95 with self-ratings of assertion and behavioral ratings
of role plays.

PRIMARY REFERENCE: Callner, D. A. and Ross, S. M. (1976). The reliability and
validity of three measures of assertion in a drug addict population, *Behavior
Therapy*, 7, 659–667. Instrument reprinted by permission of publisher and
authors.

AVAILABILITY: Dr. Steven M. Ross, Veterans Administration Medical Center,
Salt Lake City, UT 84148.

AQ-D

Please record your response to each item in the space to the left using the following scale:

$$-2 = \text{Never descriptive of me}$$
$$-1 = \text{Usually not descriptive of me}$$
$$+1 = \text{Usually descriptive of me}$$
$$+2 = \text{Always descriptive of me}$$

_____ 1. When someone says something nice to me, I have a hard time taking their compliment.

_____ 2. I usually avoid complaining about the poor service in a restaurant

_____ 3. I have no trouble telling friends not to bring drugs over to my house.

_____ 4. If I disagreed with the director of the drug program on something he said, I probably would not openly express my opinions.

_____ 5. I never have a hard time getting up enough nerve to call up girls to ask them out for dates.

_____ 6. In general, I believe that the only way to make new friends is to get out and find them yourself.

_____ 7. I have a problem with telling someone that I like them.

_____ 8. I have a hard time criticizing others even when I know that they are wrong and I am right.

_____ 9. If I knew of a person on the ward taking drugs on the sly, I probably would not bring it up in a group meeting.

_____ 10. I never feel shaky and overly nervous when I think of asking a boss for a raise.

_____ 11. In general, I am outgoing and aggressive with girls that I take out.

_____ 12. I usually take the lead when with a group of friends.

_____ 13. I often don't say some of the nice things that I am thinking about some people.

_____ 14. Anyone attempting to push ahead of me in a line is in for a good battle.

_____ 15. When it comes to drugs, I have a hard time turning them down, even when I really want to.

_____ 16. I usually hesitate to make phone calls to business establishments and institutions.

_____ 17. I usually wait for the girl to make physical advances towards me before I make physical advances towards her.

_____ 18. I believe that following the lead of others is more desirable than leading them yourself.

_____ 19. I never have a hard time saying nice things and complimenting other people.

_____ 20. If someone took the parking place that I had been waiting for, I would be mad, but I would probably drive off without saying anything.

_____ 21. Drugs allow me to be more aggressive and outgoing than I normally would be.

_____ 22. If a policeman started to give me a ticket for speeding, I would try to talk him out of it.

_____ 23. I have little trouble in starting a conversation with girls that I have just met or been introduced to.
_____ 24. Most people seem to be more aggressive and assertive than I am.
_____ 25. I never avoid asking questions for fear of sounding stupid.
_____ 26. If one of my friends was very depressed, I would go up and try to make him feel better.
_____ 27. During an argument, I usually keep my real feelings bottled up inside and do not express them.
_____ 28. If I were at a good party and a person that I just met offered me some free drugs, I would turn him down without any trouble.
_____ 29. If I were applying for a job that I had a lot of experience for, and the employer told me that I didn't have enough experience, I would try to convince him that I did.
_____ 30. Showing affection with girls has been a problem for me.
_____ 31. I tend to let my feelings be known rather than keeping them bottled up inside of me.
_____ 32. I never get embarrassed whenever I try to give someone a compliment.
_____ 33. If I stopped at the laundry to pick up my shirts and the clerk told me that some of them had been lost, I probably would just walk out and not say anything.
_____ 34. I am open and frank about my feelings.
_____ 35. I am afraid of asking girls out because I would feel rejected if they refused.
_____ 36. To be honest, people often take advantage of me.
_____ 37. I have no problem turning down drugs when they are offered to me.
_____ 38. In general, I get overly nervous whenever I have to talk to people in authority positions.
_____ 39. I would not describe myself as shy.
_____ 40. In general, I don't hesitate to openly express my opinions when in a group of people.

ASSERTION SELF-STATEMENT TEST—REVISED (ASST-R)

AUTHORS: Richard G. Heimberg, Emil J. Chiauzzi, Robert E. Becker, and Rita Madrazo-Peterson

PURPOSE: To measure self-statements in relation to assertiveness.

DESCRIPTION: The ASST-R is a 24-item instrument designed to assess the role of self-statements in assertive (or nonassertive) behaviors. Self-statements are assumed to have a crucial role in affecting assertiveness and unassertiveness, especially by cognitive and cognitive-behavior therapists. The ASST-R was devised to be used to teach these self-statements and to assess the relationship to assertiveness. The ASST-R consists of 12 positive and 12 negative self-statements. The ASST-R is viewed as a useful measure for teaching cognitive changes in problems involving nonassertive behavior.

NORMS: The ASST-R was studied with three samples including 12 psychiatric patients of mixed diagnosis randomly selected from a mental health clinic in Albany, New York; 16 "normal" adults from the center's nonprofessional staff; and 20 college students from undergraduate psychology courses at SUNY-Albany. The means for positive self-statements were: students = 44, "normal" adults = 39, psychiatric patients = 33. The means for negative self-statements were: students = 27, "normal" adults = 23, psychiatric patients = 37.

SCORING: Each item is rated for frequency on a 5-point scale and the individual items are summed for scores on the positive and negative dimensions. Total scores are not used. Positive items = 3, 5, 6, 9, 13, 14–16, 19, 21–23. Negative items = 1, 2, 4, 7, 8, 10–12, 17, 18, 20, 24.

RELIABILITY: No data were reported.

VALIDITY: The ASST-R has good known-groups validity, significantly discriminating between patients and the other two groups on negative and positive statements. There also was a significant difference between subjects evaluated as high and low in assertion on negative self-statements (but not positive statements).

PRIMARY REFERENCE: Heimberg, R. G., Chiauzzi, E. J., Becker, R. E., and Madrazo-Peterson, R. (1983). Cognitive mediation of assertive behavior: An analysis of the self-statement patterns of college students, psychiatric patients, and normal adults, *Cognitive Therapy and Research*, 7, 455–464.

AVAILABILITY: Dr. Richard Heimberg, Department of Psychology, SUNY-Albany, 1400 Washington Avenue, Albany, NY 12222.

ASST-R

It is obvious that people think a variety of things when they are responding in different situations. These thoughts, along with feelings, determine what kind of responses a person will make.

Below is a list of things which you may have thought to yourself at some time while responding in the assertive situations. Read each item and decide how frequently you may have been thinking a similar thought during the assertive situations.

Circle a number from 1 to 5 for each item. The scale is interpreted as follows:

1 = *Hardly ever* had the thought
2 = *Rarely* had the thought
3 = *Sometimes* had the thought
4 = *Often* had the thought
5 = *Very often* had the thought

Please answer as honestly as possible.

1. I was thinking that I was too nervous to say what I felt.

    1   2   3   4   5

2. I was thinking that the other person would suspect some ulterior motive if I said anything.

    1   2   3   4   5

3. I was thinking that the other person should respect an honest expression of feelings.

    1   2   3   4   5

4. I was thinking that many people fail to get involved or stand up for themselves in similar situations, so there is nothing wrong with my keeping quiet.

    1   2   3   4   5

5. I was thinking that I could benefit by expressing myself.

    1   2   3   4   5

6. I was thinking that I should act in accord with what I think is right.

    1   2   3   4   5

7. I was thinking that if I could avoid this situation, I could somehow relieve my discomfort.

    1   2   3   4   5

8. I was thinking that it would be selfish of me to let my own feelings be known.

    1   2   3   4   5

9. I was thinking that I could express myself in a calm, relaxed way.

    1   2   3   4   5

10. I was thinking that I would appear incompetent or inadequate if I tried to take a stand.

    1   2   3   4   5

11. I was thinking that something bad would happen to me if I tried to express myself.

    1   2   3   4   5

12. I was thinking that the other person wouldn't like me if I offered my opinion.

    1   2   3   4   5

13. I was thinking that my opinions and decisions should be respected if they are reasonable.

    1   2   3   4   5

14. I was thinking that since letting my feelings be known was an effective course of action in the past, I should do likewise now.

    1   2   3   4   5

15. I was thinking that I would only be hurting myself by not expressing myself.

    1   2   3   4   5

16. I was thinking that future interactions with the other person might be damaged if I didn't say what I felt now.

    1   2   3   4   5

17.   I was thinking that since similar past experiences resulted in failure or ineffectiveness, I shouldn't bother to do anything now.

1   2   3   4   5

18.   I was thinking that I would probably feel guilty later if I refused to do the person a favor.

1   2   3   4   5

19.   I was thinking that there didn't seem to be a good reason why I shouldn't speak my mind.

1   2   3   4   5

20.   I was thinking that I would become embarrassed if I let my feelings be known.

1   2   3   4   5

21.   I was thinking that if I didn't state my opinion now, it might cause problems later on.

1   2   3   4   5

22.   I was thinking that my views are important.

1   2   3   4   5

23.   I was thinking that if I didn't speak up, it will interfere with my plans.

1   2   3   4   5

24.   I was thinking that a friendly person would not impose his/her views in this situation.

1   2   3   4   5

ASSERTIVE JOB-HUNTING SURVEY (AJHS)

AUTHOR: Heather A. Becker

PURPOSE: To measure self-reported job-hunting assertiveness.

DESCRIPTION: The AJHS is a 25-item questionnaire designed to assess assertiveness in hunting for jobs—that is, the extent to which the respondent acts on his or her environment to procure information, establish contact persons in organizations, and so on. Developed originally from a pool of 35 items based on the job-hunting literature, the items on the complete instrument were designed to reflect all aspects of job-hunting including resumé writing, contacting prospective employees, soliciting recommendations, and interviewing. The AJHS can be used in classes or assertive training groups, as an outcome measure, to stimulate discussion of job-hunting assertiveness, and as a research tool for investigating correlates of assertiveness in job hunting.

NORMS: Norms for the AJHS were established on 190 college students who had applied at a university center for career planning or job assistance. (Several hundred other students also have been studied.) The norm group included 50% men and 50% women, and represented all classifications from freshman to graduate students and a wide range of academic areas. Mean responses for each item are available in the primary reference; the overall mean score was 105.55. Scores for subgroups of students are not provided.

SCORING: Items 1, 2, 4, 5, 7, 8, 10–12, 14, 15, 17, 19, 20, 22–25 are reverse-scored on the 6-point scales, with all responses then summed. This provides a range of 25 to 150, with higher scores indicating more assertive responses.

RELIABILITY: The AJHS has good internal consistency, with a coefficient alpha of .82. The instrument also has good stability, with a two-month test-retest reliability of .77.

VALIDITY: The AJHS established a form of concurrent validity, with a significant correlation between previous job-hunting experience and scores on the AJHS. The AJHS also is sensitive to change, showing significant pre- to posttest changes in two assertive job-hunting classes. No other validity data were reported.

PRIMARY REFERENCE: Becker, H. A. (1980). The Assertive Job-Hunting Survey, *Measurement and Evaluation in Guidance*, 13, 43–48. Instrument reproduced with permission of Heather Becker.

AVAILABILITY: Dr. Heather Becker, 2734 Trail of the Madrones, Austin, TX 78746

AJHS

For each of the following items, please indicate to the left of the item how likely you would be to respond in a job-hunting situation using the scale below.

1 = Very unlikely
2 = Rather unlikely
3 = Unlikely
4 = Likely
5 = Rather likely
6 = Very likely

_____ 1. Would mention only paid work experience
_____ 2. Reluctant to ask for more information
_____ 3. Would ask employers if they knew of other employers
_____ 4. Downplay my qualifications
_____ 5. Would rather use an employment agency
_____ 6. Would contact employee to learn more about organization
_____ 7. Hesitate to ask questions when interviewed
_____ 8. Avoid contacting employers because they're too busy
_____ 9. Would leave or arrange another appointment
_____ 10. Experienced employment counselor knows best
_____ 11. If employer too busy, would stop trying to contact
_____ 12. Getting job largely luck
_____ 13. Would directly contact employer, rather than personnel
_____ 14. Reluctant to contact employer unless there's opening
_____ 15. Would not apply unless had all qualifications
_____ 16. Would not ask for a second interview
_____ 17. Reluctant to contact employer unless there's opening
_____ 18. Would ask employer how to improve chances for another position
_____ 19. Feel uncomfortable asking friends for job leads
_____ 20. Better take whatever job I can get
_____ 21. If personnel didn't refer me, directly contact the person
_____ 22. Would rather interview with recruiters
_____ 23. Figure there's nothing else to do
_____ 24. Check out openings before deciding what to do
_____ 25. Reluctant to contact someone I don't know for information

ASSERTIVENESS SELF-REPORT INVENTORY (ASRI)

AUTHORS: Sharon D. Herzberger, Esther Chan, and Judith Katz

PURPOSE: To measure assertiveness.

DESCRIPTION: The ASRI is a 25-item instrument specifically developed to overcome criticisms of other measures of assertiveness: it is specific, in that items indicate the behavior, situation, and other people involved; it focuses on behavioral and affective dimensions of assertiveness; it is relatively short; it is broadly conceptualized; and details about development of the items for the scale are reported. The ASRI is simple to administer and to score. Items were generated by upper-level psychology students who were studying test construction and the construct of assertiveness. Those items that were not strongly endorsed in a preliminary study, that were correlated with social desirability, or that were not significantly correlated with the total score were dropped, leaving these 25 items.

NORMS: Initial work on the ASRI has been conducted with college students and not on clinical populations. A series of studies was conducted with 268 students (96 males and 172 females). Mean scores for males in different testing sessions ranged from 9.54 to 10.63 and for females from 9.81 to 10.71. There were no significant male-female differences.

SCORING: The total score is derived simply by adding the total number of "true" responses for items 1, 3, 4, 9, 13, 15, 16, 18–20, 22, 24 to "false" responses for remaining items.

RELIABILITY: The ASRI has good stability with a five-week test-retest correlation of .81. Data were not reported on internal consistency.

VALIDITY: The ASRI has good concurrent validity, correlating significantly with the Rathus Assertiveness Schedule. Further, the ASRI was not significantly correlated with subscales of the Buss-Durkee Aggression Inventory, suggesting that assertiveness and aggression are independent constructs. The ASRI also significantly predicted respondents' assertive solutions to specific dilemmas and peer-rated assertiveness, thus suggesting fair predictive validity.

PRIMARY REFERENCE: Herzberger, S. D., Chan, E., and Katz, J. (1984). The development of an assertiveness self-report inventory, *Journal of Personality Assessment*, 48, 317–323. Instrument reproduced with permission of Sharon D. Herzberger and the Journal of Personality Assessment.

AVAILABILITY: Journal article.

ASRI

Read each question carefully and answer all 25 of them. Circle either "True" (T) or "False" (F), whichever most represents your viewpoint.

T F   1. When my date has acted rudely at a party, I don't hesitate to let him/her know I don't like it.
T F   2. I feel guilty after I ask my neighbor to be quiet after midnight on a weeknight.
T F   3. After eating an excellent meal at a restaurant, I do not hesitate to compliment the chef.
T F   4. If I were stood up on a date I would tell the person who stood me up that I felt angry.
T F   5. When I get a terrible haircut and my hair stylist/barber asks me how I like it, I say I like it.
T F   6. I would feel self-conscious asking a question in a large lecture class.
T F   7. I usually let my friends have a larger portion of food at social gatherings and take a smaller one for myself.
T F   8. When on a date I act cheerful, even though I am depressed, so as not to upset my date's mood.
T F   9. I feel justified when I send improperly cooked food back to the kitchen in a restaurant.
T F   10. When people I don't know wear nice outfits, I hesitate to compliment them.
T F   11. I'm not likely to tell my date that I am irritated when he/she pays more attention to others and ignores me.
T F   12. I tip a consistent percentage to a waitress despite receiving poor service.
T F   13. When an interviewer cancels an appointment for the third time I tell him/her that I am annoyed.
T F   14. When a roommate makes a mess I would rather clean it up myself than confront him/her about it.
T F   15. If I received a call late at night from a casual acquaintance, I would say I was sleeping and ask not to be called so late.
T F   16. When people use my car and don't refill the tank, I let them know I feel unfairly treated.
T F   17. I find it difficult to ask a favor of a stranger.
T F   18. If my stereo were stolen, I wouldn't regret reporting it to the police even if I suspected a friend.
T F   19. If I were going out with friends for an evening and my boyfriend/girlfriend did not want me to, I would do it anyway.
T F   20. I feel comfortable engaging in discussions in a group
T F   21. I feel guilty when my boyfriend/girlfriend wants to go to a movie but we go where I wanted to instead.
T F   22. When my roommate consistently fails to take an accurate telephone message, I let him/her know I'm upset.
T F   23. When people use abusive language around me, I ignore it even though it bothers me.

T F   24. If someone makes loud noises when I am studying at the library I will express my discontent.

T F   25. I feel guilty telling my boyfriend/girlfriend that I have to do homework this evening instead of seeing him/her.

ASSERTIVENESS SELF-STATEMENT TEST (ASST)

AUTHORS: R. M. Schwartz and J. M. Gottman

PURPOSE: To measure cognitions related to assertion.

DESCRIPTION: The ASST is a 32-item instrument designed to measure cognitions—defined as self-statements—in assertion-related problems. The ASST is designed to be situation-specific rather than global and to be used when the cognitions are active in short-term memory to minimize distortion. Thus, recent situations that called for assertive behaviors can be focused on for each administration of the ASST. The ASST has two subscales relevant to the refusal of unreasonable requests: positive self-statements that facilitate (or make it easier to refuse) a request (items: 4, 5, 7, 9, 10, 12, 16, 17, 20, 23, 24, 26, 28, 30–32) and negative self-statements that interfere (or make it harder to refuse) with a request (items: 1–3, 6, 8, 11, 13–15, 18, 19, 21, 22, 25, 27, 29).

NORMS: The ASST was studied initially with undergraduate students. No other demographic data are available nor are actual norms.

SCORING: The ASST is easily scored by summing individual items for each of the subscales. The range for each subscale is from 16 to 80.

RELIABILITY: The ASST has fair internal consistency, with an alpha of .78. No data on stability are available.

VALIDITY: The ASST has good construct validity, consistently demonstrating that functional and dysfunctional groups differ in their frequency of positive and negative self-statements, and show predictable changes in self-statements (mainly a reduction in negative) as a result of psychotherapy. The ASST also has good concurrent validity, with correlations between negative self-statements and a measure of cognitive complexity and the Irrational Beliefs Test, and between the positive subscale and self-efficacy scores.

PRIMARY REFERENCE: Schwartz, R. M. and Gottman, J. M. (1976). Toward a task analysis of assertive behavior, *Journal of Consulting and Clinical Psychology*, 44, 910–920.

AVAILABILITY: Journal article.

ASST

It is obvious that people think a variety of things when they are responding in different situations. These thoughts, along with feelings, determine what kind of responses a person will make.

Below is a list of things which you may have thought to yourself at some time while responding in the assertive situations. Read each item and decide how frequently you may have been thinking a similar thought during the assertive situations.

Circle a number from 1 to 5 for each item. The scale is interpreted as follows:

1 = *Hardly ever* had the thought
2 = *Rarely* had the thought
3 = *Sometimes* had the thought
4 = *Often* had the thought
5 = *Very often* had the thought

Please answer as honestly as possible.

1. I was thinking that it was not worth the hassle to refuse.

   1   2   3   4   5

2. I was worried about what the other person would think about me if I refused.

   1   2   3   4   5

3. I was thinking that I would probably feel guilty later if I refused to do the person a favor.

   1   2   3   4   5

4. I was thinking that it is not my responsibility to help people I hardly know.

   1   2   3   4   5

5. I was thinking that there didn't seem to be a good reason why I should say yes.

   1   2   3   4   5

6. I was thinking that It was my responsibility to help those who need me.

   1   2   3   4   5

7.   I was thinking that I just don't feel like saying yes.

1   2   3   4   5

8.   I was worried that the person might become angry if I refused.

1   2   3   4   5

9.   I was thinking that this request is an unreasonable one.

1   2   3   4   5

10. I was thinking that the person could ask someone else.

1   2   3   4   5

11. I was thinking that it is better to help others than to be self-centered.

1   2   3   4   5

12. I was thinking that I will be happy later if I don't commit myself to something I don't want to do.

1   2   3   4   5

13. I was thinking that I would get embarrassed if I refused.

1   2   3   4   5

14. I was concerned that the person would think I was selfish if I refused.

1   2   3   4   5

15. I was thinking that this person really seems to need me.

1   2   3   4   5

16. I was thinking that I am perfectly free to say no.

1   2   3   4   5

17. I was thinking that if I don't say no now, I'll end up doing something I don't want to do.

1   2   3   4   5

18. I was thinking that it is always good to be helpful to other people.

    1   2   3   4   5

19. I was thinking that the person might be hurt or insulted if I refused.

    1   2   3   4   5

20. I was thinking that this person should take care of his/her own business.

    1   2   3   4   5

21. I was thinking that this request sounds pretty reasonable.

    1   2   3   4   5

22. I was thinking that people will dislike me if I always refuse.

    1   2   3   4   5

23. I was thinking that my own plans are too important.

    1   2   3   4   5

24. I was thinking that I don't have to please this person by giving in to his/her request.

    1   2   3   4   5

25. I was thinking that it is morally wrong to refuse someone who needs help.

    1   2   3   4   5

26. I was thinking that if I commit myself, it will interfere with my plans.

    1   2   3   4   5

27. I was thinking that a friendly person would not refuse in this situation.

    1   2   3   4   5

28. I was thinking that I am too busy now to say yes.

    1   2   3   4   5

29. I was afraid that there would be a scene if I said no.

    1   2   3   4   5

30.   I was thinking that since I hardly know the person, why should I go out of
      my way for him/her.

      1   2   3   4   5

31.   I was thinking that it doesn't matter what the person thinks of me.

      1   2   3   4   5

32.   I was thinking that this request is an imposition on me.

      1   2   3   4   5

AUDITORY HALLUCINATIONS QUESTIONNAIRE (AHQ)

AUTHORS: Harry H. Hustig and R. Julian Hafner

PURPOSE: To measure auditory hallucinations.

DESCRIPTION: The AHQ is a 9-item instrument (plus open-ended questions) that measures the presence and characteristics of auditory hallucinations. The AHQ also measures respondents' delusions and mood. The AHQ is filled out as a diary, three times a day at 8 A.M., 2 P.M., and 8 P.M. The first part of the diary requests respondents to write down their two most prominent delusions (referred to in the first two items). The AHQ has been used successfully with respondents diagnosed as schizophrenic, with persistent auditory hallucinations. Although each of the 9 scales is typically used as a separate scale, it may also be possible to use a total score for all scales (sum of 9 item responses) or to derive three scores, one for delusions (first 2 scales), one for hallucinations (next 4 scales), and one for mood (last 3 scales).

NORMS: The AHQ was studied initially with 12 individuals, all diagnosed as schizophrenic, with auditory hallucinations that persisted over 12 months. Eleven subjects were women (mean age of 32.6 years) whose auditory hallucinations had persisted for a mean of 4.5 years, and all reported persistent paranoid delusions of at least 2-years' duration. All respondents were receiving neuroleptic medication. Mean scores for the nine scale items, in order of their presentation on the instrument, for one week, were: delusions = 2.8, 2.8; hallucinations = 2.9, 2.2, 2.8, 3.1; and mood = 2.9, 3.0, 2.2. The mean for all 9 scales was 2.74 (total score = 24.7).

RELIABILITY: Reliability for the AHQ was determined by correlating scores made at the same time on seven occasions over 20 days, a type of test-retest reliability. The two delusion scales had a mean correlation of .84, the four hallucination scales had a mean correlation of .71, and the three mood scales had a mean correlation exceeding .74, suggesting good stability.

VALIDITY: A type of concurrent validity was determined by correlating each scale with all the others. This correlation matrix showed consistent significant relationships over time between quality of auditory relationships, mood, and strength of delusional beliefs.

PRIMARY REFERENCE: Hustig, H. H. and Hafner, R. J. (1990). Persistent auditory hallucinations and their relationship to delusions and mood, *Journal of Nervous and Mental Disease*, 178, 264–267. Instrument reprinted with permission of publisher and authors.

AVAILABILITY: Journal article.

AHQ

PLEASE START COMPLETING THIS SHEET AT ABOUT 8:00 A.M.

DATE: _____   Time at which you started filling in this page _____

PLEASE WRITE DOWN YOUR TWO MOST PROMINENT BELIEFS

Belief 1. _____

_____

Belief 2. _____

_____

Please remind yourself of *Belief 1*. Now, rate your belief as it is *right now* by circling
the correct number:

1	2	3	4	5
This is definitely true	This is very likely to be true	This is probably true	I am not sure if this is true	This is probably not true

Please remind yourself of *Belief 2*. Now, rate it in the same way:

1	2	3	4	5
This is definitely true	This is very likely to be true	This is probably true	I am not sure if this is true	This is probably not true

NOW, PLEASE DESCRIBE YOUR VOICES

Right now, my voices are saying: _____

_____

_____

THESE VOICES ARE:

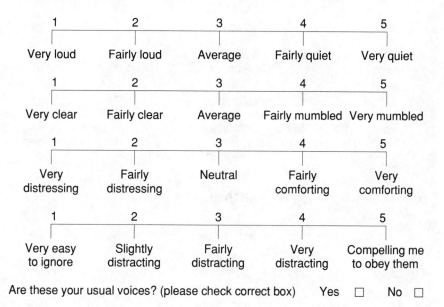

1	2	3	4	5
Very loud	Fairly loud	Average	Fairly quiet	Very quiet

1	2	3	4	5
Very clear	Fairly clear	Average	Fairly mumbled	Very mumbled

1	2	3	4	5
Very distressing	Fairly distressing	Neutral	Fairly comforting	Very comforting

1	2	3	4	5
Very easy to ignore	Slightly distracting	Fairly distracting	Very distracting	Compelling me to obey them

Are these your usual voices? (please check correct box)   Yes ☐   No ☐

If they are *not* your usual voices, please describe them, including if possible the name and sex of the person who is speaking:

_____

_____

_____

Right now, do you hear any other sounds that go along with, or are separate from, your voices?   Yes ☐   No ☐

If *yes*, please describe these sounds: _____

_____

_____

Please describe any other experiences (e.g. visions, smells, or feelings) that you are having:

_____

_____

NOW, PLEASE RATE YOUR *MOOD* AS IT IS RIGHT NOW:

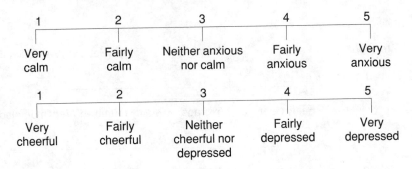

HOW *CLEAR* ARE YOUR THOUGHTS RIGHT NOW?

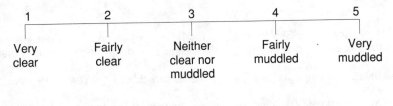

HAVE YOU TAKEN YOUR MEDICATION?   Yes ☐   No ☐

AUTHORITARIANISM SCALE (AS)

AUTHOR: Patrick C. L. Heaven

PURPOSE: To measure authoritarian behavior.

DESCRIPTION: The AS (Revised F-scale) is a 35-item instrument designed to measure authoritarianism. Much work has been done on the authoritarian personality using the original F-scale (Adorno et al., 1950). That scale, however, does not predict authoritarian behavior, but rather is most likely a measure of potential fascism. The AS was developed to address this limitation and two other weaknesses: the unilateral wording of items and a response set to particular items. The AS focuses on the multifaceted nature of authoritarianism and the items represent authoritarian behaviors. By presenting a balance of negatively and positively worded items, an acquiescent response set is controlled. The scale can be used as a short form by deleting items 3, 6, 8, 9, 10, 11, 15, 16, 17, 18, 22, 24, 26, 31, and 35; this is the recommended form for the non-Australian client.

NORMS: The AS was developed on four separate samples from New South Wales, Australia: two samples of randomly selected adults ($n = 456$) who were in their middle 40s; 48 experienced police officers, whose average age was 31.1 with a standard deviation of 6.24 years; and a purposive sample of adults ($n = 49$). Few data are presented on the samples' scores except for the police officers and a subsample of adults matched with the police according to gender, age and level of education. The average score for police was 75.71 with a standard deviation of 7.37. The matched subsample's average score was 69.85 with a standard deviation of 10.98.

SCORING: Scoring is not fully described in the primary reference. Each item is rated on the degree to which the respondent agrees. A 5-item scale can be used for responses, giving a range of scores from 35 to 165. Items 5–9, 12–14, 22–24, 31 are reverse-scored. Higher scores reflect more authoritarianism.

RELIABILITY: The internal consistency of the AS ranged from .70 to .83 for the sample of police officers and randomly selected adults, respectively. The internal consistency for the 20-item short form was .79, which was based on the sample of adults.

VALIDITY: Research on known-groups validity suggests the AS discriminates police officers' scores from the matched sample of adults. The purposive sample of 49 adults had scores on the AS which correlated with 11 behavioral dimensions of authoritarianism as rated by two close friends.

PRIMARY REFERENCE: Heaven, P. C. L. (1985). Construction and validation of a measure of authoritarian personality, *Journal of Personality Assessment*, 49, 545–551.

AVAILABILITY: Journal article.

AS

Rate each item in terms of how much you agree with the content. Please use the following scale and record your responses in the space to the left of the item.

1 = Almost never
2 = Rarely
3 = Occasionally
4 = Frequently
5 = Almost always

_____ 1. Does the idea of being a leader attract you?
_____ 2. Do you tend to feel quite confident on occasions when you are directing the activities of others?
_____ 3. Do you try to get yourself into positions of authority when you can?
_____ 4. Do you think you would make a good officer in the army?
_____ 5. Do you think you would make a poor military leader?
_____ 6. I would not vote for a political party that advocates racial discrimination.
_____ 7. Is being comfortable more important to you than getting ahead?
_____ 8. Are you satisfied to be no better than most other people at your job?
_____ 9. I am easily convinced by the opinions of others.
_____ 10. I agree with South Africa's Apartheid Policy.
_____ 11. Do you tend to boss people around?
_____ 12. Do you dislike having to tell others what to do?
_____ 13. If you are told to take charge of some situation, does this make you feel uncomfortable?
_____ 14. Would you rather take orders than give them?
_____ 15. Do you tend to be the one who makes the decisions at home?
_____ 16. Do you like to have the last word in an argument or discussion?
_____ 17. If ever a Falkland-type situation arose in Australia, I'd volunteer to fight.
_____ 18. I enjoy and feel good wearing a military uniform.
_____ 19. Do you tend to plan ahead for your job or career?
_____ 20. Is "getting on in life" important to you?
_____ 21. Are you an ambitious person?
_____ 22. Are you inclined to read of the successes of others rather than do the work of making yourself a success?
_____ 23. Are you inclined to take life as it comes without much planning?
_____ 24. Would it upset you a lot to see a child or animal suffer?
_____ 25. Do you have enemies who want to harm you?
_____ 26. Do you tend to dominate the conversation?
_____ 27. Are you argumentative?
_____ 28. Are there several people who keep trying to avoid you?
_____ 29. I often find myself disagreeing with people.
_____ 30. I can't help getting into arguments when people disagree with me.
_____ 31. Even when my anger is aroused, I don't use strong language.
_____ 32. If somebody annoys me, I am apt to tell him/her what I think.

_____ 33. When people yell at me I yell back.
_____ 34. When arguing, I tend to raise my voice.
_____ 35. Would you like other people to be afraid of you?

AUTHORITY BEHAVIOR INVENTORY (ABI)

AUTHOR: Ken Rigby

PURPOSE: To measure acceptance of authority.

DESCRIPTION: This 24-item instrument measures the acceptance of authority in the form of a behavioral inventory. As a concept, the acceptance of authority is different from accepting or liking people in general. It is similar to the notion of "authoritarian submission" found in the California F Scale, The Rokeach Dogmatism Scale and other attitude scales. As a behavioral inventory, instead of an attitude scale, the ABI is based on observable and verifiable actions or events. The current version of the ABI was developed from an earlier 14-item instrument. A respondent with higher acceptance of authority is generally considered pro-authority, is likely to follow rules, and tends to obey social demands that include the legal obligation to conform. This could encompass such activities as obeying traffic regulations and refraining from illegal drug and alcohol abuse. Clinicians may find this instrument useful with rebellious youngsters or juvenile delinquents. The relation of the ABI to antisocial personality is apparent; however, the honesty of the responses must be taken into consideration.

NORMS: The ABI has norms on a sample of social work students ($n = 100$) and nonstudents in the general public ($n = 100$) from Australia. The mean scores were 68.64 for the students and 75.78 for nonstudents. A separate sample of nonstudents had a similar mean (74.85). The mean ABI scores were not different between women and men.

SCORING: Scores are the total of each item score. Items 2, 5, 8, 9, 12, 14, 15, 17, 18, 19, 21, and 24 are reverse-scored. Scores range from 24 to 200, with higher scores indicating more positive orientation toward acceptance of authority.

RELIABILITY: Reliability was first determined by the item-total correlation. All items were significantly correlated with total scores, with a range from .12 to .67. The ABI also has good internal consistency, with an alpha of .84. From the second sample of nonstudent respondents, the alpha was .90. Data on stability are not available.

VALIDITY: Validity was estimated by correlating scores on the ABI items with a corresponding item when a rater independently evaluated the respondent. Respondents' scores were significantly correlated with the rater's evaluation, with correlations ranging from .23 to .88. Similarly, a separate study of 150 respondents found correlations between ABI scores and ratings of perceived authority by a rater who knew the person. Total scores on the ABI were significantly correlated with a measure of attitude towards authority, .71 for students and .77 for nonstudents, which supports the ABI's concurrent validity. Respondents perceived as more pro-authority had significantly higher ABI scores than subjects perceived as less pro-authority. This supports the instrument's known-groups validity. Similarly, differences were found on the ABI scores by membership in different political parties.

PRIMARY REFERENCE: Rigby, K. (1987). An authority behavior inventory, *Journal of Personality Assessment*, 51, 615–625. Instrument reproduced with permission of Ken Rigby and Lawrence Erlbaum Associates, Inc.

AVAILABILITY: Dr. Ken Rigby, School of Social Services, University of South Australia, North Terrace, Adelaide 5000, South Australia, Australia 5001.

ABI

This questionnaire is intended to assess the frequency with which you *behave* in certain ways. Answer each question as carefully as you can by placing a number on the space by each one as follows:

$$1 = \text{Never}$$
$$2 = \text{Rarely}$$
$$3 = \text{Occasionally}$$
$$4 = \text{Frequently}$$
$$5 = \text{Very frequently}$$

_____ 1. Do you listen attentively to what older people say about how you should behave?

_____ 2. Do you question the judgment of umpires or referees when you think they have made an incorrect decision?

_____ 3. When a person in authority whom you trust tells you to do something, do you do it, even though you can't see the reason for it?

_____ 4. Do you criticize people who are rude to their superiors?

_____ 5. Do you encourage young people to do what they want to do, even when it is against the wishes of their parents?

_____ 6. When you go to work, do you dress so as to be acceptable to the people who run the place?

_____ 7. Do you treat experts with respect even when you don't think much of them personally?

_____ 8. Do you support left-wing, radical policies?

_____ 9. Do you take part in demonstrations to show your opposition to policies you do not like?

_____ 10. Do you express approval for the work of school teachers?

_____ 11. Do you go to church?

_____ 12. Do you make fun of the police?

_____ 13. When things are bad, do you look for guidance from someone wiser than yourself?

_____ 14. Do you sympathize with rebels?

_____ 15. When you are in a hurry, do you break the speed limit or encourage your driver to do so, if it seems reasonably safe?

_____ 16. Do you follow doctor's orders?

_____ 17. Do you question what you hear on the news?

_____ 18. Do you cross the road against the pedestrian traffic lights?

_____ 19. Do you ask for a "second opinion" when you feel uncertain about a doctor's advice?

_____ 20. Do you stand when they play the national anthem in public?

_____ 21. Do you express contempt for politicians?

_____ 22. Do you get annoyed when people sneer at those in authority?

_____ 23. Do you show special respect for people in high positions?

_____ 24. Do you speak up against your boss or person in charge when he or she acts unfairly?

AUTOMATIC THOUGHTS QUESTIONNAIRE (ATQ)

AUTHORS: Philip C. Kendall and Steven D. Hollon

PURPOSE: To measure cognitive self-statements of depression.

DESCRIPTION: This ATQ is a 30-item instrument that measures the frequency of automatic negative statements about the self. Such negative covert statements play an important role in the development, maintenance and treatment of various psychopathologies, including depression. ATQ taps four aspects of these automatic thoughts: personal maladjustment and desire for change (PMDC), negative self-concepts and negative expectations (NSNE), low self-esteem (LSE), and Helplessness. The instrument is particularly noteworthy as it was designed to measure change in cognition due to clinical interventions.

NORMS: The ATQ was developed on a sample of 312 undergraduates. The sample had an average age of 20.22 with a standard deviation of 4.34 years. From this sample subjects were categorized as depressed or nondepressed based on scores from the Beck Depression Inventory and Minnesota Multiphasic Personality Inventory Depression scale. The average ATQ score for the depressed subsample was 79.64 with a standard deviation of 22.29. The average score for the nondepressed sample was 48.57 with a standard deviation of 10.89.

SCORING: Items are rated on the frequency of occurrence from "not at all" to "all the time." Total scores are the sum of all 30 items. Items on each factor are: PMDC: 7, 10, 14, 20, 26; NSNE: 2, 3, 9, 21, 23, 24, 28; LSE: 17, 18; Helplessness: 29, 30.

RELIABILITY: The instrument has excellent internal consistency with an alpha coefficient of .97. No information was available for test-retest reliability.

VALIDITY: The 30 items of the ATQ were selected from a pool of 100, and all significantly discriminated depressed from nondepressed subjects. This finding was repeated with another sample of depressed and nondepressed subjects. The instrument also has good concurrent validity, correlating with two measures of depression, the Beck Depression Inventory and the MMPI Depression Scale. Contrary to the initial prediction, scores were highly correlated with anxiety.

PRIMARY REFERENCE: Hollon, S. D. and Kendall, P. C. (1980). Cognitive self-statements in depression: Development of an Automatic Thoughts Questionnaire, *Cognitive Therapy and Research*, 4, 383–395. Instrument reproduced with permission of Philip C. Kendall.

AVAILABILITY: Dr. Philip C. Kendall, Division of Clinical Psychology, Temple University, Philadelphia, PA 19122

ATQ

Listed below are a variety of thoughts that pop into people's heads. Please read each thought and indicate how frequently, if at all, the thought occurred to you *over the last week*. Please read each item carefully and fill in the blank with the appropriate number, using the following scale:

1 = Not at all
2 = Sometimes
3 = Moderately often
4 = Often
5 = All the time

_____ 1.   I feel like I'm up against the world.
_____ 2.   I'm no good
_____ 3.   Why can't I ever succeed?
_____ 4.   No one understands me.
_____ 5.   I've let people down.
_____ 6.   I don't think I can go on.
_____ 7.   I wish I were a better person.
_____ 8.   I'm so weak.
_____ 9.   My life's not going the way I want it to.
_____ 10. I'm so disappointed in myself.
_____ 11. Nothing feels good anymore.
_____ 12. I can't stand this anymore.
_____ 13. I can't get started.
_____ 14. What's wrong with me?
_____ 15. I wish I were somewhere else.
_____ 16. I can't get things together.
_____ 17. I hate myself.
_____ 18. I'm worthless.
_____ 19. I wish I could just disappear.
_____ 20. What's the matter with me?
_____ 21. I'm a loser.
_____ 22. My life is a mess.
_____ 23. I'm a failure.
_____ 24. I'll never make it.
_____ 25. I feel so helpless.
_____ 26. Something has to change.
_____ 27. There must be something wrong with me.
_____ 28. My future is bleak.
_____ 29. It's just not worth it.
_____ 30. I can't finish anything.

BAKKER ASSERTIVENESS-AGGRESSIVENESS INVENTORY (AS-AGI)

AUTHORS: Cornelis B. Bakker, Marianne K. Bakker-Rabdau, and Saul Breit

PURPOSE: To measure two dimensions of assertion.

DESCRIPTION: This 36-item inventory measures assertiveness in terms of two components necessary for social functioning: the ability to refuse unreasonable requests ("assertiveness" AS), and the ability to take the initiative, make requests, or ask for favors ("aggressiveness" AG). In this measure aggressiveness differs from hostility, tending to relate more to being responsible and taking the initiative in social situations. The two instruments can also be used separately as 18-item measures.

NORMS: Normative data are available from seven different samples. From a sample of 250 college students, males had average AS and AG scores of 48.83 and 51.07, respectively, while female scores were 47.69 for the AS and 52.37 for the AG. A sample of 17 male city employee supervisors, with an average age of 40.1 with a standard deviation of 6.3 years, had AS scores of 43.85 and 47.88 for the AG. From a sample of students seeking assertiveness training the average AS and AG scores were 55.0 and 58.67 respectively, for males and 54.85 and 58.60 for females; the average ages of these males and females were 39.0 and 43.4, respectively. Additional normative data on nurses, X-Ray technicians and employees of a city water department are reported in the primary reference.

SCORING: Each item is rated on a 5-point scale from "almost always" to "almost never" according to the likelihood the respondent would behave in the specified manner. Each scale is scored separately. Those items with a plus sign before the alternative are reverse-scored as follows: 1 becomes 5, 2 becomes 4, 4 becomes 2, and 5 becomes 1. The item responses for each scale are summed with a range from 18 to 90. Higher scores indicate that the individual is less likely to exhibit assertiveness or aggressiveness.

RELIABILITY: These scales have been shown to be fairly reliable in terms of internal consistency and test-retest reliability. Internal consistency was estimated from a split-half procedure and was .73 for the AS scale and .80 for AG scale. Test-retest correlations were .75 for the AS and .88 for AG over a six-week period.

VALIDITY: Item analysis of all 36 items indicated that scores on each correlated highly with the score on the subscale of which it is a part. Research on known-groups validity indicated that both scales discriminated between a client and college sample. The scales are sensitive to measuring change as AS and AG scores changed subsequent to assertiveness training.

PRIMARY REFERENCE: Bakker, C. B., Bakker-Rabdau, M. K., and Breit S. (1978). The measurement of assertiveness and aggressiveness, *Journal of*

Personality Assessment, 42, 277–284. Instrument reproduced with permission of C. B. Bakker and the *Journal of Personality Assessment*.

AVAILABILITY: C. B. Bakker, M.D., Department of Psychiatry, Adult Development Program, Sacred Heart Medical Center, West 101 Eighth Avenue, Spokane, WA 99220.

AS-AGI

Below are several different situations. Each is followed by one way of responding. Your task is to read each question and indicate how likely you are to respond in that way, according to the following scale:

$$1 = \text{Almost always}$$
$$2 = \text{Frequently}$$
$$3 = \text{Occasionally}$$
$$4 = \text{Sometimes}$$
$$5 = \text{Almost never}$$

Record your answers in the space to the left of each item.

AS Items

_____ 1. You have set aside the evening to get some necessary work done. Just as you get started some friends drop over for a social visit.
    − You welcome them in and postpone what you had planned to do.

_____ 2. You are standing in line when someone pushes ahead of you.
    + You tell the person to get back in line behind you.

_____ 3. A friend or relative asks to borrow your car or other valuable property but you would prefer not to lend it to them.
    − You lend it to them anyway.

_____ 4. A person who has kept you waiting before is late again for an appointment.
    − You ignore it and act as if nothing has happened.

_____ 5. Someone has, in your opinion, treated you unfairly or incorrectly.
    + You confront the person directly concerning this.

_____ 6. Friends or neighbors fail to return some items they have borrowed from you.
    + You keep after them until they return them.

_____ 7. Others put pressure on you to drink, smoke pot, take drugs, or eat too much.
    + You refuse to yield to their pressure.

_____ 8. Another person interrupts you while you are speaking.
    − You wait until the other is finished speaking before you go on with your story.

_____ 9. You are asked to carry out a task that you do not feel like doing.
    + You tell the other that you don't want to do it.

_____ 10. Your sexual partner has done something that you do not like.
    − You act as if nothing bothersome has happened.

_____ 11. A salesperson has spent a great deal of time showing you merchandise but none of it is exactly what you want.
    − You buy something anyway.

_____ 12. You are invited to a party or other social event, which you would rather not attend.
    − You accept the invitation.

_____ 13. In a concert or a movie theater a couple next to you distracts you with their conversation.
           \+ You ask them to be quiet or move somewhere else.
_____ 14. In a restaurant you receive food that is poorly prepared.
           \+ You ask the waiter or waitress to replace it.
_____ 15. You receive incorrect or damaged merchandise from a store.
           \+ You return the merchandise.
_____ 16. A person who seems a lot worse off than you asks you for something you could easily do without but you don't like to.
           – You give the person what he/she asks for.
_____ 17. Someone gives you—unasked for—a negative appraisal of your behavior.
           \+ You tell the other you are not interested.
_____ 18. Friends or parents try to get information from you that you consider personal.
           – You give them the information they want.

AG Items

_____ 19. You have been appointed to a newly formed committee.
           \+ You take a leadership role.
_____ 20. You are in a bus or plane sitting next to a person you have never met.
           \+ You strike up a conversation.
_____ 21. You are a guest in a home of a new acquaintance. The dinner was so good you would like a second helping.
           \+ You go ahead and take a second helping.
_____ 22. You are being interviewed for a job you really want to get.
           – You undersell yourself.
_____ 23. You are meeting or greeting several people.
           \+ You make physical contact with each other in turn either by hugging, putting an arm around their shoulders, or slapping their backs.
_____ 24. You have observed that someone has done an excellent job at something.
           – You don't tell that person about it.
_____ 25. In a store or restaurant the personnel are very busy and many customers seem to be waiting a long time for service.
           \+ You manage to get service ahead of other customers.
_____ 26. You observe someone behave in a suspicious manner.
           – You don't do anything because it is none of your business.
_____ 27. You have parked your car but notice that you do not have the correct change for the parking meter.
           \+ You ask a passer-by for the change.
_____ 28. Someone has done or said something that arouses your curiosity.
           – You refrain from asking questions.
_____ 29. You have observed certain behaviors of a friend or acquaintance that you think need to be changed. You tell the other person about this as soon as possible.
           \+ You tell the other person about this as soon as possible

___ 30. You would like to get a raise but your boss has said nothing about it.
             − You wait for your boss to bring the matter up.

___ 31. During a social visit with a group of friends everyone participates actively in the conversation.
             + You dominate the conversation most of the time.

___ 32. During a discussion you believe that you have something worthwhile to contribute.
             + You don't bother to state it unless the others ask you to give your opinion.

___ 33. You have an opportunity to participate in a lively, no-holds barred debate.
             − You remain a listener rather than participate.

___ 34. You want a favor done by a person you do not know too well.
             − You prefer to do without rather than ask that person.

___ 35. You have moved into a new neighborhood or started a new job and you would like to make social contacts.
             − You wait for others to introduce themselves.

___ 36. You see an opportunity to get ahead but know it will take a great deal of energy.
             + You take the opportunity and forge ahead.

BARNETT LIKING OF CHILDREN SCALE (BLOCS)

AUTHORS: Mark A. Barnett and Christina S. Sinisi

PURPOSE: To measure attitudes toward children.

DESCRIPTION: The BLOCS is a 14-item instrument designed to assess the extent to which individuals have a favorable attitude toward children. The BLOCS measures general attitudes of people like parents and teachers whose attitudes could be associated with a broad range of beliefs and behaviors about children and childbearing. The BLOCS is seen as a viable measure for examining the way an individual's tendency to like or dislike children may influence his or her interactions with children in areas as diverse as teaching and child maltreatment.

NORMS: The BLOCS was studied initially with several different samples involving a total of 284 undergraduate students of whom 145 were males and 139 females. No other demographic data were reported. Females report significantly greater liking of children than males with means that range from 80.66 to 81.23 for females and 72.02 to 74.35 for males.

SCORING: The BLOCS is easily scored by reverse-scoring items 3, 6, 10, and 13 and then summing individual items for a total score. The higher the score, the more positive the attitude toward children.

RELIABILITY: The BLOCS has excellent internal consistency, with an alpha of .93. The BLOCS also has excellent stability, with a one-week test-retest reliability coefficient of .91.

VALIDITY: The BLOCS has good concurrent validity, correlating significantly with several subscales of the Hereford Childbearing Scale and with a number of independent statements of childbearing attitudes.

PRIMARY REFERENCE: Barnett, M. A. and Sinisi, C. S. (1990). The initial validation of a Liking of Children Scale, *Journal of Personality Assessment*, 55, 161–167.

AVAILABILITY: Journal article.

BLOCS

Please indicate the extent to which you agree or disagree with each of the following statements by circling the appropriate number under each statement.

Strongly disagree			Neither disagree nor agree			Strongly agree
1	2	3	4	5	6	7

1. Watching little children play gives me pleasure.

    1   2   3   4   5   6   7

2. I enjoy getting to know a child.

    1   2   3   4   5   6   7

3. I do not like talking with young children.

    1   2   3   4   5   6   7

4. I enjoy holding little children.

    1   2   3   4   5   6   7

5. I feel happy when I make a child smile.

    1   2   3   4   5   6   7

6. I do not like being around children.

    1   2   3   4   5   6   7

7. I enjoy watching children play in a park.

    1   2   3   4   5   6   7

8. Time seems to go by quickly when I interact with children.

    1   2   3   4   5   6   7

9. I like to listen to children talk to one another.

    1   2   3   4   5   6   7

10.   Children are annoying.

             1   2   3   4   5   6   7

11.   I enjoy trying to make a child smile.

             1   2   3   4   5   6   7

12.   Children are likable once you get to know them.

             1   2   3   4   5   6   7

13.   It bothers me when children get loud and active.

             1   2   3   4   5   6   7

14.   I like children.

             1   2   3   4   5   6   7

BELIEF IN PERSONAL CONTROL SCALE (BPCS)

AUTHOR: Joy L. Berrenberg

PURPOSE: To measure personal control.

DESCRIPTION: The BPCS is a 45-item instrument designed to measure three dimensions of personal control: general external control (F1) assesses the extent to which an individual believes his or her outcomes are self-produced (internality) or produced by fate or others (externality). The exaggerated control dimension (F2) measures an extreme and unrealistic belief in personal control. The God-mediated dimension (F3) measures the belief that God can be enlisted in the achievement of outcomes (distinguishing between individuals who believe they have no control over their outcomes and those who believe they control outcomes through God). Items on the three subscales are indicated on the measure itself.

NORMS: The BPCS was studied with several samples of students for a total of 404 (169 males and 235 females). Of this group, all were undergraduates except for 48 seminary graduate students and 34 psychology graduate students. For the undergraduates, means for general external control were 68.91 (SD = 8.35), for exaggerated internal control were 55.57 (SD = 7.56), and for God-mediated control were 28.27 (SD = 11.43).

SCORING: The BPCS is easily scored by summing items for each subscale score. Items marked with an asterisk are reverse-scored so that higher scores mean more internal control (F1), a more exaggerated belief in control (F2), and less belief in God as a mediator of control (F3).

RELIABILITY: The BPCS has very good to excellent internal consistency, with alphas of .85 (F1), .88 (F2), and .97 (F3). The BPCS has very good stability, with four-week test-retest correlations of .81 (F1), .85 (F2), and .93 (F3).

VALIDITY: The BPCS has excellent construct validity, with correlations in the expected directions with several other measures including Internal-External Locus of Control, the Taylor Manifest Anxiety Scale, the Feelings of Inadequacy Scale, and the Mania and Depression Scales. The 45-item BPCS is also highly correlated with an earlier 85-item version (factors correlate from .85 to .95).

PRIMARY REFERENCE: Berrenberg, J. L. (1987). The Belief in Personal Control Scale: A measure of God-mediated and exaggerated control, *Journal of Personality Assessment*, 51, 194–206.

AVAILABILITY: Dr. Joy Berrenberg, Department of Psychology, University of Colorado, 1200 Larimer Street, Denver, CO 80204.

BPCS

This questionnaire consists of items describing possible perceptions you may have of yourself, others, and life in general. Please respond to each of the statements below by indicating the extent to which that statement describes your beliefs. For each statement circle the number that best describes your feelings.

1 = Always true
2 = Often true
3 = Sometimes true
4 = Rarely
5 = Never true

Scoring
Key

*F2	1.	I can make things happen easily.	1 2 3 4 5
F1	2.	Getting what you want is a matter of knowing the right people.	1 2 3 4 5
F1	3.	My behavior is dictated by the demands of society.	1 2 3 4 5
*F2	4.	If I just keep trying, I can overcome any obstacle.	1 2 3 4 5
F3	5.	I can succeed with God's help.	1 2 3 4 5
F1	6.	I find that luck plays a bigger role in my life than my ability.	1 2 3 4 5
*F2	7.	If nothing is happening, I go out and make it happen.	1 2 3 4 5
*F2	8.	I am solely responsible for the outcomes in my life.	1 2 3 4 5
F3	9.	I rely on God to help me control my life.	1 2 3 4 5
*F2	10.	Regardless of the obstacles, I refuse to quit trying.	1 2 3 4 5
F1	11.	My success is a matter of luck.	1 2 3 4 5
F1	12.	Getting what you want is a matter of being in the right place at the right time.	1 2 3 4 5
*F2	13.	I am able to control effectively the behavior of others.	1 2 3 4 5

F3	14.	If I need help, I know that God is there for me.	1	2	3	4	5
F1	15.	I feel that other people have more control over my life than I do.	1	2	3	4	5
F1	16.	There is little that I can do to change my destiny.	1	2	3	4	5
*F2	17.	I feel that I control my life as much as is humanly possible.	1	2	3	4	5
F3	18.	God rewards me if I obey his laws.	1	2	3	4	5
F1	19.	I am not the master of my own fate.	1	2	3	4	5
*F2	20.	I continue to strive for a goal long after others would have given up.	1	2	3	4	5
F1	21.	Most things in my life I just can't control.	1	2	3	4	5
F3	22.	God helps me to control my life.	1	2	3	4	5
*F2	23.	I have more control over my life than other people have over theirs.	1	2	3	4	5
*F2	24.	I actively strive to make things happen for myself.	1	2	3	4	5
F1	25.	Other people hinder my ability to direct my life.	1	2	3	4	5
F1	26.	What happens to me is a matter of good or bad fortune.	1	2	3	4	5
*F2	27.	When something stands in my way, I go around it.	1	2	3	4	5
*F2	28.	I can be whatever I want to be.	1	2	3	4	5
*F2	29.	I know how to get what I want from others.	1	2	3	4	5
F1	30.	Fate can be blamed for my failures.	1	2	3	4	5
F3	31.	With God's help, I can be whatever I want to be.	1	2	3	4	5
F1	32.	I am the victim of circumstances beyond my control.	1	2	3	4	5
F1	33.	I can control my own thoughts.	1	2	3	4	5
*F2	34.	There is nothing that happens to me that I don't control.	1	2	3	4	5

*F2	35.	Whenever I run up against some obstacle, I strive even harder to overcome it and reach my goal.	1	2	3	4	5
F3	36.	By placing my life in God's hands, I can accomplish anything.	1	2	3	4	5
F1	37.	I am at the mercy of my physical impulses.	1	2	3	4	5
F1	38.	In this life, what happens to me is determined by my fate.	1	2	3	4	5
F3	39.	My actions are the result of God working through me.	1	2	3	4	5
F1	40.	I am the victim of social forces.	1	2	3	4	5
*F2	41.	Controlling my life involves mind over matter.	1	2	3	4	5
*F2	42.	When I want something, I assert myself in order to get it.	1	2	3	4	5
F1	43.	The unconscious mind, over which I have no control, directs my life.	1	2	3	4	5
F3	44.	If I really want something, I pray to God to bring it to me.	1	2	3	4	5
F1	45.	I am not really in control of the outcomes in my life.	1	2	3	4	5

BELIEFS ASSOCIATED WITH CHILDHOOD SEXUAL ABUSE (BACSA)

AUTHORS: Derek Jehu, Carole Klassen, and Marjorie Gazan

PURPOSE: To measure beliefs associated with sexual abuse.

DESCRIPTION: The BACSA is a 17-item instrument designed to measure common distorted beliefs associated with childhood sexual abuse. The instrument actually was developed to be used to depict changes in clients who are receiving cognitive therapy to restructure distorted beliefs that could contribute to mood disturbances such as guilt, low self-esteem, and sadness.

NORMS: No norms were reported. Initial testing of the instrument was conducted on 25 women who previously had been sexually abused. No demographic data are available.

SCORING: The BACSA is scored by simply totaling the scores (0–4) on the 5-point scale, producing a potential range of 0 to 68 with higher scores suggesting a greater degree of distortion that is clinically significant. A cut-off point of 15 (one standard deviation below the mean of 30.82 for 11 clients) is suggested, with clients scoring above 15 presumably having clinically significant distorted beliefs.

RELIABILITY: The BACSA has excellent short-term stability, with a one-week test-retest correlation of .93. No data were provided on internal consistency.

VALIDITY: The authors report good face validity and fair concurrent validity, with a .55 (p < .01) correlation with the Beck Depression Inventory.

PRIMARY REFERENCE: Jehu, D., Klassen, C., and Gazan, M. (1986). Cognitive restructuring of distorted beliefs associated with childhood sexual abuse, *Journal of Social Work and Human Sexuality*, 4, 49–69.

AVAILABILITY: Dr. Derek Jehu, Department of Psychology, University of Leicester, Leicester, LEI7RH, England.

Instruments for Practice

BACSA

Please circle one number from 0 to 4 that best indicates how strongly you believe each statement to be true in your own case. Please answer according to what your really believe yourself, not what you think you should believe.

        0 = Absolutely untrue
        1 = Mostly untrue
        2 = Partly true, partly untrue
        3 = Mostly true
        4 = Absolutely true

1. I must be an extremely rare woman to have experienced   0   1   2   3   4
    sex with an older person I was a child.

2. I am worthless and bad.   0   1   2   3   4

3. You can't depend on women; they are all weak and   0   1   2   3   4
    useless creatures.

4. No man can be trusted.   0   1   2   3   4

5. I must have permitted sex to happen because I wasn't   0   1   2   3   4
    forced into it.

6. I don't have the right to deny my body to any man who   0   1   2   3   4
    demands it.

7. Anyone who knows what happened to me sexually will   0   1   2   3   4
    not want anything more to do with me.

8. I must have been seductive and provocative when I was   0   1   2   3   4
    young.

9. It doesn't matter what happens to me in my life.   0   1   2   3   4

10. No man could care for me without a sexual relationship.   0   1   2   3   4

11. It is dangerous to get close to anyone because they   0   1   2   3   4
    always betray, exploit, or hurt you.

12. I must have been responsible for sex when I was young   0   1   2   3   4
    because it went on for so long.

13. I will never be able to lead a normal life; the damage is   0   1   2   3   4
    permanent.

14. Only bad, worthless guys would be interested in me.   0   1   2   3   4

15. It must be unnatural to feel any pleasure during molestation.   0   1   2   3   4

16. I am inferior to other people because I did not have normal experiences.   0   1   2   3   4

17. I've already been used so it doesn't matter if other men use me.   0   1   2   3   4

BODY IMAGE AVOIDANCE QUESTIONNAIRE (BIAQ)

AUTHORS: James C. Rosen, Debra Srebnik, Elaine Saltzberg, and Sally Wendt

PURPOSE: To measure behavioral tendencies that frequently accompany body-image disturbance.

DESCRIPTION: The BIAQ is a 19-item instrument designed to measure behavioral tendencies that often accompany body-image disturbance. In particular, the questionnaire deals with avoidance of situations that provoke concern about physical appearance, such as avoidance of physical intimacy, social outings, and tight-fitting clothes. Since these avoidance behaviors are common in persons with body dissatisfaction and since there are no measures of this component of the problem, the authors interviewed 40 randomly selected female residents of a university dormitory and categorized commonly reported complaints of behavioral changes associated with negative body image into the items of this questionnaire. The measure is viewed as useful for targeting changes in avoidance of these situations as a result of treatment.

NORMS: The BIAQ was tested with a sample of 353 female introductory psychology students with a mean age of 19.7 years and a mean deviation from normal weight (according to charts of the Metropolitan Life Insurance Company) of 2.01%. The mean score on the BIAQ was 31.5 with a standard deviation of 13.9 and a range of 1 to 74.

SCORING: The BIAQ is scored by simply totaling the scores on the individual, 6-point items, providing a potential range of scores from 0 to 94. Although the BIAQ comprises four factors derived through factor analysis (clothing, social activities, eating at restaurants, and grooming and weight), these factors are not scored separately.

RELIABILITY: The BIAQ has excellent internal consistency, with a Cronbach's alpha of .89, and is very stable with a two-week, test-retest reliability coefficient of .87.

VALIDITY: The BIAQ has fair to good concurrent validity, with a low but significant correlation of .22 with body size estimation, a correlation of .78 with the Body Shape Questionnaire, and correlations of .68 and .63 with the Shape Concern and Weight Concern scales respectively. The BIAQ has good known-groups validity, significantly distinguishing between clinical (bulimia nervosa) and nonclinical populations. Finally, the BIAQ has been shown to be sensitive to changes in clients with body-image disturbance.

PRIMARY REFERENCE: Rosen, J. C., Srebnik, D., Saltzberg, E., and Wendt, S. (1991). Development of a Body Image Avoidance Questionnaire, *Psychological Assessment*, 3, 32–37. Instrument reprinted by permission of authors and publisher.

AVAILABILITY: Dr. J. C. Rosen, Department of Psychology, University of Vermont, Burlington, VT 05405.

BIAQ

Circle the number which best describes how often you engage in these behaviors at the present time.

		Always	Usually	Often	Some-times	Rarely	Never
1.	I wear baggy clothes.	5	4	3	2	1	0
2.	I wear clothes I do not like.	5	4	3	2	1	0
3.	I wear darker color clothing.	5	4	3	2	1	0
4.	I wear a special set of clothing, e.g., my "fat clothes."	5	4	3	2	1	0
5.	I restrict the amount of food I eat.	5	4	3	2	1	0
6.	I only eat fruits, vegetables, and other low calories foods.	5	4	3	2	1	0
7.	I fast for a day or longer.	5	4	3	2	1	0
8.	I do not go out socially if I will be "checked out."	5	4	3	2	1	0
9.	I do not go out socially if the people I am with will discuss weight.	5	4	3	2	1	0
10.	I do not go out socially if the people I am with are thinner than me.	5	4	3	2	1	0

		Always	Usually	Often	Some-times	Rarely	Never
11.	I do not go out socially if it involves eating.	5	4	3	2	1	0
12.	I weigh myself.	5	4	3	2	1	0
13.	I am inactive.	5	4	3	2	1	0
14.	I look at myself in the mirror.	5	4	3	2	1	0
15.	I avoid physical intimacy.	5	4	3	2	1	0
16.	I wear clothes that will divert attention from my weight.	5	4	3	2	1	0
17.	I avoid going clothes shopping.	5	4	3	2	1	0
18.	I don't wear "revealing" clothes (e.g., bathing suits, tank tops, or shorts).	5	4	3	2	1	0
19.	I get dressed up or made up.	5	4	3	2	1	0

BODY SENSATIONS QUESTIONNAIRE (BSQ)

AUTHORS: Dianne L. Chambless, G. Craig Caputo, Priscilla Bright, and Richard Gallagher

PURPOSE: To measure physical sensations in agoraphobia.

DESCRIPTION: The BSQ is an 18-item instrument designed to measure body sensations associated with agoraphobia. The items on the BSQ were generated from interviews with clients and therapists involved in an agoraphobia treatment program. The BSQ contains items that clients report to be disturbing that are associated with anxiety. The BSQ can be used to help assess agoraphobia and to monitor changes due to treatment.

NORMS: The BSQ was studied initially with 175 clients applying for treatment at the Agoraphobia and Anxiety Program at Temple University; 80% were female and the sample had been agoraphobic for a median of eight years. The mean age of the group was 37.64. The mean score was 3.05 (SD = .86).

SCORING: The BSQ is easily scored by summing the individual item ratings and dividing by the number of items rated.

RELIABILITY: The BSQ has very good internal consistency, with an alpha of .87. It also has good stability, with a one-month test-retest correlation of .67.

VALIDITY: The BSQ has very good concurrent validity, correlating with other measures of agoraphobia and several measures of psychopathology such as the Beck Depression Inventory, State-Trait Anxiety Inventory, and the Neuroticism Scale of the Eysenck Personality Questionnaire. The BSQ has good known-groups validity, significantly discriminating agoraphobic clients from a "normal" control group. The BSQ also is sensitive to changes due to treatment.

PRIMARY REFERENCE: Chambless, D. L., Caputo, G. C., Bright, P., and Gallagher, R. (1984). Assessment of fear in agoraphobics: The Body Sensations Questionnaire and the Agoraphobic Cognitions Questionnaire, *Journal of Consulting and Clinical Psychology*, 52, 1090–1097. Instrument reprinted by permission of authors and publisher.

AVAILABILITY: Dr. Dianne Chambless, Department of Psychology, American University, Washington, DC 20016.

BSQ

Below is a list of specific body sensations that may occur when you are nervous or in a feared situation. Please mark down how afraid you are of these feelings. Use a five-point scale from "not worried" to "extremely frightened." Please rate all items.

1 = Not frightened or worried by this sensation
2 = Somewhat frightened by this sensation
3 = Moderately frightened by this sensation
4 = Very frightened by this sensation
5 = Extremely frightened by this sensation

____ 1. Heart palpitations
____ 2. Pressure or a heavy feeling in chest
____ 3. Numbness in arms or legs
____ 4. Tingling in the fingertips
____ 5. Numbness in another part of your body
____ 6. Feeling short of breath
____ 7. Dizziness
____ 8. Blurred or distorted vision
____ 9. Nausea
____ 10. Having "butterflies" in your stomach
____ 11. Feeling a knot in your stomach
____ 12. Having a lump in your throat
____ 13. Wobbly or rubber legs
____ 14. Sweating
____ 15. A dry throat
____ 16. Feeling disoriented and confused
____ 17. Feeling disconnected from your body: Only partly present
____ 18. Other _____

Please describe _____

_____

_____

BOREDOM PRONENESS (BP)

AUTHORS: Richard Famer and Norman D. Sundberg

PURPOSE: To measure proneness to boredom.

DESCRIPTION: The BP is a 28-item instrument designed to measure the tendency or predisposition to boredom. The BP is based on the idea that boredom is a widespread and significant problem that has been associated in research with drug use, overeating, truancy in schools, maladjustment ratings in students, job dissatisfaction, and poor functioning on the job. The BP is a useful measure for assessing boredom and then keeping track of changes over time as a result of intervention programs.

NORMS: The BP was investigated mainly with a sample of 233 college undergraduates (93 males, 140 females). The overall mean is 9.76 (SD = 4.8). The mean for males was 10.44 (SD = 4.88) and for females 9.30 (SD = 4.72). This difference was not statistically significant.

SCORING: The BP is easily scored by summing all "correct" scores. The correct score for items 1, 7, 8, 11, 13, 15, 18, 22–24 is "false." The remaining items are scored "true" to indicate boredom proneness. Higher scores indicate greater proneness to boredom.

RELIABILITY: The BP has good internal consistency, with an alpha of .79. The BP also has very good stability, with a one-week test-retest correlation of .83.

VALIDITY: The BP has very good construct validity, correlating in predicted ways with self-ratings of boredom, lack of interest in the classroom, the Job Boredom Scale, the Beck Depression Inventory, the Center for Epidemiological Studies—Depression Scale, the Hopelessness Scale, the Perceived Effort Scale, the UCLA Loneliness Scale, the Life Satisfaction Index, and two subscales of the General Causality Orientations Scale.

PRIMARY REFERENCE: Famer, R. and Sundberg, N. D. (1986). Boredom proneness—The development and correlates of a new scale, *Journal of Personality Assessment*, 50, 4–17.

AVAILABILITY: Journal article.

BP

Put an "X" below "T" (True) or "F" (False) according to how you would usually describe yourself.

T   F

____ ____ 1. It is easy for me to concentrate on my activities.
____ ____ 2. Frequently when I am working I find myself worrying about other things.
____ ____ 3. Time always seems to be passing slowly.
____ ____ 4. I often find myself at "loose ends," not knowing what to do.
____ ____ 5. I am often trapped in situations where I have to do meaningless things.
____ ____ 6. Having to look at someone's home movies or travel slides bores me tremendously.
____ ____ 7. I have projects in mind all the time, things to do.
____ ____ 8. I find it easy to entertain myself.
____ ____ 9. Many things I have to do are repetitive and monotonous.
____ ____ 10. It takes more stimulation to get me going than most people.
____ ____ 11. I get a kick out of most things I do.
____ ____ 12. I am seldom excited about my work.
____ ____ 13. In any situation I can usually find something to do or see to keep me interested.
____ ____ 14. Much of the time I just sit around doing nothing.
____ ____ 15. I am good at waiting patiently.
____ ____ 16. I often find myself with nothing to do—time on my hands.
____ ____ 17. In situations where I have to wait, such as a line or queue, I get very restless.
____ ____ 18. I often wake up with a new idea.
____ ____ 19. It would be very hard for me to find a job that is exciting enough.
____ ____ 20. I would like more challenging things to do in life.
____ ____ 21. I feel that I am working below my abilities most of the time.
____ ____ 22. Many people would say that I am a creative or imaginative person.
____ ____ 23. I have so many interests, I don't have time to do everything.
____ ____ 24. Among my friends, I am the one who keeps doing something the longest.
____ ____ 25. Unless I am doing something exciting, even dangerous, I feel half-dead and dull.
____ ____ 26. It takes a lot of change and variety to keep me really happy.
____ ____ 27. It seems that the same things are on television or the movies all the time; it's getting old.
____ ____ 28. When I was young, I was often in monotonous and tiresome situations.

BRIEF DEPRESSION RATING SCALE (BDRS)

AUTHOR: Robert Kellner

PURPOSE: To measure depression.

DESCRIPTION: The BDRS is an 8-item rating scale designed to measure depression by clinical observations. The scale was developed through a series of studies beginning with reviews of symptoms of depressed patients, and culminating in a series of validation studies. The BDRS is particularly recommended for its brevity, its sensitivity to measuring changes in depression, and its ability to detect small differences between the effects of two treatments. The BDRS is one of the few rating scales in this book, i.e., it is not a self-report measure. Its ease of use compared to many other rating scales was the primary reason for its inclusion.

NORMS: The BDRS has been studied with several samples including depressed in- and outpatients. Specific demographic information is not available nor are actual norms.

SCORING: The BDRS is easily scored by summing individual items for a total score.

RELIABILITY: The BDRS has excellent interobserver reliability with correlations that range from .91 to .94.

VALIDITY: The BDRS has excellent concurrent validity, correlating .83 with the Hamilton Depression Rating Scale. The BDRS also has good known-groups validity, significantly distinguishing between depressed in- and outpatients. The BDRS also has been found to be sensitive to differences between treatments.

PRIMARY REFERENCE: Kellner, R. (1986). The Brief Depression Rating Scale, in N. Sartorius and T. A. Ban (eds.), *Assessment of Depression*, pp. 179–183. New York: Springer-Verlag.

AVAILABILITY: Dr. Robert Kellner, University of Mexico, Department of Psychiatry, 2400 Tucker, NE, Albuquerque, NM 87131.

BDRS

Circle the appropriate number

	9	8	7	6	5	4	3	2	1
I. Depressive mood. Feeling of despair	Incapacitating	Severe distress		Moderately distressed		Slight		Cheerful*	
II. Psychophysiologic somatic symptoms**	Incapacitating	Severe symptoms or impairment		Moderate		Slight		Completely absent or normal functions	
III. Lack of interest, initiative, and activity	Totally inactive	Severe apathy, very few activities		Moderately impaired interest and initiative		Slight loss of interest and initiative		Interested and energetic	
IV. Sleep disturbance***	Apparently sleeping 1 h or less	Sleeping about 2 h a night		Sleeping 4–5 h		Slight sleep disturbance		Sleeping well*	

	1	2	3	4	5	6	7	8	9
V. Anxiety, worry, tension	Calm and relaxed		Slight		Moderate tension or anxiety		Severe distress		Incapacitating
VI. Appearance	Appears cheerful*		Sad appearance at times		Sad appearance, but can be made to smile		Sad appearance, does not smile at all		Continuous expression of utmost despair
VII. Depressive beliefs	Confident* and optimistic		Occasional brief depressional beliefs		Frequent beliefs of no hope or unworthiness		Has some depressive psychotic delusions		Most thought are delusional
VIII. Suicidal thoughts or behavior	No suicidal thoughts.		Occasional thoughts of suicide. Does not want to die		Intermittent thought of suicide. No plans		Frequent suicidal preoccupations and wishes to die		Evidence of serious risk and a recent suicide attempt

* If excessive, please comment.

** Including appetite, sexual interest, gastric symptoms, etc. Rate the symptom which is most severe.

*** If any of the following is reported: difficulty in falling asleep, waking up early, restless sleep, or nightmares, rate the sleep disturbances as "slightly moderate" or "severe" even if the total number of hours slept is adequate.

If in doubt whether to rate *severity* of the symptoms or behavior or *frequency* of occurrence, rate *severity* of the symptom or behavior.

The usual period rated is the *past* week; the rating period can be made longer or shorter, depending on the design of the study.

For the symptoms which do not have specific rating instructions the rating cues should be interpreted as follows:

9—Incapacitating—The patient is unable to carry out everyday tasks (not only related to his or her occupation) because of the severity of his or her symptoms.

7—Severe—The patient is severely distressed and/or his or her performance is substantially impaired but not to the point of incapacity.

5—Moderate—This rating is made when neither "severe" not "slight" is applicable.

3—Slight—The patient either mentions spontaneously or replies to questioning that the symptom is not troublesome with statements such as "slight" or "only a little."

1—Absent—Total absence of the symptom during the period covered by rating.

Intermediate ratings—(scores 2, 4, 6, and 8) should be used only if the main cues (1, 3, 5, 7, and 9) do not adequately express the rater's opinion.

98

BRIEF SCREEN FOR DEPRESSION (BSD)

AUTHORS: A. Ralph Hakstian and Peter D. McLean

PURPOSE: To measure depression.

DESCRIPTION: The BSD is a 4-item instrument designed to serve as a screening device for depression. The BSD was designed to detect clinical levels of depression, and to tap a full range of response domains. The BSD can be used alone or as part of a battery of measures. The BSD has a cutting score of 21 to distinguish clinical from nonclinical subjects and 24 to distinguish depressed from other psychiatric subjects.

NORMS: The BSD was studied with a sample of 196 depressed subjects as diagnosed by the MMPI Depression Scale and the Depression Adjective Checklist; mean age was 39 with 72% of the sample being female; 25% had made a serious suicide attempt. A sample of 161 "normal" subjects was recruited by newspaper ads, and 107 nondepressed psychiatric patients matched with other groups was used as a control. For the depressed group, the mean was 33.88 (SD = 6.6) and for the "normal" group the mean was 13.27 (SD = 5.2).

SCORING: The BSD is scored by summing scores for items 2–4 and adding four times the item "1" score to produce an overall score.

RELIABILITY: The BSD has fair internal consistency, with alphas that range from .63 to .65. The BSD has good stability, with a one-week test-retest correlation of .73 and a three-month test-retest correlation of .54.

VALIDITY: The BSD has very good concurrent validity, correlating with the Beck Depression Inventory and the Depression Adjective Checklist. It also has excellent known-groups validity as evidenced by the cut-off scores described earlier that distinguish between depressed and nondepressed patients and between patients and "normals."

PRIMARY REFERENCE: Hakstian, A. R. and McLean, P. D. (1989). Brief Screen for Depression, *Psychological Assessment*, 1, 139–141.

AVAILABILITY: Journal article.

BSD

1. How many times during the last 2 days have you been preoccupied by thoughts of hopelessness, helplessness, pessimism, intense worry, unhappiness, and so on? (Circle number)

1	2	3	4	5
Not at all	Rarely	Frequently	Most of the time	All of the time

2. How relaxed have you been during the last 2 days, compared to how you normally are? (Circle number)

        1   2   3   4   5   6   7   8   9   10
    Quite calm   Extremely tense
    and relaxed   (i.e., wringing
    physically   hands, muscle
                                                tremors, etc.)

3. To what extent have you had difficulty starting and following through an ordinary job or task to completion during the last week compared to when you feel things have been going well? (Circle number)

        1   2   3   4   5   6   7   8   9   10
    Start and finish   Put things off/
    jobs as well as   starting and not
    most other people   finishing for a
                                                long time, if at all

4. How satisfied are you with your ability to perform your usual domestic duties (i.e., shopping, meals, dishes, home repair, cleaning up, child care, etc.)? (Circle number)

        1   2   3   4   5   6   7   8   9   10
    Very   Very
    satisfied   dissatisfied

BULIMIA TEST—REVISED (BULIT-R)

AUTHOR: Mark H. Thelen and Marcia Smith

PURPOSE: To measure bulimia in accordance with the DSM-III-R.

DESCRIPTION: This 28-item instrument is designed to measure bulimia using the definitions set forth in the Diagnostic and Statistical Manual, 3rd Edition, Revised. The BULIT-R revises and replaces the original instrument because five new criteria were adopted in the DSM-III-R and two others from the DSM-III were dropped. The new criteria are: a persistent overconcern with the shape and weight of one's body; recurring episodes of binge eating; a minimum average of two episodes a week for at least three months; lack of control of overeating behaviors during the episodes; and weight reduction behaviors, including self-induced vomiting, fasting, vigorous exercise, or the use of laxatives. The two criteria dropped in the DSM-III-R and the BULIT-R are the reference to depression and the exclusion criterion of anorexia nervosa. The instrument was developed with rigorous psycho-metric procedures using six separate samples of bulimic and control subjects. It may be used to screen clients for bulimia as well as measure change during treatment. While the BULIT-R was developed on females for whom this disorder is more common, the instrument has clinical utility with males at risk of bulimia, such as high school wrestlers or other competitive athletes who may have weight limits imposed on them.

NORMS: The mean BULIT-R score for a sample of 21 females diagnosed with bulimia was 117.95; for a sample of 100 female psychology students, it was 57.50. An independent sample of 23 bulimics and 157 controls reported means of 118.08 and 59.62, respectively.

SCORING: There are eight filler items that are not scored. BULIT-R scores are the sum of the responses to items 1, 2*, 3, 4, 5*, 7*, 8*, 9, 10*, 12*, 13*, 14*, 15*, 16*, 17*, 18, 21*, 22, 23*, 24, 25, 26*, 28*, 30*, 32*, 33, 34, 35*. Items with an asterisk are reverse-scored. The instrument has a suggested cutting score of 104, below which one would not be classified as bulimic. To reduce false negatives, a cutting score of 85 is recommended.

RELIABILITY: The BULIT-R has excellent internal consistency. From a sample of 23 female bulimics and 157 normal college females, the alpha coefficient was .97. Test-retest over a two-month period was .95 suggesting the instrument is extremely stable.

VALIDITY: The validity of the instrument is evidenced with known-group procedures where each item and total scores discriminated between subjects diagnosed with bulimia and college females enrolled in a psychology course. This discrimination was replicated in an independent sample of bulimics and "normals." Concurrent validity is seen by a correlation of .85 between

BULIT-R scores and scores on the Binge Scale. Scores on the BULIT-R correlated .99 with the original BULIT.

PRIMARY REFERENCE: Thelen, M. H., Farmer, J., Wonderlich, S., and Smith, M. (1991). A revision of the bulimia test: The BULIT-R, *Psychological Assessment*, 3, 119–124. Instrument reproduced with permission of Mark Thelen.

AVAILABILITY: Dr. Mark Thelen, Department of Psychology, 210 McAlester Hall, University of Missouri, Columbia, MO 65211.

BULIT-R

Answer each question by circling the appropriate number. Please respond to each item as honestly as possible; remember, all of the information you provide will be kept strictly confidential.

1. I am satisfied with my eating patterns.
    1. Agree
    2. Neutral
    3. Disagree a little
    4. Disagree
    5. Disagree strongly

2. Would you presently call yourself a "binge eater"?
    1. Yes, absolutely
    2. Yes
    3. Yes, probably
    4. Yes, possibly
    5. No, probably not

3. Do you feel you have control over the amount of food you consume?
    1. Most or all of the time
    2. A lot of the time
    3. Occasionally
    4. Rarely
    5. Never

4. I am satisfied with the shape and size of my body.
    1. Frequently or always
    2. Sometimes
    3. Occasionally
    4. Rarely
    5. Seldom or never

5. When I feel that my eating behavior is out of control, I try to take rather extreme measures to get back on course (strict dieting, fasting, laxatives, diuretics, self-induced vomiting, or vigorous exercise).
    1. Always
    2. Almost always
    3. Frequently
    4. Sometimes
    5. Never or my eating behavior is never out of control

6. I use laxatives or suppositories to help control my weight.
    1. Once a day or more
    2. 3–6 times a week
    3. Once or twice a week
    4. 2–3 times a month
    5. Once a month or less (or never)

7. I am obsessed about the size and shape of my body.
    1. Always
    2. Almost always
    3. Frequently
    4. Sometimes
    5. Seldom or never

8. There are times when I rapidly eat a very large amount of food.
    1. More than twice a week
    2. Twice a week
    3. Once a week
    4. 2–3 times a month
    5. Once a month or less (or never)

9. How long have you been binge eating (eating uncontrollably to the point of stuffing yourself)?
    1. Not applicable; I don't binge eat
    2. Less than 3 months
    3. 3 months to 1 year
    4. 1–3 years
    5. 3 or more years

10. Most people I know would be amazed if they knew how much food I can consume at one sitting.
    1. Without a doubt
    2. Very probably
    3. Probably
    4. Possibly
    5. No

11. I exercise in order to burn calories.
    1. More than 2 hours per day
    2. About 2 hours per day
    3. More than 1 but less than 2 hours per day
    4. One hour or less per day
    5. I exercise but not to burn calories or I don't exercise

12. Compared with women your age, how preoccupied are you about your weight and body shape?
    1. A great deal more than average
    2. Much more than average
    3. More than average
    4. A little more than average
    5. Average or less than average

13. I am afraid to eat anything for fear that I won't be able to stop.
    1. Always
    2. Almost always
    3. Frequently
    4. Sometimes
    5. Seldom or never

14. I feel tormented by the idea that I am fat or might gain weight.
    1. Always
    2. Almost always
    3. Frequently
    4. Sometimes
    5. Seldom or never

15. How often do you intentionally vomit after eating?
    1. 2 or more times a week
    2. Once a week
    3. 2–3 times a month
    4. Once a month
    5. Less than once a month or never

16. I eat a lot of food when I'm not even hungry.
    1. Very frequently
    2. Frequently
    3. Occasionally
    4. Sometimes
    5. Seldom or never

17. My eating patterns are different from the eating patterns of most people.
    1. Always
    2. Almost always
    3. Frequently
    4. Sometimes
    5. Seldom or never

18. After I binge eat I turn to one of several strict methods to try to keep from gaining weight (vigorous exercise, strict dieting, fasting, self-induced vomiting, laxatives, or diuretics).
    1. Never or I don't binge eat
    2. Rarely
    3. Occasionally
    4. A lot of the time
    5. Most or all of the time

19. I have tried to lose weight by fasting or going on strict diets.
    1. Not in the past year
    2. Once in the past year
    3. 2–3 times in the past year
    4. 4–5 times in the past year
    5. More than 5 times in the past year

20. I exercise vigorously and for long periods of time in order to burn calories.
     1. Average or less than average
     2. A little more than average
     3. More than average
     4. Much more than average
     5. A great deal more than average

21. When engaged in an eating binge, I tend to eat foods that are high in carbohydrates (sweets and starches).
     1. Always
     2. Almost always
     3. Frequently
     4. Sometimes
     5. Seldom or I don't binge

22. Compared to most people, my ability to control my eating behavior seems to be:
     1. Greater than others' ability
     2. About the same
     3. Less
     4. Much less
     5. I have absolutely no control

23. I would presently label myself a "compulsive eater" (one who engages in episodes of uncontrolled eating).
     1. Absolutely
     2. Yes
     3. Yes, probably
     4. Yes, possibly
     5. No, probably not

24. I hate the way my body looks after I eat too much.
     1. Seldom or never
     2. Sometimes
     3. Frequently
     4. Almost always
     5. Always

25. When I am trying to keep from gaining weight, I feel that I have to resort to vigorous exercise, strict dieting, fasting, self-induced vomiting, laxatives, or diuretics.
     1. Never
     2. Rarely
     3. Occasionally
     4. A lot of the time
     5. Most or all of the time

26. Do you believe that it is easier for you to vomit than it is for most people?
    1. Yes, it's no problem at all for me
    2. Yes, it's easier
    3. Yes, it's a little easier
    4. About the same
    5. No, it's less easy

27. I use diuretics (water pills) to help control my weight.
    1. Never
    2. Seldom
    3. Sometimes
    4. Frequently
    5. Very frequently

28. I feel that food controls my life.
    1. Always
    2. Almost always
    3. Frequently
    4. Sometimes
    5. Seldom or never

29. I try to control my weight by eating little or no food for a day or longer.
    1. Never
    2. Seldom
    3. Sometimes
    4. Frequently
    5. Very frequently

30. When consuming a large quantity of food, at what rate of speed do you usually eat?
    1. More rapidly than most people have ever eaten in their lives
    2. A lot more rapidly than most people
    3. A little more rapidly than most people
    4. About the same rate as most people
    5. More slowly than most people (or not applicable)

31. I use laxatives or suppositories to help control my weight
    1. Never
    2. Seldom
    3. Sometimes
    4. Frequently
    5. Very frequently

32. Right after I binge eat I feel:
    1. So fat and bloated I can't stand it
    2. Extremely fat
    3. Fat
    4. A little fat
    5. OK about how my body looks or I never binge eat

33. Compared to other people of my sex, my ability to always feel in control of how much I eat is:
    1.   About the same or greater
    2.   A little less
    3.   Less
    4.   Much less
    5.   A great deal less

34. In the last 3 months, on the average how often did you binge eat (eat uncontrollably to the point of stuffing yourself)?
    1.   Once a month or less (or never)
    2.   2–3 times a month
    3.   Once a week
    4.   Twice a week
    5.   More than twice a week

35. Most people I know would be surprised at how fat I look after I eat a lot of food.
    1.   Yes, definitely
    2.   Yes
    3.   Yes, probably
    4.   Yes, possibly
    5.   No, probably not or I never eat a lot of food

36. I use diuretics (water pills) to help control my weight.
    1.   3 times a week or more
    2.   Once or twice a week
    3.   2–3 times a month
    4.   Once a month
    5.   Never

CAREGIVER STRAIN INDEX (CSI)

AUTHOR: Betsy C. Robinson

PURPOSE: To measure caregiver strain.

DESCRIPTION: The CSI is a 13-item instrument designed to measure the strain among caregivers of physically ill and functionally impaired older adults. The CSI was developed by systematically identifying the most common stressors named by adult children caring for an elderly parent and by reviewing the literature on caregiver strain. Although most practitioners are aware of the strain involved in providing care for the elderly, this brief, easily administered and scored questionnaire should be useful in preventive clinical practice. The CSI can be read to the respondent or filled out by the respondent as he or she reads it.

NORMS: The CSI was studied initially with 85 individuals who had been named as primary caregivers by elderly ex-patients from three San Francisco hospitals. The caregivers included 38% spouses, 22% daughters or daughters-in-law, 11% sons, 14% other relatives, 12% friends, and 4% neighbors. The age range was from 22 to 83 years. The mean score was 3.529 with a standard deviation of 3.5. The authors suggest that positive responses to seven or more items on the CSI indicate a greater level of stress.

SCORING: Item scores are summed for a total score that can range from 0 to 13 with higher scores indicating greater strain.

RELIABILITY: The CSI has very good internal consistency, with an alpha of .86. No data on stability were provided.

VALIDITY: The CSI has demonstrated fairly good construct validity, correlating in the predicted direction with a number of variables measuring ex-patient characteristics (e.g., ability to perform activities of daily living), subjective perception of the caregiving relationship (e.g., caregiver perceives it is hard to give help), and emotional status of caregivers (e.g., hostility).

PRIMARY REFERENCE: Robinson, B. C. (1983), Validation of a Caregiver Strain Index, *Journal of Gerontology*, 38, 344–348.

AVAILABILITY: Journal article.

CSI

I am going to read a list of things which other people have found to be difficult in helping out after somebody comes home from the hospital. *Would you tell me whether any of these apply to you by answering "yes" or "no" for each item.*

	Yes = 1	No = 2
Sleep is disturbed (e.g., because _____ is in and out of bed or wanders around at night).	_____	_____
It is inconvenient (e.g., because helping takes so much time or it's a long drive over to help).	_____	_____
It is a physical strain (e.g., because of lifting in and out of a chair; effort or concentration is required).	_____	_____
It is confining (e.g., helping restricts free time or cannot go visiting).	_____	_____
There have been family adjustments (e.g., because helping has disrupted routine; there has been no privacy).	_____	_____
There have been changes in personal plans (e.g., had to turn down a job; could not go on vacation).	_____	_____
There have been other demands on my time (e.g., from other family members).	_____	_____
There have been emotional adjustments (e.g., because of severe arguments).	_____	_____
Some behavior is upsetting (e.g., because of incontinence; _____ has trouble remembering things; or _____ accuses people of taking things).	_____	_____
It is upsetting to find _____ has changed so much from his/her former self (e.g., he/she is a different person than he/she used to be).	_____	_____
There have been work adjustments (e.g., because of having to take time off).	_____	_____
It is a financial strain.	_____	_____
Feeling completely overwhelmed (e.g., because of worry about _____ ; concerns about how you will manage).	_____	_____

Total Score (COUNT "YES" RESPONSES)

CAREGIVER'S BURDEN SCALE (CBS)

AUTHORS: Steven H. Zarit, Karen E. Reever, and Julie Bach-Peterson

PURPOSE: To measure caregivers' feelings of burden.

DESCRIPTION: The CBS is a 29-item scale designed to measure feelings of burden experienced by caregivers of elderly persons with senile dementia. The items for the CBS were selected based on clinical experience and prior research, and covered areas most frequently mentioned by caregivers as problems. Because of the increasing aging of the population and the emphasis in the gerontological literature on finding alternatives to institutionalization for the elderly, there is a need to be aware of the potential burden on family members of caring for older relatives, especially those with dementia. The CBS provides the opportunity for a systematic assessment of caregivers' perceptions of these burdens.

NORMS: The CBS was initially studied with 29 elderly people with senile dementia and their 29 primary caregivers. The mean age of the elderly was 76 with 16 males and 13 females, all white. Of the 29 caregivers, only four were male; they had a mean age of 65 years. Respondents were recruited from a research and training center offering services to older persons. The mean score for the total sample of caregivers was 30.8 with a standard deviation of 13.3. For daughters as caregivers, the mean score was 28.3 (SD = 14.6) and for spouses as caregivers, the mean was 32.5 (SD = 13.4).

SCORING: The CBS is scored on a 5-point sliding scale with scores on the items summed for the total scores. Items 14, 16, 20, and 29 are reverse-scored and subtracted from the total. Where the spouse is not the primary caregiver, the term spouse on the CBS can be replaced with the appropriate relationship (father, mother, etc.).

RELIABILITY: No data on reliability were reported.

VALIDITY: There were no significant correlations between feelings of burden and extent of behavior impairment or duration of illness. There was a low (.48) but significant negative correlation between the CBS and the frequency of family visits, a form of concurrent validity.

PRIMARY REFERENCE: Zarit, S. H., Reever, K. E., and Bach-Peterson, J. (1980). Relatives of the impaired elderly: Correlates of feelings of burden, *The Gerontologist*, 20, 649–655.

AVAILABILITY: Dr. Steven H. Zarit, Andrus Gerontology Center, University of Southern California, Los Angeles, CA 90007.

CBS

The following is a list of statements which reflect how people sometimes feel when taking care of another person. In the space to the left of each statement, please indicate how often you feel that way using the following scale:

0 = Never
1 = Rarely
2 = Sometimes
3 = Quite frequently
4 = Nearly always

_____ 1. Feel resentful of other relatives who could but who do not do things for my spouse.
_____ 2. I feel that my spouse makes requests which I perceive to be over and above what he/she needs.
_____ 3. Because of my involvement with my spouse, I don't have enough time for myself.
_____ 4. I feel stressed between trying to give to my spouse as well as to other family responsibilities, job, etc.
_____ 5. I feel embarrassed over my spouse's behavior.
_____ 6. I feel guilty about my interactions with my spouse.
_____ 7. I feel that I don't do as much for my spouse as I could or should.
_____ 8. I feel angry about my interactions with my spouse.
_____ 9. I feel that in the past, I haven't done as much for my spouse as I could have or should have.
_____ 10. I feel nervous or depressed about my interactions with my spouse.
_____ 11. I feel that my spouse currently affects my relationships with other family members and friends in a negative way.
_____ 12. I feel resentful about my interactions with my spouse.
_____ 13. I am afraid of what the future holds for my spouse.
_____ 14. I feel pleased about my interactions with my spouse.
_____ 15. It's painful to watch my spouse age.
_____ 16. I feel useful in my interactions with my spouse.
_____ 17. I feel my spouse is dependent.
_____ 18. I feel strained in my interactions with my spouse.
_____ 19. I feel that my health has suffered because of my involvement with my spouse.
_____ 20. I feel that I am contributing to the well-being of my spouse.
_____ 21. I feel that the present situation with my spouse doesn't allow me as much privacy as I like.
_____ 22. I feel that my social life has suffered because of my involvement with my spouse.
_____ 23. I wish that my spouse and I had a better relationship.
_____ 24. I feel that my spouse doesn't appreciate what I do for him/her as much as I would like.
_____ 25. I feel uncomfortable when I have friends over.
_____ 26. I feel that my spouse tries to manipulate me.

—— 27. I feel that my spouse seems to expect me to take care of him/her as if I were the only one he/she could depend on.
—— 28. I feel that I don't have enough money to support my spouse in addition to the rest of our expenses.
—— 29. I feel that I would like to be able to provide more money to support my spouse than I am able to now.

CENTER FOR EPIDEMIOLOGIC STUDIES—DEPRESSED MOOD
SCALE (CES-D)

AUTHOR: L. S. Radloff

PURPOSE: To measure depressive symptomatology in the general population.

DESCRIPTION: The CES-D is a 20-item scale that was originally designed to measure depression in the general population for epidemiological research. However it also has been shown to be useful in clinical and psychiatric settings. The scale is very easily administered and scored and was found to be easy to use by respondents in both the clinical and general populations. The CES-D measures current level of depressive symptomatology, with emphasis on the affective component—depressed mood. The CES-D items were selected from a pool of items from previously validated depression scales, from the literature, and from factor analytic studies. Because of the extensive research conducted in its development and its broad applicability, the CES-D is a particularly useful measure.

NORMS: Extensive research on the CES-D involved 3574 white respondents of both sexes from the general population plus a retest involving 1422 respondents. In addition, 105 psychiatric patients of both sexes were involved in clinical studies. An additional unspecified number of black respondents from the general population were involved in the testing. Means for the general population of white respondents ranged from 7.94 to 9.25. The mean for 70 psychiatric patients was 24.42. All results regarding reliability and validity were reported as being confirmed for subgroups: blacks and whites, both sexes, and three levels of education. No cutting scores were reported.

SCORING: The CES-D is easily scored by reverse-scoring items 4, 8, 12, and 16 and then summing the scores on all items. This produces a range of 0 to 60 with higher scores indicating greater depression.

RELIABILITY: The CES-D has very good internal consistency with alphas of roughly .85 for the general population and .90 for the psychiatric population. Split-half and Spearman-Brown reliability coefficients ranged from .77 to .92. The CES-D has fair stability with test-retest correlations that range from .51 to .67 (tested over two to eight weeks) and .32 to .54 (tested over 3 months to one year).

VALIDITY: The CES-D has excellent concurrent validity, correlating significantly with a number of other depression and mood scales. The CES-D also has good known-groups validity, discriminating well between psychiatric inpatients and the general population, and moderately among levels of severity within patient groups. The CES-D also discriminated between people in the general population who state they "need help" and those that did not, and it was shown to be sensitive to change in psychiatric patients' status after treatment. There was a very small association with social desirability response bias but it does not appear to affect the utility of CES-D.

PRIMARY REFERENCE: Radloff, L. S. (1977). The CES-D scale: A self-report depression scale for research in the general population, *Applied Psychological Measurement*, 1, 385–401. Instrument reproduced with permission of Dr. Ben Z. Locke.

AVAILABILITY: Edna L. Frazier, Program Assistant, Epidemiology and Psychopathology Branch, Division of Clinical Research, NIMH, 5600 Fishers Lane, Rm. 10C-09, Rockville, MD 20857.

CES-D

Using the scale below, indicate the number which best describes how often you felt or behaved this way—DURING THE PAST WEEK.

0 = Rarely or none of the time (less than 1 day)
1 = Some or a little of the time (1–2 days)
2 = Occasionally or a moderate amount of time (3–4 days)
3 = Most or all of the time (5–7 days)

DURING THE PAST WEEK:

___ 1. I was bothered by things that usually don't bother me.
___ 2. I did not feel like eating; my appetite was poor.
___ 3. I felt that I could not shake off the blues even with help from my family or friends.
___ 4. I felt that I was just as good as other people.
___ 5. I had trouble keeping my mind on what I was doing.
___ 6. I felt depressed.
___ 7. I felt that everything I did was an effort.
___ 8. I felt hopeful about the future.
___ 9. I thought my life had been a failure.
___ 10. I felt fearful.
___ 11. My sleep was restless.
___ 12. I was happy.
___ 13. I talked less than usual.
___ 14. I felt lonely.
___ 15. People were unfriendly.
___ 16. I enjoyed life.
___ 17. I had crying spells.
___ 18. I felt sad.
___ 19. I felt that people disliked me.
___ 20. I could not get "going."

CHINESE DEPRESSIVE SYMPTOM SCALE (CDS)

AUTHOR: Nan Lin

PURPOSE: To measure depression among Chinese in China.

DESCRIPTION: The CDS is a 22-item instrument designed to measure depressive symptoms among Chinese people in China. It was developed by adapting and translating the Center for Epidemiological Studies-Depression Scale and adding six new items based upon discussion with Chinese mental health workers. The added items were intended to tap the common idioms of psychiatric complaints that originated in the past, especially during the Cultural Revolution. The CDS can be usefully applied in cross-cultural studies or in clinical work with Chinese clients. However, its utility with Chinese living outside of China is unknown. It is reproduced here in English and Romanized Chinese.

NORMS: The CDS was administered to a random sample of 1000 adults living in Tianjin, the third largest city in China. Respondents were about equally divided between men and women, with a mean age of 43.2, 94% married, mean education of approximately seven to nine years. The mean score for the 22 items was 7.067.

SCORING: Individual items on the 4-point scales are summed to provide a range from 0 to 66 with higher scores indicating greater depressive symptoms.

RELIABILITY: The CDS has excellent internal consistency, with an alpha of .89. Data on stability were not provided.

VALIDITY: The CDS has good criterion validity, with significant correlations with four quality-of-life factors from a quality-of-life scale. The CDS was viewed as having very good predictive validity, correlating significantly with two life events scales. All validity checks indicated results were very similar to studies in North America.

PRIMARY REFERENCE: Lin, N. (1989). Measuring Depressive Symptomatology in China, *Journal of Nervous and Mental Disease*, 177, 121–131.

AVAILABILITY: Journal article.

CDS

Please place a number beside each item, to the extent it applies to you, as follows:

3 = Always
2 = From time to time
1 = Occasionally
0 = Never

_____ 1. I was bothered by things that usually don't bother me.
Yuan lai bu fan nao de shi, kai shi shi wuo fan nao.

_____ 2. I did not feel like eating; my appetite was poor.
Wou bu xiang chi dong xi, wei kou bu jia.

_____ 3. I felt that I could not shake off the blues even with the help of my family/friends.
Wou jue de xin fan, qin you de bang zhu ye bu guan yong.

_____ 4. I had trouble keeping my mind on what I was doing.
Wou bu neng ji zhong jing li zou wou yao zuo de shi.

_____ 5. I felt depressed.
Wou gan dao xie oi.

_____ 6. I felt that everything I did was an effort.
Wuo jue de zuo shen mo shi duo hen chi li.

_____ 7. I thought my life had been a failure.
Wuo jue de wuo de ren sheng jing li shi chang shi bai.

_____ 8. I felt fearful.
Wuo gan dao hai pa.

_____ 9. My sleep was restless.
Wuo shui bu hao jiao.

_____ 10. I talked less than usual.
Wuo hao xiang shuo hua bi yi qian shao le.

_____ 11. I felt lonely.
Wuo gan dao gu du.

_____ 12. People were unfriendly.
Wuo gan dao ren men dui wuo bu you hao.

_____ 13. I had crying spells.
Wuo ge yi duan shi jian jiu hui ku yi chang.

_____ 14. I felt sad.
Wuo gan dao bei shang.

_____ 15. I felt that people disliked me.
Wuo jue de bie ren bu xi huan wuo.

_____ 16. I could not get "going."
Wuo zuo ren he shi dou bu qi jin.

_____ 17. I felt I have a lot to talk about, but can't find the opportunity to say it.
Wuo jue de you hao xie hua yao shuo, dan you mei you hi shi de ji hui shuo.

_____ 18. I feel suffocated.
Wuo gan dao hen ku men.

_____ 19. I feel suspicious of others.
Wuo dui bei ren qi huai yi xin.

_____ 20. I don't think others trust me.
           Wuo jue de bie ren bu xin ren wuo.
_____ 21. I don't think I can trust others.
           Wuo jue de bu neng xin ren ta ren.
_____ 22. I remember unpleasant things from the past.
           Wuo hui xiang qi yi wang jing li guo de bu yu kuai de shi qing.

CLIENT SATISFACTION QUESTIONNAIRE (CSQ-8)

AUTHOR: C. Clifford Attkisson

PURPOSE: To assess client satisfaction with treatment.

DESCRIPTION: The CSQ-8 is an 8-item, easily scored and administered measure that is designed to measure client satisfaction with services. The items for the CSQ-8 were selected on the basis of ratings by mental health professionals of a number of items that could be related to client satisfaction and by subsequent factor analysis. The CSQ-8 is unidimensional, yielding a homogeneous estimate of general satisfaction with services. The CSQ-8 has been extensively studied, and while it is not necessarily a measure of a client's perceptions of gain from treatment, or outcome, it does elicit the client's perspective on the value of services received. Items 3, 7, and 8 can be used as a shorter scale.

NORMS: The CSQ-8 has been used with a number of populations. The largest single study involved 3268 clients from 76 clinical facilities including inpatients and outpatients. This study involved 42 Mexican Americans, 96 non-Mexican Hispanics, 361 blacks, and 2605 whites. Both sexes and a wide range of other demographic variables were included. In essence, the CSQ-8 seems to operate about the same across all ethnic groups. This also is true for a version of the CSQ-8 that was translated into Spanish. The mean scores for the four groups ranged from 26.35 to 27.23 and were not significantly different.

SCORING: The CSQ-8 is easily scored by summing the individual item scores to produce a range of 8 to 32, with higher scores indicating greater satisfaction.

RELIABILITY: The CSQ-8 has excellent internal consistency, with alphas that range from .86 to .94 in a number of studies. Test-retest correlations were not reported.

VALIDITY: The CSQ-8 has very good concurrent validity. Scores on the CSQ-8 are correlated with clients' ratings of global improvement and symptomatology, and therapists' ratings of clients' progress and likability. Scores also are correlated with drop-out rate (less satisfied clients having higher drop-out rates). The CSQ-8 has also demonstrated moderate correlations with a number of other (but not all) outcome variables, thus suggesting a modest correlation between satisfaction and treatment gain.

PRIMARY REFERENCE: Larsen, D. L., Attkisson, C. C., Hargreaves, W. A., and Nguyen, T. D. (1979). Assessment of client/patient satisfaction: Development of a general scale, *Evaluation and Program Planning*, 2, 197–207. Instrument reproduced with permission of C. Clifford Attkisson.

AVAILABILITY: Dr. C. Clifford Attkisson, Professor of Medical Psychology, Department of Psychiatry, Box 33-C, University of California, San Francisco, CA 94143.

CSQ-8

Please help us improve our program by answering some questions about the services you have received. We are interested in your honest opinions, whether they are positive or negative. *Please answer all of the questions.* We also welcome your comments and suggestions. Thank you very much; we really appreciate your help.

Circle your answer:

1. How would you rate the quality of service you have received?

4	3	2	1
Excellent	Good	Fair	Poor

2. Did you get the kind of service you wanted?

1	2	3	4
No, definitely	No, not really	Yes, generally	Yes, definitely

3. To what extent has our program met your needs?

4	3	2	1
Almost all of my needs have been met	Most of my needs have been met	Only a few of my needs have been met	None of my needs have been met

4. If a friend were in need of similar help, would you recommend our program to him or her?

1	2	3	4
No, definitely not	No, I don't think so	Yes, I think so	Yes, definitely

5. How satisfied are you with the amount of help you have received?

1	2	3	4
Quite dissatisfied	Indifferent or mildly dissatisfied	Mostly satisfied	Very satisfied

6. Have the services you received helped you to deal more effectively with your problems?

4	3	2	1
Yes, they helped a great deal	Yes, they helped somewhat	No, they really didn't help	No, they seemed to make things worse

7. In an overall, general sense, how satisfied are you with the service you have received?

4	3	2	1
Very satisfied	Mostly satisfied	Indifferent or mildly dissatfied	Quite dissatisfied

8. If you were to seek help again, would you come back to our program?

1	2	3	4
No, definitely not	No, I don't think so	Yes, I think so	Yes, definitely

CLINICAL ANXIETY SCALE (CAS)

AUTHOR: Bruce A. Thyer

PURPOSE: To measure clinical anxiety.

DESCRIPTION: The CAS is a 25-item scale that is focused on measuring the amount, degree, or severity of clinical anxiety reported by the respondent, with higher scores indicating higher amounts of anxiety. The CAS is simply worded, and easy to administer, score, and interpret. The items for the CAS were psychometrically derived from a larger number of items based on the criteria for anxiety disorders in DSM III. The CAS has a clinical cutting score of 30 (±5), and is designed to be scored and administered in the same way as the scales of the WALMYR Assessment Scales, also reproduced in this book. This instrument is particularly useful for measuring general anxiety in clinical practice.

NORMS: Initial study of the CAS was based on 41 women and 6 men (average age 40.9 years) from an agoraphobic support group, 51 men and 32 women from the U.S. Army who were attending courses in health sciences (average age 25.7 years), and 58 female and 15 male university students (average age 26.6 years). No other demographic information was available nor were actual norms.

SCORING: Like most WALMYR Assessment Scales instruments, the CAS is scored by first reverse-scoring items listed at the bottom of the page (1, 6, 7, 9, 13, 15, 16), summing these and the remaining scores, subtracting the number of completed items, multiplying this figure by 100, and dividing by the number of items completed times 4. This will produce a range from 0 to 100 with higher scores indicating greater magnitude or severity of problems.

RELIABILITY: The CAS has excellent internal consistency, with a coefficient alpha of .94. The SEM of 4.2 is relatively low, suggesting a minimal amount of measurement error. The CAS had good stability, with two-week test-retest correlations that range from .64 to .74.

VALIDITY: The CAS has good known-groups validity, discriminating significantly between groups known to be suffering from anxiety and lower-anxiety control groups. Using the clinical cutting score of 30, the CAS had a very low error rate of 6.9% in distinguishing between anxiety and control groups. No other validity information was available. Analysis of the CAS in relation to demographic variables such as age, sex, and education reveals that scores on the CAS are not affected by those factors (ethnicity was not examined).

PRIMARY REFERENCE: Hudson, W. W. (1992). *The WALMYR Assessment Scales Scoring Manual*. Tempe, AZ: WALMYR Publishing Co.

AVAILABILITY: WALMYR Publishing Co., P.O. Box 24779, Tempe, AZ 85285-4779.

CLINICAL ANXIETY SCALE (CAS)

Name: _____ Today's Date: _____

This questionnaire is designed to measure how much anxiety you are currently feeling. It is not a test, so there are no right or wrong answers. Answer each item as carefully and as accurately as you can by placing a number beside each one as follows.

    1 Rarely or none of the time
    2 A little of the time
    3 Some of the time
    4 A good part of the time
    5 Most or all of the time

---

1. ____ I feel calm.
2. ____ I feel tense.
3. ____ I feel suddenly scared for no reason.
4. ____ I feel nervous.
5. ____ I use tranquilizers or antidepressants to cope with my anxiety.
6. ____ I feel confident about the future.
7. ____ I am free from senseless or unpleasant thoughts.
8. ____ I feel afraid to go out of my house alone.
9. ____ I feel relaxed and in control of myself.
10. ____ I have spells of terror or panic.
11. ____ I feel afraid in open spaces or in the streets.
12. ____ I feel afraid I will faint in public.
13. ____ I am comfortable traveling on buses, subways or trains.
14. ____ I feel nervousness or shakiness inside.
15. ____ I feel comfortable in crowds, such as shopping or at a movie.
16. ____ I feel comfortable when I am left alone.
17. ____ I feel afraid without good reason.
18. ____ Due to my fears, I unreasonably avoid certain animals, objects or situations.
19. ____ I get upset easily or feel panicky unexpectedly.
20. ____ My hands, arms or legs shake or tremble.
21. ____ Due to my fears, I avoid social situations, whenever possible.
22. ____ I experience sudden attacks of panic which catch me by surprise.
23. ____ I feel generally anxious.
24. ____ I am bothered by dizzy spells.
25. ____ Due to my fears, I avoid being alone, whenever possible.

1, 6, 7, 9, 13, 15, 16

COGNITIVE COPING STRATEGY INVENTORY (CCSI)

AUTHORS: Robert W. Butler, Fred L. Damarin, Cynthia Beaulieu, Andrew Schwebel, and Beverly E. Thorn

PURPOSE: To measure coping strategies in acute pain.

DESCRIPTION: The CCSI is a 70-item instrument designed to measure cognitive coping strategies and catastrophizing in managing acute pain. Since most other standardized measures are used for measuring chronic pain, the CCSI is one of the few measures, if not the only one, developed for use with nonchronic or acute pain. The CCSI has seven factors; however, it can be used as a two-subscale instrument with one subscale called catastrophizing (C: items 7, 8, 11, 12, 34, 44, 50, 62, 67, 70), and the other called the cognitive coping index (CCI: remainder of items).

NORMS: The CCSI has been studied with several samples of postsurgical patients, totaling 264, including 122 men and 142 women. The mean age of the samples ranged from 45.1 to 50.3. The mean score for the CCI was 93.3 (SD = 30.7) and for catastrophizing was 19.6 (SD = 7.0).

SCORING: The scores for the CCSI are determined by adding up all items except catastrophizing and subtracting the sum of the catastrophizing items from that total for the CCI score, and simply summing subscale items (noted above) for the catastrophizing score.

RELIABILITY: The CCSI has very good internal consistency, with alphas for the subscales that range from .77 to .90. Data on stability were not available.

VALIDITY: The CCSI has good concurrent and known-groups validity, correlating with several independent and self-reported measures of pain and use of pain medication.

PRIMARY REFERENCE: Butler, R.W. (1989). Assessing cognitive coping strategies for acute postsurgical pain, *Psychological Assessment*, 1, 41–45.

AVAILABILITY: Dr. Robert Butler, Department of Psychiatry (H-620), University of California, San Diego Medical Center, 225 Dickinson Street, San Diego, CA 92103.

CCSI

The following statements describe different thoughts and behaviors that people engage in when they experience pain. For each statement you are to indicate whether it is never, some of the time, one-half of the time, most of the time, or all of the time true about the way in which you deal with your pain. You may find it helpful to think back to the most recent time you were in some degree of pain and imagine as if you were answering these questions while in pain. If the individual *content* of a test item is not similar, but the *style* in which you deal with the pain is similar to the item, you should mark the item in the true categories. Make only one response per item and try and answer each item.

	1	2	3	4	5
	Never true	Some of the time true	One half of the time true	Most of the time true	All of the time true
1. I use my imagination to change the situation or place where I am experiencing pain in order to try and make the pain more bearable.	____	____	____	____	____
2. I think of photographs or paintings that I have seen in the past.	____	____	____	____	____
3. I might attempt to imagine myself leaving my body and observing my pain in an impartial, detached manner.	____	____	____	____	____
4. I concentrate on things or people around me.	____	____	____	____	____
5. If my pain feels severely throbbing, I might tend to imagine it as only a dull ache.	____	____	____	____	____
6. I might count ceiling tiles or other objects in the room in order to occupy my mind.	____	____	____	____	____

		1	2	3	4	5
		Never true	Some of the time true	One half of the time true	Most of the time true	All of the time true
7.	I feel like I just want to get up and run away.	_____	_____	_____	_____	_____
8.	I imagine the pain becoming even more intense and hurtful.	_____	_____	_____	_____	_____
9.	I try to imagine myself in a place completely different, such as my hometown.	_____	_____	_____	_____	_____
10.	I attend to and analyze my pain as perhaps a doctor or scientist might.	_____	_____	_____	_____	_____
11.	I begin thinking of all the possible bad things that could go wrong in association with the pain.	_____	_____	_____	_____	_____
12.	If my pain feels stabbing I might try and imagine that it is only pricking.	_____	_____	_____	_____	_____
13.	I describe the pain to myself or tell others about it in order to try and make the pain less hurtful.	_____	_____	_____	_____	_____
14.	I might try and imagine myself "floating off" away from the pain but still realize that my body hurts.	_____	_____	_____	_____	_____
15.	I tell myself that the pain is really not what it seems to be, but rather some other sensation.	_____	_____	_____	_____	_____

	1	2	3	4	5
	Never true	Some of the time true	One half of the time true	Most of the time true	All of the time true

16. I "psych" myself up to deal with the pain, perhaps by telling myself that it won't last much longer. ___ ___ ___ ___ ___

17. If possible, I would try and read a book or magazine to take my mind off the pain. ___ ___ ___ ___ ___

18. I picture in my "mind's eye" a lush, green forest or other similar peaceful scene. ___ ___ ___ ___ ___

19. If a television set was available I would watch TV to distract myself from the pain. ___ ___ ___ ___ ___

20. I try and imagine that for some reason it is important for me to endure the pain. ___ ___ ___ ___ ___

21. If my pain feels burning I might try and pretend that it is only warm. ___ ___ ___ ___ ___

22. I tell myself that I don't think I can bear the pain any longer. ___ ___ ___ ___ ___

23. I try and mentally remove the pain from the part of my body that hurts by paying close attention to it. ___ ___ ___ ___ ___

24. I try and make myself busy by pretending that I am doing other things. ___ ___ ___ ___ ___

		1	2	3	4	5
		Never true	Some of the time true	One half of the time true	Most of the time true	All of the time true
25.	I use my imagination to develop pictures which help distract me.	____	____	____	____	____
26.	I imagine that the pain is really not as severe as it seems to feel.	____	____	____	____	____
27.	In general, my ability to see things visually in my "mind's eye" or imagination is quite good.	____	____	____	____	____
28.	I develop images or pictures in my mind to try and ignore the pain.	____	____	____	____	____
29.	I might concentrate on how attractive certain colors are in the room or place where I am experiencing pain.	____	____	____	____	____
30.	I might repeat a phrase such as "It's not that bad" over and over to myself.	____	____	____	____	____
31.	I imagine my pain as occurring in a situation completely different from the place where I am experiencing it.	____	____	____	____	____
32.	I might imagine that I am with a date/spouse and feel the pain but don't want to let on that it hurts too much.	____	____	____	____	____

	1	2	3	4	5
	Never true	Some of the time true	One half of the time true	Most of the time true	All of the time true

33. I might pay attention to the parts of my body that do not hurt and compare how much better they feel than where the pain is. _____ _____ _____ _____ _____

34. I find myself worrying about possibly dying. _____ _____ _____ _____ _____

35. I might think of myself as a prisoner who must withhold secrets under torture to protect my friends or country. _____ _____ _____ _____ _____

36. I might picture myself as an adventurer who has been hurt while on a journey. _____ _____ _____ _____ _____

37. I take myself very far away from the pain by using my imagination. _____ _____ _____ _____ _____

38. I might do something such as gently rub a part of my body close to where it hurts and notice the difference in the feelings. _____ _____ _____ _____ _____

39. I would focus my attention on something such as a chair or tree and think real hard about it. _____ _____ _____ _____ _____

40. I try and pretend that the pain is really only a feeling of pressure. _____ _____ _____ _____ _____

	1 Never true	2 Some of the time true	3 One half of the time true	4 Most of the time true	5 All of the time true
41. I would listen to music to help keep my mind off the pain.	___	___	___	___	___
42. I think of jokes that I have heard.	___	___	___	___	___
43. I might begin thinking about my pain as if I were conducting an experiment or writing a biology report.	___	___	___	___	___
44. I find myself expecting the worst.	___	___	___	___	___
45. I try and pretend that I am on the beach, or some-where else enjoying a summer day.	___	___	___	___	___
46. I might sit down and balance my checkbook, work crossword puzzles, or engage in hobbies if I am able.	___	___	___	___	___
47. I might attend to the pain in much the same way that a sports announcer or reporter would describe an event.	___	___	___	___	___
48. I might try and think of a difficult problem in my life and how it could be solved in order to try and forget the pain.	___	___	___	___	___
49. I concentrate on making the pain feel as if it hurts less.	___	___	___	___	___

	1	2	3	4	5
	Never true	Some of the time true	One half of the time true	Most of the time true	All of the time true

50. I tend to think that my pain is pretty awful. _____ _____ _____ _____ _____

51. I concentrate on what others might think of me and act as brave as I can. _____ _____ _____ _____ _____

52. I concentrate on convincing myself that I will deal with the pain and that it will get better in the near future. _____ _____ _____ _____ _____

53. I think of myself as being interested in pain and wanting to describe it to myself in detail. _____ _____ _____ _____ _____

54. I try and take my mind off the pain by talking to others, such as family members, about different things. _____ _____ _____ _____ _____

55. I might try and imagine being given a pain shot and my body becoming numb. _____ _____ _____ _____ _____

56. I think of and picture myself being with my spouse/boyfriend/girlfriend. _____ _____ _____ _____ _____

57. I might do mental arithmetic problems to keep my mind occupied. _____ _____ _____ _____ _____

58. I might try and think that I'm overreacting and that my pain is really not as severe as it seems. _____ _____ _____ _____ _____

	1	2	3	4	5
	Never true	Some of the time true	One half of the time true	Most of the time true	All of the time true

59. I try and sort out in my mind problems at work or home.   ____ ____ ____ ____ ____

60. I describe objects in the room to myself.   ____ ____ ____ ____ ____

61. I might begin making plans for a future event, such as a vacation, to distract me from thinking about the pain.   ____ ____ ____ ____ ____

62. I can't help but concentrate on how bad the pain actually feels.   ____ ____ ____ ____ ____

63. I work at talking myself into believing that the pain is really not all that bad and that there are others who are much worse off than me.   ____ ____ ____ ____ ____

64. I might pretend that my pain was similar to pain I have felt after a good session of exercise.   ____ ____ ____ ____ ____

65. I try and preoccupy my mind by daydreaming about various pleasant things such as clouds or sailboats.   ____ ____ ____ ____ ____

66. If my pain feels shooting I try and pretend that it is only tingling.   ____ ____ ____ ____ ____

	1	2	3	4	5
	Never true	Some of the time true	One half of the time true	Most of the time true	All of the time true
67. I find it virtually impossible to keep my mind off of my pain and how bad it hurts.	____	____	____	____	____
68. I might imagine that the pain is the result of an injury while engaging in my favorite sport.	____	____	____	____	____
69. I tell myself that I can cope with the pain without imagining or pretending anything.	____	____	____	____	____
70. I begin to worry that something might be seriously wrong with me.	____	____	____	____	____

COGNITIVE PROCESSES SURVEY (CPS)

AUTHOR: Raymond F. Martinetti

PURPOSE: To measure components of imaginal life.

DESCRIPTION: The CPS is a 39-item instrument designed to measure three components of imaginal life: degree of imaginal life (DIL—the intensity and extensity of imaginal activity), orientation toward imaginal life (OIL—the individual's emotional response to imaginal processes), and degree of suppression (DOS—the tendency to suppress feelings, especially anger and sexual ideation). The CPS may be useful for exploring the continuity of some imaginal processes between waking and sleep, and for evaluating the effectiveness of therapeutic techniques aimed at enhancing dream recall and exploration of inner states of awareness.

NORMS: The CPS was standardized on a sample of 350 college students, but actual norms were not provided. A subsequent sample of 45 men and 45 women from college psychology courses provided the following means and standard deviations: DIL—men, 30.31 (SD = 11.9), women, 42.27 (SD = 12.53); OIL—men, 28.76 (SD = 9.22), women, 38.36 (SD = 11.89); and DOS—men, 27.42 (SD = 7.70), women, 25.21 (SD = 7.01).

SCORING: The CPS is scored on a 5-point scale with scores for each subscale being a simple sum of the items on the subscale and scores for the total scale being a sum of all 39 items. Following is a guide to the subscales: OIL: items 1, 6, 7, 11, 16, 20, 21, 22, 26, 28, 32, 34, 35. DIL: items 2, 8, 9, 12, 14, 17, 19, 24, 27, 31, 33, 36, 38. DOS: items 3, 4, 5, 10, 13, 15, 18, 23, 25, 29, 30, 37, 39. Items to be reverse-scored are 1, 2, 4, 6, 8, 9, 10, 11, 12, 13, 14, 15, 17, 19, 21, 24, 25, 27, 28, 30, 31, 33, 35–39. The total range per subscale is 13 to 65 and the total range for the entire CPS is 39 to 195.

RELIABILITY: Reliability coefficients for the three subscales are reported as .78 for DIL, .75 for OIL, and .72 for DOS. The author does not state what type of reliability these coefficients measure (presumably internal consistency), nor is the reliability for the overall scale reported.

VALIDITY: No real validity data are reported. However, the author does report significant positive correlations showing that respondents with the highest imaginal life reported most dreams recalled. This may be viewed as a type of concurrent validity.

PRIMARY REFERENCE: Martinetti, R. F. (1989). Sex differences in dream recall and components of imaginal life, *Perceptual and Motor Skills*, 69, 643–649. Instrument reprinted with permission of author and publisher.

AVAILABILITY: Journal article.

CPS

Determine the extent to which you agree or disagree with each of the following statements. Place a check in the appropriate space provided to the right of each item. (SA = strongly agree, A = agree, U = undecided, D = disagree, SD = strongly disagree). Try to be as accurate as possible in giving the *first* impression you have for each statement.

		SA	A	U	D	SD
1.	I like to contemplate my innermost feelings.	—	—	—	—	—
2.	I often dream in color.	—	—	—	—	—
3.	I can't stay angry at other people for a long time.	—	—	—	—	—
4.	Masturbation is not a topic that should be openly discussed.	—	—	—	—	—
5.	A very sad novel or movie can move me to tears.	—	—	—	—	—
6.	I enjoy analyzing my own dreams.	—	—	—	—	—
7.	ESP and psychic experiences probably do not really occur.	—	—	—	—	—
8.	If I think about a song I feel as if I am really *hearing* it.	—	—	—	—	—
9.	I often experience *déjà vu* (thinking something has already happened while it is happening).	—	—	—	—	—
10.	If I had thoughts of a homosexual nature I would worry about my mental health.	—	—	—	—	—
11.	I would enjoy reading about other people's fantasies.	—	—	—	—	—
12.	I have a rich fantasy life.	—	—	—	—	—
13.	The best way to deal with disturbing thoughts is to concentrate on something completely different.	—	—	—	—	—

	SA	A	U	D	SD
14. When I listen to music I can usually visualize what it represents.	___	___	___	___	___
15. Those who try to look deeply into their own feelings are treading on dangerous ground.	___	___	___	___	___
16. I have no patience with people who claim they can predict the future.	___	___	___	___	___
17. I am more idealistic than realistic.	___	___	___	___	___
18. I think I would be sexually aroused by pornographic material.	___	___	___	___	___
19. I have had recurrent dreams at least once during my life.	___	___	___	___	___
20. People who really believe in "ghosts" are somewhat mentally disturbed.	___	___	___	___	___
21. I would rather plan my "dream house" than actually build it.	___	___	___	___	___
22. A danger of hypnosis is that the hypnotized person loses his/her free will.	___	___	___	___	___
23. A very good way of dealing with your problems is to talk to other people about them.	___	___	___	___	___
24. If I think about a food very intensely I can practically taste it.	___	___	___	___	___
25. If I had a terminal illness I would rather not know about it.	___	___	___	___	___
26. Dreams have no real meanings: They are random thoughts.	___	___	___	___	___
27. I have often wondered what becomes of a person's awareness after death.	___	___	___	___	___
28. I believe that dreams reveal truths about us.	___	___	___	___	___

		SA	A	U	D	SD
29.	I often think about my own shortcomings.	___	___	___	___	___
30.	It Is not good to openly reveal your feelings.	___	___	___	___	___
31.	My dreams tend to be quite complex.	___	___	___	___	___
32.	Daydreaming is unproductive and may even be harmful.	___	___	___	___	___
33.	I can recall past experiences in vivid detail.	___	___	___	___	___
34.	If an idea does not have practical application, it is worthless.	___	___	___	___	___
35.	I can wake up from a dream, go back to sleep, and continue the dream.	___	___	___	___	___
36.	The more you explore your motives the better is your self-understanding.	___	___	___	___	___
37.	I think everyone has private thoughts which are never publicly revealed.	___	___	___	___	___
38.	I like fictional works (books, films, etc.) better than nonfictional works.	___	___	___	___	___
39.	If I told people what I really thought of them I'd have very few friends.	___	___	___	___	___

COGNITIVE SLIPPAGE SCALE (CSS)

AUTHORS: Tracey C. Miers and Michael L. Raulin

PURPOSE: To measure cognitive impairment.

DESCRIPTION: The CSS is a 35-item scale that is designed to measure cognitive slippage, an aspect of cognitive distortion that is viewed as a primary characteristic of schizophrenia. Cognitive slippage is also viewed as central to a schizotypic personality indicative of a genetic predisposition to schizophrenia. Cognitive slippage can be manifested in several ways such as hallucinations, delusions, speech deficits, confused thinking, and attentional disorders. The CSS focuses mainly on speech deficits and confused thinking. Although the scale was developed to identify schizotypic characteristics, it may also be useful in identifying cognitive disorders among other populations.

NORMS: The scale was developed in two series of studies eventually involving 690 male and 516 female undergraduate students in introductory psychology courses. The mean score for males was 7.8 and for females 9.3; actual norms are not reported.

SCORING: The CSS is scored by assigning a score of one to the correct response and then summing these scores. The correct response is "true" on items 2, 3–5, 9, 11, 13, 15, 18, 20, 22, 24, 25, 27, 28, 30, 31, 33. The remainder are correct if answered "false."

RELIABILITY: The CSS has excellent internal consistency, with alphas of .87 for males and .90 for females. No test-retest correlations are available.

VALIDITY: The CSS has good concurrent validity in correlations with several other scales measuring schizotypic characteristics (e.g., perceptual aberration, intense ambivalence, social fear, magical ideation, somatic symptoms, and distrust). The CSS also has fair construct validity, accurately predicting scores on several scales of the MMPI between high and low scorers on the CSS. The CSS is slightly correlated with social desirability response bias suggesting that this factor cannot be totally ruled out.

PRIMARY REFERENCE: Miers, T. C. and Raulin, M. L. (1985). The development of a scale to measure cognitive slippage. Paper presented at the Eastern Psychological Association Convention, Boston, Mass., March 1985. Instrument reproduced with permission of Michael L. Raulin.

AVAILABILITY: Dr. Michael L. Raulin, SUNY-Buffalo, Psychology Department, Julian Park Hall, Buffalo, NY 14260.

CSS

Please circle either T for true or F for false for each item as it applies to you.

T F 1. My thoughts are orderly most of the time.
T F 2. I almost always feel as though my thoughts are on a different wavelength from 98% of the population.
T F 3. Often when I am talking I feel that I am not making any sense.
T F 4. Often people ask me a question and I don't know what it is that they are asking.
T F 5. Often I don't even know what it is that I have just said.
T F 6. I hardly ever find myself saying the opposite of what I meant to say.
T F 7. I rarely feel so mixed up that I have difficulty functioning.
T F 8. My thoughts are usually clear, at least to myself.
T F 9. My thoughts are more random than orderly.
T F 10. The way I perceive things is much the same as the way in which others perceive them.
T F 11. Sometimes my thoughts just disappear.
T F 12. I can usually keep my thoughts going straight.
T F 13. My thoughts are so vague and hazy that I wish that I could just reach up and pull them into place.
T F 14. I usually feel that people understand what I say.
T F 15. There have been times when I have gone an entire day or longer without speaking.
T F 16. I ordinarily don't get confused about *when* things happened.
T F 17. It's usually easy to keep the point that I am trying to make clear in my mind.
T F 18. My thoughts speed by so fast that I can't catch them.
T F 19. I usually don't feel that I'm rambling on pointlessly when I'm speaking.
T F 20. Sometimes when I try to focus on an idea, so many other thoughts come to mind that I find it impossible to concentrate on just one.
T F 21. I have no difficulty in controlling my thoughts.
T F 22. My thinking often gets "cloudy" for no apparent reason.
T F 23. I think that I am reasonably good at communicating my ideas to other people.
T F 24. I often find myself saying something that comes out completely backwards.
T F 25. My thoughts often jump from topic to topic without any logical connection.
T F 26. I'm pretty good at keeping track of time.
T F 27. Often during the day I feel as though I am being flooded by thoughts.
T F 28. The way that I process information is very different from the way in which other people do.
T F 29. I have no difficulty separating past from present.
T F 30. I often find that people are puzzled by what I say.
T F 31. My thoughts seem to come and go so quickly that I can't keep up with them.

T   F   32.   I can usually think things through clearly.
T   F   33.   I often feel confused when I try to explain my ideas.
T   F   34.   Usually my thoughts aren't difficult to keep track of.
T   F   35.   I have no difficulty in controlling my thoughts.

COGNITIVE-SOMATIC ANXIETY QUESTIONNAIRE (CSAQ)

AUTHORS: Gary E. Schwartz, Richard J. Davidson, and Daniel J. Goleman

PURPOSE: To measure cognitive and somatic components of anxiety.

DESCRIPTION: The CSAQ is a 14-item, simply worded, easy to understand measure of the cognitive and somatic aspects of anxiety. The scale is based on the assumption that there are two different aspects of anxiety—cognitive and somatic. The importance of this for practice is that therapeutic techniques for reducing anxiety may differ in their impact on these two systems. Thus, by providing information on each aspect of anxiety, this measure allows the practitioner to be more precise in selecting intervention techniques. The CSAQ is considered to be a trait measure of anxiety in that it taps relatively enduring patterns.

NORMS: The initial study was conducted on 77 respondents consisting of 44 participants in a physical exercise class and 33 volunteers who practiced cognitively-based passive meditation at least once daily. The physical exercisers were predominantly female with an average age of 27.3 years while the meditators were approximately equally divided between males and females and had an average age of 20.86 years. No real effort was made to develop norms due to the size and nature of the samples.

SCORING: The cognitive (items 1, 3, 6, 8, 9, 10, 13) and somatic items (the remainder) of the CSAQ appear in random order and are scored by totaling the sums of the scores on each item. Separate scores are computed for the cognitive and somatic scales with a range for each of 7 to 35.

RELIABILITY: No data reported.

VALIDITY: The CSAQ has good concurrent validity, correlating significantly with the State-Trait Anxiety Inventory. The CSAQ also demonstrated a type of known-groups validity in that respondents who were meditators reported less cognitive and more somatic anxiety than physical exercisers and the exercisers reported more cognitive and less somatic anxiety. The two groups did not differ on overall anxiety, supporting the idea that anxiety may not be a diffuse, undifferentiated state, but may be subdivided into component parts.

PRIMARY REFERENCE: Schwartz, G. E., Davidson, R. J., and Goleman, D. J. (1978). Patterning of cognitive and somatic processes in the self-regulation of anxiety: Effects of meditation versus exercise, *Psychosomatic Medicine, 40,* 321–328. Instrument reproduced by permission of Gary E. Schwartz and Daniel J. Goleman and the Elsevier Science Publishing Co., Inc.

AVAILABILITY: Journal article.

CSAQ

Please read the following and rate the degree to which you generally or typically experience each symptom when you are feeling anxious. Rate each item by filling in one number from 1 through 5 in the left-hand column, with 1 representing "not at all" and 5 representing "very much so." Be sure to answer every item and try to be as honest and accurate as possible in your responses.

1	2	3	4	5
Not at all				Very much so

_____ 1. Some unimportant thought runs through my mind and bothers me.
_____ 2. I perspire.
_____ 3. I imagine terrifying scenes.
_____ 4. I become immobilized.
_____ 5. My heart beats faster.
_____ 6. I can't keep anxiety-provoking pictures out of my mind.
_____ 7. I nervously pace
_____ 8. I find it difficult to concentrate because of uncontrollable thoughts.
_____ 9. I can't keep anxiety-provoking thoughts out of my mind.
_____ 10. I feel like I am losing out on things because I can't make up my mind soon enough.
_____ 11. I feel tense in my stomach.
_____ 12. I get diarrhea.
_____ 13. I worry too much over something that doesn't really matter.
_____ 14. I feel jittery in my body.

COGNITIVE TRIAD INVENTORY (CTI)

AUTHOR: Ernest Edward Beckham, William R. Leber, John T. Watkins, Jenny L. Boyer, and Jacque B. Cook

PURPOSE: To measure the cognitive triad in depressed persons.

DESCRIPTION: The CTI is a 30-item instrument designed to measure the cognitive triad hypothesized to be present in depressed persons: negative views of themselves, their worlds, and their future. Negative cognitions in these areas are hypothesized as actually leading to feelings of depression. Thus, in cognitive therapy, they would be an important target for change. The items are arranged in three subscales (negative and positive refer to scoring): view of self (items −5, −10, −13, +17, −21, +25, −29, +31, +33, −35); view of world (items +3, +8, +12, −18, +20, −23, +24, −27, −30, −34); and view of future (items +6, +9, +11, −15, −16, −19, −26, +28, −32, +36). The CTI is seen as useful for studying the role of the cognitive triad in the etiology and treatment of depression as well as how these states change over time, including after single therapy sessions.

NORMS: The CTI was initially studied on a sample of 54 patients from an outpatient mental health service in Oklahoma. All were diagnosed as depressed with a mean Beck Depression Inventory score of 21.8. The sample comprised 44 women and 10 men with a mean age of 36 years and a mean educational attainment of 13.9 years. All but two of the sample were white (the other two black), with 35.1% married, 35.1% divorced, 20.3% single, and 9.2% separated. Norms were as follows: view of self: 36.96 (SD = 14.86), view of world = 35.11 (SD = 11.21), view of future = 31.93 (SD = 13.56), and total score = 104 (SD = 34.96).

SCORING: Items on the CTI are phrased in both positive and negative terms and answered on 7-point Likert-type scales (from 1 = totally agree to 7 = totally disagree). Scores for each subscale are a sum of the items on each subscale, as indicated in the description, adding positive and negative items. To that total, add 48 to view of self, and 40 to the other two subscales. The total score is a sum of all items, with high scores representing positive views and low scores representing negative views. Items 1, 2, 4, 7, 14, and 18 are not scored.

RELIABILITY: The CTI has excellent internal consistency, with alphas of .91 for view of self, .81 for view of world, and .93 for view of future. The alpha for the total scale was .95.

VALIDITY: The authors report good face validity based on high levels of agreement regarding the meaning of the items by 16 faculty members from a university department of psychiatry and behavioral sciences. The CTI has good concurrent validity, correlating significantly (.77) with the Beck Depression Inventory. All subscales correlated significantly with external

raters' ratings of those three dimensions, and the view of self subscale
correlated significantly (.90) with a measure of self-esteem, while the view
of future subscale correlated significantly (.90) with a measure of hopelessness.

PRIMARY REFERENCE: Beckham, E. E., Leber, W. R., Watkins, J. T., Boyer,
J. L., and Cook, J. B. (1986). Development of an instrument to measure
Beck's cognitive triad: The Cognitive Triad Inventory, *Journal of Consult-
ing and Clinical Psychology*, 54, 566–567.

AVAILABILITY: Dr. E. E. Beckham, Department of Psychiatry and Behavioral
Sciences, University of Oklahoma Health Sciences Center, P.O. Box 26901,
Oklahoma City, OK 73190.

CTI

This inventory lists different ideas that people sometimes have.

For each of these ideas, show how much you agree with it by circling the answer that best describes your opinion. Be sure to *choose only one answer for each idea.* Answer the items for what you are thinking *right now.*

TA = Totally agree	SD = Slightly disagree
MA = Mostly agree	MD = Mostly disagree
SA = Slightly agree	TD = Totally disagree
N = Neutral	

1. I have many talents and skills. TA MA SA N SD MD TD

2. My job (housework, schoolwork, daily duties) is unpleasant. TA MA SA N SD MD TD

3. Most people are friendly and helpful. TA MA SA N SD MD TD

4. Nothing is likely to work out for me. TA MA SA N SD MD TD

5. I am a failure. TA MA SA N SD MD TD

6. I like to think about the good things that lie ahead for me. TA MA SA N SD MD TD

7. I do my work (job, schoolwork, housework) adequately. TA MA SA N SD MD TD

8. The people I know help me when I need it. TA MA SA N SD MD TD

9. I expect that things will be going very well for me a few years from now. TA MA SA N SD MD TD

10. I have messed up almost all the important relationships I have ever had. TA MA SA N SD MD TD

11. The future holds a lot of excitement for me. TA MA SA N SD MD TD

12. My daily activities are fun and rewarding. TA MA SA N SD MD TD

13. I can't do anything right. TA MA SA N SD MD TD

14.	People like me.	TA MA SA N SD MD TD
15.	There is nothing left in my life to look forward to.	TA MA SA N SD MD TD
16.	My current problems or concerns will always be there in one way or another.	TA MA SA N SD MD TD
17.	I am as adequate as other people I know.	TA MA SA N SD MD TD
18.	The world is a very hostile place.	TA MA SA N SD MD TD
19.	There is no reason for me to be hopeful about my future.	TA MA SA N SD MD TD
20.	The important people in my life are helpful and supportive.	TA MA SA N SD MD TD
21.	I hate myself.	TA MA SA N SD MD TD
22.	I will overcome my problems.	TA MA SA N SD MD TD
23.	Bad things happen to me a lot.	TA MA SA N SD MD TD
24.	I have a spouse or friend who is warm and supportive.	TA MA SA N SD MD TD
25.	I can do a lot of things well.	TA MA SA N SD MD TD
26.	My future is simply too awful to think about.	TA MA SA N SD MD TD
27.	My family doesn't care what happens to me.	TA MA SA N SD MD TD
28.	Things will work out well for me in the future.	TA MA SA N SD MD TD
29.	I am guilty of a great many things.	TA MA SA N SD MD TD
30.	No matter what I do, others make it difficult for me to get what I need.	TA MA SA N SD MD TD
31.	I am a worthwhile human being.	TA MA SA N SD MD TD

32. There is nothing to look forward to in the years ahead.   TA MA SA N SD MD TD

33. I like myself.   TA MA SA N SD MD TD

34. I am faced with many difficulties.   TA MA SA N SD MD TD

35. I have serious flaws in my character.   TA MA SA N SD MD TD

36. I expect to be content and satisfied as the years go by.   TA MA SA N SD MD TD

COMBAT EXPOSURE SCALE (CES)

AUTHORS: Terrence M. Keane, John A. Fairbank, Juesta M. Caddell, Rose T. Zimmering, Kathryn L. Taylor, and Catherine A. Mora

PURPOSE: To measure wartime stressors.

DESCRIPTION: The CES is a 7-item instrument designed to measure the subjective report of wartime stressors experienced by combatants. The CES was developed by deriving items from a previous combat scale and by consensus of four clinicians experienced in treating posttraumatic stress disorder (PTSD). The CES is very useful for helping understand the relationship of combat stressors interacting with other factors to produce PTSD.

NORMS: The CES was studied with three samples involving a total of 431 male, Vietnam-era veterans, with a mean age between 36.9 and 39.3 years. The mean number of years of education ranged from 13.3 to 16.3 years. The mean for a subsample of PTSD veterans was 29.37 (SD = 6.1) and for a non-PTSD veteran group was 22.8 (SD = 10.4); this difference was statistically significant.

SCORING: The CES is scored by subtracting one from the answer given on each item (e.g., an answer of 4 becomes 3). Then, from items 1, 3, 6, and 7, multiply that figure by 2. On item 3 only, if the original response is 5, subtract 2 and multiply by 2. Then sum these results for a total score. The range for the CES is from 0 to 41, with 0–8 indicating light exposure to combat, 9–16 light to moderate, 17–24 moderate, 25–32 moderate to heavy, and 33–41 heavy exposure.

RELIABILITY: The CES has very good internal consistency, with an alpha of .85. The CES also has excellent stability, with a one-week test-retest correlation of .97.

VALIDITY: The CES has good known-groups validity, significantly discriminating between veterans with and without PTSD.

PRIMARY REFERENCE: Keane, T. M. and Caddell, J. M.   (1989). Clinical evaluation of a measure to assess combat exposure, *Psychological Assessment*, 1, 53–55.

AVAILABILITY: Dr. Terrence Keane, PTSD Center (116B), V.A. Medical Center, 150 South Huntington Avenue, Boston, MA 02130.

CES

Please circle the answer that comes closest to describing your experiences.

1. Did you ever go on combat patrols or have other very dangerous duty?

1	2	3	4	5
No	1–3X	4–12X	13–50X	51+ times

2. Were you ever under enemy fire?

1	2	3	4	5
Never	< 1 month	1–3 mos	4–6 mos	7 mos or more

3. Were you ever surrounded by the enemy?

1	2	3	4	5
No	1–2X	3–12X	13–25X	26X or more

4. What percentage of the men in your unit were killed (KIA), wounded, or missing in action (MIA)?

1	2	3	4	5
None	1–25%	26–50%	51–75%	76% or more

5. How often did you fire rounds at the enemy?

1	2	3	4	5
Never	1–2X	3–12X	13–50X	51X or more

6. How often did you see someone hit by incoming or outgoing rounds?

1	2	3	4	5
Never	1–2X	3–12X	13–50X	51X or more

7. How often were you in danger of being injured or killed (i.e., pinned down, overrun, ambushed, near miss, etc.)?

1	2	3	4	5
Never	1–2X	3–12X	13–50X	51X or more

COMPULSIVENESS INVENTORY (CI)

AUTHORS:　Donna M. Kagan and Rose L. Squires

PURPOSE:　To measure nonpathological compulsiveness.

DESCRIPTION:　The 11-item CI, based on the Leyton Obsessional Inventory, is designed to measure compulsive behaviors that are common in the "normal" population. Pathological compulsiveness is defined in terms of extreme preoccupation with thoughts or activities, a tendency toward overorganization and difficulty making decisions. This scale focuses specifically on overconcern with decisions and tasks to be completed perfectly according to rigid well-established norms. It measures three aspects of compulsivity: indecision and double checking (IDC), order and regularity (OR), detail and perfection (DP). The total score on the CI can also be used as a general measure of compulsiveness.

NORMS:　Normative data are not available from the primary references. The CI was developed on a sample of 563 college students. Three hundred and four subjects were males and 259 were female. The average age was 28.2 with a standard deviation of 7.4 years.

SCORING:　The scores on the CI are the total number of "yes" responses. Items for the subscales are: IDC: 1, 2, 3, 4, 5; DP: 6, 7, 8, 9; OR: 10, 11. Higher scores mean greater compulsiveness.

RELIABILITY:　The reliability of the CI is presented for each subscale using coefficient alpha. The internal consistency for the subscales was excellent and was .89 for the IDC, .88 for OR, and .85 for DP. Alpha for the total CI was .80. No information on stability was reported.

VALIDITY:　Criterion validity was estimated by correlating the subscales with numerous personality measures. While the results are not separately presented, the summary indicates that the CI subscales correlate with behavioral dimensions of rigidity in men and women, compulsive eating and dieting, and several other measures.

PRIMARY REFERENCES:　Kagan, D. M. and Squires, R. L. (1985). Measuring non-pathological compulsiveness, *Psychological Reports*, 57, 559–563, and Squires, R. L. and Kagan, D. M. (1985). Personality correlates of disordered eating, *International Journal of Eating Disorders*, 4, 80–85. Reprinted with permission of Donna M. Kagan and John Wiley and Sons, Inc.

AVAILABILITY:　Journal article.

CI

Please respond to each question below by circling "yes" or "no."

Yes No 1. Do you have to turn things over and over in your mind for a long time before being able to decide what to do?

Yes No 2. Do you often have to check things several times?

Yes No 3. Do you ever have to do things over again a certain number of times before they seem quite right?

Yes No 4. Do you have difficulty making up your mind?

Yes No 5. Do you have to go back and check doors, cupboards, or windows to make sure they are really shut?

Yes No 6. Do you dislike having a room untidy or not quite clean for even a short time?

Yes No 7. Do you take great care in hanging and folding your clothes at night?

Yes No 8. Do you like to keep a certain order to undressing and dressing or washing or bathing?

Yes No 9. Do you like to put your personal belongings in set places?

Yes No 10. Do you like to get things done exactly right down to the smallest detail?

Yes No 11. Are you the sort of person who has to pay a great deal of attention to details?

CONCERN ABOUT DEATH-DYING (CADD) AND COPING (C) CHECKLISTS

AUTHOR: P. S. Fry

PURPOSE: To measure fears of death and dying and coping responses.

DESCRIPTION: This instrument combines a 30-item checklist measuring seven aspects of one's fear of death and dying (CADD) and a 27-item checklist measuring six aspects of coping with these fears (C). The seven concerns about death and dying on the CADD are two types of physical pain and suffering (items 1–4 and items 5–7), fear of sensory loss (items 8–11), risk of personal safety (items 12–14), self-esteem concerns (items 15–21), uncertainty of life beyond death (items 22–27), and vacuum beyond death (items 28–30). The six coping methods on the C are internal self-control (items 1–6), two types of social support seeking (items 7–11 and items 12–15), prayer (items 16–20), preoccupying oneself with objects of attachment (items 21–24), and avoidance, denial, and escape (items 25–27). The items of the two checklists were developed from semistructured interviews with 178 elderly persons and were selected for inclusion based on ratings by a panel of experts.

NORMS: Normative data are not available.

SCORING: The checklists are easily scored by simply counting the total number of items checked as either a fear or a coping method for each of the subscales. Total scores are the sum of subscales scores, and range from 0 to 30 for the concerns about death-dying and 0 to 27 for the coping mechanisms.

RELIABILITY: Extensive reliability data are not available for these two checklists. Internal consistency is suggested by the item factor loadings, which ranged from .31 to .71 for the concerns about death-dying checklist and .34 to .94 for the coping checkllst.

VALIDITY: The items of the checklists were selected based on semi-structured interviews with the homebound elderly and based on the interrater agreement of a panel of seven experts. These two procedures, especially the interrater reliability, suggest the checklists have, at the least, face validity.

PRIMARY REFERENCE: Fry, P. S. (1990). A factor analytic investigation of home-bound elderly individuals' concerns about death and dying and their coping responses, *Journal of Clinical Psychology*, 46, 737–748. Instruments reproduced with permission of P. S. Fry and *Journal of Clinical Psychology*.

AVAILABILITY: Dr. P. S. Fry, Professor of Educational Psychology, The University of Calgary, Calgary, Alberta, Canada T2N 1N4.

CADD Checklist

Below is a list of concerns people might have about death and dying. Check all that are a concern to you.

____	1.	Thoughts of physical pain and being hurt
____	2.	Thoughts of suffocating and choking
____	3.	Thoughts of lingering indefinitely on life-supporting systems
____	4.	Thoughts of being taken off life-supporting systems
____	5.	Thoughts of unsuccessful organ transplant
____	6.	Thoughts of death by violent means
____	7.	Thoughts of being consumed by parasites
____	8.	Fear of paralysis
____	9.	Fear of blindness
____	10.	Fear of inability to hear and communicate
____	11.	Fear of darkness
____	12.	Thoughts that my belongings will be destroyed after my death
____	13.	Thoughts of burglars invading my possessions
____	14.	Thoughts of strangers taking over
____	15.	Thoughts of being permanently forgotten after death
____	16.	Thoughts of no one caring
____	17.	Thoughts that life has been useless
____	18.	Thoughts of no one attending funeral
____	19.	Thoughts of no one paying respect or tribute
____	20.	Thoughts of indignity at the hands of undertakers, bankers, and insurance agents
____	21.	Thoughts of autopsy
____	22.	Rejection by God
____	23.	Thoughts of reincarnation
____	24.	Devil and other punitive elements in life beyond death
____	25.	No admission to Heaven or other place of peace
____	26.	Thoughts of timelessness in life beyond death
____	27.	Loud noises everywhere (wind blowing, thundering) in the life beyond death
____	28.	Stillness, emptiness
____	29.	Shadows everywhere beyond death
____	30.	Darkness everywhere beyond death

C Checklist

Below is a list of ways people cope with death and dying. Check all those things that you do to cope with death and dying.

_____ 1. Reminisce on happy events of the past
_____ 2. Keep busy in things that are of interest
_____ 3. Remind myself that there is nothing to be afraid of
_____ 4. Tell myself that everything is going to be OK
_____ 5. Think happy and pleasant thoughts for the future
_____ 6. Try to relax
_____ 7. Call family member(s) into room and ask them to sit close by
_____ 8. Telephone friends or relatives and have a prolonged conversation
_____ 9. Reminisce about old times with family member or friend
_____ 10. Visit doctor or physician and ask questions about physical health problems, physical illness symptoms, or medications
_____ 11. Call child in the family (grandchild, niece, nephew) and ask him or her to spend the night
_____ 12. Go or ask to be taken to visit family members or relatives
_____ 13. Go or ask to be taken to church
_____ 14. Go or ask to be taken for a drive
_____ 15. Go or ask to be taken to the park
_____ 16. Say a prayer
_____ 17. Phone a prayer line
_____ 18. Listen to religious and sacred music
_____ 19. Watch religious programs on TV
_____ 20. Read holy books
_____ 21. Look at family picture albums
_____ 22. Look at famiiy heirlooms
_____ 23. Read old letters from family members, relatives, and friends
_____ 24. Bring out family will and read and ask questions about it
_____ 25. Stay up late till ready to fall asleep
_____ 26. Ask for a snack or something to drink
_____ 27. Watch TV or listen to radio late into the night

COSTELLO-COMREY DEPRESSION AND ANXIETY SCALES (CCDAS)

AUTHORS: C. G. Costello and Andrew L. Comrey

PURPOSE: To measure depression and anxiety.

DESCRIPTION: The CCDAS is a 14-item depression scale and a 9-item anxiety scale that can be administered separately or together. These scales were initially developed separately but eventually combined into a package for final psychometric analysis. Based on independent studies utilizing a large number of items and factor analysis, the "best" depression and anxiety items were combined to form the CCDAS. These scales are viewed more as trait than state scales. The depression scale measures a person's tendency to experience a depressive mood, while the anxiety scale measures a predisposition to develop anxious affective states.

NORMS: The CCDAS was developed in a number of studies involving several hundred male and female respondents with a wide age range and number of occupations. The sample included nonclinical and clinical populations. Although means are available on earlier versions of the scales, norms were not reported for the latest CCDAS.

SCORING: All items are scored on a 1 to 9 scale, with two categories of response depending on the item: "absolutely" to "absolutely not" and "always" to "never." Scores for the anxiety and depression scales are calculated separately by reverse-scoring items 1, 6, 7, 8, 9, and 10 on the depression scale and item 3 on the anxiety scale and then summing the items on each scale. This will produce a range of 14 to 126 on the depression scale and 9 to 81 on the anxiety scale, with higher scores on both scales representing greater depression or anxiety.

RELIABILITY: The depression scale has excellent internal consistency, with split-half reliabilities of .90; split-half reliability for the anxiety scale was .70. Both scales are fairly stable, with test-retest correlations after admission and before discharge for psychiatric patients (no time given) of .72 for anxiety and .70 for depression (it is not clear in this case if this finding means the scales are not sensitive to change).

VALIDITY: The CCDAS has fair concurrent validity; its anxiety scale is correlated with the Taylor Manifest Anxiety Scales and the depression scale is correlated with the Depression scale of the MMPI. There is a small to moderate correlation between the CCDAS and social desirability, suggesting some response bias may be present.

PRIMARY REFERENCE: Costello, C. G. and Comrey, A. L. (1967). Scales for measuring depression and anxiety, *The Journal of Psychology*, 66, 303–313. Instrument reproduced with permission of *The Journal of Psychology*.

AVAILABILITY: Journal article.

CCDAS

Please circle the number that best describes your response to each item.

Depression Scale

1. I feel that life is worthwhile.

Absolutely 9	Very definitely 8	Definitely 7	Probably 6	Possibly 5	Probably not 4	Definitely not 3	Very definitely not 2	Absolutely not 1

2. When I wake up in the morning I expect to have a miserable day.

Always 9	Almost always 8	Very frequently 7	Frequently 6	Fairly often 5	Occasionally 4	Rarely 3	Almost never 2	Never 1

3. I wish I had never been born.

Absolutely 9	Very definitely 8	Definitely 7	Probably 6	Possibly 5	Probably not 4	Definitely not 3	Very definitely not 2	Absolutely not 1

4. I feel that there is more disappointment in life than satisfaction.

Absolutely 9	Very definitely 8	Definitely 7	Probably 6	Possibly 5	Probably not 4	Definitely not 3	Very definitely not 2	Absolutely not 1

5. I want to run away from everything.

| Always 9 | Almost always 8 | Very frequently 7 | Frequently 6 | Fairly often 5 | Occasionally 4 | Rarely 3 | Almost never 2 | Never 1 |

6. My future looks hopeful and promising.

| Absolutely 9 | Very definitely 8 | Definitely 7 | Probably 6 | Possibly 5 | Probably not 4 | Definitely not 3 | Very definitely not 2 | Absolutely not 1 |

7. When I get up in the morning I expect to have an interesting day.

| Always 9 | Almost always 8 | Very frequently 7 | Frequently 6 | Fairly often 5 | Occasionally 4 | Rarely 3 | Almost never 2 | Never 1 |

8. Living is a wonderful adventure for me.

| Always 9 | Almost always 8 | Very frequently 7 | Frequently 6 | Fairly often 5 | Occasionally 4 | Rarely 3 | Almost never 2 | Never 1 |

9. I am a happy person.

| Always 9 | Almost always 8 | Very frequently 7 | Frequently 6 | Fairly often 5 | Occasionally 4 | Rarely 3 | Almost never 2 | Never 1 |

157

10. Things have worked out well for me.

Absolutely not	Very definitely not	Definitely not	Probably not	Possibly	Probably	Definitely	Very definitely	Absolutely
1	2	3	4	5	6	7	8	9

11. The future looks so gloomy that I wonder if I should go on.

Never	Almost never	Rarely	Occasionally	Fairly often	Frequently	Very frequently	Almost always	Always
1	2	3	4	5	6	7	8	9

12. I feel that life is drudgery and boredom.

Never	Almost never	Rarely	Occasionally	Fairly often	Frequently	Very frequently	Almost always	Always
1	2	3	4	5	6	7	8	9

13. I feel blue and depressed.

Never	Almost never	Rarely	Occasionally	Fairly often	Frequently	Very frequently	Almost always	Always
1	2	3	4	5	6	7	8	9

14. When I look back I think life has been good to me.

Absolutely not	Very definitely not	Definitely not	Probably not	Possibly	Probably	Definitely	Very definitely	Absolutely
1	2	3	4	5	6	7	8	9

Anxiety Scale

1. I get rattled easily.

| Always 9 | Almost always 8 | Very frequently 7 | Frequently 6 | Fairly often 5 | Occasionally 4 | Rarely 3 | Almost never 2 | Never 1 |

2. When faced with excitement or unexpected situations, I become nervous and jumpy.

| Always 9 | Almost always 8 | Very frequently 7 | Frequently 6 | Fairly often 5 | Occasionally 4 | Rarely 3 | Almost never 2 | Never 1 |

3. I am calm and not easily upset.

| Always 9 | Almost always 8 | Very frequently 7 | Frequently 6 | Fairly often 5 | Occasionally 4 | Rarely 3 | Almost never 2 | Never 1 |

4. When things go wrong I get nervous and upset instead of calmly thinking out a solution.

| Always 9 | Almost always 8 | Very frequently 7 | Frequently 6 | Fairly often 5 | Occasionally 4 | Rarely 3 | Almost never 2 | Never 1 |

5. It makes me nervous when I have to wait.

| Always 9 | Almost always 8 | Very frequently 7 | Frequently 6 | Fairly often 5 | Occasionally 4 | Rarely 3 | Almost never 2 | Never 1 |

159

6. I am a tense, "high-strung" person.

Absolutely	Very definitely	Definitely	Probably	Possibly	Probably not	Definitely not	Very definitely not	Absolutely not
9	8	7	6	5	4	3	2	1

7. I am more sensitive than most other people.

Absolutely	Very definitely	Definitely	Probably	Possibly	Probably not	Definitely not	Very definitely not	Absolutely not
9	8	7	6	5	4	3	2	1

8. My hand shakes when I try to do something.

Always	Almost always	Very frequently	Frequently	Fairly often	Occasionally	Rarely	Almost never	Never
9	8	7	6	5	4	3	2	1

9. I am a very nervous person.

Absolutely	Very definitely	Definitely	Probably	Possibly	Probably not	Definitely not	Very definitely not	Absolutely not
9	8	7	6	5	4	3	2	1

DATING AND ASSERTION QUESTIONNAIRE (DAQ)

AUTHORS: Robert W. Levenson and John M. Gottman

PURPOSE: To measure social competence.

DESCRIPTION: The 18-item DAQ was designed to measure social competence with a focus on social skills in two social situations: dating and assertion. Nine items measure the general social skills of dating and nine measure assertion. The measures are sensitive to change resulting from social skills training and, therefore, are clinically useful. The Dating items and Assertion items form two separate measures. One limitation of the DAQ is that two, and possibly three, of the items pertain to social situations for college students and would not be relevant to other clients.

NORMS: Normative data on the DAQ are limited. The two subscales were developed on samples of college students, including those volunteering for social skills training in dating ($n = 46$) and assertiveness training ($n = 46$). Posttest scores for the dating skills training group were 2.41 on the Dating subscale and 2.76 on the Assertion subscale; posttest scores for subjects in the assertiveness training were 3.02 for the Dating subscale and 3.02 for the Assertion subscale.

SCORING: Half of the items are rated on a 1 to 4 scale of how frequently the respondent performs the specified behavior. The other half are rated on a 1 to 5 scale according to how comfortable the respondent would feel in the specified situation. Separate scores are computed for the dating and assertion subscales, noted by an "A" or a "D" beside the items. To compute the assertion subscale score, add the responses to items 1, 3, 4 and 6, then divide by 4; next add the responses to items 10, 12, 15, 16 and 18, then divide that total by 5; add these two figures to get an assertion subscale score. To compute the dating subscale score add the responses to items 2, 5, 7, 8 and 9 and then divide the sum by 5; next add the responses to items 11, 13, 14 and 17, and then divide by 4. Add these two figures together for a dating subscale score. These scoring procedures are summarized as: Assertion subscale score = [(items 1 + 3 + 4 + 6) ÷ 4] + [(items 10 + 12 + 15 + 16 + 18) ÷ 5]. Dating subscale score = [(items 2 + 5 + 7 + 8 + 9) ÷ 5] + [(items 11 + 13 + 14 + 17) ÷ 4]. Both subscale scores range from one to nine.

RELIABILITY: These subscales have good to excellent reliability. Their internal consistency using coefficient alpha was .92 and .85 for the Dating and Assertive subscales, respectively. The test-retest reliability correlation was good with both scales correlating .71 over a two-week period. The subscales were only slightly less stable when tested over a six-week test-retest period.

VALIDITY: The validity of these subscales is supported by known-groups validity where significantly different scores were found between a clinical sample and a nonclinical ("normal") sample of college students. Scores were

also significantly different for people identified as having dating and assertive problems compared to a sample of "normal" college subjects. Both
instruments have been shown to be sensitive to measuring change resulting
from social skills training.

PRIMARY REFERENCE: Levenson, R. W. and Gottman, J. M. (1978). Toward
the assessment of social competence, *Journal of Consulting and Clinical
Psychology*, 46, 453–462. Instrument reproduced with permission of Robert
W. Levenson and the American Psychological Association.

AVAILABILITY: Journal article.

DAQ

We are interested in finding out something about the likelihood of your acting in certain ways. Below you will find a list of specific behaviors you may or may not exhibit. Use the following rating scale:

1 = I never do this
2 = I sometimes do this
3 = I often do this
4 = I do this almost always

Now, next to each of the items on the following list, place the number which best indicates the likelihood of your behaving in that way. Be as objective as possible.

_____ 1. Stand up for your rights (A)
_____ 2. Maintain a long conversation with a member of the opposite sex (D)
_____ 3. Be confident in your ability to succeed in a situation in which you have to demonstrate your competence (A)
_____ 4. Say "no" when you feel like it (A)
_____ 5. Get a second date with someone you have dated once (D)
_____ 6. Assume a role of leadership (A)
_____ 7. Be able to accurately sense how a member of the opposite sex feels about you (D)
_____ 8. Have an intimate emotional relationship with a member of the opposite sex (D)
_____ 9. Have an intimate physical relationship with a member of the opposite sex (D)

The following questions describe a variety of social situations that you might encounter. In each situation you may feel "put on the spot." Some situations may be familiar to you, and others may not. We'd like you to read each situation and try to imagine yourself actually in the situation. The more vividly you get a mental picture and place yourself into the situation, the better.

After each situation circle one of the numbers from 1 to 5 which best describes you, using the following scale:

1 = I would be so uncomfortable and so unable to handle this situation that I would avoid it if possible.
2 = I would feel very uncomfortable and would have a lot of difficulty handling this situation.
3 = I would feel somewhat uncomfortable and would have some difficulty in handling this situation.
4 = I would feel quite comfortable and would be able to handle this situation fairly well.
5 = I would feel very comfortable and be able to handle this situation very well.

_____ 10.   You're waiting patiently in line at the checkout when a couple of
            people cut right in front of you. You feel really annoyed and want to
            tell them to wait their turn at the back of the line. One of them says,
            "Look, you don't mind do you? But we're in a terrible hurry." (A)
_____ 11.   You have enjoyed this date and would like to see your date again.
            The evening is coming to a close and you decide to say something.
            (D)
_____ 12.   You are talking to a professor about dropping a class. You explain
            your situation, which you fabricate slightly for effect. Looking at his
            grade book the professor comments that you are pretty far behind.
            You go into greater detail about why you are behind and why you'd
            like to be allowed to withdraw from his class. He then says, "I'm
            sorry, but it's against university policy to let you withdraw this late in
            the semester." (A)
_____ 13.   You meet someone you don't know very well but are attracted to.
            You want to ask him/her out for a date. (D)
_____ 14.   You meet someone of the opposite sex at lunch and have a very
            enjoyable conversation. You'd like to get together again and decide
            to say something. (D)
_____ 15.   Your roommate has several obnoxious traits that upset you very
            much. So far, you have mentioned them once or twice, but no
            noticeable changes have occurred. You still have 3 months left to
            live together. You decide to say something. (A)
_____ 16.   You're with a small group of people who you don't know too well.
            Most of them are expressing a point of view that you disagree with.
            You'd like to state your opinion even if it means you'll probably be in
            the minority. (A)
_____ 17.   You go to a party where you don't know many people. Someone of
            the opposite sex approaches you and introduces themself. You want
            to start a conversation and get to know him/her. (D)
_____ 18.   You are trying to make an appointment with the dean. You are
            talking to his secretary face-to-face. She asks you what division you
            are in and when you tell her, she starts asking you questions about
            the nature of your problem. You inquire as to why she is asking all
            these questions and she replies very snobbishly that she is the
            person who decides if your problem is important enough to warrant
            an audience with the dean. You decide to say something. (A)

DEATH DEPRESSION SCALE (DDS)

AUTHORS: Donald I. Templer, Michael LaVoie, Hilda Chalgujian, and Shan Thomas-Dobson

PURPOSE: To measure death depression.

DESCRIPTION: The DDS is a 17-item instrument designed to measure depression about one's own impending death, the death of others, or death in general. Although there are a number of instruments designed to measure fear or anxiety about death, this is reportedly the first to measure depression about death. The DDS comprises six factors: death despair (items 8, 11, 16), death loneliness (items 4, 9, 10, 13), death dread (items 14, 15, 16), death sadness (items 2, 3), death depression (items 2, 12), and death finality (items 6, 7). The DDS is seen as a useful clinical measure to determine change over time as a function of bereavement, terminal illness, and various life events.

NORMS: The DDS was studied initially on 190 psychology course undergraduates in Fresno, California, including 62 males and 128 females with a mean age of 32.2. Actual norms are not reported.

SCORING: The DDS can be administered in a true-false format (reproduced here) or in a 5-point Likert-type format (1 = "strongly agree" to 5 = "strongly disagree"). Scores on the two formats correlate .77. Of the 17 items, all but items 11 and 12 are keyed as "true." Each item scored "correctly" (i.e., as keyed) receives a score of 1, with the score for the total scale being simply the sum of all those items. (The Likert-type format is scored the same way, with reverse-scoring of items 11 and 12, and the total score being the sum of all scores on the individual items). Higher scores signify greater death depression.

RELIABILITY: The DDS has fair internal consistency, with a Kuder-Richardson coefficient of .77. No information on stability was reported.

VALIDITY: The DDS has very good concurrent validity, with significant correlations with the Death Anxiety Scale and the Zuckerman measures of general anxiety and depression.

PRIMARY REFERENCE: Templer, D. I., LaVoie, M., Chalgujian, H., and Thomas-Dobson, S. (1990). The measurement of death depression, *Journal of Clinical Psychology*, 46, 834–839.

AVAILABILITY: Journal article.

DDS

Please circle T for true or F for false in each item as it applies to you.

T F   1. I get depressed when I think about death.

T F   2. Hearing the word death makes me sad.

T F   3. Passing by cemeteries makes me sad.

T F   4. Death means terrible loneliness.

T F   5. I become terribly sad when I think about friends or relatives who have died.

T F   6. I am terribly upset by the shortness of life.

T F   7. I cannot accept the finality of death.

T F   8. Death deprives life of its meaning.

T F   9. I worry about dying alone.

T F   10. When I die, I will completely lose my friends and loved ones.

T F   11. Death does not rob life of its meaning.

T F   12. Death is not something to be depressed by.

T F   13. When I think of death, I feel tired and lifeless.

T F   14. Death is painful.

T F   15. I dread to think of the death of friends and loved ones.

T F   16. Death is the ultimate failure in life.

T F   17. I feel sad when I dream of death.

DENTAL ANXIETY SCALE (DAS)

AUTHORS: Norman L. Corah, Elliot N. Gale, and Stephen J. Illig

PURPOSE: To measure dental anxiety.

DESCRIPTION: The DAS is a 4-item instrument designed to measure anxiety about dental treatment. Dental anxiety is conceptualized as the patient's response to the stress that is specific to the dental situation. If the dentist uses this short, easy-to-administer instrument to assess patients' anxiety, he or she will not only be prepared for it, but will be able to take measures to alleviate it.

NORMS: The DAS has been normed with two large groups (totaling 2103) of college students in undergraduate psychology courses (998 men and 1105 women). No other demographic data were available. The overall mean for the DAS was 9.07, with differences of only .44 between the two groups, though this difference was statistically significant. Women tend to score more highly (more anxiety) than men.

SCORING: The DAS is easily scored by summing individual item scores (from a = 1 to e = 5) for a total score (range of 4 to 20).

RELIABILITY: The DAS has very good internal consistency, with a reliability coefficient of .86. Data on stability were not provided.

VALIDITY: The DAS has good concurrent validity, with significant correlations with several other measures of stress and anxiety related to dental work. The DAS also is reported as being sensitive to changes in dental anxiety as a result of treatment.

PRIMARY REFERENCE: Corah, N. L., Gale, E. N., and Illig, S. J. (1969). Assessment of a Dental Anxiety Scale, *Journal of the American Dental Association*, 97, 816–818.

AVAILABILITY: Journal article.

DAS

Please circle one letter under each question that most accurately represents your feelings.

1. If you had to go to the dentist tomorrow, how would you feel about it?
    a. I would look forward to it as a reasonably enjoyable experience.
    b. I wouldn't care one way or the other.
    c. I would be a little uneasy about it.
    d. I would be afraid that it would be unpleasant and painful.
    e. I would be very frightened of what the dentist might do.

2. When you are waiting in the dentist's office for your turn in the chair, how do you feel?
    a. Relaxed.
    b. A little uneasy.
    c. Tense.
    d. Anxious.
    e. So anxious that I sometimes break out in a sweat or almost feel physically sick.

3. When you are in the dentist's chair waiting while he gets his drill ready to begin working on your teeth, how do you feel?
    a. Relaxed.
    b. A little uneasy.
    c. Tense.
    d. Anxious.
    e. So anxious that I sometimes break out in a sweat or almost feel physically sick.

4. You are in the dentist's chair to have your teeth cleaned. While you are waiting and the dentist is getting out the instruments which he will use to scrape your teeth around the gums, how do you feel?
    a. Relaxed.
    b. A little uneasy.
    c. Tense.
    d. Anxious.
    e. So anxious that I sometimes break out in a sweat or almost feel physically sick.

DENTAL FEAR SURVEY (DFS)

AUTHORS: R. A. Kleinknecht, R. K. Klepac, L. D. Alexander, and D. A. Bernstein

PURPOSE: To measure fear of dental work.

DESCRIPTION: The DFS is a 20-item instrument designed to identify the respondent's specific and unique responses to a variety of dental-related stimuli that could produce fear and/or avoidance, plus a global item (item 20) for fear of dentistry. The scale is based on learning theory as being more relevant than traditional formulations in helping both understand and treat the problem of dental fear. Three factors (subscales) were identified in several factor analyses: avoidance of dentistry (items 1 and 2); felt autonomic arousal during dentistry (items 3–7); and fear of situations and stimuli (items 8–20). The DFS is viewed as being well enough established to justify its routine use with people fearful of dental work, perhaps helping match treatments to specific problems.

NORMS: The DFS has been studied with several populations including 279 males and 239 females from the practices of dentists in Washington state, and 150 males and 267 females who were college students in Florida. Overall means for these groups ranged from 2.49 (SD = 1.35) to 2.65 (SD = 1.15) for females and 2.06 (SD = 1.07) to 2.29 (SD = .94) for males.

SCORING: The DFS is easily scored by summing individual items for subscale and total scores.

RELIABILITY: Although exact figures were not available, the DFS was reported as having "uniformly high" alpha coefficients and "robust" eight to thirteen-week test-retest correlations.

VALIDITY: The DFS has good known-groups validity, significantly distinguishing between high and low scores regarding canceled appointments, waiting room activity levels, pain reports, and palmar sweating.

PRIMARY REFERENCE: Kleinknecht, R. A., McGlynn, F. D., Thorndike, R. M., and Harkavy, J. (1984). Factor analysis of the Dental Fear Survey with cross validation, *Journal of the American Dental Association*, 108, 59–61. Instrument reproduced with permission of Pergamon Press.

AVAILABILITY: Dr. R. A. Kleinknecht, Western Washington University, Bellingham, WA 98225.

DFS

The items in this questionnaire refer to various situations, feelings, and reactions related to dental work. Please rate your feeling or reaction to these items by *circling the number* (1, 2, 3, 4, or 5) of the category which most closely corresponds to your reaction.

1. Has fear of dental work ever caused you to put off making an appointment?

1	2	3	4	5
Never	Once or twice	A few times	Often	Nearly every time

2. Has fear of dental work ever caused you to cancel or not appear for an appointment?

1	2	3	4	5
Never	Once or twice	A few times	Often	Nearly every time

When having dental work done:

3. My muscles become tense

1	2	3	4	5
Not at all	A little	Somewhat	Much	Very much

4. My breathing rate increases

1	2	3	4	5
Never	Once or twice	A few times	Often	Nearly every time

5. I perspire

1	2	3	4	5
Never	Once or twice	A few times	Often	Nearly every time

6. I feel nauseated and sick to my stomach

1	2	3	4	5
Never	Once or twice	A few times	Often	Nearly every time

7. My heart beats faster

1	2	3	4	5
Never	Once or twice	A few times	Often	Nearly every time

Following is a list of things and situations that many people mention as being somewhat anxiety or fear producing. Please rate how much fear, anxiety or unpleasantness each of them causes you. Use the numbers 1–5, from the following scale. Make a check in the appropriate space. (If it helps, try to imagine yourself in each of these situations and describe what your common reaction is.)

1	2	3	4	5
None at all	A little	Somewhat	Much	Very much

	1	2	3	4	5
8. Making an appointment for dentistry	—	—	—	—	—
9. Approaching the dentist's office	—	—	—	—	—
10. Sitting in the waiting room.	—	—	—	—	—
11. Being seated in the dental chair	—	—	—	—	—
12. The smell of the dentist's office	—	—	—	—	—
13. Seeing the dentist walk in.	—	—	—	—	—
14. Seeing the anesthetic needle.	—	—	—	—	—
15. Feeling the needle injected	—	—	—	—	—
16. Seeing the drill	—	—	—	—	—
17. Hearing the drill	—	—	—	—	—

		1	2	3	4	5
18.	Feeling the vibrations of the drill	___	___	___	___	___
19.	Having your teeth cleaned	___	___	___	___	___
20.	All things considered, how fearful are you of having dental work done	___	___	___	___	___

DIETARY INVENTORY OF EATING TEMPTATIONS (DIET)

AUTHORS: David G. Schlundt and Rose T. Zimering

PURPOSE: To measure competence in situations related to weight control.

DESCRIPTION: The DIET is a 30-item instrument designed to measure behavioral competence in six types of situations related to weight control: overeating (items 6, 9, 10, 12, 14), negative emotional eating (items 24, 25, 28–30), exercise (items 2, 11, 13, 17, 19), resisting temptation (items 3, 15, 16, 20, 26), positive social eating (items 1, 18, 21, 22, 27), and food choice (items 4, 5, 7, 8, 23). The DIET was developed by using statements generated from the work of experienced weight control clinicians regarding commonly reported problem situations. An initial total of 50 situations was grouped by expert judges into the six categories described above. Subsequent research resulted in the current 30-item version. The DIET is a useful measure for assessing behavioral competency in specific energy balance situations and prescribing specific therapeutic activities as competency deficits are found.

NORMS: The DIET was studied with 361 respondents recruited from a variety of sources including college students, nurses, subjects in a weight control program, and subjects in a high blood pressure program. The total number of subjects was 193 normal weight and 168 overweight respondents. The mean DIET total score for normal weight subjects was 56.02 (SD = 16.2) and for overweight subjects was 51.16 (SD = 18.0).

SCORING: The DIET is scored simply by using the raw data supplied by each respondent who is asked to read each situation and rate the percentage of time he or she would behave as described. That percentage figure is then the score on that item. Scores for each of the six categories are the mean of the percentages for the five items in that category, and the total score is simply the mean for all item percentages.

RELIABILITY: The DIET has good to excellent internal consistency, with an alpha for the total score of .93 and alphas for the subscales ranging from .68 to .79. Stability of the DIET is also excellent, with one-week test-retest reliability of .96 for the total scores and subscale coefficients ranging from .81 to .92.

VALIDITY: The DIET has very good known-groups validity, significantly distinguishing between normal weight and overweight respondents on the total score and the exercise, overeating, and negative emotional eating subscales. A type of construct validity also was demonstrated for respondents in the weight control program by relating DIET scores to actual behavioral patterns in predicted ways as measured by self-monitoring.

PRIMARY REFERENCE: Schlundt, D. G. and Zimering, R. T. (1988). The Dieter's Inventory of Eating Temptations: A measure of weight control competence, *Addictive Behaviors*, 13, 151–164.

AVAILABILITY: Dr. David Schlundt, 323 Wilson Hall, Vanderbilt University, Nashville, TN 37274.

DIET

Each item in this questionnaire describes a situation and a behavior that promotes weight loss or weight control. Imagine that you are in the situation described and rate the percent of the time you would behave in the way described. If you would always act in the way described then give a rating of 100%. If you would never act that way give a rating of 0%. If you would sometimes act that way then circle the number at the point on the scale that shows how often you would act as described. If you feel that you never get into a situation like the one described (it does not apply to you), then rate how often you engage in the kind of behavior described in general.

1. You're having dinner with your family and your favorite meal has been prepared. You finish the first helping and someone says, "Why don't you have some more?" What percent of the time would you turn down a second helping?

    0 - - - 10 - - - 20 - - - 30 - - - 40 - - - 50 - - - 60 - - - 70 - - - 80 - - - 90 - - - 100

2. You would like to exercise every day but it is hard to find the time because of your family and work obligations. What percent of the time would you set aside a daily time for exercise?

    0 - - - 10 - - - 20 - - - 30 - - - 40 - - - 50 - - - 60 - - - 70 - - - 80 - - - 90 - - - 100

3. You like to eat high calorie snack food (e.g., cookies, potato chips, crackers, cokes, beer, cake) while watching television. What percent of the time would you watch TV without eating a high calorie snack?

    0 - - - 10 - - - 20 - - - 30 - - - 40 - - - 50 - - - 60 - - - 70 - - - 80 - - - 90 - - - 100

4. When you eat in a good restaurant, you love to order high calorie foods. What percent of the time would you order a low calorie meal?

    0 - - - 10 - - - 20 - - - 30 - - - 40 - - - 50 - - - 60 - - - 70 - - - 80 - - - 90 - - - 100

5. When planning meals, you tend to choose high calorie foods. What percent of the time would you plan low calorie meals?

    0 - - - 10 - - - 20 - - - 30 - - - 40 - - - 50 - - - 60 - - - 70 - - - 80 - - - 90 - - - 100

6. You are at a party and there is a lot of fattening food. You have already eaten more than you should and you are tempted to continue eating. What percent of the time would you stop with what you have already eaten?

    0 - - - 10 - - - 20 - - - 30 - - - 40 - - - 50 - - - 60 - - - 70 - - - 80 - - - 90 - - - 100

7.   You like to flavor your vegetables with butter, margarine, ham, or bacon fat. What percent of the time would you choose a low calorie method of seasoning?

     0 - - - 10 - - - 20 - - - 30 - - - 40 - - - 50 - - - 60 - - - 70 - - - 80 - - - 90 - - - 100

8.   You often prepare many of your foods by frying. What percent of the time would your prepare your food in a way that is less fattening?

     0 - - - 10 - - - 20 - - - 30 - - - 40 - - - 50 - - - 60 - - - 70 - - - 80 - - - 90 - - - 100

9.   You allow yourself a snack in the evening, but you find yourself eating more than your diet allows. What percent of the time would you reduce the size of your snack?

     0 - - - 10 - - - 20 - - - 30 - - - 40 - - - 50 - - - 60 - - - 70 - - - 80 - - - 90 - - - 100

10. Instead of putting foods away after finishing a meal, you find yourself eating the leftovers. What percent of the time would you put the food away without eating any?

     0 - - - 10 - - - 20 - - - 30 - - - 40 - - - 50 - - - 60 - - - 70 - - - 80 - - - 90 - - - 100

11. You are asked by another person to go for a walk but you feel tired and kind of low. What percent of the time would you overcome these feelings and say "yes" to the walk?

     0 - - - 10 - - - 20 - - - 30 - - - 40 - - - 50 - - - 60 - - - 70 - - - 80 - - - 90 - - - 100

12. You often overeat at supper because you are tired and hungry when you get home. What percent of the time would you not overeat at supper?

     0 - - - 10 - - - 20 - - - 30 - - - 40 - - - 50 - - - 60 - - - 70 - - - 80 - - - 90 - - - 100

13. When you have errands to run that are only a couple of blocks away you usually drive the car. What percent of the time would you walk on an errand when it only involves a couple of blocks?

     0 - - - 10 - - - 20 - - - 30 - - - 40 - - - 50 - - - 60 - - - 70 - - - 80 - - - 90 - - - 100

14. You are invited to someone's house for dinner and your host is an excellent cook. You often overeat because the food tastes so good. What percent of the time would you not overeat as a dinner guest?

     0 - - - 10 - - - 20 - - - 30 - - - 40 - - - 50 - - - 60 - - - 70 - - - 80 - - - 90 - - - 100

15.   You like to have something sweet to eat on your coffee break. What percent of the time would you only have coffee?

0 - - - 10 - - - 20 - - - 30 - - - 40 - - - 50 - - - 60 - - - 70 - - - 80 - - - 90 - - - 100

16.   When you cook a meal you snack on the food. What percent of the time would you wait until the meal is prepared to eat?

0 - - - 10 - - - 20 - - - 30 - - - 40 - - - 50 - - - 60 - - - 70 - - - 80 - - - 90 - - - 100

17.   You planned to exercise after work today but you feel tired and hungry when the time arrives. What percent of the time would you exercise anyway?

0 - - - 10 - - - 20 - - - 30 - - - 40 - - - 50 - - - 60 - - - 70 - - - 80 - - - 90 - - - 100

18.   There is a party at work for a co-worker and someone offers you a piece of cake. What percent of the time would you turn it down?

0 - - - 10 - - - 20 - - - 30 - - - 40 - - - 50 - - - 60 - - - 70 - - - 80 - - - 90 - - - 100

19.   You would like to climb the stairs instead of taking the elevator. What percent of the time would you take the stairs to go one or two flights?

0 - - - 10 - - - 20 - - - 30 - - - 40 - - - 50 - - - 60 - - - 70 - - - 80 - - - 90 - - - 100

20.   You are happy and feeling good today. You are tempted to treat yourself by stopping for ice cream. What percent of the time would you find some other way to be nice to yourself?

0 - - - 10 - - - 20 - - - 30 - - - 40 - - - 50 - - - 60 - - - 70 - - - 80 - - - 90 - - - 100

21.   You are at a friend's house and your friend offers you a delicious looking pastry. What percent of the time would you refuse this offer?

0 - - - 10 - - - 20 - - - 30 - - - 40 - - - 50 - - - 60 - - - 70 - - - 80 - - - 90 - - - 100

22.   You feel like celebrating. You are going out with friends to a good restaurant. What percent of the time would you celebrate without overeating?

0 - - - 10 - - - 20 - - - 30 - - - 40 - - - 50 - - - 60 - - - 70 - - - 80 - - - 90 - - - 100

23.   You finished your meal and you still feel hungry. There is cake and fruit available. What percent of the time would you choose the fruit?

0 - - - 10 - - - 20 - - - 30 - - - 40 - - - 50 - - - 60 - - - 70 - - - 80 - - - 90 - - - 100

24. You are at home feeling lonely, blue, and bored. You are craving
     something to eat. What percent of the time would you find another way of
     coping with these feelings besides eating?

     0 - - - 10 - - - 20 - - - 30 - - - 40 - - - 50 - - - 60 - - - 70 - - - 80 - - - 90 - - - 100

25. Today you did something to hurt your ankle. You want to get something to
     eat to make yourself feel better. What percent of the time would you find
     some other way to take your mind off your mishap?

     0 - - - 10 - - - 20 - - - 30 - - - 40 - - - 50 - - - 60 - - - 70 - - - 80 - - - 90 - - - 100

26. When you spend time alone at home you are tempted to snack. You are
     spending an evening alone. What percent of the time would you resist the
     urge to snack?

     0 - - - 10 - - - 20 - - - 30 - - - 40 - - - 50 - - - 60 - - - 70 - - - 80 - - - 90 - - - 100

27. You are out with a friend at lunch time and your friend suggests that you
     stop and get some ice cream. What percent of the time would you resist
     the temptation?

     0 - - - 10 - - - 20 - - - 30 - - - 40 - - - 50 - - - 60 - - - 70 - - - 80 - - - 90 - - - 100

28. You just had an upsetting argument with a family member. You are
     standing in front of the refrigerator and you feel like eating everything in
     sight. What percent of the time would you find some other way to make
     yourself feel better?

     0 - - - 10 - - - 20 - - - 30 - - - 40 - - - 50 - - - 60 - - - 70 - - - 80 - - - 90 - - - 100

29. You are having a hard day at work and you are anxious and upset. You
     feel like getting a candy bar. What percent of the time would you find a
     more constructive way to calm down and cope with your feelings?

     0 - - - 10 - - - 20 - - - 30 - - - 40 - - - 50 - - - 60 - - - 70 - - - 80 - - - 90 - - - 100

30. You just had an argument with your (husband, wife, boyfriend, girlfriend).
     You are upset, angry, and you feel like eating something. What percent of
     the time would you talk the situation over with someone or go for a walk
     instead of eating?

     0 - - - 10 - - - 20 - - - 30 - - - 40 - - - 50 - - - 60 - - - 70 - - - 80 - - - 90 - - - 100

DIETING BELIEFS SCALE (DBS)

AUTHORS: Stephen Stotland and David C. Zuroff

PURPOSE: To measure weight locus of control.

DESCRIPTION: The DBS is a 16-item instrument designed to measure locus of control regarding weight loss. Weight locus of control (WLOC) is defined as the expectancy that one can affect or control one's own weight. Internal weight locus of control is the belief that one's own behaviors or attributes determine one's weight, while the belief that one's weight is determined by factors outside one's control is considered to be external weight locus of control. The DBS comprises three factors: internal WLOC (I; items 8, 9, 10, 11, 13, 15), external-outside of control WLOC (E-O; items 3, 4, 5, 8, 14), and external-environmental WLOC (E-E; items 6, 7, 14, 16). The DBS is viewed as potentially useful for research and practice involving treatment programs for weight loss.

NORMS: The DBS was studied with 100 undergraduate, female psychology students in a Canadian university. The sample generally was of "normal" weight. The mean DBS score was 67.5 (SD = 8.7), with a range of scores from 45 to 86.

SCORING: The DBS is easily scored by summing individual item scores for the total score and scores on individual factors. Items 3–7, 12, 14, and 16 are reverse-scored. The scale is scored in the internal direction so that higher scores represent more internal weight locus of control.

RELIABILITY: The DBS has fair internal consistency, with an alpha of .68. The DBS has very good stability, with a six-week test-retest correlation of .81.

VALIDITY: The DBS has very good concurrent validity, with significant correlations with the Weight Locus of Control Scale, a number of weight-related variables, and several psychological variables including the Restraint Scale. The DBS is not correlated with social desirability response set.

PRIMARY REFERENCE: Stotland, S. and Zuroff, D. C. (1990). A new measure of weight locus of control: The Dieting Beliefs Scale, *Journal of Personality Assessment*, 54, 191–203.

AVAILABILITY: Journal article.

DBS

Please respond to the following statements by indicating how well each statement describes your beliefs. Place a number from 1 (*not at all descriptive of my beliefs*) to 6 *(very descriptive of my beliefs)* in the space provided before each statement.

1	2	3	4	5	6
Not at all descriptive of my beliefs					Very descriptive of my beliefs.

_____ 1.   By restricting what one eats, one can lose weight.
_____ 2.   When people gain weight it is because of something they have done or not done.
_____ 3.   A thin body is largely a result of genetics.
_____ 4.   No matter how much effort one puts into dieting, one's weight tends to stay about the same.
_____ 5.   One's weight is, to a great extent, controlled by fate.
_____ 6.   There is so much fattening food around that losing weight is almost impossible.
_____ 7.   Most people can only diet successfully when other people push them to do it.
_____ 8.   Having a slim and fit body has very little to do with luck.
_____ 9.   People who are overweight lack the willpower necessary to control their weight.
_____ 10. Each of us is directly responsible for our weight.
_____ 11. Losing weight is simply a matter of wanting to do it and applying yourself.
_____ 12. People who are more than a couple of pounds overweight need professional help to lose weight.
_____ 13. By increasing the amount one exercises, one can lose weight.
_____ 14. Most people are at their present weight because that is the weight level that is natural for them.
_____ 15. Unsuccessful dieting is due to lack of effort.
_____ 16. In order to lose weight people must get a lot of encouragement from others.

DISSOCIATIVE EXPERIENCES SCALE (DES)

AUTHORS: Eve M. Bernstein and Frank W. Putman

PURPOSE: To measure dissociation.

DESCRIPTION: The DES is a 28-item instrument designed to measure dissociation, the lack of "normal" integration of thoughts, experiences, and feelings into the stream of consciousness and memory. Dissociation is viewed not only as a problem in and of itself, but as related to a number of other psychiatric disorders. The DES is based on the assumption that dissociation lies along a continuum from minor dissociations of everyday life to major psychopathology. The DES was developed by using data from interviews with people meeting DSM-III criteria for dissociative disorders and consultations with clinical experts. Items identifying dissociation of moods and impulses were excluded so that experiences of dissociation would not be confused with alternations in mood and impulse related to affective disorders. The DES is viewed as an excellent research and clinical measure, perhaps the only one available to examine dissociation.

NORMS: The DES was studied originally with 31 college students (18 to 22 years), 34 "normal" adults, 14 alcoholics, 24 phobic clients, 29 agoraphobics, 10 posttraumatic stress disorder clients, 20 schizophrenics, and 20 clients with multiple personality disorder. The median scores for the eight groups were: "normals"—4.38, alcoholics—4.72, phobics—6.04, agoraphobics—7.41, adolescents—14.11, schizophrenics—20.63, PTSD—31.25, and multiple personality disorder—57.06. Most of these differences were statistically significant from each other.

SCORING: The DES originally (as with the median scores above) was scored by measuring the subject's slash mark to the nearest 5mm from the left-hand anchor point of each 100mm line. The overall score reflected in the norms above was simply a sum of the 28 item scores. The newer scale reprinted here is scored by simply adding up the circled figures (percentages) for each item for a total score. Higher scores equal greater dissociation.

RELIABILITY: The DES has very good split-half reliability, with coefficients for the eight groups ranging from .71 to .96, and with six of these being .90 or above. The DES also has very good stability, with a four- to eight-week test-retest reliability coefficient of .84.

VALIDITY: The DES has fairly good construct validity, not correlating with some theoretically unrelated variables (such as social class and sex), and with significant correlations (using Kendall's coefficient of concordance) to show a high degree of agreement among item scores in the differentiation of diagnostic groups. The DES also yielded a predicted continuum of scores with steady progression from "normal" subjects to multiple personality disorder subjects.

PRIMARY REFERENCE: Bernstein, E. M. and Putman, F. W. (1986). Development, reliability, and validity of a dissociation scale, *Journal of Nervous and Mental Disease*, 174, 727–735.
AVAILABILITY: Primary reference.

DES

This questionnaire consists of twenty-eight questions about experiences that you may have in your daily life. We are interested in how often you have these experiences. It is important, however, that your answers show how often these experiences happen to you when you *are not* under the influence of alcohol or drugs.

To answer the questions, please determine to what degree the experience described in the question applies to you and circle the number to show what percentage of the time you have the experience.

1. Some people have the experience of driving or riding in a car or bus or subway and suddenly realizing that they don't remember what has happened during all or part of the trip. Circle a number to show what percentage of the time this happens to you.

    0%   10   20   30   40   50   60   70   80   90   100%

2. Some people find that sometimes they are listening to someone talk and they suddenly realize that they did not hear part or all of what was said. Circle a number to show what percentage of the time this happens to you.

    0%   10   20   30   40   50   60   70   80   90   100%

3. Some people have the experience of finding themselves in a place and having no idea how they got there. Circle a number to show what percentage of the time this happens to you.

    0%   10   20   30   40   50   60   70   80   90   100%

4. Some people have the experience of finding themselves dressed in clothes that they don't remember putting on. Circle a number to show what percentage of the time this happens to you.,

    0%   10   20   30   40   50   60   70   80   90   100%

5. Some people have the experience of finding new things among their belongings that they do not remember buying. Circle a number to show what percentage of the time this happens to you.

    0%   10   20   30   40   50   60   70   80   90   100%

6. Some people sometimes find that they are approached by people that they do not know who call them by another name or insist that they have met them before. Circle a number to show what percentage of the time this happens to you.

    0%   10   20   30   40   50   60   70   80   90   100%

7.   Some people sometimes have the experience of feeling as though they are standing next to themselves or watching themselves do something and they actually see themselves as if they were looking at another person. Circle a number to show what percentage of the time this happens to you.

0%   10   20   30   40   50   60   70   80   90   100%

8.   Some people are told that they sometimes do not recognize friends or family members. Circle a number to show what percentage of the time this happens to you.

0%   10   20   30   40   50   60   70   80   90   100%

9.   Some people find that they have no memory for some important events in their lives (for example, a wedding or graduation). Circle a number to show what percentage of the time this happens to you.

0%   10   20   30   40   50   60   70   80   90   100%

10.   Some people have the experience of being accused of lying when they do not think that they have lied. Circle a number to show what percentage of the time this happens to you.

0%   10   20   30   40   50   60   70   80   90   100%

11.   Some people have the experience of looking in a mirror and not recognizing themselves. Circle a number to show what percentage of the time this happens to you.

0%   10   20   30   40   50   60   70   80   90   100%

12.   Some people have the experience of feeling that other people, objects, and the world around them are not real. Circle a number to show what percentage of the time this happens to you.

0%   10   20   30   40   50   60   70   80   90   100%

13.   Some people have the experience of feeling that their body does not seem to belong to them. Circle a number to show what percentage of the time this happens to you.

0%   10   20   30   40   50   60   70   80   90   100%

14.   Some people have the experience of sometimes remembering a past event so vividly that they feel as if they were reliving that event. Circle a number to show what percentage of the time this happens to you.

0%   10   20   30   40   50   60   70   80   90   100%

15. Some people have the experience of not being sure whether things that they remember happening really did happen or whether they just dreamed them. Circle a number to show what percentage of the time this happens to you.

    0%   10   20   30   40   50   60   70   80   90   100%

16. Some people have the experience of being in a familiar place but finding it strange and unfamiliar. Circle a number to show what percentage of the time this happens to you.

    0%   10   20   30   40   50   60   70   80   90   100%

17. Some people find that when they are watching television or a movie they become so absorbed in the story that they are unaware of other events happening around them. Circle a number to show what percentage of the time this happens to you.

    0%   10   20   30   40   50   60   70   80   90   100%

18. Some people find that they become so involved in a fantasy or daydream that it feels as though it were really happening to them. Circle a number to show what percentage of the time this happens to you.

    0%   10   20   30   40   50   60   70   80   90   100%

19. Some people find that they sometimes are able to ignore pain. Circle a number to show what percentage of the time this happens to you.

    0%   10   20   30   40   50   60   70   80   90   100%

20. Some people find that they sometimes sit staring off into space, thinking of nothing, and are not aware of the passage of time. Circle a number to show what percentage of the time this happens to you.

    0%   10   20   30   40   50   60   70   80   90   100%

21. Some people sometimes find that when they are alone they talk out loud to themselves. Circle a number to show what percentage of the time this happens to you.

    0%   10   20   30   40   50   60   70   80   90   100%

22. Some people find that in one situation they may act so differently compared with another situation that they feel almost as if they were two different people. Circle a number to show what percentage of the time this happens to you.

    0%   10   20   30   40   50   60   70   80   90   100%

23. Some people sometimes find that in certain situations they are able to do things with amazing ease and spontaneity that would usually be difficult for them (for example, sports, work, social situations, etc.). Circle a number to show what percentage of the time this happens to you.

0%   10   20   30   40   50   60   70   80   90   100%

24. Some people sometimes find that they cannot remember whether they have done something or have just thought about doing that (for example, not knowing whether they have just mailed a letter or have just thought about mailing it). Circle a number to show what percentage of the time this happens to you.

0%   10   20   30   40   50   60   70   80   90   100%

25. Some people find evidence that they have done things that they do not remember doing. Circle a number to show what percentage of the time this happens to you.

0%   10   20   30   40   50   60   70   80   90   100%

26. Some people sometimes find writings, drawings, or notes among their belongings that they must have done but cannot remember doing. Circle a number to show what percentage of the time this happens to you.

0%   10   20   30   40   50   60   70   80   90   100%

27. Some people sometimes find that they hear voices inside their head that tell them to do things or comment on things that they are doing. Circle a number to show what percentage of the time this happens to you.

0%   10   20   30   40   50   60   70   80   90   100%

28. Some people sometimes feel as if they are looking at the world through a fog so that people and objects appear far away or unclear. Circle a number to show what percentage of the time this happens to you.

0%   10   20   30   40   50   60   70   80   90   100%

DYSFUNCTIONAL ATTITUDE SCALE (DAS)

AUTHOR: Arlene Weissman

PURPOSE: To measure cognitive distortion.

DESCRIPTION: The DAS is a 40-item instrument designed to identify cognitive distortions—particularly the distortions that may underlie or cause depression. Based on the cognitive therapy model of Aaron Beck, the items on the DAS were constructed so as to represent seven major value systems: approval, love, achievement, perfectionism, entitlement, omnipotence, and autonomy. Two 40-item parallel forms of the DAS, which are highly correlated and have roughly the same psychometric properties, were derived from an original pool of 100 items. Although the overall score on the DAS is considered the key measure, practitioners can also examine areas where the respondent is emotionally vulnerable or strong by analyzing responses to specific items. Clinical work can then be directed at correcting the distortions underlying the depression, rather than only at the depressive symptoms per se.

NORMS: The DAS was developed in a series of studies ultimately involving some 216 male and 485 female, predominantly white, undergraduate students. Other research involved 105 depressed out-patients, 30 manic-depressive outpatients and their spouses, and 107 depressed patients. No actual norms were reported since the number of DAS items varied among these studies. For nonclinical respondents, the mean score is approximately 113.

SCORING: The DAS is easily scored by using zeros for items omitted, assigning a score of 1 (on a 7-point scale) to the adaptive end of the scale, and simply summing up the scores on all items. With no items omitted, scores on the DAS range from 40 to 280 with lower scores equaling more adaptive beliefs (few cognitive distortions).

RELIABILITY: The DAS has very good internal consistency, with alphas on the form of the DAS reproduced here ranging from .84 to .92. The DAS also has excellent stability, with test-retest correlations over eight weeks of .80 to .84.

VALIDITY: The DAS has excellent concurrent validity, significantly correlating with a number of other measures of depression and depressive-distortions such as the Beck Depression Inventory, the Profile of Mood States, and the Story Completion Test. The DAS also has good known-groups validity, significantly distinguishing between groups diagnosed as depressed or not depressed on the Beck Depression Inventory. The DAS also was found to be sensitive to change following clinical intervention with depressed outpatients.

PRIMARY REFERENCE: Weissman, A. N. (1980). Assessing depressogenic attitudes: A validation study. Paper presented at the 51st Annual Meeting of the Eastern Psychological Association, Hartford, Connecticut. Instrument reproduced with permission of Arlene N. Weissman.

AVAILABILITY: Dr. Arlene Weissman, Towers, Perrin, Forster, and Crosby, 1500 Market Street, Philadelphia, PA 19102.

DAS

This questionnaire lists different attitudes or beliefs which people sometimes hold. Read *each* statement carefully and decide how much you agree or disagree with the statement.

For each of the attitudes, indicate to the left of the item the number that *best describes how you think.* Be sure to choose only one answer for each attitude. Because people are different, there is no right answer or wrong answer to these statements. Your answers are confidential, so please do not put your name on this sheet.

To decide whether a given attitude is typical of your way of looking at things, simply keep in mind what you are like *most of the time.*

1 = Totally agree
2 = Agree very much
3 = Agree slightly
4 = Neutral
5 = Disagree slightly
6 = Disagree very much
7 = Totally disagree

_____ 1. It is difficult to be happy unless one is good looking, intelligent, rich, and creative.

_____ 2. Happiness is more a matter of my attitude towards myself than the way other people feel about me.

_____ 3. People will probably think less of me if I make a mistake.

_____ 4. If I do not do well all the time, people will not respect me.

_____ 5. Taking even a small risk is foolish because the loss is likely to be a disaster.

_____ 6. It is possible to gain another person's respect without being especially talented at anything.

_____ 7. I cannot be happy unless most people I know admire me.

_____ 8. If a person asks for help, it is a sign of weakness.

_____ 9. If I do not do as well as other people, it means I am a weak person.

_____ 10. If I fail at my work, then I am a failure as a person.

_____ 11. If you cannot do something well, there is little point in doing it at all.

_____ 12. Making mistakes is fine because I can learn from them.

_____ 13. If someone disagrees with me, it probably indicates he does not like me.

_____ 14. If I fail partly, it is as bad as being a complete failure.

_____ 15. If other people know what you are really like, they will think less of you.

_____ 16. I am nothing if a person I love doesn't love me.

_____ 17. One can get pleasure from an activity regardless of the end result

_____ 18. People should have a chance to succeed before doing anything.

_____ 19. My value as a person depends greatly on what others think of me.

_____ 20. If I don't set the highest standards for myself, I am likely to end up a second-rate person.

_____ 21. If I am to be a worthwhile person, I must be the best in at least one way.

_____ 22. People who have good ideas are better than those who do not.

_____ 23. I should be upset if I make a mistake.

_____ 24. My own opinions of myself are more important than others' opinions of me.

_____ 25. To be a good, moral, worthwhile person I must help everyone who needs it.

_____ 26. If I ask a question, it makes me look stupid.

_____ 27. It is awful to be put down by people important to you.

_____ 28. If you don't have other people to lean on, you are going to be sad.

_____ 29. I can reach important goals without pushing myself.

_____ 30. It is possible for a person to be scolded and not get upset.

_____ 31. I cannot trust other people because they might be cruel to me.

_____ 32. If others dislike you, you cannot be happy.

_____ 33. It is best to give up your own interests in order to please other people.

_____ 34. My happiness depends more on other people than it does on me.

_____ 35. I do not need the approval of other people in order to be happy.

_____ 36. If a person avoids problems, the problems tend to go away.

_____ 37. I can be happy even if I miss out on many of the good things in life.

_____ 38. What other people think about me is very important.

_____ 39. Being alone leads to unhappiness.

_____ 40. I can find happiness without being loved by another person.

EATING ATTITUDES TEST (EAT)

AUTHORS: David M. Garner and Paul E. Garfinkel

PURPOSE: To measure symptoms of anorexia nervosa.

DESCRIPTION: The 40-item EAT was designed to measure a broad range of behaviors and attitudes characteristic of anorexia nervosa. Each item is a symptom frequently observed in the disorder. The instrument has a rough cutting score of 30, above which scores indicate anorectic eating concerns. The EAT is helpful in identifying clients with serious eating concerns even if they do not show the weight loss classic to this disorder.

NORMS: The EAT was initially developed using two samples of patients diagnosed as manifesting anorexia nervosa ($n = 32$ and $n = 34$). The average age of the onset of the disorder was 18.4 years. Two "normal" control groups were also used which were composed of Canadian college students ($n = 34$ and $n = 59$). The "normal" control subjects and anorectics were from similar socioeconomic backgrounds, and the average age for the four groups was approximately 22.4 years old. Average EAT scores for one of the anorectic samples was 58.9 with a standard deviation of 13.3. The "normal" control sample of 59 had a mean of 15.6 with a standard deviation of 9.3. A group of clinically recovered anorectics ($n = 9$) had a mean of 11.4 and a standard deviation of 5.1.

SCORING: The 40 items are scored in terms of how frequently the person experiences them. Items 1, 18, 19, 23, and 39 are scored as follows: $6 = 3$, $5 = 2$, $4 = 1$, and 3, 2, and $1 = 0$. The remaining items are scored as follows: $1 = 2$, $2 = 2$, $3 = 1$, and 4, 5, and $6 = 0$. Items 2–17, 20–22, 24–26, 28–38, 40 when marked "Always" and items 1, 18, 19, 23, and 39 when marked "Never" indicate anorexia. Total scores are the sum of the item values, and range from 0 to 120.

RELIABILITY: This instrument has excellent internal consistency, with a coefficient alpha of .94 for a combined sample of anorectics and normals. For the anorectic subjects alone, the coefficient was .79.

VALIDITY: A 23-item prototype of this instrument was tested for known-groups validity. Scores differed significantly for a sample of anorectics and "normals." This finding was replicated in a separate sample. The EAT was shown to be independent of the Restraint Scale, weight fluctuation, extroversion, and neuroticism. Post hoc analysis of a group of recovered anorectics indicated that scores were in the normal range, suggesting the scale is sensitive to change.

PRIMARY REFERENCE: Garner, D. M. and Garfinkel, P. E. (1979). The Eating Attitudes Test: An index of the symptoms of anorexia nervosa, *Psychological Medicine*, 9, 273–279. Instrument reproduced with permission of David Garner.

AVAILABILITY: Dr. David Garner, 200 Elizabeth Street, Bell Wing H-639, Toronto, Ontario M5G 2C4, Canada or The Free Press.

EAT

Please indicate on the line at left the answer which applies best to each of the numbered statements. All of the results will be *strictly* confidential. Most of the questions directly relate to food or eating, although other types of questions have been included. Please answer each question carefully. Thank you.

1 = Always
2 = Very often
3 = Often
4 = Sometimes
5 = Rarely
6 = Never

____ 1. Like eating with other people.
____ 2. Prepare foods for others but do not eat what I cook.
____ 3. Become anxious prior to eating.
____ 4. Am terrified about being overweight.
____ 5. Avoid eating when I am hungry.
____ 6. Find myself preoccupied with food.
____ 7. Have gone on eating binges where I feel that I may not be able to stop.
____ 8. Cut my food into small pieces.
____ 9. Aware of the calorie content of foods that I eat.
____ 10. Particularly avoid foods with a high carbohydrate content (e.g., bread, potatoes, rice, etc.).
____ 11. Feel bloated after meals.
____ 12. Feel that others would prefer if I ate more.
____ 13. Vomit after I have eaten.
____ 14. Feel extremely guilty after eating.
____ 15. Am preoccupied with a desire to be thinner.
____ 16. Exercise strenuously to burn off calories.
____ 17. Weigh myself several times a day.
____ 18. Like my clothes to fit tightly.
____ 19. Enjoy eating meat.
____ 20. Wake up early in the morning.
____ 21. Eat the same foods day after day.
____ 22. Think about burning my calories when I exercise.
____ 23. Have regular menstrual periods.
____ 24. Other people think that I am too thin.
____ 25. Am preoccupied with the thought of having fat on my body.
____ 26. Take longer than others to eat my meals.
____ 27. Enjoy eating at restaurants.
____ 28. Take laxatives.
____ 29. Avoid foods with sugar in them.
____ 30. Eat diet foods.
____ 31. Feel that food controls my life.
____ 32. Display self control around food.
____ 33. Feel that others pressure me to eat.

____ 34. Give too much time and thought to food.
____ 35. Suffer from constipation.
____ 36. Feel uncomfortable after eating sweets.
____ 37. Engage in dieting behavior.
____ 38. Like my stomach to be empty.
____ 39. Enjoy trying new rich foods.
____ 40. Have the impulse to vomit after meals.

EATING QUESTIONNAIRE—REVISED (EQ-R)

AUTHORS: Donald A. Williamson, C. J. Davis, Anthony J. Goreczny, Sandra J. McKenzie, and Philip Watkins

PURPOSE: To measure bulimia.

DESCRIPTION: The EQ-R is a 15-item instrument designed to assess the symptoms of bulimia. The EQ-R is in a symptom checklist format that allows documentation of eating and purging habits, and can be used to differentiate binge eaters and obesity. The EQ-R is short, easy to utilize, can be used with total score or individual items, and can be used both to screen for bulimia and binge eating or to assess treatment outcome.

NORMS: The EQ-R was studied with 561 women, including 104 diagnosed with bulimia nervosa, 45 bulimic binge eaters, 36 diagnosed as obese, and 376 diagnosed as "normal" (with no eating disorders). The "normal" group was recruited from undergraduate psychology classes, while the clinical subjects were referred to an outpatient eating disorders program for treatment of bulimia or obesity. The means for the groups were: 32.18 for the nonclinical group, 47.98 for the bulimia nervosa group, 45.53 for the simple bulimia group, and 37.94 for the obese group.

SCORING: The EQ-R is easily scored by summing the item scores (from a = 1 to e = 5) for a total score. Items 7 and 10 are reverse-scored.

RELIABILITY: The EQ-R has very good internal consistency, with an alpha of .87. The EQ-R has excellent stability, with a two-week test-retest correlation of .90.

VALIDITY: The EQ-R has very good concurrent validity, correlating with the Eating Attitudes Test and the BULIT. The EQ-R also has good known-groups validity, significantly distinguishing between the bulimic groups, the obese group, and the nonclinical group.

PRIMARY REFERENCE: Williamson, D. A., Davis, C. J., Goreczny, A. J., McKenzie, S. J., and Watkins, P. (1989). The Eating Questionnaire-Revised: A symptom checklist for bulimia, in P. A. Keller and S. R. Heyman (eds.), *Innovations in Clinical Practice*, Vol. 8, pp. 321–326. Sarasota, FL: Professional Resource Exchange, Inc. Instrument reprinted by permission.

AVAILABILITY: Professional Resource Exchange, Inc., P.O. Box 15560, Sarasota, FL 34277-1560.

EQ-R

In the space provided indicate the letter of the answer that best describes your eating behavior.

_____ 1. How often do you binge eat? (a) seldom; (b) once or twice a month; (c) once a week; (d) almost every day (e) every day.

_____ 2. What is the average length of a bingeing episode? (a) less than 15 minutes; (b) 15–30 minutes; (c) 30 minutes to 1 hour; (d) 1 hour to 2 hours; (e) more than 2 hours (if e, please indicate length of episode _____).

_____ 3. Which of the following statements best applies to your binge eating? (a) I don't eat enough to satisfy me; (b) I eat until I've had enough to satisfy me; (c) I eat until my stomach feels full; (d) I eat until my stomach is painfully full; (e) I eat until I can't eat anymore.

_____ 4. Do you ever vomit after a binge? (a) never; (b) about 25% of the time; (c) about 50% of the time; (d) about 75% of the time; (e) about 100% of the time.

_____ 5. Which of the following best applies to your eating behavior when binge eating? (a) I eat much more slowly than usual; (b) I eat somewhat more slowly than usual; (c) I eat at about the same speed as I usually do; (d) I eat somewhat faster than usual; (e) I eat very rapidly.

_____ 6. How much are you concerned about your binge eating? (a) not bothered at all; (b) bothers me a little; (c) moderately concerned; (d) a major concern; (e) the most important concern in my life.

_____ 7. Which best describes the control you feel over your eating during a binge? (a) never in control; (b) in control about 25% of the time; (c) in control about 50% of the time; (d) in control about 75% of the time; (e) always in control.

_____ 8. Which of the following describes your feelings immediately after a binge? (a) I feel very good; (b) I feel good; (c) I feel fairly neutral, not too nervous or uncomfortable; (d) I am moderately nervous and/or uncomfortable; (e) I am very nervous and/or uncomfortable.

_____ 9. Which most accurately describes your mood immediately after a binge? (a) very happy; (b) moderately happy; (c) neutral; (d) moderately depressed; (e) very depressed.

_____ 10. Which of the following best describes the situation in which you typically binge? (a) always completely alone; (b) alone but around unknown others (e.g., restaurant); (c) only around others who know about my bingeing; (d) only around friends and family; (e) in any situation.

_____ 11. Which of the following best describes any weight changes you have experienced in the last year? (a) 0–5 lbs; (b) 5–10 lbs; (c) 10–20 lbs; (d) 20–30 lbs; (e) more than 30 lbs.

_____ 12. On a day that you binge, how many binge episodes typically occur during that day? (a) 0; (b) 1; (c) 2; (d) 3; (e) 4 or more.

_____ 13. How often do you use restrictive diets/fasts? (a) never; (b) one time per month; (c) two times per month; (d) one time per week; (e) almost always.

_____ 14. How often do you use laxatives to lose weight? (a) never; (b) 1–3 times per month; (c) one time per week; (d) one time per day; (e) more than one time per day (if e, please indicate frequency _____).

_____ 15. How often do you use diuretics to lose weight? (a) never; (b) 1–3 times per month; (c) one time per week; (d) one time per day; (e) more than one time per day (if e, please indicate frequency _____).

EATING SELF-EFFICACY SCALE (ESES)

AUTHORS: Shirley M. Glynn and Audrey J. Ruderman

PURPOSE: To measure eating self-efficacy.

DESCRIPTION: The ESES is a 25-item instrument designed to assess the individual's self-efficacy regarding eating (and overeating) behavior. Eating self-efficacy refers to the individual's confidence in his or her ability to cope, in this instance, in the area of eating. Previous research suggests that people's perceptions of self-efficacy with regard to eating may be an important influence on dieting and weight loss success. The ESES has two factors, eating as a function of negative affects (NA: items 2, 4, 5, 8, 11–15, 17, 18, 20, 22, 23, and 25) and eating as a function of socially acceptable circumstances (SA: remaining 10 items). Since few, if any, other scales on eating self-efficacy are available, the ESES may have important predictive and therapeutic applications.

NORMS: The ESES was first studied with 328 college introductory psychology students to reduce an original 79-item version to the current 25-item version. The ESES was then studied with 484 female undergraduates in introductory psychology courses. No other demographic data were provided. The mean on the ESES was 80.9 (SD = 26.5, median = 80). The NA mean was 42.15 (SD = 20.03) and the SA mean was 38.92 (SD = 11.47). The possible range of the total scale is 25–185. In a separate study of 618 subjects (303 male and 315 females), the mean for males was 74.24 (SD = 30.28) and for females 88.43 (SD = 29.39). The difference was statistically significant, with females reporting greater difficulty controlling their eating.

SCORING: The ESES is scored by simply adding up item scores (1 to 7) for the subscale scores (NA = 15 items, SA = 10 items) and summing all items for a total score. The higher the score, the greater the problem with self-efficacy for eating.

RELIABILITY: The ESES has excellent internal consistency, with an alpha of .92 for the entire scale, .94 for NA, and .85 for SA. The ESES also has very good stability, with a test-retest correlation of .70.

VALIDITY: The ESES has good predictive and construct validity. Scores on the ESES were significantly related to weight loss among weight loss program participants. The ESES also was significantly related in predicted directions with percentage overweight, Restraint Scale scores, previous and current dieting experience and to self-esteem.

PRIMARY REFERENCE: Glynn, S. M. and Ruderman, A. J. (1986). The development and validation of an Eating Self-Efficacy Scale, *Cognitive Therapy and Research*, 10, 403–420, Plenum Publishing Corp.

AVAILABILITY: Journal article.

ESES

For numbers 1–25 you should rate the likelihood that you would have difficulty controlling your overeating in each of the situations, using this scale:

1	2	3	4	5	6	7

No difficulty controlling eating   Moderate difficulty controlling eating   Most difficulty controlling eating

Please complete every item and record your answer in the space to the left.

How difficult is it to control your....

_____ 1. Overeating after work or school
_____ 2. Overeating when you feel restless
_____ 3. Overeating around holiday time
_____ 4. Overeating when you feel upset
_____ 5. Overeating when tense
_____ 6. Overeating with friends
_____ 7. Overeating when preparing food
_____ 8. Overeating when irritable
_____ 9. Overeating as part of a social occasion dealing with food—like at a restaurant or dinner party
_____ 10. Overeating with family members
_____ 11. Overeating when annoyed
_____ 12. Overeating when angry
_____ 13. Overeating when you are angry at yourself
_____ 14. Overeating when depressed
_____ 15. Overeating when you feel impatient
_____ 16. Overeating when you want to sit back and enjoy some food
_____ 17. Overeating after an argument
_____ 18. Overeating when you feel frustrated
_____ 19. Overeating when tempting food is in front of you
_____ 20. Overeating when you want to cheer up
_____ 21. Overeating when there is a lot of food available to you (refrigerator is full)
_____ 22. Overeating when you feel overly sensitive
_____ 23. Overeating when nervous
_____ 24. Overeating when hungry
_____ 25. Overeating when anxious or worried

EGO IDENTITY SCALE (EIS)

AUTHORS: Allen L. Tan, Randall J. Kendis, Judith Fine, and Joseph Porac

PURPOSE: To measure ego identity.

DESCRIPTION: The EIS is a 12-item scale that measures Erik Erikson's concept of ego identity. The authors reviewed Erikson's characterization of ego identity achievement and developed 41 pairs of forced-choice items with one item representing ego identity and one representing ego diffusion. Ego identity was defined as acceptance of self, a sense of direction. Identity diffusion implies doubts about one's self, lack of sense of continuity over time, and inability to make decisions and commitments. This pool of 41 items was reduced to 12 on the basis of their ability to discriminate between higher and lower scorers across all 41 items, and imperviousness to social desirability response set.

NORMS: A series of studies to develop the EIS was conducted involving 249 undergraduate students. No other demographic data or norms were reported.

SCORING: The EIS is scored by assigning a score of 1 to each statement that reflects ego identity and that is circled by the respondent, then summing the scores. The items that reflect ego identity are 1a, 2b, 3b, 4a, 5b, 6b, 7b, 8a, 9b, 10b, 11a, 12a.

RELIABILITY: The EIS has only fair internal consistency, with a split-half reliability coefficient of .68. No other reliability information was reported.

VALIDITY: The EIS correlated significantly and in predicted directions with four personality variables: internal control, intimacy, dogmatism, and extent to which an individual derives his or her values from his or her own life experiences. These correlations provide some evidence of construct validity. The EIS also correlated significantly with indices of political and occupational commitment.

PRIMARY REFERENCE: Tan, A. L., Kendis, R. J., Fine, J. T., and Porac, J. (1977). A Short Measure of Eriksonian Ego Identity, *Journal of Personality Assessment*, 41, 279–284. Instrument reproduced with permission of Allen Tan, Randall Kendis, and Judith Fine.

AVAILABILITY: Journal article or Dr. Randall Kendis, 10171 Kingbird Avenue, Fountain Valley, CA 92708 (stamped, self-addressed envelope).

EIS

On these pages, you will see 12 PAIRS of statements. Each pair consists of an *a* statement and a *b* statement. Read each of them carefully, and choose which of the two describes you better. If it is statement *a* then circle the letter *a* that appears before the statement. If it is statement *b*, then circle the letter *b* that precedes the statement. Make sure that you make a choice on every one of the 12 pairs of statements.

1. a.   I enjoy being active in clubs and youth groups.
   b.   I prefer to focus on hobbies which I can do on my own time, at my own pace.

2. a.   When I daydream, it is primarily about my past experiences.
   b.   When I daydream, it is primarily about the future and what it has in store for me.

3. a.   No matter how well I do a job, I always end up thinking that I could have done better.
   b.   When I complete a job that I have seriously worked on, I usually do not have doubts as to its quality.

4. a.   I will generally voice an opinion, even if I appear to be the only one in a group with that point of view.
   b.   If I appear to be the only one in a group with a certain opinion, I try to keep quiet in order to avoid feeling self-conscious.

5. a.   Generally speaking, a person can keep much better control of himself and of situations if he maintains an emotional distance.
   b.   A person need not feel loss of control, of himself, and of situations simply because he becomes intimately involved with another person.

6. a.   I have doubts as to the kind of person my abilities will enable me to become.
   b.   I try to formulate ideas now which will help me achieve my future goals.

7. a.   My evaluation of self-worth depends on the success or failure of my behavior in a given situation.
   b.   My self-evaluation, while flexible, remains about the same in most situations.

8. a.   While there may be disadvantages to competition, I agree that it is sometimes necessary and even good.
   b.   I do not enjoy competition

9. a.   There are times when I don't know what is expected of me.
   b.   I have a clear vision of how my life will unfold ahead of me.

10. a.   What I demand of myself and what others demand of me are often in
          conflict.
     b.   Most of the time, I don't mind doing what others demand of me
          because they are things I would probably have done anyway.

11. a.   When confronted with a task that I do not particularly enjoy, I find that
          I usually can discipline myself enough to perform them.
     b.   Often, when confronted with a task, I find myself expending my
          energies on other interesting but unrelated activities instead of
          concentrating on completing the task.

12. a.   Because of my philosophy of life, I have faith in myself, and in
          society in general.
     b.   Because of the uncertain nature of the individual and society, it is
          natural for me not to have a basic trust in society, in others, or even
          in myself.

EMOTIONAL ASSESSMENT SCALE (EAS)

AUTHORS: Charles R. Carlson, Frank L. Collins, Jean F. Stewart, James Porzelius, Jeffrey A. Nitz, and Cheryl O. Lind

PURPOSE: To measure emotional reactivity.

DESCRIPTION: The EAS is a 24-item instrument designed to measure immediate emotional responses to a full range of emotions at the same time. Based on work involving emotional responses in psychophysiological research, the EAS examines eight emotional states that are viewed as fundamental and consistent across cultures. The eight emotions are anger (items 4, 12, 20), anxiety (items 6, 14, 22), disgust (items 3, 11, 19), fear (items 2, 9, 17), guilt (items 5, 13, 15), happiness (items 8, 16, 24), sadness (items 7, 21, 23), and surprise (items 1, 10, 18). The EAS is a very useful instrument for measuring momentary levels and changes in emotions. It can be filled out in less than a minute, and can be used in a variety of clinical settings and situations.

NORMS: The EAS was studied initially with 120 persons from an undergraduate psychology course with an age range of 18 to 34 and 62% female, 38% male. The following means and standard deviations were reported: anger—mean = 14.6 (SD = 18.9); anxiety—mean = 32.4 (SD = 24.5); disgust—mean = 9.7 (SD = 13.3); fear—mean = 13.0 (SD = 14.5); guilt—mean = 12.6 (SD = 14.5); happiness—mean = 38.8 (SD = 23.8); sadness—mean = 19.1 (SD = 19.6); and surprise—mean = 10.7 (SD = 10.4).

SCORING: The EAS is scored by simply measuring the number of millimeters from the left endpoint to the slash mark located along the 100mm line. The three items composing each emotion are then summed for the score for that emotion. No total score is used.

RELIABILITY: The EAS has good to excellent reliability, with inter-item reliability for the emotions ranging from .70 to .91 and split-half reliability for the whole measure of .94. No data on stability were reported.

VALIDITY: The EAS has very good concurrent validity, with several of the subscales correlating with existing measures such as the POMS, Beck Depression Inventory, and the State-Trait Anxiety Inventory (State form). Subscales of the EAS also were found in subsequent research to be sensitive to changes in externally induced stress levels.

PRIMARY REFERENCE: Carlson, C. R., Collins, F. L., Stewart, J. F., Porzelius, J., Nitz, J. A., and Lind, C. O. (1989). The assessment of emotional reactivity: A scale development and validation study, *Journal of Psychopathology and Behavioral Assessment*, 11, 313–325. Plenum Publishing Corp.

AVAILABILITY: Dr. Charles Carlson, Department of Psychology, University of Kentucky, Lexington, KY 40506.

EAS

For each word listed, place a slash (/) somewhere on the appropriate line to indicate how you are feeling at this moment.

Least possible   Most possible

1. Surprised _____

2. Afraid _____

3. Disgusted _____

4. Angry _____

5. Guilty _____

6. Anxious _____

7. Sad _____

8. Delighted _____

9. Scared _____

10. Astonished _____

11. Repulsed _____

Least possible   Most possible

12. Mad

13. Ashamed

14. Worried

15. Disturbed

16. Joyful

17. Frightened

18. Amazed

19. Sickened

20. Annoyed

21. Humiliated

22. Nervous

23. Hopeless

24. Happy

EMOTIONAL/SOCIAL LONELINESS INVENTORY (ESLI)

AUTHORS: Harry Vincenzi and Fran Grabosky

PURPOSE: To measure emotional and social loneliness and isolation.

DESCRIPTION: The ESLI is a 15-item instrument designed to measure both loneliness and isolation from social and emotional points of view. The 15 items are presented in a paired format to contrast one's perception of his/her social network with his/her feelings about it. The ESLI has four factors that differentiate social loneliness (items 1–8, first set of questions), emotional loneliness (items 1–8, second set), social loneliness (items 9–15, first set), and emotional loneliness (items 9–15, second set). The ESLI can be used to help researchers and clinicians distinguish between social and emotional components of loneliness and isolation.

NORMS: The ESLI was studied initially with two samples. The first contained 95 respondents, including 33 masters-level psychology students, 33 high school students, and 26 in an adult psychotherapy program. The second sample included 229 respondents, 65 from a clinical population, 65 undergraduates, and 99 high school students. Both samples contained males and females. No other demographic data were reported. The following means were reported for the second sample ($n = 228$) with the scores for the clinical sample ($n = 65$) in parentheses: emotional isolation—5.3 (12.0), social isolation—7.3 (11.0), emotional loneliness—8.4 (14.0), and social loneliness—7.0 (11.9).

SCORING: Scores for the subscale and total scale are obtained by simply summing the pertinent item scores.

RELIABILITY: The ESLI has good internal consistency, with alphas for the subscales that range from .80 to .86. The ESLI has very good stability, with a two-week test-retest reliability of .80 for the total score.

VALIDITY: The ESLI has good known-groups validity, significantly distinguishing between the clinical and nonclinical groups on all four subscales. No other validity data were reported.

PRIMARY REFERENCE: Vincenzi, H. and Grabosky, F. (1987). Measuring the emotional/social aspects of loneliness and isolation, *Journal of Social Behavior and Personality*, 2, 257–270.

AVAILABILITY: Journal article.

ESLI

The purpose of this questionnaire is to help you explore what is TRUE in your life versus how you FEEL at this time. For example, you may have a mate, but due to a poor relationship, you don't feel like you have a mate. Please use the last two weeks as a guideline to answer these questions.

Please respond to each question by circling the response that best describes you. Please respond to *both* categories for each question.

Usually true = 3 Often true = 2 Sometimes true = 1 Rarely true = 0

WHAT IS TRUE IN MY LIFE AT THIS TIME.	WHAT I FEEL IN MY LIFE AT THIS TIME.
1. I don't have a close friend.	I don't feel like I have a close friend.
0 1 2 3	0 1 2 3
2. People take advantage of me when I'm involved with them.	I'm atraid to trust others.
0 1 2 3	0 1 2 3
3. I don't have a mate (or boyfriend/girlfriend).	I don't feel like I have a mate (or boyfriend/girlfriend).
0 1 2 3	0 1 2 3
4. I don't want to burden others with my problems.	Those close to me feel burdened by me when I share my problems.
0 1 2 3	0 1 2 3
5. There is nobody in my life who depends on me.	I don't feel needed or important to others.
0 1 2 3	0 1 2 3
6. I don't have any relationships that involve sharing personal thoughts.	I don't feel I can share personal thoughts with anyone.
0 1 2 3	0 1 2 3

7. There is no one in my life that   I don't feel understood.
    tries to understand me.

    0   1   2   3   0   1   2   3

8. Nobody in my life really wants to   I don't feel safe to reach out to
    be involved with me.   others.

    0   1   2   3   0   1   2   3

9. I spend a lot of time alone.   I feel lonely.

    0   1   2   3   0   1   2   3

10. I am not part of a social group or   I don't feel part of a social group
    organization.   or organization.

    0   1   2   3   0   1   2   3

11. I haven't spoken to anyone today.   I don't feel like I made contact
                                             with anyone today.

    0   1   2   3   0   1   2   3

12. I don't have much in common to   I don't feel I have anything to say
    talk about with those around me.   to people.

    0   1   2   3   0   1   2   3

13. When I'm with others I don't   I don't feel I'm being myself with
    disclose much about myself.   others.

    0   1   2   3   0   1   2   3

14. I don't take social risks.   I fear embarrassing myself around
                                             others.

    0   1   2   3   0   1   2   3

15. People don't see me as an   I don't feel I am interesting.
    interesting person.

    0   1   2   3   0   1   2   3

EVALUATION OF OTHERS QUESTIONNAIRE (EOOQ)

AUTHOR: Jeremy Shapiro

PURPOSE: To measure judgment about others.

DESCRIPTION: This 38-item checklist measures one's evaluation of other people in general. Four aspects are assessed: achievement-relatedness (A-R), social skills (SS), subjective well-being (SWB), and kindness/morality (KM). The EOOQ is based on two theoretical perspectives: cognitive theory, which holds that the evaluation of others relates to one's own evaluation and self-concept, and social comparison theory which contends that positive evaluations of others result in a low self-evaluation. The EOOQ may serve as a useful tool when working with a depressed client, especially if the intervention is cognitively oriented or includes interpersonal skills training. The version presented here relates to the evaluation of others in general, and not a specific individual. If use of the instrument warrants anchoring to a specific individual, then the reliability and validity data may not pertain.

NORMS: Actual norms are not available.

SCORING: Each adjective is rated from zero ("has none of the characteristic") to 10 ("has a very great amount of the characteristic"). Adjectives which are themselves negative (e.g., "sad") are reverse-scored. Scores on the four subscales are the sum of the following items: A-R = 4 + 9 + 17 + 20 + 24 + 25 + 28 + 36 + 38; SS = 1 + 5 + 7 + 12 + 13 + 16 + 22 + 30 + 33; SWB = 2 + 11 + 14 + 18 + 21 + 27 + 31 + 37; KM = 3 + 6 + 8 + 10 + 15 + 19 + 23 + 26 + 29 + 32 + 34 + 35. Dividing each of the separate subscale scores by the number of items in that subscale produces a score ranging from zero to 10, with higher scores reflecting more positive evaluation of others.

RELIABILITY: No reliability data are reported.

VALIDITY: The study of evaluation of others with a sample of depressed respondents provides some evidence of concurrent validity. Scores on the SWB and A-R subscales correlated with depression and dependency. SWB scores also correlated with self-criticism.

PRIMARY REFERENCE: Shapiro, J. P. (1988). Relationship between dimension of depression experience and evaluation beliefs about people in general, *Personality and Social Psychology Bulletin*, 14, 388–400. Instrument reproduced with permission of Jeremy Shapiro.

AVAILABILITY: Jeremy Shapiro, Ph.D., Child Guidance Center, 2525 East 22nd Street, Cleveland, OH 44115.

Instruments for Practice

EOOQ

Listed below are a number of words that can be used to describe people. In the space provided, please indicate how you think people in general rate on these characteristics, using a scale from 0 to 10. A "0" would mean that you think most people have none of the characteristics described by the word. A "10" would mean people in general have a very great amount of this characteristic. A "5" would mean a moderate amount.

_____ 1. Charming

_____ 2. Sad

_____ 3. Kind

_____ 4. Creative

_____ 5. Good sense of humor

_____ 6. Hypocritical

_____ 7. Friendly

_____ 8. Trustworthy

_____ 9. Wise

_____ 10. Phony

_____ 11. Sad

_____ 12. Attractive

_____ 13. Shy

_____ 14. Anxious

_____ 15. Cruel

_____ 16. Fun to be with

_____ 17. Intelligent

_____ 18. Happy with themselves

_____ 19. Snobby

_____ 20. Hardworking

_____ 21. Happy with their lives

_____ 22. Good-looking

_____ 23. Ethical

_____ 24. Competent

_____ 25. Efficient

_____ 26. Conceited

_____ 27. Moody

_____ 28. Knowledgeable

_____ 29. Dishonest

_____ 30. Likable

_____ 31. Depressed

_____ 32. Helpful

_____ 33. Easy to get along with

_____ 34. Selfish

_____ 35. Loving

_____ 36. Accomplished

_____ 37. Psychologically healthy

_____ 38. Talented

FEAR OF AIDS SCALE (FAS)

AUTHORS: Richard A. Bouton, Peggy E. Gallagher, Paul A. Garlinghouse, Terri Leal, Leslie D. Rosenstein, and Robert K. Young

PURPOSE: To measure fear of AIDS.

DESCRIPTION: The FAS is a 14-item instrument designed to measure attitudes toward the fear of AIDS. The scale was developed using Thurstone's method of equal-appearing intervals, and went through a rigorous process of external judgments to reduce the original 40 items to the current 14 items. Given the major catastrophe of AIDS and its presence in so many segments of the population, the FAS can be very useful in work both with clients and other helping professionals.

NORMS: The FAS was administered to 524 students (males = 266, females = 258) enrolled in introductory psychology classes at the University of Texas at Austin. No other demographic information was provided. The mean scores were 32.21 for males and 31.39 for females; the difference was not significant.

SCORING: The FAS is scored by assigning scores to the five choices (0 = "strongly agree" to 4 = "strongly disagree"). Items 2, 3, 4, 6, 8, 10, 12, and 14 are reverse-scored, and all items are summed for the total score. The possible range in scores is from 0 to 56 with higher scores indicating greater fear of AIDS.

RELIABILITY: The FAS has good internal consistency, with an alpha of .80. No data on stability were presented.

VALIDITY: The FAS is said to have good factorial validity, although other forms of validity are not available. Scores on the FAS are relatively independent of scores on the Homophobia Scale, suggesting that fear of AIDS is not just another way of expressing homophobia.

PRIMARY REFERENCE: Bouton, R. A., Gallagher, P. E., Garlinghouse, P. A., Leal, T., Rosenstein, L. D., and Young, R. K. (1987). Scales for measuring fear of AIDS and homophobia, *Journal of Personality Assessment*, 51, 606–614.

AVAILABILITY: Journal article.

FAS

Please indicate the extent to which you agree or disagree with each of the statements below.

		Strongly agree	Agree	Unde-cided	Dis-agree	Strongly disagree
1.	I wouldn't mind being in the same room with a friend who had AIDS.	____	____	____	____	____
2.	A centralized file containing the names of all people known to have the AIDS virus should be created.	____	____	____	____	____
3.	If I found out a friend had AIDS, I would be afraid to hug him/her.	____	____	____	____	____
4.	I would object to sending my non-infected child to a school which had a child who has AIDS.	____	____	____	____	____
5.	I believe public officials when they say AIDS cannot be transmitted through casual contact.	____	____	____	____	____
6.	I am afraid that I will get AIDS.	____	____	____	____	____
7.	AIDS children should be allowed to attend public school.	____	____	____	____	____
8.	Compared with other public health problems, I think AIDS is a very minor problem.	____	____	____	____	____
9.	If I found out that my lover had AIDS, I would still have sex with him/her.	____	____	____	____	____

	Strongly agree	Agree	Unde-cided	Dis-agree	Strongly disagree
10. The seriousness of AIDS is greatly overblown by the media.	____	____	____	____	____
11. AIDS will become a severe and widespread epidemic.	____	____	____	____	____
12. I am worried about catching AIDS in a public restroom.	____	____	____	____	____
13. Even if a friend had AIDS, I wouldn't mind touching him/her.	____	____	____	____	____
14. If I found out a friend or lover had AIDS I would be afraid to kiss him/her.	____	____	____	____	____

FEAR-OF-INTIMACY SCALE (FIS)

AUTHORS: Carol J. Descutner and Mark Thelen

PURPOSE: To measure fear of intimacy.

DESCRIPTION: The FIS is a 35-item instrument designed to measure fear of intimacy, defined as the inhibited capacity of an individual, because of anxiety, to exchange thoughts and feelings of personal significance with another individual who is highly valued. The FIS is based on the idea that intimacy exists only with the communication of personal information about which one has strong feelings and with high regard for the intimate other. The FIS is viewed as useful for research on this topic as well as for evaluating treatment outcomes when problems with intimacy are the focus.

NORMS: The FIS was studied initially in several stages including 175 male and 285 female introductory psychology students. The mean age for a subsample of 129 from this group was 19.1 years. The mean score on the FIS was 78.75 (SD = 21.82); there was no statistically significant difference between men and women.

SCORING: The FIS is easily scored by summing individual item responses for a total score. Items 3, 6–8, 10, 14, 17–19, 21, 22, 25, 27, 29, and 30 are reverse-scored.

RELIABILITY: The FIS has excellent internal consistency, with an alpha of .93. The FIS also has excellent stability, with a one-month test-retest correlation of .89.

VALIDITY: The FIS has good construct validity in comparison with a number of measures with which it should and should not be correlated. These included positive correlations with the UCLA Loneliness Scale and negative correlations with the Jourard Self-Disclosure Questionnaire, Miller Social Intimacy Scale and Need for Cognition, as well as several items of self-report data on relationships. The FIS is correlated significantly with social desirability.

PRIMARY REFERENCE: Descutner, C. J. and Thelen, M. H. (1991). Development and validation of a Fear-of-Intimacy Scale, *Psychological Assessment*, 3, 218–225.

AVAILABILITY: Dr. Mark Thelen, University of Missouri, 210 McAlester Hall, Columbia, MO 65211.

FIS

Part A Instructions: Imagine you are in a *close, dating* relationship. Respond to the following statements as you would *if you were in that close relationship*. Rate how characteristic each statement is of you on a scale of 1 to 5 as described below, and put your response in the space to the left of the statement.

1 = Not at all characteristic of me
2 = Slightly characteristic of me
3 = Moderately characteristic of me
4 = Very characteristic of me
5 = Extremely characteristic of me

Note. In each statement "O" refers to the person who would be in the close relationship with you.

_____ 1. I would feel uncomfortable telling O about things in the past that I have felt ashamed of.
_____ 2. I would feel uneasy talking with O about something that has hurt me deeply.
_____ 3. I would feel comfortable expressing my true feelings to O.
_____ 4. If O were upset I would sometimes be afraid of showing that I care.
_____ 5. I might be afraid to confide my innermost feelings to O.
_____ 6. I would feel at ease telling O that I care about him/her.
_____ 7. I would have a feeling of complete togetherness with O.
_____ 8. I would be comfortable discussing significant problems with O.
_____ 9. A part of me would be afraid to make a long-term commitment to O.
_____ 10. I would feel comfortable telling my experiences, even sad ones, to O.
_____ 11. I would probably feel nervous showing O strong feelings of affection.
_____ 12. I would find it difficult being open with O about my personal thoughts.
_____ 13. I would feel uneasy with O depending on me for emotional support.
_____ 14. I would not be afraid to share with O what I dislike about myself.
_____ 15. I would be afraid to take the risk of being hurt in order to establish a closer relationship with O.
_____ 16. I would feel comfortable keeping very personal information to myself.
_____ 17. I would not be nervous about being spontaneous with O.
_____ 18. I would feel comfortable telling O things that I do not tell other people.
_____ 19. I would feel comfortable trusting O with my deepest thoughts and feelings.
_____ 20. I would sometimes feel uneasy if O told me about very personal matters.
_____ 21. I would be comfortable revealing to O what I feel are my shortcomings and handicaps.
_____ 22. I would be comfortable with having a close emotional tie between us.
_____ 23. I would be afraid of sharing my private thoughts with O.
_____ 24. I would be afraid that I might not always feel close to O.
_____ 25. I would be comfortable telling O what my needs are.
_____ 26. I would be afraid that O would be more invested in the relationship than I would be.

_____ 27. I would feel comfortable about having open and honest
           communication with O.
_____ 28. I would sometimes feel uncomfortable listening to O's personal
           problems.
_____ 29. I would feel at ease to completely be myself around O.
_____ 30. I would feel relaxed being together and talking about our personal
           goals.

Part B Instructions: Respond to the following statements as they apply to your past
relationships. Rate how characteristic each statement is of you on a scale of 1 to 5
as described in the instructions for Part A.

_____ 31. I have shied away from opportunities to be close to someone.
_____ 32. I have held back my feelings in previous relationships.
_____ 33. There are people who think that I am afraid to get close to them.
_____ 34. There are people who think that I am not an easy person to get to
           know.
_____ 35. I have done things in previous relationships to keep me from
           developing closeness.

FEAR OF NEGATIVE EVALUATION (FNE)

AUTHORS: David Watson and Ronald Friend

PURPOSE: To measure social anxiety.

DESCRIPTION: This 30-item instrument was designed to measure one aspect of social anxiety, the fear of receiving negative evaluations from others. Scores on the FNE essentially reflect a fear of the loss of social approval. Items on the measure include signs of anxiety and ineffective social behaviors that would incur disapproval by others. The FNE is also available in a shorter, 12-item form (Leary, 1983). Both versions are reproduced here. The Brief FNE is composed of the original FNE items which correlated above .50 with the total FNE score. The Brief FNE and the original FNE are highly correlated.

NORMS: The FNE was originally developed on a sample of 297 college students, of which 92 were excluded from data analysis because of attrition or missing information. No demographic data are presented. The mean FNE score was 13.97 for males ($n = 60$) and 16.1 for females ($n = 146$). The Brief FNE has a different scoring system. The mean Brief FNE score was 35.7 with a standard deviation of 8.1 for a sample of 150 college students.

SCORING: The FNE items are answered "true" or "false." Items 2, 3, 5, 7, 9, 11, 13, 14, 17, 19, 20, 22, 24, 25, 28, 29 and 30 are keyed "true" while the other items are keyed for "false" responses. A value of 1 is assigned to each item answer which matches the key and 0 for answers which do not match the key. Scores are the sum of all item values, and range from 0 to 30.

The Brief FNE is rated on a five point scale in terms of how characteristic each item is of the respondent. Items 2, 4, 7 and 10 are reverse-scored. Total scores are the sum of the item responses and range from 12 to 60.

RELIABILITY: Internal consistency of the FNE was first determined by correlating each item with the total FNE score. The average item to total score correlation was .72. Internal consistency using Kuder-Richardson formula 20 was excellent, with correlations of .94 for a sample of 205 college students and .96 for a separate sample of 154 subjects. The FNE was shown to be stable with a test-retest correlation of .78 over a one-month period and .94 from a separate sample of 29 subjects. The Brief FNE has excellent internal consistency, with a Cronbach's alpha of .90. The Brief FNE is also considered stable with a test-retest correlation of .75 over a four week period.

VALIDITY: A type of known-groups validity was demonstrated by comparing a sample of subjects who scored in the upper 25 percentile of the FNE with subjects from the lower 25 percentile. The results, which only approach statistical significance, suggest the high FNE group sought more approval from others and avoided disapproval. The groups also differed on measures of uneasiness. Scores on the FNE correlated with measures of social approval, locus of control, desirability, autonomy, dependence, dominance, abasement, exhibitionism, and other measures of anxiety. The Brief FNE was evaluated for validity first by correlating scores with the full-length FNE; this correlation was .96. Criterion-related validity was shown with scores on the Brief FNE correlating with anxiety, avoidance, the degree to which respondents said that they were well presented, and the degree to which respondents were bothered by an unfavorable evaluation from others.

PRIMARY REFERENCES: Watson, D. and Friend, R. (1969). Measurement of social-evaluative anxiety, *Journal of Consulting and Clinical Psychology*, 33, 448–457. Leary, M. R. (1983). A brief version of the Fear of Negative Evaluation scale, *Personality and Social Psychology Bulletin*, 9, 371–375. Instrument reproduced with permission of D. Watson and the American Psychological Association.

AVAILABILITY: Journal articles.

FNE

For the following statements, please answer each in terms of whether it is true or false for you. Circle T for true or F for false.

T F 1. I rarely worry about seeming foolish to others.
T F 2. I worry about what people will think of me even when I know it doesn't make any difference.
T F 3. I become tense and jittery if I know someone is sizing me up.
T F 4. I am unconcerned even if I know people are forming an unfavorable impression of me.
T F 5. I feel very upset when I commit some social error.
T F 6. The opinions that important people have of me cause me little concern.
T F 7. I am often afraid that I may look ridiculous or make a fool of myself.
T F 8. I react very little when other people disapprove of me.
T F 9. I am frequently afraid of other people noticing my shortcomings.
T F 10. The disapproval of others would have little effect on me.
T F 11. If someone is evaluating me I tend to expect the worst.
T F 12. I rarely worry about what kind of impression I am making on someone.
T F 13. I am afraid that others will not approve of me.
T F 14. I am afraid that people will find fault with me.
T F 15. Other people's opinions of me do not bother me.
T F 16. I am not necessarily upset if I do not please someone.
T F 17. When I am talking to someone, I worry about what they may be thinking about me.
T F 18. I feel that you can't help making social errors sometimes, so why worry about it.
T F 19. I am usually worried about what kind of impression I make.
T F 20. I worry a lot about what my superiors think of me.
T F 21. If I know someone is judging me, it has little effect on me.
T F 22. I worry that others will think I am not worthwhile.
T F 23. I worry very little about what others may think of me.
T F 24. Sometimes I think I am too concerned with what other people think of me.
T F 25. I often worry that I will say or do the wrong things.
T F 26. I am often indifferent to the opinions others have of me.
T F 27. I am usually confident that others will have a favorable impression of me.
T F 28. I often worry that people who are important to me won't think very much of me.
T F 29. I brood about the opinions my friends have about me.
T F 30. I become tense and jittery if I know I am being judged by my superiors.

BRIEF FNE

For the following statements please indicate how characteristic each is of you using the following rating scale:

1 = Not at all characteristic of me
2 = Slightly characteristic of me
3 = Moderately characteristic of me
4 = Very characteristic of me
5 = Extremely characteristic of me

Please record your answers in the spaces to the left of the items.

____ 1. I worry about what other people will think of me even when I know it doesn't make any difference.
____ 2. I am unconcerned even if I know people are forming an unfavorable impression of me.
____ 3. I am frequently afraid of other people noticing my shortcomings.
____ 4. I rarely worry about what kind of impression I am making on someone.
____ 5. I am afraid that people will not approve of me.
____ 6. I am afraid that people will find fault with me.
____ 7. Other people's opinions of me do not bother me.
____ 8. When I am talking to someone, I worry about what they may be thinking about me.
____ 9. I am usually worried about what kind of impression I make.
____ 10. If I know someone is judging me, it has little effect on me.
____ 11. Sometimes I think I am too concerned with what other people think of me.
____ 12. I often worry that I will say or do the wrong things.

FEAR QUESTIONNAIRE (FQ)

AUTHORS: I. M. Marks and A. M. Mathews

PURPOSE: To measure fear in phobic patients.

DESCRIPTION: This 24-item instrument was developed in three research and treatment facilities in order to assess the outcome of work with phobic patients. The form is general enough to be useful with any phobic disorder, but has added precision because it allows the practitioner to specify the phobia that is the focus of treatment, which is called the main target phobia rating. The form includes fifteen questions on different types of phobias, which can be used as subscales measuring agoraphobia (Ag), blood-injury phobia (BI) and social phobia (SP). The FQ also includes 5 items measuring anxiety and depression symptoms (ADS) associated with phobia. Finally, along with the target phobia at the beginning of the form, the FQ ends with another global phobia index.

NORMS: Normative data are reported on all aspects of the FQ. For the main target phobia, the mean score for a sample of 20 phobic inpatients was 7. The mean score on the 15-item total phobia scale was 47 for the 20 patients. Extensive additional data on large samples are available.

SCORING: All items are rated on a scale from 1 to 8 with higher scores reflecting more severe phobic responses. The total phobia rating is the sum of the scores for items 2 through 16. The three subscales are composed of the following items: Ag: 5, 6, 8, 12, 15; BI: 2, 4, 10, 13, 16; SP: 3, 7, 9, 11, 14. The ADS score is the sum of items 18 through 22.

RELIABILITY: This instrument has good test-retest reliability. For the three subscales combined the correlation was .82 for a one-week period. The test-retest correlation was also excellent for the Main Target Phobia (.93), and good for the global phobia rating (.79) and the anxiety-depression subscale (.82). Internal consistency data are not reported.

VALIDITY: The validity of the FQ has been supported by several studies. The FQ has been shown to discriminate between phobics and nonphobics on all aspects of the measure. Most important for the purposes of monitoring clients, the FQ has been shown to be sensitive, with scores changing over the course of intervention.

PRIMARY REFERENCE: Marks, I. M. and Mathews, A. M. (1978). Brief standard self-rating for phobic patients, *Behaviour Research and Therapy*, 17, 263–267. Instrument reproduced with permission of I. M. Marks and A. M. Mathews.

AVAILABILITY: Journal article.

FQ

Choose a number from the scale below to show how much you would avoid each of the situations listed below because of fear or other unpleasant feelings. Then write the number you chose in the blank opposite each situation.

0	1	2	3	4	5	6	7	8
Would not avoid it		Slightly avoid it		Definitely avoid it		Markedly avoid it		Always avoid it

_____ 1. Main phobia you want treated (describe in your own words)
_____ 2. Injections or minor surgery
_____ 3. Eating or drinking with other people
_____ 4. Hospitals
_____ 5. Traveling alone by bus or coach
_____ 6. Walking alone in busy streets
_____ 7. Being watched or stared at
_____ 8. Going into crowded shops
_____ 9. Talking to people in authority
_____ 10. Sight of blood
_____ 11. Being criticized
_____ 12. Going alone far from home
_____ 13. Thought of injury or illness
_____ 14. Speaking or acting to an audience
_____ 15. Large open spaces
_____ 16. Going to the dentist
_____ 17. Other situations (describe)

Now choose a number from the scale below to show how much you are troubled by each problem listed, and write the number in the blank.

0	1	2	3	4	5	6	7	8
Hardly at all		Slightly troublesome		Definitely troublesome		Markedly troublesome		Very severely troublesome

_____ 18. Feeling miserable or depressed
_____ 19. Feeling irritable or angry
_____ 20. Feeling tense or panicky
_____ 21. Upsetting thoughts coming into your mind
_____ 22. Feeling you or your surroundings are strange or unreal
_____ 23. Other feelings (describe)

How would you rate the present state of your phobic symptoms on the scale below? Please circle one number between 0 and 8.

0	1	2	3	4	5	6	7	8
No phobias present		Slightly disturbing/ not really disturbing		Definitely disturbing/ disabling		Markedly disturbing/ disabling		Very severely disturbing/ disabling

FEAR SURVEY SCHEDULE-II (FSS-II)

AUTHOR: James H. Geer

PURPOSE: To measure responses to commonly occurring fears.

DESCRIPTION: The 51-item FSS-II is designed to measure fear responses. The FSS-II is one of the most widely-used fear schedules in the behavior therapy literature. The instrument lists potential fear evoking situations and stimuli. A client rates his or her level of discomfort or distress. The items included on the FSS-II were first empirically selected from a pool of 111. Each item was then examined to determine its correlation with total scores. All items, except number 15, correlated with total scores for male and female college students, with item 15 reaching significance for females. Total scores on this FSS reflect general fear.

NORMS: Mean scores on the sample mentioned above were 75.78 with a standard deviation of 33.84 for males and 100.16 with a standard deviation of 36.11 for females. These means were significantly different. In a separate study, 1814 college students enrolled in an introductory psychology class had means and standard deviations of 81.81 and 33.64 for males and 108.47 and 36.78 for females. These means were also significantly different.

SCORING: Each item is rated on a 7-point scale of intensity of fear. Scores are the sum of the item scores and range from 51 to 357. Higher scores indicate greater fear.

RELIABILITY: The FSS-II is a very reliable instrument, with an internal consistency coefficient of .94 using Kuder-Richardson formula 20. The instrument is reported to be stable, although the reliability data are not as direct as test-retest reliability data.

VALIDITY: The FSS has good concurrent validity, with significant correlations between the FSS and emotionality and anxiety, while the scores are not associated with scores on measures of introversion and extroversion. Known-groups validity data indicate that groups categorized according to FSS scores differ on five relevant criteria: the time it took subjects to approach a frightening stimulus, the distance between the subjects and the stimulus, subjects' ratings of experienced fear, experimenter's rating of the fear the subjects presented, and an affect adjective checklist completed by the subjects.

PRIMARY REFERENCE: Geer, J. H. (1965). The development of a scale to measure fear, *Behaviour Research and Therapy*, 3, 45–53. Instrument reproduced with permission of James H. Geer.

AVAILABILITY: Journal article.

FSS-II

Below are 51 different stimuli that can cause fear in people. Please rate how much fear you feel using the following rating scale and record your answer in the space provided:

1 = None
2 = Very little fear
3 = A little fear
4 = Some fear
5 = Much fear
6 = Very much fear
7 = Terror

____ 1. Sharp objects
____ 2. Being a passenger in a car
____ 3. Dead bodies
____ 4. Suffocating
____ 5. Failing a test
____ 6. Looking foolish
____ 7. Being a passenger in an airplane
____ 8. Worms
____ 9. Arguing with parents
____ 10. Rats and mice
____ 11. Life after death
____ 12. Hypodermic needles
____ 13. Being criticized
____ 14. Meeting someone for the first time
____ 15. Roller coasters
____ 16. Being alone
____ 17. Making mistakes
____ 18. Being misunderstood
____ 19. Death
____ 20. Being in a fight
____ 21. Crowded places
____ 22. Blood
____ 23. Heights
____ 24. Being a leader
____ 25. Swimming alone
____ 26. Illness
____ 27. Being with drunks
____ 28. Illness or injury to loved ones
____ 29. Being self-conscious
____ 30. Driving a car
____ 31. Meeting authority
____ 32. Mental illness
____ 33. Closed places
____ 34. Boating
____ 35. Spiders
____ 36. Thunderstorms
____ 37. Not being a success
____ 38. God
____ 39. Snakes
____ 40. Cemeteries
____ 41. Speaking before a group
____ 42. Seeing a fight
____ 43. Death of a loved one
____ 44. Dark places
____ 45. Strange dogs
____ 46. Deep water
____ 47. Being with a member of the opposite sex
____ 48. Stinging insects
____ 49. Untimely or early death
____ 50. Losing a job
____ 51. Auto accidents

FREQUENCY OF SELF REINFORCEMENT QUESTIONNAIRE
(FSRQ)

AUTHOR: Elaine M. Heiby

PURPOSE: To measure skill at self-reinforcement.

DESCRIPTION: The FSRQ (also known as the Self-Reinforcement Questionnaire, SRQ) is a 30-item instrument designed to assess respondents' en-
couraging, supporting, and valuing themselves and their own efforts.
Self-reinforcement is seen as a generalized response set with a low frequency
of self-reinforcement viewed as a possible causative factor in depression.
Thus, use of this measure would be in conjunction with clinical work on
increasing a client's skills at, and the frequency of, self-reinforcement. Items
on the FSRQ were initially selected from a pool of 100 items, based on
judgments of content validity by 10 clinicians. Research on the FSRQ is
continuing with a shorter form available from the author.

NORMS: The FSRQ has been studied with several samples of educated adults
and undergraduate college students. Actual norms on the latest version of
the FSRQ are not available.

SCORING: The FSRQ is easily scored by reverse-scoring negatively worded
items and summing the individual items to obtain an overall score. The range
of scores is from 0 to 90 with higher scores indicating greater frequency of
self-reinforcement. Scores below 17 suggest deficits in self-reinforcement
skills, dependence upon others for approval, and possible vulnerability to
depression.

RELIABILITY: The FSRQ has very good internal consistency, with split-half
reliability of .87. The FSRQ has excellent stability, with an eight week
test-retest correlation of .92.

VALIDITY: The FSRQ has good concurrent validity as demonstrated by correlations between FSRQ scores and self-monitoring of self-reinforcement
and experimenter ratings of respondents' tendency to engage in self-reinforcement. The FSRQ is not correlated with social desirability response set,
and is sensitive to change following training in self-reinforcement skills. The
FSRQ is also reported as having good construct validity as demonstrated by
negative correlations with self-punishment, the Beck Depression Inventory
and measures of cognitive distortion.

PRIMARY REFERENCE: Heiby, E. M. (1983). Assessment of frequency of self-
reinforcement, *Journal of Personality and Social Psychology*, 44, 263–
270. Instrument reproduced with permission of Elaine M. Heiby and the
American Psychological Association.

AVAILABILITY: Dr. Elaine M. Heiby, University of Hawaii, Department of
Psychology, Honolulu, HI 96822.

FSRQ

Below are a number of statements about beliefs or attitudes people have. Indicate how descriptive the statements are for you by rating each item, as indicated below. There are no right or wrong answers. Your answers are confidential, so do not put your name on this sheet. Thank you!

Rate each item for how much of the time it is descriptive for you. In the blank before each item, rate:

0 = Never descriptive of me
1 = A little of the time descriptive of me
2 = Some of the time descriptive of me
3 = Most of the time descriptive of me

_____ 1. When I fail at something, I am still able to feel good about myself.
_____ 2. I can stick to a boring task that I need to finish without someone pushing me.
_____ 3. I have negative thoughts about myself.
_____ 4. When I do something right, I take time to enjoy the feeling.
_____ 5. I have such high standards for what I expect of myself that I have a hard time meeting my standards.
_____ 6. I seem to blame myself and be very critical of myself when things go wrong.
_____ 7. I can have a good time doing some things alone.
_____ 8. I get upset with myself when I make mistakes.
_____ 9. My feelings of self-confidence go up and down.
_____ 10. When I succeed at small things, it helps me to go on.
_____ 11. If I do not do something absolutely perfectly, I don't feel satisfied.
_____ 12. I get myself through hard things mostly by thinking I'll enjoy myself afterwards.
_____ 13. When I make mistakes, I take time to criticize myself.
_____ 14. I encourage myself to improve at something by feeling good about myself.
_____ 15. I put myself down so that I will do things better in the future.
_____ 16. I think talking about what you've done right is bragging.
_____ 17. I find that I feel better when I silently praise myself.
_____ 18. I can keep working at something hard to do when I stop to think of what I've already done.
_____ 19. The way I keep up my self-confidence is by remembering any successes I have had.
_____ 20. The way I achieve my goals is by rewarding myself every step along the way.
_____ 21. Praising yourself is being selfish.
_____ 22. When someone criticizes me, I lose my self-confidence.
_____ 23. I criticize myself more often than others criticize me.
_____ 24. I feel I have a lot of good qualities.
_____ 25. I silently praise myself even when other people do not praise me.
_____ 26. Any activity can provide some pleasure no matter how it comes out.

_____ 27. If I don't do the best possible job, I don't feel good about myself.
_____ 28. I should be upset if I make a mistake
_____ 29. My happiness depends more on myself than it depends on other people.
_____ 30. People who talk about their own better points are just bragging.

FRIENDLINESS–UNFRIENDLINESS SCALE (SACRAL)

AUTHOR: John M. Reisman

PURPOSE: To measure friendliness as related to self-concept, accessibility, rewardingness, and alienation.

DESCRIPTION: This 20-item instrument measures friendliness-unfriendliness. Friendliness is a complex set of skills and beliefs about one's self that relates to loneliness, shyness, social skills deficits, and feelings of alienation. For some clients whose problems relate to loneliness and depression, friendliness is a more important assessment than the actual number of friends. Items in the SACRAL were selected from a pool of 40 items based on the ability to discriminate between respondents categorized into high-SACRAL and low-SACRAL groups according to total scores. The short form reported here correlated .94 with the 40-item version. There are four subscales composed of the following items: self-concept (S: items 1, 5, 9, 13, 17); accessibility (AC: items 2, 6, 10, 14, 18); rewardingness (R: items 3, 7, 11, 15, 19); and alienation (AL: items 4, 8, 12, 16, 20). The total score measuring overall friendliness is derived by adding scores for S, AC, R, and AL.

NORMS: A sample of 25 undergraduates had a mean and standard deviation of 42.2 and 15.0, respectively. Scores tended to range from 27 to 57. For a subsample of respondents categorized as high in friendliness, the mean was 113 and standard deviation was 8.8 ($n = 17$). A subsample of respondents considered low in friendliness had a mean of 81 and a standard deviation of 9.0. Both sets of norms are based on the 40-item version and not the 20-item version.

SCORING: Items 9, 10, 11, 14, 15, 17, 18, and 19 are scored in the positive direction. Responses of 0 or 1 are scored as 0. All other items are reverse-scored, with responses of 3 or 4 both being scored as 0.

RELIABILITY: Reliability data are not presented in the primary reference.

VALIDITY: There is evidence of construct validity. This is seen in a 94% agreement rate between subjects' SACRAL scores and the assessment of raters of subject responses in a laboratory setting. Concurrent validity is seen by associations between SACRAL subscale scores and ratings of satisfaction with oneself and one's friends, scores on a measure of the value of friends for being supportive, helpful, and stimulating. Respondents with high and low scores on the SACRAL had significantly different ratings on interpersonal judgment.

PRIMARY REFERENCE: Reisman, J. M. and Billingham, S. (1989). SACRAL: Additional correlates of a self-report measure of friendliness-unfriendliness, *Journal of Personality Assessment*, 53, 113–121. Instrument reproduced with permission of John M. Reisman.

AVAILABILITY: The Free Press.

SACRAL

The following statements sample how people feel about themselves and other people. There are no right or wrong answers. *What is important is what you personally believe or feel is true of yourself.* Read each statement carefully, then mark how much you agree or disagree with it. Circle 4 if you agree very much. Circle 3 if you somewhat agree. Circle 1 if you somewhat disagree. Circle 0 if you disagree very much.

1. There are many times when you don't think well of yourself.   4   3   1   0

2. A lot of the ideas and opinions of other people don't make   4   3   1   0
    much sense.

3. You often don't give compliments to someone who might   4   3   1   0
    deserve them.

4. You find it hard to be really yourself, even with your friends.   4   3   1   0

5. You are a shy person.   4   3   1   0

6. Even if you don't hear from a friend for several days and   4   3   1   0
    don't know why, you don't try to get in touch.

7. When your friends need advice, it is not always easy for you   4   3   1   0
    to give them suggestions or ideas about what to do.

8. You like to spend your time alone and to be by yourself.   4   3   1   0

9. You are very pleasant and agreeable.   4   3   1   0

10. If someone comes to talk with you, you always stop   4   3   1   0
    whatever it is you're doing and give your attention to the
    person.

11. If there is a new person around, you introduce yourself and   4   3   1   0
    your friends.

12. If you have time for fun and relaxation, you prefer to read or   4   3   1   0
    watch television or do something by yourself.

13. You lose your temper easily.   4   3   1   0

14. It's easy for you to start a conversation with a stranger and   4   3   1   0
    keep it going.

15. When your friends are sick, you always send them a little present or give them a call.   4 3 1 0

16. People often take your actions and comments the wrong way.   4 3 1 0

17. You think of yourself as a very friendly person.   4 3 1 0

18. People often come to you with their personal problems.   4 3 1 0

19. If you see someone who needs help, you drop whatever you're doing and lend a hand.   4 3 1 0

20. Good friends are hard for you to find.   4 3 1 0

FROST MULTIDIMENSIONAL PERFECTIONISM SCALE (FMPS)

AUTHORS: Randy O. Frost, Patricia Martin, Cathleen Lahart, and Robin Rosenblate

PURPOSE: To measure perfectionism.

DESCRIPTION: The FMPS is a 35-item instrument designed to measure the several components of perfectionism. Since few if any existing measures tap all major dimensions of perfectionism, the FMPS was developed. Perfectionism in general was viewed as having high standards of performance accompanied by overly critical evaluations of one's own behavior. Perfectionism also was viewed as either underlying or being related to several other psychological disorders. A total of 67 items was generated from other measures, and reduced to 35 items in a series of studies. The 35 items comprise six factors: concern over mistakes (CM, items 9, 10, 13, 14, 18, 21, 23, 25, 34); personal standards (PS, items 4, 6, 12, 16, 19, 24, 30); parental expectations (PE, items 1, 11, 15, 20, 26); parental criticism (PC, items 3, 5, 22, 35); doubts about actions (D, items 17, 28, 32, 33); and organization (O, items 2, 7, 8, 27, 29, 31). The FMPS is viewed as a useful measure both for research and therapeutic practice in helping pinpoint and evaluate change in the different components of perfectionism.

NORMS: A series of four studies was undertaken to develop the FMPS. The total number of subjects involved 576 female undergraduate students. No other demographic information was provided, nor were actual norms (means and standard deviations).

SCORING: The subscale and total scores are derived simply by summing individual item scores. The possible range from the 35 5-point Likert-type items is from 35 to 175, with higher scores suggesting greater amounts of perfectionism.

RELIABILITY: The FMPS has good to excellent reliability, with alphas that range from .77 to .93 for the subscales. The alpha for the total scale was .90. No test-retest data were provided.

VALIDITY: The FMPS has good concurrent validity, significantly correlating with three other perfectionism scales, the BURNS, EDI, and IBT. The overall FMPS and/or several of its subscales have good construct validity, correlating with a variety of measures of psychopathology including the Brief Symptom Inventory, the Depressive Experiences Questionnaire, several measures of compulsivity, and with procrastination.

PRIMARY REFERENCE: Frost, R. O., Martin, P., Lahart, C., and Rosenblate, R. (1990). The dimensions of perfectionism, *Cognitive Therapy and Research*, 14, 449–468. Instrument reprinted with permission of Randy O. Frost and Plenum Publishing Corp.

AVAILABILITY: Dr. Randy O. Frost, Department of Psychology, Smith College, Northampton, MA 01063.

FMPS

Please circle the number that best corresponds to your agreement with each statement below. Use this rating system:

Strongly disagree   1   2   3   4   5   Strongly agree

		Strongly disagree				Strongly agree
1.	My parents set very high standards for me.	1	2	3	4	5
2.	Organization is very important to me.	1	2	3	4	5
3.	As a child, I was punished for doing things less than perfectly.	1	2	3	4	5
4.	If I do not set the highest standards for myself, I am likely to end up a second rate person.	1	2	3	4	5
5.	My parents never tried to understand my mistakes.	1	2	3	4	5
6.	It is important to me that I be thoroughly competent in everything I do.	1	2	3	4	5
7.	I am a neat person.	1	2	3	4	5
8.	I try to be an organized person.	1	2	3	4	5
9.	If I fail at work/school, I am a failure as a person.	1	2	3	4	5
10.	I should be upset if I make a mistake.	1	2	3	4	5
11.	My parents wanted me to be the best at everything.	1	2	3	4	5
12.	I set higher goals than most people.	1	2	3	4	5

		Strongly disagree				Strongly agree
13.	If someone does a task at work/school better than I, then I feel like I failed the whole task.	1	2	3	4	5
14.	If I fail partly, it is as bad as being a complete failure.	1	2	3	4	5
15.	Only outstanding performance is good enough in my family.	1	2	3	4	5
16.	I am very good at focusing my efforts on attaining a goal.	1	2	3	4	5
17.	Even when I do something very carefully, I often feel that it is not quite right.	1	2	3	4	5
18.	I hate being less than best at things.	1	2	3	4	5
19.	I have extremely high goals.	1	2	3	4	5
20.	My parents have expected excellence from me.	1	2	3	4	5
21.	People will probably think less of me if I make a mistake.	1	2	3	4	5
22.	I never felt like I could meet my parents' expectations.	1	2	3	4	5
23.	If I do not do as well as other people, it means I am an inferior human being.	1	2	3	4	5
24.	Other people seem to accept lower standards from themselves than I do.	1	2	3	4	5
25.	If I do not do well all the time, people will not respect me.	1	2	3	4	5
26.	My parents have always had higher expectations for my future than I have.	1	2	3	4	5

		Strongly disagree				Strongly agree
27.	I try to be a neat person.	1	2	3	4	5
28.	I usually have doubts about the simple everyday things I do.	1	2	3	4	5
29.	Neatness is very important to me.	1	2	3	4	5
30.	I expect higher performance in my daily tasks than most people.	1	2	3	4	5
31.	I am an organized person.	1	2	3	4	5
32.	I tend to get behind in my work because I repeat things over and over.	1	2	3	4	5
33.	It takes me a long time to do something "right."	1	2	3	4	5
34.	The fewer mistakes I make, the more people will like me.	1	2	3	4	5
35.	I never felt like I could meet my parents' standards.	1	2	3	4	5

GENERALIZED CONTENTMENT SCALE (GCS)

AUTHOR: Walter W. Hudson

PURPOSE: To measure nonpsychotic depression.

DESCRIPTION: The GCS is a 25-item scale that is designed to measure the degree, severity, or magnitude of nonpsychotic depression. In contrast to many measures of depression, the GCS focuses largely on affective aspects of clinical depression, examining respondents' feelings about a number of behaviors, attitudes, and events associated with depression. The GCS has three cutting scores. The first is a score of 30 (±5); scores below this point indicate absence of a clinically significant problem in this area. Scores above 30 suggest the presence of a clinically significant problem. The second cutting score is 50 (±5), with clients scoring above 50 often found to have some suicidal ideation. The third cutting score is 70. Scores above this point nearly always indicate that clients are experiencing severe stress with a clear possibility that suicide may be being considered. The practitioner should be aware of and investigate this possibility. Another advantage of the GCS is that it is one of several scales of the WALMYR Assessment Scales package reproduced here, all of which are administered and scored the same way.

NORMS: This scale was developed with 2140 respondents, including single and married individuals, clinical and nonclinical populations, high school and college students and nonstudents. Respondents were primarily Caucasian, but also included Japanese and Chinese Americans, and a smaller number of members of other ethnic groups. The GCS is not recommended for use with children under the age of 12. Actual norms are not available.

SCORING: Like most WALMYR Assessment Scales instruments, the GCS is scored by first reverse-scoring items listed at the bottom of the page (5, 8, 9, 11–13, 15, 16, 21–24), summing these and the remaining scores, subtracting the number of completed items, multiplying this figure by 100, and dividing by the number of items completed times 6. This will produce a range from 0 to 100 with higher scores indicating greater magnitude or severity of problems.

RELIABILITY: The GCS has a mean alpha of .92, indicating excellent internal consistency, and an excellent (low) SEM of 4.56. The GCS also has excellent short-term stability, with a two-hour test-retest correlation of .94.

VALIDITY: The GCS has good concurrent validity, correlating in two studies .85 and .76 with the Beck Depression Inventory and .92 and .81 for two samples using the Zung Depression Inventory. The GCS has excellent known-groups validity, discriminating significantly between members of a group judged to be clinically depressed and those judged not to be depressed. The GCS also has good construct validity, correlating poorly with a number of measures with which it should not correlate, and correlating at high levels with several measures with which it should, such as self-esteem, happiness, and sense of identity.

PRIMARY REFERENCE: Hudson, W. W. (1992). *The WALMYR Assessment Scales Scoring Manual.* Tempe, AZ: WALMYR Publishing Co.

AVAILABILITY: WALMYR Publishing Co., P.O. Box 24779, Tempe, AZ 85285-4779.

GENERALIZED CONTENTMENT SCALE (GCS)

Name: _____ Today's Date: _____

This questionnaire is designed to measure the way you feel about your life and surroundings. It is not a test, so there are no right or wrong answers. Answer each item as carefully and as accurately as you can by placing a number beside each one as follows.

1 = None of the time
2 = Very rarely
3 = A little of the time
4 = Some of the time
5 = A good part of the time
6 = Most of the time
7 = All of the time

1. ____ I feel powerless to do anything about my life.
2. ____ I feel blue.
3. ____ I think about ending my life.
4. ____ I have crying spells.
5. ____ It is easy for me to enjoy myself.
6. ____ I have a hard time getting started on things that I need to do.
7. ____ I get very depressed.
8. ____ I feel there is always someone I can depend on when things get tough.
9. ____ I feel that the future looks bright for me.
10. ____ I feel downhearted.
11. ____ I feel that I am needed.
12. ____ I feel that I am appreciated by others.
13. ____ I enjoy being active and busy.
14. ____ I feel that others would be better off without me.
15. ____ I enjoy being with other people.
16. ____ I feel that it is easy for me to make decisions.
17. ____ I feel downtrodden.
18. ____ I feel terribly lonely.
19. ____ I get upset easily.
20. ____ I feel that nobody really cares about me.
21. ____ I have a full life.
22. ____ I feel that people really care about me.
23. ____ I have a great deal of fun.
24. ____ I feel great in the morning.
25. ____ I feel that my situation is hopeless.

5, 8, 9, 11, 12, 13, 15, 16, 21, 22, 23, 24.

GENERALIZED EXPECTANCY FOR SUCCESS SCALE (GESS)

AUTHORS: Bobbi Fibel and W. Daniel Hale

PURPOSE: To measure locus of control of success.

DESCRIPTION: The GESS is a 30-item measure that assesses the generalized expectancy of being successful. The construct is defined as the belief that in most situations one is able to obtain desired goals. The concept is related to anxiety and the negative cognitions often associated with depression, and suicidal ideation. Factor analysis suggests that the instrument measures three aspects of generalized expectancy: general efficacy (GE), long-range career-oriented expectancy (LRCOE), personal problem solving (PPS), and a fourth factor that has no consistent theme. Items were selected based, in part, on not correlating with social desirability.

NORMS: The instrument was developed with three samples of college students. The samples were reported to be predominantly middle-class, Caucasian college students (207 females and 132 males). For males, the mean was 112.32 with a standard deviation of 13.8, a median of 113.14 and a mode of 112. For females, the mean was 112.15 with a standard deviation of 13.23, a median of 112.8 and a mode of 109.

SCORING: Each item is rated in terms of how much it applies to the respondent. Items reflecting failure are reverse-scored (numbers 1, 2, 4, 6, 7, 8, 14, 15, 17, 18, 24, 27, 28). Scores are the sum of the item ratings, and range from 30 to 150. Higher scores reflect an internal locus of control of success. Items for the factors are: GE: 4, 8, 9, 10, 12, 13, 15, 16, 21, 22; LRCOE: 14, 17, 24, 25, 26, 29, 30; PPS: 3, 5, 6, 11, 19, 20, 23, 28.

RELIABILITY: The GESS has excellent reliability for the total score. Data were not presented for factors. Internal consistency using coefficient alpha was .90 for females and .91 for males. Test-retest reliability for a six-week period was .83 for both genders.

VALIDITY: The validity of the GESS has been tested primarily with concurrent validity procedures. Scores correlate significantly with depression, hopelessness, and suicidal ideation. Scores were not associated with social desirability for men, but were correlated for females.

PRIMARY REFERENCE: Fibel, B. and Hale, W. D. (1978). The Generalized Expectancy for Success Scale—A new measure, *Journal of Consulting and Clinical Psychology*, 46, 924–931. Instrument reproduced with permission of W. Daniel Hale and the American Psychological Association.

AVAILABILITY: Journal article.

Instruments for Practice

GESS

Please indicate the degree to which you believe each statement would apply to you personally by indicating to the left of the item the appropriate number, according to the following key:

1 = Highly improbable
2 = Improbable
3 = Equally improbable and probable, not sure
4 = Probable
5 = Highly probable

In the future I expect that I will
_____ 1. find that people don't seem to understand what I am trying to say.
_____ 2. be discouraged about my ability to gain the respect of others.
_____ 3. be a good parent.
_____ 4. be unable to accomplish my goals.
_____ 5. have a stressful marital relationship.
_____ 6. deal poorly with emergency situations.
_____ 7. find my efforts to change situations I don't like are ineffective.
_____ 8. not be very good at learning new skills.
_____ 9. carry through my responsibilities successfully.
_____ 10. discover that the good in life outweighs the bad.
_____ 11. handle unexpected problems successfully.
_____ 12. get the promotions I deserve.
_____ 13. succeed in the projects I undertake.
_____ 14. not make any significant contributions to society.
_____ 15. discover that my life is not getting much better.
_____ 16. be listened to when I speak.
_____ 17. discover that my plans don't work out too well.
_____ 18. find that no matter how hard I try, things just don't turn out the way I would like.
_____ 19. handle myself well in whatever situation I'm in.
_____ 20. be able to solve my own problems.
_____ 21. succeed at most things I try.
_____ 22. be successful in my endeavors in the long run.
_____ 23. be very successful working out my personal life.
_____ 24. experience many failures in my life.
_____ 25. make a good first impression on people I meet for the first time.
_____ 26. attain the career goals I have set for myself.
_____ 27. have difficulty dealing with my superiors.
_____ 28. have problems working with others.
_____ 29. be a good judge of what it takes to get ahead.
_____ 30. achieve recognition in my profession.

GERIATRIC DEPRESSION SCALE (GDS)

AUTHORS: T. L. Brink, J. A. Yesavage, O. Lum, P. Heersema, V. Huang, T. L. Rose, M. Adey, and V. O. Leirer

PURPOSE: To measure depression in the elderly.

DESCRIPTION: The GDS is a 30-item instrument to rate depression in the elderly. The GDS is written in simple language and can be administered in an oral or written format. If administered orally, the practitioner may have to repeat the question in order to get a response that is clearly yes or no. Translations are available in Spanish, Hebrew, Romanian, Russian, and French. The main purpose for development of the GDS was to provide a screening test for depression in elderly populations that would be simple to administer and not require special training for the interviewer. The GDS has been used successfully with both physically healthy and ill samples of the elderly.

NORMS: The initial data for the GDS came from two groups of elderly people. The first ($n = 40$) were individuals recruited from senior centers and housing projects who were functioning well with no history of mental problems. The second group ($n = 60$) comprised elderly under treatment—inpatient and outpatient—for depression. No other demographic data are reported. The authors state that 0 to 10 on the GDS is normal; 11 to 20 indicates moderate or severe depression.

SCORING: Of the 30 items, 20 indicate the presence of depression when answered positively while 10 (items 1, 5, 7, 9, 15, 19, 21, 27, 29, 30) indicate depression when answered negatively. The GDS is scored by totaling one point counted for each depressive answer and zero points counted for a nondepressed answer.

RELIABILITY: The GDS has excellent internal consistency with an alpha of .94 and split-half reliability of .94. The GDS also has excellent stability, with a one-week test-retest correlation of .85.

VALIDITY: The GDS has excellent concurrent validity, with correlations of .83 between the GDS and Zung's Self-Rating Depression Scale and .84 with the Hamilton Rating Scale for Depression. The GDS also has good known-groups validity in distinguishing significantly among respondents classified as normal, mildly depressed, and severely depressed. The GDS also has distinguished between depressed and nondepressed physically ill elderly and between depressed and nondepressed elderly undergoing cognitive treatment for senile dementia.

PRIMARY REFERENCE: Yesavage, J. A., Brink, T. L., Rose, T. L., and Leirer, V. O. (1983). Development and validation of a geriatric depression screening scale: A preliminary report, *Journal of Psychiatric Research*, 17, 37–49. Instrument reproduced with permission of T. L. Brink and Jerome Yesavage.

AVAILABILITY: Dr. T. L. Brink, Clinical Gerontologist, 1044 Sylvan Drive, San Carlos, CA 94070 or Dr. Jerome Yesavage, V. A. Medical Center, Palo Alto, CA 94305.

GDS

Please circle the best answer for how you felt over the past week.

Yes No   1.   Are you basically satisfied with your life?
Yes No   2.   Have you dropped many of your activities and interests?
Yes No   3.   Do you feel that your life is empty?
Yes No   4.   Do you often get bored?
Yes No   5.   Are you hopeful about the future?
Yes No   6.   Are you bothered by thoughts you can't get out of your head?
Yes No   7.   Are you in good spirits most of the time?
Yes No   8.   Are you afraid that something bad is going to happen to you?
Yes No   9.   Do you feel happy most of the time?
Yes No   10. Do you often feel helpless?
Yes No   11. Do you often get restless and fidgety?
Yes No   12. Do you prefer to stay at home, rather than going out and doing new things?
Yes No   13. Do you frequently worry about the future?
Yes No   14. Do you feel you have more problems with memory than most?
Yes No   15. Do you think it is wonderful to be alive now?
Yes No   16. Do you often feel downhearted and blue?
Yes No   17. Do you feel pretty worthless the way you are now?
Yes No   18. Do you worry a lot about the past?
Yes No   19. Do you find life very exciting?
Yes No   20. Is it hard for you to get started on new projects?
Yes No   21. Do you feel full of energy?
Yes No   22. Do you feel that your situation is hopeless?
Yes No   23. Do you think that most people are better off than you are?
Yes No   24. Do you frequently get upset over little things?
Yes No   25. Do you frequently feel like crying?
Yes No   26. Do you have trouble concentrating?
Yes No   27. Do you enjoy getting up in the morning?
Yes No   28. Do you prefer to avoid social gatherings?
Yes No   29. Is it easy for you to make decisions?
Yes No   30. Is your mind as clear as it used to be?

GOLDFARB FEAR OF FAT SCALE (GFFS)

AUTHOR: Lori A. Goldfarb

PURPOSE: To measure the fear of gaining weight.

DESCRIPTION: The 10-item GFFS measures one of the underlying emotional experiences of eating disorders, the fear of becoming fat. The instrument can also be used to assess weight phobia. It is also useful in identifying clients at risk of bulimia or anorexia as well as in assessing the state of those already suffering from these disorders.

NORMS: The GFFS was developed on student and clinical samples. The mean score was 25.5 for 98 high school females. A sample of randomly selected college students had a mean of 18.33, while a small sample of anorectic patients ($N = 7$) had a mean of 35.0. A third sample of college females had a mean of 30 for a group of diagnosed bulimics, 23.9 for "repeat dieters," and 17.3 for nondieting females.

SCORING: Each item is rated on a scale from 1 to 4, "very untrue" to "very true." Scores are the sum of each item, and range from 10 to 40 with high scores indicating more fear of gaining weight.

RELIABILITY: The GFFS has been shown to have very good reliability. The internal consistency reliability using coefficient alpha was .85. Over a one-week period, the GFFS has excellent stability, with a test-retest correlation of .88.

VALIDITY: The validity data generally are positive. There were significantly different scores for samples of anorectic patients and college females; the scores also differed between bulimic and repeat dieters and nondieters. Both of these studies reflect known-groups validity. Correlations between the GFFS and state-trait anxiety, depression, neuroticism, maladjustment, and control and achievement orientations demonstrate concurrent validity. The GFFS was negatively correlated with self-esteem.

PRIMARY REFERENCE: Goldfarb, L. A., Dykens, E. M., and Gerrard, M. (1985). The Goldfarb Fear of Fat Scale, *Journal of Personality Assessment*, 49, 329–332. Instrument reproduced with permission of Lori A. Goldfarb and the *Journal of Personality Assessment*.

AVAILABILITY: Journal article.

GFFS

Please read each of the following statements and select the number which best represents your feelings and beliefs.

$$1 = \text{Very untrue}$$
$$2 = \text{Somewhat untrue}$$
$$3 = \text{Somewhat true}$$
$$4 = \text{Very true}$$

_____ 1. My biggest fear is of becoming fat.
_____ 2. I am afraid to gain even a little weight.
_____ 3. I believe there is a real risk that I will become overweight someday.
_____ 4. I don't understand how overweight people can live with themselves.
_____ 5. Becoming fat would be the worst thing that could happen to me.
_____ 6. If I stopped concentrating on controlling my weight, chances are I would become very fat.
_____ 7. There is nothing that I can do to make the thought of gaining weight less painful and frightening.
_____ 8. I feel like all my energy goes into controlling my weight.
_____ 9. If I eat even a little, I may lose control and not stop eating.
_____ 10. Staying hungry is the only way I can guard against losing control and becoming fat.

HARDINESS SCALE (HS)

AUTHOR: Paul T. Bartone, Robert J. Ursano, Kathleen M. Wright, and Larry H. Ingraham

PURPOSE: To measure resiliency to stress.

DESCRIPTION: The HS is a 45-item instrument designed to measure dispositional resilience, the hardiness of one's personality. Hardiness is considered to relate to how one approaches and interprets experiences. Three components of hardiness serve as subscales of the HS: commitment, which refers to imputed meaning and purpose to self, others, and work; control, a sense of autonomy and influence on one's future; and challenge, a zest and excitement for life which is perceived as opportunities for growth. Hardiness has been shown to relate to how people process and cope with stressful events. In stressful situations, hardiness has been shown to be associated with high levels of well-being.

NORMS: Normative data are currently being developed by Paul Bartone. Published norms are not available, though the HS was studied originally with 164 military disaster assistance officers, 93% of whom were male, 85% white, with a median age of 34.

SCORING: The HS is scored by first reverse-scoring items 3–7, 9–12, 14, 16, 18, 20, 23, 24, 26, 29, 31, 32, 34, 35, 37, 38, 40, 41, and 43–45. Each subscale is then scored by summing the subscale items as follows: Commitment = 1 + 7 + 8 + 9 + 17 + 18 + 23 + 24 + 25 + 31 + 37 + 39 + 41 + 44 + 45. Control = 2 + 3 + 4 + 10 + 11 + 13 + 14 + 19 + 22 + 26 + 28 + 29 + 34 + 42 + 43. Challenge = 5 + 6 + 12 + 15 + 16 + 20 + 21 + 27 + 30 + 32 + 33 + 35 + 36 + 38 + 40. An HS short form is available by deleting items 3, 9, 11, 12, 14, 16, 18, 23, 28, 35, 37, 38, 40, 43, and 44. Higher scores indicate more hardiness.

RELIABILITY: The internal consistency (alpha) coefficients were .62, .66, and .82 for the challenge, control, and commitment subscales, respectively. As a total summated scale, the HS had an alpha of .85. The internal consistency of the 30-item short form ranged from .56 to .82 for the subscales. Internal consistency of the summated 30-item form was .83. Data on stability are not available.

VALIDITY: The 45-item HS was developed from a pool of 76 items. Scale scores correlated .93 with total scores on the 76-item version. The three-subscale structure was supported with principal components factor analysis. Scores on the 30-item short form correlated .82 with scores on the 45-item version. HS scores were predictive of mental and physical health. Scores are sensitive to measuring change due to the level of stressful events.

PRIMARY REFERENCE: Bartone, P., Ursano, R. J., Wright, K. M., and Ingraham, L.H. (1989). The impact of a military air disaster on the health of assistance workers, *Journal of Nervous and Mental Disease*, 177, 317–328. Instrument is in the public domain and reprinted with permission of Paul T. Bartone.

AVAILABILITY: Captain Paul T. Bartone, Ph.D., SGRD-UWI-A, Department of Military Psychiatry, Walter Reed Army Institute of Research, Washington, DC 20307.

HS

Below are statements about life that people often feel differently about. Circle a number to show how you feel about each one. Read the items carefully, and indicate how much you think each one is true in general. There are no right or wrong answers; just give your own honest opinions.

Not at all true	A little true	Quite true	Completely true
0	1	2	3

1. Most of my life gets spent doing things that are worthwhile. 1 2 3 4 5

2. Planning ahead can help avoid most future problems. 1 2 3 4 5

3. Trying hard doesn't pay, since things still don't turn out right. 1 2 3 4 5

4. No matter how hard I try, my efforts usually accomplish nothing. 1 2 3 4 5

5. I don't like to make changes in my everyday schedule. 1 2 3 4 5

6. The "tried and true" ways are always best. 1 2 3 4 5

7. Working hard doesn't matter, since only the bosses profit by it. 1 2 3 4 5

8. By working hard you can always achieve your goals. 1 2 3 4 5

9. Most working people are simply manipulated by their bosses. 1 2 3 4 5

10. Most of what happens in life is just meant to be. 1 2 3 4 5

11. It's usually impossible for me to change things at work. 1 2 3 4 5

12. New laws should never hurt a person's paycheck. 1 2 3 4 5

13. When I make plans, I'm certain I can make them work. 1 2 3 4 5

14. It's very hard for me to change a friend's mind about something. 1 2 3 4 5

15. It's exciting to learn something about myself. 1 2 3 4 5

16. People who never change their minds usually have good judgment.   1 2 3 4 5

17. I really look forward to my work.   1 2 3 4 5

18. Politicians run our lives.   1 2 3 4 5

19. If I'm working on a difficult task, I know when to seek help.   1 2 3 4 5

20. I won't answer a question until I'm really sure I understand it.   1 2 3 4 5

21. I like a lot of variety in my work.   1 2 3 4 5

22. Most of the time, people listen carefully to what I say.   1 2 3 4 5

23. Daydreams are more exciting than reality for me.   1 2 3 4 5

24. Thinking of yourself as a free person just leads to frustration.   1 2 3 4 5

25. Trying your best at work really pays off in the end.   1 2 3 4 5

26. My mistakes are usually very difficult to correct.   1 2 3 4 5

27. It bothers me when my daily routine gets interrupted.   1 2 3 4 5

28. It's best to handle most problems by just not thinking of them.   1 2 3 4 5

29. Most good athletes and leaders are born, not made.   1 2 3 4 5

30. I often wake up eager to take up my life wherever it left off.   1 2 3 4 5

31. Lots of times, I don't really know my own mind.   1 2 3 4 5

32. I respect rules because they guide me.   1 2 3 4 5

33. I like it when things are uncertain or unpredictable.   1 2 3 4 5

34. I can't do much to prevent it if someone wants to harm me.   1 2 3 4 5

35. People who do their best should get full support from society.   1 2 3 4 5

36. Changes in routine are interesting to me.   1 2 3 4 5

37. People who believe in individuality are only kidding   1 2 3 4 5
    themselves.

38. I have no use for theories that are not closely tied to   1 2 3 4 5
    facts.

39. Most days, life is really interesting and exciting for me.   1 2 3 4 5

40. I want to be sure someone will take care of me when I'm   1 2 3 4 5
    old.

41. It's hard to imagine anyone getting excited about   1 2 3 4 5
    working.

42. What happens to me tomorrow depends on what I do   1 2 3 4 5
    today.

43. If someone gets angry at me, it's usually no fault of mine.   1 2 3 4 5

44. It's hard to believe people who say their work helps   1 2 3 4 5
    society.

45. Ordinary work is just too boring to be worth doing.   1 2 3 4 5

HENDRICK SEXUAL ATTITUDE SCALE (HSAS)

AUTHORS: Susan Hendrick and Clyde Hendrick

PURPOSE: To measure four attitudes of sexuality.

DESCRIPTION: The HSAS is a 43-item instrument which measures four dimensions of sexuality: permissiveness (HSAS-P); sexual practices (HSAS-SP); communion in the relationship (HSAS-C); and instrumentality (HSAS-I). The instrument was developed from a pool of 150 items. The four-subscale structure was supported by two independent factor analyses with two samples. When using this scale one needs to be mindful of gender differences on some scores, such as HSAS-P and HSAS-I, and differences on all four subscales due to race and ethnicity. With couples in treatment, it is important to compare their scores with those of the gender-specific norms before determining if the discrepancies between their scores are meaningful.

NORMS: Because of the differences due to gender and race/ethnicity, extensive norms for men and women are reported in the primary reference. From a sample of 341 women, the mean scores on the HSAS-P, HSAS-SP, HSAS-C, and HSAS-I were 4.0, 2.1, 1.9, and 2.6, respectively. From a sample of 466 men, mean scores for the same subscales were 3.0, 2.0, 1.9, and 3.2, respectively. The primary reference also provides additional normative data categorized by ethnicity.

SCORING: After reverse-scoring items 19, 20, and 21, subscale scores are the sum of the item ratings, divided by the number of items in each subscale (HSAS-P: items 1–21, HSAS-SP: items 22–28, HSAS-C: 29–37, and HSAS-I: 38–43). Higher scores reflect more permissive sexual attitudes.

RELIABILITY: The four subscales of the HSAS have good to excellent internal consistency and test-retest reliability. In a study of 807 subjects the standardized alpha was .94, .71, .80, and .80 for the HSAS-P, HSAS-SP, HSAS-C, and HSAS-I, respectively. Test-retest correlations over a four-week period were .88, .80, .67, and .66 for the same subscales.

VALIDITY: The validity of the HSAS has been estimated with concurrent validity procedures. Scores on the subscales tend to correlate with other measures of sex and love and sensation seeking. Known-groups validity is suggested by differences in scores between persons reporting to be currently in love with those not currently in love on three of the four subscales.

PRIMARY REFERENCE: Hendrick, S. and Hendrick, C. (1987). Multidimensionality of sexual attitudes, *The Journal of Sex Research*, 23, 502–526. Instrument reproduced with permission of *The Journal of Sex Research*, a publication for the Scientific Study of Sex.

AVAILABILITY: Susan Hendrick, Ph.D., Department of Psychology, Texas Tech University, Lubbock, TX 79409.

HSAS

Using the following scale, please rate each item and record your response on the space next to that item.

1 = Strongly agree
2 = Moderately agree
3 = Neutral
4 = Moderately disagree
5 = Strongly disagree

_____ 1.   I do not need to be committed to a person to have sex with him/her.
_____ 2.   Casual sex is acceptable.
_____ 3.   I would like to have sex with many partners.
_____ 4.   One-night stands are sometimes very enjoyable.
_____ 5.   It is okay to have ongoing sexual relationships with more than one person at a time.
_____ 6.   It is okay to manipulate someone into having sex as long as no future promises are made.
_____ 7.   Sex as a simple exchange of favors is okay if both people agree to it.
_____ 8.   The best sex is with no strings attached.
_____ 9.   Life would have fewer problems if people could have sex more freely.
_____ 10. It is possible to enjoy sex with a person and not like that person very much.
_____ 11. Sex is more fun with someone you don't love.
_____ 12. It is all right to pressure someone into having sex.
_____ 13. Extensive premarital sexual experience is fine.
_____ 14. Extramarital affairs are all right as long as one's partner doesn't know about them.
_____ 15. Sex for its own sake is perfectly all right.
_____ 16. I would feel comfortable having intercourse with my partner in the presence of other people.
_____ 17. Prostitution is acceptable.
_____ 18. It is okay for sex to be just good physical release.
_____ 19. Sex without love is meaningless.
_____ 20. People should at least be friends before they have sex together.
_____ 21. In order for sex to be good, it must also be meaningful.
_____ 22. Birth control is part of responsible sexuality.
_____ 23. A woman should share responsibility for birth control.
_____ 24. A man should share responsibility for birth control.
_____ 25. Sex education is important for young people.
_____ 26. Using "sex toys" during lovemaking is acceptable.
_____ 27. Masturbation is all right.
_____ 28. Masturbating one's partner during intercourse can increase the pleasure of sex.
_____ 29. Sex gets better as a relationship progresses.
_____ 30. Sex is the closest form of communication between two people.
_____ 31. A sexual encounter between two people deeply in love is the ultimate human interaction.

_____ 32. Orgasm is the greatest experience in the world.

_____ 33. At its best, sex seems to be the merging of two souls.

_____ 34. Sex is a very important part of life.

_____ 35. Sex is usually an intensive, almost overwhelming experience.

_____ 36. During sexual intercourse, intense awareness of the partner is the best frame of mind.

_____ 37. Sex is fundamentally good.

_____ 38. Sex is best when you let yourself go and focus on your own pleasure.

_____ 39. Sex is primarily the taking of pleasure from another person.

_____ 40. The main purpose of sex is to enjoy oneself.

_____ 41. Sex is primarily physical.

_____ 42. Sex is primarily a bodily function, like eating.

_____ 43. Sex is mostly a game between males and females.

HOMOPHOBIA SCALE (HS)

AUTHORS: Richard A. Bouton, Peggy E. Gallagher, Paul A. Garlinghouse, Terri Leal, Leslie D. Rosenstein, and Robert K. Young

PURPOSE: To measure homophobia.

DESCRIPTION: The HS is a 7-item instrument designed to measure homophobia. The scale was developed by using Thurstone's method of equal-appearing intervals, and went through a rigorous process of external judgments to reduce the original 30 items to the current 7. Given the large number of homosexually-oriented people and the prevalence of negative attitudes about them, the HS can be useful in work both with clients and other helping professionals.

NORMS: The HS was administered to 524 students (266 males, 258 females) enrolled in introductory psychology classes at the University of Texas at Austin. No other demographic information was provided. The mean score for males was 15.8 and for females 13.8; the difference was statistically significant.

SCORING: The HS is scored by assigning scores of 0, 1, 2, 3, and 4 to the five choices (strongly agree through strongly disagree). Negative items are reverse-scored (items 2, 5, 6, and 7) and all items are summed for the total score. The possible range is 0 to 28 with high scores indicating greater homophobia.

RELIABILITY: The HS has excellent internal consistency, with an alpha of .89. Data on stability were not available.

VALIDITY: The HS is said to have good factorial validity, although other types of validity are not available. Scores on the HS are relatively independent of scores on the Fear of AIDS Scale.

PRIMARY REFERENCE: Bouton, R. A., Gallagher, P. E., Garlinghouse, P. A., Leal, T., Rosenstein, L. D., and Young, R. K. (1987). Scales for measuring fear of AIDS and homophobia, *Journal of Personality Assessment*, 51, 606–614.

AVAILABILITY: Journal article.

HS

Please indicate the extent to which you agree or disagree with each statement by placing a checkmark on the appropriate line.

	Strongly agree	Agree	Unde-cided	Dis-agree	Strongly disagree
1. Homosexuals contribute positively to society.	___	___	___	___	___
2. Homosexuality is disgusting.	___	___	___	___	___
3. Homosexuals are just as moral as heterosexuals.	___	___	___	___	___
4. Homosexuals should have equal civil rights.	___	___	___	___	___
5. Homosexuals corrupt young people.	___	___	___	___	___
6. Homosexuality is a sin.	___	___	___	___	___
7. Homosexuality should be against the law.	___	___	___	___	___

HUNGER SATIETY SCALES (H-SS)

AUTHOR: Paul E. Garfinkel

PURPOSE: To measure the sensation of hunger and satiety.

DESCRIPTION: The H-SS is comprised of two 9-item measures developed for research on anorexia. The point of departure for the instrument is that anorectic patients have a distorted view of hunger signals—they become unable to perceive hunger and therefore eat less frequently; because they feel unable to stop eating, they are unable to recognize satiation. The hunger scale measures one's response to signs of hunger and the satiety scale assesses one's response to signs to stop eating. The instruments do not provide continuous scores, so comparison must be in terms of change from misperception to correct perception on each item.

NORMS: The instrument was originally developed on a sample of 11 female anorexia nervosa patients who had a weight loss greater than 25 percent. These subjects ranged in ages from 16 to 23 years. Eleven undergraduate females were selected to serve as a comparison group. These subjects were matched with the clinical sample on age, religion, social class and height.

SCORING: Scores are not summed on the H-SS. Each item is an individual index. Comparisons can be made by examining changes in the alternatives chosen as indicative of respondent's "feelings at the moment."

RELIABILITY: Reliability data are not available.

VALIDITY: Known-groups validity is evident from the fact that the anorectics and matched controls responded differently. Anorectics tended to have a stronger urge to eat and to be more preoccupied with food and more anxious when hungry. The control group experienced satiety as a fullness in the stomach while anorectic patients experienced satiety without appropriate physical sensations.

PRIMARY REFERENCE: Garfinkel, P. E. (1974). Perception of hunger and satiety in anorexia nervosa, *Psychological Medicine*, 4, 309–315. Instruments reproduced with permission of Paul Garfinkel.

AVAILABILITY: Journal article.

H-SS

This questionnaire is about hunger. For each heading circle as many of the answers as are appropriate to how you feel now. You may leave a section out or answer more than once. At the end add any general comments about your usual feelings of hunger.

I. Gastric sensations:
   1. feeling of emptiness
   2. rumbling
   3. ache
   4. pain
   5. tenseness
   6. nausea
   7. no gastric sensations to provide information for hunger

II. Mouth and throat sensations:
   1. emptiness
   2. dryness
   3. salivation
   4. unpleasant taste or sensation
   5. pleasant
   6. tightness

III. Cerebral sensations:
   1. headache
   2. dizziness
   3. faintness
   4. spots before the eyes
   5. ringing in ears

IV. General overall sensations:
   1. weakness
   2. tiredness
   3. restlessness
   4. cold
   5. warmth
   6. muscular spasms

V. Mood when hungry:
   1. nervous
   2. irritable
   3. tense
   4. depressed
   5. apathetic
   6. cheerful
   7. excited
   8. calm
   9. relaxed
   10. contented

VI. Urge to eat:
   1. no urge to eat
   2. mild—would eat if food were available but can wait comfortably
   3. fairly strong—want to eat soon, waiting is fairly uncomfortable
   4. so strong you want to eat now, waiting is very uncomfortable

VII. Preoccupation with thoughts of food.
   1. not at all—no thoughts of food
   2. mild—only occasional thoughts of food
   3. moderate—many thoughts of food but can concentrate on other things
   4. very preoccupied—most of thoughts are of food and it is difficult to concentrate on other things

VIII. Time of day or night when hungriest:

IX. Other comments about hunger:

This questionnaire is about fullness. For each heading circle as many answers as are appropriate to how you've felt since completing the meal. You may leave a section out or answer more than once. At the end add any general comments about your feelings of fullness.

I. One most important reason for stopping eating:
   1. no more food available
   2. eat until feeling of satisfaction
   3. "diet-limit" set for figure or health

II. Gastric sensation at end of eating:
   1. full stomach
   2. distended
   3. bloated
   4. nausea
   5. ache
   6. pain
   7. feeling of emptiness
   8. no stomach sensations to provide information for stopping

III. Cerebral sensations at end of eating:
   1. headache
   2. dizziness
   3. faintness
   4. spots before the eyes
   5. ringing in ears

IV. General overall sensations at end of eating:
   1. weakness
   2. tiredness
   3. restlessness
   4. cold
   5. warmth
   6. muscular spasms

V. Mood at end of eating:
   1. nervous
   2. irritable
   3. tense
   4. depressed
   5. apathetic
   6 cheerful
   7. excited
   8. calm
   9. relaxed
   10. contented

VI. Urge to eat at end of eating:
   1. no urge to eat
   2. mild—would eat if food were available
   3. moderate—want to eat again soon, waiting is fairly uncomfortable
   4. strong—want to eat again now, waiting is very uncomfortable

VII. Preoccupation with thoughts of food:
1. not at all—no thoughts of food
2. mild—only occasional thoughts of food
3. moderate—many thoughts of food but can concentrate on other things
4. very preoccupied—most of thoughts are of food and it is difficult to concentrate on other things

VIII. Will power required to stop eating:
1. none—stopping is an abrupt process
2. none—stopping a gradual process
3. some—will power required since the urge to eat is still present
4. considerable will power is required.

IX. Other comments about feeling full:

HYPERCOMPETITIVE ATTITUDE SCALE (HAS)

AUTHORS: Richard M. Ryckman, Max Hammer, Linda M. Kaczor, and Joel A. Gold

PURPOSE: To measure hypercompetitiveness.

DESCRIPTION: The HAS is a 26-item instrument designed to measure hyper-competitiveness—the need to compete and win at any cost as a way of maintaining self-worth. The construct includes manipulation, aggressiveness, and exploitation and denigration of others across a wide range of situations. The HAS is based on psychoanalyst Karen Horney's construct of hypercompetitiveness. Based on an initial pool of 65 items, subsequent research produced the current 26-item scale. The HAS is seen as useful in business and industry as either a screening instrument or as a way of singling out individuals who may need special help. The HAS also may prove useful in clinical situations as both an assessment and an evaluation device.

NORMS: The HAS has been evaluated in a series of studies ultimately involving 642 subjects. All were undergraduates in psychology classes at the University of Maine. The one study that reported mean scores involved 53 male and 51 female students. No other demographic data were provided. The mean scores for the HAS ranged from 71.87 to 72.07 (with standard deviations ranging from 12.18 to 14.12).

SCORING: The HAS is scored on a 5-point scale with the total score being a sum of all item scores. The following items are reverse-scored: 3, 5, 6, 10, 13, 15, 16, 18–20, 24–26. Higher scores indicate stronger hypercompetitive attitudes.

RELIABILITY: The HAS has excellent internal consistency, with an alpha of .91. The HAS also has very good stability, with a six-week test-retest correlation of .81.

VALIDITY: The HAS has good concurrent and construct validity. It is correlated with the Win-at-Any-Cost Sports Competition Scale, is positively correlated with neuroticism, and is negatively correlated with self-esteem and self-actualization. The HAS also was positively correlated with mistrust, dogmatism, calloused sexual attitudes toward women, and to perceptions that violence is manly. The HAS is not correlated with social desirability response set.

PRIMARY REFERENCE: Ryckman, R. M., Hammer, M., Kaczor, L. M., and Gold, J. A. (1990). Construction of a Hypercompetitive Attitude Scale, *Journal of Personality Assessment, 55,* 630–639.

AVAILABILITY: Journal article.

HAS

Please read each of the statements very carefully so that you understand what is being asked. Then ask yourself how true the statement is as it applies to you. Rate your answer to that statement on the 5-point scale and record your answer in the space to the left of the item. The categories for each score are as follows:

1 = Never true of me
2 = Seldom true of me
3 = Sometimes true of me
4 = Often true of me
5 = Always true of me

_____ 1. Winning in competition makes me feel more powerful as a person.
_____ 2. I find myself being competitive even in situations which do not call for competition.
_____ 3. I do not see my opponents in competition as my enemies.
_____ 4. I compete with others even if they are not competing with me.
_____ 5. Success in athletic competition does not make me feel superior to others.
_____ 6. Winning in competition does not give me a greater sense of worth.
_____ 7. When my competitors receive rewards for their accomplishment, I feel envy.
_____ 8. I find myself turning a friendly game or activity into a serious contest or conflict.
_____ 9. It's a dog-eat-dog world. If you don't get the better of others, they will surely get the better of you.
_____ 10. I do not mind giving credit to someone for doing something that I could have done just as well or better.
_____ 11. If I can disturb my opponent in some way in order to get the edge in competition, I will do so.
_____ 12. I really feel down when I lose in athletic competition.
_____ 13. Gaining praise from others is not an important reason why I enter competitive situations.
_____ 14. I like the challenge of getting someone to like me who is already going with someone else.
_____ 15. I do not view my relationships in competitive terms.
_____ 16. It does not bother me to be passed by someone while I am driving on the roads.
_____ 17. I can't stand to lose an argument.
_____ 18. In school, I do not feel superior whenever I do better on tests than other students.
_____ 19. I feel no need to get even with a person who criticizes or makes me look bad in front of others.
_____ 20. Losing in competition has little effect on me.
_____ 21. Failure or loss in competition makes me feel less worthy as a person.
_____ 22. People who quit during competition are weak.
_____ 23. Competition inspires me to excel.
_____ 24. I do not try to win arguments with members of my family.

_____ 25. I believe that you can be a nice guy and still win or be successful in competition.

_____ 26. I do not find it difficult to be fully satisfied with my performance in a competitive situation.

HYPOCHONDRIASIS SCALE FOR INSTITUTIONAL GERIATRIC PATIENTS (HSIG)

AUTHOR: T. L. Brink, J. Bryant, J. Belanger, D. Capri, S. Jasculca, C. Janakes, and C. Oliveira

PURPOSE: To measure beliefs about physical health in geriatric patients.

DESCRIPTION: The HSIG is a 6-item scale that can be administered in written or oral form. The practitioner may have to repeat questions in order to get a clear yes or no answer. The HSIG is actually a test of attitudes rather than behavior so that it is possible for a respondent to score high on the HSIG (higher scores indicating higher hypochondriasis), and yet have no somatic complaints. The 6 items for the scale were selected from a pool of 27 questions on the basis of their ability to distinguish between respondents known to be hypochondriacal and those known not to be. The scale is available in Spanish and French.

NORMS: Initial study was conducted on a sample of 69 patients at three extended-care facilities for the elderly. The mean score for those identified by staff as hypochondriacal was 3.9 and the mean score for nonhypochondriacal patients was 1.56. No other demographic data were available.

SCORING: Each item is answered yes or no. For each hypochondriacal answer, the item is scored as one point; these items are then summed for a total score with a range of 0 to 6. Hypochondriacal answers are "yes" to items 3, 5, and 6 and "no" to items 1, 2, and 4. Scores under 3 are considered nonhypochondriacal.

RELIABILITY: No reliability data were reported.

VALIDITY: The HSIG significantly distinguished between geriatric patients identified by staff consensus as hypochondriacal and those not so identified. No other validity data are available.

PRIMARY REFERENCE: Brink, T. L., Bryant, J., Belanger, J., Capri, D., Jasculca, S., Janakes, C., and Oliveira, C. (1978). Hypochondriasis in an institutional geriatric population: Construction of a scale (HSIG), *Journal of the American Geriatrics Society*, 26, 552–559. Instrument reproduced with permission of T. L. Brink.

AVAILABILITY: Dr. T. L. Brink, Clinical Gerontologist, 1044 Sylvan Drive, San Carlos, CA 94070.

HSIG

Please circle either "Yes" or "No" for each question as it applies to you.

Yes No 1. Are you satisfied with your health most of the time?

Yes No 2. Do you ever feel completely well?

Yes No 3. Are you tired most of the time?

Yes No 4. Do you feel your best in the morning?

Yes No 5. Do you frequently have strange aches and pains that you cannot identify?

Yes No 6. Is it hard for you to believe it when the doctor tells you that there is nothing physically wrong with you?

ILLNESS ATTITUDE SCALE (IAS)

AUTHOR: Robert Kellner

PURPOSE: To measure hypochondriasis.

DESCRIPTION: The IAS is a 28-item instrument designed to measure attitudes, fears and beliefs associated with the psychopathology of hypochondriasis and that of abnormal illness behavior. The IAS comprises several subscales: worry about illness (W: items 1–3); concern about pain (CP: items 4–6); health habits (HH: items 7–9); hypochondriacal beliefs (HB: items 10–12); thanatophobia (Th: items 13–15); disease phobia (DP: items 16–18); bodily preoccupation (BP: items 19–21); treatment experience (TE: items 22–24); and effects of symptoms (ES: items 26–28). Items 15a and 25 are not scored. The IAS is a useful measure for monitoring changes in hypochondriacal attitudes and fears due to treatment.

NORMS: The IAS has been studied with a number of samples involving several hundred people. These included hundreds of nonsymptomatic or "normal" respondents, samples of hypochondriacal patients, nonhypochondriacal psychiatric patients, a sample of elderly, and several samples of students. A wide range of demographic characteristics were reported including variations in income and employment, both genders, and different ethnicities. Mean scores are available from the author for most of these groups. Several of the subscales significantly distinguish among groups based on sex, medical problem, presence of hypochondriasis, and so on.

SCORING: The IAS is easily scored by summing item responses for each subscale. Subscale scores range from 3 to 15; higher scores indicate more pathology.

RELIABILITY: The IAS has fair to excellent stability, with one- to four-week test-retest correlations for the subscales for "normal" respondents that range from .62 to .92. All correlations except one were .75 or higher. Data on internal consistency are not available.

VALIDITY: The IAS has good known-groups validity, significantly distinguishing between patients known to have hypochondriacal symptoms and those known not to have such symptoms. The IAS also has fair concurrent validity, with significant correlations between most subscales and self-ratings of depression, anxiety, and anger. The IAS also is sensitive to changes due to treatment.

PRIMARY REFERENCE: Kellner, R., Slocumb, J., Wiggins, R. N., Abbott, P. J., Winslow, W. W., and Pathak, D. (1985). Hostility, somatic symptoms and hypochondriacal fears and beliefs, *Journal of Nervous and Mental Disease*, 173, 554–560.

AVAILABILITY: Dr. Robert Kellner, Department of Psychiatry, University of New Mexico, 2400 Tucker Avenue, Albuquerque, NM 87131.

IAS

Please answer all questions which can be checked by circling the response that is best for you. Circle one answer even if you cannot answer accurately. Answer the other few questions with a few words or sentences. Do not think long before answering. Work quickly!

		1	2	3	4	5
1.	Do you worry about your health?	No	Rarely	Some-times	Often	Most of the time
2.	Are you worried that you may get a serious illness in the future?	No	Rarely	Some-times	Often	Most of the time
3.	Does the thought of a serious illness scare you?	No	Rarely	Some-times	Often	Most of the time
4.	If you have a pain, do you worry that it may be caused by a serious illness?	No	Rarely	Some-times	Often	Most of the time
5.	If a pain lasts for a week or more, do you see a physician?	No	Rarely	Some-times	Often	Most of the time
6.	If a pain lasts a week or more, do you believe that you have a serious illness?	No	Rarely	Some-times	Often	Most of the time
7.	Do you avoid habits which may be harmful to you such as smoking?	No	Rarely	Some-times	Often	Most of the time
8.	Do you avoid foods which may not be healthy?	No	Rarely	Some-times	Often	Most of the time
9.	Do you examine your body to find whether there is something wrong?	No	Rarely	Some-times	Often	Most of the time
10.	Do you believe that you have a physical disease but the doctors have not diagnosed it correctly?	No	Rarely	Some-times	Often	Most of the time

11.	When your doctor tells you that you have no physical disease to account for your symptoms, do you refuse to believe him?	No	Rarely	Some-times	Often	Most of the time
12.	When you have been told by a doctor what he found, do you soon begin to believe that you may have developed a new illness?	No	Rarely	Some-times	Often	Most of the time
13.	Are you afraid of news which reminds you of death (such as funerals, obituary notices)?	No	Rarely	Some-times	Often	Most of the time
14.	Does the thought of death scare you?	No	Rarely	Some-times	Often	Most of the time
15.	Are you afraid that you may die soon?	No	Rarely	Some-times	Often	Most of the time
15a.	Has your doctor told you that you have an illness now? If yes, what illness?	Yes	No			
15b.	How often do you worry about this illness?	Not at all	Rarely	Some-times	Often	Most of the time
16.	Are you afraid that you may have cancer?	No	Rarely	Some-times	Often	Most of the time
17.	Are you afraid that you may have heart disease?	No	Rarely	Some-times	Often	Most of the time
18.	Are you afraid that you may have another serious illness? Which illness?	No	Rarely	Some-times	Often	Most of the time
19.	When you read or hear about an illness, do you get symptoms similar to those of the illness?	No	Rarely	Some-times	Often	Most of the time

20.	When you notice a sensation in your body, do you find it difficult to think of something else?	No	Rarely	Some-times	Often	Most of the time
21.	When you feel a sensation in your body do you worry about it?	No	Rarely	Some-times	Often	Most of the time
22.	How often do you see a doctor?	Almost never	Only very rarely	About 4 times a year	About once a month	About once a week
23.	How many different doctors, chiropractors or other healers have you seen in the past year?	None	1	2 or 3	4 or 5	6 or more
24.	How often have you been treated during the past year? (For example, drugs, change of drugs, surgery, etc.)	Not at all	Once	2 or 3 times	4 or 5 times	6 or more times
25.	If yes, what were the treatments?					

_____

_____

The next three questions concern your bodily symptoms (for example, pain, aches, pressure in your body, breathing difficulties, tiredness, etc.).

26.	Do your bodily symptoms stop you from working?	No	Rarely	Some-times	Often	Most of the time
27.	Do your bodily symptoms stop you from concentrating on what you are doing?	No	Rarely	Some-times	Often	Most of the time
28.	Do your bodily symptoms stop you from enjoying yourself?	No	Rarely	Some-times	Often	Most of the time

ILLNESS BEHAVIOR INVENTORY (IBI)

AUTHORS: Ira Daniel Turkat and Loyd S. Pettegrew

PURPOSE: To measure illness behavior.

DESCRIPTION: The IBI is a 20-item scale designed to assess the behaviors performed or reported by a respondent that indicate he or she is physically ill or in physical discomfort. The items were initially developed based on observations of patients in inpatient and ambulatory clinical settings. Two dimensions of illness behavior are measured by this instrument: work-related illness behavior with items related to the curtailment of work behaviors and activities when ill, and social illness behavior with items related to frequent discussion or complaints about being ill and acting more ill than one feels. This measure may be useful in work with clients who exhibit excessive or inappropriate illness behavior and as a screening device for clinical practice since it correlates well with a variety of factors related to medical utilization.

NORMS: Several different samples were used to examine aspects of this measure including 40 graduate nursing students, 32 undergraduate linguistic students, 50 lower back pain patients, a group of diabetic neuropathy patients (number unknown), 152 healthy college students and 63 female undergraduates. No other demographic information was provided. The IBI is in a relatively early stage of development, and work on standardization is only beginning.

SCORING: Scores on each of the six-point Likert-type scales are simply totaled to provide a range from 20 to 120. Higher scores indicate greater illness behavior.

RELIABILITY: The IBI has excellent internal consistency; the work items have an alpha of .89 and the 11 social items have an alpha of .88. No data for the measure as a whole were reported. The IBI also has excellent stability, with two-week test-retest reliabilities of .97 for work-related items, .93 for social items, and .90 overall.

VALIDITY: The IBI has good concurrent validity in that it correlates significantly with a number of illness behavior measures and treatment outcome meas ures in chronically ill samples. The IBI also has good known-groups validity in distinguishing between patients independently assessed as either high or low illness behavior patients. Finally, the IBI also demonstrates good predictive validity by predicting several illness behaviors in a healthy sample.

PRIMARY REFERENCE: Turkat, I. D. and Pettegrew, L. S. (1983). Development and validation of the illness behavior inventory, *Journal of Behavioral Assessment*, 5, 35–45. Instrument reproduced with permission of Ira D. Turkat and L. S. Pettegrew, and Plenum Press.

AVAILABILITY: Dr. Loyd S. Pettegrew, Department of Communications. University of South Florida, Tampa, FL 33620.

IBI

Please put a number beside each item indicating the extent to which you agree or disagree as follows:

1 = Strongly disagree
2 = Disagree
3 = Somewhat disagree
4 = Somewhat agree
5 = Agree
6 = Strongly agree

_____ 1.   I see doctors often.
_____ 2.   When ill, I have to stop work completely.
_____ 3.   I stay in bed when I feel ill.
_____ 4.   I work fewer hours when I'm ill.
_____ 5.   I do fewer chores around the house when I'm ill.
_____ 6.   I seek help from others when I'm ill.
_____ 7.   When ill, I work slower.
_____ 8.   I leave work early when I'm ill.
_____ 9.   I complain about being ill when I feel ill.
_____ 10. I avoid certain aspects of my job when I'm ill.
_____ 11. I take rest periods when I'm ill.
_____ 12. Most people who know me are aware that I take medication.
_____ 13. Even if I don't feel ill at certain times, I find that I talk about my illness anyway.
_____ 14. Others often behave towards me as if I'm ill.
_____ 15. Although I very seldom bring up the topic of my illness, I frequently find myself involved in conversation about my illness with others.
_____ 16. Others seem to act as if I am more ill than I really am.
_____ 17. My illness or aspects of it are a frequent topic of conversation.
_____ 18. When I'm ill people can tell by the way I act.
_____ 19. Often I act more ill than I really am.
_____ 20. I have large medical bills.

ILLNESS BEHAVIOR QUESTIONNAIRE (IBQ)

AUTHORS: I. Pilowsky and N. D. Spence

PURPOSE: To measure the ways individuals experience and respond to their health status.

DESCRIPTION: The IBQ is a 62-item instrument designed to measure a respondent's attitudes, ideas, affects, and attributions in relation to illness. The IBQ consists of seven major subscales derived through factor analysis, each of which has at least five items. The seven scales of the IBQ are general hypochondriasis (GH), disease conviction (DC), psychologic versus somatic perceptions of illness (PIS), affective inhibition (AI), affective disturbance (AD), denial (D), and irritability (I). The IBQ also generates scores on the Whiteley Index of Hypochondriasis (WH) and two other minor factors. The IBQ is written in easily understood language, is easily scored, and translations in several languages are available. Some of the scales have cut-off points for the detection of "abnormality." The IBQ is useful for examining illness behavior in general and for identifying physical complaints that are manifestations of a psychiatric disorder. A manual providing further details is available from the author.

NORMS: Data on the IBQ have been developed in several studies including 231 pain clinic patients, 147 general practice patients, 217 general hospital patients, and 540 patients from a general hospital psychiatric ward. The respondents are from both the United States and Australia. Norms are available in the manual for all these groups.

SCORING: The IBQ is very easily hand-scored by using the scoring key available in the manual. The scoring key on the questionnaire describes which items on the IBQ belong to which subscale and the meaning of a "yes" or "no" on each item. The "correct" answers and the items for each subscale are shown in the left-hand column of the questionnaire. These items are summed to obtain the subscale scores. For the Whiteley Index of Hypochondriasis, a "yes" answer to items 1, 2, 9, 10, 16, 21, 24, 33, 34, 38, 39, and 41 and a "no" answer to item 8 are the "correct" scores.

RELIABILITY: The IBQ has very good stability, with one- to twelve-week test-retest correlations that range from .67 to .85 for the subscales; only one correlation (for affective inhibition) is below .76. No data on internal consistency were reported.

VALIDITY: The IBQ has good face and content validity. The affective disturbance subscale has very good concurrent validity, correlating significantly with several measures of depression and anxiety. The subscales of the IBQ also have good known-groups validity, distinguishing predictably in several studies between criterion groups, for example, psychiatric versus pain patients. In addition, there were high levels of agreement between the scores of patients and the patients' responses as perceived by spouses.

PRIMARY REFERENCE: Pilowsky, I. (1983). Manual for the Illness Behavior Questionnaire. University of Adelaide, Department of Psychiatry. Instrument reproduced with permission of I. Pilowsky.

AVAILABILITY: Professor I. Pilowsky, University of Adelaide, Department of Psychiatry, Royal Adelaide Hospital, Adelaide, South Australia 5001.

IBQ

Please circle the answer that applies most to you—"Yes" or "No"—for each statement.

Scoring Key				
	Yes	No	1.	Do you worry a lot about your health?
DC-Yes	Yes	No	2.	Do you think there is something seriously wrong with your body?
DC-Yes	Yes	No	3.	Does your illness interfere with your life a great deal?
I-No	Yes	No	4.	Are you easy to get along with when you are ill?
	Yes	No	5.	Does your family have a history of illness?
	Yes	No	6.	Do you think you are more liable to illness than other people?
DC-No	Yes	No	7.	If the doctor told you that he could find nothing wrong with you would you believe him?
	Yes	No	8.	Is it easy for you to forget about yourself and think about all sorts of other things?
GH-Yes	Yes	No	9.	If you feel ill and someone tells you that you are looking better, do you become annoyed?
DC-Yes	Yes	No	10.	Do you find that you are often aware of various things happening in your body?
P/S-Yes	Yes	No	11.	Do you ever think of your illness as a punishment for something you have done wrong in the past?
AD-Yes	Yes	No	12.	Do you have trouble with your nerves?
	Yes	No	13.	If you feel ill or worried, can you be easily cheered up by the doctor?
	Yes	No	14.	Do you think that other people realize what it's like to be sick?
	Yes	No	15.	Does it upset you to talk to the doctor about your illness?
PS-No	Yes	No	16.	Are you bothered by many pains and aches?
I-Yes	Yes	No	17.	Does your illness affect the way you get on with your family or friends a great deal?
AD-Yes	Yes	No	18.	Do you find that you get anxious easily?
	Yes	No	19.	Do you know anybody who has had the same illness as you?
GH-Yes	Yes	No	20.	Are you more sensitive to pain than other people?
GH-Yes	Yes	No	21.	Are you afraid of illness?
AI-No	Yes	No	22.	Can you express your personal feelings easily to other people?
	Yes	No	23.	Do people feel sorry for you when you are ill?
GH-Yes	Yes	No	24.	Do you think that you worry about your health more than most people?
	Yes	No	25.	Do you find that your illness affects your sexual relations?

Scoring
Key

	Yes	No		
D-No	Yes	No	26.	Do you experience a lot of pain with your illness?
D-No	Yes	No	27.	Except for your illness, do you have any problems in your life?
	Yes	No	28.	Do you care whether or not people realize you are sick?
GH-Yes	Yes	No	29.	Do you find that you get jealous of other people's good health?
GH-Yes	Yes	No	30.	Do you ever have silly thoughts about your health which you can't get out of your mind, no matter how hard you try?
D-No	Yes	No	31.	Do you have any financial problems?
GH-Yes	Yes	No	32.	Are you upset by the way people take your illness?
	Yes	No	33.	Is it hard for you to believe the doctor when he tells you there is nothing for you to worry about?
	Yes	No	34.	Do you often worry about the possibility that you have got a serious illness?
DC-No	Yes	No	35.	Are you sleeping well?
AI-Yes	Yes	No	36.	When you are angry, do you tend to bottle up your feelings?
GH-Yes	Yes	No	37.	Do you often think that you might suddenly fall ill?
GH-Yes	Yes	No	38.	If a disease is brought to your attention (through the radio, television, newspapers, or someone you know), do you worry about getting it yourself?
	Yes	No	39.	Do you get the feeling that people are not taking your illness seriously enough?
	Yes	No	40.	Are you upset by the appearance of your face or body?
DC-Yes	Yes	No	41.	Do you find that you are bothered by many different symptoms?
	Yes	No	42.	Do you frequently try to explain to others how you are feeling?
D-No	Yes	No	43.	Do you have any family problems?
P/S-Yes	Yes	No	44.	Do you think there is something the matter with your mind?
	Yes	No	45.	Are you eating well?
P/S-No	Yes	No	46.	Is your bad health the biggest difficulty of your life?
AD-Yes	Yes	No	47.	Do you find that you get sad easily?
	Yes	No	48.	Do you worry or fuss over small details that seem unimportant to others?
	Yes	No	49.	Are you always a cooperative patient?
	Yes	No	50.	Do you often have the symptoms of a very serious disease?
	Yes	No	51.	Do you find that you get angry easily?
	Yes	No	52.	Do you have any work problems?
AI-Yes	Yes	No	53.	Do you prefer to keep your feelings to yourself?
Ad-Yes	Yes	No	54.	Do you often find that you get depressed?

Scoring Key				
D-Yes	Yes	No	55.	Would all your worries be over if you were physically healthy?
I-Yes	Yes	No	56.	Are you more irritable towards other people?
P/S-Yes	Yes	No	57.	Do you think that your symptoms may be caused by worry?
AI-Yes	Yes	No	58.	Is it easy for you to let people know when you are cross with them?
AD-Yes	Yes	No	59.	Is it hard for you to relax?
D-No	Yes	No	60.	Do you have personal worries which are not caused by physical illness?
I-Yes	Yes	No	61.	Do you often find that you lose patience with other people?
AI-Yes	Yes	No	62.	Is it hard for you to show people your personal feelings?

IMPACT OF EVENT SCALE (IES)

AUTHOR: Mardi J. Horowitz

PURPOSE: To measure the stress associated with traumatic events.

DESCRIPTION: The 15-item IES assesses the experience of posttraumatic stress for any specific life event and its context, such as the death of a loved one. The instructions intentionally do not define the traumatic event. This is to be done by the practitioner and the respondent during the course of treatment. The IES is a relatively direct measure of the stress associated with a traumatic event. The IES measures two categories of experience in response to stressful events: intrusive experience, such as ideas, feelings, or bad dreams; and avoidance, the recognized avoidance of certain ideas, feelings, and situations. Because the IES has been shown to be sensitive to change, it is appropriate for monitoring clients' progress in treatment.

NORMS: Normative data are available on two samples. One was a sample of 35 outpatients who sought treatment to cope with the death of a parent. The second was a field sample of 37 adult volunteers who had a recently deceased parent. The average age of the outpatient sample was 31.4 with a standard deviation of 8.7 years. The mean score and standard deviation on the intrusive subscale was 21.02 and 7.9, respectively. Mean score on the avoidance subscale was 20.8 with a standard deviation of 10.2. The mean intrusive subscale score for the field sample was 13.5 with a standard deviation of 9.1. The avoidance subscale mean was 9.4 with a standard deviation of 9.6. All of the above data were assessed two months after the stressful event had occurred.

SCORING: Items are rated according to how frequently the intrusive or avoidance reaction occurred. Responses are scored from 0 to 5 with higher scores reflecting more stressful impact. Scores for the intrusive subscale range from 0 to 35 and are the sum of the ratings on the following items: 1, 4, 5, 6, 10, 11, 14. Scores range from 0 to 40 for the avoidance subscale, computed by adding the ratings on the following items: 2, 3, 7, 8, 9, 12, 13, 15. A cutoff point of 26 is suggested, with scores above that suggesting moderate to severe impact.

RELIABILITY: Based on two separate samples, the subscales of the IES show very good internal consistency, with coefficients ranging from .79 to .92, with an average of .86 for the intrusive subscale and .90 for the avoidance subscale. No data on stability were reported.

VALIDITY: The known-groups validity of the IES has been supported with significant differences in the scores of outpatients seeking treatment for bereavement and three field samples. The subscales indicate the IES is sensitive to change as scores changed over the course of the treatment.

PRIMARY REFERENCES: Horowitz, M. J., Wilner, N., and Alvarez, W. (1979). Impact of event scale: A measure of subjective stress. *Psychosomatic Medicine*, 41, 209–218; Zilberg, N. J., Weiss, D. S., and Horowitz, M. J. (1982). Impact of event scale: A cross-validation study and some empirical evidence supporting a conceptual model of stress response syndromes, *Journal of Consulting and Clinical Psychology*, 50, 407–414. Instrument reproduced with permission of M. J. Horowitz and the American Psychological Association.

AVAILABILITY: Mardi J. Horowitz, M.D., Professor of Psychiatry, University of California, 401 Parnassus Avenue, San Francisco, CA 94143.

IES

Below is a list of comments made by people about stressful life events and the context surrounding them. Read each item and decide how frequently each item was true for you during the past seven (7) days, for the event and its context, about which you are dealing in treatment. If the item did not occur during the past seven days, choose the "Not at all" option. Indicate on the line at the left of each comment the number that best describes that item. Please complete each item.

0 = Not at all
1 = Rarely
3 = Sometimes
5 = Often

_____   1. I thought about it when I didn't mean to.
_____   2. I avoided letting myself get upset when I thought about it or was reminded of it.
_____   3. I tried to remove it from memory.
_____   4. I had trouble falling asleep or staying asleep, because of pictures or thoughts that came into my mind.
_____   5. I had waves of strong feelings about it.
_____   6. I had dreams about it.
_____   7. I stayed away from reminders of it.
_____   8. I felt as if it hadn't happened or wasn't real.
_____   9. I tried not to talk about it.
_____ 10. Pictures about it popped into my mind.
_____ 11. Other things kept making me think about it.
_____ 12. I was aware that I still had a lot of feelings about it, but I didn't deal with them.
_____ 13. I tried not to think about it.
_____ 14. Any reminder brought back feelings about it.
_____ 15. My feelings about it were kind of numb.

INDEX OF ALCOHOL INVOLVEMENT (IAI)

AUTHOR: Gordon MacNeil
PURPOSE: To measure alcohol abuse.
DESCRIPTION: The IAI is a 25-item instrument designed to measure the degree or magnitude of problems of alcohol abuse. The items of the IAI were constructed to be a sample of all possible items that would indicate the presence or absence of difficulties regarding alcohol use. The IAI is a very easy-to-use measure for assessing self-reported alcohol abuse. Another advantage of the IAI is that it is one of some 20 instruments of the WALMYR Assessment Scales (WAS) package reproduced here, all of which are administered and scored the same way.
NORMS: The IAI was studied with 305 undergraduate students at a large western university. The mean age was 24 years; 87% were white, 13% were minorities. Females were approximately 60% of the sample. Actual norms are not available.
SCORING: Like most WAS instruments, the IAI is scored by first reverse-scoring items listed at the bottom of the page (5, 20, 23), summing these and the remaining scores, subtracting the number of completed items, multiplying this figure by 100, and dividing by the number of items completed times 6. This will produce a range from 0 to 100 with higher scores indicating greater problems with alcohol.
RELIABILITY: The IAI has excellent internal consistency, with an alpha of .90. Data on stability were not reported.
VALIDITY: The IAI has very good factorial and construct validity. It was correlated in predicted directions and amounts with a number of other scales of the WAS including the Generalized Contentment Scale, Index of Clinical Stress, the Partner Abuse Scale (Physical and Non-Physical), the Non-Physical Abuse of Partner Scale, and the Physical Abuse of Partner Scale.
PRIMARY REFERENCE: MacNeil, G. (1991). A short-form scale to measure alcohol abuse, *Research on Social Work Practice*, 1, 68–75.
AVAILABILITY: WALMYR Publishing Co., P.O. Box 24779, Tempe, AZ 85285-4779.

INDEX OF ALCOHOL INVOLVEMENT (IAI)

Name: _____Today's Date: _____

This questionnaire is designed to measure your use of alcohol. It is not a test, so there are no right or wrong answers. Answer each item as carefully and as accurately as you can by placing a number beside each one as follows.

1 = Never
2 = Very rarely
3 = A little of the time
4 = Some of the time
5 = A good part of the time
6 = Most of the time
7 = Always

1. ____ When I have a drink with friends, I usually drink more than they do.
2. ____ My family or friends tell me I drink too much.
3. ____ I feel that I drink too much alcohol.
4. ____ After I've had one or two drinks, it is difficult for me to stop drinking.
5. ____ When I am drinking, I have three or fewer drinks.
6. ____ I feel guilty about what happened when I have been drinking.
7. ____ When I go drinking, I get into fights.
8. ____ My drinking causes problems with my family or friends.
9. ____ My drinking causes problems with my work.
10. ____ After I have been drinking, I cannot remember things that happened when I think about them the next day.
11. ____ After I have been drinking, I get the shakes.
12. ____ My friends think I have a drinking problem.
13. ____ I drink to calm my nerves or make me feel better.
14. ____ I drink when I am alone.
15. ____ I drink until I go to sleep or pass out.
16. ____ My drinking interferes with obligations to my family or friends.
17. ____ I have one or more drinks when things are not going well for me.
18. ____ It is hard for me to stop drinking when I want to.
19. ____ I have one or more drinks before noon.
20. ____ My friends think my level of drinking is acceptable.
21. ____ I get mean and angry when I drink.
22. ____ My friends avoid me when I am drinking.
23. ____ I avoid drinking to excess.
24. ____ My personal life gets very troublesome when I drink.
25. ____ I drink 3 to 4 times a week.

5, 20, 23.

INDEX OF ATTITUDES TOWARD HOMOSEXUALS (IAH)

AUTHORS: Walter W. Hudson and Wendell Ricketts

PURPOSE: To measure homophobia.

DESCRIPTION: The IAH is a 25-item instrument designed to measure the degree or magnitude of a problem clients may have with homophobia, the fear of being in close quarters with homosexuals. Unlike most of the other scales in this book, the IAH is not designed to measure necessarily a personal or social problem; scores on the IAH are not indicative of a clinical disorder. The score on the IAH reflects the degree of comfort the respondent feels when in the presence of homosexuals. An advantage of the IAH is that it is one of some 20 instruments of the WALMYR Assessment Scales package reproduced here, all of which are administered and scored the same way.

NORMS: Not available. The IAH has a cutting point of 50; scores below 50 reflect an increasingly nonhomophobic response and scores over 50 represent increasing degrees of a homophobic response.

SCORING: Like most WALMYR Assessment Scales instruments, the IAH is scored by first reverse-scoring items listed at the bottom of the page (3, 4, 6, 9, 10, 12–15, 17, 19, 21, 24), summing these and the remaining scores, subtracting the number of completed items, multiplying this figure by 100, and dividing by the number of items completed times 4. This will produce a range from 0 to 100 with higher scores indicating greater magnitude or severity of problems.

RELIABILITY: The IAH has excellent internal consistency, with alphas in excess of .90. Data on stability were not available.

VALIDITY: The IAH is reported to have excellent content, construct, and factorial validity, with most validity correlations over .60.

PRIMARY REFERENCE: Hudson, W. W. (1992). *The WALMYR Assessment Scales Scoring Manual*. Tempe, AZ: WALMYR Publishing Co.

AVAILABILITY: WALMYR Publishing Co., P.O. Box 24779, Tempe, AZ 85285-4779.

INDEX OF ATTITUDES TOWARD HOMOSEXUALS (IAH)

Name: _____Today's Date: _____

This questionnaire is designed to measure the way you feel about working or associating with homosexuals. It is not a test, so there are no right or wrong answers. Answer each item as carefully and as accurately as you can by placing a number beside each one as follows.

1 = Strongly Agree
2 = Agree
3 = Neither agree nor disagree
4 = Disagree
5 = Strongly disagree

1. ____ I would feel comfortable working closely with a male homosexual.
2. ____ I would enjoy attending social functions at which homosexuals were present.
3. ____ I would feel uncomfortable if I learned that my neighbor was homosexual.
4. ____ If a member of my sex made a sexual advance toward me I would feel angry.
5. ____ I would feel comfortable knowing that I was attractive to members of my sex.
6. ____ I would feel uncomfortable being seen in a gay bar.
7. ____ I would feel comfortable if a member of my sex made an advance toward me.
8. ____ I would be comfortable if I found myself attracted to a member of my sex.
9. ____ I would feel disappointed if I learned that my child was homosexual.
10. ____ I would feel nervous being in a group of homosexuals.
11. ____ I would feel comfortable knowing that my clergyman was homosexual.
12. ____ I would be upset if I learned that my brother or sister was homosexual.
13. ____ I would feel that I had failed as a parent if I learned that my child was gay.
14. ____ If I saw two men holding hands in public I would feel disgusted.
15. ____ If a member of my sex made an advance toward me I would be offended.
16. ____ I would feel comfortable if I learned that my daughter's teacher was a lesbian.
17. ____ I would feel uncomfortable if I learned that my spouse or partner was attracted to members of his or her sex.
18. ____ I would feel at ease talking with a homosexual person at a party.
19. ____ I would feel uncomfortable if I learned that my boss was homosexual.
20. ____ It would not bother me to walk through a predominantly gay section of town.
21. ____ It would disturb me to find out that my doctor was homosexual.
22. ____ I would feel comfortable if I learned that my best friend of my sex was homosexual.
23. ____ If a member of my sex made an advance toward me I would feel flattered.
24. ____ I would feel uncomfortable knowing that my son's male teacher was homosexual.
25. ____ I would feel comfortable working closely with a female homosexual.

3, 4, 6, 9, 10, 12, 13, 14, 15, 17, 19, 21, 24.

INDEX OF CLINICAL STRESS (ICS)

AUTHOR: Neil Abell

PURPOSE: To measure subjective stress.

DESCRIPTION: The ICS is a 25-item instrument designed to measure the degree or magnitude of problems clients have with personal stress. The items were designed to reflect the range of perceptions associated with subjective stress; the items were developed not as responses to specifically identified stressor events, but as general indicators of affective states associated with the experience of stress. The ICS enables a practitioner to explore perceived stress without the problems associated with life events indices. Another advantage of the ICS is that it is one of some 20 instruments of the WALMYR Assessment Scales package (WAS) reproduced here, all of which are administered and scored the same way.

NORMS: The ICS was studied initially with 205 patients and family members recruited at a family practice residency program in a regional medical center in a midsized southern community. The mean age was 33 years, 72.1% were female, 27.9% were male, 62.6% were married, and the rest were single, divorced, or widowed; 81.9% were white, 16.2% were black, and the rest were other minorities. The mean ICS score was 28.96 (SD = 18.73). However, this score was based on 5-point scales for responses; currently, 7-point responses are recommended.

SCORING: Like most WALMYR Assessment Scales instruments, the ICS is scored by first reverse-scoring items listed at the bottom of the page (5, 8, 11, 13), summing these and the remaining scores, subtracting the number of completed items, multiplying this figure by 100, and dividing by the number of items completed times 6. This will produce a range from 0 to 100 with higher scores indicating greater magnitude or severity of problems.

RELIABILITY: The ICS has excellent internal consistency, with an alpha of .96. Data on stability were not reported.

VALIDITY: The ICS has good factorial validity and fair beginning construct validity, correlating in the predicted direction with the Generalized Contentment Scale and the Index of Family Relations.

PRIMARY REFERENCE: Abell, N. (1991). The Index of Clinical Stress: A brief measure of subjective stress for practice and research, *Social Work Research and Abstracts*, 27, 12–15.

AVAILABILITY: WALMYR Publishing Co., P.O. Box 24779, Tempe, AZ 85285-4779.

INDEX OF CLINICAL STRESS (ICS)

Name: _____ Today's Date: _____

This questionnaire is designed to measure the way you feel about the amount of personal stress that you experience. It is not a test, so there are no right or wrong answers. Answer each item as carefully and as accurately as you can by placing a number beside each one as follows.

    1 = None of the time
    2 = Very rarely
    3 = A little of the time
    4 = Some of the time
    5 = A good part of the time
    6 = Most of the time
    7 = All of the time

---

1. ____ I feel extremely tense.
2. ____ I feel very jittery.
3. ____ I feel like I want to scream.
4. ____ I feel overwhelmed.
5. ____ I feel very relaxed.
6. ____ I feel so anxious I want to cry.
7. ____ I feel so stressed that I'd like to hit something.
8. ____ I feel very calm and peaceful.
9. ____ I feel like I am stretched to the breaking point.
10. ____ It is very hard for me to relax.
11. ____ It is very easy for me to fall asleep at night.
12. ____ I feel an enormous sense of pressure on me.
13. ____ I feel like my life is going very smoothly.
14. ____ I feel very panicked.
15. ____ I feel like I am on the verge of a total collapse.
16. ____ I feel that I am losing control of my life.
17. ____ I feel that I am near a breaking point.
18. ____ I feel wound up like a coiled spring.
19. ____ I feel that I can't keep up with all the demands on me.
20. ____ I feel very much behind in my work.
21. ____ I feel tense and angry with those around me.
22. ____ I feel I must race from one task to the next.
23. ____ I feel that I just can't keep up with everything.
24. ____ I feel as tight as a drum.
25. ____ I feel very much on edge.

5, 8, 11, 13.

INDEX OF SELF-ESTEEM (ISE)

AUTHOR: Walter W. Hudson

PURPOSE: To measure problems with self-esteem.

DESCRIPTION: The ISE is a 25-item scale designed to measure the degree, severity, or magnitude of a problem the client has with self-esteem. Self-esteem is considered as the evaluative component of self-concept. The ISE is written in very simple language, is easily administered, and easily scored. Because problems with self-esteem are often central to social and psychological difficulties, this instrument has a wide range of utility for a number of clinical problems. The ISE has two cutting scores. The first is a score of 30 (±5); scores below this point indicate absence of a clinically significant problem in this area. Scores above 30 suggest the presence of a clinically significant problem. The second cutting score is 70. Scores above this point nearly always indicate that clients are experiencing severe stress with a clear possibility that some type of violence could be considered or used to deal with problems. The practitioner should be aware of this possibility. Another advantage of the ISE is that it is one of some 20 scales of the WALMYR Assessment Scales package reproduced here, all of which are administered and scored the same way.

NORMS: This scale was derived from tests of 1745 respondents, including single and married individuals, clinical and nonclinical populations, college students and nonstudents. Respondents included Caucasians, Japanese and Chinese Americans, and a smaller number of members of other ethnic groups. The ISE is not recommended for use with children under the age of 12. Actual norms are not available.

SCORING: Like most WALMYR Assessment Scales instruments, the ISE is scored by first reverse-scoring items listed at the bottom of the page (3–7, 14, 15, 18, 21–23, 25), summing these and the remaining scores, subtracting the number of completed items, multiplying this figure by 100, and dividing by the number of items completed times 6. This will produce a range from 0 to 100 with higher scores indicating greater magnitude or severity of problems.

RELIABILITY: The ISE has a mean alpha of .93, indicating excellent internal consistency, and an excellent (low) SEM of 3.70. The ISE also has excellent short-term stability with a two-hour test-retest correlation of .92.

VALIDITY: The ISE has good known-groups validity, significantly distinguishing between clients judged by clinicians to have problems in the area of self-esteem and those judged not to. Further, the ISE has very good construct validity, correlating poorly with measures with which it should not and correlating well with a range of other measures with which it should correlate highly, e.g., depression, happiness, sense of identity, and scores on the Generalized Contentment Scale (depression).

PRIMARY REFERENCE: Hudson, W. W. (1992). *The WALMYR Assessment Scales Scoring Manual*. Tempe, AZ: WALMYR Publishing Co.

AVAILABILITY: WALMYR Publishing Co., P. O. Box 24779, Tempe, AZ 85285-4779.

INDEX OF SELF-ESTEEM (ISE)

Name: _____ Today's Date: _____

This questionnaire is designed to measure how you see yourself. It is not a test, so there are no right or wrong answers. Please answer each item as carefully and as accurately as you can by placing a number beside each one as follows.

    1 = None of the time
    2 = Very rarely
    3 = A little of the time
    4 = Some of the time
    5 = A good part of the time
    6 = Most of the time
    7 = All of the time

1. _____ I feel that people would not like me if they really knew me well.
2. _____ I feel that others get along much better than I do.
3. _____ I feel that I am a beautiful person.
4. _____ When I am with others I feel they are glad I am with them.
5. _____ I feel that people really like to talk with me.
6. _____ I feel that I am a very competent person.
7. _____ I think I make a good impression on others.
8. _____ I feel that I need more self-confidence.
9. _____ When I am with strangers I am very nervous.
10. _____ I think that I am a dull person.
11. _____ I feel ugly.
12. _____ I feel that others have more fun than I do.
13. _____ I feel that I bore people.
14. _____ I think my friends find me interesting.
15. _____ I think I have a good sense of humor.
16. _____ I feel very self-conscious when I am with strangers.
17. _____ I feel that if I could be more like other people I would have it made.
18. _____ I feel that people have a good time when they are with me.
19. _____ I feel like a wallflower when I go out.
20. _____ I feel I get pushed around more than others.
21. _____ I think I am a rather nice person.
22. _____ I feel that people really like me very much.
23. _____ I feel that I am a likeable person.
24. _____ I am afraid I will appear foolish to others.
25. _____ My friends think very highly of me.

3, 4, 5, 6, 7, 14, 15, 18, 21, 22, 23, 25.

INDEX OF SEXUAL SATISFACTION (ISS)

AUTHOR: Walter W. Hudson
PURPOSE: To measure problems in sexual satisfaction.
DESCRIPTION: The ISS is a 25-item measure of the degree, severity or magnitude of a problem in the sexual component of a couple's relationship. The ISS measures the respondent's feelings about a number of behaviors, attitudes, events, affect states, and preferences that are associated with the sexual relationship between partners. The items were written with special concern about being nonoffensive and not imposing on the rights or privacy of the client. The ISS has two cutting scores. The first is a score of 30 (±5); scores below this point indicate absence of a clinically significant problem in this area. Scores above 30 suggest the presence of a clinically significant problem. The second cutting score is 70. Scores above this point nearly always indicate that clients are experiencing severe stress with a clear possibility that some type of violence could be considered or used to deal with problems. The practitioner should be aware of this possibility. Another advantage of the ISS is that it is one of some 20 scales of the WALMYR Assessment Scales package reproduced here, all of which are administered and scored the same way.
NORMS: The scale was developed from tests of 1738 respondents, including single and married individuals, clinical and nonclinical populations, high school and college students and nonstudents. Respondents were primarily Caucasian, but also include Japanese and Chinese Americans, and a smaller number of members of other ethnic groups. Actual norms are not available.
SCORING: Like most WALMYR Assessment Scales instruments, the ISS is scored by first reverse-scoring items listed at the bottom of the page (1–3, 9, 10, 12, 16, 17, 19, 21–23), summing these and the remaining scores, subtracting the number of completed items, multiplying this figure by 100, and dividing by the number of items completed times 6. This will produce a range from 0 to 100 with higher scores indicating greater magnitude or severity of problems.
RELIABILITY: The ISS has a mean alpha of .92, indicating excellent internal consistency, and a (low) SEM of 4.24. The ISS also has excellent short-term stability, with a two-hour test-retest correlation of .94.
VALIDITY: The ISS has excellent concurrent validity, correlating significantly with the Locke-Wallace Marital Adjustment Scale and the Index of Marital Satisfaction. It has excellent known-groups validity, significantly distinguishing between people known to have problems with sexual satisfaction and those known not to. The ISS also has excellent construct validity, correlating poorly with those measures with which it should not correlate

and correlating highly with several measures with which it should correlate such as measures of marital satisfaction and problems.

PRIMARY REFERENCE: Hudson, W. W. (1992). *The WALMYR Assessment Scales Scoring Manual.* Tempe, AZ: WALMYR Publishing Co.

AVAILABILITY: WALMYR Publishing Co., P.O. Box 24779, Tempe, AZ 85285-4779.

INDEX OF SEXUAL SATISFACTION (ISS)

Name: _____ Today's Date: _____

This questionnaire is designed to measure the degree of satisfaction you have in the sexual relationship with your partner. It is not a test, so there are no right or wrong answers. Answer each item as carefully and as accurately as you can by placing a number beside each one as follows.

1 = None of the time
2 = Very rarely
3 = A little of the time
4 = Some of the time
5 = A good part of the time
6 = Most of the time
7 = All of the time

1. ____ I feel that my partner enjoys our sex life.
2. ____ Our sex life is very exciting.
3. ____ Sex is fun for my partner and me.
4. ____ Sex with my partner has become a chore for me.
5. ____ I feel that our sex is dirty and disgusting.
6. ____ Our sex life is monotonous.
7. ____ When we have sex it is too rushed and hurriedly completed.
8. ____ I feel that my sex life is lacking in quality.
9. ____ My partner is sexually very exciting.
10. ____ I enjoy the sex techniques that my partner likes or uses.
11. ____ I feel that my partner wants too much sex from me.
12. ____ I think that our sex is wonderful.
13. ____ My partner dwells on sex too much.
14. ____ I try to avoid sexual contact with my partner.
15. ____ My partner is too rough or brutal when we have sex.
16. ____ My partner is a wonderful sex mate.
17. ____ I feel that sex is a normal function of our relationship.
18. ____ My partner does not want sex when I do.
19. ____ I feel that our sex life really adds a lot to our relationship.
20. ____ My partner seems to avoid sexual contact with me.
21. ____ It is easy for me to get sexually excited by my partner.
22. ____ I feel that my partner is sexually pleased with me.
23. ____ My partner is very sensitive to my sexual needs and desires.
24. ____ My partner does not satisfy me sexually.
25. ____ I feel that my sex life is boring.

1, 2, 3, 9, 10, 12, 16, 17, 19, 21, 22, 23.

INTERACTION AND AUDIENCE ANXIOUSNESS SCALES
(IAS and AAS)

AUTHOR: Mark R. Leary

PURPOSE: To measure social anxiety.

DESCRIPTION: The IAS (15 items) and AAS (12 items) are designed to measure two forms of social anxiety. These two measures of anxiety deviate from other instruments that assess anxious feelings and anxious behavior. They start from the position that a person who has anxious feelings may still interact socially despite feeling distressed. These instruments define social anxiety as the experiential state of anxiety resulting from being evaluated in social settings. Two classes of social anxiety are measured: interaction anxiety (IA), which concerns social responses that are contingent upon others' behavior, and audience anxiousness (AA), when social responses are not contingent upon others' behaviors. The measures can be used separately or together.

NORMS: A sample of 363 college students was used to develop the IAS and AAS. Demographic data and norms are not reported in the primary reference. Data are reported for a clinical sample of 13 students seeking professional help for interpersonal problems, speech majors ($n = 12$) and students selected from a pool of volunteers ($n = 17$). The mean IAS and AAS scores were 54.9 and 43.1, respectively, for those seeking professional help. The speech majors had mean IAS and AAS scores of 33.6 and 28.2 respectively, while the third sample's means were 38.1 and 39.3. Little information is available on sampling procedures or demographic characteristics.

SCORING: Each item is rated on a 5-point scale from "uncharacteristic or not true" to "characteristic or true." Items 3, 6, 10, and 15 on the IAS and 2 and 8 on the AAS are reverse-scored. Scores are the sum of the item ratings. For the IAS, scores range from 15 to 75. For the AAS, scores range from 12 to 60.

RELIABILITY: The reliability of these two instruments is excellent. The internal consistency using coefficient alphas was .88 for both the IAS and AAS. Both measures had very good test-retest reliability, correlating .80 for the IAS and .84 for the AAS over a four-week period.

VALIDITY: These instruments also have strong evidence of validity. Concurrent validity was indicated with IAS scores correlating with the Social Avoidance and Distress Scale, social anxiety, shyness, confidence as a speaker, fear of negative evaluation, sociability, public self-consciousness, and self-esteem. The AAS was also correlated with these criteria. There is also evidence of known-groups validity with differences between IAS and AAS scores for the clinical sample and the other two samples presented in the section on Norms. Scores are fairly independent of social desirability.

PRIMARY REFERENCE: Leary, M. R. (1983). Social anxiousness: The construct
and its measurement, *Journal of Personality Assessment*, 47, 66–75. Instruments reproduced with permission of Mark R. Leary.
AVAILABILITY: Journal article.

IAS

Below are fifteen statements. Please read each one and consider how characteristic
it is of you. Rate each statement using the following scale and record your answer
in the space to the left of the statement.

     1 = Uncharacteristic of me or not true
     2 = Somewhat uncharacteristic of me or somewhat not true
     3 = Neither uncharacteristic nor characteristic
     4 = Somewhat characteristic of me or somewhat true
     5 = Characteristic of me or true

____ 1. I often feel nervous even in casual get-togethers.

____ 2. I usually feel uncomfortable when I am in a group of people I don't
know.

____ 3. I am usually at ease when speaking to a member of the opposite sex.

____ 4. I get nervous when I must talk to a teacher or boss.

____ 5. Parties often make me feel anxious and uncomfortable.

____ 6. I am probably less shy in social interactions than most people.

____ 7. I sometimes feel tense when talking to people of my own sex if I
don't know them very well.

____ 8. I would be nervous if I was being interviewed for a job.

____ 9. I wish I had more confidence in social situations.

____ 10. I seldom feel anxious in social situations.

____ 11. In general, I am a shy person.

____ 12. I often feel nervous when talking to an attractive member of the
opposite sex.

____ 13. I often feel nervous when calling someone I don't know very well on
the telephone.

____ 14. I get nervous when I speak to someone in a position of authority.

____ 15. I usually feel relaxed around other people, even people who are
quite different from me.

AAS

Below are twelve statements. Please read each one and consider how characteristic it is of you. Rate each statement using the following scale and record your answer in the space to the left of the statement.

1 = Uncharacteristic of me or not true
2 = Somewhat uncharacteristic of me or somewhat not true
3 = Neither uncharacteristic nor characteristic
4 = Somewhat characteristic or somewhat true
5 = Characteristic of me or true

_____ 1. I usually get nervous when I speak in front of a group.

_____ 2. I enjoy speaking in public.

_____ 3. I tend to experience "stage fright" when I must appear before a group.

_____ 4. I would be terrified if I had to appear before a large audience.

_____ 5. I get "butterflies" in my stomach when I must speak or perform before others.

_____ 6. I would feel awkward and tense if I knew someone was filming me with a movie camera.

_____ 7. My thoughts become jumbled when I speak before an audience.

_____ 8. I don't mind speaking in front of a group if I have rehearsed what I am going to say.

_____ 9. I wish I did not get so nervous when I speak in front of a group.

_____ 10. If I was a musician, I would probably get "stage fright" before a concert.

_____ 11. When I speak in front of others, I worry about making a fool out of myself.

_____ 12. I get nervous when I must make a presentation at school or work.

INTERNAL CONTROL INDEX (ICI)

AUTHOR: Patricia Duttweiler

PURPOSE: To measure locus of control.

DESCRIPTION: The ICI is a 28-item instrument designed to measure where a person looks for, or expects to obtain, reinforcement. An individual with an external locus of control believes that reinforcement is based on luck or chance, while an individual with an internal locus of control believes that reinforcement is based on his or her own behavior. Locus of control is viewed as a personality trait that influences human behavior across a wide range of situations related to learning and achievement. There are two factors contained in the ICI, one that is called self-confidence, and a second that is called autonomous behavior (behavior independent of social pressure).

NORMS: The ICI was developed and tested with several samples of junior college, university undergraduate, and continuing education students. The total N involved 1365 respondents of both sexes. Means are available that are broken down by age, group, sex, race, and educational and socio-economic level and range from 99.3 to 120.8.

SCORING: Each item is scored on a 5-point scale from A ("rarely") to E ("usually"). Half of the items are worded so that high internally oriented respondents are expected to answer half at the "usually" end of the scale and the other half at the "rarely" end. The "rarely" response is scored as 5 points on items 1, 2, 4, 6, 8, 11, 14, 17, 19, 22, 23, 24, 26, and 27; for the remainder of the items, the response "usually" is scored as 5 points. This produces a possible range of scores from 28 to 140 with higher scores reflecting higher internal locus of control.

RELIABILITY: The ICI has very good internal consistency, with alphas of .84 and .85. No test-retest correlations were reported.

VALIDITY: The ICI has fair concurrent validity, with a low but significant correlation with Mirels' Factor I of the Rotter I-E Scale.

PRIMARY REFERENCE: Duttweiler, P. C. (1984). The Internal Control Index: A newly developed measure of locus of control, *Educational and Psychological Measurement*, 44, 209–221. Instrument reproduced with permission of Patricia Duttweiler and *Educational and Psychological Measurement*.

AVAILABILITY: Journal article.

ICI

Please read each statement. Where there is a blank, decide what your normal or usual attitude, feeling, or behavior would be:

> A = Rarely (less than 10% of the time)
> B = Occasionally (about 30% of the time)
> C = Sometimes (about half the time)
> D = Frequently (about 70% of the time)
> E = Usually (more than 90% of the time)

Of course, there are always unusual situations in which this would not be the case, but think of what you would do or feel in most normal situations.

Write the letter that describes your usual attitude or behavior in the *space provided on the response sheet.*

1. When faced with a problem I _____ try to forget it.

2. I _____ need frequent encouragement from others for me to keep working at a difficult task.

3. I _____ like jobs where I can make decisions and be responsible for my own work.

4. I _____ change my opinion when someone I admire disagrees with me.

5. If I want something I _____ work hard to get it.

6. I _____ prefer to learn the facts about something from someone else rather than have to dig them out for myself.

7. I _____ will accept jobs that require me to supervise others.

8. I _____ have a hard time saying "no" when someone tries to sell me something I don't want.

9. I _____ like to have a say in any decisions made by any group I'm in.

10. I _____ consider the different sides of an issue before making any decisions.

11. What other people think _____ has a great influence on my behavior.

12. Whenever something good happens to me I _____ feel it is because I've earned it.

13. I _____ enjoy being in a position of leadership.

14. I _____ need someone else to praise my work before I am satisfied with what I've done.

15. I _____ am sure enough of my opinions to try and influence others.

16. When something is going to affect me I _____ learn as much about it as I can.

17. I _____ decide to do things on the spur of the moment.

18. For me, knowing I've done something well is _____ more important than being praised by someone else.

19. I _____ let other peoples' demands keep me from doing things I want to do.

20. I _____ stick to my opinions when someone disagrees with me.

21. I _____ do what I feel like doing not what other people think I ought to do.

22. I _____ get discouraged when doing something that takes a long time to achieve results.

23. When part of a group I _____ prefer to let other people make all the decisions.

24. When I have a problem I _____ follow the advice of friends or relatives.

25. I _____ enjoy trying to do difficult tasks more than I enjoy trying to do easy tasks.

26. I _____ prefer situations where I can depend on someone else's ability rather than just my own.

27. Having someone important tell me I did a good job is _____ more important to me than feeling I've done a good job.

28. When I'm involved in something I _____ try to find out all I can about what is going on even when someone else is in charge.

INTERNAL VERSUS EXTERNAL CONTROL OF WEIGHT SCALE (IECW)

AUTHORS: Lester L. Tobias and Marian L. MacDonald

PURPOSE: To measure locus of control pertaining to weight loss.

DESCRIPTION: The 5-item IECW is similar to other measures of locus of control in that it attempts to measure the degree to which respondents consider achievement of a goal as contingent or noncontingent on their own behavior. The scale was initially developed to test the effectiveness of internal perceptions to facilitate weight reduction. The instrument is relevant to weight reduction treatment that emphasizes clients' taking responsibility for their treatment. While the IECW registers change toward an internal control orientation as a consequence of treatment, the perceived responsibility itself is insufficient to facilitate weight loss. Consequently, the IECW needs to be used along with other measures of treatment effectiveness.

NORMS: The IECW was developed on 100 undergraduate females whose weights were at least ten percent more than their desirable weight, who expressed a belief that the weight problem was related to eating and activity patterns, and declared a desire to change. The sample's average age was 19.2 years, ranging from 17 to 26. The average weight of the sample was 161.8 pounds. The average IECW score before any experimental manipulation was approximately 1.04.

SCORING: Items are arranged in a forced-choice format; one alternative reflects an internal orientation and the other reflects an external orientation. External choices (the first alternative in items 1, 3, and 5, the second alternative in items 2 and 4) are scored "1." Total scores are the sum of the internal alternatives selected by the respondent. Scores range from 0 to 5.

RELIABILITY: The reliability of the IECW was determined using test-retest correlations over a ten-week period. The correlation coefficient was .52, which is low but acceptable because of the long period between administrations. Internal consistency data were not reported.

VALIDITY: The instrument lacks validity data. Scores did not differ between pre- and post-weight reduction program. Criterion validity to determine if scores actually correlate with weight reduction has not been established.

PRIMARY REFERENCE: Tobias, L. L. and MacDonald, M. L. (1977). Internal locus of control and weight loss: An insufficient condition, *Journal of Consulting and Clinical Psychology*, 45, 647–653. Instrument reproduced with permission of the American Psychological Association.

AVAILABILITY: Journal article.

IECW

Each item consists of two statements; choose the statement with which you *agree most* by placing a check in the blank to the left of that statement.

1. ____ Overweight problems are mainly a result of hereditary or physiological factors.
   ____ Overweight problems are mainly a result of lack of self-control.

2. ____ Overweight people will lose weight only when they can generate enough internal motivation.
   ____ Overweight people need some tangible external motivation in order to reduce.

3. ____ Diet pills can be a valuable aid in weight reduction.
   ____ A person who loses weight with diet pills will gain the weight back eventually.

4. ____ In overweight people, hunger is caused by the expectation of being hungry.
   ____ In overweight people, hunger is caused by stomach contractions and low blood sugar levels.

5. ____ Overweight problems can be traced to early childhood and are very resistant to change.
   ____ Overweight problems can be traced to poor eating habits which are relatively simple to change.

INTERPERSONAL DEPENDENCY INVENTORY (IDI)

AUTHORS: Robert M. A. Hirschfield, G. L. Klerman, H. G. Gough, I. Barrett, S. J. Korchin, and P. Chodoff.

PURPOSE: To measure interpersonal dependency.

DESCRIPTION: The IDI is a 48-item instrument designed to measure the thoughts, behaviors, and feelings revolving around the need to associate closely with valued people. The theoretical base for the IDI is a blend of psychoanalytic, social learning, and attachment theories emphasizing the importance of excess dependency for a range of emotional and behavioral disorders. Based on an initial pool of 98 items, the 48-item scale was developed using factor analysis. This resulted in three subscales: Emotional reliance on others (items 3, 6, 7, 9, 12, 15, 16, 19, 22, 26, 29, 33, 35, 38, 40, 43, 45, 47), lack of self-confidence (items 2, 5, 10, 13, 17, 19, 20, 23, 24, 27, 30, 32, 36, 29, 41, 44, 46) and assertion of autonomy (items 1, 4, 8, 11, 14, 18, 21, 25, 28, 31, 34, 37, 42, 48).

NORMS: Research on the IDI has involved three samples. The first is a predominantly white group of 88 university males and 132 university females with a mean age of 24. The second involved 76 male and 104 female psychiatric patients, predominantly white. The third involved 19 male and 47 female psychiatric patients (mean age of 31) and 64 male and 57 female nonpsychiatric community residents (mean age of 41). Means for these groups on the IDI ranged from 176.3 to 210.3; however, a new scoring system has replaced the one used in determining these figures so that the mean for "normal" samples averages around 50.

SCORING: The IDI is scored by summing the responses from each of the three subscales to yield scores for each one. Items 10, 23, and 44 on the self-confidence subscale are rescored by subtracting the item response from 5. The scores on the three subscales can be summed for the overall score. A new, more complicated scoring system for the total score, utilizing weighted scores and producing means of around 50 for normal samples, is available from the author.

RELIABILITY: The IDI has good internal consistency, with split-half reliabilities that range from .72 to .91. No test-retest data were reported.

VALIDITY: The IDI has fairly good concurrent validity, with the first two subscales correlating significantly with measures of general neuroticism (the Maudley Personality Inventory) and anxiety, interpersonal sensitivity, and depression (Symptom Checklist-90). The IDI also distinguishes between psychiatric patients and normals. However, the first two subscales are also correlated with the social desirability scale of the MMPI, suggesting that respondents tend to respond based on what they believe is socially desirable.

PRIMARY REFERENCE: Hirschfield, R. M. A., Klerman, G. L., Gough, H. G., Barrett, J., Korchin, S. J., and Chodoff, P. (1977). A measure of interpersonal dependency, *Journal of Personality Assessment*, 41, 610–618. Instrument reproduced by permission of the authors and the *Journal of Personality Assessment*.

AVAILABILITY: Dr. Harrison G. Gough, Institute of Personality Assessment and Research, University of California, Berkeley, CA 94720.

IDI

Please read each statement and decide whether or not it is characteristic of your attitudes, feelings, or behavior. Then assign a rating to every statement, using the values given below:

> 4 = very characteristic of me
> 3 = quite characteristic of me
> 2 = somewhat characteristic of me
> 1 = not characteristic of me

---- 1. I prefer to be by myself.
---- 2. When I have a decision to make, I always ask for advice.
---- 3. I do my best work when I know it will be appreciated.
---- 4. I can't stand being fussed over when I am sick.
---- 5. I would rather be a follower than a leader.
---- 6. I believe people could do a lot more for me if they wanted to.
---- 7. As a child, pleasing my parents was very important to me.
---- 8. I don't need other people to make me feel good.
---- 9. Disapproval by someone I care about is very painful for me.
---- 10. I feel confident of my ability to deal with most of the personal problems I am likely to meet in life.
---- 11. I'm the only person I want to please.
---- 12. The idea of losing a close friend is terrifying to me.
---- 13. I am quick to agree with the opinions expressed by others.
---- 14. I rely only on myself.
---- 15. I would be completely lost if I didn't have someone special.
---- 16. I get upset when someone discovers a mistake I've made.
---- 17. It is hard for me to ask someone for a favor.
---- 18. I hate it when people offer me sympathy.
---- 19. I easily get discouraged when I don't get what I need from others.
---- 20. In an argument, I give in easily.
---- 21. I don't need much from people.
---- 22. I must have one person who is very special to me.
---- 23. When I go to a party, I expect that the other people will like me.
---- 24. I feel better when I know someone else is in command.
---- 25. When I am sick, I prefer that my friends leave me alone.
---- 26. I'm never happier than when people say I've done a good job.
---- 27. It is hard for me to make up my mind about a TV show or movie until I know what other people think.
---- 28. I am willing to disregard other people's feelings in order to accomplish something that's important to me.
---- 29. I need to have one person who puts me above all others.
---- 30. In social situations I tend to be very self-conscious.
---- 31. I don't need anyone.
---- 32. I have a lot of trouble making decisions by myself.
---- 33. I tend to imagine the worst if a loved one doesn't arrive when expected.

_____ 34. Even when things go wrong I can get along without asking for help from my friends.

_____ 35. I tend to expect too much from others.

_____ 36. I don't like to buy clothes by myself.

_____ 37. I tend to be a loner.

_____ 38. I feel that I never really get all that I need from people.

_____ 39. When I meet new people, I'm afraid that I won't do the right thing.

_____ 40. Even if most people turned against me, I could still go on if someone I love stood by me.

_____ 41. I would rather stay free of involvements with others than to risk disappointments.

_____ 42. What people think of me doesn't affect how I feel.

_____ 43. I think that most people don't realize how easily they can hurt me.

_____ 44. I am very confident about my own judgment.

_____ 45. I have always had a terrible fear that I will lose the love and support of people I desperately need.

_____ 46. I don't have what it takes to be a good leader.

_____ 47. I would feel helpless if deserted by someone I love.

_____ 48. What other people say doesn't bother me.

INTIMACY SCALE (IS)

AUTHORS: Alexis J. Walker and Linda Thompson

PURPOSE: To assess intimacy.

DESCRIPTION: The IS is a 17-item instrument designed to measure general intimacy or affection. The IS is actually part of a broader instrument that taps several dimensions of intimacy but is reported on by its authors as a separate scale. Intimacy is defined simply as family members' caring about each other, and includes such elements of emotional closeness as affection, altruism, enjoyment, satisfaction, a feeling the relationship is important, openness, respect, solidarity, and commitment.

NORMS: The IS was studied initially with 166 female college undergraduates of whom 68% were aged 20 to 25; 166 mothers of the students, most of whom were aged 40 to 49 (63%) and were middle class, with 73% on their first marriages; and 148 grandmothers, 40% of whom were between the ages of 60 and 69 and 40% of whom were between the ages of 70 and 79, 52% of whom were married and 45% widowed. The mean IS score for mothers was 6.21 (SD = .69) and the mean IS score for daughters was 6.04 (SD = 1.00).

SCORING: The IS is scored by summing and then averaging (dividing by 17) item scores to create individual scores. The possible range is 1 to 7 with higher scores reflecting greater intimacy.

RELIABILITY: The IS has excellent internal consistency, with alphas that range from .91 to .97. No stability data were reported.

VALIDITY: Although actual validity data are not reported in the primary reference, the IS was correlated with distal and proximal aid to the mother from the mother's report and with proximal aid to the mother from the daughter's report.

PRIMARY REFERENCE: Walker, A. J. and Thompson, L. (1983). Intimacy and intergenerational aid and contact among mothers and daughters, *Journal of Marriage and the Family*, 45, 841–849, a publication of the National Council on Family Relations.

AVAILABILITY: Journal article.

IS

Please indicate your perception of your relationship using the following scale:

1 = Never
2 = Occasionally
3 = Sometimes
4 = Often
5 = Frequently
6 = Almost always
7 = Always

Record your perception in the space to the left of each item.

_____ 1. We want to spend time together.
_____ 2. She shows that she loves me.
_____ 3. We're honest with each other.
_____ 4. We can accept each other's criticism of our faults and mistakes.
_____ 5. We like each other.
_____ 6. We respect each other.
_____ 7. Our lives are better because of each other.
_____ 8. We enjoy the relationship.
_____ 9. She cares about the way I feel.
_____ 10. We feel like we are a unit.
_____ 11. There's a great amount of unselfishness in our relationship.
_____ 12. She always thinks of my best interest.
_____ 13. I'm lucky to have her in my life.
_____ 14. She always makes me feel better.
_____ 15. She is important to me.
_____ 16. We love each other.
_____ 17. I'm sure of this relationship.

INVENTORY TO DIAGNOSE DEPRESSION (IDD)

AUTHORS: Mark Zimmerman, William Coryell, Caryn Corenthal, and Sheila Wilson

PURPOSE: To measure major depression disorder.

DESCRIPTION: The IDD is a 22-item instrument designed to diagnose major depressive disorder (MDD). The IDD differs from other depression scales in three ways. First, it covers the entire range of symptoms used in DSM-III to diagnose MDD. Second, the IDD not only can quantify the severity of depression but can be used to decide the presence or absence of a symptom. And third, the IDD assesses symptom duration.

NORMS: The IDD was studied initially with 220 psychiatric inpatients and 15 "normal" controls including 94 men and 141 women; 42.1% were single, 31.9% married, and the rest divorced, separated, or widowed. The mean years of education was 12.7 (81.3% high school graduates and 16.2% college graduates); 62.1% were diagnosed with MDD, 11.1% with schizophrenia, and the rest scattered among several diagnoses (including 15 "normals"). The mean score on the IDD for patients diagnosed as MDD was 42.6 (SD = 11.8) and for nondepressed subjects 19.0 (SD = 15.7). This difference was statistically significant.

SCORING: To quantify the severity of depression, the item scores are totaled, with higher scores showing greater severity. A score of 0 or 1 on each item represents no disturbance (0) or subclinical severity (1), and a score of 2 or more is counted as a symptom.

RELIABILITY: The IDD has excellent internal consistency, with an alpha of .92. The IDD also has excellent stability, with a one-day test-retest correlation of .98.

VALIDITY: The IDD has excellent concurrent validity, correlating significantly with other scales of depression (Beck Depression Inventory, Carrol Rating Scale, and the HRS). The IDD also discriminates significantly between different levels of depression, and was highly accurate (over 80% in diagnostic sensitivity). The IDD also was sensitive to clinical change.

PRIMARY REFERENCE: Zimmerman, M., Coryell, W., Corenthal, C., and Wilson, S. (1986). A self-report scale to diagnose major depressive disorder, *Archives of General Psychiatry*, 43, 1076–1081.

AVAILABILITY: Dr. Mark Zimmerman, Medical College of Pennsylvania, Eastern Pennsylvania Psychiatric Institute, 32000 Henry Avenue, Philadelphia, PA 19129.

IDD

1. On this questionnaire are groups of 5 statements.
2. Read each group of statements carefully. Then pick out the one statement in each group that best describes the way you have been feeling the PAST WEEK. Circle the number next to the statement you picked.
3. For every group in which you circled #1, 2, 3, or 4, answer the follow-up question as to whether you have been feeling that way for more or less than 2 weeks by circling either "more" or "less" as appropriate.

1. 0 I do not feel sad or depressed.
    1 I occasionally feel sad or down.
    2 I feel sad most of the time, but I can snap out of it.
    3 I feel sad all the time, and I can't snap out of it.
    4 I am so sad or unhappy that I can't stand it.

If you circled #1, 2, 3, or 4: Have you been feeling sad or down for more or less than 2 weeks?   more   less

2. 0 My energy level is normal.
    1 My energy level is occasionally a little lower than normal.
    2 I get tired more easily or have less energy than usual.
    3 I get tired from doing almost anything.
    4 I feel tired or exhausted almost all of the time.

If you circled #1, 2, 3, or 4: Has your energy level been lower than usual for more or less than 2 weeks?   more   less

3. 0 I have not been feeling more restless and fidgety than usual.
    1 I feel a little more restless or fidgety than usual.
    2 I have been very fidgety, and I have some difficulty sitting still in a chair.
    3 I have been extremely fidgety, and I have been pacing a little bit almost every day.
    4 I have been pacing more than an hour per day, and I can't sit still.

If you circled #1, 2, 3, or 4: Have you felt restless and fidgety for more or less than 2 weeks?   more   less

4. 0 I have not been talking or moving more slowly than usual.
    1 I am talking a little slower than usual.
    2 I am speaking slower than usual, and it takes me longer to respond to questions, but I can still carry on a normal conversation.
    3 Normal conversations are difficult because it is hard to start talking.
    4 I feel extremely slowed down physically, like I am stuck in mud.

If you circled #1, 2, 3, or 4: Have you felt slowed down for more or less than 2 weeks?   more   less

5. 0 I have not lost interest in my usual activities.
    1 I am a little less interested in 1 or 2 of my usual activities.
    2 I am less interested in several of my usual activities.
    3 I have lost most of my interest in almost all of my usual activities.
    4 I have lost all interest in all of my usual activities.

If you circled #1, 2, 3, or 4: Has your interest in your usual
activities been low for more or less than 2 weeks?   more   less

6. 0 I get as much pleasure out of my usual activities as usual.
    1 I get a little less pleasure from 1 or 2 of my usual activities.
    2 I get less pleasure from several of my usual activities.
    3 I get almost no pleasure from most of the activities which I usually enjoy.
    4 I get no pleasure from any of the activities which I usually enjoy.

If you circled #1, 2, 3, or 4: Has your enjoyment in your usual
activities been low for more or less than 2 weeks?   more   less

7. 0 I have not noticed any recent change in my interest in sex.
    1 I am only slightly less interested in sex than usual.
    2 There is a noticeable decrease in my interest in sex.
    3 I am much less interested in sex now.
    4 I have lost all interest in sex.

If you circled #1, 2, 3, or 4: Has your interest in sex been low for
more or less than 2 weeks?   more   less

8. 0 I have not been feeling guilty.
    1 I occasionally feel a little guilty.
    2 I often feel guilty.
    3 I feel quite guilty most of the time.
    4 I feel extremely guilty most of the time.

If you circled #1, 2, 3, or 4: Have you had guilt feelings for more or
less than 2 weeks?   more   less

9. 0 I do not feel like a failure.
    1 My opinion of myself is occasionally a little low.
    2 I feel I am inferior to most people.
    3 I feel like a failure.
    4 I feel I am a totally worthless person.

If you circled #1, 2, 3, or 4: Have you been down on yourself for
more or less than 2 weeks?   more   less

10.   0   I haven't had any thoughts of death or suicide.
        1   I occasionally think life is not worth living.
        2   I frequently think of dying in passive ways (such as going to sleep and
              not waking up), or that I'd be better off dead.
        3   I have frequent thoughts of killing myself, but I would not carry them out.
        4   I would kill myself if I had the chance.

If you circled #1, 2, 3, or 4: Have you been thinking about dying or
killing yourself for more or less than 2 weeks?   more   less

11.   0   I can concentrate as well as usual.
        1   My ability to concentrate is slightly worse than usual.
        2   My attention span is not as good as usual and I am having difficulty
              collecting my thoughts, but this hasn't caused any problems.
        3   My ability to read or hold a conversation is not as good as it usually is.
        4   I cannot read, watch TV, or have a conversation without
              great difficulty.

If you circled #1, 2, 3, or 4: Have you had problems concentrating
for more or less than 2 weeks?   more   less

12.   0   I make decisions as well as I usually do.
        1   Decision making is slightly more difficult than usual.
        2   It is harder and takes longer to make decisions, but I do make them.
        3   I am unable to make some decisions.
        4   I can't make any decisions at all.

If you circled #1, 2, 3, or 4: Have you had problems making
decisions for more or less than 2 weeks?   more   less

13.   0   My appetite is not less than normal.
        1   My appetite is slightly worse than usual.
        2   My appetite is clearly not as good as usual, but I still eat.
        3   My appetite is much worse now.
        4   I have no appetite at all, and I have to force myself to eat even a little.

If you circled #1, 2, 3, or 4: Has your appetite been decreased for
more or less than 2 weeks?   more   less

14.   0   I haven't lost any weight.
        1   I've lost less than 5 pounds.
        2   I've lost between 5 and 10 pounds.
        3   I've lost between 11 and 25 pounds.
        4   I've lost more than 25 pounds.

If you circled #1, 2, 3, or 4: Have you been dieting and deliberately
trying to lose weight?   Y or N

If you circled #1, 2, 3, or 4: Have you been losing weight for more
or less than 2 weeks?   more   less

15.   0   My appetite is not greater than normal.
       1   My appetite is slightly greater than usual.
       2   My appetite is clearly greater than usual.
       3   My appetite is much greater than usual.
       4   I feel hungry all the time.

If you circled #1, 2, 3, or 4: Has your appetite been increased for
more or less than 2 weeks?   more   less

16.   0   I haven't gained any weight.
       1   I've gained less than 5 pounds.
       2   I've gained between 5 and 10 pounds.
       3   I've gained between 11 and 25 pounds.
       4   I've gained more than 25 pounds.

If you circled #1, 2, 3, or 4: Have you been gaining weight for
more or less than 2 weeks?   more   less

17.   0   I am not sleeping less than normal.
       1   I occasionally have slight difficulty sleeping.
       2   I clearly don't sleep as well as usual.
       3   I sleep about half my normal amount of time.
       4   I sleep less than 2 hours per night.

If you circled #1, 2, 3, or 4: Which of these sleep problems have
you experienced? (circle all which apply)
       1   I have difficulty falling asleep.
       2   My sleep is fitful and restless in the middle of the night.
       3   I wake up earlier than usual and cannot fall back to sleep.

If you circled #1, 2, 3, or 4: Have you been having sleep problems
for more or less than 2 weeks?   more   less

18.   0   I am not sleeping more than normal.
       1   I occasionally sleep more than usual.
       2   I frequently sleep at least 1 hour more than usual.
       3   I frequently sleep at least 2 hours more than usual.
       4   I frequently sleep at least 3 hours more than usual.

If you circled #1, 2, 3, or 4: Have you been sleeping extra for more
or less than 2 weeks?   more   less

19.   0   I do not feel anxious, nervous, or tense.
       1   I occasionally feel a little anxious.
       2   I often feel anxious.
       3   I feel very anxious most of the time.
       4   I feel terrified and near panic.

If you circled #1, 2, 3, or 4: Have you been feeling anxious,
nervous, or tense for more or less than 2 weeks?   more   less

20.   0   I do not feel discouraged about the future.
      1   I occasionally feel a little discouraged about the future.
      2   I often feel discouraged about the future.
      3   I feel very discouraged about the future most of the
          time.
      4   I feel that the future is hopeless and that things will never improve.

If you circled #1, 2, 3, or 4: Have you been feeling discouraged
than usual for more or less than 2 weeks?   more   less

21.   0   I do not feel irritated or annoyed.
      1   I occasionally get a little more irritated than usual.
      2   I get irritated or annoyed by things that usually don't bother me.
      3   I feel irritated or annoyed almost all the time.
      4   I feel so depressed that I don't get irritated at all by things that used to
          bother me.

If you circled #1, 2, 3, or 4: Have you been feeling more irritable
than usual for more or less than 2 weeks?   more   less

22.   0   I am not worried about my physical health.
      1   I am occasionally concerned about bodily aches and pains.
      2   I am worried about my physical health.
      3   I am very worried about my physical health.
      4   I am so worried about my physical health that I cannot think about
          anything else.

If you circled #1, 2, 3, or 4: Have you been worried about your
physical health for more or less than 2 weeks?   more   less

IRRATIONAL VALUES SCALE (IVS)

AUTHOR: A. P. MacDonald

PURPOSE: To measure endorsement of irrational values.

DESCRIPTION: The IVS is a 9-item scale that was designed to measure a respondent's endorsement of nine irrational values that are based on the work of Albert Ellis. The underlying assumption is the belief that high endorsement of certain values or ideas would lead to neurosis. (Although eleven values were studied, two values were dropped because they did not possess adequate psychometric properties.) The IVS was seen as providing construct validity for Ellis's ideas because it was related to several measures of psychopathology. The scale might prove useful in clinical programs where the goal is to challenge and refute the clients' unrealistic, dysfunctional, or irrational ideas.

NORMS: Initial study of the IVS was based on three samples of undergraduates including 101 males and 80 females. No work on standardization was reported.

SCORING: The scores on 9-point Likert-type scales are totaled, producing a range of 9 to 81.

RELIABILITY: Internal consistency of the IVS is fairly good, with alphas of .73 and .79 reported. No test-retest data were reported.

VALIDITY: The IVS has good concurrent validity, correlating significantly with several measures including the California Personality Inventory, Eysenck Neuroticism Scale, Taylor Manifest Anxiety Scale, and the MacDonald-Tseng Internal-External Locus of Control Scale. Also, the IVS was not correlated with the Marlowe-Crowne Social Desirability Scale, indicating the IVS is free from social desirability response set.

PRIMARY REFERENCE: MacDonald, A. P. and Games, Richard G. (1972). Ellis' irrational values, *Rational Living*, 7, 25–28. Instrument reproduced with permission of Dr. A. P. MacDonald.

AVAILABILITY: Journal article.

IVS

People have different opinions. We are interested in knowing your opinions concerning the following issues. There are no right or wrong answers for the items; we are interested in opinions only. Please indicate your own opinion by circling a number from one to nine on the scale provided for each statement. In case of doubt, circle the number which comes closest to representing your true opinion. Please do not leave any blanks.

1. It is essential that one be loved or approved by virtually everyone in his community.

    Completely   Completely
    disagree   agree
        1   2   3   4   5   6   7   8   9

2. One must be perfectly competent, adequate, and achieving to consider oneself worthwhile.

    Completely   Completely
    disagree   agree
        1   2   3   4   5   6   7   8   9

3. Some people are bad, wicked, or villainous and therefore should be blamed and punished.

    Completely   Completely
    disagree   agree
        1   2   3   4   5   6   7   8   9

4. It is a terrible catastrophe when things are not as one wants them to be.

    Completely   Completely
    disagree   agree
        1   2   3   4   5   6   7   8   9

5. Unhappiness is caused by outside circumstances and the individual has no control over it.

    Completely   Completely
    disagree   agree
        1   2   3   4   5   6   7   8   9

6. Dangerous or fearsome things are causes for great concern, and their possibility must be continually dwelt upon.

    Completely   Completely
    disagree   agree
        1   2   3   4   5   6   7   8   9

7. One should be dependent on others and must have someone stronger on whom to rely.

    Completely   Completely
    disagree   agree
        1   2   3   4   5   6   7   8   9

8. One should be quite upset over people's problems and disturbances.

    Completely   Completely
    disagree   agree
        1   2   3   4   5   6   7   8   9

9. There is always a right or perfect solution to every problem, and it must be found or the results will be catastrophic.

    Completely   Completely
    disagree   agree
        1   2   3   4   5   6   7   8   9

IRRITABILITY/APATHY SCALE (IAS)

AUTHORS: Alistair Burns, Susan Folstein, Jason Brandt, and Marshall Folstein

PURPOSE: To measure apathy and irritability in Alzheimer and Huntington's disease patients.

DESCRIPTION: The IAS is actually composed of two 5-item rating scales, an irritability scale and an apathy scale. These two characteristics are seen as prominent in a number of psychiatric disorders, but also in diseases such as Alzheimer and Huntington's. However, most previous measures of these constructs were not useful for severely cognitively impaired patients. The IAS is viewed as an advance in measurement since it utilizes a rating system by relevant others and focuses on measuring specific defined tracts.

NORMS: The IAS was studied with 31 Alzheimer (AD) and 26 Huntington's (HD) patients from clinics at the Johns Hopkins Hospital. The AD subjects were 93% white and 7% black with 18 women and 13 men with a mean age of 70.3. HD patients were 69% white and 31% black with 11 women and 15 men and a mean age of 48.3. The mean irritability score for the AD group was 9.6, with 58% scoring above the cut-off point, and the mean score for the HD group was 8.2 with 58% above the cut-off point. The mean apathy score for the AD group was 14.7 with 48% above the cut-off point, while the mean apathy score for the HD group was 15.1 with 48% above the cut-off point.

SCORING: Irritability is scored by summing all items for a maximum total of 17. Irritability was defined as present (the cut-off point) if the patient was rated at 2 or above on the 5-point irritability scale. Apathy is scored by summing all items for a maximum total of 25. Apathy was defined as present (the cut-off point) if a majority of the items were endorsed (a rating of 3 or above on questions 2, 4, and 5 and a rating of 4 or 5 on questions 1 and 3).

RELIABILITY: Both scales have fair to good internal consistency. The alpha for all 5 items on the irritability scale is .82 and for all 5 items on apathy is .78. Interrater reliabilities were excellent: 1.00 for irritability and .85 for apathy. Both scales are also very stable with one- to two-week test-retest reliabilities of .81 for irritability and .76 for apathy.

VALIDITY: The IAS has good concurrent validity, correlating .87 for the HD group with the behavioral abnormalities scale of the Psychogeriatric Dependency Rating Scale. The IAS also has good known-groups validity, significantly distinguishing both the AD and HD group on both scales from a group of "normals." Neither scale was correlated with a measure of aggression.

PRIMARY REFERENCE: Burns, A., Folstein, S., Brandt, J., and Folstein, M. (1990). Clinical assessment of irritability, aggression and apathy in Huntington and Alzheimer Disease, *Journal of Nervous and Mental Disease*, 178, 20–26.

AVAILABILITY: Journal article.

IAS

Please answer the following questions about your _____ according to how he/she is now, compared with how he/she was before his/her health problems began. (It may be necessary to emphasize that the questionnaire relates to behavior since the onset of the illness and not in the very recent past. An open-ended question such as "what effect has your _____ illness had on him/her" may be used.)

Irritability

1. How irritable would you say he/she was? *Score*

1	2	3	4	5	
Not at all irritable				Extremely irritable	_____

	Never (score = 1)	Some-times (score = 2)	Always (score = 3)
2. Does he/she sulk after he/she is angry?	_____	_____	_____
3. Does he/she "pout" if he/she does not get his/her own way?	_____	_____	_____
4. Does he/she get into arguments?	_____	_____	_____
5. Does he/she raise his/her voice in anger?	_____	_____	_____

Apathy

1. Has his/her interest in everyday events changed? *Score*

1	2	3	4	5	
Much more interested		Just the same		Much less interested	_____

2. How long does he/she stay lying in bed or sitting in a chair doing nothing during the day?

1	2	3	4	5	
No more than anyone else				All the time	_____

3. How active is he/she in day to day activities?

1	2	3	4	5	
Very active		Normal		Very inactive	_____

4. How busy does he/she keep himself/herself?   *Score*

1	2	3	4	5
Same hobbies as usual	Less so but still has hobbies	Prefers doing nothing but does with prompting	Prefers watching TV or watches others doing things	If left alone does nothing

                                                                                  _____

5. Does the patient seem withdrawn from things?

1	2	3	4	5
Not at all	A little more than usual	More than usual	Much more than usual	Yes, definitely

                                                                                  _____

JOB INTERVIEW SELF-STATEMENT SCHEDULE (JISSS)

AUTHORS: Richard G. Heimberg, Kevin E. Keller, and Theresa Peca-Baker

PURPOSE: To measure social-evaluative anxiety in job interviews.

DESCRIPTION: The JISSS is a 50-item instrument designed to measure positive and negative cognitions and their relation to evaluative anxiety in job interview situations. The JISSS is based on the idea that social-evaluative anxiety about performance in job interviews may inhibit effective performance, and that internal dialogues (self-statements) contribute to the presence or absence of anxiety. Thus, the JISSS uses an essentially cognitive perspective to examine self-statements that could affect job interview performance. The JISSS has two subscales, negative self-statement (items 1, 4, 9, 11, 13, 15, 16, 20–24, 26, 27, 29, 34, 37, 38, 40, 42–46, 48) and positive self-statement (items 2, 3, 5–8, 10, 12, 14, 17–19, 25, 28, 30–33, 35, 36, 39, 41, 47, 49, 50). It also provides two scores, one for assessing the frequency of occurrence of self-statements ("how often") and the other for assessing the impact of self-statements ("help or hinder").

NORMS: The JISSS was studied with two samples of undergraduate psychology students totaling 303 (200 women, 103 men), with a mean age of 18+. No other demographic information was provided. Means on the positive subscale ranged from 308.72 to 337.70 (SD = 74.5 to 80.3) and the negative subscale ranged from 190.77 to 205.08 (SD = 62.2 to 71.8). In one out of three trials, women had a significantly higher negative score than men.

SCORING: The two scores for the JISSS are derived by multiplying frequency ratings by impact ratings and summing across all subscale items.

RELIABILITY: The JISSS has excellent internal consistency, with alphas of .91 and .92 for both subscales. The JISSS has fair to good stability, with three- to four-week test-retest correlations of .57 for the negative subscale and .73 for the positive subscale.

VALIDITY: The JISSS has good concurrent validity, with significant correlations in predicted directions with interview anxiety as measured by the A-State portion of the State-Trait Anxiety Inventory. The JISSS was not related to social desirability or general fears of negative evaluation. The JISSS also has good known-groups validity, significantly distinguishing between groups of high- and low-interview-anxious subjects.

PRIMARY REFERENCE: Heimberg, R. G., Keller, K. E., and Peca-Baker, T. (1986). Cognitive assessment of social-evaluative anxiety in the job interview: Job Interview Self-Statement Schedule, *Journal of Counseling Psychology*, 33, 190–195.

AVAILABILITY: Dr. Richard Heimberg, Department of Psychology, SUNY-Albany, 1400 Washington Avenue, Albany, NY 12222.

JISSS

While you answer this questionnaire, you are to imagine that you are being interviewed for a job and that you and the interviewer are the only persons present. Items in this questionnaire were made up to be like thoughts you may have during the job interview. Answer the following two questions about each item:

a. *How often*
   How often would this thought occur to you in a job interview?

   1 = Never
   2 = Seldom
   3 = Sometimes
   4 = Often
   5 = Constantly

b. *Help or Hinder*
   Should this thought occur to you, to what extent would it help or hinder your interview performance?

   1 = Not at all
   2 = A little
   3 = Some
   4 = A lot
   5 = A great deal

Use the key above in marking your answers on the blanks next to each question.

1. I am being humiliated.
   ____ a. How often?
   ____ b. Help or hinder?

2. I really have good qualifications for this job.
   ____ a. How often?
   ____ b. Help or hinder?

3. I'm usually better at things than most people so I have a better chance of getting hired.
   ____ a. How often?
   ____ b. Help or hinder?

4. I can't think of a thing to say.
   ____ a. How often?
   ____ b. Help or hinder?

5. I feel like I dressed right for this interview.
   ____ a. How often?
   ____ b. Help or hinder?

6. When I leave I will feel like I have done my best.
   _____ a. How often?
   _____ b. Help or hinder?

7. I would be very happy in this job.
   _____ a. How often?
   _____ b. Help or hinder?

8. I would be very good at this job.
   _____ a. How often?
   _____ b. Help or hinder?

9. I'm not expressing myself clearly.
   _____ a. How often?
   _____ b. Help or hinder?

10. I make a good impression on people.
    _____ a. How often?
    _____ b. Help or hinder?

11. I feel less qualified when I think about the other applicants.
    _____ a. How often?
    _____ b. Help or hinder?

12. I am feeling and coming across as confident.
    _____ a. How often?
    _____ b. Help or hinder?

13. I am afraid that I'll never be hired for anything.
    _____ a. How often?
    _____ b. Help or hinder?

14. I am really looking my best today.
    _____ a. How often?
    _____ b. Help or hinder?

15. I am not coming across as knowing enough about the position.
    _____ a. How often?
    _____ b. Help or hinder?

16. The interviewer has already made up his/her mind.
    _____ a. How often?
    _____ b. Help or hinder?

17. I am looking forward to meeting the people who work here.
    _____ a. How often?
    _____ b. Help or hinder?

18. This job would give me a good chance to get ahead.
____ a.   How often?
____ b.   Help or hinder?

19. The interviewer and I are on the same wavelength.
____ a.   How often?
____ b.   Help or hinder?

20. I wish I had more interview experience.
____ a.   How often?
____ b.   Help or hinder?

21. My voice is shaky
____ a.   How often?
____ b.   Help or hinder?

22. The interviewer doesn't like "people like me."
____ a.   How often?
____ b.   Help or hinder?

23. I am saying all the wrong things.
____ a.   How often?
____ b.   Help or hinder?

24. This interview is not going well.
____ a.   How often?
____ b.   Help or hinder?

25. The interviewer is pleased with my qualifications.
____ a.   How often?
____ b.   Help or hinder?

26. I am freezing up under the pressure.
____ a.   How often?
____ b.   Help or hinder?

27. I am afraid that they will find out later that I'm not as competent as I have claimed.
____ a.   How often?
____ b.   Help or hinder?

28. I am expressing myself well.
____ a.   How often?
____ b.   Help or hinder?

29. I'm nervous and the interviewer knows it.
____ a.   How often?
____ b.   Help or hinder?

30. I'm doing a good job answering the interviewer's questions.
    ___ a. How often?
    ___ b. Help or hinder?

31. I will be myself and that should be plenty.
    ___ a. How often?
    ___ b. Help or hinder?

32. This sounds interesting and exciting.
    ___ a. How often?
    ___ b. Help or hinder?

33. I expect the interviewer to like me.
    ___ a. How often?
    ___ b. Help or hinder?

34. I don't know what this person wants from me.
    ___ a. How often?
    ___ b. Help or hinder?

35. I really can do this job.
    ___ a. How often?
    ___ b. Help or hinder?

36. The more interviews I go on, the better I get.
    ___ a. How often?
    ___ b. Help or hinder?

37. I sound like I don't know what I am talking about.
    ___ a. How often?
    ___ b. Help or hinder?

38. I won't be able to say what I want before the interview ends.
    ___ a. How often?
    ___ b. Help or hinder?

39. The future looks promising.
    ___ a. How often?
    ___ b. Help or hinder?

40. I forgot the questions I was going to ask.
    ___ a. How often?
    ___ b. Help or hinder?

41. This place needs someone like me.
    ___ a. How often?
    ___ b. Help or hinder?

42. I won't be able to answer an important question.
     _____ a.   How often?
     _____ b.   Help or hinder?

43. I will cost myself this job by doing something stupid.
     _____ a.   How often?
     _____ b.   Help or hinder?

44. I am not qualified.
     _____ a.   How often?
     _____ b.   Help or hinder?

45. This is stressful.
     _____ a.   How often?
     _____ b.   Help or hinder?

46. I am not going to get this job.
     _____ a.   How often?
     _____ b.   Help or hinder?

47. This is what I want and my attitude shows it.
     _____ a.   How often?
     _____ b.   Help or hinder?

48. I sound stupid.
     _____ a.   How often?
     _____ b.   Help or hinder?

49. This job is perfect for me and I am perfect for this job.
     _____ a.   How often?
     _____ b.   Help or hinder?

50. I would feel terrific if I got this job.
     _____ a.   How often?
     _____ b.   Help or hinder?

LIFE EVENTS QUESTIONNAIRE (LEQ)

AUTHOR: T. S. Brugha

PURPOSE: To measure stressful life events.

DESCRIPTION: The LEQ is a 12-item instrument measuring common life events that tend to be threatening. The instrument was designed to overcome the labor-intense time and expense of more lengthy interviews. The LEQ is useful in making an assessment for an Axis IV diagnosis with the DSM-IV. The instrument is acceptable to psychiatric patients and the general population. The instrument has high sensitivity and is more likely to produce false positives (identify as a stressful event one that may not be) than false negatives (failing to identify a stressful event that is present). The client identifies stressful events over the past six months, with the specific months written in at the top of the questionnaire. Once a client has successfully identified the stressful events, the specific LEQ items may serve as a good point of departure in developing a self-anchored rating scale.

NORMS: No normative data are available.

SCORING: Each item of the LEQ may be scored 1 if it is checked and 0 if not. A total score would be the sum of all items, although scores will tend to be skewed due to the nature of the instrument.

RELIABILITY: The test-retest reliability of the LEQ is reported as .84 for a three-month period and .66 for a six-month period. Data on internal consistency are not available.

VALIDITY: Concurrent validity estimates were derived from the concordance between inpatient psychotic patients' identification of stressful events and those identified by a significant other; there was a 90% agreement when assessed at a three-month period and a 70% agreement when assessed at six months. The authors also used an extensive interview of stressful events as a base rate and showed that the LEQ was sensitive to the identification of stressful events.

PRIMARY REFERENCE: Brugha, T. S., and Cragg, D. (1990). The list of threatening experiences: The reliability and validity of a brief Life Events Questionnaire, *Acta Psychiatrica Scandinavica*, 82, 77–81. Instrument reproduced with permission of T. S. Brugha.

AVAILABILITY: Dr. T. S. Brugha, Department of Psychiatry, Clinical Sciences Building, Leicester Royal Infirmary, P.O. Box 65, Leicester, LE27LX England.

LEQ

Have any of the following life events or problems happened to you during the last 6 months? Please check the box or boxes corresponding to the month or months in which any event happened or began.

MONTHS

You yourself suffered a serious illness, injury, or an assault.						
A serious illness, injury, or assault happened to a close relative.						
Your parent, child, or spouse died.						
A close family friend or another relative (aunt, cousin, grandparent) died.						
You had a separation due to marital difficulties.						
You broke off a steady relationship.						
You had a serious problem with a close friend, neighbor, or relative.						
You became unemployed or you were seeking work unsuccessfully for more than one month.						
You were sacked from your job.						
You had a major financial crisis.						
You had problems with the police and a court appearance.						
Something you valued was lost or stolen.						

LIFE SATISFACTION INDEX-Z (LSIZ)

AUTHORS: Bernice Neugarten, Robert J. Havighurst, and Sheldon S. Tobin

PURPOSE: To measure the psychological well-being of the elderly.

DESCRIPTION: The LSIZ is an 18-item instrument designed to measure the life satisfaction of older people. The LSIZ was developed from a rating scale that was designed to be used by interviewers rating respondents and it may be administered as a self-report instrument orally or in writing. Items for the LSIZ were selected on the basis of their correlations with the original rating scale and their ability to discriminate between high and low scorers on the rating scale. Based on research on this instrument, it is recommended that the LSIZ be used mainly with individuals over 65.

NORMS: Initial study of the LSIZ was conducted with a sample of 60 people reported to represent a wide range of age from 65 years, both sexes, and all social classes. The mean score on the original instrument was 12.4; however, this instrument included two more items than the current LSIZ.

SCORING: The LSIZ is easily scored by assigning one point to each item that is "correctly" checked and summing these scores. A correct score is "agree" on items 1, 2, 4, 6, 8, 9, 11, 12, 13, 14, 17. Other items are correct if the respondent answers "disagree."

RELIABILITY: No data were reported, but the rating scales from which the LSIZ was developed had excellent inter-observer agreement.

VALIDITY: The LSIZ showed a moderate correlation with the instrument from which it was developed, the Life Satisfaction Rating Scale, indicating some degree of concurrent validity. The LSIZ also demonstrated a form of known-groups validity by successfully discriminating between high and low scorers on the Life Satisfaction Rating Scale.

PRIMARY REFERENCE: Neugarten, B. L., Havighurst, R. J, and Tobin, S. S. (1961). The measurement of life satisfaction, *Journal of Gerontology*, 16, 134–143. Instrument reproduced with permission of Bernice Neugarten and Robert J. Havighurst.

AVAILABILITY: Journal article.

LSIZ

Here are some statements about life in general that people feel different ways about.
Read each statement on the list and indicate at left the number that best describes
how you feel about the statement.

1 = Agree
2 = Disagree
3 = Unsure

_____ 1. As I grow older, things seem better than I thought they would be.
_____ 2. I have gotten more of the breaks in life than most of the people I
          know.
_____ 3. This is the dreariest time of my life.
_____ 4. I am just as happy as when I was younger.
_____ 5. My life could be happier than it is now.
_____ 6. These are the best years of my life.
_____ 7. Most of the things I do are boring or monotonous.
_____ 8. I expect some interesting and pleasant things to happen to me in the
          future.
_____ 9. The things I do are as interesting to me as they ever were.
_____ 10. I feel old and somewhat tired.
_____ 11. As I look back on my life, I am fairly well satisfied.
_____ 12. I would not change my past life even if I could.
_____ 13. Compared to other people my age, I make a good appearance.
_____ 14. I have made plans for things I'll be doing in a month or a year from
          now.
_____ 15. When I think back over my life, I didn't get most of the important
          things I wanted.
_____ 16. Compared to other people, I get down in the dumps too often.
_____ 17. I've gotten pretty much what I expected out of life.
_____ 18. In spite of what some people say, the lot of the average man is
          getting worse, not better.

LIKING PEOPLE SCALE (LPS)

AUTHOR: Erik E. Filsinger

PURPOSE: To measure interpersonal orientation.

DESCRIPTION: This 15-item instrument measures one aspect of interpersonal orientation, the general liking of other people. Interpersonal orientation plays a significant role in one's social development and adjustment. The theoretical point of departure of the LPS is that the degree of liking people influences whether one approaches or avoids social interaction. The instrument has utility, then, for monitoring intervention in cases of social isolation, shyness, and antisocial behavior. Scores on the instrument do not appear to be significantly different for males and females, although females score slightly higher than males.

NORMS: Normative data are reported for three samples. One hundred and forty college students (57 males and 83 females) from diverse demographic backgrounds had a mean of 59.4 with a standard deviation of 8.14. A second sample of college students had mean scores of 57.64 for males ($n = 15$) and 59.86 for females ($n = 58$). A third sample of randomly selected adults had a mean score of 52.27 for males and 55.35 for females.

SCORING: Respondents rate each item in terms of their agreement or disagreement. Ratings are quantified from 1 to 5 as follows: a = 1, b = 2, c = 3, d = 4, and e = 5. Items 4, 6, 8, 9, 10, and 15 are reverse-scored; total scores are the sum of all the items, with a range of 15 to 75. High scores indicate more liking of people.

RELIABILITY: The reliability of the LPS was estimated using Cronbach's alpha to test internal consistency. The LPS had good to very good internal consistency from two samples of college students (.85 and .75 respectively). Coefficient alpha was .78 from the random sample of adults. No data on stability were reported.

VALIDITY: The instrument generally has good validity evidence. In three separate samples the LPS was shown to have good concurrent validity, correlating with the amount of time spent alone, the number of close friends, scores on a misanthropy measure, and social anxiety. The instrument has also been shown to correlate with four measures of affiliation motivation, with social self-esteem, and with the ability to judge others.

PRIMARY REFERENCE: Filsinger, E. E. (1981). A measure of interpersonal orientation: The Liking People Scale, *Journal of Personality Assessment*, 45, 295–300. Instrument reproduced with permission of Erik E. Filsinger.

AVAILABILITY: Journal article.

LPS

The following questions ask your feeling about a number of things. Since we are all different, some people may think and feel one way; other people think and feel another way. There is no such thing as a "right" or "wrong" answer. The idea is to read each question and then fill out your answer. Try to respond to every question, even if it does not apply to you very well. The possible answers for each question are:

a = Strongly agree
b = Moderately agree
c = Neutral
d = Moderately disagree
e = Strongly disagree

_____ 1. Sometimes when people are talking to me, I find myself wishing that they would leave.
_____ 2. My need for people is quite low.
_____ 3. One of the things wrong with people today is that they are too dependent upon other people.
_____ 4. My happiest experiences involve other people.
_____ 5. People are not important for my personal happiness.
_____ 6. Personal character is developed in the stream of life.
_____ 7. I could be happy living away from people.
_____ 8. It is important to me to be able to get along with other people.
_____ 9. No matter what I am doing, I would rather do it in the company of other people.
_____ 10. There is no question about it—I like people.
_____ 11. Personal character is developed in solitude.
_____ 12. In general, I don't like people.
_____ 13. Except for my close friends, I don't like people.
_____ 14. A person only has a limited amount of time and people tend to cut into it.
_____ 15. People are the most important thing in my life.

LONELINESS RATING SCALE (LRS)

AUTHORS: Joseph J. Scalise, Earl J. Ginter, and Lawrence H. Gerstein

PURPOSE: To measure affective components of loneliness.

DESCRIPTION: The LRS is a 40-item instrument in two parts: Part A measures the frequency of certain affects and Part B measures the intensity or impact of the affective experience. The LRS is composed of four factors derived from factor analysis: depletion (a loss of vigor, exhaustion), isolation (an interpersonal segregation), agitation (restlessness, frustration, antagonism), and dejection (a feeling of discouragement or despondency). The original items for the LRS were based on a list of words solicited from students about how they felt when they were lonely, plus review of the loneliness literature. The LRS thus allows measurement of how often a respondent experiences each of the four dimensions of the measure, and of the impact the experience of those feelings has.

NORMS: The LRS was developed with a sample of 277 males and 486 females, largely university students. The median age was 21 years with a range of 11 to 72 years. Means and standard deviations are reported for all four subscales for both men and women. There is a significant difference between male and female scores on all of the subscales except agitation. In all instances, women scored higher suggesting greater frequency and intensity of the three dimensions when lonely.

SCORING: Eight separate scores are derived from the LRS—four frequency scores and four intensity scores. Scores for each factor are obtained by simply adding up the numbers circled for the items that make up a factor (depletion: 4, 9, 11, 14, 18, 21, 22, 25, 26, 37; isolation: 6, 7, 20, 23, 28, 29, 31, 35, 39, 40; agitation: 3, 8, 12, 13, 15, 17, 24, 32, 33, 34; dejection: 1, 25, 10, 16, 19, 27, 30, 36, 38). If a person circles "never" for frequency, the corresponding intensity (Part B) portion should not be completed. Scores for the frequency dimensions range from 0 to 30 and scores for intensity from 0 to 50.

RELIABILITY: The frequency dimensions have very good internal consistency, with alphas that range from .82 to .89. Stability of the LRS is also good with six-week test-retest reliabilities ranging from .61 to .71 for frequency and .65 to .70 for intensity while four-week test-retest reliability was .72 to .81 for frequency and .73 to .78 for intensity.

VALIDITY: The only validity information available showed correlations of .25 to .46 with the UCLA Loneliness Scale, thus suggesting a moderate degree of concurrent validity.

PRIMARY REFERENCE: Scalise, J. J., Ginter, E. J., and Gerstein, L. H. (1984). A multidimensional loneliness measure: The Loneliness Rating Scale (LRS),

Journal of Personality Assessment, 48, 525–530. Instrument reproduced with permission of J. J. Scalise.

AVAILABILITY: Dr. Joseph J. Scalise, Department of Psychology and Counselor Education, Nicholls State University, Thibodaux, LA 70310.

LRS

This is not a test. We are only interested in finding out how you feel when you experience loneliness.

There are 40 two-part questions. In the first part of the question, several words are used to describe loneliness. Indicate which word most describes how you feel by placing the appropriate number of the following scale to the left of each statement.

$$0 = \text{Never}$$
$$1 = \text{Occasionally}$$
$$2 = \text{Frequently}$$
$$3 = \text{Always}$$

In the second part, you are asked to indicate on a scale of 1 to 5 how much this feeling affects you by writing the appropriate number on the right hand side of the statement.

1	2	3	4	5
Bothersome				Overwhelming

If your answer to the first part of the statement is "never," skip the second part of the statement.

_____ 1. When I experience loneliness, I feel *low.*
The feeling of being *low* is: _____

_____ 2. When I experience loneliness, I feel *sad.*
The feeling of being *sad* is: _____

_____ 3. When I experience loneliness, I feel *angry.*
The feeling of being *angry* is: _____

_____ 4. When I experience loneliness, I feel *depressed.*
The feeling of being *depressed* is: _____

_____ 5. When I experience loneliness, I feel *drained.*
The feeling of being *drained* is: _____

_____ 6. When I experience loneliness, I feel *unloved.*
The feeling of being *unloved* is: _____

_____ 7. When I experience loneliness, I feel *worthless.*
The feeling of being *worthless* is: _____

_____ 8. When I experience loneliness, I feel *nervous.*
The feeling of being *nervous* is: _____

_____   9. When I experience loneliness, I feel *empty*.
           The feeling of being *empty* is: _____

_____ 10. When I experience loneliness, I feel *blue*.
           The feeling of being *blue* is: _____

_____ 11. When I experience loneliness, I feel *hollow*.
           The feeling of being *hollow* is: _____

_____ 12. When I experience loneliness, I feel *humiliated*.
           The feeling of being *humiliated* is: _____

_____ 13. When I experience loneliness, I feel *guilty*.
           The feeling of being *guilty* is: _____

_____ 14. When I experience loneliness, I feel *secluded*.
           The feeling of being *secluded* is: _____

_____ 15. When I experience loneliness, I feel *tormented*.
           The feeling of being *tormented* is: _____

_____ 16. When I experience loneliness, I feel *self-pity*.
           The feeling of *self-pity* is: _____

_____ 17. When I experience loneliness, I feel *aggressive*.
           The feeling of being *aggressive* is: _____

_____ 18. When I experience loneliness, I feel *alienated*.
           The feeling of being *alienated* is: _____

_____ 19. When I experience loneliness, I feel *hurt*.
           The feeling of being *hurt* is: _____

_____ 20. When I experience loneliness, I feel *hopeless*.
           The feeling of being *hopeless* is: _____

_____ 21. When I experience loneliness, I feel *broken*.
           The feeling of being *broken* is: _____

_____ 22. When I experience loneliness, I feel *withdrawn*.
           The feeling of being *withdrawn* is: _____

_____ 23. When I experience loneliness, I feel *disliked*.
           The feeling of being *disliked* is: _____

_____ 24. When I experience loneliness, I feel *hostile*.
           The feeling of being *hostile* is: _____

_____ 25. When I experience loneliness, I feel *numb*.
           The feeling of being *numb* is: _____

_____ 26. When I experience loneliness, I feel *passive*.
The feeling of being *passive* is: _____

_____ 27. When I experience loneliness, I feel *confused*.
The feeling of being *confused* is: _____

_____ 28. When I experience loneliness, I feel *abandoned*.
The feeling of being *abandoned* is: _____

_____ 29. When I experience loneliness, I feel *unacceptable*.
The feeling of being *unacceptable* is: _____

_____ 30. When I experience loneliness, I *feel discouraged*.
The feeling of being *discouraged* is: _____

_____ 31. When I experience loneliness, I feel *faceless*.
The feeling of being *faceless* is: _____

_____ 32. When I experience loneliness, I feel *sick*.
The feeling of being *sick* is: _____

_____ 33. When I experience loneliness, I feel *scared*.
The feeling of being *scared* is: _____

_____ 34. When I experience loneliness, I feel *tense*.
The feeling of being *tense* is: _____

_____ 35. When I experience loneliness, I feel *deserted*.
The feeling of being *deserted* is: _____

_____ 36. When I experience loneliness, I feel *miserable*.
The feeling of being *miserable* is: _____

_____ 37. When I experience loneliness, I feel *detached*.
The feeling of being *detached* is: _____

_____ 38. When I experience loneliness, I feel *unhappy*.
The feeling of being *unhappy* is: _____

_____ 39. When I experience loneliness, I feel *excluded*.
The feeling of being *excluded* is: _____

_____ 40. When I experience loneliness, I feel *useless*.
The feeling of being *useless* is: _____

LOVE ATTITUDES SCALE (LAS)

AUTHORS: Clyde Hendrick and Susan S. Hendrick

PURPOSE: To measure love styles/attitudes.

DESCRIPTION: The LAS is a 42-item instrument designed to measure attitudes about love. Six styles of love form the subscales of the LAS: eros (E: passionate love, items 1–7), ludus (L: game-playing love, items 8–14), storge (S: friendship love, items 15–21), pragma (P: logical, "shopping list" love, items 22–28), mania (M: possessive, dependent love, items 29–35), and agape (A: all-giving selfless love, items 36–42). The LAS has two versions, the most recent (reprinted here) being relationship-specific. The LAS is a useful measure for both research and practice involving issues around love.

NORMS: The LAS has been studied with several samples involving a total of 536 male and 607 female college students taking introductory psychology courses. For the current version of the LAS, means were: E = 2.08, L = 3.56, S = 2.42, P = 3.09, M = 2.94, A = 2.20. There are significant differences between men and women on all but the eros and agape subscales.

SCORING: The LAS is scored by summing the 5-point Likert-type item responses, with A ("strongly agree") being given 1 point. Lower scores indicate greater agreement with the scale. It is recommended that only the subscale scores be used.

RELIABILITY: The LAS has good internal consistency, with alphas for the subscales that range from .74 to .84. Data on stability were not reported on the new scale, but four- to six-week test-retest correlations on the older version of the LAS were reported as ranging from .70 to .82.

VALIDITY: Although no data on validity were reported for the relationship-specific version of the LAS, the older, more general version, which is very similar to the newer version, is reported as having good concurrent validity. The LAS is related to sex-role attitudes, self-disclosure and sensation-seeking, sexual attitudes, religious beliefs, and whether individuals currently are in love.

PRIMARY REFERENCE: Hendrick, C. and Hendrick, S. S. (1990). A relationship-specific version of the Love Attitudes Scale, *Journal of Social Behavior and Personality*, 5, 239–254. Instrument reprinted by permission of authors and the American Psychological Association.

AVAILABILITY: Journal article.

LAS

Listed below are several statements that reflect different attitudes about love. For each statement fill in the blank using the response that indicates how much you agree or disagree with that statement. The items refer to a specific love relationship. Whenever possible, answer the questions with your current partner in mind. If you are not currently dating anyone, answer the questions with your most recent partner in mind. If you have never been in love, answer in terms of what you think your responses would most likely be.

For each statement:

A = Strongly agree with the statement
B = Moderately agree with the statement
C = Neutral—neither agree nor disagree
D = Moderately disagree with the statement
E = Strongly disagree with the statement

_____ 1. My partner and I were attracted to each other immediately after we first met.
_____ 2. My partner and I have the right physical "chemistry" between us.
_____ 3. Our lovemaking is very intense and satisfying.
_____ 4. I feel that my partner and I were meant for each other.
_____ 5. My partner and I became emotionally involved rather quickly.
_____ 6. My partner and I really understand each other.
_____ 7. My partner fits my ideal standards of physical beauty/handsomeness.
_____ 8. I try to keep my partner a little uncertain about my commitment to him/her.
_____ 9. I believe that what my partner doesn't know about me won't hurt him/her.
_____ 10. I have sometimes had to keep my partner from finding out about other partners.
_____ 11. I could get over my affair with my partner pretty easily and quickly.
_____ 12. My partner would get upset if he/she knew of some of the things I've done with other people.
_____ 13. When my partner gets too dependent on me, I want to back off a little.
_____ 14. I enjoy playing the "game of love" with my partner and a number of other partners.
_____ 15. It is hard for me to say exactly when our friendship turned into love.
_____ 16. To be genuine, our love first required *caring* for a while.
_____ 17. I expect to always be friends with my partner.
_____ 18. Our love is the best kind because it grew out of a long friendship.
_____ 19. Our friendship merged gradually into love over time.
_____ 20. Our love is really a deep friendship, not a mysterious, mystical emotion.
_____ 21. Our love relationship is the most satisfying because it developed from a good friendship.
_____ 22. I considered what my partner was going to become in life before I committed myself to him/her.

_____ 23.   I tried to plan my life carefully before choosing my partner.

_____ 24.   In choosing my partner, I believed it was best to love someone with a similar background.

_____ 25.   A main consideration in choosing my partner was how he/she would reflect on my family.

_____ 26.   An important factor in choosing my partner was whether or not he/she would be a good parent.

_____ 27.   One consideration in choosing my partner was how he/she would reflect on my career.

_____ 28.   Before getting very involved with my partner, I tried to figure out how compatible his/her hereditary background would be with mine in case we ever had children.

_____ 29.   When things aren't right with my partner and me, my stomach gets upset.

_____ 30.   If my partner and I break up, I would get so depressed that I would even think of suicide.

_____ 31.   Sometimes I get so excited about being in love with my partner that I can't sleep.

_____ 32.   When my partner doesn't pay attention to me, I feel sick all over.

_____ 33.   Since I've been in love with my partner, I've had trouble concentrating on anything else.

_____ 34.   I cannot relax if I suspect that my partner is with someone else.

_____ 35.   If my partner ignores me for a while, I sometimes do stupid things to try to get his/her attention back.

_____ 36.   I try to always help my partner through difficult times.

_____ 37.   I would rather suffer myself than let my partner suffer.

_____ 38.   I cannot be happy unless I place my partner's happiness before my own.

_____ 39.   I am usually willing to sacrifice my own wishes to let my partner achieve his/hers.

_____ 40.   Whatever I own is my partner's to use as he/she chooses.

_____ 41.   When my partner gets angry with me, I still love him/her fully and unconditionally.

_____ 42.   I would endure all things for the sake of my partner.

MAGICAL IDEATION SCALE (MIS)

AUTHORS: Mark Eckblad and Loren J. Chapman

PURPOSE: To measure magical thinking.

DESCRIPTION: This 30-item instrument was designed to measure the magical ideations characteristic of schizotypical disorders. The MIS is also considered a general measure of a proneness to psychosis. Magical ideation is defined as the belief in what general Western culture would consider invalid causation, such as superstitiousness, clairvoyance, telepathy, and so on. The focus of the MIS is not on the credibility of these forms of causation, but the respondent's personal beliefs and experiences.

NORMS: The MIS has normative data from a total of 1,512 undergraduate college students. The mean score was 8.56 with a standard deviation of 5.24 for males ($n = 682$). Females ($n = 830$) have a mean of 9.69 and a standard deviation of 5.93.

SCORING: Respondents indicate whether the item is true or false regarding their personal experience. Items 7, 12, 13, 16 18, 22, 23 are scored 1 if answered false. All other items are scored 1 if answered true. Total scores range from 0 to 30; higher scores reflect more reported experiences of magical ideation.

RELIABILITY: The MIS has very good internal consistency, with correlations of .82 and .85 for males and females respectively. Data on stability were not available.

VALIDITY: The items of the MIS were first judged as to whether or not they were congruent with a specified definition of magical ideation; this represents logical content validity. The instrument then went through several revisions in order to make certain it was not associated with social desirability and an acquiescence response set. Concurrent validity is supported with correlations between scores on the MIS and measures of perceptual aberration, physical anhedonism, and psychotism. Known-groups validity was evident with differences on psychotic and psychotic-like symptoms for subjects whose MIS scores were two standard deviations above the mean and a control group.

PRIMARY REFERENCE: Eckblad, M. and Chapman, L. J. (1983). Magical ideation as an indicator of schizotypy, *Journal of Consulting and Clinical Psychology* 51, 215–225. Instrument reproduced with permission of Mark Eckblad and Loren Chapman, and the American Psychological Association.

AVAILABILITY: The Free Press.

MIS

Indicate whether each item is true or false of your experiences by circling the T or the F to the left of the item.

T F 1. Some people can make me aware of them just by thinking about me.
T F 2. I have had the momentary feeling that I might not be human.
T F 3. I have sometimes been fearful of stepping on sidewalk cracks.
T F 4. I think I could learn to read others' minds if I wanted to.
T F 5. Horoscopes are right too often for it to be a coincidence.
T F 6. Things sometimes seem to be in different places when I get home, even though no one has been there.
T F 7. Numbers like 13 and 7 have no special powers.
T F 8. I have occasionally had the silly feeling that a TV or radio broadcaster knew I was listening to him.
T F 9. I have worried that people on other planets may be influencing what happens on earth.
T F 10. The government refuses to tell us the truth about flying saucers.
T F 11. I have felt that there were messages for me in the way things were arranged, like in a store window.
T F 12. I have never doubted that my dreams are the products of my own mind.
T F 13. Good luck charms don't work.
T F 14. I have noticed sounds on my records that are not there at other times.
T F 15. The hand motions that strangers make seem to influence me at times.
T F 16. I almost never dream about things before they happen.
T F 17. I have had the momentary feeling that someone's place has been taken by a look-alike.
T F 18. It is not possible to harm others merely by thinking bad thoughts about them.
T F 19. I have sometimes sensed an evil presence around me, although I could not see it.
T F 20. I sometimes have a feeling of gaining or losing energy when certain people look at me or touch me.
T F 21. I have sometimes had the passing thought that strangers are in love with me.
T F 22. I have never had the feeling that certain thoughts of mine really belonged to someone else.
T F 23. When introduced to strangers, I rarely wonder whether I have known them before.
T F 24. If reincarnation were true, it would explain some unusual experiences I have had.
T F 25. People often behave so strangely that one wonders if they are part of an experiment.
T F 26. At times I perform certain little rituals to ward off negative influences.

T   F   27. I have felt that I might cause something to happen just by thinking too much about it.
T   F   28. I have wondered whether the spirits of the dead can influence the living.
T   F   29. At times I have felt that a professor's lecture was meant especially for me.
T   F   30. I have sometimes felt that strangers were reading my mind.

MATHEMATICS ANXIETY RATING SCALE—REVISED (MARS-R)

AUTHORS: Barbara S. Plake and Clair S. Parker

PURPOSE: To measure anxiety about math.

DESCRIPTION: This 24-item instrument is designed to measure anxiety related to involvement in statistics and mathematic courses. The instrument is a revised version of a 98-item scale by Richardson and Suinn (1972). The current version is more focused on situation-specific (state) anxiety, general (trait) anxiety, and test anxiety. The instrument forms two subscales: learning math anxiety (LMA), which pertains to the process of learning math and statistics, and mathematic evaluation anxiety (MEA), which measures anxiety over being tested about math and statistics.

NORMS: Data are reported on 170 college students enrolled in three introductory statistics classes at a large, urban, midwestern university. The mean MARS-R score was 59.84 with a standard deviation of 20.55.

SCORING: Respondents rate each item on a 5-point scale from "low anxiety" to "high anxiety." Scores are the sum of the item ratings, and range from 24 to 120 for the total scale.

RELIABILITY: The reliability of the revised form has been tested for internal consistency using coefficient alpha. The scale has excellent reliability, with an alpha of .98. No data are presented on stability.

VALIDITY: There are mixed findings regarding the MARS-R. Scores were not correlated with achievement anxiety, but were correlated with Spielberger's State-Trait Anxiety measures. Concurrent validity was established with correlations between the MARS-R and math achievement, and with significant correlations with the 98-item version.

PRIMARY REFERENCE: Plake, B. S. and Parker, C. S. (1982). The development and validation of a revised version of the Mathematics Anxiety Rating Scale, *Educational and Psychological Measurement*, 42, 551–557. Instrument reproduced with permission of Richard M. Suinn, the Rocky Mountain Behavioral Science Institute, Inc., and *Educational and Psychological Measurement*.

AVAILABILITY: Journal article.

MARS-R

Please rate each item in terms of how anxious you feel during the event specified.
Use the following scale and record your answer in the space to the left of the item:

$$1 = \text{Low anxiety}$$
$$2 = \text{Some anxiety}$$
$$3 = \text{Moderate anxiety}$$
$$4 = \text{Quite a bit of anxiety}$$
$$5 = \text{High anxiety}$$

Learning Mathematics Anxiety

____ 1. Watching a teacher work an algebraic equation on the blackboard.
____ 2. Buying a math textbook.
____ 3. Reading and interpreting graphs or charts.
____ 4. Signing up for a course in statistics.
____ 5. Listening to another student explain a math formula.
____ 6. Walking into a math class.
____ 7. Looking through the pages in a math text.
____ 8. Starting a new chapter in a math book.
____ 9. Walking on campus and thinking about a math course.
____ 10. Picking up a math textbook to begin working on a homework assignment.
____ 11. Reading the word "statistics."
____ 12. Working on an abstract mathematical problem, such as: "if x = outstanding bills, and y = total income, calculate how much you have left for recreational expenditures."
____ 13. Reading a formula in chemistry.
____ 14. Listening to a lecture in a math class.
____ 15. Having to use the tables in the back of a math book.
____ 16. Being told how to interpret probability statements.

Mathematics Evaluation Anxiety

____ 1. Being given a homework assignment of many difficult problems which is due the next class meeting.
____ 2. Thinking about an upcoming math test one day before.
____ 3. Solving square root problem.
____ 4. Taking an examination (quiz) in a math course.
____ 5. Getting ready to study for a math test.
____ 6. Being given a "pop" quiz in a math class.
____ 7. Waiting to get a math test returned in which you expected to do well.
____ 8. Taking an examination (final) in a math course.

MAUDSLEY OBSESSIONAL-COMPULSIVE INVENTORY (MOC)

AUTHORS: R. J. Hodgson and S. Rachman

PURPOSE: To measure obsessional-compulsive complaints.

DESCRIPTION: The MOC is a 30-item inventory designed to measure different types of obsessive-compulsive ritual. Sixty-five items based on a review of the literature and interviews with obsessive-compulsive patients made up a first questionnaire. Following pretesting, the current 30-item questionnaire was developed. Factor analysis revealed four factors: checking (C: items 6, 8, 14, 15, 20, 22, 26); cleaning (CL: items 1, 4, 5, 9, 13, 17, 19, 21, 24, 26, 27); slowness (S: items 2, 4, 8, 16, 23, 25, 29); and doubting (D: items 3, 7, 10–12, 18, 30). (Items 2 and 8 on the S factor are negatively related to the factor; some items load on more than one factor.) The MOC is viewed as a valuable measure for evaluating change in therapy on specific obsessive-compulsive dimensions.

NORMS: The MOC was studied initially with 100 obsessional patients in England, Scotland, and Wales, plus 50 nonobsessional neurotic individuals. No other demographic data were provided. The total mean score for the obsessional patients was 18.86 (SD = 4.92) and for the neurotics 9.27 (SD = 5.43). The mean checking score was 6.10 (SD = 2.21) for obsessionals and 2.84 (SD = 2.29) for neurotics. The mean for cleaning was 5.55 (SD = 3.04) for obsessionals and 2.38 (SD = 1.97) for neurotics. The slowness mean was 3.63 (SD = 1.93) for obsessionals and 2.27 (SD = 1.09) for neurotics, and the doubting mean was 5.39 (SD = 1.60) for obsessionals and 3.69 (SD = 1.99) for neurotics.

SCORING: The MOC is scored simply by totaling the number of questions that are answered in the obsessional direction for each factor and summing these for the total score. For example, a "true" response for item 1 would count as one point because it is in the "obsessional direction" where a "false" response to item 1 would not count in the score.

RELIABILITY: The MOC has fair internal consistency, with an alpha of .80 for the cleaning subscale and alphas of .70 for the remaining subscales. No overall alpha was reported. The MOC has very good stability, with a one-month test-retest reliability coefficient of .80.

VALIDITY: The MOC has fair concurrent validity, correlating .60 with the Leyton Obsessional Inventory. The MOC also is reported to be sensitive to change as a result of therapy and has good known-groups validity in distinguishing between patients with obsessive-compulsive and neurotic disorders.

PRIMARY REFERENCE: Hodgson, R. J. and Rachman, S. (1977). Obsessional-compulsive complaints, *Behavior Research and Therapy*, 15, 389–395. Instrument reprinted with permission of Pergamon Press.

AVAILABILITY: Journal article.

MOC

Please answer each question by putting a circle around T for "true" or F for "false" in response to each question. There are no right or wrong answers, and no trick questions. Work quickly and do not think too long about the exact meaning of the question.

T	F	1.	I avoid using public telephones because of possible contamination.
T	F	2.	I frequently get nasty thoughts and have difficulty in getting rid of them.
T	F	3.	I am more concerned than most people about honesty.
T	F	4.	I am often late because I can't seem to get through everything on time.
T	F	5.	I don't worry unduly about contamination if I touch an animal.
T	F	6.	I frequently have to check things (e.g., gas or water taps, doors, etc.) several times.
T	F	7.	I have a very strict conscience.
T	F	8.	I find that almost every day I am upset by unpleasant thoughts that come into my mind against my will.
T	F	9.	I do not worry unduly if I accidently bump into somebody.
T	F	10.	I usually have serious doubts about the simple everyday things I do.
T	F	11.	Neither of my parents was very strict during my childhood.
T	F	12.	I tend to get behind in my work because I repeat things over and over again.
T	F	13.	I use only an average amount of soap.
T	F	14.	Some numbers are extremely unlucky.
T	F	15.	I do not check letters over and over again before mailing them.
T	F	16.	I do not take a long time to dress in the morning.
T	F	17.	I am not excessively concerned about cleanliness.
T	F	18.	One of my major problems is that I pay too much attention to detail.
T	F	19.	I can use well-kept toilets without any hesitation.
T	F	20.	My major problem is repeated checking.
T	F	21.	I am not unduly concerned about germs and diseases.
T	F	22.	I do not tend to check things more than once.
T	F	23.	I do not stick to a very strict routine when doing ordinary things.
T	F	24.	My hands do not feel dirty after touching money.
T	F	25.	I do not usually count when doing a routine task.
T	F	26.	I take rather a long time to complete my washing in the morning.
T	F	27.	I do not use a great deal of antiseptics.
T	F	28.	I spend a lot of time every day checking things over and over again.
T	F	29.	Hanging and folding my clothes at night does not take up a lot of time.
T	F	30.	Even when I do something very carefully I often feel that it is not quite right.

MCGILL PAIN QUESTIONNAIRE (MPQ)

AUTHOR: Ronald Melzack

PURPOSE: To measure pain.

DESCRIPTION: The MPQ is a 21-item instrument designed to obtain quantitative measures of complex qualitative pain experiences. It consists of 78 adjectives arranged into 20 groups: 10 groups measure the sensory quality of pain (SQ: items 1–10), 5 groups measure the affective quality of pain (AQ: items 11–15), 1 set of adjectives measures the evaluative quality of pain, the overall intensity of the pain experience (EQ: item 16), and 4 groups measure miscellaneous pain (MP: items 17–20); 1 item measures present pain intensity (PPI: item 21). The human figure on the MPQ is used to indicate the location of one's pain, and additional items provide useful qualitative information. A French version also is available.

NORMS: Norms are available in the primary references for several samples presenting different types of pain, such as menstrual pain, arthritis, and back pain.

SCORING: Several methods of scoring the MPQ are described in the primary references. The most important is the pain rating index (PRI) that is obtained for the SQ, AQ, EQ, and MP separately as well as for a total score. The PRI is obtained by adding the rank values of the words selected by the respondent in each set and for the total of the first 20 items. A second score is the overall intensity of pain (PPI, item 21). A third score is simply the total of the number of items checked for each set; scores are the total of the items, divided by the number of items composing the subscales. The total score—the sum of the subscales—also can be used.

RELIABILITY: The author notes that several studies have shown the MPQ to provide a reliable measure of pain experience.

VALIDITY: There is strong support for the validity of the MPQ. The different scoring procedures have moderate to high correlations, and the subscales also are correlated. The MPQ also is sensitive to changes due to pain management training, and has shown known-groups validity by distinguishing among different forms of pain (e.g., low back pain in people with and without organic symptoms).

PRIMARY REFERENCES: Melzack, R. (1975). The McGill pain questionnaire: Major properties and scoring methods, *Pain*, 1, 277–299. Melzack, R. (1983). *Pain Measurement and Assessment.* New York: Raven Press. Instrument reproduced with permission of Ronald Melzack.

AVAILABILITY: Ronald Melzack, Ph.D., Professor, Department of Psychology, McGill University, 1205 Dr. Penfield Avenue, Montreal, Quebec, Canada H3A 1B1.

MPQ

Check every item that describes your pain. Indicate on the figure the areas where you are experiencing pain.

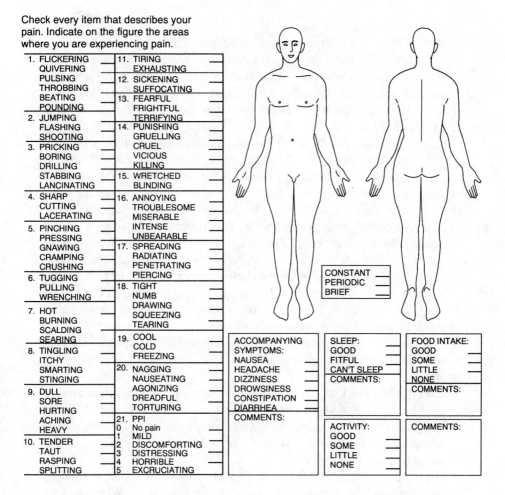

1. FLICKERING		11. TIRING	
QUIVERING		EXHAUSTING	
PULSING		12. SICKENING	
THROBBING		SUFFOCATING	
BEATING		13. FEARFUL	
POUNDING		FRIGHTFUL	
2. JUMPING		TERRIFYING	
FLASHING		14. PUNISHING	
SHOOTING		GRUELLING	
3. PRICKING		CRUEL	
BORING		VICIOUS	
DRILLING		KILLING	
STABBING		15. WRETCHED	
LANCINATING		BLINDING	
4. SHARP		16. ANNOYING	
CUTTING		TROUBLESOME	
LACERATING		MISERABLE	
5. PINCHING		INTENSE	
PRESSING		UNBEARABLE	
GNAWING		17. SPREADING	
CRAMPING		RADIATING	
CRUSHING		PENETRATING	
6. TUGGING		PIERCING	
PULLING		18. TIGHT	
WRENCHING		NUMB	
7. HOT		DRAWING	
BURNING		SQUEEZING	
SCALDING		TEARING	
SEARING		19. COOL	
8. TINGLING		COLD	
ITCHY		FREEZING	
SMARTING		20. NAGGING	
STINGING		NAUSEATING	
9. DULL		AGONIZING	
SORE		DREADFUL	
HURTING		TORTURING	
ACHING		21. PPI	
HEAVY		0 No pain	
10. TENDER		1 MILD	
TAUT		2 DISCOMFORTING	
RASPING		3 DISTRESSING	
SPLITTING		4 HORRIBLE	
		5 EXCRUCIATING	

CONSTANT
PERIODIC
BRIEF

ACCOMPANYING SYMPTOMS:	SLEEP:	FOOD INTAKE:
NAUSEA	GOOD	GOOD
HEADACHE	FITFUL	SOME
DIZZINESS	CAN'T SLEEP	LITTLE
DROWSINESS	COMMENTS:	NONE
CONSTIPATION		COMMENTS:
DIARRHEA		
COMMENTS:	ACTIVITY:	COMMENTS:
	GOOD	
	SOME	
	LITTLE	
	NONE	

MCMULLIN ADDICTION THOUGHT SCALE (MAT)

AUTHOR: Rian F. McMullin

PURPOSE: To measure irrational thoughts in chemically dependent clients.

DESCRIPTION: The MAT is a 42-item instrument designed to measure irrational cognitions of chemically dependent clients both for assessment and evaluation purposes. The MAT has five core types: not my fault (I; items 1, 4, 8, 11, 17, 19, 28, 29); I am powerful enough to control it (II; items 2, 14–16, 18, 23, 26, 30, 36, 39); drinking is good, pleasant, fun (III; items 3, 6, 10, 13, 22, 27, 31, 38, 41); I am not an alcoholic/don't have a problem (IV; items 5, 7, 25, 32, 35, 42); and I need to drink (V; items 9, 12, 20, 21, 24, 33, 34, 37, 40). The MAT is a very useful measure for keeping track of changes over time, especially as a result of cognitive-behavioral treatment.

NORMS: The MAT was studied with several samples in chemical dependency treatment centers in the United States and Australia: 275 subjects participated; 75% were male with an age range from 17 to 78. Norms are divided into very high, high, average, low, and very low scores for each factor. Very high (a) and high (b) scores were as follows for each subscale: I = 8 (a) and 6, 7 (b); II = 8–10 (a) and 5–7 (b); III = 8, 9 (a) and 6, 7 (b); IV = 5, 6 (a) and 3, 4 (b); and V = 8, 9 (a) and 6, 7 (b). Very low scores were 0 on subscales II and IV and 0, 1 on the other subscales.

SCORING: The MAT is easily scored by summing item responses for each subscale score and the total score.

RELIABILITY: Data were not available.

VALIDITY: The MAT has good predictive validity, showing significant reductions in irrational thoughts given longer periods of sobriety. The MAT also has good known-groups validity, significantly distinguishing between a recovered and nonrecovered sample. The MAT also is sensitive to changes due to treatment.

PRIMARY REFERENCE: McMullin, R. E. and Gehlaar, M. (1990). *Thinking and drinking: An exposé of drinkers' distorted beliefs*. Wheelers Hill, Victoria, Australia: Marlin Publications.

AVAILABILITY: Dr. Rian McMullin, Castle Medical Center, P.O. Box 10747, Hilo, HI 96721.

MAT

Using the following scale, record your answer in the space to the left of each item:

> 0 = Strongly disagree
> 1 = Disagree
> 2 = Neutral
> 3 = Agree
> 4 = Strongly agree

How many of the following thoughts do you believe right now?

____ 1. I am not responsible for my drinking or drugging.
____ 2. I can stop drinking or drugging through will power alone.
____ 3. A little booze is good for me.
____ 4. I can't stop drinking or drugging, so why bother trying.
____ 5. A couple of drinks or a little drug can't hurt me.
____ 6. I need to drink or drug to have fun.
____ 7. It's normal to drink alcohol or use drugs the way I have in the past.
____ 8. Bad feelings (fear, sadness, anger, etc.) caused me to drink or drug too much.
____ 9. The best way to stop feeling bad is to take a drink or drug.
____ 10. Being intoxicated or high feels good.
____ 11. I can't hold my liquor or my drug as well as others.
____ 12. I need to drink or drug to be more self-confident.
____ 13. Drinking or drugging is a good way to remove boredom.
____ 14. I can cure my drinking or drugging by a *little* self-discipline.
____ 15. I can become a social drinker or a social user, if I try hard enough.
____ 16. It's my fault that I am an alcoholic or an addict.
____ 17. Something inside of me took over and made me drink or drug.
____ 18. Addiction is just a bad habit.
____ 19. Outside catastrophes (losing a job, spouse leaving, etc.) causes people to drink or drug.
____ 20. I can cope better with life by drinking or drugging.
____ 21. Drinking or drugging is a good way to get back at someone.
____ 22. Wanting a drink or drug is the same as needing one.
____ 23. One can be cured of any addiction.
____ 24. It's necessary to stop withdrawal symptoms by taking another drink or drug.
____ 25. My drinking or drugging problem was not that serious.
____ 26. I can predict what I will do when I drink or drug.
____ 27. I am a better lover when I drink or drug.
____ 28. Social pressure made me use drink or drugs too much.
____ 29. I needed to take a drink or drug to keep emotions from overpowering me.
____ 30. I can be sober without help if I try hard enough.
____ 31. I needed a drink or drug to feel better.
____ 32. A person who works hard earns a drink or drug.
____ 33. Drinking or drugging is a good way to escape from life's stresses.

_____ 34. I should be happy all the time.
_____ 35. I am not an alcoholic or an addict.
_____ 36. You can't tell me anything about my drinking or drugging that I don't know.
_____ 37. We should get what we want in life.
_____ 38. Intoxication or getting high uncovers an individual's real personality.
_____ 39. Psychological problems cause alcoholism and addiction.
_____ 40. The best way to handle problems is not to think about them.
_____ 41. I am more creative when I am drinking or drugging.
_____ 42. There are more important things in life than my drinking or drugging problem.

MEDICAL OUTCOME SCALE (MOS)
(A version of the SF-36)

AUTHORS: Anita L. Stewart, Ron D. Hays, and John Ware, Jr.

PURPOSE: To measure six aspects of health.

DESCRIPTION: This 20-item instrument measures six aspects of health: physical functioning (PF), role functioning (RF), social functioning (SF), mental health (MH), health perceptions (HP), and Pain. Physical functioning assesses limitations due to one's health condition. Role and social functioning are defined by limitations due to health problems. Mental health is defined in terms of psychological distress and well-being. Health perception assesses rates of one's current health in general, and Pain is designed to ascertain one's physical discomfort. PF is composed of six items (3, 4, 5, 6, 7, 8). The RF is a two-item scale (9, 10). MH is composed of five items (12, 13, 14, 15, 16). HP also has 5 items (1, 17, 18, 19, 20). The other subscales are single-item indices. The MOS takes only three to four minutes to complete.

NORMS: Based on a national urban sample of adults ($N = 8294$), the means and standard deviations for the PF, RF, SF, MH, HP, and Pain were 78.5 (30.8), 77.5 (38.3), 87.2 (23.6), 72.6 (20.2), 63.0 (26.8), and 31.4 (2.77), respectively.

SCORING: Item scores for each response are coded and displayed in parentheses. Thus, subscale scores are either the indices score or the sum of item scores, and all range from 0 to approximately 100. For the SF index, however, the score must be multiplied by 5 in order to range from 0 to 100. Higher scores reflect better functioning.

RELIABILITY: For the multi-item scales the alpha coefficients were PF = .86, RF = .81, MH = .88, HP = .87. Internal consistency was similar for a sample of "normal" persons, persons with depression, and for persons with physical health conditions. Data on stability were not available.

VALIDITY: Concurrent validity was evidenced by the correlation between scale scores. There was also criterion validity as established by correlations between MOS scores and education and age. Known-groups validity is illustrated by different scores on the MOS for different samples in poor health compared to the general population.

PRIMARY REFERENCE: Stewart, A. L., Hays, R. D., and Ware, J. E. (1988). The MOS short-form general health survey, *Medical Care*, 26, 724–735. Instrument reproduced with permission of Anita L. Stewart, Ph.D., and J. B. Lippincott Company.

AVAILABILITY: Journal article.

MOS

Please check the answer that most applies to you.

1. In general, would you say your health is:

    [ ] Excellent (20)

    [ ] Very Good (15)

    [ ] Good (10)

    [ ] Fair (5)

    [ ] Poor (0)

2. How much bodily pain have you had during the past 4 weeks?

    [ ] None (100)

    [ ] Very mild (75)

    [ ] Mild (50)

    [ ] Moderate (25)

    [ ] Severe (0)

For how long (if at all) has your health limited you in each of the following activities?
(Check one box on each line.)

	Limited for more than 3 months (0)	Limited for 3 months or less (8.3)	Not limited at all (16.6)
3. The kinds or amounts of vigorous activities you can do, like lifting heavy objects, running, or participating in strenuous sports	[ ]	[ ]	[ ]
4. The kinds or amounts of moderate activities you can do, like moving a table, carrying groceries, or bowling	[ ]	[ ]	[ ]

	Limited for more than 3 months (0)	Limited for 3 months or less (8.3)	Not limited at all (16.6)
5. Walking uphill or climbing a few flights of stairs	[ ]	[ ]	[ ]
6. Bending, lifting, or stooping	[ ]	[ ]	[ ]
7. Walking one block	[ ]	[ ]	[ ]
8. Eating, dressing, bathing, or using the toilet	[ ]	[ ]	[ ]

	Yes, for more than 3 months (0)	Yes, for 3 months or less (25)	No (50)
9. Does your health keep you from working at a job, doing work around the house, or going to school?	[ ]	[ ]	[ ]
10. Have you been unable to do certain kinds or amounts of work, housework, or school-work because of your health?	[ ]	[ ]	[ ]

For each of the following questions, please check the box for the one answer that comes closest to the way you have been feeling during the past month. (Check one box on each line)

	All of the time (0)	Most of the time (4)	A good bit of the time (8)	Some of the time (12)	A little of the time (16)	None of the time (20)
11. How much of the time, during the past month, has your health limited your social activities (like visiting with friends or close relatives)?	[ ]	[ ]	[ ]	[ ]	[ ]	[ ]

		All of the time (0)	Most of the time (4)	A good bit of the time (8)	Some of the time (12)	A little of the time (16)	None of the time (20)
12.	How much of the time, during the past month, have you been a very nervous person?	[ ]	[ ]	[ ]	[ ]	[ ]	[ ]
13.	During the past month, how much of the time have you felt calm and peaceful?	[ ]	[ ]	[ ]	[ ]	[ ]	[ ]
14.	How much of the time, during the past month, have you felt downhearted and blue?	[ ]	[ ]	[ ]	[ ]	[ ]	[ ]
15.	During the past month, how much of the time have you been a happy person?	[ ]	[ ]	[ ]	[ ]	[ ]	[ ]
16.	How often, during the past month, have you felt so down in the dumps that nothing could cheer you up?	[ ]	[ ]	[ ]	[ ]	[ ]	[ ]

Please check the box that best describes whether each of the following statements is true or false for you. (Check one box on each line)

		Definitely true (60)	Mostly true (5)	Not sure (10)	Mostly false (15)	Definitely false (20)
17.	I am somewhat ill	[ ]	[ ]	[ ]	[ ]	[ ]
18.	I am as healthy as anybody I know	[ ]	[ ]	[ ]	[ ]	[ ]

	Definitely true (60)	Mostly true (5)	Not sure (10)	Mostly false (15)	Definitely false (20)
19. My health is excellent	[ ]	[ ]	[ ]	[ ]	[ ]
20. I have been feeling bad lately	[ ]	[ ]	[ ]	[ ]	[ ]

MENSTRUAL SYMPTOM QUESTIONNAIRE (MSQ)

AUTHOR: Margaret Chesney

PURPOSE: To measure spasmodic and congestive menstrual pain.

DESCRIPTION: This 25-item instrument is designed to measure two types of menstrual pain: spasmodic, which begins on the first day of menstruation and is experienced as spasms, and congestive, which occurs during the premenstrual cycle and is experienced as heaviness or dull aching pains in abdomen, breasts, and ankles. The MSQ supports the theory that there are two types of dysmenorrhea. The instrument is very useful in classifying types of menstrual pain and selecting appropriate interventions. Since these two types of menstrual pain occur separately, once the client's pain is classified, the half of the items that assess the particular type of dysmenorrhea should be used.

NORMS: The MSQ was developed on a sample of 56 undergraduate college students who described themselves as having menstrual discomfort. Normative data are not presented.

SCORING: On the first 24 items respondents are asked to indicate the degree to which they experience the symptom by selecting one of the five alternatives. Spasmodic items (2, 4, 6, 7, 8, 10, 12, 14, 15, 18, 21, 24) are scored from 1 to 5 for each alternative as indicated on the instrument. Congestive items (1, 3, 5, 9, 11, 13, 16, 17, 19, 20, 22, 23) are reverse-scored. Item 25 is scored by assigning 5 points if the respondent checked Type 1 and 1 point if she checked Type 2. Total scores are the sum of all 25 items. Higher MSQ scores reflect spasmodic menstrual pain, while lower scores reflect congestive menstrual pain. Scores range from 29 to 125 with 77 as a mid-point between the two types of pain. Scores closer to 77 indicate an absence of either type of menstrual pain.

RELIABILITY: Test-retest correlations provide the primary support for reliability. Over a two-week period, items 1 through 24 had a test-retest correlation of .78. The test-retest correlation for item 25, was .93. Total MSQ scores correlated .87 for this same period, indicating that the instrument is stable. No internal consistency data were reported.

VALIDITY: The MSQ was developed from a pool of 51 items. Based on factor analysis, items were included on the MSQ if they had factor loadings of .35 or greater. Twelve items were related to spasmodic pain and 12 were related to congestive pain. Scores on the forced-choice item, number 25, correlated .49 with spasmodic pain scores and −.39 with congestive pain scores, suggesting concurrent validity.

PRIMARY REFERENCE: Chesney, M. A. and Tasto, D. L. (1975). The development of the Menstrual Symptom Questionnaire, *Behaviour Research and*

Therapy, 13, 237–244. Instrument reproduced with permission of Margaret Chesney.

AVAILABILITY: Journal article.

MSQ

For each of the 24 items below please indicate how often you have had the experience, using the following scale. Please record your answers in the space to the left of the items.

1 = Never
2 = Rarely
3 = Sometimes
4 = Often
5 = Always

_____ 1. I feel irritable, easily agitated, and am impatient a few days *before* my period.

_____ 2. I have cramps that *begin* on the first day of my period.

_____ 3. I feel depressed for several days *before* my period.

_____ 4. I have abdominal pain or discomfort which begins one day *before* my period.

_____ 5. For several days *before* my period I feel exhausted, lethargic, or tired.

_____ 6. I only know that my period is coming by looking at the calendar.

_____ 7. I take a prescription drug for the pain *during* my period.

_____ 8. I feel weak and dizzy *during* my period.

_____ 9. I feel tense and nervous *before* my period.

_____ 10. I have diarrhea *during* my period.

_____ 11. I have backaches several days *before* my period.

_____ 12. I take aspirin for the pain *during* my period.

_____ 13. My breasts feel tender and sore a few days *before* my period.

_____ 14. My lower back, abdomen, and the inner sides of my thighs *begin* to hurt or be tender on the first day of my period.

_____ 15. *During* the first day or so of my period, I feel like curling up in bed, using a hot water bottle on my abdomen, or taking a hot bath.

_____ 16. I gain weight *before* my period.

_____ 17. I am constipated *during* my period.

_____ 18. *Beginning* on the first day of my period, I have pains which may diminish or disappear for several minutes and then reappear.

_____ 19. The pain I have with my period is not intense, but a continuous dull aching.

_____ 20. I have abdominal discomfort for more than one day *before* my period.

_____ 21. I have backaches which *begin* the same day as my period.

_____ 22. My abdominal area feels bloated for a few days *before* my period.

_____ 23. I feel nauseous *during* the first day or so of my period.

_____ 24. I have headaches for a few days *before* my period.

For the final question please read each of the two descriptions and indicate the type most closely experienced by you.

25.   TYPE 1   The pain begins on the first day of menstruation, often coming within an hour of the first signs of menstruation. The pain is most severe the first day and may or may not continue on subsequent days. Felt as spasms, the pain may lessen or subside for awhile and then reappear. A few women find this pain so severe as to cause vomiting, fainting or dizziness; some others report that they are most comfortable in bed or taking a hot bath. This pain is limited to the lower abdomen, back and inner sides of the thighs.

      TYPE 2   There is advanced warning of the onset of menstruation during which the woman feels an increasing heaviness, and a dull aching pain in the lower abdomen. This pain is sometimes accompanied by nausea, lack of appetite, and constipation. Headaches, backaches, and breast pain are also characteristic of this type of menstrual discomfort.

                 The type that most closely fits my experience is TYPE____

MICHIGAN ALCOHOLISM SCREENING TEST (MAST)

AUTHOR: Melvin L. Selzer

PURPOSE: To detect alcoholism.

DESCRIPTION: The MAST is a 24-item instrument designed to detect alcoholism. The items on the MAST were selected on the basis of review of several other approaches to investigating alcohol abuse. A few items were developed to be sufficiently neutral that persons reluctant to see themselves as problem drinkers may reveal their alcoholic symptoms. The MAST was developed with the understanding that lack of candor of respondents may be a problem, and was validated in a way that attempted to minimize such failures. Although the MAST was originally designed to be administered orally by professionals and nonprofessionals, it may also be completed by the respondent, although it is not known what effect this may have on its validity. The MAST has been found to be superior as a screening device to a search of records from medical, legal, and social agencies. Where the MAST is used for screening purposes, clinical confirmation is suggested. A short form of 13 items also is available (items 1, 3, 5, 6, 7, 8, 10, 13, 15, 19, 20, 23, and 24).

NORMS: The MAST was administered to several groups: 103 controls, 116 hospitalized alcoholics, 99 people arrested for drunk driving, 110 people arrested for being drunk and disorderly, and 98 people under review for revocation of their driver's licenses because of excessive accidents and moving violations. The groups were largely white and male with mean ages that ranged from 25 to 44 years. Scores on the MAST for all five groups are available in the primary references.

SCORING: Although the scoring of the MAST appears complicated, it is fairly easy once mastered. Each item on the MAST is assigned a weight of 1 to 5, with 5 considered diagnostic of alcoholism. Weights for the items are listed in the left-hand column of the instrument. Negative responses to items 1, 4, 6, and 7 are considered alcoholic responses, and positive responses to the other items are considered alcoholic responses. An overall score of 3 points or less is considered to indicate nonalcoholism, 4 points is suggestive of alcoholism, and 5 points or more indicates alcoholism.

RELIABILITY: The long and short forms of the MAST have excellent internal consistencies, with alphas of .95 and .93, respectively. No data on stability were reported.

VALIDITY: The MAST has excellent known-groups validity, being able to classify most respondents as alcoholic or nonalcoholic; only 15 out of 526 people originally classified as nonalcoholic subsequently were found to be alcoholic. In fact, even when respondents were instructed in advance to lie about their drinking problems, the MAST correctly identified 92% of 99 hospitalized alcoholics as having severe alcoholic problems. Low correlations with the Deny-Bad subscale of the Crowne-Marlowe Social Desirability Scale suggest the effect of denial on MAST scores is weak.

PRIMARY REFERENCES: Selzer, M. L. (1971). The Michigan Alcoholism Screening Test: The quest for a new diagnostic instrument, *American Journal of Psychiatry*, 127, 89–94. Selzer, M. L., Vinokur, A., and van Rooijen, L. (1975). A self-administered Short Michigan Alcoholism Screening Test, *Journal of Studies on Alcohol*, 36, 117–126. Instrument reproduced with permission of *American Journal of Psychiatry*.

AVAILABILITY: Journal article.

MAST

Please circle either Yes or No for each item as it applies to you.

Yes No (2)   1. Do you feel you are a normal drinker?
Yes No (2)   2. Have you ever awakened the morning after some drinking the night before and found that you could not remember a part of the evening before?
Yes No (1)   3. Does your wife, husband, a parent, or other near relative ever worry or complain about your drinking?
Yes No (2)   4. Can you stop drinking without a struggle after one or two drinks?
Yes No (1)   5. Do you ever feel guilty about your drinking?
Yes No (2)   6. Do friends or relatives think you are a normal drinker?
Yes No (2)   7. Are you able to stop drinking when you want to?
Yes No (5)   8. Have you ever attended a meeting of Alcoholics Anonymous (AA)?
Yes No (1)   9. Have you ever gotten into physical fights when drinking?
Yes No (2) 10. Has drinking ever created problems between you and your wife, husband, a parent, or other near relative?
Yes No (2) 11. Has your wife, husband, a parent, or other near relative ever gone to anyone for help about your drinking?
Yes No (2) 12. Have you ever lost friends or girlfriends/boyfriends because of your drinking?
Yes No (2) 13. Have you ever gotten into trouble at work because of drinking?
Yes No (2) 14. Have you ever lost a job because of drinking?
Yes No (2) 15. Have you ever neglected your obligations, your family, or your work for two or more days in a row because you were drinking?
Yes No (1) 16. Do you drink before noon fairly often?
Yes No (2) 17. Have you ever been told you have liver trouble? Cirrhosis?
Yes No (5) 18. After heavy drinking, have you ever had delirium tremens (DTs) or severe shaking, or heard voices, or seen things that weren't really there?
Yes No (5) 19. Have you ever gone to anyone for help about your drinking?
Yes No (5) 20. Have you ever been in a hospital because of drinking?
Yes No (2) 21. Have you ever been a patient in a psychiatric hospital or on a psychiatric ward of a general hospital where drinking was part of the problem that resulted in hospitalization?
Yes No (2) 22. Have you ever been seen at a psychiatric or mental health clinic, or gone to a doctor, social worker, or clergyman for help with any emotional problem where drinking was part of the problem?
Yes No (2) 23. Have you ever been arrested for drunken driving while intoxicated or driving under the influence of alcoholic beverages?
Yes No (2) 24. Have you ever been arrested, even for a few hours, because of other drunken behavior?

MILLER SOCIAL INTIMACY SCALE (MSIS)

AUTHORS: Rickey S. Miller and Herbert M. Lefcourt

PURPOSE: To measure the level of social intimacy.

DESCRIPTION: The MSIS is a 17-item instrument (items 4–20) designed to measure closeness with others. It is based on the findings of several studies that show intimacy to be an important predictor of healthy psychological and physical functioning, especially in regard to marriage, relationships with others, bereavement, and response to stress. The initial item pool of 30 was generated by intensive interviews with university undergraduates; subsequent tests produced the current 17 items, 6 of which are frequency items and 11 of which measure intensity. The MSIS is structured to permit an assessment of intimacy in the context of friendship or marriage.

NORMS: The 252 respondents who participated in the developmental research on the MSIS included 72 male and 116 female unmarried undergraduate students (mean age 21.3 years), 17 (n = 34) married couples (mean age 24.3) who were also students, and a married clinic sample of 15 couples (n = 30) seeking conjoint marital therapy (mean age 36.3 years). Mean scores for the groups were: unmarried males 134.9, unmarried females 139.3, married males 152.5, married females 156.2, clinic males 124.5, and clinic females 133.8.

SCORING: The original instrument, scored on a 10-point scale, has been revised to the 5-point scale reproduced here. Items 1, 2, 3, 21, and 22 are not scored. Items 5 and 17 are reverse-scored, then the individual items are summed (A = 1, E = 5) to produce an overall score for the MSIS, with higher scores indicating greater amounts of social intimacy.

RELIABILITY: The MSIS has excellent internal consistency, with alphas in two samples of .86 and .91. The MSIS is also extremely stable, with a two-month test-retest correlation of .96 and .84 over a one-month interval.

VALIDITY: The MSIS has good known-groups validity, significantly distinguishing between couples seeking marital therapy and those not seeking it, and between married and unmarried students. It also has established construct validity by correlating or not correlating in predicted directions with several other measures such as the UCLA Loneliness Scale, the Interpersonal Relationship Scale, the Tennessee Self-Concept Scale, and the Personality Research Form. Responses on the MSIS are not affected by social desirability response set.

PRIMARY REFERENCE: Miller, R. S. and Lefcourt, H. M. (1982). The assessment of social intimacy, *Journal of Personality Assessment*, 46, 514–518. Instrument reproduced with permission of Rickey S. Miller and Herbert M. Lefcourt.

AVAILABILITY: Dr. Herbert M. Lefcourt, Department of Psychology, University of Waterloo, University Avenue, Waterloo, Ontario, Canada N2L 3G1.

MSIS

A number of phrases are listed below that describe the kind of relationships people have with others. Indicate, by circling the appropriate letters in the answer field, how you would describe your current relationship with your closest friend. This friend can be of either sex and should be someone whom you consider to be your closest friend at this time. While it is not necessary to specify the name of this friend, please indicate his/her sex in question 1.

Remember that you are to indicate the kind of relationship you have *now* with your *closest friend*.

1. Sex of your closest friend: M:_____   F_____

2. Your marital status: single_____   married_____   common-law_____
                           separated or divorced_____   widowed_____

3. Is the friend you describe your spouse?   Yes_____   No_____

		Very rarely		Some of the time		Almost always
4.	When you have leisure time how often do you choose to spend it with him/her alone?	A	B	C	D	E
5.	How often do you keep very personal information to yourself and do not share it with him/her?	A	B	C	D	E
6.	How often do you show him/her affection?	A	B	C	D	E
7.	How often do you confide very personal information to him/her?	A	B	C	D	E
8.	How often are you able to understand his/her feelings?	A	B	C	D	E
9.	How often do you feel close to him/her?	A	B	C	D	E

		Not much		A little		A great deal
10.	How much do you like to spend time alone with him/her?	A	B	C	D	E
11.	How much do you feel like being encouraging and supportive to him/her when he/she is unhappy?	A	B	C	D	E
12.	How close do you feel to him/her most of the time?	A	B	C	D	E
13.	How important is it to you to listen to his/her personal disclosures?	A	B	C	D	E
14.	How satisfying is your relationship with him/her?	A	B	C	D	E
15.	How affectionate do you feel towards him/her?	A	B	C	D	E
16.	How important is it to you that he/she understand your feelings?	A	B	C	D	E
17.	How much damage is caused by a typical disagreement in your relationship with him/her?	A	B	C	D	E
18.	How important is it to you that he/she be encouraging and supportive to you when you are unhappy?	A	B	C	D	E
19.	How important is it to you that he/she show you affection?	A	B	C	D	E
20.	How important is your relationship with him/her in your life?	A	B	C	D	E

21. You have just described the relationship you have now with your closest friend. We are interested in knowing *how long* this person has been your closest friend. Please check the appropriate category:
        less than a month _____ 1–4 months _____ 5–8 months _____
        9–12 months _____ over a year _____

22. Recall your *previous* closest friend. Are you less close _____ just as close _____ or closer _____ with the current friend you described on this scale?

MISSISSIPPI SCALE (MS)

AUTHORS: Terrance Keane, J. M. Caddell, and K. L. Taylor

PURPOSE: To assess combat-related posttraumatic stress disorder.

DESCRIPTION: The MS is a 35-item instrument designed to measure posttraumatic stress disorder (PTSD) resulting from combat. The MS covers the full domain of PTSD symptoms and various associated features as delineated in the DSM-III-R. Factor analysis suggests the MS assesses six aspects of combat-related PTSD: intrusive memories and depression, problems with interpersonal adjustment, lability of affect and memory, ruminative features, problems sleeping, and other interpersonal problems. The MS is also available in forms appropriate for spouses and civilians.

NORMS: Means and standard deviations are available from three samples of Vietnam veterans: combat veterans with PTSD (*n* = 30), noncombat psychiatric patients (*n* = 30), and well-adjusted veterans (*n* = 32). The means (and standard deviations) are 130 (18), 86 (26), and 76 (18) for the respective three samples.

SCORING: Items 2, 6, 11, 17, 19, 22, 24, 27, 30, and 34 are reverse-scored. Total scores are the sum of all item scores. Scores range from 35 to 175 with higher scores reflecting higher PTSD symptoms.

RELIABILITY: The MS has excellent reliability. The alpha coefficient of internal consistency is .94 and the average item-to-total correlation is .58. Test-retest reliability over a one-week period is .97.

VALIDITY: The MS has some evidence of concurrent validity. Scores on the MS correlated .25 with combat exposure, which may seem low but may suggest there is a threshold of exposure sufficient to become the antecedent of PTSD. From this perspective, a correlation of this magnitude is acceptable. The MS has excellent evidence of known-groups validity, with scores differentiating PTSD patients from psychiatric patients and a well-adjusted sample; MS scores correctly classified 90% of the subjects. There was agreement between the MS and the structured clinical interview of the DSM-III-R, with a coefficient of agreement (kappa) of .75. The concordance rate between the MS and diagnosis in the community was .53, indicating a greater likelihood of a false positive score with the MS (i.e., failing to identify a patient who indeed is suffering from PTSD).

PRIMARY REFERENCE: Keane, T. M., Caddell, J. M., and Taylor K. L. (1988) Mississippi Scale for combat-related posttraumatic stress disorder: Three studies in reliability and validity, *Journal of Consulting and Clinical Psychology*, 56, 85–90. Instrument reproduced with permission of Terrance Keane.

AVAILABILITY: Terrance Keane, Ph.D., National Center for PTSD, V.A. Medical Center, 150 S. Huntington Avenue, Boston, MA 02130.

MS

Please circle the number that best describes how you feel about each statement.

1. Before I entered the military, I had more close friends than I have now.

1	2	3	4	5
Not at all true	Slightly true	Somewhat true	Very true	Extremely true

2. I do not feel guilt over things that I did in the military.

1	2	3	4	5
Never true	Rarely true	Sometimes true	Usually true	Always true

3. If someone pushes me too far, I am likely to become violent.

1	2	3	4	5
Very unlikely	Unlikely	Somewhat unlikely	Very likely	Extremely likely

4. If something happens that reminds me of the military, I become very distressed and upset.

1	2	3	4	5
Never	Rarely	Sometimes	Frequently	Very frequently

5. The people who know me best are afraid of me.

1	2	3	4	5
Never true	Rarely true	Sometimes true	Usually true	Always true

6. I am able to get emotionally close to others.

1	2	3	4	5
Never	Rarely	Sometimes	Frequently	Very frequently

7. I have nightmares over experiences in the military that really happened.

1	2	3	4	5
Never	Rarely	Sometimes	Frequently	Very frequently

8.   When I think of some of the things I did in the military, I wish I were dead.

1	2	3	4	5
Never true	Rarely true	Sometimes true	Usually true	Always true

9.   It seems as if I have no feelings.

1	2	3	4	5
Not at all true	Slightly true	Somewhat true	Very true	Extremely true

10.   Lately, I have felt like killing myself.

1	2	3	4	5
Not at all true	Slightly true	Somewhat true	Very true	Extremely true

11.   I fall asleep, stay asleep, and awaken only when the alarm goes off.

1	2	3	4	5
Never	Rarely	Sometimes	Frequently	Very frequently

12.   I wonder why I am still alive when others died in the military.

1	2	3	4	5
Never	Rarely	Sometimes	Frequently	Very frequently

13.   Being in certain situations makes me feel as though I am back in the military.

1	2	3	4	5
Never	Rarely	Sometimes	Frequently	Very frequently

14.   My dreams at night are so real that I waken in a cold sweat and force myself to stay awake.

1	2	3	4	5
Never	Rarely	Sometimes	Frequently	Very frequently

15. I feel like I cannot go on.

1	2	3	4	5
Not at all true	Slightly true	Somewhat true	Very true	Extremely true

16. I do not laugh or cry at the same things other people do.

1	2	3	4	5
Not at all true	Slightly true	Somewhat true	Very true	Extremely true

17. I still enjoy doing many things that I used to enjoy.

1	2	3	4	5
Never true	Rarely true	Sometimes true	Usually true	Always true

18. Daydreams are very real and frightening.

1	2	3	4	5
Never true	Rarely true	Sometimes true	Usually true	Always true

19. I have found it easy to keep a job since my separation from the military.

1	2	3	4	5
Not at all true	Slightly true	Somewhat true	Very true	Extremely true

20. I have trouble concentrating on tasks.

1	2	3	4	5
Never true	Rarely true	Sometimes true	Usually true	Always true

21. I have cried for no good reason.

1	2	3	4	5
Never	Rarely	Sometimes	Frequently	Very frequently

22. I enjoy the company of others.

1	2	3	4	5
Never	Rarely	Sometimes	Frequently	Very frequently

23. I am frightened by my urges.

1	2	3	4	5
Never	Rarely	Sometimes	Frequently	Very frequently

24. I fall asleep easily at night.

1	2	3	4	5
Never	Rarely	Sometimes	Frequently	Very frequently

25. Unexpected noises make me jump.

1	2	3	4	5
Never	Rarely	Sometimes	Frequently	Very frequently

26. No one understands how I feel, not even my family.

1	2	3	4	5
Not at all true	Slightly true	Somewhat true	Very true	Extremely true

27. I am an easy-going, even-tempered person.

1	2	3	4	5
Never	Rarely	Sometimes	Frequently	Very frequently

28. I feel there are certain things that I did in the military that I can never tell anyone, because no one would ever understand.

1	2	3	4	5
Not at all true	Slightly true	Somewhat true	Very true	Extremely true

29. There have been times when I used alcohol (or other drugs) to help me sleep or to make me forget about things that happened while I was in the service.

1	2	3	4	5
Never	Rarely	Sometimes	Frequently	Very frequently

30. I feel comfortable when I am in a crowd.

1	2	3	4	5
Never	Rarely	Sometimes	Frequently	Very frequently

31. I lose my cool and explode over minor everyday things.

1	2	3	4	5
Never	Rarely	Sometimes	Frequently	Very frequently

32. I am afraid to go to sleep at night.

1	2	3	4	5
Never	Rarely	Sometimes	Frequently	Very frequently

33. I try to stay away from anything that will remind me of things which happened while I was in the military.

1	2	3	4	5
Never	Rarely	Sometimes	Frequently	Very frequently

34. My memory is as good as it ever was.

1	2	3	4	5
Not at all true	Slightly true	Somewhat true	Very true	Extremely true

35. I have a hard time expressing my feelings, even to the people I care about.

1	2	3	4	5
Not at all true	Slightly true	Somewhat true	Very true	Extremely true

MOBILITY INVENTORY FOR AGORAPHOBIA (MI)

AUTHORS: Dianne L. Chambless, G. Craig Caputo, Susan E. Jasin, Edward J. Gracely, and Christine Williams

PURPOSE: To measure severity of agoraphobic avoidance behavior.

DESCRIPTION: The MI is a 27-item instrument designed to measure agoraphobic avoidance behavior and frequency of panic attacks. Twenty-six of the items measure avoidance, with each item rated for avoidance both when the client is alone and when accompanied. The final item gives a definition of panic and asks the respondent to report the number of panic experiences during the previous week. The MI was developed by using items from the Fear Survey Schedule, items obtained in interviews with agoraphobic clients, and from observations of avoidance behavior and panic attacks in agoraphobic clients. The MI provides clinically useful information both in total score form as well as in interpretation of scores on individual items.

NORMS: Two samples were used in development of the MI. The first consisted of 159 clients applying for treatment at a clinic specializing in agoraphobia and anxiety (88% female, mean age 34.6) and 23 nonagoraphobic controls with similar demographic characteristics. The second sample involved 83 agoraphobic clients, including significantly more males. Norms for all of these groups on each item are available in the primary reference. When averaged across all situations, the mean score for agoraphobics for avoidance when accompanied ranges from 2.41 to 2.64 and the mean score for avoidance when alone ranges from 3.30 to 3.35

SCORING: Each item on the MI is scored on a 1 to 5 basis and each item can be interpreted independently. The MI does not use a mean score averaged across all situations for avoidance when accompanied by another and avoidance when alone. To derive these scores simply add the rating for the "when accompanied" column and divide by the number of items answered. Do the same procedures for the items in the "when alone" column.

RELIABILITY: The MI has excellent internal consistency, with alphas that range from .91 to .97. The MI also has excellent stability, with overall test-retest reliabilities over 31 days of .89 and .90 for avoidance when alone and .75 and .86 for avoidance when accompanied.

VALIDITY: The MI has very good concurrent validity, correlating significantly with the agoraphobic factor of the Fear Questionnaire, the Beck Depression Inventory, and the Trait form of the State-Trait Anxiety Inventory. The MI also has good known-groups validity, significantly distinguishing between agoraphobic and non-clinical and social phobic respondents. Finally, the MI also has been found in two studies to be sensitive to changes following treatment for agoraphobia.

PRIMARY REFERENCE: Chambless, D. L., Caputo, G. C., Jasin, S. E., Gracely, E. J., and Williams, C. (1985). The Mobility Inventory for Agoraphobia, *Behavioral Research and Therapy*, 23, 35–44. Instrument reproduced with permission of Pergamon Press.
AVAILABILITY: Journal article.

MI

Please indicate the degree to which you avoid the following places or situations because of discomfort or anxiety. Rate your amount of avoidance when you are with a trusted companion and when you are alone. Do this by using the following scale.

1 = Never avoid
2 = Rarely avoid
3 = Avoid about half the time
4 = Avoid most of the time
5 = Always avoid

(You may use numbers halfway between those listed when you think it is appropriate. For example, 3-1/2 or 4-1/2.)

Write your score in the blanks for each situation or place under both conditions: when accompanied, and when alone. Leave blank those situations that do not apply to you.

Places	When accompanied	When alone
Theaters	_____	_____
Supermarkets	_____	_____
Classrooms	_____	_____
Department stores	_____	_____
Restaurants	_____	_____
Museums	_____	_____
Elevators	_____	_____
Auditoriums or stadiums	_____	_____
Parking garages	_____	_____
High places	_____	_____
Tell how high _____	_____	_____
Enclosed spaces (e.g., tunnels)	_____	_____
Open spaces	_____	_____
Outside (e.g., fields, wide streets, courtyards)	_____	_____
Inside (e.g., large rooms, lobbies)	_____	_____
Riding in:		

Places	When accompanied	When alone
Buses	_____	_____
Trains	_____	_____
Subways	_____	_____
Airplanes	_____	_____
Boats	_____	_____
Driving or riding in car:		
At any time	_____	_____
On expressways	_____	_____
Situations:		
Standing in lines	_____	_____
Crossing bridges	_____	_____
Parties or social gatherings	_____	_____
Walking on the street	_____	_____
Staying at home alone	NA	_____
Being far way from home	_____	_____
Other (specify)	_____	_____

We define a *panic attack* as:
  (1) a high level of anxiety accompanied by
  (2) strong body reactions (heart palpitations, sweating, muscle tremors, dizziness, nausea) with
  (3) the temporary loss of the ability to plan, think, or reason and
  (4) the intense desire to escape or flee the situation. (Note, this is different from high anxiety or fear alone.)

Please indicate the total number of panic attacks you have had in the last 7 days. _____

MOOD-RELATED PLEASANT EVENTS SCHEDULE
(MRPES)

AUTHORS: Douglas J. MacPhillamy and Peter M. Lewinsohn

PURPOSE: To measure frequency and enjoyment of pleasant events.

DESCRIPTION: The MRPES is a 49-item instrument designed to measure how frequently one engages in pleasant events and how much enjoyment one derives from those events. As part of the 320-item Pleasant Event Schedule (PES), the MRPES contains events that are related to mood. The frequency and enjoyment scores may be used separately or by multiplying the frequency by the enjoyment to create a product score. In addition to these total scores, the MRPES has two useful subscales, the pleasant social interactions subscale (items 12, 14, 15, 42, and 49) and the competence and independence subscale (items 11, 19, 25, 28, 33, 35, and 45). The MRPES is useful in identifying pleasant events that may serve as reinforcement in behavior therapy and as an assessment of change in enjoyment, as would be relevant when working with a person who is depressed.

NORMS: Normative data are available for males and females from a sample of 464 normal adults. The mean frequency score for males was 1.31 with a standard deviation of .27. For females, the mean and standard deviation were 1.37 and .25, respectively. For males, total enjoyment scores had a mean and standard deviation of 1.47 and .29, respectively; for females, 1.54 and .26. The mean and standard deviation of the total product score were 2.06 and .63 for males and 2.18 and .59 for females.

SCORING: The frequency and enjoyment scores are derived by simply summing the item scores and dividing by the total number of items. Product scores are derived by multiplying the item frequency score by the enjoyment score, summing the results, and dividing by the number of items. Computerized scoring procedures are available from the authors. Frequency and enjoyment scores have a range of 0 to 2 and product scores have a range of 0 to 4. Higher scores reflect more frequent participation in pleasant events and more enjoyment derived from those events.

RELIABILITY: Internal consistency information is not available for the MRPES, but is reported for the 320-item PES. This longer version has excellent internal consistency, with alpha coefficients of .96, .98, and .97 for the frequency, enjoyment, and product scores, respectively. Test-retest reliability is available for the MRPES for one-month (.69), two-month (.49), and three-month (.50) periods. The test-retest reliability suggests adequate stability for the MRPES.

VALIDITY: Most of the validity data available examine the 320-item PES, which has excellent construct and concurrent validity. The 320-item PES also has known-groups validity, with scores discriminating people who are depressed from those who are not. The MRPES itself seems slightly affected by an irrelevant response set, most likely a "yea-saying" response set. Scoring procedures are available from the authors which help minimize this limitation.

PRIMARY REFERENCE: MacPhillamy, D. J. and Lewinsohn, P. M. (1982). The Pleasant Events Schedule: Studies on reliability, validity and scale inter-correlation, *Journal of Consulting and Clinical Psychology*, 50, 363–380. Instrument reproduced with permission of Peter Lewinsohn.

AVAILABILITY: Peter M. Lewinsohn, Ph.D., Research Scientist, Oregon Research Institute, 1715 Franklin Blvd., Eugene, OR 97403-1983.

MRPES

This schedule is designed to find out about the things you have enjoyed during the past month. The schedule contains a list of events or activities that people some-times enjoy. You will be asked to go over the list twice, the first time rating each event on how many times it has happened in the past month and the second time rating each event on how pleasant it has been for you. Please rate every event. There are no right or wrong answers.

Below is a list of activities, events, and experiences. HOW OFTEN HAVE THESE EVENTS HAPPENED IN YOUR LIFE IN THE PAST MONTH? Please answer this question by rating each item on the following scale:

0 = This has not happened in the past 30 days.
1 = This has happened *a few times* (1 to 6) in the past 30 days.
2 = This has happened *often* (7 or more) in the past 30 days.

Place your rating in the space to the far left of the item, under the column headed "Frequency." Important: Some items will list *more than one event*; for those items, mark how often you have done *any* of the listed events.

Frequency Enjoyment

_____	_____	1.	Being in the country
_____	_____	2.	Meeting someone new of the same sex
_____	_____	3.	Planning trips or vacations
_____	_____	4.	Reading stories, novels, poems, or plays
_____	_____	5.	Driving skillfully
_____	_____	6.	Breathing clean air
_____	_____	7.	Saying something clearly
_____	_____	8.	Thinking about something good in the future
_____	_____	9.	Laughing
_____	_____	10.	Being with animals
_____	_____	11.	Having a frank and open conversation
_____	_____	12.	Going to a party
_____	_____	13.	Combing or brushing my hair
_____	_____	14.	Being with friends
_____	_____	15.	Being popular at a gathering
_____	_____	16.	Watching wild animals
_____	_____	17.	Sitting in the sun
_____	_____	18.	Seeing good things happen to my family or friends
_____	_____	19.	Planning or organizing something
_____	_____	20.	Having a lively talk
_____	_____	21.	Having friends come to visit
_____	_____	22.	Wearing clean clothes
_____	_____	23.	Seeing beautiful scenery
_____	_____	24.	Eating good food
_____	_____	25.	Doing a good job
_____	_____	26.	Having spare time

Frequency Enjoyment

Frequency	Enjoyment		
_____	_____	27.	Being noticed as sexually attractive
_____	_____	28.	Learning to do something new
_____	_____	29.	Complimenting or praising someone
_____	_____	30.	Thinking about people I like
_____	_____	31.	Kissing
_____	_____	32.	Feeling the presence of the Lord in my life
_____	_____	33.	Doing a project in my own way
_____	_____	34.	Having peace and quiet
_____	_____	35.	Being relaxed
_____	_____	36.	Sleeping soundly at night
_____	_____	37.	Petting, necking
_____	_____	38.	Amusing people
_____	_____	39.	Being with someone I love
_____	_____	40.	Having sexual relations with a partner
_____	_____	41.	Watching people
_____	_____	42.	Being with happy people
_____	_____	43.	Smiling at people
_____	_____	44.	Being with my husband or wife
_____	_____	45.	Having people show interest in what I have said
_____	_____	46.	Having coffee, tea, a Coke, etc., with friends
_____	_____	47.	Being complimented or told I have done well
_____	_____	48.	Being told I am loved
_____	_____	49.	Seeing old friends

Now please go over the list once again. This time the question is, HOW PLEASANT, ENJOYABLE, OR REWARDING WAS EACH EVENT DURING THE PAST MONTH? Please answer this question by rating each event on the following scale:

0 = This was *not* pleasant. (Use this rating for events
that were either neutral or unpleasant.)
1 = This event was *somewhat* pleasant. (Use this rating
for events that were *mildly* or *moderately* pleasant.)
2 = This event was *very* pleasant. (Use this rating for
events that were *strongly or extremely* pleasant.)

Important: If an event has happened to you *more than once* in the past month, try to rate roughly how pleasant it was *on the average.* If an event has *not* happened to you during the past month, then rate it according to how much fun you *think* it would have been. (If you haven't done any of the events in such an item, give it the average rating of the events in that item which you *would like to have done.*)

Place your ratings in the space immediately to the left of each item, under the column headed "Enjoyment." Now go back to the list of events, start with item 1, and go through the entire list rating each event on *roughly how pleasant it was (or would have been) during the past 30 days.* Please make sure that you rate each item.

MOOD SURVEY (MS)

AUTHORS: Bill Underwood and William J. Froming

PURPOSE: To measure happy and sad moods.

DESCRIPTION: The MS is an 18-item instrument that assesses happy and sad moods as traits, that is, as long-term personality characteristics. Happy and sad moods are treated as endpoints on a continuum in an attempt to identify people who differ in average mood level taken over a long period of time. Conceptual analysis of moods suggested three dimensions on which initial construction of the MS was based: the average level of a person's mood, frequency of mood change, and the intensity with which people react to mood experiences. The MS actually possesses two primary subscales: level of mood (LM) and reactivity to situations (RS).

NORMS: Several studies were carried out to identify the psychometric properties of the MS. All were based on undergraduate students in an introductory psychology class (796 females and 591 males). No additional demographic data were reported nor were specific norms.

SCORING: Individual item scores on the 6-point Likert scales are simply totaled along with the responses to three questions asking respondents to estimate mood level, frequency of mood change, and intensity of mood reactions on 99-point scales. The LM subscale consists of items 2, 4, 6, 8, 10, 11, 13, 15, and 16 with items 6, 11, 13, and 15 reverse-scored. The RS subscale consists of items 1, 5, 7, 9, 12, 14, 17, and 18 with items 5, 9, and 14 reverse-scored.

RELIABILITY: Test-retest reliability over three weeks is .80 for the level subscale and .85 for reactivity, indicating good stability. For a seven-week period, test-retest reliability was .63 for level and .83 for reactivity. No data on internal consistency were available.

VALIDITY: The MS has good concurrent validity, correlating significantly with a number of other measures such as the Beck Depression Inventory and the Mood Adjective Checklist. The MS also showed stronger correlations with personality measures than did other, state measures of mood. Further, the subscales of the MS were found to correlate or not correlate in the predicted directions with other mood scales, establishing a form of construct validity.

PRIMARY REFERENCE: Underwood, B. and Froming, W. J. (1980). The Mood Survey: A personality measure of happy and sad moods, *Journal of Personality Assessment*, 44, 404–414. Instrument reproduced with permission of William J. Froming and *Journal of Personality Assessment*.

AVAILABILITY: Dr. William J. Froming, Department of Psychology, University of Florida, Gainesville, FL 32611.

MS

Below are a number of statements about your experience of moods. We would like you to consider your usual behavior when you respond. Using the scale, indicate the appropriate number to the left of each question and try to be as honest as you can.

1 = Strongly disagree
2 = Moderately disagree
3 = Somewhat disagree
4 = Somewhat agree
5 = Moderately agree
6 = Strongly agree

_____ 1. I may change from happy to sad and back again several times in a single week.
_____ 2. I usually feel quite cheerful.
_____ 3. I'm frequently "down in the dumps."
_____ 4. I generally look at the sunny side of life.
_____ 5. Compared to my friends, I'm less up and down in my mood states.
_____ 6. I'm not often really elated.
_____ 7. Sometimes my moods swing back and forth very rapidly.
_____ 8. I usually feel as though I'm bubbling over with joy.
_____ 9. My moods are quite consistent; they almost never vary.
_____ 10. I consider myself a happy person.
_____ 11. Compared to my friends, I think less positively about life in general.
_____ 12. I'm a very changeable person.
_____ 13. I am not as cheerful as most people.
_____ 14. I'm not as "moody" as most people I know.
_____ 15. My friends often seem to feel I am unhappy.
_____ 16. If 1 = extremely sad, 50 = neutral, and 99 = extremely happy, how happy are you in general?
_____ 17. If 1 = hardly ever and 99 = extremely frequently, how frequently do your moods change?
_____ 18. If 1 = not at all and 99 = extremely intensely, how intensely do you react to mood experiences?

MULTIDIMENSIONAL BODY-SELF RELATIONS
QUESTIONNAIRE (MBSRQ)

AUTHOR: Thomas F. Cash

PURPOSE: To measure body image.

DESCRIPTION: The MBSRQ is a 69-item instrument designed to measure self-attitudinal aspects of the body-image construct. The MBSRQ contains a number of subscales based on factor analysis: appearance evaluation (AE: items 5, 11, 21, 30, 39, *42, *48), appearance orientation (AO: items 1, 2, 12, 13, 22, *23, 31, *32, *40, 41, *49, 50), fitness evaluation (FE: items 24, *33, 51), fitness orientation (FO: items 3, 4, *6, 14, *15, *16, *25, 26, *34, 35, *43, 44, 53), health evaluation (HE: items 7, *17, 27, *30, *45, 54), health orientation (HO: items 8, 9, 18, 19, *28, 29, *38, 52), illness orientation (IO: items *37, 46, *47, 55, 56), body areas satisfaction (BAS: items 61–68), subjective weight (SW: items 59 and 60), and weight preoccupation (WP: items 10, 28, 57, 58). The MBSRQ offers a wide range of information that can be useful in assessing a number of dimensions of body image.

NORMS: The MBSRQ was studied with a sample of 2066 (996 males, 1070 females) based upon a stratified random sample of the U.S. population. The means for the factors described above are as follows: AE—males 3.49, females 3.36; AO—males 3.60, females 3.91; FE—males 3.72, females 3.48; FO—males 3.41, females 3.20; HE—males 3.95, females 3.86; HO—males 3.61, females 3.75; IO—males 3.18, females 3.21; BAS—males 4.12, females 3.80; SW—males 3.26, females 3.53; WP—males 9.87, females 12.14.

SCORING: All items with asterisks as noted above are reverse-scored, then items on the respective factors are summed for the subscale scores. Subjective weight is scored by summing items 59 and 60 and dividing by 2. Weight preoccupation is scored by summing items 10, 20, 57, 58 and dividing by 4.

RELIABILITY: The first seven factors of the MBSRQ have very good internal consistency, with alphas that range from .75 to .90. All subscales have good to excellent stability, with test-retest correlations that range from .49 to .91.

VALIDITY: The MBSRQ has demonstrated its validity in numerous studies in which subscales have been correlated with a number of other health and body image instruments.

PRIMARY REFERENCE: Cash, T. F. and Pruzinsky, T. (eds.). (1990). *Body Images: Development, Deviance and Change*. New York: Guilford.

AVAILABILITY: Dr. Thomas Cash, Department of Psychology, Old Dominion University, Norfolk, VA 23529.

MBSRQ

The following pages contain a series of statements about how people might think, feel, or behave. You are asked to indicate *the extent to which each statement pertains to you personally.*

Your answers to the items in the questionnaire are anonymous, so please do not write your name on any of the materials. In order to complete the questionnaire, read each statement carefully and decide how much it pertains to you personally. Using the scale below, indicate your answer by entering it to the left of the number of the statement.

1	2	3	4	5
Definitely disagree	Mostly disagree	Neither agree nor disagree	Mostly agree	Definitely agree

There are no right or wrong answers. Just give the answer that is most accurate for you. Remember, your responses are anonymous, so please be *completely honest*. Please give an answer to all of the items.

_____ 1. Before going out in public, I always notice how I look.
_____ 2. I am careful to buy clothes that will make me look my best.
_____ 3. I would pass most physical-fitness tests.
_____ 4. It is important that I have superior physical strength.
_____ 5. My body is sexually appealing.
_____ 6. I am not involved in a regular exercise program.
_____ 7. I am in control of my health.
_____ 8. I know a lot about things that affect my physical health.
_____ 9. I have deliberately developed a healthy life-style.
_____ 10. I constantly worry about being or becoming fat.
_____ 11. I like my looks just the way they are.
_____ 12. I check my appearance in a mirror whenever I can.
_____ 13. Before going out, I usually spend a lot of time getting ready.
_____ 14. My physical endurance is good.
_____ 15. Participating in sports is unimportant to me.
_____ 16. I do not actively do things to keep physically fit.
_____ 17. My health is a matter of unexpected ups and downs.
_____ 18. Good health is one of the most important things in my life.
_____ 19. I don't do anything that I know might threaten my health.
_____ 20. I am very conscious of even small changes in my weight.
_____ 21. Most people would consider me good looking.
_____ 22. It is important that I always look good.
_____ 23. I use very few grooming products.
_____ 24. I easily learn physical skills.
_____ 25. Being physically fit is not a strong priority in my life.
_____ 26. I do things to increase my physical strength.
_____ 27. I am seldom physically ill.
_____ 28. I take my health for granted.

_____ 29.   I often read books and magazines that pertain to health.
_____ 30.   I like the way I look without my clothes.
_____ 31.   I am self-conscious if my grooming isn't right.
_____ 32.   I usually wear whatever is handy without caring how it looks.
_____ 33.   I do poorly in physical sports or games.
_____ 34.   I seldom think about my athletic skills.
_____ 35.   I work to improve my physical stamina.
_____ 36.   From day to day, I never know how my body will feel.
_____ 37.   If I am sick, I don't pay much attention to my symptoms.
_____ 38.   I make no special effort to eat a balanced and nutritious diet.
_____ 39.   I like the way my clothes fit me.
_____ 40.   I don't care what people think about my appearance.
_____ 41.   I take special care with my hair grooming.
_____ 42.   I dislike my physique.
_____ 43.   I don't care to improve my abilities in physical activities.
_____ 44.   I try to be physically active.
_____ 45.   I often feel vulnerable to sickness.
_____ 46.   I pay close attention to my body for any signs of illness.
_____ 47.   If I'm coming down with a cold or flu, I just ignore it and go on as usual.
_____ 48.   I am physically unattractive.
_____ 49.   I never think about my appearance.
_____ 50.   I am always trying to improve my physical appearance.
_____ 51.   I am very well coordinated.
_____ 52.   I know a lot about physical fitness.
_____ 53.   I play a sport regularly throughout the year.
_____ 54.   I am a physically healthy person.
_____ 55.   I am very aware of small changes in my physical health.
_____ 56.   At the first sign of illness, I seek medical advice.
_____ 57.   I am on a weight-loss diet.

For the remainder of the items use the response scale given with the item, and enter your answer in the space beside the item.

_____ 58.   I have tried to lose weight by fasting or going on crash diets.

     1.   Never
     2.   Rarely
     3.   Sometimes
     4.   Often
     5.   Very often

_____ 59.   I think I am:

     1.   Very underweight
     2.   Somewhat underweight
     3.   Normal weight
     4.   Somewhat overweight
     5.   Very overweight

____ 60.   From looking at me, most other people would think I am:

        1.   Very underweight
        2.   Somewhat underweight
        3.   Normal weight
        4.   Somewhat overweight
        5.   Very overweight

61–69.   Use this 1–5 scale to indicate how satisfied you are with each of the following areas of your body:

1	2	3	4	5
Very dissatisfied	Mostly dissatisfied	Neither satisfied nor dissatisfied	Mostly satisfied	Very satisfied

____ 61.   Face (facial features, complexion)
____ 62.   Hair (color, thickness, texture)
____ 63.   Lower torso (buttocks, hips, thighs, legs)
____ 64.   Mid torso (waist, stomach)
____ 65.   Upper torso (chest or breasts, shoulders, arms)
____ 66.   Muscle tone
____ 67.   Weight
____ 68.   Height
____ 69.   Overall appearance

MULTIDIMENSIONAL DESIRE FOR CONTROL SCALES (MDCS)

AUTHOR: Lynda A. Anderson

PURPOSE: To measure desire for control in clinical health care interactions.

DESCRIPTION: This 17-item instrument is designed to measure three dimensions of clients' desire for control in clinical interactions, which is considered facilitative in promoting effective patient-health care. While the development of the MDCS was based on patients in diabetes management, the instrument has utility in other health care contexts. It helps determine whether one's patient prefers a prescriptive clinician-directed clinical interaction or a participatory role in his or her health care. The MDCS assesses three dimensions of control: personal control (PC), clinician control (CC), and shared control (SC) between patient and clinician.

NORMS: Normative data are available for three samples of males in treatment for non–insulin dependent diabetes mellitus. The three samples had ns of 110, 50, and 109; for all three samples, the majority of respondents were African-American. For the sample of 110 men, the PC, CC, and SC have the following means and standard deviations: 2.20 (SD = .95), 4.19 (SD = .78), 4.02 (SD = .99), respectively. The sample of 50 had the following means and standard deviations for PC, CC, and SC: 2.14 (SD = 1.01); 4.11 (SD = .88); and 4.06 (SD = .97). The sample of 109 had similar scores.

SCORING: Each item is rated on a 7-point Likert-type scale ranging from "strongly agree" to "strongly disagree." The three scales are the sum of each item score as follows: PC = 5 + 9 + 10 + 12 + 13 + 15 + 16; CC = 1 + 2 + 3 + 4 + 8 + 11; SC = 6 + 7 + 14 + 17. Lower scores reflect more control by the patient, clinician, or shared control by patient and clinician.

RELIABILITY: Internal consistency of the MDCS is fair to good. For the sample of 110 patients, the alpha coefficients were .79, .76, .75 for PC, CC, and SC respectively. For the sample of 109 the alpha coefficients were .81, .80, and .75 for the three scales. Data on stability were not available.

VALIDITY: The MDCS has good factorial validity supported by an exploratory factor analysis on the sample of 110 patients and a confirmatory factor analysis from the sample of 109 patients. Concurrent validity is evidenced by correlations with the Multidimensional Health Locus of Control Scales. The PC was slightly associated with social desirability, although social desirability was uncorrelated with scores on the CC and SC. PC scores also correlated with a measure of the role of patient while the CC and SC correlated with scores on a measure of the role of the doctor, and shared roles between the patient and clinician. The PC correlated with measures of affective and behavioral satisfaction, and CC scores correlated with affective, behavioral, and cognitive satisfaction. The SC was unassociated with satisfaction.

PRIMARY REFERENCE: Anderson, L. A., DeVellis, R. F., Boyles, B., and Feussner, J. R. (1989). Patients' perception of their clinical interactions: Development of the Multidimensional Desire for Control Scales, *Health Education Research*, 4, 383–397.

AVAILABILITY: Lynda A. Anderson, Ph.D., University of Michigan, School of Public Health, 1420 Washington Heights, Ann Arbor, MI 48109-2029.

MDCS

The following items ask about your beliefs regarding your clinical care. Please answer each item by rating your degree of agreement or disagreement using the following scale, and record your answer in the space to the left of each item.

1 = Strongly agree
2 = Somewhat agree
3 = Slightly agree
4 = Neither agree nor disagree
5 = Slightly disagree
6 = Somewhat disagree
7 = Strongly disagree

_____ 1. The doctor, not I, will decide what information I receive about my medical care.

_____ 2. The doctor will make the decisions for me regarding a treatment program for my diabetes.

_____ 3. The doctor, not I, will direct my medical care.

_____ 4. I will defer decisions about my treatment to the expert advice of the doctor.

_____ 5. I, not the doctor, will decide what type of diet program I need to follow.

_____ 6. The doctor and I will make decisions about my medical care together, on an equal basis.

_____ 7. The doctor and I will be equal partners in establishing the treatment goals for my illness.

_____ 8. The doctor will try to influence the choices I make about my treatment program.

_____ 9. I, not the doctor, will decide what information I get about my treatment program.

_____ 10. If my diabetes gets out of control, I will decide what should be done to change my treatment program.

_____ 11. The doctor, not I, will begin discussions of my laboratory test results.

_____ 12. I will decide the best way to meet my treatment goals, regardless of how they are established.

_____ 13. I will decide what my medical care program is going to be.

_____ 14. The doctor and I will supervise my treatment program together.

_____ 15. I, not the doctor, will be in charge of my medical care.

_____ 16. Even in a medical crisis, I will make the decision about my medical care.

_____ 17. The doctor will give me a choice about what glucose testing method I should use at home.

MULTIDIMENSIONAL HEALTH LOCUS OF CONTROL SCALES
(MHLC)

AUTHORS: Kenneth A. Wallston, Barbara Studler Wallston, and Robert DeVellis

PURPOSE: To measure locus of control of health-related behavior.

DESCRIPTION: This 18-item instrument measures three dimensions of locus of control of reinforcement as it pertains to health. Specifically, the MHLC assesses people's belief that their health is or is not determined by their own behavior. These issues of internal and external control have been extensively studied in regard to numerous clinical problems. The MHLC looks at beliefs about three sources of control over health, with each subscale containing six items: internality of health locus of control (IHLC), powerful other locus of control (POLC), and chance locus of control (CHLC). The MHLC has parallel forms (Forms A and B) designed to be alternated for use as repeated measures, or the two forms may be combined to create longer (12 items) and more reliable subscales. Further information on scoring and application of the scales is available from the authors.

NORMS: Normative data are available on samples of chronic patients (*n* = 609), college students (*n* = 749), healthy adults (*n* = 1287) and persons involved in preventive health behaviors (*n* = 720). The IHLC, CHLC, and POLC scales had average scores of 25.78, 17.64, and 22.54 for the chronic patients, and 26.68, 16.72, and 17.87 for college students. Healthy adults had average scores of 25.55, 16.21, and 19.16 for the IHLC, CHLC, and POLC, respectively, while the sample of persons involved in preventive health behaviors had average scores of 27.38, 15.52, and 18.44.

SCORING: All items are arranged on 6-point Likert scales ranging from "strongly agree" to "strongly disagree." Scores for each subscale are the sums of the following items: IHLC: 1, 6, 8, 12, 13, 17; POLC: 3, 5, 7, 10, 14, 18; CHLC: 2, 4, 9, 11, 15, 16. Higher scores reflect externality.

RELIABILITY: The items were empirically selected from a pool of 88 items, with fairly stringent criteria. The internal consistency reliability using Cronbach's alpha ranged from .67 to .77 for all six scales, the three dimensions, and two parallel forms. When the parallel forms were combined to make 12-item scales the alphas ranged from .83 to .86 for the three scales. Data on stability were not available.

VALIDITY: The MHLC Scales have fairly good criterion validity, correlating with subjects' state of health. The scales also correlate with other measures of locus of control, including the Multidimensional Locus of Control Scales for Psychiatric Patients. Except for the chance locus of control scale, the scales were not correlated with social desirability.

PRIMARY REFERENCE: Wallston, K. A., Wallston, B. S., and DeVellis, R. (1978). Development of the Multidimensional Health Locus of Control (MHLC) Scales, *Health Education Monographs*, 6, 160–170. Instrument reproduced with permission of Kenneth A. Wallston, Ph.D.

AVAILABILITY: Kenneth A. Wallston, Professor, Health Care Research Project, Vanderbilt University, School of Nursing, Nashville, TN 37240.

MHLC

Form A

This is a questionnaire designed to determine the way in which different people view certain important health-related issues. Each item is a belief statement with which you may agree or disagree. Each statement can be rated on a scale which ranges from strongly disagree (1) to strongly agree (6). For each item we would like you to record the number that represents the extent to which you disagree or agree with the statement. The more strongly you agree with a statement, then the higher will be the number you record. The more strongly you disagree with a statement, then the lower will be the number you record. Please make sure that you answer every item and that you record *only one* number per item. This is a measure of your personal beliefs; obviously, there are no right or wrong answers.

Please answer these items carefully, but do not spend too much time on any one item. As much as you can, try to respond to each item independently. When making your choice, do not be influenced by your previous choices. It is important that you respond according to your actual beliefs and not according to how you feel you should believe or how you think we want you to believe.

> 1 = Strongly disagree
> 2 = Moderately disagree
> 3 = Slightly disagree
> 4 = Slightly agree
> 5 = Moderately agree
> 6 = Strongly agree

1. If I get sick, it is my own behavior which determines how soon I get well again.
2. No matter what I do, if I am going to get sick, I will get sick.
3. Having regular contact with my physician is the best way for me to avoid illness.
4. Most things that affect my health happen to me by accident.
5. Whenever I don't feel well, I should consult a medically trained professional.
6. I am in control of my health.
7. My family has a lot to do with my becoming sick or staying healthy.
8. When I get sick, I am to blame.
9. Luck plays a big part in determining how soon I will recover from an illness.
10. Health professionals control my health.
11. My good health is largely a matter of good fortune.
12. The main thing which affects my health is what I myself do.
13. If I take care of myself, I can avoid illness.
14. When I recover from an illness, it's usually because other people (for example, doctors, nurses, family, friends) have been taking good care of me.
15. No matter what I do, I'm likely to get sick.

____ 16.   If it's meant to be, I will stay healthy.
____ 17.   If I take the right actions, I can stay healthy.
____ 18.   Regarding my health, I can only do what my doctor tells me to do.

Form B

This is a questionnaire designed to determine the way in which different people view certain important health-related issues. Each item is a belief statement with which you may agree or disagree. Each statement can be rated on a scale which ranges from strongly disagree (1) to strongly agree (6). For each item we would like you to record the number that represents the extent to which you disagree or agree with the statement. The more strongly you agree with a statement, then the higher will be the number you record. The more strongly you disagree with a statement, then the lower will be the number you record. Please make sure that you answer every item and that you record *only one* number per item. This is a measure of your personal beliefs; obviously, there are no right or wrong answers.

Please answer these items carefully, but do not spend too much time on any one item. As much as you can, try to respond to each item independently. When making your choice, do not be influenced by your previous choices. It is important that you respond according to your actual beliefs and not according to how you feel you should believe or how you think we want you to believe.

> 1 = Strongly disagree
> 2 = Moderately disagree
> 3 = Slightly disagree
> 4 = Slightly agree
> 5 = Moderately agree
> 6 = Strongly agree

____ 1.   If I become sick, I have the power to make myself well again.
____ 2.   Often I feel that no matter what I do, if I am going to get sick, I will get sick.
____ 3.   If I see an excellent doctor regularly, I am less likely to have health problems.
____ 4.   It seems that my health is greatly influenced by accidental happenings.
____ 5.   I can only maintain my health by consulting health professionals.
____ 6.   I am directly responsible for my health.
____ 7.   Other people play a big part in whether I stay healthy or become sick.
____ 8.   Whatever goes wrong with my health is my own fault.
____ 9.   When I am sick, I just have to let nature run its course.
____ 10.   Health professionals keep me healthy.
____ 11.   When I stay healthy, I'm just plain lucky.
____ 12.   My physical well-being depends on how well I take care of myself.
____ 13.   When I feel ill, I know it is because I have not been taking care of myself properly.
____ 14.   The type of care I receive from other people is what is responsible for how well I recover from an illness.

___ 15. Even when I take care of myself, it's easy to get sick.
___ 16. When I become ill, it's a matter of fate.
___ 17. I can pretty much stay healthy by taking good care of myself.
___ 18. Following doctor's orders to the letter is the best way for me to stay healthy.

MULTIDIMENSIONAL LOCUS OF CONTROL SCALES FOR PSYCHIATRIC PATIENTS (MLOCP)

AUTHOR: Hanna Levenson

PURPOSE: To measure locus of control of adjustment and empowerment.

DESCRIPTION: This 24-item multidimensional instrument measures the belief that reinforcement is contingent upon one's own behavior or on events which are not contingent upon one's behavior, such as chance or luck. According to social learning theory, a person who has an internal locus of control is more adjusted than one who considers consequences as the result of external events. Moreover, the author of this instrument believes that one of the goals of treatment is the development of internal control, signifying competence and mastery over one's environment. The three dimensions of locus of control assessed are internal locus of control (ILC), powerful others control (POC) and chance control (CC). Factor analysis has generally supported the dimensionality of the instrument.

NORMS: Normative data are based on 165 consecutively admitted psychiatric patients. Ninety-five were male and 70 were female, and approximately 66 percent of the sample was white, while the rest were black. The average age of the sample was 37 years old. Data also are available on 96 "normal" subjects, although little demographic information is reported. The mean scores for the ILC, POC, and CC were 35.4, 23.8, and 21.7, respectively, for the sample of psychiatric patients. The ILC, POC, and CC average scores were 35.5. 16.7, and 13.9 for the nonclinical sample. Data also are reported for patients' diagnoses. Males and females do not seem to score differently on the subscales.

SCORING: Each item is rated on a 6-point scale from "strongly disagree" to "strongly agree." The three subscales are summed separately, and the items grouped according to scales. Total scale scores range from 8 to 48. Higher scores reflect more externality. Scale items are: ILC: 1, 4, 5, 9, 18, 19, 21, 23; POC: 3, 8, 11, 13, 15, 17, 20, 22; CC: 2, 6, 7, 10, 12, 14, 16, 24.

RELIABILITY: For two of the three scales, the internal consistency reliability was good. Alphas were .67, .82, and .79 for the ILC, POC, and CC, respectively. Test-retest reliability over a five-day interval was .74 and .78 for the POC and CC, but only .08 for the ILC.

VALIDITY: The validity of this instrument is established primarily through known-groups procedures. Scores on the POC and CC scales discriminated between neurotic and psychotic patients, with a range of specific differences occurring between specific types of disorders.

PRIMARY REFERENCE: Levenson, H. (1973). Multidimensional locus of control in psychiatric patients, *Journal of Consulting and Clinical Psychology*,

41, 397–404. Instrument reproduced with permission of the American Psychological Association.

AVAILABILITY: Journal article.

MLOCP

Indicate the extent to which you agree with each of the statements below using the following scale:

1 = Strongly agree
2 = Moderately agree
3 = Slightly agree
4 = Slightly disagree
5 = Moderately disagree
6 = Strongly disagree

_____ 1. Whether or not I get to be a leader depends mostly on my ability.
_____ 2. To a great extent my life is controlled by accidental happenings.
_____ 3. I feel like what happens in my life is mostly determined by powerful people.
_____ 4. My behavior will determine when I am ready to leave the hospital.
_____ 5. When I make plans, I am almost certain to make them work.
_____ 6. Often there is no chance of protecting my personal interests from bad luck happenings.
_____ 7. When I get what I want it's usually because I'm lucky.
_____ 8. Even if I were a good leader, I would not be made a leader unless I play up to those in positions of power.
_____ 9. How many friends I have depends on how nice a person I am.
_____ 10. I have often found that what is going to happen will happen.
_____ 11. My life is chiefly controlled by powerful others.
_____ 12. It is impossible for anyone to say how long I'll be in the hospital.
_____ 13. People like myself have very little chance of protecting our interests when they conflict with those of powerful other people.
_____ 14. It's not always wise for me to plan too far ahead because many things turn out to be a matter of good or bad fortune.
_____ 15. Getting what I want means I have to please those people above me.
_____ 16. Whether or not I get to be a leader depends on whether I'm lucky enough to be in the right place at the right time.
_____ 17. If important people were to decide they didn't like me, I probably wouldn't make many friends.
_____ 18. I can pretty much determine what will happen in my life.
_____ 19. I am usually able to protect my personal interests.
_____ 20. How soon I leave the hospital depends on other people who have power over me.
_____ 21. When I get what I want, it's usually because I worked hard for it.
_____ 22. In order to have my plans work, I make sure that they fit in with the desires of people who have power over me.
_____ 23. My life is determined by my own actions.
_____ 24. It's chiefly a matter of fate whether or not I have a few friends or many friends.

MULTIDIMENSIONAL SCALE OF PERCEIVED SOCIAL SUPPORT (MSPSS)

AUTHORS: Gregory D. Zimet, Nancy W. Dahlem, Sara G. Zimet, and Gordon K. Farley

PURPOSE: To measure perceived social support.

DESCRIPTION: The MSPSS is a 12-item instrument designed to measure perceived social support from three sources: family, friends, and a significant other. The MSPSS assesses the extent to which respondents perceive social support from each of those sources and is divided into three subscales: family (items 3, 4, 8, 11); friends (items 1, 2, 5, 6, 7, 9, 12); and significant other (items 1, 2, 5, 10). The MSPSS is short, easy to use, self-explanatory, and time effective.

NORMS: The MSPSS has been studied with a variety of diverse samples. The most recent study involves 154 students in a two- or four-year college on a large urban campus. The mean age of the 122 women and 32 men was 26.5 (range from 18 to 51 years); the students were characterized as from ethnically and socioeconomically diverse backgrounds. Means for this group were 5.58 (SD = 1.07) for the total score, 5.31 (SD = 1.46) for the family subscale, 5.50 (SD = 1.25) for the friends subscale, and 5.94 (SD = 1.34) for the significant other subscale.

SCORING: The MSPSS is easily scored by summing individual item scores for the total and subscale scores and dividing by the number of items. Higher scores reflect higher perceived support.

RELIABILITY: The MSPSS has excellent internal consistency, with alphas of .91 for the total scale and .90 to .95 for the subscales. The authors claim good test-retest reliability as well.

VALIDITY: The MSPSS has good factorial validity and has good concurrent validity, correlating with depression, and with degree of coronary artery disease in Type A patients (inverse correlations). The authors also claim good construct validity for the MSPSS. The MSPSS is not correlated with the Marlow-Crowne Social Desirability Scale.

PRIMARY REFERENCE: Zimet, G. D., Dahlem, N. W., Zimet, S. G., and Farley, G. K. (1988). The Multidimensional Scale of Perceived Social Support, *Journal of Personality Assessment*, 52, 30–41.

AVAILABILITY: Dr. Gregory D. Zimet, Rainbow Babies and Children's Hospital, Room 373, 2101 Adelbert Road, Cleveland, OH 44106.

MSPSS

We are interested in how you feel about the following statements. Read each statement carefully. Indicate how you feel about each statement by circling the appropriate number using the following scale:

1 = Very strongly disagree
2 = Strongly disagree
3 = Mildly disagree
4 = Neutral
5 = Mildly agree
6 = Strongly agree
7 = Very strongly agree

1. There is a special person who is around when I am in need.   1 2 3 4 5 6 7

2. There is a special person with whom I can share joys and sorrows.   1 2 3 4 5 6 7

3. My family really tries to help me.   1 2 3 4 5 6 7

4. I get the emotional help and support I need from my family.   1 2 3 4 5 6 7

5. I have a special person who is a real source of comfort to me.   1 2 3 4 5 6 7

6. My friends really try to help me.   1 2 3 4 5 6 7

7. I can count on my friends when things go wrong.   1 2 3 4 5 6 7

8. I can talk about my problems with my family.   1 2 3 4 5 6 7

9. I have friends with whom I can share my joys and sorrows.   1 2 3 4 5 6 7

10. There is a special person in my life who cares about my feelings.   1 2 3 4 5 6 7

11. My family is willing to help me make decisions.   1 2 3 4 5 6 7

12. I can talk about my problems with my friends.   1 2 3 4 5 6 7

MULTIDIMENSIONAL SUPPORT SCALE (MDSS)

AUTHORS: Helen R. Winefield, Anthony H. Winefield, and Marika Tigge-mann

PURPOSE: To measure social support in young adults.

DESCRIPTION: The MDSS is a 19-item instrument designed to measure social support—including frequency and adequacy of emotional, practical, and informational support—in young adults. The MDSS is structured to examine support from three sources—confidants, peers, and supervisors. The MDSS has five factors reflecting sources of support rather than types: confidant availability (section A: items 1a, 2a, 4a, 4b, 5a, 6a, 7a), supervisor adequacy (section C: items 1b, 2b, 3b, 4b, 5b, 6b), supervisor availability (section C: items 1a, 2a, 4a, 5a, 6a), peer adequacy (section B: items 1b, 2b, 3b, 4b, 5b, 6b), and peer availability (section B: items 1a, 2a, 4a, 5a, 6a). On the items above "a" refers to frequency/availability rating and "b" is the adequacy/satisfaction rating.

NORMS: The MDSS was studied with 483 adults living in Australia, with a mean age of 23.6 years (SD = 1.1), 51.3% female, with 24.3% of the males and 42.7% of the females being married; 84.4% of the sample was employed, the remainder being either students (10.1%) or unemployed (4.8%). Actual norms were not reported.

SCORING: The MDSS is scored by simply summing item scores for the individual factors and total scores, using a 4-point scale for frequency and a 3-point scale for satisfaction.

RELIABILITY: The MDSS has very good internal consistency, with alphas for the subscales that range from .81 to .90. No data on stability were reported.

VALIDITY: The MDSS has good concurrent validity, with significant correlations with three measures of psychological well-being: Rosenberg's Self-Esteem and Depressive Affect scales and the General Health Questionnaire. The MDSS was a better predictor of psychological well-being than measures of health, financial distress, and stressful life events.

PRIMARY REFERENCE: Winefield, H. R., Winefield, A. H., and Tiggemann, M. (1992). Social support and psychological well-being in young adults: The MultiDimensional Support Scale, *Journal of Personality Assessment*, 58, 198–210.

AVAILABILITY: Journal article.

MDSS

Below are some questions about the kind of help and support you have available to you in coping with your life at present. The questions refer to three different groups of people who might have been providing support to you IN THE LAST MONTH. For each item, please *circle the alternative* which shows your answer.

A.   Firstly, think of your *family and close friends, especially the 2–3 who are most important to you.*

	Never	Some-times	Often	Usually/ always	Would have liked them to do this		
					More often	Less often	Just right
1. How often did they really listen to you when you talked about your concerns or problems?	1	2	3	4	1	2	3
2. How often did you feel that they were really trying to understand your problems?	1	2	3	4	1	2	3
3. How often did they try to take your mind off your problems by telling jokes or chattering about other things?	1	2	3	4	1	2	3
4. How often did they really make you feel loved?	1	2	3	4	1	2	3
5. How often did they help you in practical ways, like doing things for you or lending you money?	1	2	3	4	1	2	3

	Never	Some-times	Often	Usually/always	Would have liked them to do this		
					More often	Less often	Just right
6. How often did they answer your questions or give you advice about how to solve your problems?	1	2	3	4	1	2	3
7. How often could you use them as examples of how to deal with your problems?	1	2	3	4	1	2	3

B. Now, think of *other people of about your age that you know, who are like you in being employed, unemployed, or studying.*

	Never	Some-times	Often	Usually/always	More often	Less often	Just right
1. How often did they really listen to you when you talked about your concerns or problems?	1	2	3	4	1	2	3
2. How often did you feel that they were really trying to understand your problems?	1	2	3	4	1	2	3
3. How often did they try to take your mind off your problems by telling jokes or chattering about other things?	1	2	3	4	1	2	3
4. How often did they help you in practical ways, like doing things for you or lending you money?	1	2	3	4	1	2	3

	Never	Some-times	Often	Usually/always	Would have liked them to do this		
					More often	Less often	Just right
5. How often did they answer your questions or give you advice about how to solve your problem?	1	2	3	4	1	2	3
6. How often could you use them as examples of how to deal with your problems?	1	2	3	4	1	2	3

C. Lastly, think about the *people in some sort of* authority over you. If you are employed, this means your supervisors at work. If you are unemployed, it means your local employment service staff. If you are a fulltime student, it means your lecturers and tutors. Depending on which ones are relevant for you, answer for the 2–3 that you see most.

	Never	Some-times	Often	Usually/always	More often	Less often	Just right
1. How often did they really listen to you when you talked about your concerns or problems?	1	2	3	4	1	2	3
2. How often did you feel that they were really trying to understand your problems?	1	2	3	4	1	2	3
3. How often did they try to take your mind off your problems by telling jokes or chattering about other things?	1	2	3	4	1	2	3
4. How often did they fulfill their responsibilities towards you in helpful practical ways?	1	2	3	4	1	2	3

	Never	Some-times	Often	Usually/always	Would have liked them to do this		
					More often	Less often	Just right
5. How often did they answer your questions or give you advice about how to solve your problems?	1	2	3	4	1	2	3
6. How often could you use them as examples of how to deal with your problems?	1	2	3	4	1	2	3

NEGATIVE ATTITUDES TOWARD MASTURBATION
INVENTORY (NAMI)

AUTHORS: Paul R. Abramson and Donald L. Mosher

PURPOSE: To measure guilt over masturbation.

DESCRIPTION: This 30-item instrument measures negative attitudes toward masturbation. Negative attitudes can emerge from a lack of information or from inadequate information about sexuality; additionally, negative attitudes may develop from conditioned emotional reactions. Negative attitudes tend to be related to a lower frequency of masturbation and to sexual inexperience. Negative attitudes are considered evidence of guilt over masturbation. Knowledge of negative attitudes toward masturbation can assist in therapeutic work on sexuality and the treatment of some orgasmic disorders.

NORMS: Normative data are reported on 95 male and 99 female college students. The mean NAMI was 72.06 with a standard deviation of 15.29 for males and 72.44 with a standard deviation of 16.36 for females. The difference between males and females on NAMI scores was not significant.

SCORING: Each item is rated on a 5-point Likert-type scale by recording a number from (1) strongly disagree to (5) strongly agree in the space to the left of the item. Items 3, 5, 8, 11, 13, 14–17, 22, 27, 29, are reverse-scored. Total scores are the sum of all items and range from 30 to 150 with higher scores indicating more negative attitudes.

RELIABILITY: This instrument has acceptable evidence of internal consistency. The reliability, calculated according to the Spearman-Brown formula, was .75. All items except one had significant correlations with total scores. Estimates of test-retest reliability are not available.

VALIDITY: The NAMI shows strong evidence of concurrent validity. Correlations were found between NAMI and sexual guilt, sexual experiences, and frequency of masturbation for females. For males the NAMI only correlated with two of the criteria, sexual guilt and frequency of masturbation.

PRIMARY REFERENCE: Abramson, P. R. and Mosher, D. L. (1975). Development of a measure of negative attitudes toward masturbation, *Journal of Consulting and Clinical Psychology*, 43, 485–490. Instrument reproduced with permission of Dr. Paul R. Abramson and the American Psychological Association.

AVAILABILITY: Dr. Paul R. Abramson, Department of Psychology, UCLA, Los Angeles, CA 90024.

NAMI

Below are thirty statements regarding masturbation. Please indicate the extent to which you agree with each by placing the appropriate number to the left of the statement. The numbers are based on the following scale:

1 = Strongly disagree
2 = Disagree
3 = Neither agree nor disagree
4 = Agree
5 = Strongly agree

_____ 1. People masturbate to escape from feelings of tension and anxiety.
_____ 2. People who masturbate will not enjoy sexual intercourse as much as those who refrain from masturbation.
_____ 3. Masturbation is a private matter which neither harms nor concerns anyone else.
_____ 4. Masturbation is a sin against yourself.
_____ 5. Masturbation in childhood can help a person develop a natural, healthy attitude toward sex.
_____ 6. Masturbation in an adult is juvenile and immature.
_____ 7. Masturbation can lead to homosexuality.
_____ 8. Excessive masturbation is physically impossible, as it is a needless worry.
_____ 9. If you enjoy masturbating too much, you may never learn to relate to the opposite sex.
_____ 10. After masturbating, a person feels degraded.
_____ 11. Experience with masturbation can potentially help a woman become orgastic in sexual intercourse.
_____ 12. I feel guilty about masturbating.
_____ 13. Masturbation can be a "friend in need" when there is no "friend in deed."
_____ 14. Masturbation can provide an outlet for sex fantasies without harming anyone else or endangering oneself.
_____ 15. Excessive masturbation can lead to problems of impotence in men and frigidity in women.
_____ 16. Masturbation is an escape mechanism which prevents a person from developing a mature sexual outlook.
_____ 17. Masturbation can provide harmless relief from sexual tensions.
_____ 18. Playing with your own genitals is disgusting.
_____ 19. Excessive masturbation is associated with neurosis, depression, and behavioral problems.
_____ 20. Any masturbation is too much.
_____ 21. Masturbation is a compulsive, addictive habit which once begun is almost impossible to stop.
_____ 22. Masturbation is fun.
_____ 23. When I masturbate, I am disgusted with myself.
_____ 24. A pattern of frequent masturbation is associated with introversion and withdrawal from social contacts.

_____ 25. I would be ashamed to admit publicly that I have masturbated.

_____ 26. Excessive masturbation leads to mental dullness and fatigue.

_____ 27. Masturbation is a normal sexual outlet.

_____ 28. Masturbation is caused by an excessive preoccupation with thoughts about sex.

_____ 29. Masturbation can teach you to enjoy the sensuousness of your own body.

_____ 30. After I masturbate, I am disgusted with myself for losing control of my body.

NETWORK ORIENTATION SCALE (NOS)

AUTHORS: Alan Vaux, Philip Burda, and Doreen Stewart

PURPOSE: To measure negative network orientation.

DESCRIPTION: The NOS is a 20-item instrument designed to measure negative network orientation—the perspective that it is inadvisable, useless, or risky to seek help from others. The NOS is based on social support theory, but does not focus on the fact that a person may suffer from lack of social support; rather, the NOS measures the individual's unwillingness to maintain, nurture, or utilize those supports that he or she has. Items for the NOS were generated rationally after clarification of the basic construct of negative network orientation and were intended to reflect beliefs that it is useless, inadvisable, or dangerous to draw on network resources. The NOS is seen as not only a useful research device, but one that could be valuable in assessing client potential for involvement in therapy or in other community helping resources.

NORMS: The NOS initially was studied on four samples of college students and one of community adults. Ethnicity/cultural characteristics were mixed, including U.S. whites and blacks and foreign students. The mean age of the students ranged from 22 to 25 and of the community adults ranged from 30 to 60. The proportion of women in the samples ranged from 30% to 73%. Actual norms were not provided.

SCORING: Items using both positive and negative wording are used to minimize acquiescence in responding. Items 3, 5, 8, 10, 12, 13, 15, 17, 18, and 20 are negatively worded and are reverse-scored. All items are then summed for a total score, with higher scores indicating a more negative orientation.

RELIABILITY: The NOS has very good internal consistency, with alphas that range from .60 to .88 (mean alpha = .74). Stability was shown to be good in two of three tests including test-retest correlations of .85, .87, and .18 over one, two, and three-week intervals, respectively.

VALIDITY: The NOS has good concurrent validity and fair construct validity. Negative network expectations were associated with reports of smaller support networks, less available supportive behavior, and less positive appraisals of support. Positive network orientations were associated with personality factors such as nurturance, affiliation, trust, and a feminine sex-role orientation.

PRIMARY REFERENCE: Vaux, A., Burda, P., and Stewart, D. (1986). Orientation toward utilization of support resources, *Journal of Community Psychology*, 11, 159–170.

AVAILABILITY: Journal article.

NOS

Below is a list of statements concerning relationships with other people. Please indicate the extent to which you agree or disagree with each statement. (Using the scale below, circle one number corresponding to each statement.)

1 = Strongly agree
2 = Agree
3 = Disagree
4 = Strongly disagree

		SA	A	D	SD
1.	Sometimes it is necessary to talk to someone about your problems.	1	2	3	4
2.	Friends often have good advice to give.	1	2	3	4
3.	You have to be careful who you tell personal things to.	1	2	3	4
4.	I often get useful information from other people.	1	2	3	4
5.	People should keep their problems to themselves.	1	2	3	4
6.	It's easy for me to talk about personal and private matters.	1	2	3	4
7.	In the past, friends have really helped me out when I've had a problem.	1	2	3	4
8.	You can never trust people to keep a secret.	1	2	3	4
9.	When a person gets upset they should talk it over with a friend.	1	2	3	4
10.	Other people never understand my problems.	1	2	3	4
11.	Almost everyone knows someone they can trust with a personal secret.	1	2	3	4
12.	If you can't figure out your problems, nobody can.	1	2	3	4
13.	In the past, I have rarely found other people's opinions helpful when I have a problem.	1	2	3	4
14.	It really helps when you are angry to tell a friend what happened.	1	2	3	4

		SA	A	D	SD
15.	Some things are too personal to talk to anyone about.	1	2	3	4
16.	It's fairly easy to tell who you can trust, and who you can't.	1	2	3	4
17.	In the past, I have been hurt by people I confided in.	1	2	3	4
18.	If you confide in other people, they will take advantage of you.	1	2	3	4
19.	It's okay to ask favors of people.	1	2	3	4
20.	Even if I need something, I would hesitate to borrow it from someone.	1	2	3	4

NONCONTINGENT OUTCOME INSTRUMENT (NOI)

AUTHOR: Jeremy P. Shapiro

PURPOSE: To measure pessimism regarding uncontrolled events.

DESCRIPTION: The NOI is a 10-item instrument designed as an index of the respondent's pessimism regarding the occurrence of relatively uncontrolled events in the lives of people in general. The respondent is asked to estimate the frequency or probability of 10 events whose occurrence is basically beyond the control of individuals. This measure may be used as an estimate of the extent of pessimism and negativity in an individual's perceptions of the lives of others, and may be especially useful with depressed clients.

NORMS: The NOI was initially studied with 65 men and 49 women who were students in an introductory college psychology class. The age range was from 18 to 23. No other demographic data are provided. Means and standard deviations for each item are reported for men and women separately in the original article, but no overall norms for the measure as a whole are provided.

SCORING: Each item provides an exact percentage figure for each client. Presumably, these items can be tallied across subjects. In addition, the scores on each item could be totaled for an overall score which could range hypothetically from 0 to 1000.

RELIABILITY: Split-half reliability for the NOI was very good for women with a correlation of .87, but poor for men (.40).

VALIDITY: There was a significant correlation for men with scores on a self-criticism scale. For women, the NOI was significantly correlated with scales measuring dependency, self-criticism, and efficacy. The NOI was not correlated with overall depression for either group.

PRIMARY REFERENCE: Shapiro, J. P. (1988). Relationships between dimensions of depressive experience and perceptions of the lives of people in general, *Journal of Personality Assessment*, 52, 297–308.

AVAILABILITY: Journal article.

NOI

Please answer the following questions. It is impossible to know the exact right answers, so just state your best judgment. All the questions refer to people of all ages in America.

1. What percentage of people do you think will have cancer at some time in their lives? _____%

2. What percentage of people do you think will at some time get into an automobile accident that is not their fault? _____%

3. What percentage of people do you think will be the victim of a violent crime at some time in their lives? _____%

4. What do you think the probability is that there will be a major economic depression in the next 25 years? _____%

5. What percentage of married couples do you think have experienced or will experience infertility (inability to have a child)? _____%

6. What percentage of people do you think will be the victim of a nonviolent crime (e.g., burglary) at some time in their lives? _____%

7. What percentage of people do you think have one or more serious medical problems? _____%

8. What do you think the probability is that there will be a nuclear war in the next 50 years? _____%

9. What percentage of people do you think will die before the age of 50? _____%

10. What percentage of people do you think will at some time have an accident in their home that will require a trip to a doctor? _____%

OBSESSIVE-COMPULSIVE SCALE (OCS)

AUTHORS: Gerald D. Gibb, James R. Bailey, Randall H. Best, and Thomas T. Lambirth

PURPOSE: To measure degree of compulsivity.

DESCRIPTION: This 20-item instrument measures a concept that is widely discussed in clinical practice, but for which there are few systematic measurement tools. The focus of the OCS is on a general tendency toward obsessive thoughts and compulsive behaviors. The scale is a general measure of this disorder, and does not provide separate scores for obsessive thoughts and compulsive behaviors. The true-false format makes the OCS easy to complete, and the instrument has a validity check (see below).

NORMS: The OCS was developed using 114 college students with mean scores of 11.15 and 11.24 for males and females, respectively. The mean for a clinical sample ($N = 57$) was 11.22.

SCORING: Items 1, 2, 4, 6, 7, 8, 16, 17, 18, and 21 are assigned 1 point if answered "true." Items 5, 9, 10, 11, 12, 13, 14, 19, 20, and 22 are assigned 1 point if answered "false." Scores range from 0 to 20, with higher scores indicating more compulsivity. Items 3 and 15 are validity checks, and if answered incorrectly, the OCS score should not be considered valid.

RELIABILITY: This instrument has evidence of internal consistency and test-retest reliability. The internal consistency was estimated by correlating each item with the total, and these correlations were significant. The test-retest reliability correlation was .82 over a three-week period indicating good stability.

VALIDITY: The OCS has several estimates of concurrent validity: scores correlated with clinicians' ratings of client's compulsivity, with Comrey's Order Scale, and with a measure of flexibility.

PRIMARY REFERENCE: Gibb, G. D., Bailey, J. R., Best, R. H., and Lambirth, T. T. (1983). The measurement of the obsessive compulsive personality, *Educational and Psychological Measurement*, 43, 1233–1237. Instrument reproduced with permission of Gerald D. Gibb.

AVAILABILITY: Lt. Gerald D. Gibb, MSC, USNR, Psychological Sciences Department, Naval Aerospace Medical Research Library, Naval Air Station, Pensacola, FL 32508.

OCS

Please indicate whether each statement below is true or false for you by circling the T or the F to the left of the question.

T F 1. I feel compelled to do things I don't want to do.
T F 2. I usually check things that I know I have already done.
T F 3. I can walk 30 miles in an hour.
T F 4. I often do things I don't want to do because I cannot resist doing them.
T F 5. I seldom keep a daily routine.
T F 6. I feel compelled always to complete what I am doing.
T F 7. I often feel the need to double check what I do.
T F 8. I'd rather do things the same way all the time.
T F 9. I seldom have recurring thoughts.
T F 10. I seldom am compelled to do something I don't want to do.
T F 11. I don't feel uncomfortable and uneasy when I don't do things my usual way.
T F 12. If I don't feel like doing something it won't bother me not to do it.
T F 13. I usually never feel the need to be organized.
T F 14. I am uneasy about keeping a rigid time schedule.
T F 15. My birthday comes once a year.
T F 16. I am often compelled to do some things I do not want to do.
T F 17. I like to keep a rigid daily routine.
T F 18. I believe there is a place for everything and everything in its place.
T F 19. I seldom check things I know I have already done.
T F 20. I am not obsessed with details.
T F 21. I often have recurring thoughts.
T F 22. I like to do things differently each time.

PANIC ATTACK COGNITIONS QUESTIONNAIRE (PACQ)

AUTHORS: George A. Clum, Susan Broyles, Janet Borden, and Patti Lou Watkins

PURPOSE: To measure cognitions associated with panic attacks.

DESCRIPTION: The PACQ is a 23-item instrument designed to measure negative or catastrophic cognitions associated with panic attacks. The items for the PACQ were derived from the DSM-III, the Agoraphobic Cognition Questionnaire, and interviews with clients. Since negative cognitions are viewed as a key part of the problem in panic disorders, the PACQ is viewed as especially useful for clinical and research work with panic attacks.

NORMS: The PACQ was studied initially with 103 subjects including 63 females and 40 males, with a mean age of 32 years. All subjects responded to an offer for a free evaluation of problem anxiety, and met DSM-III criteria for at least one anxiety disorder diagnosis. The group was divided into those with and without panic attacks. The means for subjects with and without panic attacks were not reported although there were significant differences between the groups.

SCORING: The PACQ is easily scored by summing the ratings across all items. The potential range for the scale is 23 to 92, with higher scores indicating more domination of negative cognitions during or after a panic attack.

RELIABILITY: The PACQ has very good internal consistency, with an alpha of .88. No data on stability were reported.

VALIDITY: The PACQ has fair known-groups validity, significantly distinguishing between individuals suffering from panic attacks and those with anxiety disorders not suffering from panic attacks.

PRIMARY REFERENCE: Clum, G. A., Broyles, S., Borden, J., and Watkins, P. L. (1990). Validity and reliability of the Panic Attack Symptoms and Cognition Questionnaire, *Journal of Psychopathology and Behavioral Assessment*, 12, 233–245, Plenum Publishing Corp.

AVAILABILITY: Dr. George A. Clum, Psychology Department, Virginia Tech, Blacksburg, VA 24011.

PACQ

Frightening thoughts often accompany or follow panic attacks. Think of your last panic attack. Using the scale below, rate each of the following thoughts according to the degree to which you thought it during and after this panic attack. Remember to rate each thought twice, once for during and once for after your last attack.

1 = Not at all
2 = Some, but not much
3 = Quite a lot
4 = Totally dominated your thoughts

		During	After
1.	I am going to die.	___	___
2.	I am going insane.	___	___
3.	I am losing control.	___	___
4.	This will never end.	___	___
5.	I am really scared.	___	___
6.	I am having a heart attack.	___	___
7.	I am going to pass out.	___	___
8.	I don't know what people will think.	___	___
9.	I won't be able to get out of here.	___	___
10.	I don't understand what is happening to me.	___	___
11.	People will think I am crazy.	___	___
12.	I will always be this way.	___	___
13.	I am going to throw up.	___	___
14.	I must have a brain tumor.	___	___
15.	I am going to act foolish.	___	___
16.	I am going blind.	___	___
17.	I will hurt someone.	___	___
18.	I am going to have a stroke.	___	___
19.	I am going to scream.	___	___
20.	I will be paralyzed by fear.	___	___
21.	Something is really physically wrong with me.	___	___
22.	I will not be able to breathe.	___	___
23.	Something terrible will happen.	___	___

PANIC ATTACK SYMPTOMS QUESTIONNAIRE (PASQ)

AUTHORS: George A. Clum, Susan Broyles, Janet Borden, and Patti Lou Watkins

PURPOSE: To measure symptoms of a panic attack.

DESCRIPTION: The PASQ is a 33-item (plus one open-ended item) instrument designed to measure duration of symptoms (and, hence, severity) experienced during panic attacks. The items for the PASQ were taken from the DSM-III description of panic disorder symptoms, from symptoms reported in the literature, and from interviews with clients. Given the recent proliferation of research and clinical work with clients who suffer from panic attacks, the PASQ is viewed as very useful for both research and clinical work.

NORMS: The PASQ was studied initially with 103 subjects including 63 females and 40 males, with a mean age of 32 years. All subjects responded to an offer for a free evaluation of problem anxiety, and met DSM-III criteria for at least one anxiety disorder diagnosis. The group was divided into those with panic attacks and those without. The mean for subjects with panic attacks was 87.53 and for those without panic attacks was 70.1. This difference was statistically significant.

SCORING: The PASQ is easily scored by summing the ratings across all items. The potential range for the 33 items is 0 to 165, with higher scores indicating greater duration of symptoms.

RELIABILITY: The PASQ has very good internal consistency, with an alpha of .88. No data on stability were reported.

VALIDITY: The PASQ has excellent known-groups validity, significantly distinguishing between individuals suffering from panic attacks and those with anxiety disorders not suffering from panic attacks.

PRIMARY REFERENCE: Clum, G. A., Broyles, S., Borden, J., and Watkins, P. L. (1990). Validity and reliability of the Panic Attack Symptoms and Cognition Questionnaire, *Journal of Psychopathology and Behavioral Assessment*, 12, 233–245, Plenum Publishing Corp.

AVAILABILITY: Dr. George A. Clum, Psychology Department, Virginia Tech, Blacksburg, VA 24061.

PASQ

The symptoms listed below are frequently experienced during a panic attack. Using the scale below for your most recent attack, circle the number corresponding to the length of time you experienced any of the symptoms listed.

0 = Did not experience this
1 = Fleetingly (1 second to 1 minute)
2 = Briefly (1 minute to 10 minutes)
3 = Moderately (10 minutes to 1 hour)
4 = Persistently (1 hour to 24 hours)
5 = Protractedly (1 day to 2 days or longer)

1.	Heart beating rapidly		0 1 2 3 4 5
2.	Pain in chest		0 1 2 3 4 5
3.	Heart pounding in chest		0 1 2 3 4 5
4.	Difficulty in swallowing (lump in throat)		0 1 2 3 4 5
5.	Feeling of suffocation		0 1 2 3 4 5
6.	Choking sensation		0 1 2 3 4 5
7.	Hands or feet tingle		0 1 2 3 4 5
8.	Face feels hot		0 1 2 3 4 5
9.	Sweating		0 1 2 3 4 5
10.	Trembling or shaking inside		0 1 2 3 4 5
11.	Hands or body trembling or shaking		0 1 2 3 4 5
12.	Numbness in hands or feet		0 1 2 3 4 5
13.	Feeling that you are not really you or are disconnected from your body		0 1 2 3 4 5
14.	Feeling that things around you are unreal, as if in a dream		0 1 2 3 4 5
15.	Nausea		0 1 2 3 4 5
16.	Breathing rapidly (as if unable to catch your breath)		0 1 2 3 4 5
17.	Cold hands or feet		0 1 2 3 4 5

18. Dry mouth   0 1 2 3 4 5

19. Sinking feeling in stomach   0 1 2 3 4 5

20. Nerves feeling "wired"   0 1 2 3 4 5

21. Feeling physically immobilized   0 1 2 3 4 5

22. Blurred or distorted vision   0 1 2 3 4 5

23. Pressure in chest   0 1 2 3 4 5

24. Shortness of breath   0 1 2 3 4 5

25. Dizziness   0 1 2 3 4 5

26. Feeling faint   0 1 2 3 4 5

27. Butterflies in stomach   0 1 2 3 4 5

28. Stomach knotted   0 1 2 3 4 5

29. Tightness in chest   0 1 2 3 4 5

30. Legs feeling wobbly or rubbery   0 1 2 3 4 5

31. Feeling disoriented or confused   0 1 2 3 4 5

32. Cold clamminess   0 1 2 3 4 5

33. Sensitivity to loud noises   0 1 2 3 4 5

34. Other (please list)   _____

_____

How many times have you experienced these attacks:

    in the past week   _____

    in the past month   _____

    in the past six months   _____

    in the past year   _____

PATIENT REACTIONS ASSESSMENT (PRA)

AUTHORS: John P. Galassi, Rachel Schanberg, and William B. Ware

PURPOSE: To measure perceived qualities of health care providers.

DESCRIPTION: The PRA is a 15-item instrument composed of three subscales designed to measure perceived quality of information (I; items 1, 5, 10, 11, 14) and affective behaviors of health care providers (A; items 3, 6, 9, 12, 15), and the client's perceived ability to initiate communication (C; items 2, 4, 7, 8, 13). The PRA is based on the assumption that provider information giving and affective behaviors are related to clients' satisfaction, compliance, and understanding of their condition. Client communication is also viewed as important in overall health care provision. The PRA can be viewed as a measure of the perceived quality of the relationship in a medical setting.

NORMS: The PRA was studied with 197 patients at a cancer center in North Carolina including 79 men, 116 women, and 2 who did not specify gender. The sample was 86.3% white, 7.6% black, and .6% Native American. Seventy-eight percent of the sample was married. The most frequent types of cancer were melanoma, breast, and lymphoma. The mean for the total PRA was 88.16 (SD = 12.85); for the I subscale, 29.24 (SD = 4.54); for the A subscale, 30.49 (SD = 4.95); and for the C subscale, 28.43 (SD = 6.32).

SCORING: The PRA is scored by first reverse-scoring items 2, 4, 7, 8, 12, 13, 15 and then summing item responses for a total score and subscale scores.

RELIABILITY: The PRA has excellent internal consistency, with an overall alpha of .91 and alphas that range from .87 to .91 for the subscales. There were no data on stability.

VALIDITY: The PRA has fair known-groups validity, significantly distinguishing a group of caregivers perceived by counseling professionals as having more effective relationships from those seen as having less effective relationships.

PRIMARY REFERENCE: Galassi, J. P., Schanberg, R., and Ware, W. B. (1992). The Patient Reactions Assessment: A brief measure of quality of the patient-provider relationship, *Psychological Assessment*, 4, 346–351.

AVAILABILITY: The Free Press.

PRA

Think about your *recent* contacts with the medical professional who *primarily* examined you in clinic today. Then answer the following questions by circling the number that best describes how you feel about your *recent* contacts with that person. Use the following key to guide your answers:

1 = Very strongly disagree
2 = Strongly disagree
3 = Disagree
4 = Unsure
5 = Agree
6 = Strongly agree
7 = Very strongly agree

1. I understand the possible side effects of treatment.   1   2   3   4   5   6   7

2. If this person tells me something that is different from what I was told before, it is difficult for me to ask about it in order to get it straightened out.   1   2   3   4   5   6   7

3. He/she is warm and caring toward me.   1   2   3   4   5   6   7

4. If I don't understand something the person says, I have difficulty asking for more information.   1   2   3   4   5   6   7

5. The person told me what he/she hopes the treatment will do for me.   1   2   3   4   5   6   7

6. This person makes me feel comfortable about discussing personal or sensitive issues.   1   2   3   4   5   6   7

7. It is hard for me to tell the person about new symptoms.   1   2   3   4   5   6   7

8. It is hard for me to ask about how my treatment is going.   1   2   3   4   5   6   7

9. This person really respects me.   1   2   3   4   5   6   7

10. I understand pretty well the medical plan for helping me.   1   2   3   4   5   6   7

11. After talking to this person, I have a good idea of what changes to expect in my health over the next weeks and months.   1   2   3   4   5   6   7

12. When I talk to this person, I sometimes end up feeling insulted.   1 2 3 4 5 6 7

13. I have difficulty asking this person questions.   1 2 3 4 5 6 7

14. The treatment procedure was clearly explained to me.   1 2 3 4 5 6 7

15. This individual *doesn't* seem interested in me as a person.   1 2 3 4 5 6 7

PERCEIVED GUILT INDEX—STATE (PGI-S)
PERCEIVED GUILT INDEX—TRAIT (PGI-T)

AUTHORS: John R. Otterbacher and David C. Munz

PURPOSE: To measure the state and trait of guilt.

DESCRIPTION: The PGI-S and the PGI-T make up an instrument that measures the emotional experience of guilt as a state at the moment (PGI-S) and as a generalized self-concept (PGI-T). The instruments are quite different from others in this volume as they are scored as a single index and the score value is based on ratings from a sample of college students. The instrument was developed by having undergraduates ($n = 80$) develop an item pool of adjectives and phrases describing guilt. A second sample of college students rated each item in terms of its intensity of guilt, and 83 items were selected based on the median ratings. A final sample of college students then rated the items on a semantic differential and 11 items were selected as a uni-dimensional index of the emotional experience of guilt. The instrument is particularly useful in settings where one needs to monitor a client's guilt reaction to specific events or situations. When the PGI-T and PGI-S instruments are used together, the trait scale should be administered first.

NORMS: Normative data are not available. The score values for all the items were based on a sample of 55 undergraduate students.

SCORING: There are two ways to score the PGI, as single indexes for the specific trait and state word selected, and as a score assessing one's guilt reaction to a particular situation which is compared to how one "normally" feels. Scores for the PGI-S and PGI-T are determined by assigning the item score value. The score values for each item are: 1 = 6.8, 2 = 1.1, 3 = 4.3, 4 = 9.4, 5 = 2.0, 6 = 7.8, 7 = 5.9, 8 = 3.4, 9 = 8.6, 10 = 5.3, 11 = 10.4. Since the respondent is instructed to select one item, the score is simply the item score value corresponding to the item.

The second method of scoring the PGI is more complicated. First assign the respondent the appropriate item scores as described above, then subtract the PGI-T from the PGI-S score, and add 10 to the result. The constant 10 is used to eliminate confusion over minus and positive signs. Moreover, scores above 10 indicate an intensity of guilt greater than what one normally feels, while scores below 10 represent a guilt reaction less than one's usual experience.

RELIABILITY: Reliability for the two scales is reported in terms of test-retest correlations over a four-week period. Scores were not correlated for the PGI-S scale, as would be expected of a state measurement. The PGI-T was only slightly correlated (.30). Data on internal consistency were not available.

VALIDITY: As a measure of one's guilt reaction (i.e., the second scoring method), the PGI-S and PGI-T have been shown to be sensitive to assessing changes occurring as a consequence of sacramental confession. Concurrent validity is demonstrated by differences in the relationship between state and trait guilt scores for groups where guilt increased and decreased over a four-week period.

PRIMARY REFERENCE: Otterbacher, J. R. and Munz, D. C. (1973). State-trait measure of experiential guilt, *Journal of Consulting and Clinical Psychology*, 40, 115–121. Instruments reproduced with permission of David C. Munz and the American Psychological Association.

AVAILABILITY: David C. Munz, Ph.D., Department of Psychology, St. Louis University, St. Louis, MO 63104.

PGI-S

Below is a list of words and phrases people use to describe how they feel at different times. Please check the word or phrase that best describes the way you feel *at this moment*. So that you will become familiar with the general range of feeling that they cover or represent, carefully read the entire list before making your selection. Again, check only *one* word or phrase, that which best describes the way you feel *at this moment*.

_____ 1. Reproachable
_____ 2. Innocent
_____ 3. Pent up
_____ 4. Disgraceful
_____ 5. Undisturbed
_____ 6. Marred
_____ 7. Chagrined
_____ 8. Restrained
_____ 9. Degraded
_____ 10. Fretful
_____ 11. Unforgivable

PGI-T

Below is a list of words and phrases people use to describe how *guilty* they feel at different times. Please check the word or phrase which best describes the way you *normally feel*. So that you will become familiar with the general range of feeling that they cover or represent, carefully read this entire list before making your selection. Again, check only *one* word or phrase, that which best describes how *guilty* you *normally feel*.

_____ 1. Reproachable
_____ 2. Innocent
_____ 3. Pent up
_____ 4. Disgraceful
_____ 5. Undisturbed
_____ 6. Marred
_____ 7. Chagrined
_____ 8. Restrained
_____ 9. Degraded
_____ 10. Fretful
_____ 11. Unforgivable

PERCEIVED SOCIAL SUPPORT—FRIEND SCALE (PSS-Fr)
PERCEIVED SOCIAL SUPPORT—FAMILY SCALE (PSS-Fa)

AUTHORS: Mary E. Procidano and Kenneth Heller

PURPOSE: To measure fulfillment of social support from friends and family.

DESCRIPTION: The PSS-Fr and PSS-Fa are two 20-item instruments designed to measure the degree one perceives his/her needs for support as fulfilled by friends and family. Social support varies between friends and family in that one's network of friends is comparatively less long-term than the family networks and requires more social competence in maintenance than is demanded of one's family network. In part, this difference is because people assume the family network is their birthright. The items of the instruments presented here were developed from a pool of 84 items and were selected by magnitude of items to total correlations. Factor analysis suggests the instruments each measure a single domain.

NORMS: Normative data were derived from a sample of 222 (mean age = 19 years) undergraduate psychology students. The mean and standard deviation for the PSS-Fr and PSS-Fa were 15.15 (SD = 5.08) and 13.40 (SD = 4.83).

SCORING: The PSS-Fr and PSS-Fa are scored "yes," "no," and "don't know" ("don't know" is scored 0 on both scales). On the PSS-Fr an answer of "no" is scored +1 for items 2, 6, 7, 15, 18, and 20. For the remaining items "yes" is scored +1. For the PSS-Fa, answers of "no" to items 3, 4, 16, 19, and 20 are scored +1, and for all other items a "yes" answer is scored +1. Scale scores are the total of item scores and range from 0 to 20 for the PSS-Fr and the PSS-Fa. Higher scores reflect more perceived social support.

RELIABILITY: The PSS has excellent internal consistency, with an alpha of .90. The test-retest coefficient of stability over a one-month period was .83. The reliability data are based on the original 20-item PSS before the items were anchored for separate perceived support from friends and family. Alphas for the final PSS-Fa ranged from .88 to .91 and .84 to .90 for the PSS-Fr.

VALIDITY: Both the PSS-Fr and PSS-Fa have good concurrent validity. Scores are correlated with psychological distress and social competence. Both measures were associated with psychological symptoms. Scores on the PSS-Fr were predicted by length of time one was a member of one's social network and the degree of reciprocity in the relationship. Scores on the PSS-Fa were predicted by intangible and tangible support from family members. Correlations also were noted with the California Personality Inventory and interpersonal dependency. Subjects categorized as high and low in perceived support differed in the verbal disclosure which supports the instruments' known-groups validity. Clinical and nonclinical samples also differed on both measures.

PRIMARY REFERENCE: Procidano, M. E. and Heller, K. (1983). Measures of perceived social support from friends and from family: Three validation studies, *American Journal of Community Psychology*, 11, 1–24. Instrument reprinted with permission of Mary Procidano and Plenum Publishing Corp.

AVAILABILITY: Dr. Mary Procidano, Department of Psychology, Fordham University, Bronx, NY 10458-5198.

PSS-Fr

The statements which follow refer to feelings and experiences which occur to most people at one time or another in their relationships with *friends.* For each statement there are three possible answers: Yes, No, Don't know. Please circle the answer you choose for each item.

Yes No Don't know 1. My friends give me the moral support I need.

Yes No Don't know 2. Most other people are closer to their friends than I am.

Yes No Don't know 3. My friends enjoy hearing about what I think.

Yes No Don't know 5. I rely on my friends for emotional support.

Yes No Don't know 6. If I felt that one or more of my friends were upset with me, I'd just keep it to myself.

Yes No Don't know 7. I feel that I'm on the fringe in my circle of friends.,

Yes No Don't know 8. There is a friend I could go to if I were just feeling down, without feeling funny about it later.

Yes No Don't know 9. My friends and I are very open about what we think about things.

Yes No Don't know 10. My friends are sensitive to my personal needs.

Yes No Don't know 11. My friends come to me for emotional support.

Yes No Don't know 12. My friends are good at helping me solve problems.

Yes No Don't know 13. I have a deep sharing relationship with a number of friends.

Yes No Don't know 14. My friends get good ideas about how to do things or make things from me.

Yes No Don't know 15. When I confide in friends, it makes me feel uncomfortable.

Yes No Don't know 16. My friends seek me out for companionship.

Yes No Don't know 17. I think that my friends feel that I'm good at helping them solve problems.

Yes No Don't know 18. I don't have a relationship with a friend that is as intimate as other people's relationships with friends.

Yes No Don't know 19. I've recently gotten a good idea about how to do something from a friend.

Yes No Don't know 20. I wish my friends were much different.

PSS-Fa

The statements which follow refer to feelings and experiences which occur to most people at one time or another in their relationships with their *families*. For each statement there are three possible answers: Yes, No, Don't know. Please circle the answer you choose for each item.

Yes No Don't know 1. My family gives me the moral support I need.

Yes No Don't know 2. I get good ideas about how to do things or make things from my family.

Yes No Don't know 3. Most other people are closer to their family than I am.

Yes No Don't know 4. When I confide in the members of my family who are closest to me, I get the idea that it makes them uncomfortable.

Yes No Don't know 5. My family enjoys hearing about what I think.

Yes No Don't know 6. Members of my family share many of my interests.

Yes No Don't know 7. Certain members of my family come to me when they have problems or need advice.

Yes No Don't know 8. I rely on my family for emotional support.

Yes No Don't know 9. There is a member of my family I could go to if I were just feeling down, without feeling funny about it later.

Yes No Don't know 10. My family and I are very open about what we think about things.

Yes No Don't know 11. My family is sensitive to my personal needs.

Yes No Don't know 12. Members of my family come to me for emotional support.

Yes No Don't know 13. Members of my family are good at helping me solve problems.

Yes No Don't know 14. I have a deep sharing relationship with a number of members of my family.

Yes No Don't know 15. Members of my family get good ideas about how to do things or make things from me.

Yes No Don't know 16. When I confide in members of my family, it makes me uncomfortable.

Yes No Don't know 17. Members of my family seek me out for companionship.

Yes No Don't know 18. I think that my family feels that I'm good at helping them solve problems.

Yes No Don't know 19. I don't have a relationship with a member of my family that is as close as other people's relationships with family members.

Yes No Don't know 20. I wish my family were much different.

PERSONAL ASSERTION ANALYSIS (PAA)

AUTHORS: Bonnie L. Hedlund and Carol U. Lindquist

PURPOSE: To distinguish among passive, aggressive, and assertive behavior.

DESCRIPTION: The PAA is a 30-item instrument designed to assess passive, aggressive, and assertive behavior and to help determine an individual's need for assertion training. The PAA asks respondents to report what they actually do rather than what they know how to do. A pool of 87 items was collected from a number of available assertion inventories. Through use of factor analysis, the PAA was reduced to 30 items and three factors, each with 10 items; three factor analyses with different samples confirm the presence of the three factors—passive (items 3, 6, 11, 13, 16, 21, 25, 26, 27, 29), aggressive (items 5, 7, 10, 12, 15, 17, 22, 23, 24, 30), and assertive (items 1, 2, 4, 8, 9, 14, 18, 19, 20, 28).

NORMS: Three separate samples were used in developing and validating the PAA. The first was a sample of 120 undergraduates (mean age 19); the second a sample of 200 undergraduates (mean age 23.3); the third sample of 275 included 68 male and 76 female adolescents (mean age 17.5), 25 male and 32 female alcoholics (mean age 43), 5 females and 7 males involved in spouse abuse, and 10 males and 17 females who reported they were satisfied in their marriages (mean age 40). The means for the second sample were 23.45 for aggression, 18.97 for assertion, and 21.20 for passivity. The means for the third sample were 29.23 for aggression, 22.12 for assertion, and 27.37 for passivity. There were no differences between males and females.

SCORING: The individual items are summed for each subscale; a low score indicates more of that type of behavior. Each subscale ranges from 0 to 40.

RELIABILITY: The PAA has fairly good stability with a one-week test-retest correlation of .70 for aggression and assertion and .82 for passivity. No internal consistency data were reported.

VALIDITY: The PAA demonstrates a fair degree of construct validity. The PAA subscales correlated in predicted directions with some measures with which they should correlate, including a number of personality tests of assertion and aggression, taped role-play situations, peer ratings, and global self-ratings. There were small but significant correlations between the assertion and aggression subscales and the Marlowe-Crowne Social Desirability Scale, indicating a small effect of social desirability on responses to the PAA.

PRIMARY REFERENCE: Hedlund, B. L. and Lindquist, C. U. (1984). The development of an inventory for distinguishing among passive, aggressive, and assertive behavior, *Behavioral Assessment*, 6, 379–390. Instrument reproduced with permission of Bonnie L. Hedlund and Carol U. Lindquist.

AVAILABILITY: Dr. Bonnie L. Hedlund or Dr. Carol U. Lindquist, Department of Psychology, California State University, Fullerton, CA 92634.

PAA

Please read the following statements: Each one describes a situation and a response. Try to imagine a situation in your life that is as close to the one described as possible, then rate the response according to its similarity with what you *might* do in the actual situation.

1 = Just like me
2 = Sometimes like me
3 = Not usually like me
4 = Not at all like me

_____ 1. You'd like a raise, so you make an appointment with your boss to explain the reasons you feel you should receive one.

_____ 2. You usually take the lead when you are in a group of people.

_____ 3. Because of a high-pressure salesperson, you buy a camera that meets most but not all of your requirements.

_____ 4. You're working on a project with a friend but you seem to be doing all the work. You say, "I'd like to see if we could find a different way to divide the responsibility. I feel I'm doing most of the work."

_____ 5. After waiting in a restaurant for 20 minutes, you loudly tell the host of your dissatisfaction and leave.

_____ 6. A very important person you have long admired comes to speak in your town. Afterwards you are too hesitant to go and meet him/her.

_____ 7. Your parents have been after you to spend more time with them. You tell them to stop nagging you.

_____ 8. Your neighbor's stereo is disturbing you. You call and ask if he/she would please turn it down.

_____ 9. A repairman overcharges you. You explain that you feel the charges are excessive and ask for the bill to be adjusted.

_____ 10. A person cuts in front of you in line, so you push him/her out of line.

_____ 11. When you're feeling warm towards your parent/spouse, it is difficult for you to express this to them.

_____ 12. You are delayed getting home because you stayed at a friend's too long. When your parent/spouse is angry, you tell him/her it's none of his/her business.

_____ 13. When trying to talk to someone of the opposite sex, you get nervous.

_____ 14. In a job interview you are able to state your positive points as well as your negative points.

_____ 15. You are driving to an appointment with a friend and she/he has a flat tire. While she/he is changing the tire, you tell her/him how dumb it was to let the tires get worn.

_____ 16. You accept your boss's opinion about your lack of ability to handle responsibility, but later complain to some friends about his/her unfairness.

_____ 17. You are arguing with a person and she/he pushes you, so you push her/him back.

_____ 18. In a discussion with a small group of people, you state your position and are willing to discuss it, but you don't feel that you have to win.

_____ 19. The person next to you in a movie is explaining the plot of the movie to his/her companion. You ask them to please be quiet because they are distracting you from the movie.

_____ 20. When you see a new person you would like to meet, you usually try to start a conversation with him/her.

_____ 21. Your neighbor wants to use your car. Even though you'd rather she/he didn't, you say yes.

_____ 22. A friend of yours is arguing with someone much larger than she/he is. You decide to help your friend by saying, "I'm really tired of listening to you mouth off."

_____ 23. A person cuts in front of you in line, so you say, "Who do you think you are? Get out of my way."

_____ 24. You are talking to a friend and she/he doesn't appear to be listening. You tell her/him that you are sick and tired of her/him not listening to you.

_____ 25. Speaking before a group makes you so nervous that you have a great deal of trouble speaking clearly.

_____ 26. You are waiting for a car to pull out of a parking place so that you can park. Someone comes up behind you and honks. You drive on.

_____ 27. You find it hard to express contradictory opinions when dealing with an authority figure.

_____ 28. Your spouse/boyfriend/girlfriend is supposed to take you out. Fifteen minutes before you are to leave, she/he calls and cancels. You tell her/him that you are very disappointed.

_____ 29. In a group situation, you usually wait to see what the majority of the people want before giving your opinion.

_____ 30. You have arranged to meet a friend, but she/he doesn't arrive. At the first opportunity, you call her/him and demand an explanation.

PERSONAL STYLE INVENTORY (PSI)

AUTHORS: Clive J. Robins and Alice G. Luten

PURPOSE: To measure sociotropy and autonomy in depression.

DESCRIPTION: The PSI is a 60-item instrument designed to measure sociotropy and autonomy as they are related to depression. Sociotropy is defined as social dependency, a person's investment in positive interchange with others. Autonomy, or individuality is defined as a person's investment in preserving and increasing his or her independence. Each characteristic is hypothesized to be related to different clinical presentations among depressed clients. Highly sociotropic individuals, when depressed, primarily feel deprived and exhibit clinical features consistent with this sense of deprivation (e.g., thoughts of loss, crying). This pattern is consistent with the concept of reactive depression. When highly autonomous people are depressed, they primarily feel defeated (e.g., pessimistic about treatment, self-blaming, feeling like a failure). This pattern is consistent with the picture of endogenous depression. The PSI is very useful for understanding depression and perhaps for keeping track over time of differentially targeted intervention efforts. The PSI consists of six subscales that comprise the two main subscales, sociotropy and autonomy. Sociotropy includes subscales for concern about what others think (items 1, 7, 13, 19, 25, 31, 36, 43, 49, 55), dependency (items 3, 9, 15, 21, 27, 33, 39, 45, 51, 57), and pleasing others (items 5, 11, 17, 23, 29, 35, 41, 47, 53, 59). Autonomy includes the subscales perfectionism/self-criticism (items 2, 8, 14, 20, 26, 32, 38, 44, 50, 56), need for control/freedom from outside control (items 4, 10, 16, 22, 28, 34, 44, 46, 52, 58), and defensive separation (items 6, 12, 18, 24, 30, 36, 42, 48, 54, 60).

NORMS: The PSI was studied with 13 male and 37 female psychiatric inpatients diagnosed with some variation of depression. The mean age was 44.12 years, 58% were married, 26% were separated or divorced, 4% widowed, and 12% never married. Twenty percent had less than a high school diploma, 18% completed high school, and 62% had some college or a college degree. The mean score on the sociotropy scale was 127.65 (SD = 18.36) and on autonomy was 117.27 (SD = 17.29). There were no significant differences between men and women.

SCORING: The PSI subscales are easily scored by summing item scores, with "strongly disagree" equaling a score of 1 to "strongly agree" equaling a score of 6. Scores on each of the sets of three subscales can be summed to produce overall sociotropy and autonomy scores. Obtaining a single total score is not recommended.

RELIABILITY: The PSI has very good internal consistency, with alphas of .88 for sociotropy and .83 for autonomy. The PSI has very good stability, with five- to thirteen-week test-retest reliabilities of .80 for sociotropy and .76 for autonomy.

VALIDITY: The PSI has very good concurrent and predictive validity, correlating in predicted directions with an Index of Clinical Features that comprised 19 clinical features that are hypothesized to be differentially related to sociotropy or autonomy.

PRIMARY REFERENCE: Robins, C. J. and Luten, A. G. (1991). Sociotropy and autonomy: Differential patterns of clinical presentation in unipolar depression, *Journal of Abnormal Psychology*, 100, 71–77.

AVAILABILITY: Dr. Clive Robins, Duke University Medical Center, Box 3903, Durham, NC 27710

PSI

Here are a number of statements about personal characteristics. Please read each one carefully, and indicate whether you agree or disagree, and to what extent, by circling a number.

		Strongly disagree	Dis- agree	Slightly disagree	Slightly agree	Agree	Strongly agree
1.	I am very sensitive to criticism by others.	1	2	3	4	5	6
2.	I often find that I don't live up to my own standards and ideals.	1	2	3	4	5	6
3.	I find it difficult to be separated from people I love.	1	2	3	4	5	6
4.	I resent it when people try to direct my behavior or activities.	1	2	3	4	5	6
5.	I often put other people's needs before my own.	1	2	3	4	5	6
6.	I don't like relying on others for help.	1	2	3	4	5	6
7.	I worry a lot that people may criticize me.	1	2	3	4	5	6

		Strongly disagree	Dis-agree	Slightly disagree	Slightly agree	Agree	Strongly agree
8.	The standards and goals I set for myself are usually higher than those of other people.	1	2	3	4	5	6
9.	It is hard for me to break off a relationship even if it is making me unhappy.	1	2	3	4	5	6
10.	I rarely trust the advice of others when making a big decision.	1	2	3	4	5	6
11.	I am very sensitive to the effects I have on the feelings of other people.	1	2	3	4	5	6
12.	When I'm feeling blue, I don't like to be offered sympathy.	1	2	3	4	5	6
13.	I am very sensitive to signs of possible rejection by others.	1	2	3	4	5	6
14.	It is hard for me to accept my own weaknesses and limitations.	1	2	3	4	5	6
15.	It is hard for me to take charge of my own affairs without help from other people.	1	2	3	4	5	6

	Strongly disagree	Dis-agree	Slightly disagree	Slightly agree	Agree	Strongly agree
16. I am very upset when other people or circumstances interfere with my plans.	1	2	3	4	5	6
17. I worry a lot about hurting or offending people.	1	2	3	4	5	6
18. I don't like people to invade my privacy.	1	2	3	4	5	6
19. I am easily persuaded by others.	1	2	3	4	5	6
20. I tend to be very self-critical.	1	2	3	4	5	6
21. I need other people's help in order to cope with life's problems.	1	2	3	4	5	6
22. I try to maintain control over my feelings at all times.	1	2	3	4	5	6
23. I try to please other people too much.	1	2	3	4	5	6
24. It is hard for me to have someone dependent on me.	1	2	3	4	5	6

		Strongly disagree	Dis- agree	Slightly disagree	Slightly agree	Agree	Strongly agree
25.	It is very important to me to be liked or admired by others.	1	2	3	4	5	6
26.	I believe in doing something well or not doing it at all.	1	2	3	4	5	6
27.	I never really feel secure in a close relationship because I am concerned that I might lose the other person.	1	2	3	4	5	6
28.	I am easily bothered by other people making demands of me.	1	2	3	4	5	6
29.	I often feel responsible for solving other people's problems.	1	2	3	4	5	6
30.	I can be completely independent of other people.	1	2	3	4	5	6
31.	I am very concerned with how people react to me.	1	2	3	4	5	6
32.	I should be able to excel at anything if I try hard enough.	1	2	3	4	5	6

		Strongly disagree	Dis- agree	Slightly disagree	Slightly agree	Agree	Strongly agree
33.	I find it difficult if I have to be alone all day.	1	2	3	4	5	6
34.	I often try to change other people's behavior.	1	2	3	4	5	6
35.	I feel I have to be nice to other people.	1	2	3	4	5	6
36.	I tend to keep other people at a distance.	1	2	3	4	5	6
37.	I get very uncomfortable when I'm not sure whether or not someone likes me.	1	2	3	4	5	6
38.	I usually view my performance as either a complete success or a complete failure.	1	2	3	4	5	6
39.	It is very hard for me to get over the feeling of loss when a relationship has ended.	1	2	3	4	5	6
40.	It is hard for me to take instructions from people who have authority over me.	1	2	3	4	5	6

		Strongly disagree	Dis-agree	Slightly disagree	Slightly agree	Agree	Strongly agree
41.	I am too apologetic to other people.	1	2	3	4	5	6
42.	It is hard for me to open up and talk about my feelings and other personal things.	1	2	3	4	5	6
43.	I often censor what I say because the other person may disapprove or disagree.	1	2	3	4	5	6
44.	I judge myself as a person based on the quality of the work that I do.	1	2	3	4	5	6
45.	I like to be certain that there is somebody close I can contact in case something unpleasant happens to me.	1	2	3	4	5	6
46.	When making a big decision, I usually feel that advice from others is intrusive.	1	2	3	4	5	6
47.	It is hard for me to say "no" to other people's requests.	1	2	3	4	5	6

	Strongly disagree	Dis-agree	Slightly disagree	Slightly agree	Agree	Strongly agree
48. It is hard for me to express admiration or affection.	1	2	3	4	5	6
49. It is hard for me to be a nonconformist.	1	2	3	4	5	6
50. It bothers me when I feel that I am only average and ordinary.	1	2	3	4	5	6
51. I become upset when something happens to me and there's nobody around to talk to.	1	2	3	4	5	6
52. I become upset more than most people I know when limits are placed on my personal independence and freedom.	1	2	3	4	5	6
53. I often let people take advantage of me.	1	2	3	4	5	6
54. It is difficult for me to make a long-term commitment to a relationship.	1	2	3	4	5	6

		Strongly disagree	Dis- agree	Slightly disagree	Slightly agree	Agree	Strongly agree
55.	I am most comfortable when I know my behavior is what others expect of me.	1	2	3	4	5	6
56.	I feel bad about myself when I am not actively accomplishing things.	1	2	3	4	5	6
57.	I become very upset when a friend breaks a date or forgets to call me as planned.	1	2	3	4	5	6
58.	I resent it when others assume responsibility for my plans.	1	2	3	4	5	6
59.	It is hard for me to let people know when I am angry with them.	1	2	3	4	5	6
60.	In relationships, people are often too demanding of one another.	1	2	3	4	5	6

PHYSICAL SELF-EFFICACY SCALE (PSE)

AUTHORS: Richard M. Ryckman, Michael A. Robbins, Billy Thornton, and Peggy Cantrell

PURPOSE: To measure perceived physical competence.

DESCRIPTION: The PSE is a 22-item instrument that is based on the assumption that people's expectations about their own efficacy have important effects on cognitive, affective, and behavioral patterns. The PSE also is based on the assumption that there are a variety of arenas in which individuals must achieve mastery if they are to perceive themselves as efficacious. One of these arenas is physical self-concept. The PSE is designed to measure individual differences in perceived physical competence and feelings of confidence in displaying physical skills to others. The instrument was based on a pool of 90 items; those items that were not highly correlated with social desirability response set but were related to two primary factors were selected to form the PSE. The final form has two subscales, perceived physical ability (PPA): (items 1, 2, 4, 6, 8, 12, 13, 19*, 21*, 22*) and physical self-presentation confidence (PSPC): (items 3*, 5, 7, 9*, 10, 11*, 14*, 15, 16, 17*, 18, 20*), plus an overall PSE scale. The PSE is useful for diagnostic and assessment purposes in medical and clinical settings and in athletic programs.

NORMS: A series of studies was conducted in the development of the PSE, eventually involving some 950 undergraduate students. Demographic data and actual norms were not reported.

SCORING: The PSE is scored by first reverse-scoring the items with asterisks (noted above), then summing the scores on the individual items within each factor for the subscale scores and summing the two subscale scores for the overall PSE score. The scores on the PPA range from 10 to 60, on PSPC from 12 to 72, and overall scores from 22 to 132. Higher scores on all three indicate greater self-efficacy.

RELIABILITY: The PSE has good internal consistency, with alphas of .84 for PPA, .74 for PSPC, and .81 for the overall PSE. The PSE is also a very stable instrument with six-week test-retest correlations of .89 for PPA, .69 for PSPC, and .80 for the PSE as a whole.

VALIDITY: The PSE has good concurrent validity, correlating significantly with a number of other measures such as the Tennessee Physical Self-Concept Scale, the Texas Social Behavior Inventory (self-esteem), the Self-Consciousness Scale, and the Taylor Manifest Anxiety Scale. The PSE also has good predictive validity, predicting a number of scores on other instruments as well as sports and physically related activities (e.g., respondents with higher PSE scores outperform respondents with lower PSE scores).

PRIMARY REFERENCE: Ryckman, R. M., Robbins, M. A., Thornton, B., and
    Cantrell, P. (1982). Development and validation of a Physical Self-Efficacy
    Scale, *Journal of Personality and Social Psychology*, 42, 891–900. Instru-
    ment reproduced with permission of Richard M. Ryckman and the American
    Psychological Association.
AVAILABILITY: Dr. Richard M. Ryckman, Department of Psychology, Uni-
    versity of Maine, Orono, ME 04469.

PSE

Please place one number to the left of the column for each item as follows:

1 = Strongly agree
2 = Agree
3 = Somewhat agree
4 = Somewhat disagree
5 = Disagree
6 = Strongly disagree

_____ 1. I have excellent reflexes.
_____ 2. I am not agile and graceful.
_____ 3. I am rarely embarrassed by my voice.
_____ 4. My physique is rather strong.
_____ 5. Sometimes I don't hold up well under stress.
_____ 6. I can't run fast.
_____ 7. I have physical defects that sometimes bother me.
_____ 8. I don't feel in control when I take tests involving physical dexterity.
_____ 9. I am never intimidated by the thought of a sexual encounter.
_____ 10. People think negative things about me because of my posture.
_____ 11. I am not hesitant about disagreeing with people bigger than I.
_____ 12. I have poor muscle tone.
_____ 13. I take little pride in my ability in sports.
_____ 14. Athletic people usually do not receive more attention than I.
_____ 15. I am sometimes envious of those better looking than myself.
_____ 16. Sometimes my laugh embarrasses me.
_____ 17. I am not concerned with the impression my physique makes on others.
_____ 18. Sometimes I feel uncomfortable shaking hands because my hand is clammy.
_____ 19. My speed has helped me out of some tight spots.
_____ 20. I find that I am not accident prone.
_____ 21. I have a strong grip.
_____ 22. Because of my agility, I have been able to do things that many others could not do.

PROBLEM-SOLVING INVENTORY (PSI)

AUTHOR: P. Paul Heppner

PURPOSE: To assess respondents' perception of their problem-solving behaviors and attitudes.

DESCRIPTION: The PSI is a 35-item instrument designed to measure how individuals believe they generally react to personal problems in their daily lives. The term "problems" refers to personal problems such as getting along with friends, feeling depressed, choosing a career, or deciding whether to get divorced. Although the PSI does not measure actual problem-solving skills, it does measure the evaluative awareness of one's problem solving abilities or style. The PSI comprises three subscales based on factor analysis: problem solving confidence (items 5, 10, 11*, 12, 19, 23, 24, 27, 33, 34*, 35), approach-avoidance style (items 1*, 2*, 4*, 6, 7, 8, 13*, 15*, 16, 17*, 18, 20, 21*, 28, 30, 31), and personal control (3*, 14*, 25*, 26*, 32*). In addition, the total score is viewed as a single, general index of problem-solving perception. This is one of the few standardized measures that addresses this central concern of helping professionals with clients' coping and problem-solving skills.

NORMS: The PSI was developed and tested with several samples of white, introductory psychology students (402 males, 498 females); 25 black male and 59 black female students; 26 male and 42 female counseling center clients; 306 undergraduates across all four academic years; and four populations of adults including 101 "normals," 77 inpatient alcoholic males, 29 elderly, and 90 female university extension staff members. Norms for all these groups are available. The means on the total PSI range from 74.0 for the female extension staff members to 98.0 for male counseling center clients.

SCORING: The PSI can be self-scored by the client, or scored by the practitioner either directly or using a computer (computer answer sheets are available). Items with asterisks (see above) are reverse-scored. Then the scores for the items on each factor are summed. The three factor scores are summed for the total score. Items 9, 22, and 29 are filler items and not scored. Lower scores reflect greater perceived problem-solving abilities.

RELIABILITY: The PSI has good to excellent internal consistency, with alphas ranging from .72 to .85 on the subscales and .90 for the total measure. The PSI has excellent stability with two-week test-retest correlations for the subscales and total measure that range from .83 to .89.

VALIDITY: Extensive testing of the PSI reveals good validity in several areas. Concurrent validity was established by significant correlations between the PSI and scores on a self-rating scale of one's problem-solving skill. Construct validity has been demonstrated in a number of studies by establishing that the PSI is correlated with other measures with which it should be correlated and is not correlated with those with which it theoretically should not be. Several personality measures were used in these studies, such as Rotter's Internal-External Scale and the Myers-Briggs Type Indicator. The PSI has been found to distinguish significantly between groups such as clinical and nonclinical, or those with higher and lower scores on measures of psychological disturbance, thus establishing known-groups validity. The PSI is sensitive to clinical changes and also is not affected by social desirability response set.

PRIMARY REFERENCE: Heppner, P. P. and Petersen. C. H. (1982). The development and implications of a personal problem-solving inventory, *Journal of Counseling Psychology*, 29, 66–75. Instrument reproduced with permission of P. Paul Heppner.

AVAILABILITY: Dr. P. Paul Heppner, University of Missouri-Columbia, Psychology Department, 210 McAlester Hall, Columbia, MO 65211.

PSI

Read each statement, and indicate the extent to which you agree or disagree with that statement, using the following options:

1 = Strongly agree
2 = Moderately agree
3 = Slightly agree
4 = Slightly disagree
5 = Moderately disagree
6 = Strongly disagree

_____ 1. When a solution to a problem was unsuccessful, I did not examine why it didn't work.
_____ 2. When I am confronted with a complex problem, I do not bother to develop a strategy to collect information so I can define exactly what the problem is.
_____ 3. When my first efforts to solve a problem fail, I become uneasy about my ability to handle the situation.
_____ 4. After I have solved a problem, I do not analyze what went right or what went wrong.
_____ 5. I am usually able to think up creative and effective alternatives to solve a problem.
_____ 6. After I have tried to solve a problem with a certain course of action, I take time and compare the actual outcome to what I think should have happened.
_____ 7. When I have a problem, I think up as many possible ways to handle it as I can until I can't come up with any more ideas.
_____ 8. When confronted with a problem, I consistently examine my feelings to find out what is going on in a problem situation.
_____ 9. When I am confused with a problem, I do not try to define vague ideas or feelings into concrete or specific terms.
_____ 10. I have the ability to solve most problems even though initially no solution is immediately apparent.
_____ 11. Many problems I face are too complex for me to solve.
_____ 12. I make decisions and am happy with them later.
_____ 13. When confronted with a problem, I tend to do the first thing that I can think to solve it.
_____ 14. Sometimes I do not stop and take time to deal with my problems, but just kind of muddle ahead.
_____ 15. When deciding on an idea or possible solution to a problem, I do not take time to consider the chances of each alternative being successful.
_____ 16. When confronted with a problem, I stop and think about it before deciding on a next step.
_____ 17. I generally go with the first good idea that comes to my mind.
_____ 18. When making a decision, I weigh the consequences of each alternative and compare them against each other.

____ 19. When I make plans to solve a problem, I am almost certain that I can make them work.

____ 20. I try to predict the overall result of carrying out a particular course of action.

____ 21. When I try to think up possible solutions to a problem, I do not come up with very many alternatives.

____ 22. In trying to solve a problem, one strategy I often use is to think of past problems that have been similar.

____ 23. Given enough time and effort, I believe I can solve most problems that confront me.

____ 24. When faced with a novel situation I have confidence that I can handle problems that may arise.

____ 25. Even though I work on a problem, sometimes I feel like I am groping or wandering, and am not getting down to the real issue.

____ 26. I make snap judgments and later regret them.

____ 27. I trust my ability to solve new and difficult problems.

____ 28. I have a systematic method for comparing alternatives and making decisions.

____ 29. When I try to think of ways of handling a problem, I do not try to combine different ideas together.

____ 30. When confronted with a problem, I don't usually examine what sort of external things in my environment may be contributing to my problem.

____ 31. When I am confronted by a problem, one of the first things I do is survey the situation and consider all the relevant pieces of information.

____ 32. Sometimes I get so charged up emotionally that I am unable to consider many ways of dealing with my problem.

____ 33. After making a decision, the outcome I expected usually matches the actual outcome.

____ 34. When confronted with a problem, I am unsure of whether I can handle the situation.

____ 35. When I become aware of a problem, one of the first things I do is to try to find out exactly what the problem is.

PROCRASTINATION ASSESSMENT SCALE—STUDENTS (PASS)

AUTHORS: Linda J. Solomon and Esther D. Rothblum

PURPOSE: To measure procrastination.

DESCRIPTION: The PASS is a 44-item instrument designed to measure the frequency of cognitive-behavioral antecedents of procrastination. The PASS was developed to measure three areas: (1) the prevalence of academic procrastination, (2) the reasons for academic procrastination, and (3) to compare scores on the PASS with behavioral indices of procrastination and other related constructs. The PASS is divided into two parts; the first part measures the prevalence of procrastination in six academic areas, and the second part assesses reasons for procrastination. The PASS is useful in both identifying potential focal areas for intervention, and in tracking changes in procrastination over time.

NORMS: The PASS was investigated with 323 university students (101 males, 222 females) enrolled in introductory psychology courses; 90% were between the ages of 18 to 21; 85% were freshmen, 13% sophomores, and the remaining subjects were juniors and seniors. Norms were reported in percentages: 46% always or nearly always procrastinate on a paper, 27.6% procrastinate on studying for exams, 30.1% procrastinate on reading weekly assignments, 10.6% procrastinate on administrative tasks, 23% on attendance tasks, and 10.2% on school activities in general. In addition, 23.7% reported that procrastination was always or nearly always a problem when writing a paper, 21.2% said it was a problem when studying for exams, and 23.7% said it was a problem when doing weekly readings. There were no significant sex differences in procrastination. Regarding reasons for procrastination, 49.5% of the variance reflects fear of failure, and 18% reflects aversiveness of the task and laziness. Females were more likely to fear failure than were males.

SCORING: Scores on the 5-point Likert-type scale (a = 1 to e = 5) are summed for each academic task (scores range from 2 to 10) and across the six areas of academic functioning (ranging from 12 to 60). Scores on reasons for procrastination and interest in changing are summed as separate subscales. A total score can be obtained by summing all subscale scores.

RELIABILITY: The most recent research shows low levels of internal consistency for the PASS with split-half correlations of .58 for men and .31 for women regarding procrastination frequency. The correlation for procrastination as a problem was .26 overall and for reasons for procrastination was .80. The stability of the PASS was fair with one-month test-retest correlations of .74 for prevalence and .56 for reasons for procrastination. For the total score, the test-retest correlation was .80.

VALIDITY: The PASS has very good concurrent validity, with significant correlations with the Beck Depression Inventory, Ellis Scale of Irrational Cognitions, Rosenberg Self-Esteem Scale, and the Delay Avoidance Scale. Significant correlations also were found between the number of self-paced quizzes and PASS scores and between the PASS and total grade point averages (higher PASS scores correlated with lower GPAs).

PRIMARY REFERENCE: Solomon, L. J. and Rothblum, E. D. (1984). Academic Procrastination: Frequency and cognitive behavioral correlates, *Journal of Counseling Psychology*, 31, 503–509.

AVAILABILITY: The Free Press.

PASS

AREAS OF PROCRASTINATION

For each of the following activities, please rate the degree to which you delay or procrastinate. Rate each item on an a to e scale according to how often you wait until the last minute to do the activity. Then, indicate on an a to e scale the degree to which you feel procrastination on that task is a problem. Finally, indicate on an a to e scale the degree to which you would like to decrease your tendency to procrastinate on each task. Mark your answers by circling the appropriate letter below each question.

I.   *Writing a Term Paper*

1.   To what degree do you procrastinate on this task?

Never procrastinate	Almost never	Sometimes	Nearly always	Always procrastinate
a	b	c	d	e

2.   To what degree is procrastination on this task a problem for you?

Not at all a problem	Almost never	Sometimes	Nearly always	Always a problem
a	b	c	d	e

3.   To what extent do you want to decrease your tendency to procrastinate on this task?

Do not want to decrease		Somewhat		Definitely want to decrease
a	b	c	d	e

II. *Studying for Exams*

4.   To what degree do you procrastinate on this task?

Never procrastinate	Almost never	Sometimes	Nearly always	Always procrastinate
a	b	c	d	e

5.   To what degree is procrastination on this task a problem for you?

Not at all a problem	Almost never	Sometimes	Nearly always	Always a problem
a	b	c	d	e

6. To what extent do you want to decrease your tendency to procrastinate on this task?

				Definitely
Do not want				want to
to decrease		Somewhat		decrease
a	b	c	d	e

III. *Keeping Up Weekly Reading Assignments*

7. To what degree do you procrastinate on this task?

Never	Almost		Nearly	Always
procrastinate	never	Sometimes	always	procrastinate
a	b	c	d	e

8. To what degree is procrastination on this task a problem for you?

Not at all a	Almost		Nearly	Always a
problem	never	Sometimes	always	problem
a	b	c	d	e

9. To what extent do you want to decrease your tendency to procrastinate on this task?

				Definitely
Do not want				want to
to decrease		Somewhat		decrease
a	b	c	d	e

IV. *Academic Administrative Tasks: Filling Out Forms, Registering for Classes, Getting ID Card, etc.*

10. To what degree do you procrastinate on this task?

Never	Almost		Nearly	Always
procrastinate	never	Sometimes	always	procrastinate
a	b	c	d	e

11. To what degree is procrastination on this task a problem for you?

Not at all a	Almost		Nearly	Always a
problem	never	Sometimes	always	problem
a	b	c	d	e

12. To what extent do you want to decrease your tendency to procrastinate on this task?

				Definitely want to decrease
Do not want to decrease		Somewhat		
a	b	c	d	e

V. *Attendance Tasks: Meeting with Your Advisor, Making an Appointment with a Professor, etc.*

13. To what extent do you procrastinate on this task?

Never procrastinate	Almost never	Sometimes	Nearly always	Always procrastinate
a	b	c	d	e

14. To what extent is procrastination on this task a problem for you?

Not at all a problem	Almost never	Sometimes	Nearly always	Always a problem
a	b	c	d	e

15. To what extent do you want to decrease your tendency to procrastinate on this task?

				Definitely want to decrease
Do not want to decrease		Somewhat		
a	b	c	d	e

VI. *School Activities in General*

16. To what extent do you procrastinate on these activities?

Never procrastinate	Almost never	Sometimes	Nearly always	Always procrastinate
a	b	c	d	e

17. To what extent is procrastination on these activities a problem for you?

Not at all a problem	Almost never	Sometimes	Nearly always	Always a problem
a	b	c	d	e

18. To what extent do you want to decrease your tendency to procrastinate on these activities?

Do not want to decrease		Somewhat		Definitely want to decrease
a	b	c	d	e

REASONS FOR PROCRASTINATION

Think of the last time the following situation occurred. It's near the end of the semester. The term paper you were assigned at the beginning of the semester is due very soon. You have not begun work on this paper. There are reasons why you have been procrastinating on this task.

Rate each of the following reasons on a 5-point scale according to how much it reflects why you procrastinated at the time. Mark your answers by writing the letter a to e in the space to the left of each statement.

Use the scale:

Not at all reflects why I procrastinated		Somewhat reflects		Definitely reflects why I procrastinated
a	b	c	d	e

____ 19. You were concerned the professor wouldn't like your work.

____ 20. You had a hard time knowing what to include and what not to include in your paper.

____ 21. You waited until a classmate did his/hers, so that he/she could give you some advice.

____ 22. You had too many other things to do.

____ 23. There's some information you needed to ask the professor, but you felt uncomfortable approaching him/her.

____ 24. You were worried you would get a bad grade.

____ 25. You resented having to do things assigned by others.

____ 26. You didn't think you knew enough to write the paper.

____ 27. You really disliked writing term papers.

____ 28. You felt overwhelmed by the task.

____ 29. You had difficulty requesting information from other people.

____ 30. You looked forward to the excitement of doing this task at the last minute.

____ 31. You couldn't choose among all the topics.

____ 32. You were concerned that if you did well, your classmates would resent you.

____ 33. You didn't trust yourself to do a good job.

____ 34. You didn't have enough energy to begin the task.

____ 35. You felt it just takes too long to write a term paper.

____ 36. You liked the challenge of waiting until the deadline.

____ 37. You knew that your classmates hadn't started the paper either.

_____ 38. You resented people setting deadlines for you.

_____ 39. You were concerned you wouldn't meet your own expectations.

_____ 40. You were concerned that if you got a good grade, people would have higher expectations of you in the future.

_____ 41. You waited to see if the professor would give you some more information about the paper.

_____ 42. You set very high standards for yourself and you worried that you wouldn't be able to meet those standards.

_____ 43. You just felt too lazy to write a term paper.

_____ 44. Your friends were pressuring you to do other things.

PROCRASTINATION SCALE (PS)

AUTHOR: Bruce W. Tuckman

PURPOSE: To measure procrastination.

DESCRIPTION: The PS is a 35-item instrument designed to measure tendencies of procrastination. Procrastination is viewed as the lack or absence of self-regulated performance, the tendency to put off or completely avoid an activity under one's control. From an original 72 items, factor analysis resulted in the present 35-item scale. Subsequent factor analysis revealed 16 items that could be used as a short form PS (items 1, 2, 3, 4, 7, 9, 11, 18, 22–25, 28, 29, 32, 34). The PS is a useful scale for research or for evaluating changes in clients being treated for problems involving procrastination.

NORMS: The PS was studied with 183 college juniors and seniors between the ages of 19 and 22 who were preparing to become teachers. Actual norms were not provided.

SCORING: The PS is easily scored by summing the item responses on a scale from 1 to 4 ("That's me for sure" = 4) for a total score, with higher scores equaling greater tendencies to procrastination. Items 6, 8, 13, 17, 25, 27, 29, 30, 33, 34 are reverse-scored.

RELIABILITY: The PS has excellent internal consistency, with an alpha of .90 for the 35-item scale and .86 for the 16-item scale. No data on stability were reported.

VALIDITY: The PS has good concurrent validity, correlating negatively with the General Self-Efficacy Scale and a behavioral measure of self-regulated performance.

PRIMARY REFERENCE: Tuckman, B. W. (1991). The development and concurrent validity of the Procrastination Scale, *Educational and Psychological Measurement*, 51, 473–480.

AVAILABILITY: Journal article.

PS

Indicate how you feel about each statement by placing the appropriate letter in the blank.

A = That's me for sure
B = That's my tendency
C = That's *not* my tendency
D = That's *not* me for sure

____ 1. I needlessly delay finishing jobs, even when they're important.
____ 2. I postpone starting in on things I don't like to do.
____ 3. When I have a deadline, I wait till the last minute.
____ 4. I delay making tough decisions.
____ 5. I stall on initiating new activities.
____ 6. I'm on time for appointments.
____ 7. I keep putting off improving my work habits.
____ 8. I get right to work, even on life's unpleasant chores.
____ 9. I manage to find an excuse for not doing something.
____ 10. I avoid doing those things which I expect to do poorly.
____ 11. I put the necessary time into even boring tasks, like studying.
____ 12. When I get tired of an unpleasant job, I stop.
____ 13. I believe in "keeping my nose to the grindstone."
____ 14. When something's not worth the trouble, I stop.
____ 15. I believe that things I don't like doing should not exist.
____ 16. I consider people who make me do unfair and difficult things to be rotten.
____ 17. When it counts, I can manage to enjoy even studying.
____ 18. I am an incurable time waster.
____ 19. I feel that it's my absolute right to have other people treat me fairly.
____ 20. I believe that other people don't have the right to give me deadlines.
____ 21. Studying makes me feel entirely miserable.
____ 22. I'm a time waster now but I can't seem to do anything about it.
____ 23. When something's too tough to tackle, I believe in postponing it.
____ 24. I promise myself I'll do something and then drag my feet.
____ 25. Whenever I make a plan of action, I follow it.
____ 26. I wish I could find an easy way to get myself moving.
____ 27. When I have trouble with a task, it's usually my own fault.
____ 28. Even though I hate myself if I don't get started, it doesn't get me going.
____ 29. I always finish important jobs with time to spare.
____ 30. When I'm done with my work, I check it over.
____ 31. I look for a loophole or shortcut to get through a tough task.
____ 32. I still get stuck in neutral even though I know how important it is to get started.
____ 33. I never met a job I couldn't "lick."
____ 34. Putting something off until tomorrow is not the way I do it.
____ 35. I feel that work burns me out.

Copyright © 1990 Bruce W. Tuckman.

PROVISION OF SOCIAL RELATIONS (PSR)

AUTHORS: R. Jay Turner, B. Gail Frankel, and Deborah M. Levin

PURPOSE: To measure social support.

DESCRIPTION: The PSR is a 15-item instrument designed to measure components of social support. Based initially on the conceptualization by Weiss of five components of social support (attachment, social integration, reassurance of worth, reliable alliance, and guidance), factor analysis revealed the PSR to have essentially two dimensions, family support (items 4, 7, 10, 11, 12, 14) and friend support (items 1, 2, 3, 5, 6, 8, 9, 13, 15). The PSR is one of the few instruments that examines the environmental variable of social support (or, at least, the respondent's perceptions of it), a key element for assessment and intervention in many clinical approaches.

NORMS: The PSR was developed in a series of studies involving 200 university students, 523 discharged psychiatric patients in Canada (59% female), and 989 (54% female) psychiatrically disabled community residents located in interviews with 11,000 households in Ontario, Canada. Actual norms are not available.

SCORING: The PSR is scored by reverse-scoring items 7 and 15 and then summing the item scores on each of the subdimensions to get a score for that dimension. A total score can be obtained by summing the scores on the two subdimensions. Higher scores reflect more social support.

RELIABILITY: The PSR has good internal consistency, with alphas that range from .75 to .87. No test-retest correlations were reported.

VALIDITY: The PSR has good concurrent validity, correlating significantly with the Kaplan Scale of Social Support. The PSR is negatively correlated with several measures of psychological distress, indicating that the PSR is not confounded by item content measuring psychological distress.

PRIMARY REFERENCE: Turner, R. J., Frankel, B. G., and Levin, D. M. (1983). Social support: Conceptualization, measurement, and implications for mental health, *Research in Community and Mental Health*, 3, 67–111. Instrument reproduced with permission of JAI Press, Inc. and B. Gail Frankel.

AVAILABILITY: Journal article.

PSR

We would like to know something about your relationships with other people. Please read each statement below and decide how well the statement describes you. For each statement, show your answer by indicating to the left of the item the number that best describes how you feel. The numbers represent the following answers.

1 = Very much like me
2 = Much like me
3 = Somewhat like me
4 = Not very much like me
5 = Not at all like me

_____ 1. When I'm with my friends, I feel completely able to relax and be myself.
_____ 2. I share the same approach to life that many of my friends do.
_____ 3. People who know me trust me and respect me.
_____ 4. No matter what happens, I know that my family will always be there for me should I need them.
_____ 5. When I want to go out to do things I know that many of my friends would enjoy doing these things with me.
_____ 6. I have at least one friend I could tell anything to.
_____ 7. Sometimes I'm not sure if I can completely rely on my family.
_____ 8. People who know me think I am good at what I do.
_____ 9. I feel very close to some of my friends.
_____ 10. People in my family have confidence in me.
_____ 11. My family lets me know they think I am a worthwhile person.
_____ 12. People in my family provide me with help in finding solutions to my problems.
_____ 13. My friends would take the time to talk over my problems, should I ever want to.
_____ 14. I know my family will always stand by me.
_____ 15. Even when I am with my friends I feel alone.

PURSUING–DISTANCING SCALE (P-D)

AUTHORS: Donald M. Bernstein, John Santelli, Karen Alter-Reid, and Vincent Androsiglio

PURPOSE: To measure interpersonal pursuing and distancing.

DESCRIPTION: The P-D is an 80-item scale designed to measure the construct of interpersonal pursuing and distancing. Although the scale is longer than almost all in this book, it is included here because of its easy and speedy administration. Pursuing and distancing are related to the general construct of interpersonal contact or preferred amount of "space" among people. Pursuing is said to represent the forces of connectedness and togetherness, while distancing represents the forces of individuality and depends upon privacy and avoidance of emotional involvement for self-protection. The P-D reflects the manner in which pursuing and distancing are expressed behaviorally. The P-D is viewed as useful not only for research on these constructs but as a tool for clinicians who explore these topics with their clients.

NORMS: The P-D has been studied with several samples, including 36 pairs of twins, 95 psychology students, 203 Indians, 161 Thais (all English speaking), and 61 nonstudent American adults. The mean age of the samples ranged from 23 to 39. The scores were fairly equally distributed. Across all American samples, pursuing scores average 22 (SD = 5.5) and distancing scores average 19.5 (SD = 5.7). There were no significant differences due to sex.

SCORING: The P-D is easily responded to by circling "YES" next to an item if it applies to the respondent, or "NO" if it does not. The scores for pursuing and distancing are easily obtained by summing the number of items of each type found self-descriptive by the subject. The pursuing items are: 1, 2, 3, 6, 8, 11, 12, 13, 16, 19, 21, 22, 24, 26, 27, 31, 32, 34, 37, 38, 44, 45, 47, 49, 50, 54, 55, 57, 58, 60, 63, 65, 68, 69, 70, 73, 75, 76, 79, 80. The remaining items are distancing. The scale has six subscales for which scoring keys are available from the authors. The subscales are: cognitive style, emotional style, social style, communicative style, sensation selling, and anality.

RELIABILITY: Internal consistency for the P-D was determined by finding the correlation of each item with the total score for that item's form (pursuing and distancing). The mean correlation for all items was .31, suggesting rather weak internal consistency. No data on stability are available.

VALIDITY: The P-D is said to have very good construct validity, as revealed by significant correlations in predicted ways with instruments measuring sex role, assertiveness, sensation-seeking, introversion-extraversion, and by clinicians' ratings of client characteristics.

PRIMARY REFERENCE: Bernstein, D. M., Santelli, J., Alter-Reid, K., and Androsiglio, V. (1985). Pursuing and Distancing: The construct and its measurement, *Journal of Personality Assessment*, 49, 273–281.
AVAILABILITY: Dr. Donald M. Bernstein, Psychology Department, Fairleigh Dickinson University, Teaneck, NJ 07666.

P-D

Please circle "Yes" on the answer sheet for each item that applies to you, and circle "No" if the item does not apply to you. You must pick one or the other; *never mark both "Yes" and "No" for the same item.* On occasion, you may feel that two seemingly contradictory items apply or do not apply to you. In those instances make the response that best describes you for each separate item regardless of the apparent contradiction. That is, it's OK to make the same response to contradictory statements if you see both statements as characterizing you.

Yes	No	1.	When I talk to people I like to make frequent eye contact.
Yes	No	2.	If my feelings were badly hurt I would not hesitate to show them.
Yes	No	3.	When something good happens to me, I can't wait to tell someone about it.
Yes	No	4.	When I greet family and friends I'm glad when the hugging and kissing are over.
Yes	No	5.	After a fight I usually remain silent and aloof.
Yes	No	6.	I enjoy gambling.
Yes	No	7.	I tend to hold back praise or compliments.
Yes	No	8.	I usually talk to the person sitting next to me on the train or bus.
Yes	No	9.	I am more comfortable when situations are clear-cut and unambiguous.
Yes	No	10.	I find it difficult to say "I love you" to someone.
Yes	No	11.	I am inclined to be optimistic.
Yes	No	12.	I like to spend a lot of my time playing games that involve other people.
Yes	No	13.	I often prefer to buy things on impulse.
Yes	No	14.	When I come home from work or school I relax by watching a good TV program.
Yes	No	15.	I tend to avoid disclosing information of a personal nature.
Yes	No	16.	I like to take spontaneous vacations with as little planning as possible.
Yes	No	17.	I find entertaining at my house a burden.
Yes	No	18.	When I listen to a song I focus my attention mainly on the lyrics.
Yes	No	19.	I can easily say "I'm sorry."
Yes	No	20.	I tend to avoid using intuition.
Yes	No	21.	I prefer not to wear a watch.
Yes	No	22.	I find it easy to trust people.
Yes	No	23.	When I recall a work of art it is mainly in terms of its technical aspects.
Yes	No	24.	I tend to speak my mind even if feelings get ruffled.
Yes	No	25.	I tend to describe events as the orderly sequence of specific details.
Yes	No	26.	I prefer to initiate sexual activity with my partner.
Yes	No	27.	I make friends quickly.
Yes	No	28.	When I take a trip I'm mainly interested in reaching my destination.
Yes	No	29.	I think a great deal about the past and future.

Yes   No   30.   I prefer to save my money.
Yes   No   31.   If someone owed me money I would ask for it back.
Yes   No   32.   At a party I rapidly become involved with other people.
Yes   No   33.   I like movies with clear-cut plots.
Yes   No   34.   If I disagree with someone I will let them know what I think.
Yes   No   35.   I find it difficult to say "I'm angry with you" to someone.
Yes   No   36.   After a heated argument I usually refrain from discussing the topic more.
Yes   No   37.   I enjoy movies that make me cry.
Yes   No   38.   I prefer to try new things.
Yes   No   39.   If a restaurant served me something ill-prepared I would probably not send it back.
Yes   No   40.   I become uncomfortable when people around me are emotional.
Yes   No   41.   I often find myself looking elsewhere while talking to someone.
Yes   No   42.   If I were badly injured I would control my feelings.
Yes   No   43.   When something good happens to me I often wait awhile before telling someone about it.
Yes   No   44.   When I greet family and friends I like to hug and kiss.
Yes   No   45.   I usually make up soon after a fight.
Yes   No   46.   I don't enjoy gambling.
Yes   No   47.   I give praise or compliments freely.
Yes   No   48.   When I take a train or bus I read the paper or a book during the trip.
Yes   No   49.   I have little difficulty dealing with ambiguity and uncertainty.
Yes   No   50.   I would find it easy to say "I love you" to someone.
Yes   No   51.   I'm inclined to be pessimistic.
Yes   No   52.   I like to spend most of my time reading good books.
Yes   No   53.   I consider my finances and research prices before making most purchases.
Yes   No   54.   When I come home from work or school I unwind by engaging in conversation.
Yes   No   55.   I find it easy to tell people about myself.
Yes   No   56.   I like to take planned vacations where I know what will happen in advance.
Yes   No   57.   I like to entertain people at my house.
Yes   No   58.   When I hear a song it is mainly the melody that holds my attention.
Yes   No   59.   I find it difficult to say "I'm sorry."
Yes   No   60.   I am inclined to be intuitive.
Yes   No   61.   I prefer to wear a watch.
Yes   No   62.   I find it difficult to trust people.
Yes   No   63.   When I recall a work of art it is in terms of the impression it made on me.
Yes   No   64.   I avoid telling people what's on my mind if I think it may hurt their feelings.
Yes   No   65.   I tend to describe events in terms of general impressions.
Yes   No   66.   I would rather have my partner initiate sexual activity.
Yes   No   67.   I make friends slowly.
Yes   No   68.   Traveling to a destination is as enjoyable as getting there.

Yes No 69. I am mainly concerned with the present.
Yes No 70. I prefer to spend my money.
Yes No 71. If someone owed me money I would be hesitant to ask for it back.
Yes No 72. At a party I wait to be approached by people.
Yes No 73. I prefer impressionistic, abstract movies.
Yes No 74. I avoid making waves.
Yes No 75. I would find it easy to say "I'm angry with you" to someone.
Yes No 76. After a heated argument I often continue discussing the topic.
Yes No 77. I rarely react emotionally to a movie.
Yes No 78. I prefer to do things I'm familiar with.
Yes No 79. If a restaurant served me something ill-prepared I would send it back.
Yes No 80. I remain at ease when people around me are emotional.

QUESTIONNAIRE OF EXPERIENCES OF DISSOCIATION (QED)

AUTHOR: Kevin C. Riley

PURPOSE: To measure dissociation.

DESCRIPTION: The QED is a 26-item instrument designed to measure dissociation or the failure to integrate thoughts, feelings, and actions into consciousness. Dissociation is viewed as the mechanism underlying the syndrome of hysteria and symptoms such as conversion reaction, fugue states, and multiple personality. The items for the QED were drawn from the clinical literature on people suffering from the above problems. The QED is viewed as a useful measure for clinicians working with problems related to dissociation.

NORMS: The QED has been studied with large, nonclinical samples (760 women, 450 men), and smaller samples of clinical respondents (somatization disorder, $n = 21$, and multiple personality disorder, $n = 3$). No other demographic information is available. The "normal" group had a mean of 9.92, the somatization disorder group's mean was 13.9, and the multiple personality group's mean was 24.6.

SCORING: The QED is scored by simply scoring one point for each dissociation response and summing these up. Higher scores show greater dissociation. "Correct" (dissociative) answers are "true" for all items except items 7, 10, 15, 17, 18, 20, 21, and 23–26.

RELIABILITY: The QED has fairly good internal consistency, with an alpha of .77. No data on stability are available.

VALIDITY: The QED has good face validity. There are no other real validity data; however, the fact that the two clinical groups, somatization and multiple personality disorder as described above, believed to be at risk for dissociation, have elevated scores on the QED suggests some degree of known-groups validity.

PRIMARY REFERENCE: Riley, K. C. (1988). Measurement of Dissociation, *Journal of Nervous and Mental Disease*, 176, 449–450.

AVAILABILITY: Journal article.

QED

Listed below are a number of statements about experiences you may or may not have had. Read each one and indicate your response by circling the appropriate letter (T = True, F = False). There are no "right" or "wrong" answers.

T F   1. I often feel as if things were not real.
T F   2. Occasionally, I feel like someone else.
T F   3. Sometimes my mind blocks, goes totally empty.
T F   4. I often wonder who I really am.
T F   5. At one or more times, I have found myself staring intently at myself in the mirror as though looking at a stranger.
T F   6. I often feel that I am removed from my thoughts and actions.
T F   7. I rarely feel confused, like in a daze.
T F   8. I have had periods where I could not remember where I had been the day (or days) before.
T F   9. When I try to speak words, they don't come out right.
T F 10. I have never come to without knowing where I was or how I got there.
T F 11. As I was growing up, people often said that I seemed to be off in a world of my own.
T F 12. Sometimes I feel like my body is undergoing a transformation.
T F 13. Sometimes I feel as if there is someone inside of me directing my actions.
T F 14. Sometimes my limbs move on their own.
T F 15. When I was a child, I rarely sat and daydreamed in school.
T F 16. Sometimes I have problems understanding others' speech.
T F 17. I am rarely bothered by forgetting where I put things.
T F 18. My mind has never gone blank on me.
T F 19. I have a rich and exciting fantasy life.
T F 20. I never find myself staring off into space without thinking of anything.
T F 21. I daydream very little.
T F 22. My soul sometimes leaves my body.
T F 23. I do not think that I would be able to hypnotize myself.
T F 24. When I was a child, I never had imaginary companions.
T F 25. I have never gone into a trance, like hypnosis.
T F 26. I have never had periods of déjà vu, that is, found myself in a new position with the distinct sense that I had been there or experienced it before.

RAPE AFTERMATH SYMPTOM TEST (RAST)

AUTHOR: Dean G. Kilpatrick

PURPOSE: To measure responses to rape.

DESCRIPTION: The RAST is a 70-item instrument designed to measure fear and other symptoms commonly experienced by female victims after a rape experience. The RAST was constructed using items from instruments that were considered successful in detecting rape-related symptoms—the Derogatis SCL–9O-R and the Veronen-Kilpatrick Modified Fear Survey. A major value of the RAST is it is relatively brief (in comparison to the other measures) and thus may enhance assessment and evaluation efficiency.

NORMS: The RAST was studied initially with 204 adult, female rape victims and 173 nonvictims, matched for age, race, and residential neighborhood. Roughly 56–57% of each group was white, 40–43% black, and 0.6–2% other. There was a broad range of educational and marital status represented in the samples. The means for the RAST varied dramatically for the rape group depending on the length of time that had transpired since the rape. From 6 to 21 days after the rape ($n = 131$), the mean was 101.80 (SD = 43.17). Six months after the rape ($n = 103$), the mean was 60.70 (SD = 38.17). One year after the rape ($n = 75$), the mean was 60.73 (SD = 40.57), and three years after the rape ($n = 12$), the mean was 46.00 (SD = 32.57).

SCORING: The RAST is easily scored by simply summing individual item scores for a total score. The possible range is from 0 to 280 with higher scores indicating more psychological symptoms and fear-producing stimuli.

RELIABILITY: The RAST has excellent internal consistency, with an alpha of .95. It also has excellent stability, with a 2.5-month test-retest correlation of .85 (for nonvictims).

VALIDITY: The RAST has excellent known-groups validity, significantly distinguishing between victims and nonvictims at all the time periods described above. No other validity data were available.

PRIMARY REFERENCE: Kilpatrick, D. G., Best, C. L., Veronen, L. J., Ruff, M. H., Ruff, G. A., and Allison, J. C. (1985). The aftermath of rape: A 3-year longitudinal study. Paper presented at the annual convention of the American Psychological Association, Los Angeles, California.

AVAILABILITY: Dr. Dean Kilpatrick, Crime Victims Research and Treatment Center, Department of Psychiatry and Behavioral Sciences, Medical University of South Carolina, Charleston, SC 29425.

RAST

Using the following key, complete the two sections below:

0 = Not at all
1 = A little
2 = A fair amount
3 = Much
4 = Very much

SECTION 1

The items in this section refer to things and experiences that may cause fear or unpleasant feelings. Circle the number that describes how much you are disturbed by each item nowadays.

1.	Parking lots	0	1	2	3	4
2.	Being in a car alone	0	1	2	3	4
3.	Being on an elevator alone	0	1	2	3	4
4.	Automobiles	0	1	2	3	4
5.	Darkness	0	1	2	3	4
6.	Strange shapes	0	1	2	3	4
7.	Closed spaces	0	1	2	3	4
8.	Going out with new people	0	1	2	3	4
9.	Entering room where people are seated	0	1	2	3	4
10.	Answering the phone	0	1	2	3	4
11.	Seeing other people injected	0	1	2	3	4
12.	Journeys by bus	0	1	2	3	4
13.	Enclosed places	0	1	2	3	4
14.	Being criticized	0	1	2	3	4
15.	Being awakened at night	0	1	2	3	4
16.	Being in a strange place	0	1	2	3	4

17.	Walking on a dimly lit street	0	1	2	3	4
18.	Being alone	0	1	2	3	4
19.	Sound of doorbell	0	1	2	3	4
20.	Sudden noises	0	1	2	3	4
21.	A man's penis	0	1	2	3	4
22.	Sexual intercourse	0	1	2	3	4
23.	Stopping at a stoplight	0	1	2	3	4
24.	Blind dates	0	1	2	3	4
25.	Dreams	0	1	2	3	4
26.	Strangers	0	1	2	3	4
27.	Door slamming	0	1	2	3	4
28.	People talking about you	0	1	2	3	4
29.	Sleeping alone	0	1	2	3	4
30.	People behind you	0	1	2	3	4
31.	Shadows	0	1	2	3	4
32.	Testifying in court	0	1	2	3	4
33.	Journeys by train	0	1	2	3	4
34.	Journeys by car	0	1	2	3	4
35.	Crowds	0	1	2	3	4
36.	Angry people	0	1	2	3	4
37.	Talking to police	0	1	2	3	4
38.	Large open spaces	0	1	2	3	4
39.	Nude men	0	1	2	3	4
40.	Voices	0	1	2	3	4

SECTION 2

Below is a list of problems and complaints that people sometimes have. Read each one carefully and circle the number from the previous key (0 = not at all, 1 = a little, 2 = a fair amount, 3 = much, 4 = very much) that best describes how much discomfort that problem has caused you during the past _____, including today.

1.	Feeling low in energy or slowed down	0	1	2	3	4
2.	Feeling of being caught or trapped	0	1	2	3	4
3.	Feeling lonely	0	1	2	3	4
4.	Feelings of worthlessness	0	1	2	3	4
5.	Feeling afraid in open spaces or in the streets	0	1	2	3	4
6.	Feeling afraid to go out of your house alone	0	1	2	3	4
7.	Feeling afraid to travel on buses, subways, or trains	0	1	2	3	4
8.	Having to avoid certain things, places, or activities because they frighten you	0	1	2	3	4
9.	Feeling uneasy in crowds such as shopping or at a movie	0	1	2	3	4
10.	Feeling nervous when you are left alone	0	1	2	3	4
11.	Trouble falling asleep	0	1	2	3	4
12.	Awakening in the early morning	0	1	2	3	4
13.	Sleep that is restless or disturbed	0	1	2	3	4
14.	Suddenly scared for no reason	0	1	2	3	4
15.	Feeling fearful	0	1	2	3	4
16.	Spells of terror or panic	0	1	2	3	4
17.	Feeling so restless you couldn't sit still	0	1	2	3	4
18.	The feeling that something bad is going to happen to you	0	1	2	3	4
19.	Thoughts and images of a frightening nature	0	1	2	3	4
20.	Feeling that most people cannot be trusted	0	1	2	3	4

21. Feeling that you are watched or talked about by others   0 1 2 3 4

22. Feeling that people will take advantage of you if you let them   0 1 2 3 4

23. Feeling shy or uneasy with the opposite sex   0 1 2 3 4

24. Feeling others do not understand you or are unsympathetic   0 1 2 3 4

25. Feeling uneasy when people are watching or talking about you   0 1 2 3 4

26. Feeling very self-conscious with others   0 1 2 3 4

27. Hearing voices other people do not hear   0 1 2 3 4

28. Feeling lonely even when you are with people   0 1 2 3 4

29. Having thoughts about sex that bother you a lot   0 1 2 3 4

30. The idea that something is wrong with your mind   0 1 2 3 4

RATHUS ASSERTIVENESS SCHEDULE (RAS)

AUTHOR: Spencer A. Rathus

PURPOSE: To measure assertiveness.

DESCRIPTION: This 30-item instrument was designed to measure assertiveness, or what the author called social boldness. Respondents are asked to rate 30 social situations according to how characteristic each is of their own experience. This widely used instrument provides the practitioner with clients' impressions of their own assertiveness and frankness, and can be used to provide positive feedback to clients during treatment, which is especially important in working with assertiveness problems. The RAS does not seem to be affected by social desirability.

NORMS: Data are reported for a sample of 68 undergraduates which also were used in the reliability analysis. The subjects had an age range from 17 to 27 years. The mean RAS was .294 with a standard deviation of 29.121. At an eight week post test the mean was 1.62 with a standard deviation of 27.632.

SCORING: Items are rated in terms of how descriptive the item is of the respondent. Ratings are from +3 to −3. Seventeen items, indicated by an asterisk on the scale, are reverse-scored. Scores are determined by summing item ratings, and can range from −90 to +90. Negative scores reflect nonassertiveness and positive scores reflect assertiveness.

RELIABILITY: The RAS has evidence of good internal consistency and stability. Split-half reliability was .77. Test-retest reliability over an eight-week period was .78.

VALIDITY: The RAS has good concurrent validity. Scores on the instrument have been shown to correlate with measures of boldness, outspokenness, assertiveness, aggressiveness, and confidence. Strong concurrent validity also is seen in the correlation between RAS scores and trained raters' rankings of assertiveness. Also, the RAS has been shown to possess construct validity: 19 of the 30 items correlated with external measures of assertiveness and 28 were negatively correlated with a measure of niceness.

PRIMARY REFERENCE: Rathus, S. A. (1973). A 30-item schedule for assessing assertive behavior, *Behavior Therapy*, 4, 398–406. Instrument reproduced with permission of Academic Press.

AVAILABILITY: Journal article.

RAS

Indicate how characteristic or descriptive each of the following statements is of you by using the code given below.

+3 = Very characteristic of me, extremely descriptive
+2 = Rather characteristic of me, quite descriptive
+1 = Somewhat characteristic of me, slightly descriptive
−1 = Somewhat uncharacteristic of me, slightly nondescriptive
−2 = Rather uncharacteristic of me, quite nondescriptive
−3 = Very uncharacteristic of me, extremely nondescriptive

____ 1. Most people seem to be more aggressive and assertive than I am. *
____ 2. I have hesitated to make or accept dates because of "shyness." *
____ 3. When the food served at a restaurant is not done to my satisfaction, I complain about it to the waiter or waitress.
____ 4. I am careful to avoid hurting other people's feelings, even when I feel that I have been injured. *
____ 5. If a salesman has gone to considerable trouble to show me merchandise that is not quite suitable, I have a difficult time saying "No." *
____ 6. When I am asked to do something, I insist upon knowing why.
____ 7. There are times when I look for a good, vigorous argument.
____ 8. I strive to get ahead as well as most people in my position.
____ 9. To be honest, people often take advantage of me. *
____ 10. I enjoy starting conversations with new acquaintances and strangers.
____ 11. I often don't know what to say to attractive persons of the opposite sex. *
____ 12. I will hesitate to make phone calls to business establishments and institutions. *
____ 13. I would rather apply for a job or for admission to a college by writing letters than by going through with personal interviews. *
____ 14. I find it embarrassing to return merchandise. *
____ 15. If a close and respected relative were annoying me, I would smother my feelings rather than express my annoyance. *
____ 16. I have avoided asking questions for fear of sounding stupid. *
____ 17. During an argument I am sometimes afraid that I will get so upset that I will shake all over. *
____ 18. If a famed and respected lecturer makes a statement which I think is incorrect, I will have the audience hear my point of view as well.
____ 19. I avoid arguing over prices with clerks and salesmen. *
____ 20. When I have done something important or worthwhile, I manage to let others know about it.
____ 21. I am open and frank about my feelings.
____ 22. If someone has been spreading false and bad stories about me, I see him/her as soon as possible to "have a talk" about it.
____ 23. I often have a hard time saying "No." *
____ 24. I tend to bottle up my emotions rather than make a scene. *
____ 25. I complain about poor service in a restaurant and elsewhere.

_____ 26. When I am given a compliment, I sometimes just don't know what to say. *

_____ 27. If a couple near me in a theater or at a lecture were conversing rather loudly, I would ask them to be quiet or to take their conversation elsewhere.

_____ 28. Anyone attempting to push ahead of me in a line is in for a good battle.

_____ 29. I am quick to express an opinion.

_____ 30. There are times when I just can't say anything. *

RATIONAL BEHAVIOR INVENTORY (RBI)

AUTHORS: Clayton T. Shorkey and Victor C. Whiteman

PURPOSE: To measure irrational and absolutist beliefs.

DESCRIPTION: The RBI is a 37-item instrument that provides an overall index of irrationality, or the tendency to hold irrational and absolutist beliefs. The RBI is based on the work of Albert Ellis on cognitive therapy and the assumption that irrational beliefs underlie emotional disorders. The RBI was specifically constructed to be used for assessment, treatment planning, and evaluation in rational-behavior and cognitive-behavior therapy. It has been extensively studied by a number of investigators. The RBI presents one overall score plus 11 factors: (1) catastrophizing, (2) guilt, (3) perfectionism, (4) need for approval, (5) caring and helping, (6) blame and punishment, (7) inertia and avoidance, (8) independence, (9) self-downing, (10) projected misfortune, and (11) control of emotions. Each factor has three or four items, and separate factor scores as well as the overall score give a clear picture of the extent of an individual's irrational or dysfunctional beliefs in several areas.

NORMS: The RBI has been studied with a number of different clinical and nonclinical samples. The initial studies were conducted on 414 undergraduate students and 127 mental health professionals attending workshops by Albert Ellis. For undergraduates, the mean total rationality score was 26.35. There were no statistically significant differences between males and females except on one subscale. For the two groups of mental health professionals, total RBI scores prior to the Ellis workshop were 28.45 and 27.62. Normative data are available for other groups as well.

SCORING: The RBI is somewhat difficult to score and it is recommended that the scoring guide available with the instrument be used. Basically, each item on the RBI is assigned a cutting point of 3 or 4, and the number of points assigned to that item is based on that cutting point. Once the score for each factor is determined by summing the scores on each item on the factor, the overall score is determined by summing the scores for all eleven factors. This results in a possible range of 0 to 38 with higher scores indicating greater irrationality.

RELIABILITY: The RBI has good internal consistency and homogeneity. Each factor was measured by a Guttman scale with a coefficient of reproducibility of .60 or more. The total RBI had a split-half reliability of .73. The RBI has good stability, with a .82 test-retest correlation after three days and .71 after ten days.

VALIDITY: A number of studies have demonstrated good concurrent and known-groups validity for the RBI. The RBI is significantly correlated in predicted directions with several measures of trait and state anxiety in clinical and nonclinical samples. The RBI has been found to be significantly correlated to several other personality measures, such as anomie, authoritarianism, dogmatism, self-esteem, and to measures of psychiatric symptomatology. Further, the RBI has been found to distinguish between clinical and nonclinical samples in several studies, and is also sensitive to changes from both workshops and therapy. Finally, the RBI does not appear to be influenced by social desirability response set.

PRIMARY REFERENCE: Shorkey, C. T. and Whiteman, V. L. (1977). Development of the Rational Behavior Inventory: Initial validity and reliability, *Educational and Psychological Measurement*, 37, 527–534. Instrument reproduced with permission of Clayton T. Shorkey.

AVAILABILITY: Educational Testing Service, Princeton, NJ 08540.

RBI

For each of the following questions, please follow the scale and indicate the numbered response that most clearly reflects your opinion. Work quickly and answer each question.

1 = Strongly disagree
2 = Disagree
3 = Neutral
4 = Agree
5 = Strongly agree

_____ 1. Helping others is the very basis of life.
_____ 2. It is necessary to be especially friendly to new colleagues and neighbors.
_____ 3. People should observe moral laws more strictly than they do.
_____ 4. I find it difficult to take criticism without feeling hurt.
_____ 5. I often spend more time trying to think of ways of getting out of things than it would take me to do them.
_____ 6. I tend to become terribly upset and miserable when things are not the way I would like them to be.
_____ 7. It is impossible at any given time to change one's emotions.
_____ 8. It is sinful to doubt the Bible.
_____ 9. Sympathy is the most beautiful human emotion.
_____ 10. I shrink from facing a crisis or difficulty.
_____ 11. I often get excited or upset when things go wrong.
_____ 12. One should rebel against doing unpleasant things, however necessary, if doing them is unpleasant.
_____ 13. I get upset when neighbors are very harsh with their little children.
_____ 14. It is realistic to expect that there should be no incompatibility in marriage.
_____ 15. I frequently feel unhappy with my appearance.
_____ 16. A person should be thoroughly competent, adequate, talented, and intelligent in all possible respects.
_____ 17. What others think of you is most important.
_____ 18. Other people should make things easier for us, and help with life's difficulties.
_____ 19. I tend to look to others for the kind of behavior they approve as right or wrong.
_____ 20. I find that my occupation and social life tend to make me unhappy.
_____ 21. I usually try to avoid doing chores which I dislike doing.
_____ 22. Some of my family and/or friends have habits that bother and annoy me very much.
_____ 23. I tend to worry about possible accidents and disasters.
_____ 24. I like to bear responsibility alone.
_____ 25. I get terribly upset and miserable when things are not the way I like them to be.
_____ 26. I worry quite a bit over possible misfortunes.
_____ 27. Punishing oneself for all errors will prevent future mistakes.

_____ 28. One can best help others by criticizing them and sharply pointing out the error of their ways.

_____ 29. Worrying about a possible danger will help ward it off or decrease its effects.

_____ 30. I worry about little things.

_____ 31. Certain people are bad, wicked, or villainous and should be severely blamed and punished for their sins.

_____ 32. A large number of people are guilty of bad sexual conduct.

_____ 33. One should blame oneself severely for all mistakes and wrongdoings.

_____ 34. It makes me very uncomfortable to be different.

_____ 35. I worry over possible misfortunes.

_____ 36. I prefer to be independent of others in making decisions.

_____ 37. Because a certain thing once strongly affected one's life, it should indefinitely affect it.

RAULIN INTENSE AMBIVALENCE SCALE (RIAS)

AUTHOR: Michael L. Raulin

PURPOSE: To measure intense ambivalence.

DESCRIPTION: The RIAS is a 45-item scale designed to measure intense ambivalence. Ambivalence is defined as the existence of simultaneous or rapidly interchangeable positive and negative feelings toward the same object or activity, with both positive and negative feelings being strong. Although the RIAS was developed on the assumption that intense ambivalence is an important feature in schizophrenia, development of the instrument with diverse populations suggests broader utility. The 45 true/false items were chosen from a wide range of potential items. In designing the scale, particular attention was placed on minimizing social desirability response set.

NORMS: Several studies were carried out in the development of RIAS. The first set involved 384 male and 475 female undergraduate students. The second involved 89 male and 8 female inpatients diagnosed as schizophrenic, 13 male and 18 female inpatients diagnosed as depressed, 66 male and 131 female psychology clinic clients with a range of nonpsychotic disorders, and a "normal" control group of 104 male and 39 females from the general population. Mean scores on the RIAS were 16.23 for the depressed patients, 13.93 for the clinic clients, and 10.82 for the "normal" controls. For the college students, mean scores ranged from 8.45 to 10.51.

SCORING: The RIAS is scored by assigning a score of one to the correct responses and summing them. The correct responses are "true" to items 1, 4, 5, 7–22, 24, 26, 27, 30–32, 34, 35, 37, 38, 40, 42, 43, 45, and "false" for the remainder of the items.

RELIABILITY: The RIAS has excellent internal consistency, with alphas that range from .86 to .94. It also has excellent stability, with test-retest correlations of .81 for time periods of ten to twelve weeks.

VALIDITY: The RIAS was not correlated with age, education, and social class suggesting these variables do not affect responses. The RIAS has good known-groups validity, distinguishing between college students rated as ambivalent or not ambivalent and among depressed, schizophrenic and clinic clients, and "normal" controls. The RIAS also has some concurrent validity, correlating with two other scales of schizotypy (indicating a genetic predisposition for schizophrenia).

PRIMARY REFERENCE: Raulin, M. L. (1984). Development of a scale to measure intense ambivalence, *Journal of Consulting and Clinical Psychology*, 52, 63–72. Instrument reproduced with permission of Michael L. Raulin and the American Psychological Association.

AVAILABILITY: Dr. Michael L. Raulin, SUNY-Buffalo, Psychology Department, Julian Park Hall, Buffalo, NY 14260.

RIAS

Circle either T for true or F for false for each item as it applies to you.

T F   1. Very often, even my favorite pastimes don't excite me.
T F   2. I feel I can trust my friends.
T F   3. Small imperfections in a person are rarely enough to change love into hatred.
T F   4. There have been times when I have hated one or both of my parents for the affection they have expressed for me.
T F   5. Words of affection almost always make people uncomfortable.
T F   6. I don't mind too much the faults of people I admire.
T F   7. Love and hate tend to go together.
T F   8. Honest people will tell you that they often feel chronic resentment toward the people they love.
T F   9. Everything I enjoy has its painful side.
T F   10. Love never seems to last very long.
T F   11. My strongest feelings of pleasure usually seem to be mixed with pain.
T F   12. Whenever I get what I want, I usually don't want it at all any more.
T F   13. I have always experienced dissatisfaction with feelings of love.
T F   14. I worry the most when things are going the best.
T F   15. I often get very angry with people just because I love them so much.
T F   16. I start distrusting people if I have to depend on them too much.
T F   17. I can think of someone right now whom I thought I liked a day or two ago, but now strongly dislike.
T F   18. The people around me seem to be very changeable.
T F   19. It is hard to imagine two people loving one another for many years.
T F   20. The closer I get to people, the more I am annoyed by their faults.
T F   21. I find that the surest way to start resenting someone is to just start liking them too much.
T F   22. Often I feel like I hate even my favorite activities.
T F   23. I usually know when I can trust someone.
T F   24. Everyone has a lot of hidden resentment toward his loved ones.
T F   25. I usually know exactly how I feel about people I have grown close to.
T F   26. I have noticed that feelings of tenderness often turn into feelings of anger.
T F   27. I always seem to be the most unsure of myself at the same time that I am most confident of myself.
T F   28. My interest in personally enjoyed hobbies and pastimes has remained relatively stable.
T F   29. I can usually depend on those with whom I am close.
T F   30. My experiences with love have always been muddled with great frustration
T F   31. I usually find that feelings of hate will interfere when I have grown to love someone.

T	F	32.	A sense of shame has often interfered with my accepting words of praise from others.
T	F	33.	I rarely feel rejected by those who depend on me.
T	F	34.	I am wary of love because it is such a short-lived emotion.
T	F	35.	I usually experience doubt when I have accomplished something that I have worked on for a long time.
T	F	36.	I rarely doubt the appropriateness of praise that I have received from others in the past.
T	F	37.	I often feel as though I cannot trust people whom I have grown to depend on.
T	F	38.	I usually experience some grief over my own feelings of pleasure.
T	F	39.	It is rare for me to love a person one minute and hate them the next minute.
T	F	40.	I doubt if I can ever be sure exactly what my true interests are.
T	F	41.	I can't remember ever feeling love and hate for the same person at the same time.
T	F	42.	Love is always painful for me.
T	F	43.	Close relationships never seem to last long.
T	F	44.	I never had much trouble telling whether my parents loved me or hated me.
T	F	45.	Most people disappoint their friends.

REACTION INVENTORY INTERFERENCE (RII)

AUTHORS: David R. Evans and Shahe S. Kazarian

PURPOSE: To measure obsessional thoughts and compulsive acts.

DESCRIPTION: The RII is a 40-item instrument designed to identify obsessional thoughts and compulsive acts that interfere with an individual's daily activities. Items for the RII were selected empirically by asking students in an introductory psychology class to identify bothersome obsessional ruminations and compulsive acts. Those on which there was agreement were included as items on the RII. Although factor analysis revealed nine factors, the overall score of the scale appears to have the most value for identifying obsessive-compulsive behavior. The RII is considered a state measure in that it does not assume that the obsessive-compulsive thoughts and acts are enduring dispositions.

NORMS: An initial study, used to refine the RII, was conducted with 25 male and 25 female undergraduate students in an introductory psychology class in Canada. A second study was conducted with 172 members of another introductory psychology class in Canada. No other demographic data or norms were presented.

SCORING: The items are rated on a scale of 0 to 4 and those individual scores are simply totaled to produce the "degree of obsessionality" for each respondent. Scores can range from 0 to 160.

RELIABILITY: The RII demonstrates excellent internal consistency using item-test correlations to produce an overall reliability figure of .95. Data on test-retest reliability were not reported.

VALIDITY: The RII was significantly correlated with the Leyton Obsessional Inventory, suggesting good concurrent validity. No other validity data were available.

PRIMARY REFERENCE: Evans, D. R. and Kazarian, S. S. (1977). Development of a state measure of obsessive compulsive behavior, *Journal of Clinical Psychology*, 33, 436–439. Instrument reproduced with permission of David R. Evans, Shahe S. Kazarian, and the American Psychological Association.

AVAILABILITY: Dr. David R. Evans, Psychology Department, University of Western Ontario, London, Ontario, Canada N6A 5C2.

RII

The items in this questionnaire describe thoughts or acts that may interfere with other things or waste your time. Please indicate how much each problem bothers you by writing the appropriate number in the space next to each item.

1 = Not at all
2 = A little
3 = A fair amount
4 = Much
5 = Very much

____ 1. Eating many times a day
____ 2. Constantly checking your watch
____ 3. Repeatedly worrying about finishing things on time
____ 4. Continually thinking about the future
____ 5. Worrying about your appearance over and over again
____ 6. Repeatedly wondering if you are capable
____ 7. Always worrying about your work piling up
____ 8. Constantly wondering whether you will fail at things
____ 9. Repeatedly worrying about your job situation
____ 10. Continually worrying about catching up with your work
____ 11. Frequently being concerned about how you interact with others
____ 12. Always wasting time wandering around
____ 13. Worrying about everyday decisions over and over again
____ 14. Continually worrying about how well you are doing
____ 15. Worrying about being evaluated all the time
____ 16. Always doubting your intelligence or ability
____ 17. Wondering if you are doing the right thing over and over again
____ 18. Continually pondering about the world at large
____ 19. Repeatedly worrying about how you are performing
____ 20. Always checking several times whether you have done something like locking a door
____ 21. Often worrying about your cleanliness or tidiness
____ 22. Always being indecisive
____ 23. Washing your hands many times each day
____ 24. Repeatedly experiencing a tune (number, word) running through your mind
____ 25. Brooding all the time
____ 26. Constantly counting unimportant things
____ 27. Repeatedly asking people for advice
____ 28. Spending time worrying about trivial details all the time
____ 29. Repeatedly being unable to get started on things
____ 30. Constantly thinking about your family
____ 31. Swearing all the time
____ 32. Continually playing with an object (pen, pencil, keys)
____ 33. Repeatedly thinking about things you don't do well
____ 34. Always thinking about the "rat race"
____ 36. Constantly worrying about what people above you think about you

_____ 37. Frequently thinking about getting to sleep
_____ 38. Always being concerned about improving yourself
_____ 39. Repeatedly checking to see if you have done something correctly
_____ 40. Constantly thinking about yourself

REASONS FOR LIVING INVENTORY (RFL)

AUTHOR: Marsha M. Linehan

PURPOSE: To measure adaptive characteristics in suicide.

DESCRIPTION: This 48-item inventory assesses a range of beliefs that differentiate suicidal from nonsuicidal individuals and can be viewed as a measure of an individual's commitment to various reasons for not committing suicide. The RFL is one of the few instruments that approach the topic from the perspective of adaptive coping skills that are absent in the suicidal person. It is based on a cognitive-behavioral theory which assumes that cognitive patterns mediate suicidal behavior. While slightly longer than other instruments in this book, the RFL has six short subscales that are potentially very useful in working with suicidal clients: suicidal and coping belief (SCB), responsibility to family (RF), child-related concerns (CRC), fear of suicide (FS), fear of social disapproval (FSD), and moral objections (MO). Total scores may be used, although more value in guiding intervention is found by using the subscales.

NORMS: The scale was developed on a sample of 193 non-clinical adults and a sample of 244 psychiatric inpatients. The non-clinical sample had an average age of 36 years. Mean scores on the SCB, RF, CRC, FS, FSD, and MO were 4.55, 3.86, 3.66, 2.38, 2.34, and 3.02, respectively. The clinical sample was categorized into three subsamples according to past suicidal behaviors: nonsuicidal ($n = 78$), suicidal ideations ($n = 89$), and parasuicidal ($n = 77$). The average scores on the SCB, RF, CC, FS, FSD, and MO were as follows for each of the three subsamples: nonsuicidal subjects: 4.82, 4.49, 3.89, 3.07, 3.13, and 3.54; suicidal ideation: 4.82, 4.49, 3.89, 3.07, 3.13, and 3.54; parasuicidal: 3.56, 3.55, 2.69, 2.94, 2.82, and 2.73. Mean scores on the total RFL scale were 4.25, 3.28, and 3.28 for the nonsuicidal, suicidal ideation, and parasuicidal subsamples. Scores are not significantly different for men and women.

SCORING: Each subscale score is calculated by averaging the individual item ratings within that subscale; for example on the SCB the item total is divided by 24. The total score is obtained by summing each item score and dividing by 48. By using average scores for each subscale, comparison across subscales is possible. Subscale items are: SCB: 2, 3, 4, 8, 10, 12, 13, 14, 17, 19, 20, 22, 24, 25, 29, 32, 35, 36, 37, 39, 40, 42, 44, 45; RF: 1, 7, 9, 16, 30, 47, 48; CC: 11, 21, 28; FS: 6, 15, 18, 26, 33, 38, 46; FSD: 31, 41, 43; MO: 5, 24, 27, 34. Higher scores indicate more reasons for living.

RELIABILITY: Reliability was based on a variety of samples, and estimated using Cronbach's alpha. Correlations ranged from .72 to .89, indicating fairly high internal consistency. No data on stability were reported.

VALIDITY: Probably the biggest limitation of this inventory is a lack of predictive validity. The subscale with the strongest concurrent validity is the SCB which correlated with suicidal ideation and likelihood of suicide in the "normal" sample. In the clinical sample the SCB correlated with suicidal ideation, likelihood of suicide, suicidal threats, and suicidal solutions. The RF also correlated with these suicidal behaviors in the clinical sample, but showed less evidence of validity with the nonclinical sample. The CC was correlated with three of the four criteria for the clinical sample. Evidence of known-groups validity also supports the instrument.

PRIMARY REFERENCE: Linehan, M. M., Goldstein, J. L., Nielsen, S. L., and Chiles, J. A. (1983). Reasons for staying alive when you are thinking of killing yourself: The Reasons for Living Inventory, *Journal of Consulting and Clinical Psychology*, 51, 276–286. Instrument reproduced with permission of Marsha M. Linehan and the American Psychological Association.

AVAILABILITY: Dr. Marsha M. Linehan, Department of Psychology NI-25, University of Washington, Seattle, WA 98195.

RFL

Many people have thought of suicide at least once. Others have never considered it. Whether you have considered it or not, we are interested in the reasons you would have for *not* committing suicide if the thought were to occur to you or if someone were to suggest it to you.

Below are reasons people sometimes give for not committing suicide. We would like to know how important each of these possible reasons would be to you at this time in your life as a reason to *not* kill yourself. Please rate this in the space at the left on each question.

Each reason can be rated from 1 (not at all important) to 6 (extremely important). If a reason does not apply to you or if you do not believe the statement is true, then it is not likely important and you should put a 1. Please use the whole range of choices so as not to rate only at the middle (2, 3, 4, 5) or only at the extremes (1, 6).

Even if you never have considered suicide or firmly believe you never would seriously consider killing yourself, it is still important that you rate each reason. In this case, rate on the basis of why killing yourself is not or would never be an alternative for you.

In each space put a number to indicate the importance to you of each for *not* killing yourself.

1 = Not at all *important*
2 = Quite *unimportant*
3 = Somewhat *unimportant*
4 = Somewhat *important*
5 = Quite *important*
6 = Extremely *important*

_____ 1. I have a responsibility and commitment to my family.
_____ 2. I believe I can learn to adjust or cope with my problems.
_____ 3. I believe I have control over my life and destiny.
_____ 4. I have a desire to live.
_____ 5. I believe only God has the right to end a life.
_____ 6. I am afraid of death.
_____ 7. My family might believe I did not love them.
_____ 8. I do not believe that things get miserable or hopeless enough that I would rather be dead.
_____ 9. My family depends upon me and needs me.
_____ 10. I do not want to die.
_____ 11. I want to watch my children as they grow.
_____ 12. Life is all we have and is better than nothing.
_____ 13. I have future plans I am looking forward to carrying out.
_____ 14. No matter how badly I feel, I know that it will not last.
_____ 15. I am afraid of the unknown.
_____ 16. I love and enjoy my family too much and could not leave them.

_____ 17. I want to experience all that life has to offer and there are many experiences I haven't had yet which I want to have.
_____ 18. I am afraid that my method of killing myself would fail.
_____ 19. I care enough about myself to live.
_____ 20. Life is too beautiful and precious to end it.
_____ 21. It would not be fair to leave the children for others to take care of.
_____ 22. I believe I can find other solutions to my problems.
_____ 23. I am afraid of going to hell.
_____ 24. I have a love of life.
_____ 25. I am too stable to kill myself.
_____ 26. I am a coward and do not have the guts to do it.
_____ 27. My religious beliefs forbid it.
_____ 28. The effect on my children could be harmful.
_____ 29. I am curious about what will happen in the future.
_____ 30. It would hurt my family too much and I would not want them to suffer.
_____ 31. I am concerned about what others would think of me.
_____ 32. I believe everything has a way of working out for the best.
_____ 33. I could not decide where, when, and how to do it.
_____ 34. I consider it morally wrong.
_____ 35. I still have many things left to do.
_____ 36. I have the courage to face life.
_____ 37. I am so inept that my method would not work.
_____ 38. I am afraid of the actual "act" of killing myself (the pain, blood, violence).
_____ 39. I believe killing myself would not really accomplish or solve anything.
_____ 40. I have hope that things will improve and the future will be happier.
_____ 41. Other people would think I am weak and selfish.
_____ 42. I have an inner drive to survive.
_____ 43. I would not want people to think I did not have control over my life.
_____ 44. I believe I can find a purpose in life, a reason to live.
_____ 45. I see no reason to hurry death along.
_____ 46. I am so inept that my method would not work.
_____ 47. I would not want my family to feel guilty afterwards.
_____ 48. I would not want my family to think I was selfish or a coward.

REID-GUNDLACH SOCIAL SERVICE SATISFACTION SCALE
(R-GSSSS)

AUTHORS: P. Nelson Reid and James P. Gundlach

PURPOSE: To assess the extent of consumer satisfaction with social services.

DESCRIPTION: The R-GSSSS is a 34-item instrument that provides an overall satisfaction-with-service score plus three subscales dealing with consumers' reactions to social services regarding the following: (1) relevance (the extent to which a service corresponds to the client's perception of his or her problem and needs); (2) impact (the extent to which services reduce the problem); and (3) gratification (the extent to which services enhance the client's self-esteem and contribute to a sense of power and integrity). The relevance subscale consists of items 1 through 11; the impact subscale is composed of items 12 through 21, and the gratification subscale consists of items 22 through 34. The R-GSSSS is designed for use with a wide range of social services. When necessary, the term "social worker" on individual items can be replaced by the appropriate professional designation.

NORMS: The initial study was conducted with 166 heads of households of low-income families who had a high rate of use of social services. The respondents were 81% female, 47% married, and 52.5% were between the ages of 19 and 29. The sample contained fairly equal numbers of white and black respondents; 2.4% were Mexican-American. Actual norms were not available.

SCORING: The instrument is scored by adding the individual item scores and dividing by the number of items in the scale. Thus, the sum of all scores is divided by 34 for the total score, the relevance subscale is divided by 11, the impact subscale is divided by 10, and the gratification subscale is divided by 13. This results in all scales having a range of scores of 1 (minimum satisfaction) to 5 (maximum satisfaction). Items 3, 6, 9, 10, 13, 16, 17, 18, 20, 22, 23, 26, 27, 28, 29, 30, 31, and 33 are reverse-scored.

RELIABILITY: Internal consistency of the scale was very good with a total alpha of .95; the three subscales had alphas ranging from .82 to .86. The authors' analyses reveal the three subscales to be sufficiently independent to justify using all three as measures of different aspects of consumer satisfaction. Data on stability were not available.

VALIDITY: The scales have high face validity. Other forms of validity infor-mation are not reported. However, race, marital status, and type of service utilized were significantly related to satisfaction in predictable ways. Blacks and Mexican-Americans, single consumers, and those utilizing AFDS and Medicaid reported lower satisfaction levels.

PRIMARY REFERENCE: Reid, P. N., and Gundlach, J. H. (1983). A scale for the measurement of consumer satisfaction with social services, *Journal of*

Social Service Research, 7, 37–54. Instrument reproduced with permission of P. N. Reid and Haworth Press.

AVAILABILITY: Dr. Nelson Reid, North Carolina State University, Department of Social Work, Box 8107, Raleigh, NC 27965-8107.

R-GSSSS

Using the scale from one to five described below, please indicate on the line at the left of each item the number that comes closest to how you feel.

1 = Strongly agree
2 = Agree
3 = Undecided
4 = Disagree
5 = Strongly disagree

____ 1.   The social worker took my problems very seriously.
____ 2.   If I had been the social worker I would have dealt with my problems in just the same way.
____ 3.   The worker I had could never understand anyone like me.
____ 4.   Overall the agency has been very helpful to me.
____ 5.   If a friend of mine had similar problems I would tell them to go to the agency.
____ 6.   The social worker asks a lot of embarrassing questions.
____ 7.   I can always count on the worker to help if I'm in trouble.
____ 8.   The social agency will help me as much as they can.
____ 9.   I don't think the agency has the power to really help me.
____ 10. The social worker tries hard but usually isn't too helpful.
____ 11. The problem the agency tried to help me with is one of the most important in my life.
____ 12. Things have gotten better since I've been going to the agency.
____ 13. Since I've been using the agency my life is more messed up than ever.
____ 14. The agency is always available when I need it.
____ 15. I got from the agency exactly what I wanted.
____ 16. The social worker loves to talk but won't really do anything for me.
____ 17. Sometimes I just tell the social worker what I think she wants to hear.
____ 18. The social worker is usually in a hurry when I see her.
____ 19. No one should have any trouble getting some help from this agency.
____ 20. The worker sometimes says things I don't understand.
____ 21. The social workers are always explaining things carefully.
____ 22. I never looked forward to my visits to the social agency.
____ 23. I hope I'll never have to go back to the agency for help.
____ 24. Every time I talk to my worker I feel relieved.
____ 25. I can tell the social worker the truth without worrying.
____ 26. I usually feel nervous when I talk to my worker.
____ 27. The social worker is always looking for lies in what I tell her.
____ 28. It takes a lot of courage to go to the agency.
____ 29. When I enter the agency I feel very small and insignificant.
____ 30. The agency is very demanding.
____ 31. The social worker will sometimes lie to me.
____ 32. Generally the social worker is an honest person.
____ 33. I have the feeling that the worker talks to other people about me.
____ 34. I always feel well treated when I leave the social agency.

RESTRAINT SCALE (RS)

AUTHOR: C. Peter Herman

PURPOSE: To measure efforts to control eating.

DESCRIPTION: This 10-item instrument measures one aspect of dieting behavior, the ability to restrain from eating in order to maintain a particular weight. The scale ranges from the extreme of someone who has never given a moment's thought about dieting to someone who is overly concerned with dieting. The instrument may be useful with both obese clients attempting to reduce weight and with anorectic and bulimic clients.

NORMS: The instrument was developed on a sample of 57 female college students. Normative data are not presented.

SCORING: The RS score is the sum of all 10 items. For items 1 through 4 and item 10 the alternatives are scored as follows: a = 0, b = 1, c = 2, d = 3, e = 4. Items 5 through 9 are scored as follows: a = 0, b = 1, c = 2, d = 3. Scores can range from zero to 35 with higher scores indicating more concern over dieting.

RELIABILITY: Reliability data are not available from primary reference.

VALIDITY: This instrument was tested for criterion validity by creating two groups, one of restrained eaters and one of nonrestrained eaters. Different eating patterns were then observed for the two groups. The findings tend to be consistent for men and women, with slightly higher scores found for women. Similar differences in eating patterns were found with subjects who were categorized as obese, normal, and skinny according to their scores on the RS. These findings are evidence of known-groups validity. Concurrent validity is evidenced by an association between weight gain and the RS.

PRIMARY REFERENCE: Herman, C. P. (1978). Restrained eating. *Psychiatric Clinics of North America*, 1, 593–607. Instrument reproduced with permission of C. P. Herman.

AVAILABILITY: Journal article.

RS

Please answer the following items by circling the alternatives below the question.

1. How often are you dieting?
   a. Never   b. Rarely   c. Sometimes   d. Often   e. Always

2. What is the maximum amount of weight (in pounds) that you have ever lost in one month?
   a. 0–4   b. 5–9   c. 10–14   d. 15–19   e. 20+

3. What is your maximum weight gain within a week?
   a. 0–1   b. 1.1–2   c. 2.1–3   d. 3.1–5   e. 5.1+

4. In a typical week, how much does your weight fluctuate?
   a. 0–1   b. 1.1–2   c. 2.1–3   d. 3.1–5   e. 5.1+

5. Would a weight fluctuation of 5 pounds affect the way you live your life?
   a. Not at all   b. Slightly   c. Moderately   d. Very Much

6. Do you eat sensibly in front of others and splurge alone?
   a. Never   b. Rarely   c. Often   d. Always

7. Do you give too much time and thought to food?
   a. Never   b. Rarely   c. Often   d. Always

8. Do you have feelings of guilt after overeating?
   a. Never   b. Rarely   c. Often   d. Always

9. How conscious are you of what you are eating?
   a. Not at all   b. Slightly   c. Moderately   d. Extremely

10. How many pounds over your desired weight were you at your maximum weight?
    a. 0–1   b. 1–5   c. 6–10   d. 11–20   e. 21+

REVISED KINSHIP SCALE (KS)

AUTHORS: Kent G. Bailey and Gustavo R. Nava

PURPOSE: To measure psychological kinship.

DESCRIPTION: The KS is a 20-item instrument designed to measure feelings of deep affiliation and love in interpersonally close relationships. The instrument is based on the notion that feelings of kinship with family members and genetically unrelated significant others derive from a human heritage of attachment, bonding, and sociality. Respondents complete the KS in relation to any person as a stimulus by filling in the blanks on the instrument. This person could be a family member, partner in an interpersonal relationship, or even the clinician, since clinicians are incorporated into a client's psychological kinship. The current KS was revised from an original 60-item instrument. Based on a sample of female college students, factor analyses suggest that there are four subscales of the KS: family love (FL = 1 + 3 + 4 + 6 + 7 + 10 + 11 + 16 + 19 + 20); practical support (PS = 5 + 8 + 15 + 18); emotional intimacy (EI = 12 + 13 + 14 + 17); and intellectual intimacy (II = 2 + 9). The FL can be used as a short-form measure of psychological kinship.

NORMS: Norms are reported separately for women and men, and, of course, vary according to the stimulus person. A sample of 144 unmarried college women had a mean KS score of 84.8 with a standard deviation of 9.7 when evaluating their relationship with the parent to whom they were closest, and a mean and standard deviation of 86.6 and 9.3 for the boyfriend. A sample of single college men had means (and standard deviations) of 80.6 (9.6) and 84.6 (8.8) for their closest parent and girlfriend. Means are not reported for the short form or other subscales.

SCORING: Each item is rated on a 1 to 5 scale ranging from "unimportant" to "very important." Total scores are the sum of each item, and range from 20 to 100 for the KS and 10 to 50 for the short form.

RELIABILITY: Reliability of the revised KS is not reported; however, the 60-item version had excellent internal consistency, with an odd-even correlation of .95.

VALIDITY: This instrument has good concurrent validity, as seen in its correlations with measures of love, liking, and attachment for both samples of women and men when evaluating their closest parent and boyfriend/girlfriend. With the exception of the practical support factor, the subscales also correlated with those measures for both closest parent and boyfriend/girlfriend. Further, mean total scores correlated with five measures of the relationship, of time spent together, time one would want to spend together, reliance on others for emotional support, and perceived caring. For women the total KS scores correlated with two of these five variables.

PRIMARY REFERENCE: Nava, G. R. and Bailey, K. G. (1991). Measuring psychological kinship: Scale refinement and validation, *Psychological Reports*, 68, 215–227. Instrument reprinted with permission of Kent G. Bailey and Clinical Psychology Publishing Company, Inc.

AVAILABILITY: Dr. Kent G. Bailey, Department of Psychology, Virginia Commonwealth University, 806 Franklin Street, Richmond, VA 23284-2018.

KS

This questionnaire is about what you consider important in your relations with other people. Think about _____. Then consider how important each of the following items is in your relationship with this person. Use the following scale and record your rating in the space next to each item:

$$5 = \text{\textit{Very important} to you}$$
$$4 = \text{\textit{Important} to you}$$
$$3 = \text{You are \textit{not sure}}$$
$$2 = \text{\textit{Unimportant} to you}$$
$$1 = \text{\textit{Very unimportant} to you}$$

How important is it for _____:

____ 1. To hug me if I need it.
____ 2. To share my beliefs and values.
____ 3. To feel love for me.
____ 4. To remember me ten years from now.
____ 5. To give me a birthday present.
____ 6. To still like me even if I do something wrong.
____ 7. To be available when I need him/her.
____ 8. To care about my financial situation.
____ 9. To make specific suggestions about how to deal with my personal problems.
____ 10. To treat me like a member of the family.
____ 11. To be a loving person.
____ 12. To be someone I could cry in front of.
____ 13. To be concerned about my health.
____ 14. To be willing to accept a loan from me.
____ 15. To post bail for me if I am in jail.
____ 16. To feel that I am important in his/her life.
____ 17. To be willing to care for me if I am sick.
____ 18. To lend me money if I am in need.
____ 19. To think of me as a "loved one."
____ 20. To share a strong feeling of "kinship" with me.

REVISED MARTIN-LARSEN APPROVAL MOTIVATION (RMLAM)

AUTHOR: Harry J. Martin

PURPOSE: To measure the need for approval from others.

DESCRIPTION: This 20-item instrument assesses the need for favorable evaluations from others. It is considered revised because the present form controls for an acquiescence response bias, which has a problem with earlier forms of the instrument. It is similar to the Marlowe-Crowne Social Desirability Scale, although the RMLAM more directly taps the construct in terms of the desire to receive positive evaluations and social reinforcement (approval), as well as the need to avoid negative evaluations and social punishment (criticism and rejection.). The instrument focuses on social situations and interpersonal behaviors. The RMLAM also is available in a shorter 10-item form (items 2, 4, 5, 6, 10, 12, 13, 16, 18, and 19).

NORMS: Mean and standard deviation scores are available from a sample of college students ($n = 123$). The average score was 53.6 with a standard deviation of 9.02. The mean and standard deviation for the shorter 10-item version was 26.3 and 5.37, respectively. Scores do not seem to be influenced by gender.

SCORING: Items are rated on a 5-point scale from "disagree strongly" to "agree strongly." Items 2, 12, 13, 16, and 19 are reverse-scored. Total scores are the sum of the items and range from 20 to 100 for the 20-item version; higher scores indicate stronger need for social approval.

RELIABILITY: The reliability of the RMLAM was estimated in terms of internal consistency and test-retest reliability. For the long and short forms, alpha was .75 and .67 respectively. Test-retest correlations for a one-week period were .72 and .94 for the two forms.

VALIDITY: Scores on the long version correlated with faking on the MMPI, and clinical defensiveness. The short form correlated with clinical defensiveness but was not associated with faking on the MMPI. Both long and short forms correlated with neuroticism and the Marlowe-Crowne Social Desirability Scale.

PRIMARY REFERENCE: Martin, H. J. (1984). A revised measure of approval motivation and its relationship to social desirability, *Journal of Personality Assessment*, 48, 508–519. Instrument reproduced with permission of the *Journal of Personality Assessment*.

AVAILABILITY: Journal article.

RMLAM

Below are twenty statements. Please rate how much you agree with each using the following scale. Please record your answer in the space to the left of the statement.

1 = Disagree strongly
2 = Disagree
3 = No opinion
4 = Agree
5 = Agree strongly

_____ 1. Depending upon the people involved, I react to the same situation in different ways.

_____ 2. I would rather be myself than be well thought of.

_____ 3. Many times I feel like just flipping a coin in order to decide what I should do.

_____ 4. I change my opinion (or the way that I do things) in order to please someone else.

_____ 5. In order to get along and be liked, I tend to be what people expect me to be.

_____ 6. I find it difficult to talk about my ideas if they are contrary to group opinion.

_____ 7. One should avoid doing things in public which appear to be wrong to others, even though one knows that he/she is right.

_____ 8. Sometimes I feel that I don't have enough control over the direction that my life is taking.

_____ 9. It is better to be humble than assertive when dealing with people.

_____ 10. I am willing to argue only if I know that my friends will back me up.

_____ 11. If I hear that someone expresses a poor opinion of me, I do my best the next time that I see this person to make a good impression.

_____ 12. I seldom feel the need to make excuses or apologize for my behavior.

_____ 13. It is not important to me that I behave "properly" in social situations.

_____ 14. The best way to handle people is to agree with them and tell them what they want to hear.

_____ 15. It is hard for me to go on with my work if I am not encouraged to do so.

_____ 16. If there is any criticism or anyone says anything about me, I can take it.

_____ 17. It is wise to flatter important people.

_____ 18. I am careful at parties and social gatherings for fear that I will do or say things that others won't like.

_____ 19. I usually do not change my position when people disagree with me.

_____ 20. How many friends you have depends on how nice a person you are.

REVISED UCLA LONELINESS SCALE (RULS)

AUTHORS: Dan Russell, Letitia Peplau, and Carolyn Cutrona

PURPOSE: To measure loneliness.

DESCRIPTION: The RULS is a 20-item scale designed to measure loneliness in a variety of populations. This and earlier versions have been used in a number of studies that show loneliness is a common and distressing problem for many people. Loneliness has been linked with any number of other problems including personality characteristics (shyness, feelings of alienation), alcohol abuse, adolescent delinquent behavior, suicide, and physical illness. This version of the scale was undertaken to eliminate response bias, social desirability response set, and lack of clarity regarding distinctiveness from related constructs. The RULS has a number of potential uses for practice in identifying lonely individuals whose loneliness is a problem in and of itself or as related to other problems.

NORMS: A number of studies have been carried out with earlier versions of the RULS. With this version, 399 undergraduate students (171 males, 228 females) from three campuses provided the basis for the research. The mean for male students was 37.06 and for females, 128. The mean for students who were not dating was 43.1 which was significantly different from students who were dating casually (34.0) and romantically involved (32.7).

SCORING: After reverse-scoring items 1, 4–6, 9, 10, 15, 16, 19, 20, the scores on all 20 items are summed, producing a possible range of 20 to 80 with higher scores indicating greater loneliness.

RELIABILITY: The RULS has excellent internal consistency, with an alpha of .94. No test-retest data are reported.

VALIDITY: The RULS has good concurrent validity, correlating with a number of mood and personality measures (e.g., the Beck Depression Inventory, the Texas Social Behavior Inventory), and particularly with a self-labeling loneliness index. In addition, people who were more lonely on the RULS reported more limited social activities and relationships and more emotions theoretically linked to loneliness. Finally, results showed the RULS to be unaffected by social desirability response set as measured by the Marlowe-Crowne Social Desirability Inventory.

PRIMARY REFERENCE: Russell, D., Peplau, L. A., and Cutrona, C. E. (1980). The Revised UCLA Loneliness Scale: Concurrent and discriminant validity evidence, *Journal of Personality and Social Psychology*, 39, 472–480. Instrument reproduced with permission of Letitia A. Peplau.

AVAILABILITY: Professor Letitia A. Peplau, Department of Psychology, UCLA, Los Angeles, CA 90024.

RULS

Indicate how often you have felt the way described in each statement using the following scale:

> 4 = "I have felt this way *often*"
> 3 = "I have felt this way *sometimes.*"
> 2 = "I have felt this way *rarely.*"
> 1 = "I have *never* felt this way."

_____ 1. I feel in tune with the people around me.

_____ 2. I lack companionship.

_____ 3. There is no one I can turn to.

_____ 4. I do not feel alone.

_____ 5. I feel part of a group of friends.

_____ 6. I have a lot in common with the people around me.

_____ 7. I am no longer close to anyone.

_____ 8. My interests and ideas are not shared by those around me.

_____ 9. I am an outgoing person.

_____ 10. There are people I feel close to.

_____ 11. I feel left out.

_____ 12. My social relationships are superficial.

_____ 13. No one really knows me well.

_____ 14. I feel isolated from others.

_____ 15. I can find companionship when I want it.

_____ 16. There are people who really understand me.

_____ 17. I am unhappy being so withdrawn.

_____ 18. People are around me but not with me.

_____ 19. There are people I can talk to.

_____ 20. There are people I can turn to.

ROLE PERCEPTION SCALE (RPS)

AUTHORS: Mary Sue Richardson and Judith Landon Alpert

PURPOSE: To measure perception of roles.

DESCRIPTION: This 40-item instrument is designed to measure four aspects of one's perception of roles: innovation (items 1–10), involvement (items 11–20), affectivity (items 21–30), and competition (31–40). The instrument is intended to be used in conjunction with a projective technique where the respondent first writes brief stories in response to the roles of work, marriage, parenting, the combination of work and marriage roles, and the combination of the work and parenting roles. Respondents are given the first sentence and instructed to write a brief story (in 5 minutes or less) which addresses four concerns: what led up to the event in the story, a description of what is happening at the moment, a description of what the character is thinking and feeling at the moment, and the outcome of the story. Respondents answer the RPS in response to the character in the story; the RPS has two forms, one for male and one for female characters in the story. The RPS can be used with any role, such as a client in an identity crisis or struggling to adapt to a change in life. The RPS is particularly useful to clinicians working with clients troubled by role transitions, including marriage, parenthood, divorce, retirement, widowhood, or caring for a sick loved one. Evidence of the RPS's reliability and validity, however, is limited to the roles mentioned above.

NORMS: Norms are reported for role engagement (RE), which combines the scores on innovation, involvement, and affectivity. Norms are based on 88 female and 46 male college students. For males, RE means (and standard deviations) were $-.532$ (.89), $-.058$ (.92), $-.174$ (.95), $-.213$ (.91), and .374 (.74) for the roles of work, marriage, parenting, work-marriage, and work-parenting, respectively. The means (and standard deviations) for the competition subscale were .129 (1.0), .02 (.84), .041 (.96), .022 (.96), and .232 (.76) for the same five roles. Female means (and standard deviations) for the RE were $-.298$ (.95), .089 (.93), $-.200$ (.98), .38 (.77), and .344 (.92) for the roles of work, marriage, parenting, work-marriage, and work-parenting, respectively. Competition means (and standard deviations) for females were .085 (92), $-.11$ (.86), $-.26$ (86), .235 (.88), and $-.188$ (.84) for the same five roles.

SCORING: Items 1, 4–6, 10, 12, 15, 18–20, 21, 25–27, 30, 33, 34, 36, 39, and 40 are scored 1 if the respondent answered "false." A "true" response on the other items is scored as 1. Scores are then summed for each subscale and divided by the number of items answered. Higher scores reflect more innovation, involvement, affectivity, and competition in the particular role.

RELIABILITY: A prototype of the RPS had an internal consistency coefficient of .91. No other reliability information is available.

VALIDITY: The validity of the RPS is primarily supported with factor analysis where items of the affectivity, innovation, and involvement subscales loaded together to form the RE which was independent of the competition subscale.

PRIMARY REFERENCE: Richardson, M. S. and Alpert, J. L. (1980). Role perceptions: Variations by sex and roles, *Sex Roles*, 6, 783–793. Instrument reproduced with permission of Mary Sue Richardson and Judith Landon Alpert.

AVAILABILITY: Mary Sue Richardson, Ph.D., Department of Applied Psychology, 400 East Building, Washington Square, New York, NY 10003.

RPS

Please indicate whether each statement is True or False for the main character in your story. Record your answer in the space to the left of each statement by writing "T" if it is true of the main character or "F" if the statement is false for the main character.

_____ 1. She (he) has very little to say about how her (his) day is spent.

_____ 2. What she (he) does is different on different days.

_____ 3. Her (his) activities from day to day are varied.

_____ 4. She (he) is not able to do unusual things.

_____ 5. She (he) is expected to follow set rules.

_____ 6. She (he) seldom tries out new ideas.

_____ 7. She (he) thinks up unusual activities for others to do.

_____ 8. She (he) thinks about different ideas every day.

_____ 9. She (he) can choose what she (he) will do each day.

_____ 10. She (he) is involved in the same kind of activities every day.

_____ 11. She (he) seldom feels bored.

_____ 12. She (he) probably wouldn't be there if she (he) didn't have to be.

_____ 13. She (he) is often curious.

_____ 14. She (he) puts a lot of energy into what she (he) does.

_____ 15. She (he) only does what she (he) has to do.

_____ 16. She (he) wants to do what she (he) is doing.

_____ 17. She (he) seldom daydreams.

_____ 18. She (he) is thinking about something else.

_____ 19. She (he) would rather be doing something other than what she (he) is doing.

_____ 20. She (he) doesn't really care.

_____ 21.   She (he) feels discouraged.

_____ 22.   She (he) enjoys her (his) life.

_____ 23.   She (he) feels happy.

_____ 24.   She (he) often feels like smiling.

_____ 25.   She (he) is often thinking "it's unfair."

_____ 26.   She (he) thinks it's hopeless.

_____ 27.   Something is troubling her (him).

_____ 28.   She (he) often thinks that her (his) life is good.

_____ 29.   She (he) seldom has headaches.

_____ 30.   She (he) often feels like arguing.

_____ 31.   She (he) tries hard to be best.

_____ 32.   Winning is very important to her (him).

_____ 33.   She (he) doesn't mind losing.

_____ 34.   She (he) seldom competes with others.

_____ 35.   She (he) tries to do things better than other people.

_____ 36.   She (he) doesn't care about whether others get things done first.

_____ 37.   She (he) usually tries to get things done before others.

_____ 38.   She (he) compares what she (he) does with what others do.

_____ 39.   She (he) doesn't care if she (he) wins or loses.

_____ 40.   She (he) doesn't feel pressured to compete.

Note: Parentheses indicate changes for male form.

SATISFACTION WITH LIFE SCALE (SWLS)

AUTHORS: Ed Diener, Robert A. Emmons, Randy J. Larsen, and Sharon Griffin

PURPOSE: To assess subjective life satisfaction.

DESCRIPTION: The 5-item SWLS, as part of a body of research on subjective well-being, refers to the cognitive-judgmental aspects of general life satisfaction. Thus, in contrast to measures that apply some external standard, the SWLS reveals the individual's own judgment of his or her quality of life. This instrument is very short and unidimensional. Because satisfaction with life is often a key component of mental well-being, the SWLS may have clinical utility with a wide range of clients, including adolescents undergoing identity crises or adults experiencing midlife crisis.

NORMS: The SWLS was developed on a sample of 176 undergraduates from the University of Illinois. The mean was 23.5 with a standard deviation of 6.43. The researchers also report a mean of 25.8 for a sample of 53 elderly citizens from a midwestern city; the mean age for this sample was 75 years and 32 of the 53 were female.

SCORING: Each item is scored from 1 to 7 in terms of "strongly disagree" to "strongly agree." Item scores are summed for a total score, which ranges from 5 to 35, with higher scores reflecting more satisfaction with life.

RELIABILITY: The 5 items on the SWLS were selected from a pool of 48 based on factor analysis. The instrument's internal consistency is very good, with an alpha of .87. The instrument appears to have excellent test-retest reliability, with a correlation of .82 for a two-month period, suggesting it is very stable.

VALIDITY: The SWLS has been tested for concurrent validity using two samples of college students. Scores correlated with nine measures of subjective well-being for both samples. The scale was not correlated with a measure of affect intensity. The SWLS has also been shown to correlate with self-esteem, a checklist of clinical symptoms, neuroticism, and emotionality. Scores on the SWLS also correlated with independent ratings of life satisfaction among the elderly.

PRIMARY REFERENCE: Diener, E., Emmons, R. A., Larsen, R. J., and Griffin, S. (1985). The satisfaction with life scale, *Journal of Personality Assessment*, 49, 71–75. Instrument reproduced with permission of Ed Diener.

AVAILABILITY: Dr. Ed Diener, Associate Professor, Psychology Department, University of Illinois, 603 E. Daniel, Champaign, IL 61820.

SWLS

Below are five statements with which you may agree or disagree. Using the scale below, indicate your agreement with each item by placing the appropriate number on the line preceding that item. Please be open and honest in your responding.

> 1 = Strongly disagree
> 2 = Disagree
> 3 = Slightly disagree
> 4 = Neither agree nor disagree
> 5 = Slightly agree
> 6 = Agree
> 7 = Strongly agree

____ 1. In most ways my life is close to my ideal.

____ 2. The conditions of my life are excellent.

____ 3. I am satisfied with my life.

____ 4. So far I have gotten the important things I want in life.

____ 5. If I could live my life over, I would change almost nothing.

SCALE FOR THE ASSESSMENT OF NEGATIVE SYMPTOMS (SANS)
SCALE FOR THE ASSESSMENT OF POSITIVE SYMPTOMS (SAPS)

AUTHOR: Nancy C. Andreasen

PURPOSE: To assess negative and positive symptoms of psychopathology.

DESCRIPTION: These two instruments assess negative and positive symptoms of psychopathology, primarily the symptomatology of schizophrenia. Both are rating scales, used by practitioners to assess clients. The SANS is a 25-item scale that has five subscales: affective flattening, alogia, avolition and apathy, anhedonia and asociality, and impairment of attention. The SAPS is a 35-item scale with four subscales: hallucination, delusions, bizarreness, and positive formal thought disorder; the SAPS concludes with a global assessment of inappropriate affect. For both instruments, each subscale also contains a global rating index. The symptoms are considered within the time frame of one month, although this may be changed to measure more immediate responses to treatment (e.g., a one-week period in response to medication). The SANS and SAPS are designed to be used in conjunction with structured interviews, although information may be derived from direct clinical observations, observations by family members, reports from treatment personnel or the patient himself or herself.

NORMS: Means and standard deviations reported by Schuldberg et al. (1991) are from a sample of more than 390 outpatients from a mental health center and are for composite or total scores on a 22-item version of the SANS and composite scores on the first 34 items of the SAPS. The SANS had a mean of 25.5 and a standard deviation of 16.1; at a two-year follow-up the mean was 17.6 and the standard deviation was 9.0. The SAPS had a mean of 4.8 and a standard deviation of 9.3; at the two-year follow-up the mean was 8.2 with a standard deviation of 11.7. For patients with a diagnosis of schizophrenia the mean on the SANS was 32.4 and the standard deviation was 15.9, and the SAPS had a mean of 18.9 and a standard deviation of 12.9.

SCORING: The SANS and SAPS may be scored in a variety of ways. Subscale scores are the sum of all items, including the global rating item. Global items may be used by summing each to form the global summary score. Total scores for negative and positive symptoms are the sum of all items in each of the instruments to form the composite score. Total scores for the SANS range from 0 to 125 and 0 to 175 for the SAPS. Higher scores reflect more severe negative and positive symptomatology.

RELIABILITY: The reliability is very good for both the SANS and the SAPS. Using intraclass correlations coefficients on the bases of 19 patients rated, using from three to five raters, reliabilities ranged from .83 to .92 for the global summary and total scores (Schuldberg et al., 1991). Internal consistency for the global summary scores was moderate, .47 for the SANS and

.58 for the SAPS, due in part to the limited number of items. Internal consistency for the total scores was .90 for the SANS and .86 for the SAPS. Test-retest reliability over a two-year period was also very good considering the long time period, ranging from .40 to .50.

VALIDITY: Factor analysis suggests the SANS and SAPS measure two fairly independent dimensions of schizophrenic symptomatology. Outpatients diagnosed with schizophrenia had less severe negative and positive symptoms than persons hospitalized for schizophrenia, while patients without a diagnosis of schizophrenia had less severe symptoms than either group of persons with schizophrenia.

PRIMARY REFERENCES: Andreasen, N. C. (1982). Negative symptoms of schizophrenia: Definition and reliability, *Archives of General Psychiatry*, 39, 784–788. Andreasen, N. C. and Olsen, S. (1982). Negative v. positive schizophrenia: Definition and validation, *Archives of General Psychiatry*, 39, 789–794. Schuldberg, D., Quinlan, D. M., Morgenstern, H., and Glazer, W. (1990). Positive and negative symptoms in chronic psychiatric outpatients: Reliability, stability, and factor structure, *Psychological Assessment*, 2, 262–268. Instruments reproduced with permission of Nancy C. Andreasen.

AVAILABILITY: Nancy C. Andreasen, M.D., Ph.D., University of Iowa Hospitals and Clinics, MH-CRC 2911 JPP, 200 Hawkins Drive, Iowa City, IA 52242-1057.

SANS

Rate the patient on each item using the following scale:

0 = None
1 = Questionable
2 = Mild
3 = Moderate
4 = Marked
5 = Severe

AFFECTIVE FLATTENING OR BLUNTING

1. *Unchanging Facial Expression*
   The patient's face appears wooden, changes less
   than expected as emotional content of discourse
   changes.

   0 1 2 3 4 5

2. *Decreased Spontaneous Movements*
   The patient shows few or no spontaneous
   movements, does not shift position, move
   extremities, etc.

   0 1 2 3 4 5

3. *Paucity of Expressive Gestures*
   The patient does not use hand gestures, body
   position, etc., as an aid to expressing his ideas.

   0 1 2 3 4 5

4. *Poor Eye Contact*
   The patient avoids eye contact or "stares through"
   interviewer even when speaking.

   0 1 2 3 4 5

5. *Affective Nonresponsivity*
   The patient fails to smile or laugh when prompted.

   0 1 2 3 4 5

6. *Lack of Vocal Inflections*
   The patient fails to show normal vocal emphasis
   patterns, is often monotonic.

   0 1 2 3 4 5

7. *Global Rating of Affective Flattening*
   This rating should focus on overall severity of
   symptoms, especially unresponsiveness, eye
   contact, facial expression, and vocal inflections.

   0 1 2 3 4 5

ALOGIA

8. *Poverty of Speech*
   The patient's replies to questions are restricted in
   amount, tend to be brief, concrete, and unelaborated.

   0 1 2 3 4 5

9. *Poverty of Content of Speech*   0 1 2 3 4 5
    The patient's replies are adequate in amount but
    tend to be vague, overconcrete, or overgeneralized,
    and convey little information.

10. *Blocking*   0 1 2 3 4 5
    The patient indicates, either spontaneously or with
    prompting, that his train of thought was interrupted.

11. *Increased Latency of Response*   0 1 2 3 4 5
    The patient takes a long time to reply to questions;
    prompting indicates the patient is aware of the
    question.

12. *Global Rating of Alogia*   0 1 2 3 4 5
    The core features of alogia are poverty of speech
    and poverty of content.

AVOLITION-APATHY

13. *Grooming and Hygiene*   0 1 2 3 4 5
    The patient's clothes may be sloppy or soiled, and
    he may have greasy hair, body odor, etc.

14. *Impersistence at Work or School*   0 1 2 3 4 5
    The patient has difficulty seeking or maintaining
    employment, completing school work, keeping
    house, etc. If an inpatient, cannot persist at ward
    activities, such as OT, playing cards, etc.

15. *Physical Anergia*   0 1 2 3 4 5
    The patient tends to be physically inert. He may sit
    for hours and does not initiate spontaneous activity.

16. *Global Rating of Avolition-Apathy*   0 1 2 3 4 5
    Strong weight may be given to one or two prominent
    symptoms if particularly striking.

ANHEDONIA-ASOCIALITY

17. *Recreational Interests and Activities*   0 1 2 3 4 5
    The patient may have few or no interests. Both the
    quality and quantity of interests should be taken into
    account.

18. *Sexual Activity*   0 1 2 3 4 5
    The patient may show a decrease in sexual interest
    and activity, or enjoyment when active.

19. *Ability to Feel Intimacy and Closeness* 0 1 2 3 4 5
The patient may display an inability to form close or
intimate relationships, especially with the opposite
sex and family.

20. *Relationships with Friends and Peers* 0 1 2 3 4 5
The patient may have few or no friends and may
prefer to spend all of his time isolated.

21. *Global Rating of Anhedonia-Asociality* 0 1 2 3 4 5
This rating should reflect overall severity, taking into
account the patient's age, family status, etc.

ATTENTION

22. *Social Inattentiveness* 0 1 2 3 4 5
The patient appears uninvolved or unengaged. He
may seem "spacy."

23. Inattentiveness During Mental Status Testing 0 1 2 3 4 5
Tests of "serial 7s" (at least five subtractions) and
spelling "world" backwards:
Score: 2 = 1 error; 3 = 2 errors; 4 = 3 errors

24. *Global Rating of Attention* 0 1 2 3 4 5
This rating should assess the patient's overall
concentration, clinically and on tests.

SAPS

HALLUCINATIONS

1. *Auditory Hallucinations* 0 1 2 3 4 5
The patient reports voices, noises, or other sounds
that no one else hears.

2. *Voices Commenting* 0 1 2 3 4 5
The patient reports a voice which makes a running
commentary on his behavior or thoughts.

3. *Voices Conversing* 0 1 2 3 4 5
The patient reports hearing two or more voices
conversing.

4. *Somatic or Tactile Hallucinations* 0 1 2 3 4 5
The patient reports experiencing peculiar physical
sensations in the body.

5. *Olfactory Hallucinations*   0 1 2 3 4 5
   The patient reports experiencing unusual smells
   which no one else notices.

6. *Visual Hallucinations*   0 1 2 3 4 5
   The patient sees shapes or people that are not
   actually present.

7. *Global Rating of Hallucinations*   0 1 2 3 4 5
   This rating should be based on the duration and
   severity of the hallucinations and their effects on the
   patient's life.

DELUSIONS

8. *Persecutory Delusions*   0 1 2 3 4 5
   The patient believes he is being conspired against or
   persecuted in some way.

9. *Delusions of Jealousy*   0 1 2 3 4 5
   The patient believes his spouse is having an affair
   with someone.

10. *Delusions of Guilt or Sin*   0 1 2 3 4 5
    The patient believes that he has committed some
    terrible sin or done something unforgivable.

11. *Grandiose Delusions*   0 1 2 3 4 5
    The patient believes he has special powers or
    abilities.

12. *Religious Delusions*   0 1 2 3 4 5
    The patient is preoccupied with false beliefs of a
    religious nature.

13. *Somatic Delusions*   0 1 2 3 4 5
    The patient believes that somehow his body is
    diseased, abnormal, or changed.

14. *Delusions of Reference*   0 1 2 3 4 5
    The patient believes that insignificant remarks or
    events refer to him or have some special meaning.

15. *Delusions of Being Controlled*   0 1 2 3 4 5
    The patient feels that his feelings or actions are
    controlled by some outside force.

16. *Delusions of Mind Reading*   0 1 2 3 4 5
    The patient feels that people can read his mind or
    know his thoughts.

17. *Thought Broadcasting*   0 1 2 3 4 5
     The patient believes that his thoughts are broadcast
     so that he himself or others can hear them.

18. *Thought Insertion*   0 1 2 3 4 5
     The patient believes that thoughts that are not his
     own have been inserted into his mind.

19. *Thought Withdrawal*   0 1 2 3 4 5
     The patient believes that thoughts have been taken
     away from his mind.

20. *Global Rating of Delusions*   0 1 2 3 4 5
     This rating should be based on the duration and
     persistence of the delusions and their effect on the
     patient's life.

BIZARRE BEHAVIOR

21. *Clothing and Appearance*   0 1 2 3 4 5
     The patient dresses in an unusual manner or does
     other strange things to alter his appearance.

22. *Social and Sexual Behavior*   0 1 2 3 4 5
     The patient may do things considered inappropriate
     according to usual social norms (e.g., masturbating
     in public).

23. *Aggressive and Agitated Behavior*   0 1 2 3 4 5
     The patient may behave in an aggressive, agitated
     manner, often unpredictably.

24. *Repetitive or Stereotyped Behavior*   0 1 2 3 4 5
     The patient develops a set of repetitive action or
     rituals that he must perform over and over.

25. *Global Rating of Bizarre Behavior*   0 1 2 3 4 5
     This rating should reflect the type of behavior and
     the extent to which it deviates from social norms.

POSITIVE FORMAL THOUGHT DISORDER

26. *Derailment*   0 1 2 3 4 5
     A pattern of speech in which ideas slip off track onto
     ideas obliquely related or unrelated.

27. *Tangentiality*   0 1 2 3 4 5
     Replying to a question in an oblique or irrelevant
     manner.

28. *Incoherence*   0 1 2 3 4 5
A pattern of speech which is essentially
incomprehensible at times.

29. *Illogicality*   0 1 2 3 4 5
A pattern of speech in which conclusions are
reached which do not follow logically.

30. *Circumstantiality*   0 1 2 3 4 5
A pattern of speech which is very indirect and
delayed in reaching its goal idea.

31. *Pressure of Speech*   0 1 2 3 4 5
The patient's speech is rapid and difficult to interrupt;
the amount of speech produced is greater than that
considered normal.

32. *Distractible Speech*   0 1 2 3 4 5
The patient is distracted by nearby stimuli which
interrupt his flow of speech.

33. *Clanging*   0 1 2 3 4 5
A pattern of speech in which sounds rather than
meaningful relationships govern word choice.

34. *Global Rating of Positive Formal Thought Disorder*   0 1 2 3 4 5
This rating should reflect the frequency of
abnormality and degree to which it affects the
patient's ability to communicate.

INAPPROPRIATE AFFECT

35. *Inappropriate Affect*   0 1 2 3 4 5
The patient's affect is inappropriate or incongruous,
not simply flat or blunted.

SELF-ATTITUDE INVENTORY (SAI)

AUTHORS: Maurice Lorr and Richard A. Wunderlich

PURPOSE: To measure self-esteem.

DESCRIPTION: The SAI is a 32-item instrument designed to measure self-esteem. The SAI actually is composed of two subscales: confidence (items 1A, 3A, 5B, 7A, 9A, 11A, 13B, 15A, 17B, 19A, 21B, 23B, 25A, 27B, 29A, 31B), and popularity or social approval (items 2A, 4B, 6B, 8B, 10B, 12B, 14A, 16A, 18A, 20A, 22A, 24B, 26B, 28B, 30A, 32B). The SAI is presented in a paired-choice format to minimize response bias. Because of the importance of self-esteem to a number of theoretical formulations of problematic behaviors, activities, and feelings, these two brief subscales that focus on specific components of self-esteem are viewed as particularly useful, especially in evaluating the effectiveness of counseling for disturbed children.

NORMS: The SAI was studied with several samples of high school boys totaling 924, plus a sample of 45 psychiatric patients and 50 "normal" adults. No other demographic data are available nor are actual norms.

SCORING: The SAI is easily scored by simply adding up the number of items circled that agree with items described above (i.e., if 1A is circled, it is one point toward the total confidence score). The maximum score on each scale is 16, with higher scores showing greater self-esteem.

RELIABILITY: The SAI has good internal consistency, with alphas that range from .80 to .86 for confidence and from .69 to .81 for popularity. No test-retest data are reported.

VALIDITY: The SAI has good concurrent validity, correlating with the Rosenberg Self-Esteem Scale. The SAI also has good known-groups validity, significantly distinguishing between psychiatric patients and "normal" adults.

PRIMARY REFERENCE: Lorr, M. and Wunderlich, R. A. (1986). Two objective measures of self-esteem, *Journal of Personality Assessment*, 50, 18–23.

AVAILABILITY: Dr. Maurice Lorr, Life Cycle Institute, Catholic University, Washington, DC 20064.

SAI

Below are a number of statements that describe how people feel about themselves and how they relate to others. You will notice that each numbered item has two possible answers labeled A and B. Read each statement and select the one (either A or B) you agree with most. Then draw a circle around the A or the B, whichever describes you best. Be sure to circle *one* answer for each item.

1. A. I usually feel confident in my abilities.
    B. I often lack confidence in my abilities.

2. A. I have few doubts that I am popular.
    B. I have real doubts about my popularity.

3. A. I usually expect to succeed in things I try.
    B. Only occasionally do I expect to succeed in things I try.

4. A. Not many people think well of me.
    B. Most people think well of me.

5. A. There are only a few things I can do that I am proud of.
    B. There are a fair number of things I can do that I am proud of.

6. A. I seldom feel approved or noticed by people I like.
    B. I usually get both approval and attention from people I like.

7. A. I feel sure of myself in most circumstances.
    B. I feel sure of myself only in a few situations.

8. A. Few people say they like being with me.
    B. Most people say they like being with me.

9. A. I can usually accomplish everything I set out to do.
    B. Often I am unable to accomplish what I set out to do.

10. A. People seldom go out of their way to include me in their affairs.
    B. People often go out of their way to include me in their affairs.

11. A. I feel as capable as most people I know.
    B. I feel less capable than a fair number of people I know.

12. A. Few people consider me to be an interesting person.
    B. I feel that a lot of people consider me to be an interesting person.

13. A. I feel unsure whether I can handle what the future brings.
    B. I feel sure I can handle whatever the future is likely to bring.

14. A. A fair number of people seem to look up to me.
    B. Very few people seem to look up to me.

15. A. I tend to be optimistic when I take on a new job.
    B. I tend to expect failure when I take on a new job.

16. A. A fair number of persons say positive things about me.
    B. Relatively few people say nice things about me.

17. A. I seldom feel satisfied with myself.
    B. I usually feel pleased with myself.

18. A. I feel accepted by most people important to me.
    B. I feel accepted only by some people important to me.

19. A. Most people I know would rate me as a self-assured person.
    B. Few people I know would rate me as a self-assured person.

20. A. I seem to get more social invitations than my friends do.
    B. I seem to get fewer social invitations than my friends do.

21. A. I often feel I can't do anything right.
    B. Usually I can do whatever I set my mind to.

22. A. Often people confide in me.
    B. It is seldom that people confide in me.

23. A. I have a record of fewer successes than failures.
    B. I have a record of more successes than failures.

24. A. Only a few people enjoy associating with me.
    B. Many people like to associate with me.

25. A. I usually expect to win when competing with others.
    B. I seldom expect to win when competing with others.

26. A. Few people tell me they enjoy my company.
    B. Most people say they enjoy my company.

27. A. I probably think less favorably of myself than the ordinary person does.
    B. I think more favorably of myself than the ordinary person does.

28. A. Not many people seem to value my friendship.
    B. Quite a few persons appear to value my friendship.

29. A. There are very few things I would change about myself.
    B. There are many things about myself I wish I could change.

30. A. I am often asked to voice my opinion in a group discussion.
    B. I am seldom asked to express an opinion in a group discussion.

31.   A.   I seldom reach the goals I set for myself.
      B.   I usually reach the goals I set for myself.

32.   A.   My acquaintances don't seem to follow my suggestions.
      B.   My acquaintances usually follow my suggestions.

SELF-CONSCIOUSNESS SCALE (SCS)

AUTHOR: Michael F. Scheier

PURPOSE: To measure individual differences in private and public self-consciousness and social anxiety.

DESCRIPTION: The SCS is a 22-item scale that was revised from an earlier version to make it appropriate for non–college populations. The SCS is focused on the assessment of an individual's self-consciousness in both public and private situations. Public self-consciousness refers to the tendency to think about those aspects of oneself that are matters of public display (items 2, 5, 10, 13, 16, 18, 20); private self-consciousness refers to the tendency to think about more covert or hidden aspects of the self (items 1, 4, 6, 8, 12, 14, 17, 19, 21). The scale also includes a measure of social anxiety, an apprehensiveness about being evaluated by others (items 3, 7, 9, 11, 15, 22). Extensive research on the original instrument shows that public and private self-consciousness mediate a wide range of behaviors and cognitions.

NORMS: Norms for the revised SCS are based on a sample of 213 undergraduate men, 85 undergraduate women, 42 middle-aged men who had recently undergone coronary artery bypass surgery. and 396 women between the ages of 45 and 50 who were involved in a longitudinal study of menopause. For the undergraduate students, means for the men were 15.5 on private self-consciousness, 13.5 on public self-consciousness, and 8.8 on social anxiety. Means for the undergraduate women were 17.3 for private, 14.2 for public and 8.6 for social anxiety. The means were significantly different for men and women on private self-consciousness. For middle-aged men the mean for private self-consciousness was 13.5; for middle-aged women, the mean was 10.8 for public self-consciousness and 7.3 for social anxiety.

SCORING: The SCS is scored by summing scores, which range from 0 to 3, for each item. This produces a total possible range of 0 to 66.

RELIABILITY: The SCS has fairly good internal consistency, with an alpha of .75 for private self-consciousness, .84 for public self-consciousness, and .79 for social anxiety. The scale also demonstrates good stability, with test-retest correlations of .76 for private, .74 for public, and .77 for social anxiety.

VALIDITY: Since the original scale had demonstrated good validity, the main source of validity information to date is a form of concurrent validity, correlations of the revised scale with the original. All three subscales correlate in the low to mid .80s with the original scale.

PRIMARY REFERENCE: Scheier, M. F. and Carver, C. S. (1985). The Self-Consciousness Scale: A revised version for use with the general population,

Journal of Applied Social Psychology, 15, 687–699. Instrument reproduced by permission of Dr. Michael F. Scheier.
AVAILABILITY: Dr. Michael F. Scheier, Department of Psychology, Carnegie-Mellon University, Pittsburgh, PA 15213.

SCS

Please put a number next to each item indicating the extent to which that item is like you.

0 = Not at all like me
1 = A little like me
2 = Somewhat like me
3 = A lot like me

_____ 1. I'm always trying to figure myself out.
_____ 2. I'm concerned about my style of doing things.
_____ 3. It takes me time to get over my shyness in new situations.
_____ 4. I think about myself a lot.
_____ 5. I care a lot about how I present myself to others.
_____ 6. I often daydream about myself.
_____ 7. It's hard for me to work when someone is watching me.
_____ 8. I never take a hard look at myself.
_____ 9. I get embarrassed very easily.
_____ 10. I'm self-conscious about the way I look.
_____ 11. It's easy for me to talk to strangers.
_____ 12. I generally pay attention to my inner feelings.
_____ 13. I usually worry about making a good impression.
_____ 14. I'm constantly thinking about my reasons for doing things.
_____ 15. I feel nervous when I speak in front of a group.
_____ 16. Before I leave my house, I check how I look.
_____ 17. I sometimes step back (in my mind) in order to examine myself from a distance.
_____ 18. I'm concerned about what other people think of me.
_____ 19. I'm quick to notice changes in my mood.
_____ 20. I'm usually aware of my appearance.
_____ 21. I know the way my mind works when I work through a problem.
_____ 22. Large groups make me nervous.

SELF-CONTROL QUESTIONNAIRE (SCQ)

AUTHOR: Lynn P. Rehm

PURPOSE: To measure self-control behaviors and cognitions.

DESCRIPTION: The SCQ is a 40-item instrument designed to measure depression-related self-control behaviors and cognitions. The SCQ was developed to evaluate the effectiveness of a self-control therapy program for depression. Items for the SCQ were derived from deficits in self-control behavior that are hypothesized to be contributory factors in depression. The SCQ is not only useful as an outcome measure, but may be useful as an assessment of vulnerability to depression.

NORMS: The SCQ has been studied with a sample of 101 clinically depressed community volunteers and with undefined samples of "normal" and pregnant women. No other demographic data are available nor are actual norms.

SCORING: The SCQ is scored on a 5-point scale (0 to 4) from A ("very characteristic of me, extremely descriptive") to E ("very uncharacteristic of me, extremely undescriptive"). As shown on the questionnaire, 19 items (marked "A") are phrased to reflect positive, nondepressive attitudes and 21 items (marked "E") to reflect negative, depressive attitudes. The latter should be reverse-scored ($A = 4, E = 0$). The total score is then the sum of all items.

RELIABILITY: The SCQ has very good internal consistency, with alphas that range from .82 to .88. The SCQ also is very stable with a five-week, test-retest correlation of .86.

VALIDITY: The SCQ has fair concurrent validity, with a correlation of .42 with the more general Rosenberg Self-Control Schedule. Correlations with the Beck Depression Inventory range from .16 to .31. The SCQ has good predictive validity, predicting post-partum depression in pregnant women. The SCQ also is very sensitive to changes due to clinical treatment.

PRIMARY REFERENCE: O'Hara, M. W., Rehm, L. P., and Campbell, S. B. (1982), Predicting depressive symptomatology: Cognitive-behavioral models and post-partum depression, *Journal of Abnormal Psychology*, 91 457–461.

AVAILABILITY: Dr. Lynn P. Rehm, Department of Psychology, University of Houston, TX 77204.

SCQ

Please read each of the following statements and indicate just how characteristic or descriptive of you the statement is by using the letters of the code given below:

A = *Very characteristic of me, extremely descriptive*
B = Rather characteristic of me, quite descriptive
C = Somewhat characteristic of me, slightly undescriptive
D = Rather uncharacteristic of me, quite undescriptive
E = *Very uncharacteristic of me, extremely undescriptive*

(E) ____ 1. Rewarding myself for progress toward a goal is unnecessary and may actually spoil me.

(A) ____ 2. Concentrating on the final goals as well as the immediate results of my efforts can help me feel better about my work.

(E) ____ 3. When things are going well, I often feel that something bad is just around the corner and there's nothing I can do about it.

(A) ____ 4. I am aware of my accomplishments each day.

(A) ____ 5. Thinking about how well I'm doing so far is what keeps me trying.

(A) ____ 6. When I do something right, I take time to enjoy the feeling.

(A) ____ 7. It usually works best for me to save my special treats until after I carry out what I intended to accomplish.

(A) ____ 8. What is most important is how I feel about my actions, not what other think.

(E) ____ 9. There is nothing I can do to change things that are upsetting me.

(A) ____ 10. The way to achieve my goals is to reward myself along the way, in order to keep up my own efforts.

(E) ____ 11. Punishing myself for only making partial gains toward a goal is the smart way to keep pressure on and get the job done.

(A) ____ 12. I get myself through hard things largely by planning on enjoying myself afterwards.

(E) ____ 13. I depend heavily on other people's opinions to evaluate objectively what I do.

(A) ____ 14. When I don't feel like doing anything, sometimes it helps if I take time out to do something I really enjoy.

(E) ____ 15. I always seem to remember the bad things that happen to me more than the good.

(A) ____ 16. It's success at the little things that encourages me to go on trying.

(A) ____ 17. To get good results, I have to observe what I'm actually doing in order to decide what I need to do next.

(E) ____ 18. The things in life that are most important depend on chance more than anything I can do.

(A) ____ 19. Planning each step of what I have to do helps me to get things done well.

(E) ____ 20. It's no use trying to change most of the things that make me miserable.

(E) ____ 21. My mood is unrelated to my behavior.

(E) ____ 22. There isn't anything to do when I want something important other than be patient and hope for good luck.

(E) ____ 23. Activities which fail to lead to something immediately should be dropped in favor of those that do so.

(E) ____ 24. My goals seem distant and unreachable.

(E) ____ 25. I think talking about what you've done right or well is just boastful and tooting your own horn.

(E) ____ 26. Unless I set and reach very high goals, my efforts are likely to be wasted.

(E) ____ 27. When I feel blue, the best thing to do is focus on all the negative things happening to me.

(A) ____ 28. Judging what I've done realistically is necessary for me to feel good about myself.

(E) ____ 29. How I feel about myself has a lot to do with what I'm accomplishing.

(E) ____ 30. I shouldn't dwell on things I've done well in hopes of feeling good about myself.

(A) ____ 31. When there is some goal I'd like to reach, I find it best to list specifically what I have to do to get there.

(A) ____ 32. My mood changes in relation to what I'm doing.

(A) ____ 33. It's just as important to think about what will happen later as a result of my actions, as it is to watch for immediate effects.

(E) ____ 34. I'd just be fooling myself if I tried to judge my reactions myself.

(E) ____ 35. Keeping watch on what I do wrong is more helpful than watching what I do correctly.

(E) ____ 36. Criticizing myself is often the best way to help me get through a difficult task.

(A) ____ 37. Not only what goes on around us, but also the things we say and do to ourselves determine how we feel from day to day.

(A) ____ 38. I encourage myself to improve by treating myself to something special whenever I make progress.

(E) ____ 39. It's more helpful to receive criticism than praise for my actions.

(A) ____ 40. I'd be unlikely to change for the better if I didn't silently praise myself or feel good for every step in the right direction.

SELF-CONTROL SCHEDULE (SCS)

AUTHOR: Michael Rosenbaum

PURPOSE: To measure self-control.

DESCRIPTION: The SCS is a 36-item instrument designed to assess individual tendencies to apply self-control methods to the solution of behavioral problems. The SCS was developed on the basis of a cognitive-behavioral formulation of self-control in which self-controlling responses were assumed to be cued by an internal event (e.g., anxiety, disruptive thought) that affects the effective performance of some behavior. The behaviors for the measure were derived from the literature on stress-handling methods and coping-skills therapies. The initial list of 60 items was pared down to the current 36 by expert opinion and initial research on the SCS. The SCS can be used to predict success in cognitive-behavior therapy, as an indicator of changes in therapy, as a predictor of adherence to prescribed medical regimens, and to assess the client's repertoire of self-control skills.

NORMS: The SCS has been studied with several samples of Israeli and American college students amounting to several hundred subjects and including males and females. The SCS also was administered to a group of 105 Israeli men (mean age of 50.5 years) randomly selected from a group of men who were having their driver's licenses renewed and 290 male and 356 female residents of Eugene, Oregon (mean age = 63.7). The means for all samples ranged from 23 to 27 (with standard deviations from 15.2 to 25). For "normal" populations, the norm is approximately 25 (SD = 20).

SCORING: The SCS is scored by first reverse-scoring items 4, 6, 8, 9, 14, 16, 18, 19, 21, 29, and 35, and then summing all individual items. The total score of the scale could range from -108 (36×-3) to $+108$ ($36 \times +3$).

RELIABILITY: The SCS has good to excellent internal consistency, with alphas that range from .72 to .91. The SCS also has good to excellent stability, with test-retest correlations for 11 months of .77 and for four weeks of .86.

VALIDITY: The SCS has good construct validity with correlations in predicted directions with Rotter's Internal-External Scale, the Irrational Beliefs Test, and some subscales of the MMPI and the G Factor (measuring self-control as a personality pattern) of the 16 PF.

PRIMARY REFERENCE: Rosenbaum, M. (1980). A schedule for assessing self-control behaviors: Preliminary findings, *Behavior Therapy*, 11, 109–121. Instrument reprinted by permission of publisher and author.

AVAILABILITY: Dr. Michael Rosenbaum, Department of Psychology, Tel Aviv University, Tel Aviv 69978, Israel.

SCS

Indicate how characteristic or descriptive each of the following statements is of you by using the code given below.

+3 = Very characteristic of me
+2 = Rather characteristic of me
+1 = Somewhat characteristic of me
−1 = Somewhat uncharacteristic of me
−2 = Rather uncharacteristic of me
−3 = Very uncharacteristic of me

Thank you for your cooperation

1. When I do a boring job, I think about the less boring parts of the job and about the reward I will receive when I finish.   −3 −2 −1 +1 +2 +3

2. When I have to do something that makes me anxious, I try to visualize how I will overcome my anxiety while doing it.   −3 −2 −1 +1 +2 +3

3. By changing my way of thinking, I am often able to change my feelings about almost anything.   −3 −2 −1 +1 +2 +3

4. I often find it difficult to overcome my feelings of nervousness and tension without outside help.   −3 −2 −1 +1 +2 +3

5. When I am feeling depressed, I try to think about pleasant events.   −3 −2 −1 +1 +2 +3

6. I cannot help thinking about mistakes I made.   −3 −2 −1 +1 +2 +3

7. When I am faced with a difficult problem, I try to approach it in a systematic way.   −3 −2 −1 +1 +2 +3

8. I usually do what I am supposed to do more quickly when someone is pressuring me.   −3 −2 −1 +1 +2 +3

9. When I am faced with a difficult decision, I prefer to postpone it even if I have all the facts.   −3 −2 −1 +1 +2 +3

10. When I have difficulty concentrating on my reading, I look for ways to increase my concentration.   −3   −2   −1   +1   +2   +3

11. When I plan to work, I remove everything that is not relevant to my work.   −3   −2   −1   +1   +2   +3

12. When I try to get rid of a bad habit, I first try to find out all the reasons why I have the habit.   −3   −2   −1   +1   +2   +3

13. When an unpleasant thought is bothering me, I try to think about something pleasant.   −3   −2   −1   +1   +2   +3

14. If I smoked two packs of cigarettes a day, I would need outside help to stop smoking.   −3   −2   −1   +1   +2   +3

15. When I feel down, I try to act cheerful so that my mood will change.   −3   −2   −1   +1   +2   +3

16. If I have tranquilizers with me, I would take one whenever I feel tense and nervous.   −3   −2   −1   +1   +2   +3

17. When I am depressed, I try to keep myself busy with things I like.   −3   −2   −1   +1   +2   +3

18. I tend to postpone unpleasant tasks even if I could perform them immediately.   −3   −2   −1   +1   +2   +3

19. I need outside help to get rid of some of my bad habits.   −3   −2   −1   +1   +2   +3

20. When I find it difficult to settle down and do a task, I look for ways to help me settle down.   −3   −2   −1   +1   +2   +3

21. Although it makes me feel bad, I cannot help thinking about all sorts of possible catastrophes.   −3   −2   −1   +1   +2   +3

22. I prefer to finish a job that I have to do before I start doing things I really like.   −3   −2   −1   +1   +2   +3

23. When I feel physical pain, I try not to think about it.   −3   −2   −1   +1   +2   +3

24. My self-esteem increases when I am able to overcome a bad habit.   −3   −2   −1   +1   +2   +3

25. To overcome bad feelings that accompany failure, I often tell myself that it is not catastrophic and I can do anything.   −3   −2   −1   +1   +2   +3

26. When I feel that I am too impulsive, I tell myself to stop and think before I do something about it.   −3   −2   −1   +1   +2   +3

27. Even when I am terribly angry at someone, I consider my actions very carefully.   −3   −2   −1   +1   +2   +3

28. Facing the need to make a decision, I usually look for different alternatives instead of deciding quickly and spontaneously.   −3   −2   −1   +1   +2   +3

29. Usually, I first do the thing I really like to do even if there are more urgent things to do.   −3   −2   −1   +1   +2   +3

30. When I realize that I am going to be unavoidably late for an important meeting, I tell myself to keep calm.   −3   −2   −1   +1   +2   +3

31. When I feel pain in my body, I try to divert my thoughts from it.   −3   −2   −1   +1   +2   +3

32. When I am faced with a number of things to do, I usually plan my work.   −3   −2   −1   +1   +2   +3

33. When I am short of money, I decide to record all my expenses in order to budget more carefully in the future.   −3   −2   −1   +1   +2   +3

34. If I find it difficult to concentrate on a task, I divide it into smaller segments.   −3   −2   −1   +1   +2   +3

35. Quite often, I cannot overcome unpleasant thoughts that bother me.   −3   −2   −1   +1   +2   +3

36. When I am hungry and I have no opportunity to eat, I try to divert my thoughts from my stomach or try to imagine that am satisfied.   −3   −2   −1   +1   +2   +3

SELF-EFFICACY SCALE (SES)

AUTHORS: Mark Sherer, James E. Maddux, Blaise Mercandante, Steven Prentice-Dunn, Beth Jacobs, and Ronald W. Rogers.

PURPOSE: To measure general levels of belief in one's own competence.

DESCRIPTION: The SES is a 30-item instrument that measures general expectations of self-efficacy that are not tied to specific situations or behavior. The assumptions underlying this instrument are that personal expectations of mastery are a major determinant of behavioral change, and that individual differences in past experiences and attributions of success lead to different levels of generalized self-efficacy expectations. Thus, this instrument may be useful in tailoring the course of clinical intervention to the client's needs, and also as an index of progress since expectations of self-efficacy should change during the course of intervention. The SES consists of two subscales, general self-efficacy (items 2, 3, 4, 7, 8, 11, 12, 15, 16, 18, 20, 22, 23, 26, 27, 29, 30) and social self-efficacy (items 6, 10, 14, 19, 24, 28,).

NORMS: The initial studies of the SES involved 376 undergraduate students in introductory psychology classes and 150 inpatients from a Veterans Administration alcohol treatment unit. No other demographic data were provided nor were actual norms for these groups.

SCORING: Seven items (1, 5, 9, 13, 17, 21, 25) are filler items and are not scored. After items presented in a negative fashion (3, 6, 7, 8, 11, 14, 18, 20, 22, 24, 26, 29, 30) are reverse-scored, the scores for all items are summed. Before reverse-scoring, the answers are keyed as follows: A = 1, B = 2, C = 3, D = 4, E = 5. The higher the score, the higher the self-efficacy expectations.

RELIABILITY: The SES has fairly good internal consistency, with alphas of .86 for the general subscale and .71 for the social subscale. No test-retest data were reported.

VALIDITY: The SES was shown to have good criterion-related validity by accurately predicting that people with higher self-efficacy would have greater success than those who score low in self-efficacy in past vocational, educational, and monetary goals. The SES also has demonstrated construct validity by correlating significantly in predicted directions with a number of measures such as the Ego Strength Scale, the Interpersonal Competency Scale, and the Rosenberg Self-Esteem Scale.

PRIMARY REFERENCE: Sherer, M., Maddox, J. E., Mercandante, B., Prentice-Dunn, S., Jacobs, B., and Rogers, R. W. (1982). The Self-Efficacy Scale: Construction and validation, *Psychological Reports*, 51, 663-671. Instrument reproduced with permission of Mark Sherer and Ronald W. Rogers and Psychological Reports.

AVAILABILITY: Dr. Mark Sherer, 1874 Pleasant Avenue, Mobile, AL 36617.

SES

This questionnaire is a series of statements about your personal attitudes and traits. Each statement represents a commonly held belief. Read each statement and decide to what extent it describes you. There are no right or wrong answers. You will probably agree with some of the statements and disagree with others. Please indicate your own personal feelings about each statement below by marking the letter that best describes your attitude or feeling. Please be very truthful and describe yourself as you really are, not as you would like to be.

A = Disagree strongly
B = Disagree moderately
C = Neither agree nor disagree
D = Agree moderately
E = Agree strongly

_____ 1. I like to grow house plants.
_____ 2. When I make plans, I am certain I can make them work.
_____ 3. One of my problems is that I cannot get down to work when I should.
_____ 4. If I can't do a job the first time, I keep trying until I can.
_____ 5. Heredity plays the major role in determining one's personality.
_____ 6. It is difficult for me to make new friends.
_____ 7. When I set important goals for myself, I rarely achieve them.
_____ 8. I give up on things before completing them.
_____ 9. I like to cook.
_____ 10. If I see someone I would like to meet, I go to that person instead of waiting for him or her to come to me.
_____ 11. I avoid facing difficulties.
_____ 12. If something looks too complicated, I will not even bother to try it.
_____ 13. There is some good in everybody.
_____ 14. If I meet someone interesting who is very hard to make friends with, I'll soon stop trying to make friends with that person.
_____ 15. When I have something unpleasant to do, I stick to it until I finish it.
_____ 16. When I decide to do something, I go right to work on it.
_____ 17. I like science.
_____ 18. When trying to learn something new, I soon give up if I am not initially successful.
_____ 19. When I'm trying to become friends with someone who seems uninterested at first, I don't give up very easily.
_____ 20. When unexpected problems occur, I don't handle them well.
_____ 21. If I were an artist, I would like to draw children.
_____ 22. I avoid trying to learn new things when they look too difficult for me.
_____ 23. Failure just makes me try harder.
_____ 24. I do not handle myself well in social gatherings.
_____ 25. I very much like to ride horses.
_____ 26. I feel insecure about my ability to do things.
_____ 27. I am a self-reliant person.
_____ 28. I have acquired my friends through my personal abilities at making friends.

____ 29. I give up easily.
____ 30. I do not seem capable of dealing with most problems that come up in my life.

SELF-ESTEEM RATING SCALE (SERS)

AUTHORS: William R. Nugent and Janita W. Thomas

PURPOSE: To measure self-esteem.

DESCRIPTION: The SERS is a 40-item instrument that was developed to provide a clinical measure of self-esteem that can indicate not only problems in self-esteem but also positive or nonproblematic levels. The items were written to tap into a range of areas of self-evaluation including overall self-worth, social competence, problem-solving ability, intellectual ability, self-competence, and worth relative to other people. The SERS is a very useful instrument for measuring both positive and negative aspects of self-esteem in clinical practice.

NORMS: The SERS was studied initially with two samples. Sample 1 contained 246 people, of whom 91 were male and 155 female, with an average age of 32.5 years and an average of 15.7 years of formal education. Thirty-one percent were white, 11.8% black, 4.5% Hispanic, 7.7% Asian, and the rest were mixed or other groups. Sample 2 involved 107 people including 23 males and 84 females, with an average of 15.3 years of education; 93.5% were white, 4.7% black, and the rest in other groups. Actual norms were not available.

SCORING: The SERS is scored by scoring the items shown at the bottom of the measure as p/+ positively, and scoring the remaining items (N/–) negatively by placing a minus sign in front of the item score. The items are summed to produce a total score ranging from –120 to +120. Positive scores indicate more positive self-esteem and negative scores indicate more negative levels of self-esteem.

RELIABILITY: The SERS has excellent internal consistency, with an alpha of .97. The standard error of measurement was 5.67. Data on stability were not reported.

VALIDITY: The SERS was reported as having good content and factorial validity. The SERS has good construct validity, with significant correlations with the Index of Self-Esteem and the Generalized Contentment Scale (a measure of depression) as predicted, and generally low correlations with a variety of demographic variables, also as predicted.

PRIMARY REFERENCE: Nugent, W. R. and Thomas J. W. (1993). Validation of the Self-Esteem Rating Scale, *Research on Social Work Practice*, 3, 191–207.

AVAILABILITY: Journal article.

SERS

This questionnaire is designed to measure how you feel about yourself. It is not a test, so there are no right or wrong answers. Please answer each item as carefully and accurately as you can by placing a number by each one as follows:

1 = Never
2 = Rarely
3 = A little of the time
4 = Some of the time
5 = A good part of the time
6 = Most of the time
7 = Always

Please begin.

____ 1. I feel that people would *NOT* like me if they really knew me well.
____ 2. I feel that others do things much better than I do.
____ 3. I feel that I am an attractive person.
____ 4. I feel confident in my ability to deal with other people.
____ 5. I feel that I am likely to fail at things I do.
____ 6. I feel that people really like to talk with me.
____ 7. I feel that I am a very competent person.
____ 8. When I am with other people I feel that they are glad I am with them.
____ 9. I feel that I make a good impression on others.
____ 10. I feel confident that I can begin new relationships if I want to.
____ 11. I feel that I am ugly.
____ 12. I feel that I am a boring person.
____ 13. I feel very nervous when I am with strangers.
____ 14. I feel confident in my ability to learn new things.
____ 15. I feel good about myself.
____ 16. I feel ashamed about myself.
____ 17. I feel inferior to other people.
____ 18. I feel that my friends find me interesting.
____ 19. I feel that I have a good sense of humor.
____ 20. I get angry at myself over the way I am.
____ 21. I feel relaxed meeting new people.
____ 22. I feel that other people are smarter than I am.
____ 23. I do *NOT* like myself.
____ 24. I feel confident in my ability to cope with difficult situations.
____ 25. I feel that I am *NOT* very likeable.
____ 26. My friends value me a lot.
____ 27. I am afraid I will appear stupid to others.
____ 28. I feel that I am an OK person.
____ 29. I feel that I can count on myself to manage things well.
____ 30. I wish I could just disappear when I am around other people.
____ 31. I feel embarrassed to let others hear my ideas.
____ 32. I feel that I am a nice person.

___ 33. I feel that if I could be more like other people then I would feel *better* about myself.
___ 34. I feel that I get pushed around more than others.
___ 35. I feel that people like me.
___ 36. I feel that people have a good time when they are with me.
___ 37. I feel confident that I can do well in whatever I do.
___ 38. I trust the competence of others more than I trust my own abilities.
___ 39. I feel that I mess things up.
___ 40. I wish that I were someone else.

(p/+)   3,4,6,7,8,9,10,14,15,18,19,21,24,26,28,29,32,35,36,37.
(N/−)   1,2,5,11,12,13,16,17,20,22,23,25,27,30,31,33,34,38,39,40.

SELF-RATING ANXIETY SCALE (SAS)

AUTHOR: William W. K. Zung

PURPOSE: To assess anxiety as a clinical disorder and quantify anxiety symptoms.

DESCRIPTION: The SAS is a 20-item instrument consisting of the most commonly found characteristics of an anxiety disorder (5 affective and 15 somatic symptoms). Five of the items are worded symptomatically positive and 15 are worded symptomatically negative; respondents use a 4-point scale to rate how each item applied to himself or herself during the past week. The author has also developed a rating scale based on the same symptoms to be used by the clinician to rate the client (Anxiety Status Inventory or ASI), thus allowing two sources of data on the same symptoms.

NORMS: The initial study was carried out on 225 psychiatric patients including 152 male inpatients, and 23 male and 50 female outpatients with a mean age of 41 years. An additional 100 male and female "normal" (nonpatient) subjects were part of the study. However, little formal standardization work has been carried out on the SAS.

SCORING: The SAS is scored by summing the values on each item to produce a raw score ranging from 20 to 80. An SAS index is derived by dividing the raw score by 80, producing an index that ranges from .25 to 1.00 (higher scores equal more anxiety). A cutoff score of 50 is recommended, with scores over 50 suggesting the presence of clinically meaningful anxiety.

RELIABILITY: Data are not available.

VALIDITY: The SAS has fair concurrent validity, correlating significantly with the Taylor Manifest Anxiety Scale and with the clinician rating scale developed by the author (ASI). The SAS also has good known-groups validity, distinguishing between patients diagnosed as having anxiety disorders and those with other psychiatric diagnoses and between nonpatient and patient groups.

PRIMARY REFERENCE: Zung, W. K. (1971). A rating instrument for anxiety disorders, *Psychosomatics*, 12, 371–379. Instrument reproduced by permission of W. K. Zung and *Psychosomatics*, all rights reserved.

AVAILABILITY: Psykey, Inc., 7750 Daggett Street, San Diego, CA 92111.

SAS

Below are twenty statements. Please rate each using the following scale:

    1 = Some or a little of the time
    2 = Some of the time
    3 = Good part of the time
    4 = Most or all of the time

Please record your rating in the space to the left of each item.

_____   1.   I feel more nervous and anxious than usual.
_____   2.   I feel afraid for no reason at all.
_____   3.   I get upset easily or feel panicky.
_____   4.   I feel like I'm falling apart and going to pieces.
_____   5.   I feel that everything is all right and nothing bad will happen.
_____   6.   My arms and legs shake and tremble.
_____   7.   I am bothered by headaches, neck and back pains.
_____   8.   I feel weak and get tired easily.
_____   9.   I feel calm and can sit still easily.
_____ 10.   I can feel my heart beating fast.
_____ 11.   I am bothered by dizzy spells.
_____ 12.   I have fainting spells or feel like it.
_____ 13.   I can breathe in and out easily.
_____ 14.   I get feelings of numbness and tingling in my fingers, toes.
_____ 15.   I am bothered by stomach aches or indigestion.
_____ 16.   I have to empty my bladder often.
_____ 17.   My hands are usually dry and warm.
_____ 18.   My face gets hot and blushes.
_____ 19.   I fall asleep easily and get a good night's rest.
_____ 20.   I have nightmares.

SELF-RATING DEPRESSION SCALE (SDS)

AUTHOR: William W. K. Zung

PURPOSE: To assess depression as a clinical disorder and quantify the symptoms of depression.

DESCRIPTION: The SDS is a 20-item instrument developed to examine three basic aspects of depression: (1) pervasive affect, (2) physiological concomitants, and (3) psychological concomitants. The SDS consists of 10 items worded symptomatically positive and 10 items symptomatically negative. Items on the SDS were specifically selected to tap one of the three aspects of depression described above and include cognitive, affective, psychomotor, somatic, and social-interpersonal items. Respondents are asked to rate each of the 20 items on a sliding scale as to how it applies to them at the time of testing. Individual item scores as well as overall scores are considered meaningful. The author suggests the following clinical cutting scores to estimate the degree of depression: 50 to 59 (mild to moderate); 60 to 69 (moderate to severe); 70 and over (severe). A test booklet is available.

NORMS: Initial study of the SDS was conducted on 56 patients admitted to the psychiatric service of a hospital with a primary diagnosis of depression and 100 "normal" (nonpatient) subjects. Subsequent study of 22 samples reveals some support for the clinical cutting scores. However, little formal effort at standardization has been made.

SCORING: The SDS is scored by summing the values obtained on each item to produce a raw score ranging from 20 to 80. An SDS index is produced by dividing the raw score by 80 to produce a range of .25 to 1.00 (higher scores equal greater depression).

RELIABILITY: The SDS has fair internal consistency, with a split-half reliability of .73.

VALIDITY: The SDS has good known-groups validity in distinguishing between depressed and nondepressed samples, and has good concurrent validity in regard to correlations with other depression measures, such as the Beck Depression Inventory and the Hamilton Rating Scale for Depression. The SDS also is reported to be sensitive to clinical changes.

PRIMARY REFERENCE: Zung, W. K. (1965). A Self-Rating Depression Scale, *Archives of General Psychiatry*, 12, 63–70. Instrument reproduced with permission of W. K. Zung, all rights reserved.

AVAILABILITY: Psykey, Inc., 7750 Daggett Street, San Diego, CA 92111.

SDS

Below are twenty statements. Please rate each using the following scale:

1 = Some or a little of the time
2 = Some of the time
3 = Good part of the time
4 = Most or all of the time

Please record your rating in the space to the left of each item.

_____ 1.   I feel down-hearted, blue, and sad.
_____ 2.   Morning is when I feel the best.
_____ 3.   I have crying spells or feel like it.
_____ 4.   I have trouble sleeping through the night.
_____ 5.   I eat as much as I used to.
_____ 6.   I enjoy looking at, talking to, and being with attractive women/men.
_____ 7.   I notice that I am losing weight.
_____ 8.   I have trouble with constipation.
_____ 9.   My heart beats faster than usual.
_____ 10. I get tired for no reason.
_____ 11. My mind is as clear as it used to be.
_____ 12. I find it easy to do the things I used to.
_____ 13. I am restless and can't keep still.
_____ 14. I feel hopeful about the future.
_____ 15. I am more irritable than usual.
_____ 16. I find it easy to make decisions.
_____ 17. I feel that I am useful and needed.
_____ 18. My life is pretty full.
_____ 19. I feel that others would be better off if I were dead.
_____ 20. I still enjoy the things I used to do.

SELF-RIGHTEOUSNESS SCALE (SRS)

AUTHOR: Toni Falbo

PURPOSE: To measure self-righteousness.

DESCRIPTION: This 7-item instrument measures the conviction that one's beliefs or behavior are correct, especially in comparison to alternative beliefs or behaviors. It excludes self-righteousness about political issues and focuses not on specific beliefs, but on the general characteristic of self-righteousness. The SRS is not associated with anxiety, thereby distinguishing it from similar variables such as dogmatism which assumes the presence of anxiety. Two subscales can be formed; one measuring general self-righteousness (SR) and another measuring its opposite, acceptance (A). The SRS can be reworded to measure self-righteousness about a particular belief or behavior. It is useful in assessing communication style in clinical intervention with families and dyads as well as individuals.

NORMS: One hundred and twenty respondents were involved in the development of the SRS. Fifty-four were male and 66 were female, and the subjects' ages ranged from 17 to 63 years. The total SRS scores ranged from 4 to 18 with a mean of 7.45. A second sample consisted of 70 respondents (45 males and 25 females). This sample had an age range from 17 to 45 and all were involved in a demanding 10-kilometer foot race. Pretest mean scores were 9.82. The average SRS score after completing the race was 9.07.

SCORING: Each item is rated on a 5-point scale, ranging from "strongly agree" to "strongly disagree." The SR items (1, 2, 3, 4) are summed to form a total score ranging from 4 to 20. Items 3 and 4 are reverse-scored. Higher scores reflect more self-righteousness. Items 5, 6, and 7 are summed to obtain an acceptance score (A). Scores range from 3 to 15 with higher scores indicating more acceptance of others.

RELIABILITY: Reliability was separately determined for the two subscales and was generally only moderate. Internal consistency using coefficient alpha was .60 and .58 for the SR and A subscales, although all items significantly correlated with subscale scores. Stability of the SR was moderate (.54) using test-retest correlations after a ten-kilometer race. While this magnitude of a test-retest reliability coefficient is only moderate, a higher correlation would not be expected since major accomplishments, such as completing a foot race, could impact upon one's level of self-righteousness.

VALIDITY: Items of the SRS were selected from a pool of 100, based on ratings by 15 judges. Items were also selected on the basis of a lack of association with a measure of social desirability. Concurrent validity was evidenced with correlations between the SR and measures of dogmatism, and intolerance for ambiguity and state-trait anxiety. The acceptance subscale was not found to correlate with these validity criteria. Based on the theoretical notion that self-righteousness is a defense mechanism which is utilized less when one has accomplished a goal, scores on the SRS were found to be lower for subjects who were winners in the 10 kilometer race compared to subjects who simply completed the race or lost the race. The change from pretest to posttest for winners in the race was significant, suggesting the SRS is sensitive to measuring change.

PRIMARY REFERENCE: Falbo, T. and Belk, S. S. (1985). A short scale to measure self-righteousness, *Journal of Personality Assessment*, 49, 72–77. Instrument reproduced with permission of Toni Falbo and the *Journal of Personality Assessment*.

AVAILABILITY: Journal article.

SRS

Answer each item according to the following scale and record your answer to the left of each statement.

1 = Strongly agree
2 = Agree
3 = Neutral
4 = Disagree
5 = Strongly disagree

_____   1.   People who disagree with me are wrong.

_____   2.   I can benefit other people by telling them the right way to live.

_____   3.   I am excited by the free exchange of ideas.

_____   4.   I enjoy having different points of view.

_____   5.   One person's opinions are just as valid as the next.

_____   6.   Most people naturally do the right thing.

_____   7.   People generally make few mistakes because they do know what is right or wrong.

SELFISM (NS)

AUTHORS: E. Jerry Phares and Nancy Erskine

PURPOSE: To measure narcissism.

DESCRIPTION: The NS is a 28-item scale designed to measure narcissism, referred to by developers of this instrument as selfism. Selfism is viewed as an orientation, belief, or set affecting how one construes a whole range of situations that deal with the satisfaction of needs. A person who scores high on the NS views a large number of situations in a selfish or egocentric fashion. At the opposite end of the continuum are individuals who submerge their own satisfaction in favor of others. The NS samples beliefs across a broad range of situations and is not targeted toward a specific need area. Based on a review of the literature, impressionistic sources, and the work of cultural observers, the original 100 items were narrowed down to 28 based on low correlations with the Marlowe-Crowne Social Desirability Scale, high correlations with NS total scores, and a reasonable spread over the five response categories.

NORMS: A series of studies was conducted in development of the NS. The respondents included some 548 undergraduate males and 675 undergraduate females, 71 city police, and 11 campus police. No other demographic data are available. Means for 175 college females were 76.50, for 150 college males 77.91, for 71 city police 75.33, and for 11 campus police 74.73. None of these differences was statistically significant.

SCORING: The NS is scored by summing the individual item scores, each of which is on a 5-point Likert-type scale, to produce a range of 28 to 140. The following are filler items, included to disguise the purpose of the scale, and are not scored: 1, 6, 8, 12, 15, 19, 23, 26, 30, 34, 38, 39.

RELIABILITY: The NS has very good internal consistency, with split-half reliabilities of .84 for males and .83 for females. The NS also has excellent stability, with a four-week test-retest correlation of .91.

VALIDITY: The NS has fair concurrent validity, correlating significantly with the Narcissistic Personality Inventory and the Religious Attitude Scale. Also, the NS demonstrated a form of known-groups validity by correlating positively with observers' judgments of their close friends' narcissistic characteristics. The NS also distinguished between respondents who were high and low on cynicism regarding the motives of individuals in need of help.

PRIMARY REFERENCE: Phares, E. J. and Erskine, N. (1984). The measurement of selfism, *Educational and Psychological Measurement*, 44, 597–608. Instrument reproduced with permission of E. Jerry Phares.

AVAILABILITY: Dr. E. J. Phares, Department of Psychology, Kansas State University, Manhattan, KS 66506.

NS

Listed below are 40 statements that deal with personal attitudes and feelings about a variety of things. Obviously, there are no right or wrong answers—only opinions. Read each item and then decide how you *personally* feel. Mark your answers to the left of each item according to the following scheme:

5 = Strongly agree
4 = Mildly agree
3 = Agree and disagree equally
2 = Mildly disagree
1 = Strongly disagree

_____ 1. The widespread interest in professional sports is just another example of escapism.

_____ 2. In times of shortages it is sometimes necessary for one to engage in a little hoarding.

_____ 3. Thinking of yourself first is no sin in this world today.

_____ 4. The prospect of becoming very close to another person worries me a good bit.

_____ 5. The really significant contributions in the world have very frequently been made by people who were preoccupied with themselves.

_____ 6. Every older American deserves a guaranteed income to live in dignity.

_____ 7. It is more important to live for yourself rather than for other people, parents, or for posterity.

_____ 8. Organized religious groups are too concerned with raising funds these days.

_____ 9. I regard myself as someone who looks after his/her personal interests.

_____ 10. The trouble with getting too close to people is that they start making emotional demands on you.

_____ 11. Having children keeps you from engaging in a lot of self-fulfilling activities.

_____ 12. Many of our production problems in this country are due to the fact that workers no longer take pride in their jobs.

_____ 13. It's best to live for the present and not to worry about tomorrow.

_____ 14. Call it selfishness if you will, but in this world today we all have to look out for ourselves first.

_____ 15. Education is too job oriented these days; there is not enough emphasis on basic education.

_____ 16. It seems impossible to imagine the world without me in it.

_____ 17. You can hardly overestimate the importance of selling yourself in getting ahead.

_____ 18. The difficulty with marriage is that it locks you into a relationship.

_____ 19. Movies emphasize sex and violence too much.

_____ 20. If it feels right, it is right.

_____ 21. Breaks in life are nonsense. The real story is pursuing your self-interests aggressively.

_____ 22. An individual's worth will often pass unrecognized unless that person thinks of himself or herself first.

_____ 23. Consumers need a stronger voice in governmental affairs.

_____ 24. Getting ahead in life depends mainly on thinking of yourself first.

_____ 25. In general, couples should seek a divorce when they find the marriage is not a fulfilling one.

_____ 26. Too often, voting means choosing between the lesser of two evils.

_____ 27. In striving to reach one's true potential, it is sometimes necessary to worry less about other people.

_____ 28. When choosing clothes I generally consider style before matters such as comfort or durability.

_____ 29. I believe people have the right to live any damn way they please.

_____ 30. Too many people have given up reading to passively watch TV.

_____ 31. Owing money is not so bad if it's the only way one can live without depriving oneself of the good life.

_____ 32. Not enough people live for the present.

_____ 33. I don't see anything wrong with people spending a lot of time and effort on their personal appearance.

_____ 34. Physical punishment is necessary to raise children properly.

_____ 35. The Peace Corps would be a good idea if it did not delay one's getting started along the road to a personal career.

_____ 36. It simply does not pay to become sad or upset about friends, loved ones, or events that don't turn out well.

_____ 37. A definite advantage of birth control devices is that they permit sexual pleasure without the emotional responsibilities that might otherwise result.

_____ 38. Doctors seem to have forgotten that medicine involves human relations and not just prescriptions.

_____ 39. I believe that some unidentified flying objects nave actually been sent from outer space to observe our culture here on earth.

_____ 40. In this world one has to look out for oneself first because nobody else will look out for you.

SEMANTIC DIFFERENTIAL FEELING AND MOOD SCALES
(SDFMS)

AUTHORS: Maurice Lorr and Richard A. Wunderlich

PURPOSE: To measure mood states.

DESCRIPTION: The SDFMS is a 35-item semantic differential scale for measuring feeling and mood states. A semantic differential scale takes into account the bipolar language of nature and mood. The respondent simply checks off on a one-to-five scale which mood is closer to how he or she feels at the current time. The SDFMS has five factors with items on each factor indicated on the instrument: A = elated–depressed, B = relaxed–anxious, C = confident–unsure, D = energetic–fatigued, and E = good natured–grouchy.

NORMS: The SDFMS was studied initially on two samples of high school boys totaling 210 students. No other demographic data are given nor are norms.

SCORING: Each scale point is scored from 1 to 5 (from left to right on the scale). The scores on the individual scales within each factor are totaled and then divided by 7 (number of items in each factor). The scores on the five factors can be summed for an overall score.

RELIABILITY: The SDFMS has fair internal consistency, with average reliability coefficients of .74. No data on stability are available.

VALIDITY: The SDFMS has fair concurrent validity, with support from findings on the (unipolar) POMS that show four of the five mood states found with the SDFMS, and five out of six (bipolar) POMS scales corresponding closely to the SDFMS.

PRIMARY REFERENCE: Lorr, M., and Wunderlich, R. A. (1988). A Semantic Differential Mood Scale, *Journal of Clinical Psychology*, 44, 33–35.

AVAILABILITY: Dr. Maurice Lorr, Life Cycle Institute, Catholic University, Washington, DC 20064.

SDFMS

Below are some scales that describe the feelings and moods people have. Think how you feel RIGHT NOW, that is, at the present moment. Suppose the scale contrasts *sad* and *happy*. *To which* mood are you closer? Place a check mark, √, in the space that describes how you feel. You can rate yourself as *quite* happy or *slightly* happy. Or, you can rate yourself *slightly* or *quite* sad. If neither word describes how you feel, place a check mark under *neutral*.

Place your check mark in the *middle* of spaces, not on the boundaries.

			Quite	Slightly	Neutral	Slightly	Quite	
(A)	1.	Dejected						Cheerful
(C)	2.	Bold						Timid
(D)	3.	Fresh						Tired
(B)	4.	Anxious						Relaxed
(E)	5.	Friendly						Hostile
(A)	6.	Low-spirited						High-spirited
(C)	7.	Strong						Weak
(D)	8.	Lively						Weary
(B)	9.	Tense						Serene
(E)	10.	Agreeable						Grouchy
(A)	11.	Gloomy						Jolly
(C)	12.	Confident						Unsure
(D)	13.	Vigorous						Exhausted
(B)	14.	Nervous						Tranquil
(E)	15.	Good-natured						Bad-tempered
(A)	16.	Sad						Happy

			Quite	Slightly	Neutral	Slightly	Quite	
(C)	17.	Self-assured						Uncertain
(D)	18.	Energetic						Fatigued
(B)	19.	Shaky						Composed
(E)	20.	Sympathetic						Quarrelsome
(A)	21.	Depressed						Jubilant
(C)	22.	Forceful						Inadequate
(D)	23.	Ready-to-go						Sluggish
(B)	24.	Uneasy						Untroubled
(E)	25.	Genial						Irritable
(A)	26.	Despondent						Delighted
(C)	27.	Powerful						Incompetent
(D)	28.	Full of pep						Worn out
(B)	29.	Jittery						Calm
(E)	30.	Cordial						Angered
(A)	31.	Unhappy						Lighthearted
(C)	32.	Assertive						Docile
(D)	33.	Alert						Drowsy
(B)	34.	Worried						Carefree
(E)	35.	Amiable						Annoyed

SENSATION SCALE (SS)

AUTHORS: S. A. Maisto, V. J. Adesso, and R. Lauerman

PURPOSE: To measure subjective experience of physical changes following alcohol use.

DESCRIPTION: The SS is a 26-item instrument designed to measure respondents' perceptions of physiological changes following alcohol consumption. The main purpose of the SS is to examine individuals' ability to estimate their own level of intoxication. The SS generally is used as a six-category (or factor) measure: gastro-intestinal (items 1, 2, 12, 18), anesthetic (items 7, 8, 13, 14, 16, 17, 22, 23, 26), central stimulant (items 3, 9, 11, 15), impaired function (items 19, 20, 24), warmth/glow (items 4, 10, 25), and dynamic peripheral (items 5, 6, 21). The SS is recommended for use in studying changes induced by moderate alcohol intoxication, especially if a treatment goal is controlled drinking.

NORMS: The SS has been studied with several samples, including 16 males and 10 females in health-related professions who claimed no drinking-related problems and 124 male undergraduates classified as moderate to heavy drinkers. No other demographic data are reported nor are actual norms.

SCORING: The SS is scored easily by summing individual item scores for each of the six factors.

RELIABILITY: A type of stability was determined by having subjects sort the adjectives on the SS into the six categories or factors of the instrument. This resulted in agreement ratings that ranged from 76% for the dynamic peripheral factor to 97% for the gastro-intestinal factor.

VALIDITY: The SS has good known-groups validity, significantly distinguishing between subjects who have consumed an alcoholic or a nonalcoholic beverage.

PRIMARY REFERENCE: Maisto, S. A., Connors, G. J., Tucker, J. A., McCollam, J. B., and Adesso, V. J. (1980). Validation of the Sensation Scale, A measure of subjective physiological responses to alcohol, *Behavior Research and Therapy*, 18, 17–43.

AVAILABILITY: Dr. Stephen A. Maisto, V.A. Medical Center (116B), 960 Belmont Street, Brocton, MA 02401.

SS

Please circle the number that comes closest to describing how often you've experienced each sensation.

		Not at all				Moderately				A great deal	
		0	1	2	3	4	5	6	7	8	9	10
1.	Nauseous	0	1	2	3	4	5	6	7	8	9	10
2.	Stomach growling	0	1	2	3	4	5	6	7	8	9	10
3.	Ringing, buzzing	0	1	2	3	4	5	6	7	8	9	10
4.	Face flush	0	1	2	3	4	5	6	7	8	9	10
5.	Breathing changing	0	1	2	3	4	5	6	7	8	9	10
6.	Body rushes	0	1	2	3	4	5	6	7	8	9	10
7.	Limbs heavy	0	1	2	3	4	5	6	7	8	9	10
8.	Drowsy	0	1	2	3	4	5	6	7	8	9	10
9.	Light-headed	0	1	2	3	4	5	6	7	8	9	10
10.	Warm	0	1	2	3	4	5	6	7	8	9	10
11.	Head spinning	0	1	2	3	4	5	6	7	8	9	10
12.	Burning in stomach	0	1	2	3	4	5	6	7	8	9	10
13.	Face numb	0	1	2	3	4	5	6	7	8	9	10
14.	Relaxed	0	1	2	3	4	5	6	7	8	9	10
15.	Dizzy	0	1	2	3	4	5	6	7	8	9	10
16.	Numb all over	0	1	2	3	4	5	6	7	8	9	10
17.	Lips numb	0	1	2	3	4	5	6	7	8	9	10
18.	Stomach bloated	0	1	2	3	4	5	6	7	8	9	10
19.	Impaired writing	0	1	2	3	4	5	6	7	8	9	10

		Not at all			Moderately				A great deal		
		0 1 2			3 4 5 6				7 8 9 10		
20.	Impaired vision	0	1	2	3	4	5	6	7	8	9	10
21.	Heart beat changing	0	1	2	3	4	5	6	7	8	9	10
22.	Heavy	0	1	2	3	4	5	6	7	8	9	10
23.	Head numb	0	1	2	3	4	5	6	7	8	9	10
24.	Difficulty with thinking	0	1	2	3	4	5	6	7	8	9	10
25.	Cheeks warm	0	1	2	3	4	5	6	7	8	9	10
26.	Tongue thicker	0	1	2	3	4	5	6	7	8	9	10

SENSE OF SYMBOLIC IMMORTALITY SCALE (SSIS)

AUTHOR: Jean-Louis Drolet

PURPOSE: To measure the sense of one's immortality.

DESCRIPTION: This 26-item instrument is designed to measure one's inner realization of death's inevitability as a way of deriving meaning in life. The scale is based on Robert Lifton's theory which, in contrast to viewing death as the antithesis of life, asserts that developmentally, one transcends denial and fear of death and senses it as part of a continuum of life. A sense of immortality is defined as an adaptive response to the frightening reality of death. The absence of a sense of symbolic immortality is considered to thwart the capacity to derive meaning in life. The SSIS consists of five subscales in accord with Lifton's theory of the modes of experiencing symbolic immortality: biosocial mode (B = items $5 + 11 + 12 + 14 + 19 + 21 + 23 + 25$); creation mode (C = items $4 + 6 + 7 + 9 + 20 + 22 + 24$); spiritual mode (S = items $1 + 8 + 10 + 15$); transcendence mode (T = items $3 + 13 + 17 + 16$); and natural mode (N = items $2 + 16 + 18$). Total scale scores of the SSIS may also be used and seem to be the most valid. The SSIS may be useful for a client with an identity crisis and depression. A French version is also available.

NORMS: Total scores on the SSIS have a mean of 5.1 for a sample of 151 Canadian college students. Means for the B and C subscales were 4.9 and 5.3, respectively.

SCORING: Items 3, 4, 5, 6, 11, 12, 14, 17, 19, 23, and 26 are reverse-scored. Subscale scores are the sum of the subscale items divided by the number of items in the subscale. A total score is the sum of all item scores divided by 26. Scores range from 1 to 7 with higher scores indicating stronger sense of one's symbolic immortality.

RELIABILITY: The 26 items of the SSIS have excellent internal consistency, with an alpha of .91. The internal consistencies of the B, C, S, T, and N subscales were .75, .82, .64, .63, and .53, respectively. Test-retest reliability of total scores was .97 for a three-week period.

VALIDITY: The SSIS has good concurrent validity, correlating negatively with death anxiety and positively with one's sense of purpose in life. As suggested by the theory, older adults have higher scores than younger adults, which supports the known-groups validity of the SSIS.

PRIMARY REFERENCE: Drolet, J. L. (1990). Transcending death during early adulthood: Symbolic immortality, death anxiety, and purpose in life, *Journal of Clinical Psychology*, 46, 148–160. Instrument reproduced with permission of Jean-Louis Drolet.

AVAILABILITY: Dr. Jean-Louis Drolet, Department de Counseling et Orientation, Sciences de l'Education, Universite Laval, Quebec, Canada G1K-7P4.

SSIS

For each of the following statements, circle the number which most corresponds to *your feelings, way of seeing things, or way of living* at this stage in your life. Please note that the numbers always range from one to seven, number 1 indicating strong disagreement with the statement and number 7 indicating strong agreement with the statement. Try to use number 4 ("neutral") as little as possible, since this position indicates absence of judgment in either direction.

1 = Strongly disagree
2 = Disagree
3 = Slightly disagree
4 = Neutral
5 = Slightly agree
6 = Agree
7 = Strongly agree

1. I have developed a personal understanding of existence which helps me appreciate life fully.

1   2   3   4   5   6   7

2. The physical surroundings in which I live are very healthy.

1   2   3   4   5   6   7

3. Nothing interesting happens in my life.

1   2   3   4   5   6   7

4. I don't have any influence on my surroundings.

1   2   3   4   5   6   7

5. I am of no value in the eyes of society.

1   2   3   4   5   6   7

6. If I died today, I feel that absolutely no trace or influence of myself would remain.

1   2   3   4   5   6   7

7. I participate in the development of many others.

1   2   3   4   5   6   7

8. I feel that, in spite of my inevitable death, I will always be an integral part of the world.

1   2   3   4   5   6   7

9. I feel that I am doing what I want in life.

1   2   3   4   5   6   7

10. I have certain values or beliefs that help me accept or rise above my mortal condition.

1   2   3   4   5   6   7

11. I have the feeling that human nature is doomed to destruction.

1   2   3   4   5   6   7

12. Intimate relationships scare me.

1   2   3   4   5   6   7

13. Once I've decided to do something, I do it with sustained interest.

1   2   3   4   5   6   7

14. I often feel very lonely.

1   2   3   4   5   6   7

15. The eventuality of my death contributes towards giving meaning and structure to my life.

1   2   3   4   5   6   7

16. My sex life contributes greatly to my well-being.

1   2   3   4   5   6   7

17. I have difficulty undertaking new things.

1   2   3   4   5   6   7

18. I feel comfortable in my body.

1   2   3   4   5   6   7

19. My love life brings me little joy.

    1   2   3   4   5   6   7

20. I feel competent in what I do.

    1   2   3   4   5   6   7

21. If I died today, I have the feeling that I would live on in certain people I would leave behind.

    1   2   3   4   5   6   7

22. I am full of energy and vitality.

    1   2   3   4   5   6   7

23. I am not sure of who I am.

    1   2   3   4   5   6   7

24. I am satisfied with my life so far.

    1   2   3   4   5   6   7

25. I have good contact with others.

    1   2   3   4   5   6   7

26. I feel that I do not use my time well.

    1   2   3   4   5   6   7

SEPARATION-INDIVIDUATION PROCESS INVENTORY (S-IPI)

AUTHORS: R. M. Christenson and William P. Wilson

PURPOSE: To assess disturbances in the separation-individuation process.

DESCRIPTION: The S-IPI is a 39-item instrument designed to measure disturbances in the childhood processes of separation and individuation as manifested in adult pathology. Disturbances in this developmental process are
manifested in a lack of boundaries between self and others, intolerance of
aloneness, as well as trust and control issues in interpersonal relationships.
Items on the S-IPI were selected from a pool of 65 items because each
significantly differentiated a sample of patients with borderline personality
disorder and a control sample of university employees. Because of the
theoretical relationship with borderline personality disorder, the S-IPI is
particularly useful in monitoring progress with this clinically challenging
client.

NORMS: The mean and standard deviation of S-IPI scores for a sample of 20
patients diagnosed with borderline personality disorder were 201.0 and 65.6,
respectively. A sample of 180 "normal" university employees had a mean
S-IPI score of 120.6 with a standard deviation of 40.0. The authors suggest
a cutting score of 190 to distinguish persons with separation-individuation
problems from those without that problem.

SCORING: Items 7, 15, and 18 are reverse-scored. Total S-IPI scores are the
sum of all items. Scores range from 39 to 390, with higher scores indicating
more problems with individuation-separation.

RELIABILITY: The S-IPI has excellent internal consistency, with an alpha of
.92. Data on stability are not available.

VALIDITY: The S-IPI has demonstrated known-groups validity with scores
differentiating a sample of persons with DSM-III diagnoses of borderline
personality disorder from a sample of "normal" university employees. There
was some overlap in the instrument's specificity in detecting the borderline
personality, with 30% of the borderline sample and 7% of the "normals"
scoring as false positives and false negatives, respectively.

PRIMARY REFERENCE: Christenson, R. M. and Wilson, W. P. (1985). Assessing pathology in the separation-individuation process by an inventory: A
preliminary report, *Journal of Nervous and Mental Disease*, 173, 561–565.
Reproduced with permission of Randall M. Christenson, M.D.

AVAILABILITY: Randall M. Christenson, M.D., Pine Rest Christian Hospital,
300 68th Street, S.E., Grand Rapids, MI 49501-0165.

S-IPI

In this section, you are asked to rate how characteristic the following statements are about people in general. The rating is on a scale of 1 to 10 with 1 being not characteristic and 10 being very characteristic. Your rating is your opinion of how people in general feel about themselves and others, so there are no right or wrong answers. Since people's attitudes about themselves and others vary considerably, the questions vary considerably; some questions may seem a little strange or unusual to you. Please answer all the questions as best you can. Answer them fairly quickly without putting a lot of thought into them. Please write your answers in the spaces to the left.

_____ 1. When people really care for someone, they often feel worse about themselves.
_____ 2. When someone gets too emotionally close to another person, he/she often feels lost.
_____ 3. When people really get angry at someone, they often feel worthless.
_____ 4. It is when people start getting emotionally close to someone that they are most likely to get hurt.
_____ 5. People need to maintain control over others to keep from being harmed.

In this section you are asked to rate whether you think the following statements are characteristic of your feelings about yourself and other people. The rating is on a scale of 1 to 10 with 1 being not characteristic and 10 being very characteristic. Again, these are your opinions so there are no right or wrong answers. As different people often have very different thoughts about themselves and others, the statements vary considerably. Some of them may seem strange or unusual to you, but please answer all of them the best you can. Rate each statement fairly quickly without giving a lot of thought to them. Write your rating in the spaces to the left.

_____ 6. I find that people seem to change whenever I get to know them.
_____ 7. It is easy for me to see both good and bad qualities that I have at the same time.
_____ 8. I find that people either really like me or they hate me.
_____ 9. I find that others often treat me as if I am just there to meet their every wish.
_____ 10. I find that I really vacillate between really liking myself and really disliking myself.
_____ 11. When I am by myself, I feel that something is missing.
_____ 12. I need other people around me to not feel empty.
_____ 13. I sometimes feel that part of me is lost whenever I agree with someone else.
_____ 14. Like others, whenever I see someone I really respect and to whom I look up, I often feel worse about myself.
_____ 15. I find it easy to see myself as a distinct individual.
_____ 16. Whenever I realize how different I am from my parents, I feel very uneasy.

_____ 17.   In my experience, I almost always consult my mother before making an important decision.

_____ 18.   I find it relatively easy to make and keep commitments to other people.

_____ 19.   I find that when I get emotionally close to someone, I occasionally feel like hurting myself.

_____ 20.   I find that either I really like someone or I can't stand them.

_____ 21.   I often have dreams about falling that make me feel anxious.

_____ 22.   I find it difficult to form mental pictures of people significant to me.

_____ 23.   I have on more than one occasion seemed to wake up and find myself in a relationship with someone, and not be sure of how or why I am in the relationship.

_____ 24.   I must admit that when I feel lonely, I often feel like getting intoxicated.

_____ 25.   Whenever I am very angry with someone, I feel worthless.

_____ 26.   If I were to tell my deepest thoughts, I would feel empty.

_____ 27.   In my experience, people always seem to hate me.

_____ 28.   Whenever I realize how similar I am to my parents, I feel very uneasy.

_____ 29.   Often, when I am in a close relationship, I find that my sense of who I am gets lost.

_____ 30.   I find it difficult for me to see others as having both good and bad qualities at the same time.

_____ 31.   I find that the only way I can be me is to be different from other people.

_____ 32.   I find that when I get emotionally too close to someone, I sometimes feel that I have lost a part of who I am.

_____ 33.   Whenever I am away from my family, I feel very uneasy.

_____ 34.   Getting physical affection itself seems more important to me than who gives it to me.

_____ 35.   I find it difficult to really know another person well.

_____ 36.   I find that it is important for me to have my mother's approval before making a decision.

_____ 37.   I must admit that whenever I see someone else's faults, I feel better.

_____ 38.   I am tempted to try to control other people in order to keep them close to me.

_____ 39.   I must admit that whenever I get emotionally close to someone, I sometimes want to hurt them.

SESSION EVALUATION QUESTIONNAIRE (SEQ)

AUTHOR: William B. Stiles

PURPOSE: To measure the impact of clinical sessions.

DESCRIPTION: The SEQ consists of 24 bipolar adjective scales presented in a 7-point semantic differential format. It is designed to measure clients' perceptions of two dimensions of clinical sessions, depth and smoothness, and two dimensions of post-session mood, positivity and arousal. Depth refers to a session's perceived power and value and smoothness refers to a session's comfort, relaxation, and pleasantness. Positivity refers to feelings of confidence and clarity as well as happiness, while arousal refers to feeling active and excited as opposed to quiet and calm. The four dimensions were constructed on the basis of factor analyses.

NORMS: Several studies have been conducted using several different forms of the SEQ. A recent one included 72 clients and 17 counselors. The clients included 59 undergraduate students, 5 graduate students, and 8 community residents. Of these, 97% were white, 67% were female, and 33% were male. The clients' problems most typically included depression, relationship problems, low self-esteem, and insecurity. The counselors were graduate students in clinical psychology including 9 males and 8 females. Both clients and counselors used the SEQ to rate each session. No real norms are available although means for client and counselor ratings are reported.

SCORING: The four dimensions are scored separately. Scores are the sum of the item ratings, divided by the number of items that make up each dimension. Thus, depth includes four items: deep–shallow, valuable–worthless, full–empty, powerful–weak, and special–ordinary. Smoothness includes smooth–rough, comfortable–uncomfortable, easy–difficult, pleasant–unpleasant, and relaxed–tense. Positivity includes happy–sad, confident–afraid, pleased–angry, definite–uncertain, and friendly–unfriendly. Arousal includes aroused–quiet, fast–slow, moving–still, and excited–calm. Higher scores indicate greater depth, smoothness, positivity, and arousal.

RELIABILITY: The four dimensions of the SEQ have good internal consistency, with alphas that range from .78 to .91. No test-retest reliabilities are reported.

VALIDITY: No real validity data are reported although data comparing the dimensions to each other and counselor and client ratings to each other are reported. In essence, the depth and smoothness dimensions are independent of each other, while positivity and arousal were moderately correlated. Both counselor and client ratings varied greatly from session to session.

PRIMARY REFERENCE: Stiles, W. B. and Snow, J. S. (1984). Counseling session impact as seen by novice counselors and their clients, *Journal of Counseling Psychology*, 31, 3–12. Instrument reproduced with permission of William B. Stiles and the American Psychological Association.

AVAILABILITY: Dr. William B. Stiles, Department of Psychology, Miami University, Oxford, OH 45056.

SEQ

Please place an "X" on each line to show how you feel about this session.

This session was

Bad	: : : : : : :	Good
Safe	: : : : : : :	Dangerous
Difficult	: : : : : : :	Easy
Valuable	: : : : : : :	Worthless
Shallow	: : : : : : :	Deep
Relaxed	: : : : : : :	Tense
Unpleasant	: : : : : : :	Pleasant
Full	: : : : : : :	Empty
Weak	: : : : : : :	Powerful
Special	: : : : : : :	Ordinary
Rough	: : : : : : :	Smooth
Comfortable	: : : : : : :	Uncomfortable

Right now I feel:

Happy	: : : : : : :	Sad
Angry	: : : : : : :	Pleased
Moving	: : : : : : :	Still
Uncertain	: : : : : : :	Definite
Calm	: : : : : : :	Excited
Confident	: : : : : : :	Afraid
Wakeful	: : : : : : :	Sleepy
Friendly	: : : : : : :	Unfriendly
Slow	: : : : : : :	Fast
Energetic	: : : : : : :	Peaceful
Involved	: : : : : : :	Detached
Quiet	: : : : : : :	Aroused

SEVERITY OF SYMPTOMS SCALE (SSS)

AUTHORS: Benedetto Vitiello, Scott Spreat, and David Behar

PURPOSE: To measure severity of compulsive behavior in the developmentally disabled.

DESCRIPTION: The SSS is a 9-item rating scale to measure the severity of symptoms of compulsive behavior in the developmentally disabled. Compulsive behaviors are often a major problem among the developmentally disabled, and include repetitive, ritualistic behaviors that pose problems for the people performing them. The SSS is used by observers not to identify the behaviors themselves but to rate their severity. Thus, the SSS is a good measure for determining the need for treatment and for monitoring treatment success.

NORMS: The SSS was studied initially with a group of 283 mildly to profoundly developmentally disabled, all of whom were patients in a residential facility in Philadelphia. The mean age was 29.5. Patients were referred by staff members on the basis of presence of repetitive behaviors. From this group, 10 were identified as compulsive, 9 as noncompulsive but high in stereotyped behaviors, and 10 who were low in both. Overall norms are not available, although the mean for the 10 subjects identified as compulsive was 13.0.

SCORING: The SSS is easily scored by summing item scores for a total score.

RELIABILITY: The SSS has very good interrater reliability with a kappa for differential diagnosis of .82 and intraclass correlation coefficient of .82.

VALIDITY: The SSS has fair known-groups validity, significantly distinguishing between subjects previously identified as compulsive and those with neither stereotypes nor compulsive behavior.

PRIMARY REFERENCE: Vitiello, B., Spreat, S., and Behar, D. (1989). Obsessive-compulsive disorder in mentally retarded patients, *Journal of Nervous and Mental Disease*, 177, 232–236.

AVAILABILITY: Dr. B. Vitiello, NIMH, NIH 10/3D-41, Bethesda, MD 20892.

SSS

Rate the following aspects of severity of the repetitive behaviors by circling the appropriate number.

During the last week:

1. Time spent with all symptoms daily
    0 = Less than 15 minutes
    1 = 15 to 30 minutes
    2 = 30 minutes to 1 hour
    3 = 1 to 3 hours
    4 = More than 3 hours

    0 1 2 3 4

2. Subjective resistance or attempt to stop the symptoms
    0 = Not interested in stopping
    1 = Would like to stop, but didn't try
    2 = Has tried a little
    3 = Has tried hard
    4 = Has tried very hard

    0 1 2 3 4

3. Ability to stop symptoms when desired
    0 = Always
    1 = Most of the time
    2 = Only in front of other people
    3 = Very little, even when with other people
    4 = Not at all

    0 1 2 3 4

4. Interference with work/school
    0 = No work/school missed
    1 = Often late arriving at work/school
    2 = Often late completing tasks at work/school
    3 = Unable to complete tasks at work/school
    4 = Completely unable to attend work/school

    0 1 2 3 4

5. Interference with self care
   0 = No interference with daily self-care
   1 = Hygiene poor occasionally
   2 = Frequent delays in hygiene and/or dressing and/or emptying bladder or bowels
   3 = Has to be showered and/or dressed by others and/or constipated often
   4 = Completely dependent on other people for survival functions such as feeding

   0 1 2 3 4

6. Interference with social contacts and leisure activities
   0 = No interference
   1 = Has sometimes given up opportunities to see friends or play sports/hobbies
   2 = Has often refused to meet friends or to enjoy sports/hobbies
   3 = Needs to be constantly pushed in order to have any social contact
   4 = Unable to engage in any social or leisure time activities

   0 1 2 3 4

7. Slowness of walking, talking, or moving in general:
   0 = None at all
   1 = Sometimes slow in movements
   2 = Often slowed
   3 = Constantly slowed
   4 = Extremely slow, often needs help to move

   0 1 2 3 4

8. Interventions by others required:
   0 = No external intervention required
   1 = Verbal intervention from other people is sometimes necessary
   2 = Verbal intervention is often necessary
   3 = Physical intervention is necessary
   4 = Strenuous physical intervention with struggling is necessary

   0 1 2 3 4

9. Suffering and distress from symptoms or their consequences:
   0 = None at all
   1 = A little, or occasional
   2 = Moderately, often
   3 = A lot, every day
   4 = Intense, unremitting distress

   0 1 2 3 4

                                          Total severity score = _____

SEXUAL AROUSABILITY INVENTORY (SAI) AND SEXUAL AROUSABILITY INVENTORY—EXPANDED (SAI-E)

AUTHORS: Emily Franck Hoon and Dianne L. Chambless

PURPOSE: To measure sexual arousability (SAI) and sexual anxiety (SAI-E).

DESCRIPTION: The SAI is a 28-item instrument designed to measure perceived arousability to a variety of sexual experiences. This instrument was originally designed for use with females. The SAI-E is the same instrument, rated by the respondent on both arousability and anxiety dimensions. This instrument has been used with males and females. The arousability and anxiety dimensions are reported to provide independent information. Both instruments are reproduced here. The SAI has been found to discriminate between a "normal" population and individuals seeking help for sexual functioning and also to be sensitive to therapeutic changes. The SAI-E also can be valuable in helping determine if a client has an arousal or anxiety problem related to sexual dysfunctions. Items 1, 2, 5, 6, 9–12, 14–16, 18, 19, 26 can be used as one short-form version of the SAI, and the remaining items can be used as another short form.

NORMS: The SAI and SAI-E have undergone extensive testing with samples of several hundred heterosexual and homosexual women. The mean age of the samples ranged from 18.91 years to 28.20 years. Mean scores for arousability for samples of heterosexual women range from 78.93 to 99.14 and for lesbians, the mean was 92.34. The mean score for 250 heterosexual males for arousability was 90.60. For sexual anxiety, the mean score for 252 undergraduate females was 34.34.

SCORING: Both scales are scored by summing the scores on the individual items and subtracting any −1's. Higher scores mean greater arousability or anger.

RELIABILITY: The arousability scale has excellent internal consistency, with an alpha for women in two samples of .91 and .92 and split-half reliability of .92. The arousability scale is also relatively stable with an eight-week test-retest correlation of .69. The anxiety scale for women also has good internal consistency, with a split-half reliability of .94. Reliability data were not available for men.

VALIDITY: The arousability scale has good concurrent validity, correlating significantly with awareness of physiological changes during intercourse, satisfaction with sexual responsiveness, frequency of intercourse, and total episodes of intercourse before marriage. The SAI also demonstrated good known-groups validity, distinguishing between normal and sexually dysfunctional women. Sexual anxiety in the SAI-E also has been shown to demonstrate some degree of concurrent validity, with more sexually experienced women found to be significantly less anxious and with higher frequency of orgasm during intercourse also associated with lower anxiety. Validity data were not available for men.

PRIMARY REFERENCE: Hoon, E. F. and Chambless, D. (1986). Sexual Arousability Inventory (SAI) and Sexual Arousability Inventory—Expanded (SAI-E). In C. M. Davis and W. L. Yarber (eds.), *Sexuality-Related Measures: A Compendium.* Syracuse: Graphic Publishing Co. Instrument reproduced with permission of Emily Franck Hoon.

AVAILABILITY: Dr. Emily Franck Hoon, 508 NW 35 Terrace, Gainsville, FL 32607.

SAI

The experiences in this inventory may or may not be sexually arousing to you. There are no right or wrong answers. Read each item carefully and then indicate at left the number which describes how sexually aroused you feel when you have the experience, or how sexually aroused you think you would feel if you actually experienced it. *Be sure to answer every item.* If you aren't certain about an item, indicate the number that seems about right. Rate feelings of arousal according to the scale below.

-1 = Adversely affects arousal; unthinkable, repulsive, distracting
0 = Doesn't affect sexual arousal
1 = Possibly causes sexual arousal
2 = Sometimes causes sexual arousal; slightly arousing
3 = Usually causes sexual arousal; moderately arousing
4 = Almost always sexually arousing; very arousing
5 = Always causes sexual arousal; extremely arousing

_____ 1. When a loved one stimulates your genitals with mouth and tongue
_____ 2. When a loved one fondles your breasts with his/her hands
_____ 3. When you see a loved one nude
_____ 4. When a loved one caresses you with his/her eyes
_____ 5. When a loved one stimulates your genitals with his/her finger
_____ 6. When you are touched or kissed on the inner thighs by a loved one
_____ 7. When you caress a loved one's genitals with your fingers
_____ 8. When you read a pornographic or "dirty" story
_____ 9. When a loved one undresses you
_____ 10. When you dance with a loved one
_____ 11. When you have intercourse with a loved one
_____ 12. When a loved one touches or kisses your nipples
_____ 13. When you caress a loved one (other than genitals)
_____ 14. When you see pornographic pictures or slides
_____ 15. When you lie in bed with a loved one
_____ 16. When a loved one kisses you passionately
_____ 17. When you hear sounds of pleasure during sex
_____ 18. When a loved one kisses you with an exploring tongue
_____ 19. When you read suggestive or pornographic poetry
_____ 20. When you see a strip show
_____ 21. When you stimulate your partner's genitals with your mouth and tongue
_____ 22. When a loved one caresses you (other than genitals)
_____ 23. When you see a pornographic movie (stag film)
_____ 24. When you undress a loved one
_____ 25. When a loved one fondles your breasts with mouth and tongue
_____ 26. When you make love in a new or unusual place
_____ 27. When you masturbate
_____ 28. When your partner has an orgasm

SAI-E

Now rate each of the items according to how anxious you feel when you have the described experience. The meaning of anxiety is extreme uneasiness and distress. Rate feelings of anxiety according to the scale below:

-1 = Relaxing, calming
 0 = No anxiety
 1 = Possibly causes some anxiety
 2 = Sometimes causes anxiety; slightly anxiety producing
 3 = Usually causes anxiety; moderately anxiety producing
 4 = Almost always causes anxiety; very anxiety producing
 5 = Always causes anxiety; extremely anxiety producing

_____ 1. When a loved one stimulates your genitals with mouth and tongue
_____ 2. When a loved one fondles your breasts with his/her hands
_____ 3. When you see a loved one nude
_____ 4. When a loved one caresses you with his/her eyes
_____ 5. When a loved one stimulates your genitals with his/her finger
_____ 6. When you are touched or kissed on the inner thighs by a loved one
_____ 7. When you caress a loved one's genitals with your fingers
_____ 8. When you read a pornographic or "dirty" story
_____ 9. When a loved one undresses you
_____ 10. When you dance with a loved one
_____ 11. When you have intercourse with a loved one
_____ 12. When a loved one touches or kisses your nipples
_____ 13. When you caress a loved one (other than genitals)
_____ 14. When you see pornographic pictures or slides
_____ 15. When you lie in bed with a loved one
_____ 16. When a loved one kisses you passionately
_____ 17. When you hear sounds of pleasure during sex
_____ 18. When a loved one kisses you with an exploring tongue
_____ 19. When you read suggestive or pornographic poetry
_____ 20. When you see a strip show
_____ 21. When you stimulate your partner's genitals with your mouth and tongue
_____ 22. When a loved one caresses you (other than genitals)
_____ 23. When you see a pornographic movie (stag film)
_____ 24. When you undress a loved one
_____ 25. When a loved one fondles your breasts with mouth and tongue
_____ 26. When you make love in a new or unusual place
_____ 27. When you masturbate
_____ 28. When your partner has an orgasm

SEXUAL ASSAULT SYMPTOM SCALE (SASS)

AUTHORS: Libby O. Ruch, John W. Gartell, Stephanie R. Amedeo, and Barry
J. Coyne

PURPOSE: To measure trauma following rape.

DESCRIPTION: The SASS is a 32-item (plus two global emotional trauma
items) instrument designed to measure trauma in the immediate aftermath
of sexual assault. This is one of the few available self-report measures that
is relatively brief and is used to assess initial symptoms of sexual assault
trauma syndrome (i.e., immediately following the assault). The SASS has
four subscales discovered through factor analysis: disclosure shame (DS:
items 4, 7, 16, 20–22); safety fears (SF: items 1, 9, 14, 18); depression (D:
items 23–25); and self-blame (SB: items 5, 6, 13, 29). The items are read by
the clinician to the client, who then reports her response.

NORMS: The SASS was studied with 329 female victims of nonincestuous
sexual assault, age 14 and over, within 72 hours of assault, at intake in a
sexual assault treatment center. Mean age was 24.6 years. Ethnicity included
42% white, 14% Asian, 22% Polynesian, and 17% mixed and other. Actual
norms are not available, although item means and standard deviations are
reported in the primary reference.

SCORING: The SASS is easily scored by summing individual item scores and
dividing by the number of items for the subscale and total scores. Higher
scores indicate greater trauma.

RELIABILITY: The SASS has fair to good internal consistency, with alphas for
the subscales that range from .72 to .83. The alpha for the entire scale was
.69. Data on stability were not reported.

VALIDITY: The SASS has good concurrent validity, with significant correlations on all four subscales with crisis workers' ratings of clients.

PRIMARY REFERENCE: Ruch, L. O., Gartell, J. W., Amedeo, S. R., and Coyne,
B. I. (1991). The Sexual Assault Symptom Scale: measuring self-reported
sexual assault trauma in the emergency room, *Psychological Assessment*,
1, 3–8.

AVAILABILITY: Dr. Libby Ruch, Social Science Research Institute, University
of Hawaii, 2424 Maile Way, Porteus 704, Honolulu, HI 96822.

SASS

CLIENT'S EMOTIONAL CONCERNS: For each concern, please ask the client how much distress or discomfort she/he has experienced *since the assault, including right now.* Read the scale of responses for the first few questions. It is not necessary to repeat it every time. This is a report of the *client's feelings*, not an interpretation or assessment by the worker. Use the client's words as much as possible in the margins or on the reverse side of this page. Omit an item if not answered by the client and write NOA by it.

SINCE THE ASSAULT HOW MUCH HAVE YOU BEEN DISTRESSED OR UPSET BY:	Not at all	A little bit	Moderately	Quite a bit	Extremely
1. Feeling fearful about your personal safety	0	1	2	3	4
2. Feeling worried about injuries from the assault	0	1	2	3	4
3. Feeling worried about contracting a disease from the assailant	0	1	2	3	4
4. Feeling concerned about telling other people about the assault	0	1	2	3	4
5. Feeling that you didn't handle the situation as well as you might have	0	1	2	3	4
6. Feeling that you shouldn't have gotten into the situation in the first place	0	1	2	3	4
7. Feeling concerned about the reaction of other people to the assault	0	1	2	3	4
8. Feeling sad or depressed about the assault	0	1	2	3	4
9. Feeling afraid of the assailant	0	1	2	3	4
10. Feeling embarrassed about what you had to do to survive the assault	0	1	2	3	4
11. Feeling easily annoyed or irritated	0	1	2	3	4
12. Feeling angry at the assailant	0	1	2	3	4
13. Blaming yourself for things	0	1	2	3	4

SINCE THE ASSAULT HOW MUCH HAVE YOU BEEN DISTRESSED OR UPSET BY:	Not at all	A little bit	Moderately	Quite a bit	Extremely
14. Feeling fearful	0	1	2	3	4
15. Feeling others are unsympathetic or do not understand you	0	1	2	3	4
16. Feeling sad or depressed about how other people will react to the assault	0	1	2	3	4
17. Feeling angry at family or friends	0	1	2	3	4
18. Feeling nervous when you are left alone	0	1	2	3	4
19. Feeling uneasy when people are watching you or talking about you	0	1	2	3	4
20. Feeling fear or unpleasant feelings about talking to police	0	1	2	3	4
21. Feeling fear or unpleasant feelings about testifying in court	0	1	2	3	4
22. Feeling ashamed	0	1	2	3	4
23. Feeling no interest in things	0	1	2	3	4
24. Feeling hopeless about the future	0	1	2	3	4
25. Thoughts of ending your life	0	1	2	3	4
26. Trouble remembering things	0	1	2	3	4
27. Difficulty making decisions	0	1	2	3	4
28. Trouble concentrating	0	1	2	3	4
29. Feeling guilty	0	1	2	3	4
30. Feeling that most people cannot be trusted	0	1	2	3	4
31. Feeling that people will take advantage of you if you let them	0	1	2	3	4

	Not at all	A little bit	Moderately	Quite a bit	Extremely
SINCE THE ASSAULT HOW MUCH HAVE YOU BEEN DISTRESSED OR UPSET BY:					
32. Feeling angry at police or the legal system	0	1	2	3	4

EMOTIONAL TRAUMA

1. How stressful was the assault?

No stress	Little stress	Mild stress	Moderate stress	Severe stress	Very severe stress	Extreme stress
0	1	2	3	4	5	6

2. How much stress are you experiencing since the assault?

No stress	Little stress	Mild stress	Moderate stress	Severe stress	Very severe stress	Extreme stress
0	1	2	3	4	5	6

SEXUAL ATTITUDE SCALE (SAS)

AUTHORS: Walter W. Hudson, Gerald J. Murphy, and Paula S. Nurius

PURPOSE: To measure attitudes about human sexuality.

DESCRIPTION: The SAS is a 25-item instrument designed to measure liberal versus conservative attitudes toward human sexual expression. Unlike most scales in this book, the SAS reflects a value position, and is not designed necessarily to measure a personal or social problem. Scores on this scale do not necessarily reflect a clinical disorder. The SAS is perhaps of greatest utility when attitudes and discomfort about human sexuality are an issue for the client. The SAS is one of some 20 instruments of the WALMYR Assessment Scales package reproduced here, all of which are administered and scored the same way.

NORMS: Not available. The SAS has a cutting score of 50; respondents who score below 50 are presumed to be liberal in their orientation to human sexual expression, and clients scoring above 50 are presumed to be increasingly conservative in their orientation to human sexuality.

SCORING: Like most WALMYR Assessment Scales instruments, the SAS is scored by first reverse-scoring items listed at the bottom of the page (21, 22), summing these and the remaining scores, subtracting the number of completed items, multiplying this figure by 100, and dividing by the number of items completed times 4. This will produce a range from 0 to 100 with higher scores indicating greater magnitude or severity of problems.

RELIABILITY: The SAS has excellent internal consistency, with an alpha in excess of .90. Data on stability are not available.

VALIDITY: The SAS is reported to have very good content, construct, and factorial validity, with validity coefficients generally of .60 or greater.

PRIMARY REFERENCE: Hudson, W. W. (1992). *The WALMYR Assessment Scales Scoring Manual.* Tempe, AZ: WALMYR Publishing Co.

AVAILABILITY: WALMYR Publishing Co., P.O. Box 24779, Tempe, AZ 85285-4779.

SEXUAL ATTITUDE SCALE (SAS)

Name: _____Today's Date: _____

This questionnaire is designed to measure the way you feel about sexual behavior. It is not a test, so there are no right or wrong answers. Answer each item as carefully and as accurately as you can by placing a number beside each one as follows.

1 = Strongly disagree
2 = Disgree
3 = Neither agree nor disagree
4 = Agree
5 = Strongly agree

1. ____ I think there is too much sexual freedom given to adults these days.
2. ____ I think that increased sexual freedom undermines the American family.
3. ____ I think that young people have been given too much information about sex.
4. ____ Sex education should be restricted to the home.
5. ____ Older people do not need to have sex.
6. ____ Sex education should be given only when people are ready for marriage.
7. ____ Pre-marital sex may be a sign of a decaying social order.
8. ____ Extra-marital sex is never excusable.
9. ____ I think there is too much sexual freedom given to teenagers these days.
10. ____ I think there is not enough sexual restraint among young people.
11. ____ I think people indulge in sex too much.
12. ____ I think the only proper way to have sex is through intercourse.
13. ____ I think sex should be reserved for marriage.
14. ____ Sex should be only for the young.
15. ____ Too much social approval has been given to homosexuals.
16. ____ Sex should be devoted to the business of procreation.
17. ____ People should not masturbate.
18. ____ Heavy sexual petting should be discouraged.
19. ____ People should not discuss their sexual affairs or business with others.
20. ____ Severely handicapped (physically and mentally) people should not have sex.
21. ____ There should be no laws prohibiting sexual acts between consenting adults.
22. ____ What two consenting adults do together sexually is their own business.
23. ____ There is too much sex on television.
24. ____ Movies today are too sexually explicit.
25. ____ Pornography should be totally banned from our bookstores.

21, 22.

SEXUAL BEHAVIOR INVENTORY—FEMALE (SBI-F)

AUTHOR: Peter M. Bentler

PURPOSE: To assess heterosexual behavior in women.

DESCRIPTION: This 21-item instrument measures the extent to which a female has engaged in heterosexual behavior. The SBI-F was developed from 63 items dealing with various types of heterosexual behavior, using the procedure of multidimensional homogeneity scaling to assess the latent ordinal dimensions associated with observed responses to test items. The SBI-F was developed to be similar to the SBI-M (also reproduced in this book); the SBI-F also has a 10-item short form that correlates .98 with the 21-item form. This instrument can be useful in cases involving heterosexual anxieties, in developing sexual anxiety hierarchies (e.g., using the technique of systematic desensitization), or as an overall measure of change as a result of therapy. Items 1, 2, 4, 7, 8–10, 13, 14, and 16 can be used as a short form.

NORMS: Three samples of college females, totaling 389 and ranging in age from 17 to 29, were used to develop the SBI-F. Means for the three samples were 11.07, 8.01, and 13.27. No other demographic data or norms were reported.

SCORING: The SBI-F is scored by assigning 1 point to each "yes" answer and then summing the scores, producing a range of 0 to 21.

RELIABILITY: The SBI-F has excellent internal consistency, with Kuder-Richardson correlations of roughly .95. The SBI-F is also reported as having excellent ordinal scalability, with a coefficient of homogeneity of .990.

VALIDITY: No validity data were reported.

PRIMARY REFERENCE: Bentler, P. M. (1968). Heterosexual behavior assessment—II. Females, *Behaviour Research and Therapy*, 6, 27–30. Instrument reproduced with permission of Peter M. Bentler.

AVAILABILITY: Dr. P. M. Bentler, Department of Psychology, Franz Hall, UCLA, Los Angeles, CA 90024.

SBI-F

On this page you will find a series of statements which describe various sexual behaviors that a female may have engaged in. Read each statement and decide whether or not you have experienced the sexual behavior described. Then indicate your answer.

If you have engaged in the sexual behavior described in a statement at any time since your 12th birthday, circle Yes. If you have never engaged in the behavior since then, circle No. Most items refer to your behavior with other individuals; you should consider these items as referring to any individuals who were also over 12 years old.

This inventory has been devised for young and sexually inexperienced persons as well as for married and sexually experienced persons. In addition, there are great differences between people in sexual behavior preference. Thus, you will find sexual behaviors described which you have not engaged in. Please note you are asked to indicate only whether or not you have ever taken part in the sexual behavior—you are *not* asked for your attitude or feelings.

Yes No 1. I have kissed the lips of a male for one minute continuously.
Yes No 2. I have engaged in sexual intercourse with a male.
Yes No 3. I have manipulated the genitals of a male with my tongue.
Yes No 4. A male has manipulated my breasts with his hands underneath my clothes.
Yes No 5. I have manipulated the genitals of a male with my hand over his clothes.
Yes No 6. A male has manipulated my genitals with his tongue.
Yes No 7. I have engaged in mutual hand-manipulation of genitals with a male.
Yes No 8. I have had the nipples of my breasts kissed by a male.
Yes No 9. I have engaged in mutual mouth-genital manipulation with a male to the point of my orgasm and his ejaculation.
Yes No 10. I have manipulated the genitals of a male with my hand underneath his clothes.
Yes No 11. I have manipulated a male's genitals with my mouth to the point of his ejaculation.
Yes No 12. A male has manipulated my genitals with his hand over my clothes.
Yes No 13. I have engaged in heterosexual intercourse with the male using rear entry to my vagina.
Yes No 14. I have touched the genitals of a male with my lips.
Yes No 15. A male has touched my genitals with his lips.
Yes No 16. I have engaged in mutual mouth-genital manipulation with a male.
Yes No 17. I have manipulated the genitals of a male with my hand to the point of his ejaculation.
Yes No 18. A male has manipulated my genitals with his hand to the point of massive secretions.

Yes   No   19.   A male has manipulated my genitals with his hand underneath my clothes.

Yes   No   20.   I have engaged in mutual hand-manipulation of genitals with a male to the point of my orgasm and his ejaculation.

Yes   No   21.   A male has manipulated my breasts with his hands over my clothes.

SEXUAL BEHAVIOR INVENTORY—MALE (SBI-M)

AUTHOR: Peter M. Bentler

PURPOSE: To assess heterosexual behavior in men.

DESCRIPTION: This 21-item instrument measures the extent to which a male has engaged in a range of heterosexual behaviors. The SBI-M was developed from 56 items dealing with various types of heterosexual behavior using the procedure of multidimensional homogeneity scaling, which assesses the latent ordinal dimensions associated with observed responses to test items. This instrument can be useful in cases involving heterosexual anxieties, in developing sexual anxiety hierarchies (e.g., using the technique of systematic desensitization), or as an overall measure of change as a result of therapy.

NORMS: The scale was developed using two samples, the first involving 175 college males and the second a sample of 108 males. No other demographic characteristics were reported nor were actual norms, although means for the two samples were 11.14 and 14.48.

SCORING: The SBI-M is scored by assigning 1 point to each "yes" answer and then summing the scores, producing a range of 0 to 21.

RELIABILITY: The SBI-M has excellent internal consistency, with Kuder-Richardson correlations of roughly .95. The SBI-M is also reported as having close to perfect ordinal scalability, with a coefficient of homogeneity of .987.

VALIDITY: No validity data were reported.

PRIMARY REFERENCE: Bentler, P. M. (1968). Heterosexual behavior—I. Males, *Behaviour Research and Therapy*, 6, 21–25. Instrument reproduced with permission of Peter M. Bentler.

AVAILABILITY: Dr. P. M. Bentler, Department of Psychology, Franz Hall, UCLA, Los Angeles, CA 90024.

SBI-M

On this page you will find a series of statements which describe various sexual behaviors that a male may have engaged in. Read each statement and decide whether or not you have experienced the sexual behavior described. Then indicate your answer.

If you have engaged in the sexual behavior described in a statement at any time since your 12th birthday, circle Yes. If you have never engaged in the behavior since then, circle No. Most items refer to your behavior with other individuals; you should consider these items as referring to any individuals who were also over 12 years old.

This inventory has been devised for young and sexually inexperienced persons as well as for married and sexually experienced persons. In addition, there are great differences between people in sexual behavior preference. Thus, you will find sexual behaviors described which you have not engaged in. Please note you are asked to indicate only whether or not you have ever taken part in the sexual behavior—you are *not* asked for your attitude or feelings.

Yes No 1. I have kissed the lips of a female for one minute continuously.
Yes No 2. I have engaged in sexual intercourse with a female.
Yes No 3. I have manipulated the genitals of a female with my tongue.
Yes No 4. I have manipulated the breasts of a female with my hands underneath her clothes.
Yes No 5. I have manipulated the genitals of a female with my hand over her clothes.
Yes No 6. A female has manipulated my genitals with her tongue.
Yes No 7. I have engaged in mutual hand-manipulation of genitals with a female.
Yes No 8. I have kissed the nipples of the breasts of a female.
Yes No 9. I have engaged in mutual mouth-genital manipulation with a female to the point of her orgasm and my ejaculation.
Yes No 10. I have manipulated the genitals of a female with my hand underneath her clothes.
Yes No 11. A female has manipulated my genitals with her mouth to the point of my ejaculation.
Yes No 12. A female has manipulated my genitals with her hand over my clothes.
Yes No 13. I have engaged in heterosexual intercourse using rear entry to the vagina.
Yes No 14. I have touched the genitals of a female with my lips.
Yes No 15. A female has touched my genitals with her lips.
Yes No 16. I have engaged in mutual mouth-genital manipulation with a female.
Yes No 17. I have manipulated the genitals of a female with my hand to the point of massive secretions from her genitals.
Yes No 18. A female has manipulated my genitals with her hand to the point of ejaculation.

Yes No 19. A female has manipulated my genitals with her hand underneath my clothes.

Yes No 20. I have engaged in mutual hand-manipulation of genitals with a female to the point of her orgasm and my ejaculation.

Yes No 21. I have manipulated the breasts of a female with my hands over her clothes.

SIMPLE RATHUS ASSERTIVENESS SCHEDULE (SRAS)

AUTHOR: Iain A. McCormick

PURPOSE: To measure assertiveness for persons with low reading ability.

DESCRIPTION: This 30-item measure of assertiveness is based on the Rathus Assertiveness Schedule (also reproduced in this book) and is designed for persons with poor reading ability. Care was taken to make certain item content was equivalent with that of the original instrument. Because it is shorter and easier to read, the SRAS is useful in clinical work with adolescents and children as well as adults. The SRAS is more useful with teenagers than the original RAS.

NORMS: The SRAS was tested on a sample of 116 graduate students. The mean score was 94.6 with a standard deviation of 25.4 for females ($n = 82$), and 99.8 with a standard deviation of 20.1 for males ($n = 34$).

SCORING: Each item is rated on a 6-point scale from "very much like me" to "very unlike me." Items 1, 2, 4, 5, 9, 11, 12–17, 19, 23, 24, 26, and 30 are reverse-scored. The total score is the sum of all items, and can range from 30 to 180 with higher scores reflecting more assertion.

RELIABILITY: Reliability of this instrument is very good. Internal consistency was determined with odd-even correlations and was .90. The SRAS correlated .94 with the original, suggesting the two may be used as parallel forms. Data on stability were not available.

VALIDITY: There is very little validity data for this instrument. As a parallel form, much of the validity of the Rathus Assertiveness Schedule would apply. The parallel form reliability correlation can also be seen as concurrent validity data.

PRIMARY REFERENCE: McCormick, I. A. (1984). A simple version of the Rathus Assertiveness Schedule, *Behavioral Assessment* 7, 95–99, Instrument reproduced with permission of Dr. McCormick.

AVAILABILITY: Dr. I. A. McCormick, Psychology Department, Victoria University of Wellington, Private Bay, Wellington, New Zealand.

SRAS

Read each sentence carefully. Write down on each line whatever number is correct for you.

6 = Very much like me
5 = Rather like me
4 = Somewhat like me
3 = Somewhat unlike me
2 = Rather unlike me
1 = Very unlike me

_____ 1. Most people stand up for themselves more than I do.
_____ 2. At times I have not made or gone on dates because of my shyness.
_____ 3. When I am eating out and the food I am served is not cooked the way I like it, I complain to the person serving it.
_____ 4. I am careful not to hurt other people's feelings, even when I feel hurt.
_____ 5. If a person serving in a store has gone to a lot of trouble to show me something which I do not really like, I have a hard time saying "No."
_____ 6. When I am asked to do something, I always want to know why.
_____ 7. There are times when I look for a good strong argument.
_____ 8. I try as hard to get ahead in life as most people like me do.
_____ 9. To be honest, people often get the better of me.
_____ 10. I enjoy meeting and talking with people for the first time.
_____ 11. I often don't know what to say to good looking people of the opposite sex.
_____ 12. I do not like making phone calls to businesses or companies.
_____ 13. I would rather apply for jobs by writing letters than by going to talk to the people.
_____ 14. I feel silly if I return things I don't like to the store that I bought them from.
_____ 15. If a close relative that I like was upsetting me, I would hide my feelings rather than say that I was upset.
_____ 16. I have sometimes not asked questions for fear of sounding stupid.
_____ 17. During an argument I am sometimes afraid that I will get so upset that I will shake all over.
_____ 18. If a famous person were talking in a crowd and I thought he/she was wrong, I would get up and say what I thought.
_____ 19. I don't argue over prices with people selling things.
_____ 20. When I do something important or good, I try to let others know about it.
_____ 21. I am open and honest about my feelings.
_____ 22. If someone has been telling false and bad stories about me, I see him/her as soon as possible to "have a talk" about it.
_____ 23. I often have a hard time saying "No."
_____ 24. I tend not to show my feelings rather than upsetting others.
_____ 25. I complain about poor service when I am eating out or in other places.
_____ 26. When someone says I have done very well, I sometimes just don't know what to say.

_____ 27. If a couple near me in the theater were talking rather loudly, I would
          ask them to be quiet or to go somewhere else and talk.
_____ 28. Anyone trying to push ahead of me in a line is in for a good battle.
_____ 29. I am quick to say what I think.
_____ 30. There are times when I just can't say anything.

SMOKING SELF-EFFICACY QUESTIONNAIRE (SSEQ)

AUTHORS: Gep Colletti and Jay A. Supnick

PURPOSE: To measure beliefs about one's ability to resist the urge to smoke.

DESCRIPTION: The SSEQ is a 17-item instrument designed to assess the application of self-efficacy theory to smoking, that is, whether a change in one's belief about one's ability to execute a given action successfully can bring about behavior change (smoking reduction or completely quitting). Respondents are asked to read each of 17 situations and then to assess whether they could expect to control their smoking behavior and remain on a smoking reduction program in that situation. The instrument yields a total score indicating the overall strength of the self-efficacy judgment. Although still in an early stage of development, the SSEQ shows potential for clinical and research applications.

NORMS: Initial development of the SSEQ was based on 128 male and female respondents with a mean age of 39.7 who were participants in an ongoing, behaviorally oriented smoking reduction program. Twenty-nine additional respondents participated in earlier stages in the development of the scale. Means for the sample of 128 are available and broken down by sex and pre- and posttreatment scores. The overall pretreatment mean was 42.13 which rose to 72.53 after treatment.

SCORING: The SSEQ is scored by totaling respondents' confidence ratings (on a scale from 10 to 100) on each of the 17 items that apply to that respondent's personal situation. Scores are then divided by the number of items answered. This yields a mean rated confidence score with a range of 0% to 100%.

RELIABILITY: The SSEQ has an alpha coefficient of better than .90, indicating excellent internal consistency. Test-retest reliabilities were lower but significant, ranging from .41 to .62. However, these results were confounded by the fact that respondents were undergoing treatment for smoking at the time.

VALIDITY: Correlations between smoking rate and the SSEQ were statistically significant, suggesting good concurrent and predictive validity.

PRIMARY REFERENCE: Colletti, G., Supnick, J. A., and Payne, T. J. (1985). The Smoking Self-Efficacy Questionnaire (SSEQ): Preliminary scale development and validation, *Behavioral Assessment*, 7, 249–260. Instrument reproduced with permission of J. Supnick and G. Colletti.

AVAILABILITY: Dr. Jay Supnick, Department of Psychiatry, University of Rochester, Medical Center, Rochester, NY 14642.

SSEQ

The following paragraphs are descriptions of situations in which people with smoking problems often find it very difficult not to smoke. If you are trying to stop, they may be the situations in which you are likely to give up.

First, read each description and as vividly as possible try to imagine yourself in that situation. Then assess whether you expect that in this situation you could control your smoking behavior and remain on your reduction program. Write down "Yes," meaning "I could control my smoking behavior" or "No," meaning "I could not control my smoking behavior" in the blank marked "Can Do."

If you answer "Yes," then please assess how confident you are that you could control your smoking behavior. Using the numbers from the scale 10 to 100 printed below, choose one that expresses your degree of confidence, and write that number down in the blank marked "Confidence."

Some of the exact details of a situation may not apply to you, such as smoking while drinking coffee, but the description may be similar to a situation you do experience, for example, smoking while drinking alcohol. You can assess that instead. If the situation is not one you would ever experience, you can place an X in the "Can Do" blank and go on to the next item.

Confidence Scale

10	20	30	40	50	60	70	80	90	100
Quite uncertain				Moderately certain					Certain

	Can Do	Confidence

1. You just returned from an important exam and you "know" you have done poorly.   _____   _____

2. A planned date stands you up. You are disappointed and begin to blame yourself.   _____   _____

3. You have had a fight with your boyfriend, girlfriend, spouse, or any friend and you are angry and upset.   _____   _____

4. You have been out for an evening, you feel relaxed and want to end the evening with a smoke.   _____   _____

5. You have just finished dinner in a good restaurant on a special occasion. Everyone orders coffee and your friends all sit back to enjoy a cigarette.   _____   _____

		Can Do	Confidence
6.	You are out with friends who are smoking a lot. You don't want them to know that you are on a smoking reduction program.	_____	_____
7.	You just came home from a really rough day at school or work. The whole day was filled with anxiety, frustration, and failure.	_____	_____
8.	You are sitting at home alone, in a bad mood, thinking about the problems and failures in your life.	_____	_____
9.	Watching television (e.g., sport event).	_____	_____
10.	Studying.	_____	_____
11.	Reading a novel or magazine.	_____	_____
12.	Attending a sports or entertainment event.	_____	_____
13.	Talking on the phone.	_____	_____
14.	Drinking coffee or other nonalcoholic beverages.	_____	_____
15.	After a meal.	_____	_____
16.	Talking or socializing.	_____	_____
17.	Playing cards.	_____	_____

SOCIAL ADJUSTMENT SCALE—SELF REPORT (SAS-SR)

AUTHORS: Myrna M. Weissman and Eugene S. Paykel

PURPOSE: To measure adaptive social functioning.

DESCRIPTION: The SAS-SR is a 54-item instrument designed to measure adaptive functioning within a variety of social contexts. The SAS–Self Report actually is based on an earlier version involving a structured interview developed by the authors. The SAS-SR can be completed by the client, or a relevant other about the client. The authors recommend having someone knowledgeable about the measure be available to instruct a respondent about its use. The SAS-SR is a very useful way of operationalizing social adjustment. In addition to the global score, it includes subscales providing information about a number of role areas: work outside home (items 1–6), work at home (items 7–12), work as a student (items 13–18), social and leisure (items 19–29), extended family (items 30–37), marital (items 38–46), parental (items 47–50), family unit (items 51–53), and economic (item 54).

NORMS: The SAS-SR has been studied with a number of clinical and nonclinical groups. For a community sample of 399 (272 female), the overall mean was 1.59 (SD = .33). For a sample of 172 acute depressives (148 female), the overall mean was 2.53 (SD = .46). For a sample of 26 alcoholics (17 female), the mean was 2.23 (SD = .61). And for a sample of 39 schizophrenics (35 females), the mean was 1.96 (SD = .62).

SCORING: The overall adjustment score is the sum of all items divided by the number of items actually scored; the role area mean score is a sum of the items in a role area divided by the number of items actually scored in that area. For the total adjustment score, only one work area is used (one of the first three subscales). Higher scores reflect greater impairment.

RELIABILITY: The SAS-SR has fair internal consistency, with an alpha of .74. The SAS-SR has good stability, with a one-month test-retest correlation of .74.

VALIDITY: The SAS-SR has fair concurrent validity as demonstrated by correlations with the social adjustment structured interview upon which it is based. The SAS-SR has good known-groups validity, distinguishing a nonclinical, community sample from three psychiatric samples and distinguishing acutely depressed from recovered patients.

PRIMARY REFERENCE: Weissman, M. M. and Bothwell, S. (1976). Assessment of social adjustment by patient self-report, *Archives of General Psychiatry*, 33, 1111–1115.

AVAILABILITY: Dr. Myrna Weissman, College of Physicians and Surgeons, Columbia University, 722 W. 168th Street, Box 14, New York, NY 10032.

SAS-SR

We are interested in finding out how you have been doing in the last *two weeks*. We would like you to answer some questions about your work, spare time, and your family life. There are no right or wrong answers to these questions. check the answers that best describe how you have been in the last *two weeks*.

WORK OUTSIDE THE HOME
Please describe the situation that best describes you.

I am
1. ☐ a worker for pay
2. ☐ a housewife
3. ☐ a student

4. ☐ retired
5. ☐ unemployed

Do you usually work for pay more than 15 hours per week?
1. ☐ Yes
2. ☐ No

Did you work any hours for pay in the last 2 weeks?
1. ☐ Yes
2. ☐ No

Check the answer that best describes how you have been in the last 2 weeks.

1. How many days did you miss from work in the last 2 weeks?
   1. ☐ No days missed.
   2. ☐ One day.
   3. ☐ I missed about half the time.
   4. ☐ Missed more than half the time but did make at least one day.
   5. ☐ I did not work any days.
   8. ☐ I was on vacation the last two weeks.

If you have not worked any days in the past 2 weeks, go on to Question 7.

2. Have you been able to do any work in the last 2 weeks?
   1. ☐ I did my work very well.
   2. ☐ I did my work but had some minor problems.
   3. ☐ I needed help with work and did not do well about half the time.
   4. ☐ I did my work poorly most of the time.
   5. ☐ I did my work poorly all the time.

3. Have you been ashamed of how you do your work in the past 2 weeks?
   1. ☐ I never felt ashamed.
   2. ☐ Once or twice I felt a little ashamed.
   3. ☐ About half the time I felt ashamed.
   4. ☐ I felt ashamed most of the time.
   5. ☐ I felt ashamed all the time.

4. Have you had any arguments with people at work in the last 2 weeks?
    1. ☐   I had no arguments and got along very well.
    2. ☐   I usually got along well but had minor arguments.
    3. ☐   I had more than one argument.
    4. ☐   I had many arguments.
    5. ☐   I was constantly in arguments.

5. Have you felt upset, worried or uncomfortable while doing your work during the last 2 weeks?
    1. ☐   I never felt upset.
    2. ☐   Once or twice I felt upset.
    3. ☐   Half the time I felt upset
    4. ☐   I felt upset most of the time.
    5. ☐   I felt upset all of the time.

6. Have you found your work interesting these last 2 weeks?
    1. ☐   My work was almost always interesting.
    2. ☐   Once or twice my work was not interesting.
    3. ☐   Half the time my work was uninteresting.
    4. ☐   Most of the time my work was uninteresting.
    5. ☐   My work was always uninteresting.

WORK OUTSIDE THE HOME—HOUSEWIVES ANSWER QUESTIONS 7–12.
OTHERWISE, GO ON TO QUESTION 13.

7. How many days did you do some housework during the last 2 weeks?
    1. ☐   Every day.
    2. ☐   I did the housework almost every day.
    3. ☐   I did the housework about half the time.
    4. ☐   I usually did not do the housework.
    5. ☐   I was completely unable to do housework.
    8. ☐   I was away from home all of the past two weeks.

8. During the last 2 weeks, have you kept up with your housework? This includes cooking, cleaning, laundry, grocery shopping, and errands.
    1. ☐   I did my work very well.
    2. ☐   I did my work but had some minor problems.
    3. ☐   I needed help with work and did not do well about half the time.
    4. ☐   I did my work poorly most of the time.
    5. ☐   I did my work poorly all the time.

9. Have you been ashamed of how you did your housework during the last 2 weeks?
    1. ☐   I never felt ashamed.
    2. ☐   Once or twice I felt a little ashamed.
    3. ☐   About half the time I felt ashamed.
    4. ☐   I felt ashamed most of the time.
    5. ☐   I felt ashamed all the time.

10. Have you had any arguments with salespeople, tradesmen, or neighbors in the last 2 weeks?
    1. ☐ I had no arguments and got along very well.
    2. ☐ I usually got along well but had minor arguments.
    3. ☐ I had more than one argument.
    4. ☐ I had many arguments.
    5. ☐ I was constantly in arguments.

11. Have you felt upset while doing your housework during the last 2 weeks?
    1. ☐ I never felt upset.
    2. ☐ Once or twice I felt upset.
    3. ☐ Half the time I felt upset
    4. ☐ I felt upset most of the time.
    5. ☐ I felt upset all of the time.

12. Have you found your housework interesting these last 2 weeks?
    1. ☐ My work was almost always interesting.
    2. ☐ Once or twice my work was not interesting.
    3. ☐ Half the time my work was uninteresting.
    4. ☐ Most of the time my work was uninteresting.
    5. ☐ My work was always uninteresting.

FOR STUDENTS
Answer Questions 13–18 if you go to school half time or more. Otherwise go to Question 19.

What best describes your school program? (Choose one)
    1. ☐ Full time
    2. ☐ 3/4 time
    3. ☐ Half time

Check the answer that best describes how you have been the last 2 weeks.

13. How many days of classes did you miss in the last 2 weeks?
    1. ☐ No days missed.
    2. ☐ A few days missed.
    3. ☐ I missed about half the time.
    4. ☐ Missed more than half time but did make at least one day.
    5. ☐ I did not go to classes at all.
    8. ☐ I was on vacation all of the last two weeks.

14. Have you kept up with your class work in the last 2 weeks?
    1. ☐ I did my work very well.
    2. ☐ I did my work but had some minor problems.
    3. ☐ I needed help with work and did not do well about half the time.
    4. ☐ I did my work poorly most of the time.
    5. ☐ I did my work poorly all the time.

15. During the last 2 weeks have you been ashamed of how you do your schoolwork?
    1. ☐ I never felt ashamed.
    2. ☐ Once or twice I felt a little ashamed.
    3. ☐ About half the time I felt ashamed.
    4. ☐ I felt ashamed most of the time.
    5. ☐ I felt ashamed all the time.

16. Have you had any arguments with people at school in the last 2 weeks?
    1. ☐ I had no arguments and got along very well.
    2. ☐ I usually got along well but had minor arguments.
    3. ☐ I had more than one argument.
    4. ☐ I had many arguments.
    5. ☐ I was constantly in arguments.

17. Have you felt upset at school during the last 2 weeks?
    1. ☐ I never felt upset.
    2. ☐ Once or twice I felt upset.
    3. ☐ Half the time I felt upset
    4. ☐ I felt upset most of the time.
    5. ☐ I felt upset all of the time.

18. Have you found your school work interesting these last 2 weeks?
    1. ☐ My work was almost always interesting.
    2. ☐ Once or twice my work was not interesting.
    3. ☐ Half the time my work was uninteresting.
    4. ☐ Most of the time my work was uninteresting.
    5. ☐ My work was always uninteresting.

SPARE TIME—EVERYONE ANSWER QUESTIONS 19–27.

Check the answer that best describes the way you have been in the last 2 weeks.

19. How many friends have you seen or spoken to on the telephone in the last 2 weeks?
    1. ☐ Nine or more friends.
    2. ☐ Five to eight friends.
    3. ☐ Two to four friends.
    4. ☐ One friend.
    5. ☐ No friends.

20. Have you been able to talk about your feelings and problems with at least one friend during the last 2 weeks?
    1. ☐ I can always talk about my innermost feelings.
    2. ☐ I usually can talk about my feelings.
    3. ☐ About half the time I felt able to talk about my feelings.
    4. ☐ I usually was not able to talk about my feelings.
    5. ☐ I was never able to talk about my feelings.
    8. ☐ Not applicable; I have no friends.

21. How many times in the last 2 weeks have you gone out socially with other people? For example, visited friends, gone to movies, bowling, church, restaurants, invited friends to your home?
1. ☐ More than 3 times.
2. ☐ Three times.
3. ☐ Twice.
4. ☐ Once.
5. ☐ None.

22. How much time have you spent on hobbies or spare time interests during the last 2 weeks? For example, bowling, sewing, gardening, sports, reading?
1. ☐ I spent most of my spare time on hobbies almost every day.
2. ☐ I spent some spare time on hobbies some of the days.
3. ☐ I spent a little time on hobbies.
4. ☐ I usually did not spend any time on hobbies but did watch TV.
5. ☐ I did not spend any spare time on hobbies or watching TV.

23. Have you had open arguments with your friends in the past 2 weeks?
1. ☐ I had no arguments and got along very well
2. ☐ I usually got along but had minor arguments.
3. ☐ I had more than one argument.
4. ☐ I had many arguments.
5. ☐ I was constantly in arguments.
8. ☐ Not applicable; I have no friends.

24. If your feelings were hurt or offended by a friend during the last 2 weeks, how badly did you take it?
1. ☐ It did not affect me or it did not happen.
2. ☐ I got over it in a few hours.
3. ☐ I got over it in a few days.
4. ☐ I got over it in a week.
5. ☐ It will take me months to recover.
8. ☐ Not applicable; I have no friends.

25. Have you felt shy or uncomfortable with people in the last 2 weeks?
1. ☐ I always felt comfortable.
2. ☐ Sometimes I felt uncomfortable but could relax after a while.
3. ☐ About half the time I felt uncomfortable.
4. ☐ I usually felt uncomfortable.
5. ☐ I always felt uncomfortable.
8. ☐ Not applicable; I was never with people.

26. Have you felt lonely and wished for more friends during the last 2 weeks?
1. ☐ I have not felt lonely .
2. ☐ I have felt lonely a few times.
3. ☐ About half the time I felt lonely.
4. ☐ I usually felt lonely.
5. ☐ I always felt lonely and wished for more friends.

27. Have felt bored in your spare time during the last 2 weeks?
    1. ☐ I never felt bored.
    2. ☐ I usually did not feel bored.
    3. ☐ About half the time I felt bored.
    4. ☐ Most of the time I felt bored.
    5. ☐ I was constantly bored.

Are you a single, separated, or divorced person not living with a person of opposite sex; please answer below:
    1. ☐ Yes; answer questions 28 & 29.
    2. ☐ No; go to question 30.

28. How many times have you been with a date these last 2 weeks?
    1. ☐ More than 3 times.
    2. ☐ Three times.
    3. ☐ Twice.
    4. ☐ Once.
    5. ☐ Never.

29. Have you been interested in dating during the last 2 weeks? If you have not dated, would you have liked to?
    1. ☐ I was always interested in dating.
    2. ☐ Most of the time I was interested.
    3. ☐ About half the time I was interested.
    4. ☐ Most of the time I was not interested.
    5. ☐ I was completely uninterested.

FAMILY
Answer Questions 30–37 about your parents, brothers, sisters, in-laws, and children not living at home. Have you been in contact with any of them in the last 2 weeks?
    1. ☐ Yes, answer questions 30–37
    2. ☐ No, go to question 36.

30. Have you had open arguments with your relatives in the past 2 weeks?
    1. ☐ We always got along very well
    2. ☐ We usually got along very well but had some minor arguments.
    3. ☐ I had more than one argument with at least one relative.
    4. ☐ I had many arguments.
    5. ☐ I was constantly in arguments.

31. Have you been able to talk about your feelings and problems with at least one friend during the last 2 weeks?
    1. ☐ I can always talk about my feelings with at least one relative.
    2. ☐ I usually can talk about my feelings.
    3. ☐ About half the time I felt able to talk about my feelings.
    4. ☐ I usually was not able to talk about my feelings.
    5. ☐ I was never able to talk about my feelings.

32. Have you avoided contacts with your relatives these last 2 weeks?
    1. ☐ I have contacted relatives regularly.
    2. ☐ I have contacted a relative at least once.
    3. ☐ I have waited for my relatives to contact me.
    4. ☐ I avoided my relatives, but they contacted me.
    5. ☐ I have no contacts with any relatives.

33. Did you depend on your relatives for help, advice, money or friendship during the last 2 weeks?
    1. ☐ I never need to depend on them.
    2. ☐ I usually did not need to depend on them.
    3. ☐ About half the time I needed to depend on them.
    4. ☐ Most of the time I depend on them.
    5. ☐ I depend completely on them.

34. Have you wanted to do the opposite of what your relatives wanted in order to make them angry during the last 2 weeks?
    1. ☐ I never wanted to oppose them.
    2. ☐ Once or twice I wanted to oppose them.
    3. ☐ About half the time I wanted to oppose them.
    4. ☐ Most of the time I wanted to oppose them.
    5. ☐ I always opposed them

35. Have you been worried about things happening to your relatives without good reason in the last 2 weeks?
    1. ☐ I have not worried without reason.
    2. ☐ Once or twice I worried.
    3. ☐ About half the time I worried
    4. ☐ Most of the time I worried.
    5. ☐ I have worried the entire time.

EVERYONE answer Questions 36 and 37, even if your relatives are not living.

36. During the last 2 weeks, have you been thinking that you have let any of your relatives down or have been unfair to them at any time?
    1. ☐ I did not feel that I let them down at all.
    2. ☐ I usually did not feel that I let them down.
    3. ☐ About half the time I felt that I let them down.
    4. ☐ Most of the time I have felt that I let them down.
    5. ☐ I always felt that I let them down.

37. During the last 2 weeks, have you been thinking that any of your relatives have let you down or have been unfair to you at any time?
    1. ☐ I never felt that they let me down.
    2. ☐ I felt that they usually did not let me down.
    3. ☐ About half the time I felt they let me down.
    4. ☐ I usually have felt that they let me down.
    5. ☐ I am very bitter that they let me down.

Are you living with your spouse or have you been living with a person of the opposite sex in permanent relationship?
1. ☐ Yes, Please answer questions 38–46.
2. ☐ No, Go to question 47.

38. Have you had open arguments with your partner in the past 2 weeks?
1. ☐ We had no arguments and we got along very well
2. ☐ We usually got along very well but had some minor arguments.
3. ☐ We had more than one argument.
4. ☐ We had many arguments.
5. ☐ We were constantly in arguments.

39. Have you been able to talk about your feelings and problems with your partner during the last 2 weeks?
1. ☐ I could always talk about my feelings.
2. ☐ I usually could talk about my feelings.
3. ☐ About half the time I felt able to talk about my feelings.
4. ☐ I usually was not able to talk about my feelings.
5. ☐ I was never able to talk about my feelings.

40. Have you been demanding to have your own way at home during the last 2 weeks?
1. ☐ I have not insisted on always having my own way.
2. ☐ I usually have not insisted on having my own way.
3. ☐ About half the time I insisted on having my own way.
4. ☐ I usually insisted on having my own way.
5. ☐ I always insisted on having my own way.

41. Have you been bossed around by your partner these last 2 weeks?
1. ☐ Almost never.
2. ☐ Once in a while.
3. ☐ About half the time.
4. ☐ Most of the time.
5. ☐ Always.

42. How much have you felt dependent on your partner these last 2 weeks?
1. ☐ I was independent.
2. ☐ I was usually independent.
3. ☐ I was somewhat dependent.
4. ☐ I was usually dependent.
5. ☐ I depended on my partner for everything.

43. How have you felt about your partner during the last 2 weeks?
1. ☐ I always felt affection
2. ☐ I usually felt affection
3. ☐ About half the time I felt dislike and half the time affection.
4. ☐ I usually felt dislike.
5. ☐ I always felt dislike.

44. How many times have you and your partner had intercourse?
    1. ☐ More than twice a week.
    2. ☐ Once or twice a week.
    3. ☐ Once every two weeks.
    4. ☐ Less than once every two weeks but at least once in the past month.
    5. ☐ Not at all in a month or longer.

45. Have you had any problems during intercourse, such as pain, these last 2 weeks?
    1. ☐ None
    2. ☐ Once or twice.
    3. ☐ About half the time.
    4. ☐ Most of the time.
    5. ☐ Always.
    8. ☐ Not applicable; no intercourse in the last two weeks.

46. How have you felt about intercourse during the last 2 weeks?
    1. ☐ I always enjoyed it.
    3. ☐ I usually enjoyed it.
    2. ☐ About half the time I did and half the time I did not enjoy it.
    4. ☐ I usually did not enjoy it.
    5. ☐ I never enjoyed it.

CHILDREN
Have you had unmarried children, stepchildren, or foster children living at home during the last 2 weeks?
    1. ☐ Yes; answer questions 47–50.
    2. ☐ No; go to question 51.

47. Have you been interested in what your children are doing—school, play, or hobbies during the last 2 weeks?
    1. ☐ I was always interested and actively involved.
    2. ☐ I was usually interested and involved.
    3. ☐ About half the time interested and half the time not interested.
    4. ☐ I usually was disinterested.
    5. ☐ I was always disinterested.

48. Have you been able to talk and listen to your children during the last 2 weeks? Include only children over the age of 2.
    1. ☐ I was always able to communicate with them.
    2. ☐ I usually was able to communicate with them.
    3. ☐ About half the time I could communicate
    4. ☐ I was usually not able to communicate.
    5. ☐ I was completely unable to communicate.
    8. ☐ Not applicable; no children over the age of 2.

49. How have you been getting along with the children during the last 2 weeks?
    1. ☐ I had no arguments and we got along very well
    2. ☐ I usually got along very well but had some minor arguments.
    3. ☐ I had more than one argument.

4. ☐   I had many arguments.
5. ☐   I was constantly in arguments.

50. How have you felt towards your children these last 2 weeks?
1. ☐   I always felt affection.
2. ☐   I mostly felt affection.
3. ☐   About half the time I felt affection.
4. ☐   Most of the time I did not feel affection.
5. ☐   I never felt affection toward them.

FAMILY UNIT
Have you ever been married, ever lived with a person of the opposite sex, or ever had children? Please check
1. ☐   Yes; please answer questions 51–53.
2. ☐   No; go to question 54.

51. Have you worried about your partner or any of your children without any reason during the last 2 weeks, even if you are not living together now?
1. ☐   I never worried.
2. ☐   Once or twice I worried.
3. ☐   About half the time I worried
4. ☐   Most of the time I worried.
5. ☐   I always worried.
8. ☐   Not applicable; partner and children not living.

52. During the last 2 weeks, have you been thinking that you have let down your partner or any of your children at any time?
1. ☐   I did not feel I let them down.
2. ☐   I usually did not feel that I let them down.
3. ☐   About half the time I felt I let them down.
4. ☐   Most of the time I felt I let them down.
5. ☐   I let them down completely.

53. During the last 2 weeks, have you been thinking that your partner or any of your children have let you down at any time?

1. ☐   I never felt that they let me down.
2. ☐   I felt they usually did not let me down.
3. ☐   About half the time I felt they let me down.
4. ☐   I usually felt they let me down.
5. ☐   I feel bitter that they have let me down.

FINANCIAL—EVERYONE PLEASE ANSWER QUESTION 54.

54. Have you had enough money to take care of your own and your family's financial needs during the last 2 weeks?
1. ☐   I had enough money for needs
2. ☐   I usually had enough money, with minor problems.
3. ☐   About half the time I did not have enough money but did not have to borrow money.
4. ☐   I usually did not have enough money and had to borrow from others.
5. ☐   I had great financial difficulty.

SOCIAL ANXIETY THOUGHTS QUESTIONNAIRE (SAT)

AUTHOR: Lorne M. Hartman

PURPOSE: To measure the cognitive component of social anxiety.

DESCRIPTION: The SAT is a 21-item instrument designed to measure the frequency of cognitions that accompany social distress or anxiety. The basis for this instrument is the notion that cognitive factors (thoughts, images, memories, feelings) such as negative self-evaluations and evaluation of feedback from others play a role in the development, maintenance, and treatment of disorders such as social anxiety. From a pool of 117 self-statements collected from university students, the 21 items that showed the best psychometric properties were selected. Factor analysis revealed four factors, but the overall score on the SAT appears to be the most useful indicator of cognitive components of social anxiety. The four factors are: (1) thoughts of general discomfort and social inadequacy, (2) concern with others' awareness of distress; (3) fear of negative evaluations, and (4) perceptions of autonomic arousal and performance anxiety.

NORMS: Initial study of the SAT involved 28 male and 74 female undergraduates with a mean age of 21.6. No other demographic data or samples were reported. The mean score for those respondents was 42.3.

SCORING: The SAT is scored by summing the individual item scores, producing a range of 21 to 105, with higher scores indicating higher frequency of cognitions accompanying social anxiety.

RELIABILITY: The SAT has excellent internal consistency, with an alpha of .95. Test-retest correlations were not reported.

VALIDITY: The SAT has fairly good concurrent validity, showing significant correlations with the Social Avoidance and Distress Scale and the Fear of Negative Evaluation Scale. No other forms of validity were reported.

PRIMARY REFERENCE: Hartman, L. M. (1984). Cognitive components of anxiety, *Journal of Clinical Psychology*, 40, 137–139. Instrument reproduced with permission of Lorne Hartman.

AVAILABILITY: Dr. L. M. Hartman, Addiction Research Foundation, 33 Russell Street, Toronto, Ontario, Canada.

SAT

We are interested in the thoughts people have in social situations. Listed below are a variety of thoughts that pop into peoples' heads in situations that involve being with other people or talking to them. Please read each thought and indicate how frequently, if at all, the thought occurred to you *over the last week*. Please read each item carefully and, following the scale, indicate to the left of the question the number that best applies to you. Please answer each question very carefully. *In social or interpersonal situations during the past week, how often did you have the following thoughts?*

1 = Never
2 = Rarely
3 = Sometimes
4 = Often
5 = Always

____ 1.   I feel tense and uncertain.
____ 2.   I don't know what to say.
____ 3.   Maybe I sound stupid.
____ 4.   I am perspiring.
____ 5.   What will I say first?
____ 6.   Can they tell I am nervous?
____ 7.   I feel afraid.
____ 8.   I wish I could just be myself.
____ 9.   What are they thinking of me?
____ 10. I feel shaky.
____ 11. I'm not pronouncing well.
____ 12. Will others notice my anxiety?
____ 13. I feel defenseless.
____ 14. I will freeze up.
____ 15. Now they know I am nervous.
____ 16. I don't like being in this situation.
____ 17. I am inadequate.
____ 18. Does my anxiety show?
____ 19. I feel tense in my stomach.
____ 20. Others will not understand me.
____ 21. What do they think of me?

SOCIAL AVOIDANCE AND DISTRESS SCALE (SAD)

AUTHORS: David Watson and Ronald Friend

PURPOSE: To measure social anxiety.

DESCRIPTION: This 28-item measure was developed to assess anxiety in social situations. The SAD assesses two aspects of anxiety, one's experience of distress, discomfort, fear and anxiety; and the deliberate avoidance of social situations. The SAD, however, is a unidimensional measure and does not have subscales. The items are phrased to reflect anxiety and non-anxiety symptoms in an effort to control for response bias. The SAD is appropriate for general social situations rather than specific problems such as test anxiety or simple phobia.

NORMS: The SAD was developed on a sample of 297 college students. Demographic data are not available. The mean for males ($n = 60$) was 11.2 and for females ($n = 145$) the mean was 8.24. There was a significant difference between males and females, indicating that females report more social anxiety.

SCORING: Each item is answered either "true" or "false." Items 2, 5, 8, 10, 11, 13, 14, 16, 18, 20, 21, 23, 24, and 26 are keyed for "true" answers, while the other items are keyed "false." Answers which match the keyed response are given the value of 1 and answers which do not match the key are assigned the value of 0. Total scores are the sum of the item values. Scores range from 0 to 28 with higher scores indicating more anxiety.

RELIABILITY: The internal consistency of the instrument was assessed by correlating each item with the total score on the SAD. The average item to total score correlation was .77. Reliability was also determined using Kuder-Richardson Formula 20 and was excellent, with a correlation of .94. Test-retest reliability for a one-month period was .68 using a sample of 154 college students enrolled in summer school and .79 for a separate sample.

VALIDITY: The validity of the SAD was assessed by testing to see if subjects with high scores demonstrated more discomfort in a social situation than did subjects with lower scores. Additionally, comparisons were made to determine if subjects with high scores demonstrated a greater preference for being alone than did subjects with lower scores. Differences were found between the groups on these variables and are evidence of known-groups validity.

PRIMARY REFERENCE: Watson, D. and Friend, R. (1969). Measurement of social-evaluation anxiety, *Journal of Consulting and Clinical Psychology*, 33, 448–457. Instrument reprinted with permission of David Watson and the American Psychological Association.

AVAILABILITY: Journal article.

SAD

For the following statements, please answer each in terms of whether it is true or false for you. Circle T for true or F for false.

T	F	1.	I feel relaxed even in unfamiliar social situations.
T	F	2.	I try to avoid situations which force me to be very sociable.
T	F	3.	It is easy for me to relax when I am with strangers.
T	F	4.	I have no particular desire to avoid people.
T	F	5.	I often find social occasions upsetting.
T	F	6.	I usually feel calm and comfortable at social occasions.
T	F	7.	I am usually at ease when talking to someone of the opposite sex.
T	F	8.	I try to avoid talking to people unless I know them well.
T	F	9.	If the chance comes to meet new people, I often take it.
T	F	10.	I often feel nervous or tense in casual get-togethers in which both sexes are present.
T	F	11.	I am usually nervous with people unless I know them well.
T	F	12.	I usually feel relaxed when I am with a group of people.
T	F	13.	I often want to get away from people.
T	F	14.	I usually feel uncomfortable when I am in a group of people I don't know.
T	F	15.	I usually feel relaxed when I meet someone for the first time.
T	F	16.	Being introduced to people makes me tense and nervous.
T	F	17.	Even though a room is full of strangers, I may enter it anyway.
T	F	18.	I would avoid walking up and joining a large group of people.
T	F	19.	When my superiors want to talk with me, I talk willingly.
T	F	20.	I often feel on edge when I am with a group of people.
T	F	21.	I tend to withdraw from people.
T	F	22.	I don't mind talking to people at parties or social gatherings.
T	F	23.	I am seldom at ease in a large group of people.
T	F	24.	I often think up excuses in order to avoid social engagements.
T	F	25.	I sometimes take the responsibility for introducing people to each other.
T	F	26.	I try to avoid formal social occasions.
T	F	27.	I usually go to whatever social engagement I have.
T	F	28.	I find it easy to relax with other people.

SOCIAL FEAR SCALE (SFS)

AUTHORS: Michael L. Raulin and Jennifer L. Wee

PURPOSE: To measure social fear.

DESCRIPTION: The SFS is a 36-item instrument designed to measure the particular type of social fear that is believed to be a common characteristic of schizotypic individuals, those who have a possible genetic predisposition to schizophrenia. The SFS was developed to measure interpersonal aversiveness, characteristics such as social inadequacy, and a dearth of interpersonal relationships that might be present in preschizophrenics in the general population. The 36 items were selected from an item pool of 120 items based on descriptions of social fear as a schizotypic symptom.

NORMS: Development of the SFS was carried out with separate samples of undergraduate students, totaling 792 females and 670 males. No actual norms or other demographic information were reported.

SCORING: Respondents are asked to indicate whether each item is true or false as it applies to them. Items 3, 8, 16, 18, 19, 31, and 32 are considered "correct" if marked "false"; all others are "correct" if marked "true." Correct answers are assigned 1 point, and the scores are summed. The higher the score, the greater the degree of social fear.

RELIABILITY: The SFS has very good internal consistency, with alphas ranging from .85 to .88. No test-retest correlations are reported.

VALIDITY: The SFS has fair concurrent validity, correlating moderately with several other scales measuring schizotypic characteristics (e.g., perceptual aberration, intense ambivalence, somatic symptoms). High, medium, and low scores on the SFS also significantly distinguished among groups independently rated on social fear and sociability, thus suggesting some degree of known-groups validity. The SFS is slightly correlated with social desirability response bias, so this condition cannot be totally ruled out.

PRIMARY REFERENCE: Raulin, M. L. and Wee, J. L. (1984). The development and validation of a scale to measure social fear, *Journal of Clinical Psychology*, 40, 780–784. Instrument reproduced with permission of Michael L. Raulin.

AVAILABILITY: Dr. Michael L. Raulin, SUNY Buffalo, Psychology Department, Julian Park Hall, Buffalo, NY 14260.

SFS

Circle either T for true or F for false for each item as it applies to you.

T F   1.   I like staying in bed so that I won't have to see anyone.
T F   2.   I enjoy being a loner.
T F   3.   I usually prefer being with friends to being by myself.
T F   4.   Upon entering a crowded room, I often feel a strong urge to leave immediately.
T F   5.   Honest people will admit that socializing is a burden.
T F   6.   I find I can't relax unless I am alone.
T F   7.   I feel more comfortable being around animals than being around people.
T F   8.   I think I would enjoy a job that involved working with a lot of different people.
T F   9.   I like to go for days on end without seeing anyone.
T F   10.   I stay away from other people whenever possible.
T F   11.   All my favorite pastimes are things I do by myself.
T F   12.   I often tell people that I am not feeling well just to get out of doing things with them.
T F   13.   The only time I feel really comfortable is when I'm off by myself.
T F   14.   Being around other people makes me nervous.
T F   15.   I would rather eat alone than with other people.
T F   16.   I prefer traveling with friends to traveling alone.
T F   17.   I really prefer going to movies alone.
T F   18.   I almost always enjoy being with people.
T F   19.   It is rare for me to prefer sitting home alone to going out with a group of friends.
T F   20.   I often dream of being out in the wilderness with only animals as friends.
T F   21.   While talking with people I am often overwhelmed with a desire to be alone.
T F   22.   Pets are generally safer to be with than people.
T F   23.   I usually find that being with people is very wearing.
T F   24.   I often feel like leaving parties without saying goodbye.
T F   25.   Even when I am in a good mood, I prefer being alone to being with people.
T F   26.   Often I can't wait until the day is over so I can be by myself.
T F   27.   I wish people would just leave me alone.
T F   28.   I feel most secure when I am by myself.
T F   29.   When seated in a crowded place I have often felt the urge to get up suddenly and leave.
T F   30.   I often need to be totally alone for a couple of days.
T F   31.   I feel most comfortable when I am with people.
T F   32.   I like spending my spare time with other people.
T F   33.   Whenever I make plans to be with people I always regret it later.
T F   34.   The strain of being around people is so unbearable that I have to get away.
T F   35.   I would consider myself a loner.
T F   36.   I wish that I could be alone most of the time.

SOCIAL INTERACTION SELF-STATEMENT TEST (SISST)

AUTHORS: Carol R. Glass, Thomas V. Merluzzi, Joan L. Biever, and Kathryn H. Larsen

PURPOSE: To assess self-statements about social anxiety.

DESCRIPTION: The SISST is a 30-item instrument designed to measure cognitions (self-statements) associated with anxiety about social interaction. This instrument is designed for men and women who tend to have low self-confidence, inappropriate fears, worry over negative experiences, and concern about physical appearance. The SISST is based on the assumption that self-statements in specific stressful social situations are related to anxiety and competence. Thus, the SISST assesses thoughts reported by anxious individuals prior to, during, or after social interaction. The items in the SISST were derived empirically from a sample of individuals who were viewed as having high social anxiety. It consists of 15 positive (facilitative) self-statements (items 2, 4, 6, 9, 10, 12, 13, 14, 17, 18, 24, 25, 27, 28, 30) and 15 negative (inhibitory) self-statements (the remaining items). The gender of pronouns and references to males and females can be changed to produce appropriate forms for men and women.

NORMS: Initial study of the SISST was conducted on two samples. The first consisted of 40 high and 40 low socially anxious undergraduate women and the second included 32 men and 32 women selected on the basis of a random sample of undergraduate introductory psychology students, stratified by scores on the Bem Sex-Role Inventory. Means for the several subcategories of the sample are reported and range from 38.82 to 58.43 on the SISST-positive and 28.43 to 51.91 on the SISST-negative.

SCORING: The SISST is scored by summing scores (scored from 1 to 5) for the 15 positive and 15 negative items separately. Each subscale has a range of 15 to 75.

RELIABILITY: The SISST has good internal consistency, with split-half reliability coefficients of .73 for the positive and .86 for the negative subscales. No test-retest data were available.

VALIDITY: The SISST has good concurrent validity, with the subscales correlating with the Social Avoidance and Distress Scale and the Survey of Heterosocial Interactions. In addition, the SISST significantly correlated with respondents' self-evaluations of skill and anxiety immediately after role-played situations. The SISST also has good known-groups validity, with both subscales distinguishing between high and low socially anxious respondents based on scores on other measures.

PRIMARY REFERENCE: Glass, C. R., Merluzzi, T. V., Biever, J. O., and Larsen, K. H. (1982). Cognitive assessment of social anxiety: Development and validation of a self-statement questionnaire, *Cognitive Therapy and Re-*

search, 6, 37–55. Instrument reproduced with permission of Carol R. Glass and Plenum Publishing Corporation.

AVAILABILITY: Dr. Carol R. Glass, Department of Psychology, Catholic University, Washington, DC 20064.

SISST

It is obvious that people think a variety of things when they are involved in different social situations. Below is a list of things which you may have thought to yourself at some time before, during, and after the interaction in which you were engaged. Read each item and decide how frequently you may have been thinking a similar thought before, during, and after the interaction. Indicate to the left of the item the appropriate number. The scale is interpreted as follows:

1 = Hardly ever had the thought
2 = Rarely had the thought
3 = Sometimes had the thought
4 = Often had the thought
5 = Very often had the thought

Please answer as honestly as possible.

____ 1. When I can't think of anything to say I can feel myself getting very anxious.
____ 2. I can usually talk to women pretty well.
____ 3. I hope I don't make a fool of myself.
____ 4. I'm beginning to feel more at ease.
____ 5. I'm really afraid of what she'll think of me.
____ 6. No worries, no fears, no anxieties.
____ 7. I'm scared to death.
____ 8. She probably won't be interested in me.
____ 9. Maybe I can put her at ease by starting things going.
____ 10. Instead of worrying I can figure out how best to get to know her.
____ 11. I'm not too comfortable meeting women so things are bound to go wrong.
____ 12. What the heck, the worst that can happen is that she won't go for me.
____ 13. She may want to talk to me as much as I want to talk to her.
____ 14. This will be a good opportunity.
____ 15. If I blow this conversation, I'll really lose my confidence.
____ 16. What I say will probably sound stupid.
____ 17. What do I have to lose? It's worth a try.
____ 18. This is an awkward situation but I can handle it.
____ 19. Wow—I don't want to do this.
____ 20. It would crush me if she didn't respond to me.
____ 21. I've just got to make a good impression on her or I'll feel terrible.
____ 22. You're such an inhibited idiot.
____ 23. I'll probably "bomb out" anyway.
____ 24. I can handle anything.
____ 25. Even if things don't go well it's no catastrophe.
____ 26. I feel awkward and dumb; she's bound to notice.
____ 27. We probably have a lot in common.
____ 28. Maybe we'll hit it off real well.
____ 29. I wish I could leave and avoid the whole situation.
____ 30. Ah! Throw caution to the wind.

SOCIAL PROBLEM-SOLVING INVENTORY (SPSI)

AUTHORS: Thomas J. D'Zurilla and Arthur M. Nezu

PURPOSE: To measure problem-solving ability.

DESCRIPTION: The SPSI is a 70-item multidimensional measure based on a prescriptive model of problem solving that characterizes social problem solving as a complex, cognitive-affective-behavioral process that consists of a number of different components, including general motivational variables and a set of specific skills. The SPSI consists of two major scales—the Problem Orientation Scale (POS; 30 items) and the Problem-Solving Skills Scale (PSSS; 40 items)—and seven subscales (each with 10 items, as indicated on the instrument). Subsumed under the POS are the cognition subscale (CS), the emotion subscale (ES), and the behavior subscale (BS). Subsumed under the PSSS are the problem definition and formulation subscale (PDFS), the generation of alternatives subscale (GASS), the decision making subscale (DMS), and the solution implementation and verification subscale (SIVS). Although the SPSI has more items than most measures in this book, it was included because of its excellent potential for clinical use, and the centrality of the problem-solving process to many different approaches to clinical practice.

NORMS: The 70-item version of the SPSI was administered to three samples: (A) 192 undergraduates at SUNY-Stony Brook (60% female, 30% male, mean age of 19.8, 72% Caucasian, 12% Asian, 8% black, 5% Hispanic); (B) 107 undergraduates from Fairleigh Dickinson University (53% male, 47% female, mean age of 21.3, 90% Caucasian, 10% black); and (C) 45 high-stressed community residents who volunteered to participate in a stress-management research program (28 females, 17 males, mean age of 44.3, all Caucasian). The means (and standard deviation) on the SPSI and two major subscales were: (A) SPSI = 165.2 (SD = 33.24), POS = 73.56 (SD = 20.15), PSSS = 91.31 (SD = 19.88); (B) SPSI = 171.08 (SD = 35.73), POS = 77.76 (SD = 19.58), PSSS = 96.41 (SD = 25.85); and (C) SPSI = 144.64 (SD = 40.43), POS = 62.66 (SD = 17.88), PSSS = 81.96 (SD = 26.96).

SCORING: The SPSI is scored by simply summing the scores on the relevant items for each subscale, the two major scales, and the SPSI itself. The range for each subscale is from 0 to 40, for the POS is 0 to 120, for the PSSS is 0 to 160, and for the SPSI as a whole is 0 to 280. Items to be reverse-scored are indicated with an asterisk on the measure.

RELIABILITY: The SPSI has excellent internal consistency, with alphas of .94 for the POS and SPSI and .92 for the PSSS. The measure also has very good stability, with three-week test-retest correlations of .87 for the SPSI as a whole and .83 and .88 for the POS and PSSS respectively.

VALIDITY: The SPSI has excellent concurrent validity, with significant correlations between the SPSI as a whole and its two major subscales with two other problem-solving measures, the Problem-Solving Inventory and the Means-Ends Problem-Solving Procedure. The SPSI also has very good construct validity, correlating in predicted ways with several other measures, including the Internal-External Locus of Control Scale and the Scholastic Aptitude Test. The SPSI also was found to be sensitive to changes due to training in problem-solving skills, and demonstrated good predictive ability, negatively correlating with several measures of stress level, life problems, and psychological symptoms.

PRIMARY REFERENCE: D'Zurilla, T. J. and Nezu, A. M. (1992). Development and preliminary evaluation of the Social Problem-Solving Inventory (SPSI), *Psychological Assessment*, 2, 156–163.

AVAILABILITY: Journal article.

SPSI

Below is a series of statements that describe the way some people might think, feel, and behave when they are faced with problems in everyday living. We are talking about important problems that could have a significant effect on your well-being or the well-being of your loved ones, such as a health-related problem, a dispute with a family member, or a problem with your performance at work or in school. Please read each statement and carefully select one of the numbers below which indicates the extent to which the statement is true of you. Consider yourself as you *typically* think, feel, and behave when you are faced with problems in living *these days* and place the appropriate number in the parentheses ( ) next to the number of the statement.

> 0 = Not at all true of me
> 1 = Slightly true of me
> 2 = Moderately true of me
> 3 = Very true of me
> 4 = Extremely true of me

CS   *1. ( )   When I cannot solve a problem quickly and without much effort, I tend to think that I am stupid or incompetent.

PDFS   2. ( )   When I have a problem to solve, one of the things I do is examine all the information that I have about the problem and try to decide what is most relevant or important.

BS   *3. ( )   I spend too much time worrying about my problems instead of trying to solve them.

ES   *4. ( )   I usually feel threatened and afraid when I have an important problem to solve.

DMS   *5. ( )   When making decisions, I do *not* usually evaluate and compare the different alternatives carefully enough.

CS   *6. ( )   When I have a problem, I often doubt that there is a solution for it.

DMS   *7. ( )   When I am attempting to decide what is the best solution to a problem, I often fail to take into account the effect that each alternative is likely to have on the well-being of other people.

GASS   8. ( )   When I am trying to find a solution to a problem, I often think of a number of possible solutions and then try to combine different solutions to make a better solution.

ES   *9.   ( )   I usually feel nervous and unsure of myself when I have an important decision to make.

CS   10.   ( )   When my first efforts to solve a problem fail, I usually think that if I persist and do not give up too easily, I will be able to find a good solution eventually.

GASS   *11.   ( )   When I am attempting to solve a problem, I usually act on the first idea that comes to mind.

CS   12.   ( )   When I have a problem, I usually believe that there is a solution for it.

PDFS   13.   ( )   When I am faced with a large, complex problem, I often try to break it down into smaller problems that I can solve one at a time.

SIVS   *14.   ( )   After carrying out a solution to a problem, I do *not* usually take the time to compare the actual outcome with the outcome that I had anticipated when I decided on that particular solution.

BS   *15.   ( )   I usually wait to see if a problem will resolve itself first, before trying to solve it myself.

PDFS   16.   ( )   When I have a problem to solve, one of the things I do is analyze the situation and try to identify what obstacles are keeping me from getting what I want.

ED   *17.   ( )   When my first efforts to solve a problem fail, I get very angry and frustrated.

CS   *18.   ( )   When I am faced with a difficult problem, I often doubt that I will be able to solve it on my own no matter how hard I try.

SIVS   19.   ( )   I am usually quite satisfied with the outcome of my problem solutions after I carry them out.

PDFS   20.   ( )   Before trying to solve a problem, I often try to find out if the problem is being caused by some other more important problem that should be solved first.

BS   *21.   ( )   When a problem occurs in my life, I usually put off trying to solve it for as long as possible.

SIVS   *22.   ( )   After carrying out a solution to a problem, I do *not* usually take the time to evaluate all of the results carefully.

BS *23. ( ) I usually go out of my way to avoid having to deal with problems in my life.

ES *24. ( ) Difficult problems make me very upset.

DMS 25. ( ) When I am attempting to decide what is the best solution to a problem, I try to predict the overall outcome of carrying out each alternative course of action.

BS 26. ( ) I usually confront my problems "head on," instead of trying to avoid them.

GASS 27. ( ) When I am attempting to solve a problem, I often try to be creative and think of original or unconventional solutions.

GASS *28. ( ) When I am attempting to solve a problem, I usually go with the first good idea that comes to mind.

GASS 29. ( ) When I am trying to find a solution to a problem, I often think of a number of possible solutions and then later go back over them and consider how different solutions can be modified to make a better solution.

GASS *30. ( ) When I attempt to think of possible solutions to a problem, I cannot usually come up with many alternatives.

BS *31. ( ) I usually prefer to avoid problems instead of confronting them and being forced to deal with them.

DMS 32. ( ) When making decisions, I usually consider not only the immediate consequences of each alternative course of action, but also the long-term consequences.

SIVS 33. ( ) After carrying out a solution to a problem, I usually try to analyze what went right and what went wrong.

GASS 34. ( ) When I am attempting to find a solution to a problem, I usually try to think of as many different ways to approach the problem as possible.

SIVS 35. ( ) After carrying out a solution to a problem, I usually examine my feelings and evaluate how much they have changed for the better.

SIVS 36. ( ) Before carrying out a solution to a problem in the actual problematic situation, I often practice or rehearse the solution in order to increase my chances of success.

CS   37. ( )   When I am faced with a difficult problem, I usually believe that I will be able to solve the problem on my own if I try hard enough.

PDFS 38. ( )   When I have a problem to solve, one of the first things I do is get as many facts about the problem as possible.

PDFS 39. ( )   Before trying to solve a problem, I often try to find out if the problem is only one part of a bigger, more important problem that I should deal with.

BS   *40. ( )   I often put off solving problems until it is too late to do anything about them.

PDFS 41. ( )   Before trying to solve a problem, I usually evaluate the situation to determine how important the problem is for my well-being or the well-being of my loved ones.

BS   *42. ( )   I think that I spend more time avoiding my problems than solving them.

ES   *43. ( )   When I am attempting to solve a problem, I often get so upset that I cannot think clearly.

PDFS 44. ( )   Before I try to think of a solution to a problem, I usually set a specific goal that makes clear exactly what I want to accomplish.

DMS *45. ( )   When I am attempting to decide what is the best solution to a problem, I do *not* usually take the time to consider the pros and cons of each solution alternative.

SIVS 46. ( )   When the outcome of my solution to a problem is not satisfactory, I usually try to find out what went wrong and then I try again.

ES   *47. ( )   When I am working on a difficult problem, I often get so upset that I feel confused and disoriented.

ES   *48. ( )   I hate having to solve the problems that occur in my life.

SIVS 49. ( )   After carrying out a solution to a problem, I usually try to evaluate as carefully as possible how much the situation has changed for the better.

ES   *50. ( )   I am generally able to remain "cool, calm, and collected" when I am solving problems.

CS   51. ( ) When I have a problem, I usually try to see it as a
                 challenge, or opportunity to benefit in some positive way
                 from having the problem.

GASS 52. ( ) When I am attempting to solve a problem, I usually think of
                 as many alternative solutions as possible until I cannot
                 come up with any more ideas.

DMS   53. ( ) When I am attempting to decide what is the best solution to
                 a problem, I usually try to weigh the consequences of each
                 solution alternative and compare them against each other.

ES   *54. ( ) I often become depressed and immobilized when I have an
                 important problem to solve.

SIVS 55. ( ) My problem solutions are usually successful in achieving
                 my problem-solving goals.

BS   *56. ( ) When I am faced with a difficult problem, I usually try to
                 avoid the problem or I go to someone else for help in
                 solving it.

DMS   57. ( ) When I am attempting to decide what is the best solution to
                 a problem, I usually consider the effect that each
                 alternative course of action is likely to have on my personal
                 feelings.

PDFS 58. ( ) When I have a problem to solve, one of the things I do is
                 examine what sort of external circumstances in my
                 environment might be contributing to the problem.

CS   *59. ( ) When a problem occurs in my life, I usually blame myself
                 for causing it.

DMS   *60. ( ) When making decisions, I usually go with my "gut feeling"
                 without thinking too much about the consequences of each
                 alternative.

DMS   61. ( ) When making decisions, I generally use a systematic
                 method for judging and comparing alternatives.

GASS 62. ( ) When I am attempting to find a solution to a problem, I try
                 to keep in mind what my goal is at all times.

CS   *63. ( ) When my first efforts to solve a problem fail, I usually think
                 that I should give up and go look for help.

BS *64. ( ) When I have negative feelings, I tend to just go along with the mood, instead of trying to find out what problem might be causing these feelings.

GASS 65. ( ) When I am attempting to find a solution to a problem, I try to approach the problem from as many different angles as possible.

PDFS 66. ( ) When I am having trouble understanding a problem, I usually try to get more specific and concrete information about the problem to help clarify it.

CS *67. ( ) When I have a problem, I tend to dwell on the harm or loss that will result if I do not solve the problem successfully.

ES *68. ( ) When my first efforts to solve a problem fail, I tend to get discouraged and depressed.

SIVS *69. ( ) When a solution that I have carried out does not solve my problem satisfactorily, I do *not* usually take the time to examine carefully why it did not work.

DMS *70. ( ) I think that I am too impulsive when it comes to making decisions.

SOCIAL RHYTHM METRIC (SRM)

AUTHORS: Timothy Monk, Joseph F. Flaherty, Ellen Frank, and David J.
   Kupfer

PURPOSE: To measure daily social rhythm.

DESCRIPTION: This 17-item instrument is designed to measure the social
   rhythms that are important to structuring one's day. The SRM is useful when
   working with depressed clients. Fifteen events or behaviors are listed which
   are typical daily events; two items ("Activity A" and "Activity B") are left
   blank in order to isolate specific events or behaviors relevant to the respondent. The 15 events or behaviors were derived from a list of 37 daily
   activities. The theoretical basis for the SRM is that regularity of one's social
   rhythms is important to well-being. The SRM is considered useful in
   monitoring a patient's decline in depression and recovery from depression
   in terms of the regularity of events and behaviors of the day. To determine
   regularity of social rhythms, the SRM should be completed daily for an entire
   week, then averaged, with regularity defined as the average regularity of
   events. The SRM appears to be accurate whether completed throughout the
   day or retrospectively at the end of the day.

NORMS: Twelve activities occurred at least three times a week for a sample
   of 50 paid "normal" respondents. Scale scores of events had a mean of 3.44
   and a standard deviation of .91. A small sample of seven patients with
   recurrent depression reported a mean of 3.20 and a standard deviation of
   1.03.

SCORING: Scores are based on those items which occurred at least three times
   per week; items occurring less than three times per week are excluded. From
   those items occurring at least three times, the "habitual time" of occurrence
   is determined by excluding any extreme exceptions (such as going to bed
   one night at 5AM when the rest of the week one retires much earlier. Next,
   compare the times at which each event occurred; if it is within 45 minutes
   of the "habitual time," count it as a "hit" and score it 1. Now add the number
   of hits for all events occurring more than three times a week and divide by
   the number of events. Scores range from 1 to 7.

RELIABILITY: Test-retest reliability for a one-week period was .44, which is
   low but statistically significant. There were no differences in the mean scores
   for the first and second testing period. Data on internal consistency were not
   available.

VALIDITY: Validity data is limited to a comparison of SRM scores for four
   subjects with interruptions in routine. The means and standard deviations
   before the disruptive events were 1.95 and .78 and were 3.06 and .95 when
   they returned to their normal routines.

PRIMARY REFERENCE: Monk, T. H., Flaherty, J. F., Frank, E., Hoskinson, M. A., and Kupfer, D. J. (1990). The Social Rhythm Metric: An instrument to quantify the daily rhythms of life, *Journal of Nervous and Mental Disease*, 178, 120–126. Instrument reproduced with permission of Timothy H. Monk.

AVAILABILITY: Dr. T. H. Monk, Sleep Evaluation Center, Western Psychiatric Institute, 3811 O'Hara Street, Pittsburgh, PA 15213.

SRM

Fill out at end of day

ACTIVITY	Check if DID NOT DO	TIME			Check if ALONE	PEOPLE 1 = Just present 2 = Actively involved			
		Clock time	A.M.	P.M.		Spouse/ Partner	Children	Other Family Members	Other Person(s)
Out of bed									
First contact (in person or by phone) with another person									
Have morning beverage									
Have breakfast									
Go outside for the first time									
Start work, school, housework, volunteer activities, chiild or family care									
Have lunch									
Take an afternoon nap									
Have dinner									
Physical exercise									
Have an evening snack/drink									
Watch evening TV news program									
Watch another TV program									
Activity A _____									
Activity B _____									
Return home (last time)									
Go to bed									

SOCIAL SUPPORT APPRAISALS SCALE (SSA)

AUTHORS: Alan Vaux, Jeffrey Phillips, Lori Holley, Brian Thompson, Deirdre Williams, and Doreen Stewart

PURPOSE: To measure subjective appraisals of support.

DESCRIPTION: The SSA is a 23-item instrument based on the idea that social support is in fact support only if the individual believes it is available. These subjective appraisals also are viewed as related to overall psychological well-being. The SSA taps the extent to which the individual believes he or she is loved by, esteemed by, and involved with family, friends, and others.

NORMS: The SSA was studied with 10 undergraduate and community samples involving 979 respondents. The mean age ranged from mid-teens to 48. The samples were approximately 60% female, predominantly white (roughly 8% black), and roughly 50% married. Actual norms (means and standard deviations) are not reported in the primary reference.

SCORING: The SSA is scored by reverse-scoring items 3, 10, 13, 21, 22 and adding up the individual items for a total score, with lower scores indicating a stronger subjective appraisal of social support. In addition to the total score, the 8 "family" items make up an SSA-Family subscale and the 7 "friend" items make up a friend subscale. The remaining items refer to people or others in general.

RELIABILITY: The SSA has very good internal consistency, with alpha coefficients that range from .81 to .90. No data on stability were reported.

VALIDITY: The SSA was subjected to considerable evaluation of its validity resulting in very good concurrent, predictive, known-groups, and construct validity. The SSA is significantly correlated in predicted ways with a variety of measures of social support and psychological well-being, including network satisfaction, perceived support, family environment, depression, positive affect, negative affect, loneliness, life satisfaction, the SCL-90, and happiness.

PRIMARY REFERENCE: Vaux, A., Phillips, J., Holly, L., Thomson, B., Williams, D., and Stewart, D. (1986). The Social Support Appraisals (SSA) Scale: Studies of reliability and validity, *American Journal of Community Psychology*, 14, 195–219, Plenum Publishing Corp.

AVAILABILITY: Journal article.

SSA

Below is a list of statements about your relationships with family and friends. Please indicate how much you agree or disagree with each statement as being true.

(Circle one number in each row)

		Strongly agree	Agree	Dis- agree	Strongly disagree
1.	My friends respect me.	1	2	3	4
2.	My family cares for me very much.	1	2	3	4
3.	I am not important to others.	1	2	3	4
4.	My family holds me in high esteem.	1	2	3	4
5.	I am well liked.	1	2	3	4
6.	I can rely on my friends.	1	2	3	4
7.	I am really admired by my family.	1	2	3	4
8.	I am respected by other people.	1	2	3	4
9.	I am loved dearly by my family.	1	2	3	4
10.	My friends don't care about my welfare.	1	2	3	4
11.	Members of my family rely on me.	1	2	3	4
12.	I am held in high esteem.	1	2	3	4
13.	I can't rely on my family for support.	1	2	3	4
14.	People admire me.	1	2	3	4
15.	I feel a strong bond with my friends.	1	2	3	4
16.	My friends look out for me.	1	2	3	4
17.	I feel valued by other people.	1	2	3	4
18.	My family really respects me.	1	2	3	4

(Circle one number in each row)

		Strongly agree	Agree	Dis- agree	Strongly disagree
19.	My friends and I are really important to each other.	1	2	3	4
20.	I feel like I belong.	1	2	3	4
21.	If I died tomorrow, very few people would miss me.	1	2	3	4
22.	I don't feel close to members of my family.	1	2	3	4
23.	My friends and I have done a lot for one another.	1	2	3	4

SOCIAL SUPPORT BEHAVIORS SCALE (SSB)

AUTHORS: Alan Vaux, Sharon Riedel, and Doreen Stewart.

PURPOSE: To measure modes of social support.

DESCRIPTION: The SSB is a 45-item instrument designed to assess five modes of social support: emotional (items 3, 8, 12, 16, 20, 23, 27, 30, 31, 36), socializing (items 1, 2, 5, 9, 13, 18, 24), practical assistance (items 4, 6, 7, 11, 34, 37, 40, 43), financial assistance (items 14, 21, 26, 29, 32, 38, 41, 45), and advice/guidance (items 10, 15, 17, 19, 22, 25, 28, 33, 35, 39, 42, 44). The SSB is designed to assess available supportive behavior and to do so separately for family and friends. With slight changes in wording, the SSB can be used to tap supportive behaviors actually enacted in the face of some stressor. The five subscales have been confirmed through factor analysis. This is an important measure not only for the study of social support networks, but for use in clinical practice as a way of understanding real and potential supports available for clients.

NORMS: The SSB was studied initially in a series of five developmental studies involving over 300 undergraduate students. Males and females were roughly equally represented; most respondents were white with about 25% being black. Overall norms are not available since the testing strategy was to ask respondents to respond to the SSB in the face of particular stimulus problem conditions rather than as a general report of social support behaviors.

SCORING: Scores for the subscales and total scales are simply computed by summing individual item scores on the 5-point scales (possible range of 45–225). However, if the SSB is to be used to determine enacted social support, the scale is changed to a 2-point scale (0 = no, 1 = yes) and those item scores are summed as indicated above.

RELIABILITY: The SSB has very good internal consistency, with alphas that exceed .85 for several college samples. Data on stability are not available.

VALIDITY: The SSB has good concurrent validity, with significant correlations with social support network associations, support appraisals, and the Inventory of Socially Supportive Behaviors. The SSB subscales also are differentially sensitive to different types of support related to each mode of support.

PRIMARY REFERENCE: Vaux, A., Riedel, S., and Stewart, D. (1987). Modes of social support: The Social Support Behaviors (SSB) Scale, *American Journal of Community Psychiatry*, 15, 209–237, Plenum Publishing Corp.

AVAILABILITY: Journal article.

SSB

People help each other out in a lot of different ways. Suppose you had some kind of problem (were upset about something, needed help with a practical problem, were broke, or needed some advice or guidance), *how likely* would (a) members of your *family*, and (b) your *friends* be to help you out in each of the specific ways listed below. We realize you may rarely need this kind of help, but *if you did* would family and friends help in the ways indicated. Try to base your answers on your past experience with these people. Use the scale below, and circle one number under family, and one under friends, in each row.

1 = *No one* would do this
2 = *Someone might* do this
3 = *Some* family member/friend would *probably* do this
4 = *Some* family member/friend would *certainly* do this
5 = *Most* family members/friends would *certainly* do this

		(a) Family	(b) Friends
1.	Would suggest doing something, just to take-my mind off my problems.	1 2 3 4 5	1 2 3 4 5
2.	Would visit with me, or invite me over.	1 2 3 4 5	1 2 3 4 5
3.	Would comfort me if I was upset.	1 2 3 4 5	1 2 3 4 5
4.	Would give me a ride if I needed one.	1 2 3 4 5	1 2 3 4 5
5.	Would have lunch or dinner with me.	1 2 3 4 5	1 2 3 4 5
6.	Would look after my belongings (house, pets, etc.) for a while.	1 2 3 4 5	1 2 3 4 5
7.	Would loan me a car if I needed one.	1 2 3 4 5	1 2 3 4 5
8.	Would joke around or suggest doing something to cheer me up.	1 2 3 4 5	1 2 3 4 5
9.	Would go to a movie or concert with me.	1 2 3 4 5	1 2 3 4 5

		(a) Family	(b) Friends
10.	Would suggest how I could find out more about a situation.	1 2 3 4 5	1 2 3 4 5
11.	Would help me out with a move or other big chore.	1 2 3 4 5	1 2 3 4 5
12.	Would listen if I needed to talk about my feelings.	1 2 3 4 5	1 2 3 4 5
13.	Would have a good time with me.	1 2 3 4 5	1 2 3 4 5
14.	Would pay for my lunch if I was broke.	1 2 3 4 5	1 2 3 4 5
15.	Would suggest a way I might do something.	1 2 3 4 5	1 2 3 4 5
16.	Would give me encouragement to do something difficult.	1 2 3 4 5	1 2 3 4 5
17.	Would give me advice about what to do.	1 2 3 4 5	1 2 3 4 5
18.	Would chat with me.	1 2 3 4 5	1 2 3 4 5
19.	Would help me figure out what I wanted to do.	1 2 3 4 5	1 2 3 4 5
20.	Would show me that they understood how I was feeling.	1 2 3 4 5	1 2 3 4 5
21.	Would buy me a drink if I was short of money.	1 2 3 4 5	1 2 3 4 5
22.	Would help me decide what to do.	1 2 3 4 5	1 2 3 4 5
23.	Would give me a hug, or otherwise show me I was cared about.	1 2 3 4 5	1 2 3 4 5
24.	Would call me just to see how I was doing.	1 2 3 4 5	1 2 3 4 5
25.	Would help me figure out what was going on.	1 2 3 4 5	1 2 3 4 5

		(a) Family	(b) Friends
26.	Would help me out with some necessary purchase.	1 2 3 4 5	1 2 3 4 5
27.	Would not pass judgment on me.	1 2 3 4 5	1 2 3 4 5
28.	Would tell me who to talk to for help.	1 2 3 4 5	1 2 3 4 5
29.	Would loan me money for an indefinite period.	1 2 3 4 5	1 2 3 4 5
30.	Would be sympathetic if I was upset.	1 2 3 4 5	1 2 3 4 5
31.	Would stick by me in a crunch.	1 2 3 4 5	1 2 3 4 5
32.	Would buy me clothes if I was short of money.	1 2 3 4 5	1 2 3 4 5
33.	Would tell me about the available choices and options.	1 2 3 4 5	1 2 3 4 5
34.	Would loan me tools, equipment or appliances if I needed them.	1 2 3 4 5	1 2 3 4 5
35.	Would give me reasons why I should or should not do something.	1 2 3 4 5	1 2 3 4 5
36.	Would show affection for me.	1 2 3 4 5	1 2 3 4 5
37.	Would show me how to do something I didn't know how to do.	1 2 3 4 5	1 2 3 4 5
38.	Would bring me little presents of things I needed.	1 2 3 4 5	1 2 3 4 5
39.	Would tell me the best way to get something done.	1 2 3 4 5	1 2 3 4 5
40.	Would talk to other people, to arrange something for me.	1 2 3 4 5	1 2 3 4 5
41.	Would loan me money and want to "forget about it."	1 2 3 4 5	1 2 3 4 5
42.	Would tell me what to do.	1 2 3 4 5	1 2 3 4 5

		(a) Family	(b) Friends
43.	Would offer me a place to stay for a while.	1 2 3 4 5	1 2 3 4 5
44.	Would help me think about a problem.	1 2 3 4 5	1 2 3 4 5
45.	Would loan me a fairly large sum of money (say the equivalent of a month's rent or mortgage).	1 2 3 4 5	1 2 3 4 5

SOCIOPOLITICAL CONTROL SCALE (SPCS)

AUTHORS: Marc A. Zimmerman and James H. Zahniser

PURPOSE: To measure sociopolitical control.

DESCRIPTION: The SPCS is a 17-item instrument that attempts to distinguish sociopolitical control from other types of perceived control. The SPCS is based on the assumption that perceived control includes personality, cognitive, and motivational variables, all of which are built into this scale, and differs across different life spheres. The SPCS has two subscales, leadership competence (items 5–8, 14–17) and policy control (items 1–4, 9–13). This scale is especially useful for clinicians involved in some form of community practice, wherein the scale can be used to measure the sense of empowerment in clients or help in understanding the experiences of volunteers, activists, and community isolates.

NORMS: The SPCS was studied with three samples: sample 1 involved 390 undergraduates (50% female, 88% white) enrolled in an introductory psychology class; sample 2 involved 205 community residents recruited at voluntary organization meetings (55% female, 92% white, mean age = 42); sample 3 involved 143 people from four Methodist churches (52% female, 96% white, mean age = 38). On the original scales, scores were standardized and then summed producing means of 0 with deviations from 0 indicating responses above or below the average respondent.

SCORING: To simplify scoring, items on each subscale can simply be summed for a subscale score after reverse-scoring items 9–17. Thus, higher scores would indicate higher leadership competence and policy control.

RELIABILITY: The SPCS has fairly good internal consistency, with alphas for the subscales that range from .75 to .78. No data on stability were reported.

VALIDITY: The SPCS has good construct validity, with correlations in the predicted directions with locus of control measures, alienation measures, and a measure of willingness to lead. Both subscales differed across groups with different levels of participation in community activities.

PRIMARY REFERENCE: Zimmerman, M. A. and Zahniser, J. H. (1991). Refinements of sphere-specific measures of perceived control: Development of a Sociopolitical Control Scale, *Journal of Community Psychology*, 19, 189–204.

AVAILABILITY: Dr. Marc Zimmerman, Department of Health Behavior and Health Education, University of Michigan School of Public Health, Ann Arbor, MI 48109-2029.

SPCS

Please use the 6-point scale below to indicate how strongly you agree or disagree with each of the following statements as they apply to you. Place the number from 1–6 in the blank to the left of each statement.

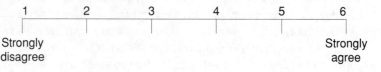

| 1 | 2 | 3 | 4 | 5 | 6 |

Strongly
disagree

Strongly
agree

_____ 1. There are plenty of ways for people like me to have a say in what our government does.

_____ 2. People like me are generally well qualified to participate in the political activity and decision making in our country.

_____ 3. I feel like I have a pretty good understanding of the important political issues which confront our society.

_____ 4. I enjoy political participation because I want to have as much say in running government as possible.

_____ 5. I am often a leader in groups.

_____ 6. I can usually organize people to get things done.

_____ 7. I would prefer to be a leader rather than a follower.

_____ 8. Other people usually follow my ideas.

_____ 9. A good many local elections aren't important enough to bother with.

_____ 10. So many other people are active in local issues and organizations that it doesn't matter much to me whether I participate or not.

_____ 11. It hardly makes any difference who I vote for because whoever gets elected does whatever he wants to do anyway.

_____ 12. Most public officials wouldn't listen to me no matter what I did.

_____ 13. Sometimes politics and government seem so complicated that a person like me can't really understand what's going on.

_____ 14. I like to wait and see if someone else is going to solve a problem so that I don't have to be bothered by it.

_____ 15. I would rather not try something I'm not good at.

_____ 16. I find it very hard to talk in front of a group.

_____ 17. I would rather someone else took over the leadership role when I 'm involved in a group project.

SOMATIC, COGNITIVE, BEHAVIORAL ANXIETY INVENTORY (SCBAI)

AUTHORS: Paul M. Lehrer and Robert L. Woolfolk

PURPOSE: To measure the components of anxiety.

DESCRIPTION: The SCBAI is a 36-item instrument designed to measure the three key components of anxiety: behavior (social avoidance), cognition (worrying), and somatic (hyperventilation). This inventory was based on previous research that showed that different types or components of anxiety do not necessarily correlate highly with each other. Items for this inventory were derived from a variety of already well-established anxiety measures as well as from the authors' clinical experiences. Separate studies decreased the size of the measure from 112 to the current items. All items load over .5 on their respective factors. The three subscales are: somatic (items 1, 2, 4, 7, 10, 13, 14, 18, 20, 23, 29, 30, 31, 33, 34, 35); behavioral (items 3, 6, 9, 12, 17, 22, 25, 26, 28); and cognitive (items 5, 8, 11, 15, 16, 19, 21, 24, 27, 32, 36). This measure is viewed as particularly valuable for therapeutic work since various types of anxiety might respond differentially to different kinds of treatment.

NORMS: The SCBAI was developed in a series of five studies. A total of 621 subjects were involved, most of whom were male and female college students, plus 70 neurotic psychiatric patients, 67 participants in a stress workshop, and 67 nonpsychotic anxious clients of several psychotherapists. Actual norms (means and standard deviations) are not reported.

SCORING: The SCBAI is scored by adding up item scores for scores on subscales as well as the total score. The higher the score, the greater the level of anxiety. Since the purpose of this measure is to focus on the components of anxiety, the total score is less a point of focus than the three subscales.

RELIABILITY: The SCBAI has excellent internal consistency, with split-half reliability coefficients of .93 for the somatic factor, .92 for the behavioral factor, and .92 for the cognitive factor. Test-retest data are not reported.

VALIDITY: The SCBAI has very good concurrent validity, with the three subscales correlating significantly with several relevant measures: the Spielberger Trait Anxiety, Eysenck Neuroticism, Eysenck Introversion, SCL-90, and the IPAT Anxiety Inventory. The SCBAI also is sensitive to change in clinical practice with the behavior subscale showing significant change following a behavioral treatment group and the cognitive subscale showing significant change following a cognitive therapy group. However, the SCBAI is also highly correlated with the Edwards Social Desirability Scale, indicating that some 25–35% of the variance in each subscale is due to social desirability.

PRIMARY REFERENCE: Lehrer, P. M. and Woolfolk, R. L. (1982). Self-report assessment of anxiety: Somatic, cognitive, and behavioral modalities, *Behavioral Assessment*, 4, 167–177.

AVAILABILITY: Dr. Paul Lehrer, Department of Psychiatry, Rutgers Medical School, Piscataway, NJ 08854.

SCBAI

Please circle the number that indicates how you feel for each item. *For example*, if you feel happy often, but not all the time, put:

I feel happy.

    0   1   2   3   4   5   (6)   7   8
    Never   Extremely often

1.   My throat gets dry.

    0   1   2   3   4   5   6   7   8
    Never   Extremely often

2.   I have difficulty in swallowing.

    0   1   2   3   4   5   6   7   8
    Never   Extremely often

3.   I try to avoid starting conversations.

    0   1   2   3   4   5   6   7   8
    Never   Extremely often

4.   My heart pounds.

    0   1   2   3   4   5   6   7   8
    Never   Extremely often

5.   I picture some future misfortune.

    0   1   2   3   4   5   6   7   8
    Never   Extremely often

6.   I avoid talking to people in authority (my boss, policemen).

    0   1   2   3   4   5   6   7   8
    Never   Extremely often

7.   My limbs tremble.

    0   1   2   3   4   5   6   7   8
    Never   Extremely often

8.   I can't get some thought out of my mind.

    0   1   2   3   4   5   6   7   8
    Never   Extremely often

9.   I avoid going into a room by myself where people are already gathered and talking.

         0   1   2   3   4   5   6   7   8
       Never   Extremely often

10.   My stomach hurts.

         0   1   2   3   4   5   6   7   8
       Never   Extremely often

11.   I dwell on mistakes that I have make.

         0   1   2   3   4   5   6   7   8
       Never   Extremely often

12.   I avoid new or unfamiliar situations.

         0   1   2   3   4   5   6   7   8
       Never   Extremely often

13.   My neck feels tight.

         0   1   2   3   4   5   6   7   8
       Never   Extremely often

14.   I feel dizzy.

         0   1   2   3   4   5   6   7   8
       Never   Extremely often

15.   I think about possible misfortunes to my loved ones.

         0   1   2   3   4   5   6   7   8
       Never   Extremely often

16.   I cannot concentrate at a task or job without irrelevant thoughts intruding.

         0   1   2   3   4   5   6   7   8
       Never   Extremely often

17.   I pass by school friends, or people I know but have not seen me for a long time, unless they speak to me first.

         0   1   2   3   4   5   6   7   8
       Never   Extremely often

18. I breathe rapidly.

```
     0     1     2     3     4     5     6     7     8
   Never                                      Extremely often
```

19. I keep busy to avoid uncomfortable thoughts.

```
     0     1     2     3     4     5     6     7     8
   Never                                      Extremely often
```

20. I can't catch my breath.

```
     0     1     2     3     4     5     6     7     8
   Never                                      Extremely often
```

21. I can't get some pictures or images out of my mind.

```
     0     1     2     3     4     5     6     7     8
   Never                                      Extremely often
```

22. I try to avoid social gatherings.

```
     0     1     2     3     4     5     6     7     8
   Never                                      Extremely often
```

23. My arms or legs feel stiff.

```
     0     1     2     3     4     5     6     7     8
   Never                                      Extremely often
```

24. I imagine myself appearing foolish with a person whose opinion of me is important.

```
     0     1     2     3     4     5     6     7     8
   Never                                      Extremely often
```

25. I find myself staying home rather than involving myself in activities outside.

```
     0     1     2     3     4     5     6     7     8
   Never                                      Extremely often
```

26. I prefer to avoid making specific plans for self-improvement.

```
     0     1     2     3     4     5     6     7     8
   Never                                      Extremely often
```

27. I am concerned that others might not think well of me.

```
     0     1     2     3     4     5     6     7     8
   Never                                      Extremely often
```

28. I try to avoid challenging jobs.

    0   1   2   3   4   5   6   7   8
Never   Extremely often

29. My muscles twitch or jump.

    0   1   2   3   4   5   6   7   8
Never   Extremely often

30. I experience a tingling sensation somewhere in my body.

    0   1   2   3   4   5   6   7   8
Never   Extremely often

31. My arms or legs feel weak.

    0   1   2   3   4   5   6   7   8
Never   Extremely often

32. I have to be careful not to let my real feelings show.

    0   1   2   3   4   5   6   7   8
Never   Extremely often

33. I experience muscular aches and pains.

    0   1   2   3   4   5   6   7   8
Never   Extremely often

34. I feel numbness in my face, limbs, or tongue.

    0   1   2   3   4   5   6   7   8
Never   Extremely often

35. I experience chest pains.

    0   1   2   3   4   5   6   7   8
Never   Extremely often

36. I have an uneasy feeling.

    0   1   2   3   4   5   6   7   8
Never   Extremely often

SPLITTING SCALE (SS)

AUTHOR: Mary-Joan Gerson

PURPOSE: To measure the characterological use of splitting as a defense mechanism.

DESCRIPTION: This 14-item instrument draws from the theories of Kernberg and Kohut who view splitting as a symptom of borderline and narcissistic personality disorders. The function of splitting is to keep ambivalence at bay. Splitting is manifested in radical shifts in evaluations both of self and other, merging of self and other, disassociated grandiosity, and exhibitionism. The defense of splitting is defined as the separation of "good" or idealized objects from "bad" or devalued objects. There does not appear to be a gender difference on the SS, even though females are diagnosed as borderline personality more frequently than males. The SS score is reportedly not associated with age.

NORMS: The SS was developed on a sample of 41 female and 34 male graduate students in psychology. The average age was 27.7 years for men and 30 for women. The mean SS was 52.97 with a standard deviation of 11.46, and ranged from 26 to 79. The SS was also developed on a sample of 113 female and 75 male patients from an urban health clinic. The age of this sample ranged from 21 to 42. Normative data are not presented.

SCORING: All items are phrased to reflect the splitting defense mechanism. Respondents are asked to rate how "true" each item is to him or her. Ratings range from 1, "not at all," to 7, "very true." Scores are the total of each item rating and range from 14 to 98. Higher scores reflect characterological use of splitting.

RELIABILITY: The reliability of the SS has been estimated through internal consistency and test-retest. The alpha coefficient was moderate (.70) but acceptable for an instrument tapping such an illusive concept. The SS was quite stable, with a test-retest correlation of .84 over a three-week period.

VALIDITY: The SS has fairly good concurrent validity evidence, with scores correlating positively with a measure of narcissistic personality, and negatively with self-esteem. The negative and positive criterion-related validity coefficients are consistent with the ego-oriented theory of this borderline defense.

PRIMARY REFERENCE: Gerson, M.-J. (1984). Splitting: The development of a measure, *Journal of Clinical Psychology*, 40, 157–162. Instrument reproduced with permission of Mary-Joan Gerson.

AVAILABILITY: Journal article.

SS

Below are fourteen questions. Please read each question and indicate in the space to the left how true each is for you using the following scale:

1 = Not at all true
2 = A little true
3 = Slightly true
4 = Somewhat true
5 = Moderately true
6 = Considerably true
7 = Very true

_____ 1. I hate to hear someone close to me being criticized.
_____ 2. When I'm with someone really terrific, I feel dumb.
_____ 3. When I'm angry, everyone around me seems rotten.
_____ 4. My friends don't know how much I'd like to be admired by people.
_____ 5. It's hard for me to get angry at people I like.
_____ 6. It's very painful when someone disappoints me.
_____ 7. I have absolutely no sympathy for people who abuse their children.
_____ 8. Sometimes I feel I could do anything in the world.
_____ 9. There are times my wife (husband)/girlfriend (boyfriend) seems as strong as iron, and at other times as helpless as a baby. (Consider your most recent relationship in the absence of an ongoing relationship.)
_____ 10. I often feel that I can't put the different parts of my personality together, so that there is one "me."
_____ 11. Sometimes I feel my love is dangerous.
_____ 12. When I'm in a new situation, there's often one person I really dislike.
_____ 13. It's hard for me to become sexually excited when I'm depressed.
_____ 14. Some people have too much power over me.

STATE-TRAIT ANGER SCALE (STAS)

AUTHORS: Charles Spielberger and Perry London

PURPOSE: To measure the state and trait of anger.

DESCRIPTION: The 30 items that make up this instrument assess anger both as an emotional state that varies in intensity, and as a relatively stable personality trait. State anger is defined as an emotional condition consisting of subjective feelings of tension, annoyance, irritation, or rage. Trait anger is defined in terms of how frequently a respondent feels state anger over time. A person high in trait anger would tend to perceive more situations as anger provoking and respond with higher state-anger scores. In this framework, anger differs from hostility, which connotes a set of attitudes that mediate aggressive behavior. The instruments were developed with rigorous psychometric procedures, including the development of long and short forms which were highly correlated, ranging from .95 for state anger to .99 for trait anger. A short form of the state-anger scale (SAS) is composed of the following items: 1, 2, 3, 7, 8, 9, 10, 11, 12, and 13. A short form of the trait-anger scale (TAS) is composed of items 1, 2, 3, 5, 6, 7, 8, 9, 11, and 14. Trait anger can also be assessed with two subscales: anger temperament and anger reaction.

NORMS: Extensive normative data are available from samples of high school students ($n = 3016$), college students ($n = 1621$), working adults ($n = 1252$), and military recruits ($n = 2360$). For a subsample of working adult women who were between 23 and 32 years old, the mean scores for the state anger, trait anger, angry temperament, and angry reaction were 13.71, 18.45, 5.99, and 9.48, respectively. For a subsample of working adult men with ages ranging from 23 to 32, the mean scores for the same scales were 14.28, 18.49, 5.9, and 9.5.

SCORING: The trait-anger items are rated on 4-point scales from "almost never" (1) to "almost always" (4). Scores are the sum of the item ratings. Subscale items are: anger temperament, 1, 2, 3, and 8; anger reaction, 5, 6, 7, and 9. The state-anger items are rated on intensity of feelings from "not at all" (1) to "very much so" (4). Scores are the sum of the state-anger items. For both state and trait anger, scores range from 10 to 40 for the 10-item short forms and from 15 to 60 for the long forms. Higher scores reflect greater anger.

RELIABILITY: The STAS has very good reliability. The internal consistency of the original 15-item trait-anger measure was .87 for a sample of 146 college students. The trait-anger measure had an internal consistency of .87 for male navy recruits and .84 for female navy recruits. The original state-anger measure has excellent internal consistency, with correlations of .93 for male and female navy recruits. The anger temperament subscale had internal consistency coefficients ranging from .84 to .89 for male and female college students and navy recruits. The angry reaction subscale had internal consistency coefficients ranging from .70 to .75 for the same samples. Internal consistency, reported for the 10-item forms using the same samples, is good to excellent. All internal consistency results are based on Cronbach's alpha.

VALIDITY: Concurrent validity support is evidenced by correlations with three measures of hostility, and measures of neuroticism, psychotism, and anxiety. Scores were not associated with state-trait curiosity or extraversion. Additional validity findings are reported in the primary reference.

PRIMARY REFERENCES: Spielberger, C. D., Jacobs, G., Russel, S., and Crane, R. S. (1983). Assessment of anger: The State-Trait Anger Scale. In J. N. Butcher and C. D. Spielberger (eds.), *Advances in Personality Assessment*, Vol. 2, pp. 159–187. Hillsdale, N.J.: Lawrence Erlbaum Associates, Inc. See also London, P. and Spielberger, C. (1983). Job stress, hassles and medical risk, *American Health*, March, 58–63. Instruments reproduced with permission of C. D. Spielberger, *American Health* and Lawrence Erlbaum Associates, Inc.

AVAILABILITY: From primary references.

SAS

A number of statements that people have used to describe how they feel are given below. Read the statements below and indicate how you feel *at the moment* by placing the appropriate number next to each item.

1 = Not at all
2 = Somewhat
3 = Moderately so
4 = Very much so

____ 1.   I am mad.
____ 2.   I feel angry.
____ 3.   I am burned up.
____ 4.   I feel irritated.
____ 5.   I feel frustrated.
____ 6.   I feel aggravated.
____ 7.   I feel like I'm about to explode.
____ 8.   I feel like banging on the table.
____ 9.   I feel like yelling at somebody.
____ 10.   I feel like swearing.
____ 11.   I am furious.
____ 12.   I feel like hitting someone.
____ 13.   I feel like breaking things.
____ 14.   I am annoyed.
____ 15.   I am resentful.

TAS

A number of statements that people have used to describe themselves are given below. Read the statements below and indicate how you *generally* feel by placing the appropriate number next to each item.

    1 = Almost never
    2 = Sometimes
    3 = Often
    4 = Almost always

_____   1.   I have a fiery temper.
_____   2.   I am quick tempered.
_____   3.   I am a hotheaded person.
_____   4.   I get annoyed when I am singled out for correction.
_____   5.   It makes me furious when I am criticized in front of others.
_____   6.   I get angry when I'm slowed down by others' mistakes.
_____   7.   I feel infuriated when I do a good job and get a poor evaluation.
_____   8.   I fly off the handle.
_____   9.   I feel annoyed when I am not given recognition for doing good work.
_____ 10.   People who think they are always right irritate me.
_____ 11.   When I get mad, I say nasty things.
_____ 12.   I feel irritated.
_____ 13.   I feel angry.
_____ 14.   When I get frustrated, I feel like hitting someone.
_____ 15.   It makes my blood boil when I am pressured.

STRESS-AROUSAL CHECKLIST (SACL)

AUTHORS: Colin Mackay and Tom Cox

PURPOSE: To measure stress and arousal.

DESCRIPTION: The 30-item SACL consists of adjectives commonly used to describe one's psychological experience of stress. The model of stress is two-dimensional. One dimension consists of feelings ranging from pleasant to unpleasant. This is a general sense of well-being. The second dimension of stress ranges from feelings of wakefulness to drowsiness, or vigorousness. The first dimension is labeled as stress while the second is labeled arousal. The stress dimension is considered a subjective experience in response to the external environment, while the arousal dimension represents ongoing somatic or autonomic activity.

NORMS: The SACL was originally tested with a sample of 145 undergraduates, although no demographic data are reported. More recent research tested the factor structure of the SACL with 72 male and 131 female second year college students. Normative data were not reported.

SCORING: The respondent rates each adjective in terms of the intensity of his or her feelings about the adjective. For the positive adjectives, the double-plus and plus ratings are scored 1 and the question mark and minus ratings are scored 0. For the negative adjectives, the question mark and minus ratings are scored 1 and the plus and double-plus ratings are scored 0. The stress subscale consists of eight negative adjectives (2, 3, 15, 21, 22, 25, 27, 28) and ten positive stress adjectives (1, 5, 6, 9, 10, 11, 12, 13, 18, 23). The arousal subscale consists of seven positive adjectives (4, 7, 14, 19, 20, 29, 30) and five negative adjectives (8, 16, 17, 24, 26). Scores are the sum of negative and positive adjectives. Stress scores range from 0 to 18; arousal scores from 0 to 12. Higher scores reflect more stress and arousal.

RELIABILITY: Reliability data are not available. Evidence of internal consistency is provided, though, by studies using factor analysis, which generally showed adjectives were correlated with other adjectives from the same subscale of stress or arousal.

VALIDITY: The SACL has evidence of known-groups validity such that scores on the stress dimension increased as a consequence of a stressful situation. Additionally, a prolonged, monotonous and repetitive task resulted in increases in stress scores and decreases in arousal scores. The SACL has also been shown to have concurrent validity, with scores correlating with various physiological measures.

PRIMARY REFERENCES: Mackay, C., Cox, T., Burrows, G., and Lazzerini, T. (1978). An inventory for the measurement of self-reported stress and arousal, *British Journal of Social and Clinical Psychology*, 17, 283–284. McCormick, I. A., Walkey, F. H., and Taylor, A. J. W. (1985). The Stress

Arousal Checklist: An independent analysis, *Educational and Psychological Measurement*, 45, 143–146. Instrument reproduced with permission of Dr. Tom Cox.

AVAILABILITY: Dr. Tom Cox, Stress Research, Department of Psychology, University of Nottingham, Nottingham, N.G. 7 2 RD, United Kingdom.

SACL

The words shown below describe different feelings and moods. Please use this list to describe your feelings *at this moment*.

If the word *definitely* describes your feelings, circle the double plus (++). If the word *more or less* describes your feelings circle the plus (+). If you do not understand the word, or *you cannot decide* whether or not it describes how you feel, circle the question mark (?). If the word *does not describe* the way you feel, circle the minus (–).

First reactions are most reliable; therefore do not spend too long thinking about each word. Please be as honest and accurate as possible.

1.	Tense	++	+	?	–	16.	Tired	++	+	?	–
2.	Relaxed	++	+	?	–	17.	Idle	++	+	?	–
3.	Restful	++	+	?	–	18.	Up-tight	++	+	?	–
4.	Active	++	+	?	–	19.	Alert	++	+	?	–
5.	Apprehensive	++	+	?	–	20.	Lively	++	+	?	–
6.	Worried	++	+	?	–	21.	Cheerful	++	+	?	–
7.	Energetic	++	+	?	–	22.	Contented	++	+	?	–
8.	Drowsy	++	+	?	–	23.	Jittery	++	+	?	–
9.	Bothered	++	+	?	–	24.	Sluggish	++	+	?	–
10.	Uneasy	++	+	?	–	25.	Pleasant	++	+	?	–
11.	Dejected	++	+	?	–	26.	Sleepy	++	+	?	–
12.	Nervous	++	+	?	–	27.	Comfortable	++	+	?	–
13.	Distressed	++	+	?	–	28.	Calm	++	+	?	–
14.	Vigorous	++	+	?	–	29.	Stimulated	++	+	?	–
15.	Peaceful	++	+	?	–	30.	Activated	++	+	?	–

STRESSFUL SITUATIONS QUESTIONNAIRE (SSQ)

AUTHORS: William F. Hodges and James P. Felling

PURPOSE: To measure apprehension and concern in stressful situations.

DESCRIPTION: This 40-item instrument was originally developed to test hypotheses regarding stress in trait anxious subjects. It measures the level of reported apprehension or concern (anxiety) in various social situations relevant to college students. The situations are those believed to involve a loss of self-esteem. Factor analysis of the instrument produced four factors which may be used as subscales to measure apprehension in physical danger (APD), apprehension in classroom and speech situations (ACSS), apprehension of social and academic failure (ASAF), and apprehension in dating situations (ADS). The last three subscales may be summed to form one measure of apprehension in ego-threatening situations, that is, situations where one fears failure. Females and males score differently only on the APD subscale.

NORMS: The SSQ was developed on a sample of 228 undergraduate college students. One-hundred and forty-one were male and 87 were female. Means and standard deviations are not reported.

SCORING: Each item is rated in terms of degree of apprehensiveness or concern from none (1) to extreme (5). Scores are the sums of the item scores. The subscales and items are: APD: 3, 7, 10, 11, 12, 13, 14, 16, 17, 18, 28, 32, 45; ACSS: 4, 5, 20, 22, 24, 29, 37, 42; ASAD: 6, 9, 44, 15, 19, 21, 23, 25, 27, 33, 35, 38; ADS: 1, 2, 34, 41. Higher scores reflect more apprehension or concern.

RELIABILITY: No reliability data were reported.

VALIDITY: The validity of the SSQ has had some support through concurrent validity procedures. Scores on the APD were not correlated with trait anxiety, but the three subscales concerning ego-threatening situations were moderately correlated. These correlations conform to the predictions of state-trait anxiety theory. A stronger concurrent validity correlation was found between the trait anxiety measure and the combined ego-threatening stressful situations than with the state anxiety measure.

PRIMARY REFERENCE: Hodges, W. F. and Felling, F. P. (1970). Types of stressful situations and their relation to trait anxiety and sex, *Journal of Consulting and Clinical Psychology*, 34, 333–337. Instrument reproduced with permission of William F. Hodges and the American Psychological Association.

AVAILABILITY: Journal article.

SSQ

Everyone is faced with situations in life that make them feel more or less apprehensive. Below is a list of situations which you may have experienced, or might be placed in some day. First, read through the entire list; then, for each situation, indicate at left the number that best describes the degree of apprehensiveness or concern you have felt or believe you would feel if in that situation. Do not skip any items. Work rapidly and put down your first impression.

1 = None at all
2 = Slight
3 = Moderate
4 = Considerable
5 = Extreme

_____ 1. Going on a blind date.
_____ 2. Asking someone for a date to a party.
_____ 3. Seeing someone bleed profusely from a cut arm.
_____ 4. Asking a teacher to clarify an assignment in class.
_____ 5. Giving a speech in front of class.
_____ 6. Introducing a friend and forgetting his name.
_____ 7. Putting iodine on an open cut.
_____ 8. Having someone angry at you.
_____ 9. Taking a test that you expect to fail.
_____ 10. Seeing a dog run over by a car.
_____ 11. Walking in a slum alone at night.
_____ 12. Giving blood at the Blood Bank.
_____ 13. Riding in an airplane in a storm.
_____ 14. Being present at an operation or watching one in a movie.
_____ 15. Belching aloud in class.
_____ 16. Having a tooth cavity filled.
_____ 17. Climbing too steep a mountain.
_____ 18. Paying respects at the open coffin of an acquaintance.
_____ 19. Being refused membership in a social club.
_____ 20. Asking a question in class.
_____ 21. Doing poorly in a course that seems easy to others.
_____ 22. Reciting a poem in class.
_____ 23. Having your date leave a dance with someone else.
_____ 24. Reciting in language class.
_____ 25. Finding the questions on a test extremely difficult.
_____ 26. Having to ask for money that was borrowed from you.
_____ 27. Forgetting lines in a school play.
_____ 28. Riding a car going 95 miles per hour.
_____ 29. Asking a teacher to explain the grading of your test.
_____ 30. Getting hurt in a fight.
_____ 31. Telling an uninvited guest to leave a party.
_____ 32. Passing a very bad traffic accident.
_____ 33. Being the only person at a party not dressed up.
_____ 34. Introducing yourself to someone attractive of the opposite sex.

____	35.	Spilling your drink on yourself at a formal dinner party.
____	36.	Having an interview for a job.
____	37.	Volunteering an answer to a question in class.
____	38.	Getting back a test you think you may have failed.
____	39.	Skiing out of control.
____	40.	Asking the person behind you to stop kicking your seat.
____	41.	Kissing a date for the first time.
____	42.	Asking a teacher to explain a question during a test.
____	43.	Asking people in a study room to make less noise.
____	44.	Being in a difficult course for which you have inadequate background.
____	45.	Participating in a psychology experiment in which you receive electric shock.

STUDENT JENKINS ACTIVITY SURVEY (SJAS)

AUTHORS: Paul R. Yarnold and Fred B. Bryant

PURPOSE: To measure Type A behavior.

DESCRIPTION: The SJAS is a 21-item instrument designed to measure Type A behaviors: coronary-prone behaviors that consist of time urgent/impatient, hard-driving/competitive, and aggressive/hostile behaviors. The SJAS has three factors or subscales: hard-driving/competitive (items 1, 8–12, 15, 16, 19–21), rapid eating (items 3, 4), and rapid speaking (items 5, 6). The three factors explain roughly 82% of the variance in SJAS scores. Because of the importance of Type A behavior as an established risk factor for coronary-artery disease and heart disease, this measure is viewed as an especially important predictor for physical health and for monitoring clinical changes in Type A behaviors. The SJAS is recommended for use primarily with young adults, particularly those in college.

NORMS: The SJAS has been extensively studied with a wide variety of college age samples. These include undergraduate samples of 1248, 4072, and 1810 American students, and 117 students in Greece. Males and females were represented in roughly equal proportions. The mean total score for 4072 undergraduates was 7.77 (SD = 3.25), while the mean for the hard-driving/competitive subscale was 2.24 (SD = 1.56). Whites have higher scores on the SJAS (more Type A) than nonwhites.

SCORING: The SJAS is scored by assigning one point for each "correct" response: 1a or b, 2a or b, 3a or b, 4a, 5a, 6a, 7c, 8a or b, 9a or b, 10a or b, 11c, 12d, 13a or b, 14a, 15c, 16c, 17a, 18c, 19c, 20a, 21a. The total score is just a sum of all item scores with a range of 0 to 21. For the subscale scores, simply sum the items on the appropriate subscale as described above. To classify respondents as Type A or Type B, find the median and classify all subjects above the median as Type A and below the median as Type B. The cutting point for the total score, above which subjects are classified as Type A is 10, and for the hard-driving/competitive subscale, the cutting point is 3.

RELIABILITY: The SJAS has only fair internal consistency, with alphas that range from .40 to .72. However, the SJAS has excellent stability, with test-retest reliabilities for two weeks that range from .90 to .96 and for three months, from .74 to .86.

VALIDITY: Although not a great deal of information on validity is available, the adult version of the SJAS has been shown to be a predictor of clinical coronary disease, suggesting good predictive validity.

PRIMARY REFERENCE: Yarnold, P. R., Mueser, K. T., Grav, B. W., and Grimm, L. G. (1986). The reliability of the student version of the Jenkins Activity Survey, *Journal of Behavioral Medicine*, 9, 401–414.

AVAILABILITY: Dr. Paul R. Yarnold, Northwestern University Medical School, 750 N. Lake Shore Drive, Room 626, Chicago, IL 60611.

SJAS

In the questions which follow there are no "correct" or "incorrect" answers; the important thing is to answer each question AS IT IS TRUE FOR YOU. Your answers are considered strictly confidential—for research purposes only. In addition, your responses are valuable only if you complete each and every question, so be sure to complete every question.

1. Is your everyday life filled mostly by:

    a)   Problems needing solutions
    b)   Challenges needing to be met
    c)   A rather predictable routine of events
    d)   Not enough things to keep me interested or busy

2. When you are under pressure or stress, do you usually:

    a)   Do something about it immediately
    b)   Plan carefully before taking any action

3. Ordinarily, how rapidly do you eat?

    a)   I'm usually the first one finished
    b)   I eat a little faster than average
    c)   I eat at about the same speed as most people
    d)   I eat more slowly than most people

4. Has your spouse or some friend ever told you that you eat too fast?

    a)   Yes, often
    b)   Yes, once or twice
    c)   No, no one has told me this

5. When you listen to someone talking, and this person takes too long to come to the point, do you feel like hurrying them along?

    a)   Frequently
    b)   Occasionally
    c)   Almost never

6. How often do you actually "put words in his mouth" in order to speed things up?

    a)   Frequently
    b)   Occasionally
    c)   Almost never

7. If you tell your spouse or a friend that you will meet them somewhere at a definite time, how often do you arrive late?

   a) Once in a while
   b) Rarely
   c) I am never late

8. Do most people consider you to be:

   a) Definitely hard-driving and competitive
   b) Probably hard-driving and competitive
   c) Probably more relaxed and easy going
   d) Definitely more relaxed and easy going

9. Nowadays, do you consider yourself to be:

   a) Definitely hard-driving and competitive
   b) Probably hard-driving and competitive
   c) Probably more relaxed and easy going
   d) Definitely more relaxed and easy going

10. How would your spouse (or closest friend) rate you?
   a) Definitely hard-driving and competitive
   b) Probably hard-driving and competitive
   c) Probably more relaxed and easy going
   d) Definitely more relaxed and easy going

11. How would your spouse (or best friend) rate your general level of activity?

   a) Too slow. Should be more active.
   b) About average. Is busy most of the time.
   c) Too active. Needs to slow down.

12. Would people who know you well agree that you have less energy than most people?

   a) Definitely yes
   b) Probably yes
   c) Probably no
   d) Definitely no

13. How was your "temper" when you were younger?

   a) Fiery and hard to control
   b) Strong, but controllable
   c) I almost never get angry

14. How often are there deadlines in your courses?

    a)   Daily or more often
    b)   Weekly
    c)   Monthly
    d)   Never

15. Do you ever set deadlines or quotas for yourself in courses or other things?

    a)   No
    b)   Yes, but only occasionally
    c)   Yes, regularly

16. In school, do you ever keep two projects moving forward at the same time by shifting back and forth rapidly from one to the other?

    a)   No, never
    b)   Yes, but only in emergencies
    c)   Yes, regularly

17. Do you maintain a regular study schedule during vacations such as Thanksgiving, Christmas, and Easter?

    a)   Yes
    b)   No
    c)   Sometimes

18. How often do you bring your work home with you at night or study materials related to your courses?

    a)   Rarely or never
    b)   Once a week or less often
    c)   More than once a week

19. When you are in a group, do the other people tend to look to you to provide leadership?

    a)   Rarely
    b)   About as often as they look to others
    c)   More often than they look to others

In the two questions immediately following, please compare yourself with the average student at your university.

20. In sense of responsibility, I am:

    a)   Much more responsible
    b)   A little more responsible
    c)   A little less responsible
    d)   Much less responsible

21.   I approach life in general

    a)   Much more seriously
    b)   A little more seriously
    c)   A little less seriously
    d)   Much less seriously

SURVEY OF HETEROSEXUAL INTERACTIONS (SHI)

AUTHORS: Craig T. Twentyman and Richard M. McFall

PURPOSE: To measure heterosexual avoidance in males.

DESCRIPTION: The SHI is a 20-item instrument designed to evaluate males' ability to handle social situations involving interaction with women. Several studies have shown the SHI to be a useful device for identifying individuals who tend to experience difficulties in heterosocial interactions. It can also be used clinically to examine changes in clients' abilities to deal with specific heterosexual problems.

NORMS: The SHI has been used in a series of studies with samples consisting solely of undergraduate males, mainly from introductory psychology classes, with the total number of subjects exceeding 2200. No other demographic data were reported. The mean SHI score for the first 604 respondents was 88.21. However, respondents rated as daters were reported as scoring above 100 on the SHI while nondaters scored below 70.

SCORING: The SHI is scored by summing the individual items (on a 1 to 7 scale) to produce the overall score, which can range from 20 to 140. Higher scores indicate more heterosocial competence or less heterosocial avoidance.

RELIABILITY: The SHI has very good internal consistency, with split-half correlations of .85, and excellent stability with a four-month test-retest correlation of .85.

VALIDITY: The SHI has very good concurrent validity, correlating significantly with reported anxiety in heterosocial situations and with self-reported behavior in social situations. The SHI also has good known-groups validity, distinguishing significantly between dating and nondating and shy and nonshy respondents. The SHI also has been found to be sensitive to changes following counseling.

PRIMARY REFERENCE: Twentyman, C., Boland, T., and McFall, R. M. (1981). Heterosocial avoidance in college males, *Behavior Modification*, 5, 523–552. Instrument reproduced with permission of Craig Twentyman and Sage Publications.

AVAILABILITY: Journal article.

SHI

This questionnaire is concerned with the social behavior of college males. We are interested in what might be broadly defined as "dating behavior." The term "date" used here is to mean any behavior in which some social activity was participated in and planned with a member of the opposite sex. Examples of this type of behavior might include going to the movies, a football game, a party, or even just getting together with some friends.

1. How many "dates" have you had in the last four weeks? Please be exact. _____
2. Estimate the average number of "dates" per month during the past year. _____
3. How many different women have you "dated" during the past year? _____
4. How would you compare yourself with other persons your age with regard to the amount of social behavior you participate in with the opposite sex?

1	2	3	4	5	6	7
Participate in less than an average amount of social behavior			Participate in an average amount of social behavior		Participate in more than an average amount of social behavior	

ITEMS

1. You want to call a woman up for a date. This is the first time you are calling her up as you only know her slightly. When you get ready to make the call, your roommate comes into the room, sits down on his bed, and begins reading a magazine. In this situation you would

1	2	3	4	5	6	7
be unable to call in every case			be able to call in some cases		be able to call in every case	

2. You are at a dance. You see a very attractive woman whom you do not know. She is standing *alone* and you would like to dance with her. You would

1	2	3	4	5	6	7
be unable to ask her in every case			be able to ask her in some cases		be able to ask her in every case	

3. You are at a party and you see two women talking. You do not know these women but you would like to know one of them better. In this situation you would

1	2	3	4	5	6	7
be unable to initiate a conversation			be able to initiate a conversation in some cases		be able to initiate a conversation in every case	

4. You are at a bar where there is also dancing. You see a couple of women sitting in a booth. One, whom you do not know, is talking with a fellow who is standing by the booth. These two go over to dance leaving the other woman sitting alone. You have seen this woman around, but do not really know her. You would like to go over and talk with her (but you wouldn't like to dance). In this situation you would

1	2	3	4	5	6	7
be unable to go over and talk to her			be able to go over and talk to her in some cases		be able to go over and talk to her in every case	

5. In a work break at your job you see a woman who also works there and is about your age. You would like to talk to her, but you do not know her. You would

1	2	3	4	5	6	7
be unable to talk to her in every case			be able to talk to her in some cases		be able to talk to her in every case	

6. You are on a crowded bus. A woman you know only *slightly* is sitting in front of you. You would like to talk to her but you notice that the fellow sitting next to her is watching you. You would

1	2	3	4	5	6	7
be unable to talk to her in every case			be able to talk to her in some cases		be able to talk to her in every case	

7. You are at a dance. You see an attractive woman whom you do not know, standing *in a group* of four women. You would like to dance. In this situation you would

1	2	3	4	5	6	7
be unable to ask her in every case			be able to ask her in some cases		be able to ask her in every case	

8. You are at a drugstore counter eating lunch. A woman whom you do not know sits down beside you. You would like to talk to her. After her meal comes she asks you to pass the sugar. In this situation you would pass the sugar

1	2	3	4	5	6	7
but be unable to initiate a conversation with her			and be able to initiate a conversation in some cases		and be able to initiate a conversation in every case	

9. A friend of yours is going out with his girlfriend this weekend. He wants you to come along and gives you the name and phone number of a woman he says would be a good date. You are not doing anything this weekend. In this situation you would

1	2	3	4	5	6	7
be unable to call in every case			be able to call in some cases		be able to call in every case	

10. You are in the library. You decide to take a break, and as you walk down the hall you see a girl whom you know only casually. She is sitting at a table and appears to be studying. You decide that you would like to ask her to get a coke with you. In this situation you would

1	2	3	4	5	6	7
be unable to ask her in every case			be able to ask her in some cases		be able to ask her in every case	

11. You want to call a woman for a date. You find this woman attractive but you do not know her. You would

1	2	3	4	5	6	7
be unable to call in every case			be able to call in some cases		be able to call in every case	

12. You are taking a class at the university. After one of your classes you see a woman whom you know. You would like to talk to her; however, she is walking with a couple of other women you do not know. You would

1	2	3	4	5	6	7
be unable to talk to her in every case			be able to talk to her in some cases		be able to talk to her in every case	

13. You have been working on a committee for the past year. There is a banquet at which you are assigned a particular seat. On one side of you there is a woman you do not know, on the other is a man you do not know. In this situation you would

1	2	3	4	5	6	7
be unable to initiate a conversation with the woman and talk only with the man			be able to initiate a conversation with the woman in some cases but talk mostly to the man		be able to initiate a conversation in every case and be able to talk equally as freely with the woman as with the man	

14. You are in the lobby of a large apartment complex waiting for a friend. As you are waiting for him to come down, a woman whom you know well walks by with another woman whom you have never seen before. The woman you know says hello and begins to talk to you. Suddenly she remembers that she left something in her room. Just before she leaves you she tells you the other woman's name. In this situation you would

1	2	3	4	5	6	7
find it very difficult to initiate a conversation with the other woman			find it only slightly difficult		find it easy to initiate and continue a conversation	

15. You are at a party at a friend's apartment. You see a woman who has come alone. You don't know her, but you would like to talk to her. In this situation you would

1	2	3	4	5	6	7
be unable to go over and talk to her			be able to go over and talk to her in some cases		be able to go over and talk to her in every case	

16. You are walking to your mailbox in the large apartment building where you live. When you get there you notice that two women are putting their names on the mailbox of the vacant apartment beneath yours. In this situation you would

1	2	3	4	5	6	7
be unable to go over and initiate a conversation			be able to go over and initiate a conversation in some cases		be able to go over and initiate a conversation in every case	

17. You are at a record store and see a woman that you once were introduced to. That was several months ago and now you have forgotten her name. You would like to talk to her. In this situation you would

1	2	3	4	5	6	7
be unable to start a conver- sation with her in every case			be able to start a conversation with her in some cases		be able to start a conversation with her in every case	

18. You are at the student union or local cafeteria where friends your age eat lunch. You have gotten your meal and are now looking for a place to sit down. Unfortunately, there are no empty tables. At one table, however, there is a woman sitting alone. In this situation you would

1	2	3	4	5	6	7
wait until another place was empty and then sit down			ask the woman if you could sit at the table but not say anything more to her		ask the woman if you could sit at the table and then initiate a conversation	

19. A couple of weeks ago you had a first date with a woman you now see walking on the street toward you. For some reason you haven't seen each other since then. You would like to talk to her but you aren't sure of what she thinks of you. In this situation you would

1	2	3	4	5	6	7
walk by without saying anything			walk up to her and say something to her in some cases		walk up to her and say some- thing in every case	

20. Generally, in most social situations involving women whom you do not know, you would

1	2	3	4	5	6	7
be unable to initiate a conversation			be able to initiate a conversation in some cases		be able to initiate a conversation in every case	

SYMPTOM QUESTIONNAIRE (SQ)

AUTHOR: Robert Kellner

PURPOSE: To measure four aspects of psychopathology and well-being.

DESCRIPTION: This 92-item instrument measures four major aspects of psychopathology: depression, anxiety, somatization, and anger-hostility. The SQ also has subscales of well-being that correspond to these four aspects, namely relaxed, contented, somatic well-being, and friendly. While longer than other instruments in the book, the checklist format and subscale structure actually provide separate and useful tools that may be administered quickly. A total of the four subscales may be used to assess total distress. Respondents simply and rapidly circle "yes" or "no" for each symptom. Some items request "true" or "false" responses in order to avoid double negatives. The SQ is quite sensitive to change over the course of treatment for persons with psychiatric disorders. It also has utility for assessing the psychological effects of persons with physical diseases. The SQ has an additional feature of assessing different time-frames of the symptoms. A respondent may indicate how he/she feels "right now," "today," or "during the past week." This is particularly useful when diurnal variations are of interest. Users need to cross-out the inappropriate time-frames that appear on the first sentence of the instructions. The SQ also is available in Spanish.

NORMS: From a sample of "normals" ($N = 50$) the means (and standard deviations) for the four symptom scales and corresponding well-being subscales are as follows: anxiety = 2.54 (2.85); relaxed = 4.7 (1.47); depression = 1.77 (2.16); contented = 5.21 (1.11); somatic = 2.82 (2.91); somatic well-being = 3.88 (1.76); hostility = 3.43 (3.32); friendly = 5.53 (1.06). For a sample of nonpsychotic-psychiatric patients, the means (and standard deviations) were: anxiety = 11.24 (5.52); relaxed = 2.53 (1.95); depressed = 10.6 (5.9); contented = 2.70 (2.16); somatic symptoms = 7.56 (5.47); somatic well-being = 2.27 (1.97); hostility = 8.0 (5.88); friendly = 3.37 (1.67).

SCORING: The SQ may be scored by hand, with transparent scoring stencils, or by a computer program. "No" is scored 0 and "yes" is scored 1. The sums of the "yes" or "true" responses compose the four symptom subscales, while the sums of the "no" or "false" responses compose the corresponding well-being subscales. Anxiety and relaxed items are: 1, 5, 8, 9*, 16*, 18, 23*, 29*, 30, 34, 36, 42, 49, 50*, 54, 59, 62, 63, 64, 68, 86, 87, 89*. Depression and contented items are: 2, 4*, 6, 7*, 24, 27, 39, 40*, 43*, 45, 47, 51*, 58, 60, 61, 66, 67, 71*, 73, 75, 76, 84, 91. Somatic and somatic well-being items are: 10*, 12, 14*, 15, 19*, 21*, 22, 28, 33, 41, 44, 46*, 52, 53, 57, 65, 72, 74, 77, 78*, 79, 85, 92. Hostility and friendly subscale items are: 3, 11, 13*, 17*, 20, 25, 26, 31*, 32, 35*, 37, 38*, 48, 55, 56, 69, 70, 80, 81, 82, 83*, 88, 90. Items with an asterisk are for the well-being subscales.

RELIABILITY: The reliability of the SQ has been estimated with several samples. Test-retest coefficients of stability over a four-week period for anxiety, depression, somatic, and hostility subscales were .71, .95, .77, and .82, respectively. Internal consistency has been assessed using split-half correlations and ranged from .75 to .95 for anxiety, .74 to .93 for depression, .57 to .84 for somatic, and .78 to .95 for hostility. These reliability estimates are based on assessing feelings over a one-week period.

VALIDITY: The SQ and subscales have excellent validity estimates determined from a variety of samples. Known-groups validity is shown by scores discriminating between psychiatric patients and "normals" in eleven different studies, as well as discriminating between different subgroups of psychiatric disorders, psychosomatic disorders, and physical diseases. Criterion-referenced validity is also reported. The SQ has been shown to be sensitive to change due to treatment, as well as to changes due to different stages of pregnancy for women undergoing amniocentesis.

PRIMARY REFERENCE: Kellner, R. (1987). A symptom questionnaire, *The Journal of Clinical Psychiatry*, 48, 268–274. Instrument reproduced with permission of Robert Kellner, M.D., Ph.D., and Physician Post-graduate Press. Copyright © 1987, Physicians Post-graduate Press.

AVAILABILITY: Dr. Robert Kellner, The University of New Mexico, School of Medicine, Department of Psychiatry, 2400 Tucker N.E., Albuquerque, NM 87131-5326.

SQ

Please describe how you have felt DURING THE PAST WEEK/TODAY/RIGHT NOW by circling the appropriate response for each word. A few times you have the choice of answering either TRUE or FALSE. Do not think long before answering. Work quickly!

1.	Nervous	Yes	No
2.	Weary	Yes	No
3.	Irritable	Yes	No
4.	Cheerful	Yes	No
5.	Tense, tensed up	Yes	No
6.	Sad, blue	Yes	No
7.	Happy	Yes	No
8.	Frightened	Yes	No
9.	Feeling calm	Yes	No
10.	Feeling healthy	Yes	No
11.	Losing temper easily	Yes	No
12.	Feeling of not enough air	True	False
13.	Feeling kind toward people	Yes	No
14.	Feeling fit	Yes	No
15.	Heavy arms or legs	Yes	No
16.	Feeling confident	Yes	No
17.	Feeling warm toward people	Yes	No
18.	Shaky	Yes	No
19.	No pains anywhere	True	False
20.	Angry	Yes	No
21.	Arms and legs feel strong	Yes	No
22.	Appetite poor	Yes	No
23.	Feeling peaceful	Yes	No
24.	Feeling unworthy	Yes	No
25.	Annoyed	Yes	No
26.	Feeling of rage	Yes	No
27.	Cannot enjoy yourself	True	False
28.	Tight head or neck	Yes	No
29.	Relaxed	Yes	No
30.	Restless	Yes	No
31.	Feeling friendly	Yes	No
32.	Feeling of hate	Yes	No
33.	Choking feeling	Yes	No
34.	Afraid	Yes	No
35.	Patient	Yes	No
36.	Scared	Yes	No
37.	Furious	Yes	No
38.	Feeling charitable, forgiving	Yes	No
39.	Feeling guilty	Yes	No
40.	Feeling well	Yes	No
41.	Feeling of pressure in head or body	Yes	No
42.	Worried	Yes	No

43.	Contented	Yes	No
44.	Weak arms or legs	Yes	No
45.	Feeling desperate, terrible	Yes	No
46.	No aches anywhere	True	False
47.	Thinking of death or dying	Yes	No
48.	Hot tempered	Yes	No
49.	Terrified	Yes	No
50.	Feeling of courage	Yes	No
51.	Enjoying yourself	Yes	No
52.	Breathing difficult	Yes	No
53.	Parts of the body feel numb or tingling	Yes	No
54.	Takes a long time to fall asleep	Yes	No
55.	Feeling hostile	Yes	No
56.	Infuriated	Yes	No
57.	Heart beating fast or pounding	Yes	No
58.	Depressed	Yes	No
59.	Jumpy	Yes	No
60.	Feeling a failure	Yes	No
61.	Not interested in things	True	False
62.	Highly strung	Yes	No
63.	Cannot relax	True	False
64.	Panicky	Yes	No
65.	Pressure on head	Yes	No
66.	Blaming yourself	Yes	No
67.	Thoughts of ending your life	Yes	No
68.	Frightening thoughts	Yes	No
69.	Enraged	Yes	No
70.	Irritated by other people	Yes	No
71.	Looking forward toward the future	Yes	No
72.	Nauseated, sick to stomach	Yes	No
73.	Feeling that life is bad	Yes	No
74.	Upset bowels or stomach	Yes	No
75.	Feeling inferior to others	Yes	No
76.	Feeling useless	Yes	No
77.	Muscle pains	Yes	No
78.	No unpleasant feeling in head or body	True	False
79.	Headaches	Yes	No
80.	Feel like attacking people	Yes	No
81.	Shaking with anger	Yes	No
82.	Mad	Yes	No
83.	Feeling of goodwill	Yes	No
84.	Feel like crying	Yes	No
85.	Cramps	Yes	No
86.	Feeling that something bad will happen	Yes	No
87.	Wound up, uptight	Yes	No
88.	Get angry quickly	Yes	No
89.	Self-confident	Yes	No
90.	Resentful	Yes	No
91.	Feeling of hopelessness	Yes	No
92.	Head pains	Yes	No

SYMPTOMS CHECKLIST (SC)

AUTHORS: Paul T. Bartone, Robert J. Ursano, Kathleen M. Wright, and Larry H. Ingraham

PURPOSE: To measure psychiatric symptoms.

DESCRIPTION: The SC is a 20-item instrument designed to measure frequency of psychiatric symptoms. The SC is based on items taken from previous measures including Stouffer's psychosomatic complaints scale and the Hopkins Symptoms Checklist. Although factor analysis showed four factors accounting for 48% of the variance (depression/withdrawal, hyperalertness, generalized anxiety, and somatic complaints), the SC typically is used as a single scale. The simplicity and brevity of the SC make it especially useful for monitoring changes in overall psychiatric symptoms.

NORMS: The SC was studied with 164 military survivor assistance officers of whom 93% were male, 85% white, 79% married, with a median age of 34. Actual norms were not provided.

SCORING: The SC is easily scored by summing item responses for a total score.

RELIABILITY: The SC has excellent internal consistency, with alphas that ranged from .90 to .93. Data on stability were not reported.

VALIDITY: The SC has good predictive validity, with respondents who had greater exposure to families affected by an air disaster and who had fewer social supports showing significantly higher SC scores.

PRIMARY REFERENCE: Bartone, P. T., Ursano, R. J., Wright, K. M., and Ingraham, L. H. (1989). The impact of a military air disaster on the health of assistance workers, *Journal of Nervous and Mental Disease*, 177, 317–328.

AVAILABILITY: Journal article.

SC

Following is a list of various troubles or complaints people sometimes have. Please indicate whether or not you experienced any of these over the past few weeks, by circling the appropriate number.

		None	A little	Often	Very often
1.	Common cold or flu.	0	1	2	3
2.	Dizziness.	0	1	2	3
3.	General aches and pains.	0	1	2	3
4.	Hands sweat and feel damp and clammy.	0	1	2	3
5.	Headaches.	0	1	2	3
6.	Muscle twitches or trembling.	0	1	2	3
7.	Nervous or tense.	0	1	2	3
8.	Rapid heart beat (not exercising).	0	1	2	3
9.	Shortness of breath (not exercising).	0	1	2	3
10.	Skin rashes.	0	1	2	3
11.	Upset stomach.	0	1	2	3
12.	Trouble sleeping.	0	1	2	3
13.	Depressed mood.	0	1	2	3
14.	Difficulty concentrating.	0	1	2	3
15.	Crying easily.	0	1	2	3
16.	Lack of appetite/loss of weight.	0	1	2	3
17.	Taking medication to sleep or calm down.	0	1	2	3
18.	Overly tired/lack of energy.	0	1	2	3
19.	Loss of interest in TV, movies, news, friends.	0	1	2	3
20.	Feeling life is pointless, meaningless.	0	1	2	3

TCU DEPRESSION (TCU-D) AND TCU DECISION-MAKING
(TCU-DM) SCALES

AUTHORS: George W. Joe, LaVerne Knezek, Deena Watson, and D. Dwayne
Simpson

PURPOSE: To measure depression and decision-making in intravenous drug
users.

DESCRIPTION: The TCU-D and TCU-DM are two parts of a 15-item instrument designed to measure depression and decision-making in intravenous
drug users. Depression is recognized as a very important problem among
intravenous drug users, while the importance of decision-making is increasing in view of the use of cognitively oriented therapies for drug use problems.
The 15-item scale actually can be used as a single scale or divided into the
two subscales: depression (items 3, 6, 10–12, 15) and decision-making
(items 1, 2, 4, 5, 7–9, 13, 14). The TCU-D and TCU-DM are viewed as useful
measures for treatment planning with drug use problems; they may also have
implications for use with other problem populations as well, especially
because of their brevity and ease of administration. These scales are part of
a package of scales of the TCU/Datar Self-Rating Scales for drug users.

NORMS: The TCU-D and TCU-DM were studied initially with 154 intravenous drug users who participated in an intravenous drug users project in
Dallas, Texas. Roughly half were black, 42% white, and 10% Hispanic; 72%
were men and 57% were unmarried. Most (54%) were unemployed. The
mean for the TCU-D was 11.4 (SD = 4.4) and for the TCU-DM was 21.3
(SD = 5.1).

SCORING: The TCU-D and TCU-DM are easily scored by summing the item
scores for each subscale. Items 3, 4, and 13 are reverse-scored.

RELIABILITY: The TCU-D and TCU-DM have fairly good internal consistency, with an alpha of .78 for depression and .77 for decision-making. No
data on stability were reported.

VALIDITY: The TCU-D has good concurrent validity, correlating .75 with the
Beck Depression Inventory. Both scales have an additional degree of concurrent validity in correlating with several behaviors: the TCU-D was
positively correlated with intravenous drug use and the TCU-DM was
negatively correlated with drug use. AIDS sex-risk behavior was positively
correlated with TCU-D and negatively correlated with TCU-DM.

PRIMARY REFERENCE: Joe, G. W., Knezek, L., Watson, D., and Simpson, D.
D. (1991). Depression and decision-making among intravenous drug users,
Psychological Reports, 68, 339–347. Instrument reproduced with permis-
sion of authors and publisher.

AVAILABILITY: Dr. D. Dwayne Simpson, Institute of Behavioral Research,
O.P.D. Box 32880, Texas Christian University, Ft. Worth, TX 76129.

TCU-D and TCU-DM

These questions ask about the way you feel or how you are. Circle the answer that tells *how much of the time* each item describes the way you have been feeling during the past week (including today).

		Never	Rarely	Some-times	Often	Almost always
1.	You make good decisions.	0	1	2	3	4
2.	You think of several different ways to solve a problem.	0	1	2	3	4
3.	You feel interested in life.	0	1	2	3	4
4.	You make decisions without thinking about consequences.	0	1	2	3	4
5.	You think about probable results of your actions.	0	1	2	3	4
6.	You feel extra tired or run down.	0	1	2	3	4
7.	You think about what causes your current problems.	0	1	2	3	4
8.	You plan ahead.	0	1	2	3	4
9.	You consider how your actions will affect others.	0	1	2	3	4
10.	You worry or brood a lot.	0	1	2	3	4
11.	You have thoughts of committing suicide.	0	1	2	3	4
12.	You feel sad or depressed.	0	1	2	3	4
13.	You have trouble making decisions.	0	1	2	3	4
14.	You analyze problems by looking at all the choices.	0	1	2	3	4
15.	You feel lonely.	0	1	2	3	4

TEMPLER DEATH ANXIETY SCALE (TDAS)

AUTHOR: Donald I. Templer

PURPOSE: To measure death anxiety.

DESCRIPTION: The TDAS is a 15-item instrument that is designed to measure respondents' anxiety about death. The TDAS includes a broad range of items and concerns about death. The instrument was carefully developed from an original pool of 40 items and has been found to be relatively free of response bias and social-desirability response set. Several factor analytic studies of the TDAS have identified a number of different factors, although essentially, the overall score is what is considered meaningful. A major advantage of the TDAS is that it has been studied and used extensively with a variety of populations. Information is available demonstrating the relationship between the TDAS and age, sex, religion, specific environmental influences, personality, physical and mental health, life expectancy, and a variety of behaviors.

NORMS: The TDAS has been tested with a variety of samples including males and females, adolescents and adults, psychiatric patients, and a number of occupational groups. Respondents total in the several thousands. Norms for some groups have been reported: means of "normal" respondents vary from 4.5 to 7.0 with TDAS scores being higher for females and psychiatric patients. For a cross-sectional sample of middle class people, the means reported were: 7.50 for youths, 7.25 for young adults, 6.85 for middle-aged, and 5.74 for elderly respondents.

SCORING: The TDAS is scored by assigning a score of one to each item correctly answered (1 = T, 2 = F, 3 = F, 4 = T, 5 = F, 6 = F, 7 = F, 8-14 = T, 15 = F), and then totaling across items.

RELIABILITY: The TDAS has fairly good internal consistency, with a Kuder-Richardson formula coefficient of .76. The TDAS also has good stability, with a three-week test-retest correlation of .83.

VALIDITY: The TDAS has good concurrent validity, correlating .74 with the Fear of Death Scale. It also has demonstrated good known-groups validity, distinguishing significantly between a group of psychiatric patients who verbalized high death anxiety and a control group.

PRIMARY REFERENCE: Lonetto, R. and Templer, D. 1. (1983). The nature of death anxiety, in C. D. Spielberger and J. N. Butcher (eds.), *Advances in Personality Assessment*, Vol 3. Hillsdale, N.J.: Lawrence Erlbaum, pp. 14–174. Instrument reproduced with permission of Donald I. Templer.

AVAILABILITY: Dr. Donald I. Templer, California School of Professional Psychology, 1350 M Street, Fresno, CA 93721.

TDAS

If a statement is true or mostly true as applied to you, circle "T."
If a statement is false or mostly false as applied to you, circle "F."

T F   1.   I am very much afraid to die.

T F   2.   The thought of death seldom enters my mind.

T F   3.   It doesn't make me nervous when people talk about death.

T F   4.   I dread to think about having to have an operation.

T F   5.   I am not at all afraid to die.

T F   6.   I am not particularly afraid of getting cancer.

T F   7.   The thought of death never bothers me.

T F   8.   I am often distressed by the way time flies so very rapidly.

T F   9.   I fear dying a painful death.

T F 10.   The subject of life after death troubles me greatly.

T F 11.   I am really scared of having a heart attack.

T F 12.   I often think about how short life really is.

T F 13.   I shudder when I hear people talking about a World War III.

T F 14.   The sight of a dead body is horrifying to me.

T F 15.   I feel that the future holds nothing for me to fear.

TEST OF NEGATIVE SOCIAL EXCHANGE (TENSE)

AUTHORS: Linda S. Ruehlman and Paul Karoly

PURPOSE: To measure negative social interactions.

DESCRIPTION: The TENSE is a 16-item instrument designed to measure negative social exchange (social interactions). It is based on the idea that the positive side of social ties—social support—has been disproportionately examined compared to negative social interactions and that few if any instruments are available that can be used in a wide variety of contexts. The TENSE was designed to measure a number of different dimensions of social interactions and applies to the general social network (not just families or peers). The TENSE has four subscales: hostility/impatience (items 1, 3, 10, 15), interference (items 5, 7, 9, 12), insensitivity (items 4, 6, 8, 11, 13), and ridicule (items 2, 14, 16).

NORMS: The TENSE was investigated with two samples involving 878 undergraduates enrolled in introductory psychology classes. Demographic information was not available for many subjects though both sexes were well represented. Means for the four subscales were 1.23 (SD = .72) for hostility/impatience (this mean is not currently valid because this subscale had 2 additional items at the time of this report), 1.07 (SD = .77) for insensitivity, .96 (SD = .80) for interference, and .88 (SD = .81) for ridicule.

SCORING: The TENSE is easily scored by summing items on each subscale and taking the mean for that subscale. Total scores are not used.

RELIABILITY: The TENSE has fair to good internal consistency, with alphas of .87 for hostility/impatience, .82 for insensitivity, .75 for interference, and .70 for ridicule. The TENSE has fair stability, with two-day test-retest correlations of .80 for hostility/impatience, .72 for insensitivity, .65 for interference, and .70 for ridicule.

VALIDITY: The TENSE has good construct validity with significant correlations in predicted directions with the Revised UCLA Loneliness Scale, Social Support and Hindrance Inventory, Inventory of Socially Supportive Behaviors, Satisfaction with Life Scale, Self-Rating Anxiety Scale, and the Beck Depression Inventory. The TENSE is negatively correlated with the Social Desirability Scale, though subsequent analyses ruled out social desirability as a potential confound.

PRIMARY REFERENCE: Ruehlman, L. S. and Karoly, P. (1991). With a little flack from my friends: Development and preliminary validation of the Test of Negative Social Exchange (TENSE), *Psychological Assessment*, 3, 97–104.

AVAILABILITY: Dr. Linda Ruehlman, Department of Psychology, Arizona State University, Tempe, AZ 85287-1104.

TENSE

The following survey concerns different types of NEGATIVE INTERACTIONS you might have had with the IMPORTANT PEOPLE IN YOUR LIFE over the PAST MONTH. Please begin by listing the first names of every *adult who currently has an impact on your life*. These important people may be those you see frequently or infrequently, they may be family or nonfamily, people you care about and/or who care about you, people you are close to, those who have some power or control over you, people you like or dislike, etc. Remember to only include ADULTS (persons 18 years of age or older) in your list.

After you have listed the names of the *important people* in your life, take a few moments to think about your interactions with them over the *past month*. Then, use the scale below to rate how often you experienced each of the following types of negative interaction with *one or more of these important people* during the past month. We are *not* concerned with how you were treated by any *one* person in particular. We'd like you to estimate *how often each negative interaction occurred* with one or more of the important people on your list. Using the following scale, select either "0," "1," "2," "3," or "4" depending on how often if happened. Write the number of your choice in the spaces to the left.

0	=	Not at all
1	=	Once or twice during the month
2	=	About once a week
3	=	Several times a week
4	=	About every day

_____ 1. Lost his or her temper with me
_____ 2. Made fun of me
_____ 3. Nagged me
_____ 4. Took advantage of me
_____ 5. Distracted me when I was doing something important
_____ 6. Took my feelings lightly
_____ 7. Was too demanding of my attention
_____ 8. Took me for granted
_____ 9. Invaded my privacy
_____ 10. Yelled at me
_____ 11. Ignored my wishes or needs
_____ 12. Prevented me from working on my goals
_____ 13. Was inconsiderate
_____ 14. Gossiped about me
_____ 15. Was angry with me
_____ 16. Laughed at me

THREAT APPRAISAL SCALE (TAS)

AUTHOR: Kenneth E. Hart

PURPOSE: To measure threat appraisal.

DESCRIPTION: The TAS is a 12-item situation-specific measure of the extent to which respondents perceive a situation as holding potential for harm to self. The TAS is rooted in cognitive-relational theory that holds that threat-appraisals are stress-relevant cognitions concerning the possibility that a taxing situation may result in damage to one's well-being. Threat appraisals are viewed as primary and secondary appraisals. Primary appraisals concern assessment of the degree to which something of personal significance is at stake and how demanding that situation may be. Secondary appraisal is the judgment of the individual's resources for coping with a stressful situation. The TAS has two subscales: primary appraisal (PA; items 1, 3, 5, 7, 9, 11) and secondary appraisal (SA; items 2, 4, 6, 8, 10, 12). The TAS may be useful in understanding the cognitions that accompany stress and as a way of monitoring changes in those cognitions as a result of therapy.

NORMS: The TAS was initially studied with 135 introductory psychology students in a large university in Houston, Texas. There were 67 men and 68 women with a mean age of 19.8 for the entire sample. No other demographic data were reported. The means for the sample were 3.8 for both subscales with standard deviations of 1.1 for PA and 1.2 for SA. The PA/SA ratio (see Scoring) mean was 1.1 (SD = 0.5).

SCORING: The TAS is scored by simply summing the individual item scores (1 to 4) for each subscale. Since the cognitive relational model proposes that perceptions of threat vary as a function of the balance between PA and SA, a PA/SA ratio score is determined by simply dividing PA scores by SA scores.

RELIABILITY: The TAS has only fair internal consistency, with an alpha of .65 for PA and .77 for SA. The alpha for the total scale was .62. No stability data were reported.

VALIDITY: The TAS has fair construct validity. It is largely uncorrelated with a variety of theoretically unrelated variables, and as a ratio measure (PA/SA) is correlated with overutilization of maladaptive coping strategies, underutilization of adaptive coping strategies, and exaggerated levels of negative emotional reactivity.

PRIMARY REFERENCE: Hart, E. K. Threat appraisals and emotional and coping responses to anger-provoking situations (unpublished manuscript).

AVAILABILITY: Dr. Kenneth E. Hart, Hofstra University, Department of Psychology, Hempstead, NY 11550.

TAS

With special reference to the stressful situation or event that you described previously, indicate the degree to which you agree or disagree with the following statements.

		Strongly disagree	Moderately disagree	Moderately agree	Strongly agree
1.	The situation was one of great importance to me.	1	2	3	4
2.	I felt in control of my emotions.	1	2	3	4
3.	The situation mattered a great deal to me.	1	2	3	4
4.	I felt in control of what it was that I was doing.	1	2	3	4
5.	The possibility existed that I might have appeared incompetent to others.	1	2	3	4
6.	I felt in control of the situation.	1	2	3	4
7.	I felt I was somehow in jeopardy.	1	2	3	4
8.	I felt confident that by putting in a lot of effort, things would be OK.	1	2	3	4
9.	The possibility existed that I might have lost the respect or approval of others.	1	2	3	4
10.	I had a great deal of confidence in my ability to solve the problem.	1	2	3	4
11.	The possibility existed that others might have thought less of me.	1	2	3	4
12.	I was confident that because of my high level of skill and general ability to solve most problems, things would be OK.	1	2	3	4

TIME URGENCY AND PERPETUAL ACTIVATION SCALE (TUPA)

AUTHORS: Logan Wright, Susan McCurdy, and Grace Rogoll

PURPOSE: To measure Type A characteristics associated with coronary heart disease.

DESCRIPTION: This 72-item instrument measures two components of Type A behavior patterns that are associated with coronary heart disease: time urgency and perpetual activation. While appearing to be longer than most instruments in this volume, the TUPA contains 25 decoy items and the scale score consists of only 47 items. The TUPA has 7 items that ascertain only time urgency (items 34, 49, 55, 63, 66, 69, 72), 9 that assess only perpetual activation (items 13, 14, 15, 18, 28, 36, 40, 45, 50), and 31 items that tap both dimensions (items 2, 3, 4, 6, 8, 9, 10, 16, 17, 20, 21, 22, 23, 25, 26, 27, 29, 31, 32, 33, 38, 41, 43, 47, 52, 57, 58, 61, 65, 67, 79). Time urgency refers to the time pressures one imposes on oneself, such as meeting deadlines and arriving on time or early for events; perpetual activation refers to excessive energy levels and being overly active, such as seen in difficulty sitting still, fast-paced behaviors, or being a "workaholic." One strong feature of the TUPA is that the items were developed from a list of time urgent and perpetual activation behaviors recorded by a sample of coronary heart disease patients; the items were then rated by another sample of patients receiving inpatient coronary care, and selected based on the correlations with structured interview assessments of time urgency and perpetual activation.

NORMS: Scores for a sample of 40 white, middle-class male noncoronary patients who were considered by their physicians as "destined" for heart disease had a mean TUPA score of 168.35 and a standard deviation of 30.14. Subjects' wives rated them slightly higher using the TUPA, with a mean of 181.06 and a standard deviation of 28.81.

SCORING: The TUPA is scored by adding the item scores for all 47 items. Total scores range from 47 to 282 with higher scores reflecting more time urgency and perpetual activation.

RELIABILITY: The 47-item TUPA has excellent internal consistency and test-retest reliability. The alpha coefficient was .91, and the coefficient of stability for a two-week interval was .90. The items forming the separate TU and PA were not sufficiently internally consistent (i.e., .54 and .73, respectively) to warrant using them as subscales.

VALIDITY: The correlations between patient ratings of the items and interview assessments of time urgency and perpetual activation may be seen as supporting the scale's concurrent validity. Scale scores correlated .43 and .45 with structured interview assessments of time urgency and perpetual activation, respectively. The sample of patients "destined" for heart disease in the opinion of their physicians had scores that correlated .61 with the physicians' rating of them on the TUPA and .57 with their wives' ratings. Total scores on two prototypes of the scale correlated with frequency of physical illness, sleep problems, respiratory illnesses, and frequency of visits to a physician. Scores on one of the prototypes were different for those who set their watches ahead from those who do not, and scores varied by the length of time it took to complete the instrument; setting a watch ahead and completion times are considered *in vivo* indicators of time urgency.

PRIMARY REFERENCE: Wright, L., McCurdy, S., and Rogoll G. (1992). The TUPA Scale: A self-report measure for the Type A subcomponent of time urgency and perpetual activation, *Psychological Assessment*, 4, 352–356. Instrument reproduced with permission of Logan Wright and the American Psychological Association.

AVAILABILITY: Dr. Logan Wright, 2701 60th Avenue NW, Norman, OK 73072.

TUPA

The following questionnaire should be completed according to how you feel at the present and as it applies to you throughout your entire life (and not just your recent past). Circle the true or untrue choice which *most* accurately describes you, the respondent. Use the following scale:

1 = *Extremely untrue* for me
2 = *Moderately untrue* for me
3 = *Slightly untrue* for me
4 = *Slightly true* for me
5 = *Moderately true* for me
6 = *Extremely true* for me

1.	I am seldom understood.	1 2 3 4 5 6
2.	During one appointment, I am already thinking about my next appointment.	1 2 3 4 5 6
3.	I schedule activities as close as possible to both sides of an appointment in order not to waste time.	1 2 3 4 5 6
4.	I hate to make a mistake dialing a phone number and have to start all over again.	1 2 3 4 5 6
5.	I have a problem with appetite.	1 2 3 4 5 6
6.	I experience a surge of energy at the beginning of a work task.	1 2 3 4 5 6
7.	The idea of speaking in front of a large crowd bothers me.	1 2 3 4 5 6
8.	I get angry, because I feel that nothing gets done at work until I get there and take control.	1 2 3 4 5 6
9.	People I know well agree that I tend to do most things in a hurry.	1 2 3 4 5 6
10.	I become impatient with people who are able to operate at a slower, less structured pace.	1 2 3 4 5 6
11.	I often have a problem saying no.	1 2 3 4 5 6
12.	I believe everyone should be required to give to charity.	1 2 3 4 5 6

13. I find it difficult to sit still and do nothing.   1 2 3 4 5 6

14. When I was in school, I held two or more offices in groups such as student council, glee club, 4-H club, sorority, or team sports.   1 2 3 4 5 6

15. People say I chew food or gum more vigorously than most people.   1 2 3 4 5 6

16. I sometimes go up stairs two at a time.   1 2 3 4 5 6

17. When driving around town, I wait until the last minute to leave and therefore must move with haste to avoid being late.   1 2 3 4 5 6

18. It is difficult for me to sit down to a long meal.   1 2 3 4 5 6

19. I seldom feel in tune with people around me.   1 2 3 4 5 6

20. In traffic, I change lanes rather than staying in a slow one.   1 2 3 4 5 6

21. I often have trouble finding time to get my hair cut or styled.   1 2 3 4 5 6

22. I have the sense that I am falling behind or that things are gaining on me.   1 2 3 4 5 6

23. I am careful to run errands in an orderly sequence, so as to do them in a minimum amount of time.   1 2 3 4 5 6

24. Living is a wonderful experience.   1 2 3 4 5 6

25. When other people talk, if they do not come to the point, I try to direct the conversation toward the central issue or otherwise keep things on track.   1 2 3 4 5 6

26. I get frustrated when fellow workers want to "visit" or casually talk with me while on the job.   1 2 3 4 5 6

27. I will take a business related phone call during a personal conversation.   1 2 3 4 5 6

28. When picking something out of a container, I dig for it quickly.   1 2 3 4 5 6

29. I usually put in an extremely full day.   1 2 3 4 5 6

30. I am not an important person.   1 2 3 4 5 6

31. I make sure the other person knows that I have   1 2 3 4 5 6
     another appointment or that I am a busy person
     during an appointment, thereby moving our meeting
     along more crisply.

32. I find it necessary to hurry much more of the time   1 2 3 4 5 6
     than my co-workers do.

33. I open things quickly and forcefully, sometimes   1 2 3 4 5 6
     ripping boxes or letters open rather than easing
     things open, or cutting them open gently with an
     opener.

34. When moving about with a group, I go first and lead   1 2 3 4 5 6
     the way, rather than standing around waiting for
     someone else to go first or figure out when to move.

35. There are times when people have control over me.   1 2 3 4 5 6

36. It is difficult for me to sit around and talk after   1 2 3 4 5 6
     finishing a meal.

37. I am sometimes a little envious of those better   1 2 3 4 5 6
     looking than me.

38. When the plans I make for the day do not go   1 2 3 4 5 6
     smoothly, I start changing them.

39. I am deeply moved by an eloquent speech.   1 2 3 4 5 6

40. More than once a week, I bring my work home with   1 2 3 4 5 6
     me at night or study materials related to my job.

41. I get angry with drivers who sit at a red light in the   1 2 3 4 5 6
     right-hand lane when I am behind them and want to
     turn right on a red light.

42. I usually have good luck in whatever I do.   1 2 3 4 5 6

43. I anticipate a green light by looking at the yellow light 1 2 3 4 5 6
     for the opposing traffic.

44. I believe most children deserve more discipline than   1 2 3 4 5 6
     they get.

45. When I must sit still, I handle an object (like a pencil), produce finger movements, move my teeth, or otherwise do not keep completely still.   1 2 3 4 5 6

46. I believe it is natural to make mistakes.   1 2 3 4 5 6

47. The only time I feel really comfortable when moving slowly is when I am sick.   1 2 3 4 5 6

48. I hate to cook.   1 2 3 4 5 6

49. I find that automated doors open too slowly, and that I often have to slow down to avoid running into them.   1 2 3 4 5 6

50. I keep my teeth pressed together, without grinding, but with my jaw muscle tense.   1 2 3 4 5 6

51. People who are lonely are lonely by choice.   1 2 3 4 5 6

52. I have more than one iron in the fire at a time.   1 2 3 4 5 6

53. There really isn't some good in everyone.   1 2 3 4 5 6

54. I sometimes forget to brush my teeth.   1 2 3 4 5 6

55. I change my route of travel on streets depending on whether or not I hit a red light (i.e., if I come to a red light and I can turn right and go a different route instead of wait through the red light, I will).   1 2 3 4 5 6

56. There is always one right solution for every problem.   1 2 3 4 5 6

57. I am demanding or hard on machinery, mechanical items, or vehicles.   1 2 3 4 5 6

58. I ease through yellow lights or edge forward when waiting for a green light.   1 2 3 4 5 6

59. I often worry about terrible things that may happen in the future.   1 2 3 4 5 6

60. I often doubt that my dreams will come true.   1 2 3 4 5 6

61. I find myself competing with fellow workers.   1 2 3 4 5 6

62. I don't enjoy gifts as much as I think I should.   1 2 3 4 5 6

63. I may be inclined to interrupt people if they are not responding in the way they should be. 1 2 3 4 5 6

64. The government refuses to tell the truth about flying saucers. 1 2 3 4 5 6

65. I have people say that I am a very busy person, one of the busiest that they have ever known. 1 2 3 4 5 6

66. I seem to anticipate that certain jobs will take less time than they eventually wind up taking. 1 2 3 4 5 6

67. I work considerably more than eight hours per day. 1 2 3 4 5 6

68. I can't take people poking fun at me. 1 2 3 4 5 6

69. When I arrive early for a meeting, I get impatient waiting for the meeting to start. 1 2 3 4 5 6

70. I have a facial grimace which I exhibit when exerting myself. 1 2 3 4 5 6

71. I enjoy pain. 1 2 3 4 5 6

72. I prepare for activities ahead of time, so I won't waste time or have to go back and get things I forgot. 1 2 3 4 5 6

TRUST IN PHYSICIAN SCALE (TPS)

AUTHORS:　Lynda A. Anderson and Robert F. Dedrick

PURPOSE:　To measure patients' trust in their physicians.

DESCRIPTION:　The TPS is an 11-item scale designed to measure patients' interpersonal trust in their primary-care physicians. This measure is based on the assumption that trust is a key ingredient defining the patient-physician relationship. Trust is defined as a person's belief that the physician's words and actions are credible, and can be relied upon, and that the physician is working in the patient's best interests. The concept of trust is recognized as dualistic, in that too little or too much may be negative. The TPS is useful in understanding patients' desires for control as well as for explaining patients' behaviors related to management of illness.

NORMS:　The TPS was studied with two samples of patients at V.A. clinics in two cities in North Carolina. Sample 1 = 160 men, mean of 11.8 years of education, mean age of 55.2, 78% married, 56.3% white. Sample 2 = 106 men, mean of 10.3 years of education, mean age of 60.9 years, 84% married and 62% white. Means ranged from 48.13 (SD = 9.86) to 57.32 (SD = 7.32).

SCORING:　The TPS is scored by reverse-scoring items 1, 5, 7, and 11 and summing all items for the total score. Higher scores reflect more of the construct (i.e., trust).

RELIABILITY:　The TPS has good to excellent internal consistency, with alphas that range from .85 to .90. No data on stability were reported.

VALIDITY:　The TPS has good construct validity, correlating in predicted directions with subscales of the Health Locus of Control Scale, with the Multidimensional Desire for Control subscales, and with patient satisfaction. The TPS also is moderately correlated with social desirability.

PRIMARY REFERENCE:　Anderson, L. A. and Dedrick, R. F. (1990). Development of the Trust in Physician Scale: A measure to assess interpersonal trust in patient-physician relationships, *Psychological Reports*, 67, 1091–1100. Instrument reproduced with permission of authors and publisher.

AVAILABILITY:　Dr. Lynda Anderson, School of Public Health, University of Michigan, 1420 Washington Heights, Ann Arbor, MI 48109.

TPS

Each item below is a statement with which you may agree or disagree. Beside each statement is a scale that ranges from strongly agree (1) to strongly disagree (5). For each item please circle the number that represents the extent to which you agree or disagree with the statement.

Please make sure that you answer every item and that you circle only one number per item. It is important that you respond according to what you actually believe and not according to how you feel you should believe or how you think we may want you to respond.

1 = Strongly agree
2 = Agree
3 = Neutral
4 = Disagree
5 = Strongly disagree

1. I doubt that my doctor really cares about me as a person.   1 2 3 4 5

2. My doctor is usually considerate of my needs and puts   1 2 3 4 5
    them first.

3. I trust my doctor so much I always try to follow his/her   1 2 3 4 5
    advice.

4. If my doctor tell me something is so, then it must be true.   1 2 3 4 5

5. I sometimes distrust my doctor's opinion and would like a   1 2 3 4 5
    second one.

6. I trust my doctor's judgments about my medical care.   1 2 3 4 5

7. I feel my doctor does *not* do everything he/she should for   1 2 3 4 5
    my medical care.

8. I trust my doctor to put my medical needs above all other   1 2 3 4 5
    considerations when treating my medical problems.

9. My doctor is a real expert in taking care of medical   1 2 3 4 5
    problems like mine.

10. I trust my doctor to tell me if a mistake was made about my 1 2 3 4 5
    treatment.

11. I sometimes worry that my doctor may not keep the   1 2 3 4 5
    information we discuss totally private.

VALUES CONFLICT RESOLUTION ASSESSMENT (VCRA)

AUTHOR: Richard T. Kinnier

PURPOSE: To measure resolution of values conflict.

DESCRIPTION: The VCRA is a 17-item instrument designed to assess the extent to which an individual is resolved about a specific values conflict. The items were constructed based on theoretical criteria found in values clarification, decision making, and related literature. The respondent first writes out an important values conflict (e.g., abortion versus adoption) that he or she is experiencing, then the decision that he or she would make at that point if forced to. Then the decision is evaluated on the 17-item scale. This is perhaps the only standardized instrument that can be used to help individuals assess their decisions and should be of value in a wide range of helping situations.

NORMS: The VCRA was studied initially with 104 graduate students (70 female and 34 male) ranging in age from 21 to 55 years (median = 32). Although actual norms are not reported, two factors were revealed: ethical-emotional resolution (items 1, 2, 6, 7, 8, 10, 11, 12, 14, 16, 17) and rational-behavioral resolution (items 3, 4, 5, 9, 13, 15).

SCORING: The VCRA is scored simply by summing item scores for the two factors and for the total score on the scale. High scores indicate better conflict resolution.

RELIABILITY: The VCRA has very good internal consistency, with alphas of .81 for ethical-emotional resolution, .76 for rational-behavioral, and .84 for the total score. The VCRA has excellent stability, with one-week test-retest correlation of .84 for ethical-emotional, .88 for rational-behavioral, and .92 for the total score.

VALIDITY: The VCRA has good construct validity, correlating significantly in predicted directions with anxiety about the conflict, self-report of conflict being resolved, and self-esteem. The VCRA also discriminates between successfully resolved conflicts and currently unresolved ones.

PRIMARY REFERENCE: Kinnier, R. T. (1987). Development of a Values Conflict Resolution Assessment, *Journal of Counseling Psychology*, 34, 34–37.

AVAILABILITY: Dr. R. T. Kinnier, Division of Psychology in Education, Payne Hall 42514, Arizona State University, Tempe, AZ 85287.

VCRA

I. CONFLICT DESCRIPTION

Read the following definitions of *values* and *values conflicts* and then describe a values conflict in your life.

Values

A person's values are his or her *beliefs about what is important in life*. Some values refer to how one should act (i.e., to be . . . honest, altruistic, competitive, self-disciplined, courageous, kind, etc.). Other values refer to what one wants to accomplish or obtain in life (i.e., to want . . . a lot of money, security, fame, a large family, meaningful friendships, world peace, equality, peace of mind, physical health, salvation, wisdom, etc.). Your values exist as a complex set of interweaving personal policies or priorities that serve as a guide for decision making. Some examples of personal value statements are: "My family always comes first," "I would rather be honest and unpopular than dishonest and popular," "I do not need to be wealthy— just comfortable," "My physical health is relatively important to me but maintaining my ideal weight is not a priority at all," "The most meaningful thing I can do with my life is to help others."

Values Conflicts

A person cannot "have it all" or "be all things." Priorities must be established and choices made. An *intra*personal values conflict occurs when an individual experiences *uncertainty about what he or she really believes or wants* and (or) when two or more *priorities or beliefs conflict or seem incompatible* to the person. The following are examples:

"I want to be very successful in my career, but I also want a more relaxing lifestyle and more time to spend with my family and friends."

"On the one hand, I don't believe in being materialistic and don't want to be. Yet, on the other hand, I am attracted to and want expensive things. I do want a bigger house, high quality car, etc."

"Generally, I want a comfortable and secure life—I want a secure job and a permanent home in a close-knit community. Yet part of me is attracted to the excitement of change, new challenges, and risk."

These are just a few general examples. Of course there are numerous idiosyncratic values conflicts. In the space provided below please describe an *important values conflict issue that you are experiencing in your life now.*

II. CONFLICT RESOLUTION

You described a values conflict in your life. Pretend that you have to resolve that conflict or make a clear decision right now. In the space provided below write the best resolution that you can *at this particular point in time.* Avoid vague responses like "I would compromise." Rather, write a concise decision or resolution so that it is clear what you would do if you were to carry it out.

_____

_____

III. QUESTIONNAIRE

The following questions refer to the specific conflict you just described and resolution you wrote. Do not change what you wrote. Evaluate *that particular resolution* exactly as written and as objectively as you can. Please respond honestly to each question by circling *one* number for each continuum.

1. *How satisfied are you* with the resolution as written?

0	1	2	3	4
Completely dissatisfied		Moderately		Very satisfied

2. To what extent is this resolution *compatible with your basic ethical, spiritual, or moral standards and principles?*

0	1	2	3	4
Not at all		Somewhat compatible		Very compatible

3. To what extent *has your actual behavior during the past few months been consistent with this resolution?*

0	1	2	3	4
Not consistent at all		Somewhat consistent		Very consistent

4. Resolving conflicts or making decisions usually involves gathering information, considering various alternatives, and critically thinking about options. During your life to what extent do you think you *have carefully analyzed and thought about your alternatives or options for this conflict?*

0	1	2	3	4
I need to do much more thinking		I need to do some more thinking		I have thought about them sufficiently

5. All decisions carry consequences. During your life to what extent have you *carefully considered possible positive and negative consequences* of living in accordance with this resolution?

0	1	2	3	4
I have not thought about possible consequences		I have thought about them to some extent		I have carefully considered possible consequences

6. Assuming that every act or decision has a positive or negative effect on society and the improvement of humankind—in your opinion what *effect (no matter how small) would this resolution have on society*?

0	1	2	3	4
More negative		Equally positive and negative		More positive

7. To what extent does the thought of carrying out this resolution *make you feel bad about yourself*?

0	1	2	3	4
Very		Somewhat		Not at all

8. Imagine, however unlikely it may seem, being in a public meeting and hearing this resolution criticized as being selfish and unhumanitarian. To what extent *could you defend that resolution in good conscience*?

0	1	2	3	4
Not defend it at all		Defend it to some extent		Defend it whole-heartedly

9. To what extent *have you thought about or made plans* regarding what you need to do in order to carry out this resolution?

0	1	2	3	4
I have not made any plans or thought about it		I have done some planning and thinking		I have planned or thought about it sufficiently

10. If most people lived in accordance with the values implied in this resolution, *how do you think the world would be changed*?

0	1	2	3	4
A worse world		No better no worse		A better world

11. To what extent *would you experience feelings of guilt* if you actually carried out this resolution?

0	1	2	3	4
Very guilty		Somewhat guilty		Not guilty at all

12. To what extent would you feel embarrassed if people who you cared about knew you wrote this particular resolution? Overall, *how embarrassed would you feel*?

0	1	2	3	4
Very embarrassed		Somewhat embarrassed		Not embar- rassed at all

13. In general, how do you think people who know you well would judge *how consistent your behavior has been* with this resolution?

0	1	2	3	4
Not consistent at all		Somewhat consistent		Very consistent

14. Sometimes people make certain decisions because they feel pressured, influenced, or manipulated by others. In such cases the decisions are not really theirs. To what extent do you think that the resolution you wrote is truly what you want or believe?

0	1	2	3	4
Not at all		Somewhat		Very much

15. To what extent do you feel committed to carrying out this resolution *during the next year*?

0	1	2	3	4
Not com- mitted at all		Somewhat committed		Very committed

16. People often tell themselves that a certain decision is better than it really is in order to avoid feeling bad about having made a mistake. To what extent do you think you are *being honest with yourself* about your evaluation of this resolution?

0	1	2	3	4
Not honest at all		Somewhat honest		Very honest

17. Try to imagine the following situation. It is sometime in the future and you only have a few months to live. Pretend that you have lived in accordance with that resolution and are now thinking about your decision and your impending death. In that context to what extent do you believe you would *regret having lived in accordance* with that resolution?

0	1	2	3	4
I would probably have many regrets		I would probably have some regrets		I would probably have few (if any) regrets

VERBAL AGGRESSIVENESS SCALE (VAS)

AUTHORS: Dominic A. Infante and Charles J. Wigley, III

PURPOSE: To measure verbal aggressiveness.

DESCRIPTION: The VAS is a 20-item instrument designed to measure verbal aggressiveness as a trait that predisposes people to attack the self-concepts of others instead of, or in addition to, their positions on topics of communication. The VAS is unidimensional, with 10 items worded negatively. Its main focus is interpersonal; verbal aggressiveness is viewed as an exchange of messages between two people where at least one person in the dyad attacks the other in order to hurt him or her psychologically. Thus, the VAS appears to hold promise in the area of family and couple counseling.

NORMS: Research on the VAS was conducted on approximately 660 undergraduate students in communication courses. Other demographic information and actual norms were not reported. However, in one study, the mean of 51.97 for males ($N = 195$) was significantly different from the mean of 46.38 for females ($N = 202$).

SCORING: The VAS is scored by reverse-scoring items 1, 3, 5, 8, 10, 12, 14, 15, 17, and 20 and then totaling the scores. This produces a range of 20 to 100.

RELIABILITY: The VAS has good internal consistency, with an alpha of .81. The VAS also has excellent stability, with a four-week test-retest correlation of .82.

VALIDITY: The VAS has fairly good concurrent validity, correlating at moderate levels with five other trait measures. Further, the VAS was significantly correlated with predicted performance for verbally aggressive messages in a variety of social influence situations, suggesting good predictive validity.

PRIMARY REFERENCE: Infante, D. A. and Wigley, C. J., III. (1986). Verbal aggressiveness: An interpersonal model and measure, *Communication Monographs*, 53, 61–69. Instrument reproduced with permission of Dominic A. Infante.

AVAILABILITY: Journal article.

VAS

This survey is concerned with how we try to get people to comply with our wishes. Indicate how often each statement is true for you personally when you try to influence other persons. Use the following scale:

1 = Almost never true
2 = Rarely true
3 = Occasionally true
4 = Often true
5 = Almost always true

_____ 1. I am extremely careful to avoid attacking individuals' intelligence when I attack their ideas.

_____ 2. When individuals are very stubborn, I use insults to soften the stubbornness.

_____ 3. I try very hard to avoid having other people feel bad about themselves when I try to influence them.

_____ 4. When people refuse to do a task I know is important, without good reason, I tell them they are unreasonable

_____ 5. When others do things I regard as stupid, I try to be extremely gentle with them.

_____ 6. If individuals I am trying to influence really deserve it, I attack their character.

_____ 7. When people behave in ways that are in very poor taste, I insult them in order to shock them into proper behavior.

_____ 8. I try to make people feel good about themselves even when their ideas are stupid.

_____ 9. When people simply will not budge on a matter of importance I lose my temper and say rather strong things to them.

_____ 10. When people criticize my shortcomings, I take it in good humor and do not try to get back at them.

_____ 11. When individuals insult me, I get a lot of pleasure out of really telling them off.

_____ 12. When I dislike individuals greatly, I try not to show it in what I say or how I say it.

_____ 13. I like poking fun at people who do things that are very stupid in order to stimulate their intelligence.

_____ 14. When I attack peoples' ideas, I try not to damage their self-concepts.

_____ 15. When I try to influence people, I make a great effort not to offend them.

_____ 16. When people do things that are mean or cruel, I attack their character in order to help correct their behavior.

_____ 17. I refuse to participate in arguments when they involve personal attacks.

_____ 18. When nothing seems to work in trying to influence others, I yell and scream in order to get some movement from them.

_____ 19. When I am not able to refute others' positions, I try to make them feel defensive in order to weaken their positions.

_____ 20. When an argument shifts to personal attacks, I try very hard to change the subject.

WAY OF LIFE SCALE (WOLS)

AUTHORS: Logan Wright, Kurt von Bussmann, Alice Friedman, Mary Khoury, Fredette Owens, and Wayne Paris

PURPOSE: To measure exaggerated social control.

DESCRIPTION: The WOLS is a 43-item instrument designed to measure non-mutuality, a measure of exaggerated social control thought to be related to the Type A behavior pattern. Nonmutuality involves a tendency to control others inappropriately in social situations. Reports of this type of behavior among Type A patients have been made mainly in clinical settings (coronary care), but include reports on domestic behaviors. The WOLS appears to have potential not only in its focus on Type A behavior, but as a measure for evaluating clinical interventions where the goal is to decrease inappropriate, social controlling behavior.

NORMS: The WOLS has been studied with several samples including 62 white, married male university faculty members, 52 middle-aged adults with chronic heart disease, 45 male undergraduates, and 30 hospitalized male patients (ages 40–55) with serious chronic heart disease. No other demographic data are available. Actual norms were not available.

SCORING: The WOLS is easily scored by scoring one point for a "true" response on items 2, 3, 7, 9, 10, 12, 15, 17–19, 21, 24, 28–30, 32, 35, and 37–40, and then summing these for the total score. The remaining items are not scored.

RELIABILITY: The WOLS has fair internal consistency, with an alpha of .63. The WOLS has very good stability, with three-week and three-month test-retest correlations of .77.

VALIDITY: The WOLS has good concurrent validity, correlating with the Jenkins Activity Scale (Type A behavior) and the Burger/Cooper Desirability of Control Scale.

PRIMARY REFERENCE: Wright, L., von Bussmann, K., Friedman, A., Khoury, M., Owens, F., and Paris, W. (1990). Exaggerated social control and its relationship to the Type A behavior pattern, *Journal of Research in Personality*, 24, 258–269.

AVAILABILITY: Journal article.

WOLS

The following questionnaire should be filled out according to how you feel at the present. Respond by circling the True or False choice which *most accurately* describes you, the respondent. The time should not exceed 5 minutes. Thank you for your time and cooperation.

True   False   1.   I am easily awakened by noise.
True   False   2.   When it's time to make a major decision like purchasing a house or a car I usually make that decision.
True   False   3.   When it's time to make a major decision about moving, I usually make that decision.
True   False   4.   My daily life is full of things that are interesting.
True   False   5.   I enjoy detective or mystery stories.
True   False   6.   I work under a great deal of tension.
True   False   7.   When it's time to discipline the children I make that decision.
True   False   8.   No one seems to understand me.
True   False   9.   When it's time to decide about social events with friends or family I usually make that decision.
True   False   10.   I like to be bossy.
True   False   11.   At times I feel like swearing.
True   False   12.   I like to get in the last word.
True   False   13.   I find it hard to keep my mind on a task.
True   False   14.   At times I feel like smashing things.
True   False   15.   I like to know the details about other people's phone conversations.
True   False   16.   I do not always tell the truth.
True   False   17.   I like to have rules and structure for handling most or all situations.
True   False   18.   I like to monitor other people to make sure things are going the way they should be.
True   False   19.   I like to make sure everything goes according to plan.
True   False   20.   I am a good mixer.
True   False   21.   I like to lead conversations or group discussions.
True   False   22.   I am liked by most people.
True   False   23.   I get angry sometimes.
True   False   24.   I may be inclined to interrupt people if they are not responding in the way they should be.
True   False   25.   I think most people would lie to get ahead.
True   False   26.   I am lacking in self confidence.
True   False   27.   I am an important person.
True   False   28.   I have a tendency to manipulate, maneuver, or control other people.
True   False   29.   I am a good leader but not particularly a good follower.
True   False   30.   I like to give directions about driving or other activities.
True   False   31.   I am happy most of the time.
True   False   32.   I am a person who, if I am going out for an evening, likes to decide where to eat, what movie to attend

True False 33. My hardest battles are with myself.
True False 34. I seem to be about as capable and smart as most others around me.
True False 35. I tend to overstructure spontaneous times such as vacations, etc., and turn them into controlled events.
True False 36. I feel useless at times.
True False 37. I have ideas about controlling other things with the children and other people such as how much food they should have on their plate, etc.
True False 38. I am seen by relatives as being a dominant member of our extended family.
True False 39. I am the one who usually decides which television channel to watch.
True False 40. I am the one who usually controls the thermostat in the house.
True False 41. Criticism or scolding hurts me terribly.
True False 42. I would rather win than lose in a game.
True False 43. I do not tire quickly.

WEST HAVEN–YALE MULTIDIMENSIONAL PAIN INVENTORY (WHYMPI)

AUTHORS: Robert D. Kerns, Dennis C. Turk, and Thomas E. Rudy

PURPOSE: To measure chronic pain.

DESCRIPTION: The WHYMPI is a three-part inventory designed to assess the impact of pain on people's lives (20 items), the responses of others to the individual's communication of pain (14 items), and the extent to which pain sufferers participate in daily activities (18 items). The WHYMPI comprises 12 subscales/factors. For the first scale, the factors are: interference (items 2, 3, 4, 8, 9, 13, 14, 17, 19), support (items 5, 10, 15), pain severity (items 1, 7, 12), self-control (items 11, 16), and negative mood (items 6, 18, 20). The second scale has three subscales: punishing responses (items 1, 4, 7, 11), solicitous responses (items 2, 5, 8, 12, 14, 15), and distracting responses (items 3, 9, 10, 13). On the third scale, there are four subscales: household chores (items 1, 5, 9, 13, 17), outdoor work (items 2, 6, 10, 14, 18), activities away from home (items 3, 7, 11, 15), and social activities (items 4, 8, 12, 16). Because of its brevity, clarity, ease of administration, and multidimensional nature, the WHYMPI is viewed as an excellent measure both for research into chronic pain and to monitor practice endeavors aimed at reducing pain.

NORMS: The WHYMPI initially was studied with 120 chronic pain patients (81.5% male) at two Veterans Administration hospitals. The mean age of the patients was 50.8 years, with a mean duration of 10.2 years of chronic pain; 68% of the patients were married. Means for subscales were as follows: interference = 3.74, support = 4.31, pain severity = 3.55, self-control = 3.63, negative mood = 3.23, punishing responses = 0.97, solicitous responses = 2.57, distracting responses = 1.72, household chores = 2.71, outdoor work = 1.19, activities away from home = 1.79, and social activities = 1.94.

SCORING: The WHYMPI is easily scored by summing item responses for the overall score and the subscale scores.

RELIABILITY: The WHYMPI has very good internal consistency, with subscale alphas that range from .70 to .90. The WHYMPI also has very good stability, with two-week test-retest correlations that range from .62 to .86.

VALIDITY: The WHYMPI was viewed as having good construct validity, based on evidence obtained from factor analysis (factorial validity). The WHYMPI also has been used as an outcome measure in several clinical studies and has been shown to be sensitive to change, predictive of depressive symptom severity, and predictive of expressions of pain and affective distress.

PRIMARY REFERENCE: Kerns, R. D., Turk, D. C., and Rudy, T. E. (1985). The West Haven–Yale Multidimensional Pain Inventory (WHYMPI), *Pain*, 23, 345–356.

AVAILABILITY: Dr. Robert D. Kerns, Psychology Service, Veterans Administration Medical Center, West Haven, CT 06516.

WHYMPI

SECTION 1

In the following 20 questions, you will be asked to describe your pain and how it affects your life. Under each question is a scale to record your answer. Read each question carefully and then *circle* a number on the scale under that question to indicate how that specific question applies to you.

1. Rate the level of your pain at the present moment.

    0   1   2   3   4   5   6
    No   Very
    pain   intense
                                                          pain

2. In general, how much does your pain problem interfere with your day-to-day activities?

    0   1   2   3   4   5   6
    No   Extreme
    interference   interference

3. Since the time you developed a pain problem, how much has your pain changed your ability to work?

    0   1   2   3   4   5   6
    No   Extreme
    change   change

    _____   Check here if you have retired for reasons other than your pain problem.

4. How much has your pain changed the amount of satisfaction or enjoyment you get from participating in social and recreational activities?

    0   1   2   3   4   5   6
    No   Extreme
    change   change

5. How supportive or helpful is your spouse (significant other) to you in relation to your pain?

    0   1   2   3   4   5   6
    Not at all   Extremely
    supportive   supportive

6. Rate your overall mood during the *past week*.

0	1	2	3	4	5	6
Extremely low mood						Extremely high mood

7. On the average, how severe has your pain been during the last week?

0	1	2	3	4	5	6
Not at all severe						Extremely severe

8. How much has your pain changed your ability to participate in recreational and other social activities?

0	1	2	3	4	5	6
No change						Extreme change

9. How much has your pain changed the amount of satisfaction you get from family-related activities?

0	1	2	3	4	5	6
No change						Extreme change

10. How worried is your spouse (significant other) about you in relation to your pain problem?

0	1	2	3	4	5	6
Not at all worried						Extremely worried

11. During the *past week* how much control do you feel that you have had over your life?

0	1	2	3	4	5	6
Not at all in control						Extremely in control

12. How much *suffering* do you experience because of your pain?

0	1	2	3	4	5	6
No suffering						Extreme suffering

13. How much has your pain changed your marriage and other family relationships?

```
   0          1          2          3          4          5          6
  No                                                              Extreme
change                                                            change
```

14. How much has your pain changed the amount of satisfaction or enjoyment you get from work?

```
   0          1          2          3          4          5          6
  No                                                              Extreme
change                                                            change
```

_____ Check here if you are not presently working.

15. How attentive is your spouse (significant other) to your pain problem?

```
   0          1          2          3          4          5          6
Not at all                                                      Extremely
attentive                                                       attentive
```

16. During the *past week* how much do you feel that you've been able to deal with your problems?

```
   0          1          2          3          4          5          6
  Not                                                           Extremely
 at all                                                            well
```

17. How much has your pain changed your ability to do household chores?

```
   0          1          2          3          4          5          6
  No                                                              Extreme
change                                                            change
```

18. During the past week how irritable have you been?

```
   0          1          2          3          4          5          6
Not at all                                                      Extremely
irritable                                                       irritable
```

19. How much has your pain changed your friendships with people other than your family?

```
   0          1          2          3          4          5          6
  No                                                              Extreme
change                                                            change
```

20. During the past week how tense or anxious have you been?

0	1	2	3	4	5	6
Not at all tense or anxious						Extremely tense or anxious

SECTION 2

In this section, we are interested in knowing how your spouse (or significant other) responds to you when he or she knows that you are in pain. On the scale listed below each question, *circle* a number to indicate *how often* your spouse (or significant other) generally responds to you in that particular way *when you are in pain*. Please answer *all* of the 14 questions.

Please identify the relationship between you and the person you are thinking of
_____.

1. Ignores me.

0	1	2	3	4	5	6
Never						Very often

2. Asks me what he/she can do to help.

0	1	2	3	4	5	6
Never						Very often

3. Reads to me.

0	1	2	3	4	5	6
Never						Very often

4. Expresses irritation at me.

0	1	2	3	4	5	6
Never						Very often

5. Takes over my jobs or duties.

0	1	2	3	4	5	6
Never						Very often

6. Talks to me about something else to take my mind off the pain.

0	1	2	3	4	5	6
Never						Very often

7.   Expresses frustration at me.

     0   1   2   3   4   5   6
  Never   Very often

8.   Tries to get me to rest.

     0   1   2   3   4   5   6
  Never   Very often

9.   Tries to involve me in some activity.

     0   1   2   3   4   5   6
  Never   Very often

10. Expresses anger at me.

     0   1   2   3   4   5   6
  Never   Very often

11. Gets me some pain medication.

     0   1   2   3   4   5   6
  Never   Very often

12. Encourages me to work on a hobby.

     0   1   2   3   4   5   6
  Never   Very often

13. Gets me something to eat or drink.

     0   1   2   3   4   5   6
  Never   Very often

14. Turns on the TV to take my mind off my pain.

     0   1   2   3   4   5   6
  Never   Very often

SECTION 3

Listed below are 18 common daily activities. Please indicate *how often* you do each of these activities by *circling* a number on the scale listed below each activity. Please complete *all* 18 questions.

1. Wash dishes.

0	1	2	3	4	5	6
Never						Very often

2. Mow the lawn.

0	1	2	3	4	5	6
Never						Very often

3. Go out to eat.

0	1	2	3	4	5	6
Never						Very often

4. Play cards or other games.

0	1	2	3	4	5	6
Never						Very often

5. Go grocery shopping.

0	1	2	3	4	5	6
Never						Very often

6. Work in the garden.

0	1	2	3	4	5	6
Never						Very often

7. Go to a movie.

0	1	2	3	4	5	6
Never						Very often

8. Visit friends.

0	1	2	3	4	5	6
Never						Very often

9. Help with the house cleaning.

0	1	2	3	4	5	6
Never						Very often

10. Work on the car.

    0   1   2   3   4   5   6
  Never   Very often

11. Take a ride in a car.

    0   1   2   3   4   5   6
  Never   Very often

12. Visit relatives.

    0   1   2   3   4   5   6
  Never   Very often

13. Prepare a meal.

    0   1   2   3   4   5   6
  Never   Very often

14. Wash the car.

    0   1   2   3   4   5   6
  Never   Very often

15. Take a trip.

    0   1   2   3   4   5   6
  Never   Very often

16. Go to a park or beach.

    0   1   2   3   4   5   6
  Never   Very often

17. Do a load of laundry.

    0   1   2   3   4   5   6
  Never   Very often

18. Work on a needed house repair.

    0   1   2   3   4   5   6
  Never   Very often

WORKING ALLIANCE INVENTORY (WAI)

AUTHOR: Adam O. Horvath

PURPOSE: To measure the working alliance between a client and clinician.

DESCRIPTION: This 36-item instrument measures three aspects of the working alliance between a client and a clinician. The aspects are (1) tasks, where the clinician and client both see in-session action and cognition as relevant and efficacious; (2) goals, where clinician and client mutually endorse and value the anticipated treatment outcome; and (3) bonds, the mutual personal attachment between the client and clinician which includes trust, acceptance, and confidence. Since these three aspects are considered to be common to all clinical treatment, the WAI may be used to evaluate treatment, regardless of theory or techniques. However, the WAI emphasizes the quality of mutuality between the clinician and the client as a primary component of effectiveness. The WAI was developed with excellent psychometric procedures from a pool of 91 items. There are two forms of the WAI, one for the clinician and one for the client. The client form is illustrated here. Each item contains a blank which is filled with either the name of the client or the clinician. A short form of the WAI is available by using only items 2, 4, 8, 12, 21, 22, 23, 24, 26, 27, 32, and 35.

NORMS: Norms are not reported in the primary references.

SCORING: Individual item responses are summed for a total score.

RELIABILITY: The WAI has very good reliability in terms of internal consistency. For example, from a sample of 29 clinician and client dyads involved in short-term treatment the client form of the WAI had alphas of .87, .82, and .68 for the goals, tasks, and bonds subscales. A separate study of 25 clinicians from a wide range of theoretical orientations reported item homogeneity coefficients ranging from .89 to .93. For the short form of the WAI, the alphas were .90 for tasks, .92 for bonds, and .90 for the goals, respectively. The composite scale of the short form has an internal consistency coefficient of .98 using Cronbach's alpha. Data on stability were not available.

VALIDITY: The WAI has very good validity. Discriminant and convergent validity were tested with the multimethod-multitrait procedure where the results support the construct validity of the WAI. The goal subscale seems to have the best discriminant validity. Concurrent validity is supported by correlations between the three subscale scores and measures of perceived attractiveness, expertness, and trustworthiness that clients feel towards clinicians, and correlates with clinicians' empathy. Scores on the tasks and goals subscales correlated with client reported outcome. Tasks subscales scores were associated with a measure of client indecision, state-trait anxiety, and change in the client's target complaint as rated by the clinician and the client.

PRIMARY REFERENCES: Horvath, A. O. and Greenberg, L. S. (1989). Development and validation of the Working Alliance Inventory, *Journal of Counseling Psychology*, 36. 223–233. Tracey, T. J. and Kokotovic, A. M. (1989). Factor structure of the Working Alliance Inventory, *Psychological Assessment*, 1, 207–210. Instrument reproduced with permission of Adam O. Horvath.

AVAILABILITY: Dr. Adam O. Horvath, Counseling Psychology Program, Faculty of Education, Simon Fraser University, Burnaby, British Columbia, Canada V5A 1S6.

WAI

Below are 36 questions about your relationship with your therapist. Using the following scale rate the degree to which you agree with each statement, and record your answer in the space to the left of the item.

1 = Not at all true
2 = A little true
3 = Slightly true
4 = Somewhat true
5 = Moderately true
6 = Considerably true
7 = Very true

____ 1. I feel uncomfortable with _____.
____ 2. _____ and I agree about the things I will need to do in therapy to help improve my situation.
____ 3. I am worried about the outcome of these sessions.
____ 4. What I am doing in therapy gives me new ways of looking at my problem.
____ 5. _____ and I understand each other.
____ 6. _____ perceives accurately what my goals are.
____ 7. I find what I am doing in therapy confusing.
____ 8. I believe _____ likes me.
____ 9. I wish _____ and I could clarify the purpose of our sessions.
____ 10. I disagree with _____ about what I ought to get out of therapy.
____ 11. I believe the time _____ and I are spending together is not spent efficiently.
____ 12. _____ does not understand what I am trying to accomplish in therapy.
____ 13. I am clear on what my responsibilities are in therapy.
____ 14. The goals of these sessions are important to me.
____ 15. I find what _____ and I are doing in therapy are unrelated to my concerns.
____ 16. I feel that the things I do in therapy will help me to accomplish the changes that I want.
____ 17. I believe _____ is genuinely concerned for my welfare.
____ 18. I am clear as to what _____ wants me to do in these sessions.
____ 19. _____ and I respect each other.
____ 20. I feel that _____ is not totally honest about his/her feelings toward me.
____ 21. I am confident in _____'s ability to help me.
____ 22. _____ and I are working towards mutually agreed upon goals.
____ 23. I feel that _____ appreciates me.
____ 24. We agree on what is important for me to work on.
____ 25. As a result of these sessions I am clearer as to how I might be able to change.
____ 26. _____ and I trust one another.
____ 27. _____ and I have different ideas on what my problems are.

____ 28.   My relationship with _____ is very important to me.
____ 29.   I have the feeling that if I say or do the wrong things, _____ will stop working with me.
____ 30.   _____ and I collaborate on setting goals for my therapy.
____ 31.   I am frustrated by the things I am doing in therapy.
____ 32.   We have established a good understanding of the kind of changes that would be good for me.
____ 33.   The things that _____ is asking me to do don't make sense.
____ 34.   I don't know what to expect as the result of my therapy.
____ 35.   I believe the way we are working with my problem is correct.
____ 36.   I feel _____ cares about me even when I do things that he/she does not approve of.

YOUNG ADULT FAMILY INVENTORY OF LIFE EVENTS AND CHANGES (YA-FILES)

AUTHORS: Hamilton I. McCubbin, Joan M. Patterson, and Janet R. Grochowski

PURPOSE: To measure stress in young adults.

DESCRIPTION: The YA-FILES is a 77-item instrument designed to measure the stressors and strains of young adults. This instrument is a modification of the Adolescent–FILES, especially with regard to 31 items referring to "College Changes." While the YA-FILES has 13 factors, the total score is recommended for use.

NORMS: The YA-FILES was studied with 184 college students, including 79 women and 82 men. No other demographic information is available. The overall mean was 196.93 (SD = 18.42).

SCORING: The YA-FILES is easily scored by simply giving a score of 1 to all "yes" answers and summing all items for the total score.

RELIABILITY: The YA-FILES has very good internal consistency, with an alpha of .85. The measure also has very good stability, with a test-retest correlation of .85.

VALIDITY: The YA-FILES has fair concurrent validity, with correlations with adolescent substance use and adolescent health locus of control. The YA-FILES also is a good predictor of college GPA.

PRIMARY REFERENCE: McCubbin, H. I. and Thompson, A. I. (eds.) (1991). *Family Assessment Inventories for Research and Practice*. Madison, WI: University of Wisconsin.

AVAILABILITY: Dr. Hamilton McCubbin, Dean, School of Family Resources and Consumer Services, Madison, WI 53706-1575.

YA-FILES

Part I - Family Life Changes

Read each family life change and decide if it happened in your family during the last 6 months. Mark one of the following responses:

Yes, the change happened to me personally
Yes, the change happened to another family member (not me)
No, the change did not happen to any member of my family

Part II - College Changes

Read each college change and decide if it happened to YOU during the last 6 months. Check YES or NO.

"FAMILY" means a group of persons who are related to each other by marriage, blood or adoption, who may or may not live with you. Family includes step-parents, step-brothers, step-sisters and foster parents.

Remember: Anytime the words parent, mother, brother, etc., are used, they also mean step-parent, step-mother, foster parent, guardian, etc.

Part I: Family Life Changes

Did this change happen in your family during the past 6 months?	YES, Happened to me personally	YES, Happened to another family member	NO, Did not happen in my family
1. Family member started new business (farm, store, etc.)	☐	☐	☐
2. Parent quit or lost a job	☐	☐	☐
3. Parents separated or divorced	☐	☐	☐
4. Parent remarried	☐	☐	☐
5. Family member was married	☐	☐	☐
6. Family member was found to have a learning disorder	☐	☐	☐
7. Parents adopted a child	☐	☐	☐
8. A member started junior high or high school	☐	☐	☐
9. Child or teenage member entered college, vocational training or armed forces	☐	☐	☐
10. Parent started school	☐	☐	☐
11. Brother or sister moved away from home	☐	☐	☐

Did this change happen in your family during the past 6 months?	YES, Happened to me personally	YES, Happened to another family member	NO, Did not happen in my family
12. Young adult member entered college, vocational training or armed forces	☐	☐	☐
13. Parent(s) started or changed to a new job	☐	☐	☐
14. Family moved to a new home	☐	☐	☐
15. Unmarried family member became pregnant	☐	☐	☐
16. Family member had an abortion	☐	☐	☐
17. Birth of a brother or sister	☐	☐	☐
18. Unmarried young adult member began having sexual intercourse	☐	☐	☐
19. Family went on welfare	☐	☐	☐
20. Damage to or loss of family property due to fire, burglary, or other disaster	☐	☐	☐
21. Brother or sister died	☐	☐	☐
22. Parent died	☐	☐	☐
23. Close family relative died	☐	☐	☐
24. Death of a close friend or family member	☐	☐	☐
25. Family member or close family friend attempted or committed suicide	☐	☐	☐
26. Family member became seriously ill or injured	☐	☐	☐
27. Family member was hospitalized	☐	☐	☐
28. Family member became physically disabled or was found to have a long-term health problem (e.g., asthma)	☐	☐	☐
29. Family member has emotional problems	☐	☐	☐
30. Grandparent(s) became seriously ill	☐	☐	☐
31. Parent(s) have more responsibility to take care of grandparent(s)	☐	☐	☐
32. Family member ran away	☐	☐	☐
33. More financial debts due to use of credit cards or charges	☐	☐	☐
34. Increased family living expenses for medical care, food, clothing, energy costs (gasoline, heating)	☐	☐	☐
35. Increase of parent's time away from family	☐	☐	☐
36. Young adult member resists doing things with family	☐	☐	☐

Did this change happen in your family during the past 6 months?	YES, Happened to me personally	YES, Happened to another family member	NO, Did not happen in my family
37. Increase in arguments between parents	☐	☐	☐
38. Teens/young adults have more arguments with one another	☐	☐	☐
39. Parent(s) and young adult(s) have increased arguments (hassles) over personal appearance (clothes, hair, etc.)	☐	☐	☐
40. Increased arguments about getting the jobs done at home	☐	☐	☐
41. Family member uses drugs (not given by doctor)	☐	☐	☐
42. Family member drinks too much alcohol	☐	☐	☐
43. Teen/young adult was suspended from or dropped out of school	☐	☐	☐
44. Parent(s) and young adults have increased arguments (hassles) over use of cigarettes, alcohol, or drugs	☐	☐	☐
45. Family member went to jail, juvenile detention, or was placed on court probation	☐	☐	☐
46. Family member was robbed or attacked (physically or sexually)	☐	☐	☐

Part II: College Changes

Did this happen in your family during the last 6 months?	YES	NO
47. Felt pressure to get good grades	☐	☐
48. Had difficulty getting needed information and help from your college advisor	☐	☐
49. Had difficulty finding a college counselor for your personal needs (e.g. academic, career, emotional, etc.)	☐	☐
50. Had difficulty getting the help you needed from a college counselor	☐	☐
51. Felt pressure to make a career choice	☐	☐
52. Felt pressure from your parents to make a career choice	☐	☐
53. Felt pressure from your parents to succeed in college	☐	☐
54. Been unable to find a quiet place to study	☐	☐
55. Been unable to use the library to study	☐	☐

56.	Been unable to use the athletic and recreational facilities when you wanted to	☐ ☐
57.	Felt financial pressures regarding how to pay for tuition, books, etc.	☐ ☐
58.	Had conflict or hassles with your roommate(s)	☐ ☐
59.	Felt the need to have more privacy	☐ ☐
60.	Felt uncertainty regarding how to act as a college student in social settings	☐ ☐
61.	Had difficulty making friends with on-campus students	☐ ☐
62.	Had difficulty making friends with commuting students	☐ ☐
63.	Had difficult making friends with students living in apartments	☐ ☐
64.	Felt lonely because you missed your family	☐ ☐
65.	Felt conflict between time to study and time to make friends and party	☐ ☐
66.	Worried about driving to class in bad weather	☐ ☐
67.	Worried about finding a place to park at school	☐ ☐
68.	Felt isolated from the college community	☐ ☐
69.	Felt your being in college has placed added strain on your family	☐ ☐
70.	Had difficult participating in social activities held at the college during evening hours or on weekends	☐ ☐
71.	Felt strain from missing contact with your high school friends	☐ ☐
72.	Been unable to study when you wanted to for as long as you wanted	☐ ☐
73.	Felt pressure to drink when you didn't want to	☐ ☐
74.	Felt pressure to use non-prescription drugs when you didn't want to	☐ ☐
75.	Worried about being sexually attractive	☐ ☐
76.	Worried about how sexually attractive to be	☐ ☐
77.	Felt confused about your priorities, values, beliefs	☐ ☐

YOUNG ADULT SOCIAL SUPPORT INVENTORY (YA-SSI)

AUTHORS: Hamilton I. McCubbin, Joan M. Patterson, and Janet R. Grochowski

PURPOSE: To measure social support.

DESCRIPTION: The YA-SSI is a 54-item instrument designed to measure social support in young adults, particularly entering college freshmen. Although the YA-SSI has not been studied with other samples, it appears to have face validity for use with young adult populations other than college students. The YA-SSI has 11 factors, but can easily serve as an overall measure of social support by using the total score.

NORMS: The YA-SSI has been studied with two samples of college students for a total of 361 subjects including both men and women. No other demographic data are available. The overall means ranged from 135.49 (SD = 16.1) to 145.4 (SD = 19.3).

SCORING: The first 12 items are not scored. The remainder of the items are assigned a 1 for "no," a 2 for "yes," and a 3 for "yes a lot." These item scores are then summed for an overall score.

RELIABILITY: The YA-SSI has excellent internal consistency, with an alpha of .89. The YA-SSI also has excellent stability, with a test-retest correlation of .90.

VALIDITY: The YA-SSI has fair predictive validity, significantly correlating with academic GPA and ratings of college friends and other relatives.

PRIMARY REFERENCE: McCubbin, H. I. and Thompson, A. I. (eds.)(1991). *Family Assessment Inventories for Research and Practice*. Madison, WI: University of Wisconsin.

AVAILABILITY: Dr. Hamilton McCubbin, Dean, School of Family Resources and Consumer Services, Madison, WI 53706-1575.

YA-SSI

Please answer the following questions:	YES	NO

1. Are one or both of your PARENTS living? ☐ ☐
2. Do you have SIBLINGS? (i.e., BROTHERS AND/OR SISTERS) ☐ ☐
3. Do you have OTHER RELATIVES such as grandparents, aunts, uncles, cousins? ☐ ☐
4. Do you have HIGH SCHOOL FRIENDS? (friendships developed during high school years) ☐ ☐
5. Do you have COLLEGE FRIENDS? (friendships develped during college) ☐ ☐
6. Do you have a paying ($) job where you have CO-WORKERS? ☐ ☐
7. Do you belong to a CHURCH OR SYNAGOGUE? ☐ ☐
8. Do you have SPIRITUAL BELIEFS? ☐ ☐
9. Do you have contact with COLLEGE FACULTY, COUNSELORS, ADMINISTRATORS? ☐ ☐
10. Do you have contacts with PROFESSIONALS OR SERVICE PROVIDERS such as doctors, nurses, barbers, diet counselors, etc.? ☐ ☐
11. Do you belong to any SPECIAL ORGANIZED GROUPS such as groups for minorities, hobbies, fitness, athletics, etc.? ☐ ☐
12. Do you watch TELEVISION, listen to the RADIO or read NEWSPAPERS, MAGAZINES, PAMPHLETS or NON-REQUIRED BOOKS? ☐ ☐

Please read each statement and then indicate how much support you receive from each of the sources listed by checking NO, YES, or YES A LOT.

I. I Have a Feeling of Being Loved or Cared About From:	NO	YES	YES A LOT
13. My parents	☐	☐	☐
14. My siblings	☐	☐	☐
15. Other relatives	☐	☐	☐
16. High school friends	☐	☐	☐
17. College friends	☐	☐	☐
18. Co-workers	☐	☐	☐
19. Church/synagogue groups	☐	☐	☐
20. My spiritual health	☐	☐	☐
21. College faculty, counselors, administrators	☐	☐	☐
22. Other professionals or service providers	☐	☐	☐
23. Special groups I belong to	☐	☐	☐
24. Reading books, watching TV, listening to music	☐	☐	☐
25. Other	☐	☐	☐

II. I Feel I Am Valued or Respected for Who I Am and What I Can Do By:	YES	NO	YES A LOT
26. My parents	☐	☐	☐
27. My siblings	☐	☐	☐
28. Other relatives	☐	☐	☐
29. High school friends	☐	☐	☐
30. College friends	☐	☐	☐
31. Co-workers	☐	☐	☐
32. Church/synagogue groups	☐	☐	☐
33. My spiritual health	☐	☐	☐
34. College faculty, counselors, administrators	☐	☐	☐
35. Other professionals or service providers	☐	☐	☐
36. Special groups I belong to	☐	☐	☐
37. Reading books, watching TV, listening to music	☐	☐	☐
38. Other	☐	☐	☐

III. I Have a Sense of Trust or Security From the "GIVE and TAKE" of Being Involved With:	YES	NO	YES A LOT
39. My parents	☐	☐	☐
40. My siblings	☐	☐	☐
41. Other relatives	☐	☐	☐
42. High school friends	☐	☐	☐
43. College friends	☐	☐	☐
44. Co-workers	☐	☐	☐
45. Church/synagogue groups	☐	☐	☐
46. My spiritual health	☐	☐	☐
47. College faculty, counselors, administrators	☐	☐	☐
48. Other professionals or service providers	☐	☐	☐
49. Special groups I belong to	☐	☐	☐
50. Reading books, watching TV, listening to music	☐	☐	☐
51. Other	☐	☐	☐

IV. When I Need To Talk or Think About How I'm Doing With My Life, I Feel Understood and Get Help From:	YES	NO	YES A LOT
52. My parents	☐	☐	☐
53. My siblings	☐	☐	☐
54. Other relatives	☐	☐	☐
55. High school friends	☐	☐	☐
56. College friends	☐	☐	☐
57. Co-workers	☐	☐	☐
58. Church/synagogue groups	☐	☐	☐
59. My spiritual health	☐	☐	☐
60. College faculty, counselors, administrators	☐	☐	☐
61. Other professionals or service providers	☐	☐	☐
62. Special groups I belong to	☐	☐	☐
63. Reading books, watching TV, listening to music	☐	☐	☐
64. Other	☐	☐	☐

		YES	NO	YES A LOT
V.	I Feel Good About Myself When I Am Able to Do Things For and Help:			
65.	My parents	☐	☐	☐
66.	My siblings	☐	☐	☐
67.	Other relatives	☐	☐	☐
68.	High school friends	☐	☐	☐
69.	College friends	☐	☐	☐
70.	Co-workers	☐	☐	☐
71.	Church/synagogue groups	☐	☐	☐
72.	My spiritual health	☐	☐	☐
73.	College faculty, counselors, administrators	☐	☐	☐
74.	Other professionals or service providers	☐	☐	☐
75.	Special groups I belong to	☐	☐	☐
76.	Reading books, watching TV, listening to music	☐	☐	☐
77.	Other	☐	☐	☐

REFERENCES

Adorno, T. W., Frenkel-Brunswick, E., Levinson, D. J., and Sanford, R. N. (1950). *The Authoritarian Personality*. New York: Harper.

American Psychiatric Association (1987). *Diagnostic and Statistical Manual—Revised*. Washington, D.C.

American Psychological Association, American Educational Research Association, and National Council on Measurement in Education (1985). *Standards For Educational and Psychological Testing*. Washington, D.C.: American Psychological Association.

Anastasi, A. (1976). Psychological Testing, 6th edition. New York: Macmillan.

Andrulis, R. S. (1977). *Adult Assessment: A Sourcebook of Tests and Measures of Human Behavior*. Springfield, Ill.: Charles C Thomas

Asarnow, J. R. and Carlson, G. A. (1982). Depression self-rating: Utility with child psychiatric inpatients, *Journal of Consulting and Clinical Psychology, 53, 491–499*.

Asher, D. R., Hymel, S., and Renshaw, P. D. (1984). Loneliness in children, *Child Development*, 55, 1457–1464.

Austin, C. D. (1981). Client assessment in context, *Social Work Research and Abstracts*, 17, 4–12.

Babbie, E. (1983). *The Practice of Social Research*, 3rd edition. Belmont, Calif.: Wadsworth.

Barlow, D. H. (ed.) (1981). *Behavioral Assessment of Adult Disorders*. New York: Guilford.

705

————— (1985). *Clinical Handbook of Psychological Disorders*. New York: Guilford.

—————, Hayes, S. C., and Nelson, R. O. (1984). *The Scientist Practitioner: Research and Accountability in Clinical and Educational Settings*. New York: Pergamon.

—————, and Hersen, M. (1984). *Single Case Experimental Designs: Strategies for Studying Behavior Change*. 2nd edition. New York: Pergamon.

Beach, S. R. H. and Arias, I. (1983). Assessment of perceptual discrepancy: Utility of the primary communication inventory, *Family Process*, 22, 309–316.

Beck, A. T., Ward, C. H., Mendelson, M., Mock, J., and Erbaugh, J. (1961). An inventory for measuring depression, *Archives of General Psychiatry*, 4, 561-571.

—————, Weissman, A., Lester, D. and Trexler, L. (1974) The measurement of pessimism: The Hopelessness Scale, *Journal of Consulting and Clinical Psychology*, 42, 861–865.

Beere, C. A. (1979). *Women and Women's Issues: A Handbook of Tests and Measures*. San Francisco: Jossey-Bass.

Bellack, A. S. and Hersen, M. (1977). The use of self-report inventories in behavioral assessment. In J. D. Cone and R. P. Hawkins (eds.), *Behavioral Assessment: New Directions in Clinical Psychology*, pp. 52–76. New York: Brunner/Mazel.

————— (eds.) (1988). *Behavioral Assessment: A Practical Handbook*. 3rd edition. New York: Pergamon.

Bernstein, D. A., and Allen, G. J. (1969). Fear Survey Schedule (II): Normative data and factor analyses based upon a large college sample. *Behavioural Research and Therapy*, 1969, 7, 403–407.

Bloom, M. (1975). *The Paradox of Helping. Introduction to the Philosophy of Scientific Practice*. New York: John Wiley.

————— and Fischer, J. (1982). *Evaluating Practice: Guidelines for the Accountable Professional*. Englewood Cliffs, N.J.: Prentice Hall.

—————, Fischer, J., and Orme, J. (1994). *Evaluating Practice: Guidelines for the Accountable Professional*, 2nd Edition. Englewood Cliffs, N.J.: Prentice Hall.

Blumenthal, M. and Dielman, T. (1975). Depression symptomatology and role function in a general population, *Archives of General Psychiatry*, 32, 985–991.

Brodsky, S. L. and Smitherman, H. O. (1983). *Handbook of Sclaes for Research in Crime and Delinquency.* New York: Plenum.

Buros, O. K. (ed.) (1978). *The Eighth Mental Measurements Yearbook,* Vols. I and II. Highland Park, N.J.: Gryphon Press.

Cattell, R. B. (1966). The scree test for the number of factors, *Multivariate Behavioral Research,* 1, 245–276.

Cautela, J. R. (1977). *Behavior Analysis Forms for Clinical Intervention.* Champaign, Ill.: Research Press.

———— (1981). *Behavior Analysis Forms for Clinical Intervention,* Vol. 2. Champaign, Ill.: Research Press.

Chang-Way, L. and Reeve, J. (1989). *Manual for the Activity-Feeling Scale II.* (Submitted for publication.)

Chun, K.-T., Cobb, S., and French, J. R., Jr. (1975). *Measures for Psychological Assessment: A Guide to 3,000 Original Sources and Their Application.* Ann Arbor, Mich.: Institute for Social Research.

Ciarlo, J. A., et al. (1986). *Assessing Mental Health Treatment Outcome Measurement Techniques.* Rockville, Md.: National Institutes of Mental Health (DHHS Publication No. (ADM) 86-1301).

Ciminero, A. R., Calhoun, K. S., and Adams, H. E. (eds.). (1977). *Handbook of Behavioral Assessment.* New York: John Wiley.

Colby, K. M. (1980). Computer Psychotherapists. In J. B. Sidowski, J. H. Johnson, and T. A. Williams (eds.), *Technology in Mental Health Care Delivery Systems,* pp. 109–117. Norwood, N.J.: Ablex.

Comrey, A. L., et al. (1973). *A Sourcebook for Mental Health Measures.* Los Angeles: Human Interaction Research Institute.

————, Barker, T., and Glaser, E. (1975). *A Sourcebook for Mental Health Measure.* Los Angeles: Human Interaction Research Institute.

———— (1978). Common methodological problems in factor analytic studies, *Journal of Consulting and Clinical Psychology,* 46, 648–659.

Cone, J. D. and Hawkins, R. P. (eds.) (1977). *Behavioral Assessment: New Directions in Clinical Psychology.* New York: Brunner/Mazel.

Conoley, J. C. and Kramer, J. J. (1989). *The Tenth Mental Measurements Yearbook.* Lincoln, Neb.: Buros Institute of Mental Measurement.

Conway, J. B. (1977). Behavioral self-control of smoking through aversion conditioning and self-management, *Journal of Consulting and Clinical Psychology,* 45, 348–357.

Corcoran, K. J. (1988). Selecting a measuring instrument. In R. M. Grinnell, Jr., *Social Work Research and Evaluation*, 3rd edition. Itasca, Ill.: F. E. Peacock.

——— (ed.) (1992). *Structuring Change: Effective Practice for Common Client Problems*. Chicago: Lyceum Books.

Cronbach, L. J. (1970). *Essentials of Psychological Testing*, 3rd edition. New York: Macmillan.

Epstein, L. H. (1976). Psychophysiological measurement in assessment. In M. Hersen and A. S. Bellack (eds.), *Behavioral Assessment: A Practical Handbook*, pp. 207–232. New York: Pergamon.

Erdman, H. P., Klein, M. H., and Greist, J. H. (1985). Direct patient computer interviewing, *Journal of Consulting and Clinical Psychology*, 53(6), 760–773.

Fenigstein, A., Scheier, M. F., and Buss, A. H. (1975). Public and private self-consciousness: Assessment and theory, *Journal of Consulting and Clinical Psychology*, 43, 522–527.

Fischer, J. (1981). The Social Work Revolution, *Social Work*, 26, 199–207.

——— (1994). Empirically based practice: The end of ideology? *Journal of Social Service Research*, 17.

——— and Gochros, H. (1975). *Planned Behavior Change: Behavior Modification in Social Work*. New York: The Free Press.

Fowler, D. (1985). Landmarks in Computer-Assisted Psychological Assessment, *Journal of Consulting and Clinical Psychology*, 53(6), 748–759.

Fredman, N. and Sherman, R. (1987). *Handbook of Measurement for Marriage and Family Therapy*. New York: Brunner/Mazel.

Gambrill, E. (1983). *Casework: A Competency-Based Approach*. Englewood Cliffs, N.J.: Prentice Hall.

Gerson, M. J. (1984). Splitting: The development of a measure, *Journal of Clinical Psychology*, 40, 157–162.

Golden, C. J., Sawicki, R. F., and Franzen, M. D. (1984). Test construction. In G. Goldstein and M. Hersen (eds.), *Handbook of Psychological Assessment*, pp. 19–37. New York: Pergamon.

Goldman, B. A. and Busch, J. C. (1978). *Directory of Unpublished Experimental Mental Measures*, Vol. II. New York: Human Sciences Press.

——— (1982). *Directory of Unpublished Experimental Mental Measures*, Vol. III. New York: Human Sciences Press.

———— and Sanders, J. L. (1974). *Directory of Unpublished Experimental Mental Measures*, Vol. I. New York: Behavioral Publications.

Goldman, J., Stein, C. L., and Guerry, S. (1983). *Psychological Methods of Clinical Assessment*. New York: Pergamon.

Goldstein, G. and Hersen M. (eds.) (1990). *Handbook of Psychological Assessment*. 2nd edition. New York: Pergamon.

Gottman, J. M. and Leiblum, S. R. (1974). *How to Do Psychotherapy and How to Evaluate It*. New York: Holt.

Grotevant, H. D. and Carlson, C. I. (eds.) (1989). *Family Assessment: A Guide to Methods and Measures*. New York: Guilford.

Hammill, D. H. D., Brown, L., and Bryant, B. R. (1989). *A Consumer's Guide to Tests in Print*. Austin, Tx.: Pro-Ed.

Haynes, S. N. (1978). *Principles of Behavioral Assessment*. New York: Gardner.

———— (1983). Behavioral assessment. In M. Hersen, A. E. Kazdin, and A. S. Bellack (eds.), *The Clinical Psychology Handbook*, pp. 397–425. New York: Pergamon.

———— and Wilson, C. C. (1979). *Behavioral Assessment*. San Francisco: Jossey-Bass.

Hersen, M. and Bellack, A. S. (eds.) (1981). *Behavioral Assessment: A Practical Handbook*. 2nd edition. New York: Pergamon.

———— (1988). *Dictionary of Behavioral Assessment Techniques*. New York: Pergamon.

Holman, A. M. (1983). *Family Assessment: Tools for Understanding and Intervention*. Beverly Hills: Sage.

Hoon, E. F. and Chambless, D. (1987). Sexual Arousability Inventory (SAI) and Sexual Arousability Inventory—Expanded (SAI-E). In C. M. Davis and W. L. Yarber (eds.), *Sexuality-Related Measures: A Compendium*. Syracuse, N.Y.: Graphic Publishing.

Hudson, W. W. (1978). First axioms of treatment, *Social Work*, 23, 65–66.

———— (1981). Development and use of indexes and scales. In R. M. Grinnell (ed.), *Social Work Research and Evaluation*. pp. 130–155. Itasca, Ill.: F. E. Peacock.

———— (1982). *The Clinical Measurement Package: A Field Manual*. Chicago: Dorsey Press.

―――― (1985). *The Clinical Assessment System*. University of Arizona, School of Social Work, Tempe, Arizona 85287 (computer program).

―――― (1992). *WALMYR Assessment Scales Scoring Manual*. Tempe, Ariz.: WALMYR Publishing Co.

Humphrey, L. L. (1982). Children's and teachers' perceptions on children's self-control: The development of two rating scales. *Journal of Consulting and Clinical Psychology*, 50, 624–633.

Jacob, T. and Tennenbaum, D. L. (1988). *Family Assessment: Rationale, Methods, and Future Directions*. New York: Plenum.

Jayaratne, S. and Levy, R. L. (1979). *Empirical Clinical Practice*. New York: Columbia University Press.

Johnson, O. G. (1976). *Tests and Measurements in Child Development* (Vols. 1 and 2). San Francisco: Jossey-Bass.

Johnson, O. G. and Bommarito, J. W. (1971). *Tests and Measurements in Child Development: A Handbook*. San Francisco: Jossey-Bass.

Johnson, S. M. and Bolstad, O. D. (1973). Methodological issues in natural observation: Some problems and solutions for field research. In L. A. Hammerlynck, L. C. Handy, and E. J. Mash (eds.), *Behavior Change: Methodology, Concepts, and Practice*. Champaign, Ill.: Research Press.

Kallman, W. M. and Feuerstein, M. (1986). Psychophysiological Procedures. In A. R. Ciminero, C. S. Calhoun, and H. E. Adams (eds.), *Handbook of Behavioral Assessment*, 2nd edition, Chapter 10. New York: John Wiley.

Kazdin, A. F. (1979). Situational specificity: The two-edged sword of behavioral assessment, *Behavioral Assessment*, 1, 57–76.

―――― (1980). *Research Design in Clinical Psychology*. New York: Harper and Row.

―――― (1982). Observer effects: Reactivity of direct observation. In D. P. Hartman (ed.), *Using Observers to Study Behavior: New Directions for Methodology of Social and Behavioral Science*, pp. 5–19. San Francisco: Jossey-Bass.

―――― (1982). *Single-Case Research Designs: Methods for Clinical and Applied Settings*. New York: Oxford University Press.

Kendall, P. C. and Hollon, S. D. (eds.) (1981). *Assessment Strategies for Cognitive-Behavioral Interventions*. New York: Academic Press.

Kestenbaum, C. J. and Williams, D. T. (eds.) (1988). *Handbook of Clinical Assessment of Children and Adolescents.* Austin, Tx.: Pro-Ed.

Kratochwill, T. R. (ed.) (1978). *Single-Subject Research: Strategies for Evaluating Change.* New York: Academic Press.

Lake, D. G., Miles, M. B., and Earle, R. B., Jr. (1973). *Measuring Human Behavior: Tools for the Assessment of Social Functioning.* New York: Teachers College Press.

Lambert, M. J., Christensen, E. R., and DeJulio, S. S. (eds.) (1983). *The Assessment of Psychotherapy Outcome.* New York: Wiley and Sons.

Lang, P. J. (1977). Physiological assessment of anxiety and fear. In D. D. Cone and R. P. Hawkins (eds.), *Behavioral Assessment: New Directions in Clinical Psychology*, pp. 178–195. New York: Brunner/ Mazel.

Lauffer, A. (1982). *Assessment Tools for Practitioners, Managers, and Trainers.* Beverly Hills, Calif.: Sage Publications.

Levitt, J. L. and Reid, W. J. (1981). Rapid-assessment instruments for practice, *Social Work Research and Abstracts*, 17, 13–19.

Levy, L. H. (1983). Trait approaches. In M. Hersen, A. E. Kazdin, and A. S. Bellack (eds.), *The Clinical Psychology Handbook*, pp. 123–142. New York: Pergamon.

Linehan, Marsha M. (1985). The reasons for living scale. In P. A. Keller and L. G. Ritt (eds.), *Innovations in Clinical Practice: A Source Book* (vol. 4). Sarasota, Fla.: Professional Resource Exchange.

Mash, L. and Terdal, L. (eds.) (1988). *Behavioral Assessment of Childhood Disorders.* 2nd edition. New York: Guilford.

Mathews, A. M., Gelder, M. G., and Johnston, D. W. (1981). *Agoraphobia: Nature and Treatment.* New York: Guilford.

McCormick, I. A. (1984). A simple version of the Rathus Assertiveness Schedule, *Behavior Assessment*, 7, 95–99.

McCubbin, H. I. and Thompson, A. I. (eds.) (1991). *Family Assessment: Inventories for Research and Practice.* Madison: University of Wisconsin.

McDonald, A. P. and Games, R. G. (1972). Ellis's irrational values, *Rational Living*, 7, 25–28.

McDowell, I. and Newell, C. (1987). *Measuring Health: A Guide to Rating Scales and Questionnaires.* New York: Oxford University Press.

McReynolds, P. (1981) (ed.). *Advances in Psychological Assessment*, Vol. V, San Francisco: Jossey-Bass.

Merluzzi, T. V., Glass, C. R., and Genest, M. (eds.) (1981). *Cognitive Assessment*. New York: Guilford.

Miller, D. C. (1977). *Handbook of Research Design and Social Measurement*, 3rd edition. New York: Longman.

Minuchin, S. (1974). *Families and Family Therapy*. Cambridge, Mass.: Harvard University Press.

Mischel, W. (1968). *Personality and Assessment*. New York: John Wiley.

———— (1981). *Introduction to Personality*. New York: Holt.

Mitchell, J. V. (ed.) (1985). The Ninth Mental Measurement Yearbook. Lincoln, Neb.: University of Nebraska Press.

Moos, R. H. (1974). *Evaluating Treatment Environments: A Social Ecological Approach*. New York: John Wiley.

———— (1975a). Assessment and impact of social climate. In P. McReynolds (ed.), *Advances in Psychological Assessment*, Vol. 3. San Francisco: Jossey-Bass.

———— (1975b). *Evaluating Correctional and Community Settings*. New York: John Wiley.

———— (1979). *Evaluating Educational Environments*. San Francisco: Jossey-Bass.

Mosher, D. L. and Sirkin, M. (1984). Measuring a macho personality constellation, *Journal of Research in Personality*, 18, 150–163.

Nay, W. R. (1979). *Multimethod Clinical Assessment*. New York: Gardner.

Nelsen, J. C. (1985). Verifying the independent variable in single-subject research, *Social Work Research and Abstracts*, 21, 3–8.

Nelson, R. O. (1981). Realistic dependent measures for clinical use, *Journal of Consulting and Clinical Psychology*, 49, 168–182.

———— and Barlow, D. H. (1981). Behavioral assessment: Basic strategies and initial procedures. In D. H. Barlow (ed.), *Behavioral Assessment of Adult Disorders*, pp. 13–43. New York: Guilford.

Nunnally, J. C. (1978). *Psychometric Theory*, 2nd edition. New York: McGraw-Hill.

Nurius, P. S. and Hudson, W. W. (1993). *Human Sources: Practice, Evaluation, and Computers*. Pacific Grove, Calif.: Brooks/Cole.

Ollendick, T. H. and Hersen, M. (1992). *Handbook of Child and Adolescent Assessment*. Des Moines, Iowa: Allyn & Bacon.

Phares, E. J. and Erskine, N. (1984). The measurement of selfism, *Educational and Psychological Measurement*, 44, 597–608.

Rathus, S. A. (1973). A 30-item schedule for assessing assertive behavior, *Behavior Therapy* 4, 398–406.

Ray, W. J. and Raczynski, J. M. (1981). Psychophysiological assessment. In M. Hersen and A. S. Bellack (eds.), *Behavioral Assessment: A Practical Handbook*, 2nd edition. New York: Pergamon.

Reckase, M. D. (1984). Scaling techniques. In G. Goldstein and M. Hersen (eds.), *Handbook of Psychological Assessment*, pp. 38–53. New York: Pergamon.

Reeve, J. and Robinson, D. T. (1987). Toward a reconceptualization of intrinsic motivation: Correlates and factor structure of the Activity-Feeling Scale, *Journal of Social Behavior and Personality*, 2, 23–36.

Rehm, L. P. (1981). Assessment of depression. In M. Hersen and A. S. Bellack (eds.), *Behavioral Assessment: A Practical Handbook*, pp. 246–295. New York: Pergamon.

Reynolds, C. R. and Kamphaus, R. W. (eds.) (1990). *Handbook of Psychological and Educational Assessment of Children*. New York: Guilford.

Richardson, F. C. and Suinn, R. M. (1972). The Mathematics Anxiety Rating Scale: Psychometric data, *Journal of Counseling Psychology*, 19, 551–554.

Roberts, R. E. and Attkisson, C. C. (1984). Assessing client satisfaction among Hispanics, *Evaluation and Program Planning*, 6, 401–413.

Robinson, J. P. and Shaver, P. R. (1973). *Measures of Social Psychological Attitudes*, revised edition. Ann Arbor, Mich.: Institute for Social Research.

Rugh, J. D., Gable R. S., and Lemke, R. R. (1986). Instrumentation for behavioral assessment. In A. R. Ciminero, K. S. Calhoun, and H. E. Adams (eds.), *Handbook of Behavioral Assessment*, 2nd edition, Chapter 4. New York: John Wiley.

Rutter, M., Tuma, A. H., and Lann, I. S. (eds.) (1988). *Assessment and Diagnosis in Child Psychology*. New York, Guilford.

Scholl, G. and Schnur, R. (1976). *Measures of Psychological, Vocational and Educational Functioning in the Blind and Visually Handicapped*. New York: American Foundation for the Blind.

Schwartz, A. and Goldiamond, I. (1975). *Social Casework: A Behavioral Approach*. New York: Columbia University Press.

Shelton, J. L. and Levy, R. L. (1981). *Behavioral Assignments and Treatment Compliance: A Handbook of Clinical Strategies*. Champaign, Research Press.

Shorkey, C. T. and Whiteman, V. (1977). Development of the Rational Behavior Inventory: Initial validity and reliability, *Educational and Psychological Measurement*, 37, 527–534.

Slack, W. V., Hicks, G. P., Reed, C. Z., and Van Cura, L. J. (1966). A computer-based medical history system, *New England Journal of Medicine*, 274, 194–198.

Smith, M. C. and Thelen, M. N. (1984) Development and validation of a test for bulimia, *Journal of Consulting and Clinical Psychology*, 52, 863–872.

Southworth, L. E., Burr, R. L., and Cox, A. E. (1981). *Screening and Evaluating the Young Infant: A Handbook of Instruments to Use from Infancy to Six Years*. Springfield, Ill.: C. C. Thomas.

Spielberger, C. D., Jacobs, G., Russel, S., and Crane, R. S. (1983). Assessment of anger: The state-trait anger scale. In J. N. Butcher and C. D. Spielberger (eds.), *Advances in Personality Assessment*, Vol. 2, pp. 159–187. Hillsdale, N.J.: Lawrence Erlbaum Associates.

Stiles, W. B. (1980). Measurement of the impact of psychotherapy sessions, *Journal of Consulting and Clinical Psychology* 48, 176–185.

Sundberg, N. D. (1977). *Assessment of Persons*. Englewood Cliffs, N.J.: Prentice Hall.

Sweetland, R. C. and Keyser, D. J. (1991). *Tests: A Comprehensive Reference*. 3rd edition. Austin, Tx.: Pro-Ed.

Tan, A. L., Kendis, R. J., Fine, J. T., and Porac, J. (1977). A short measure of Eriksonian ego identity, *Journal of Personality Assessment*, 41, 279–284.

Thomas, E. J. (1978). Research and service in single-case experimentation: Conflicts and choices, *Social Work Research and Abstracts*, 14, 20–31.

Thompson, C. (ed.) (1989). *The Instruments of Psychiatric Research*. New York: John Wiley.

Thyer, B., Papsdorf, J., Himle, D., and Bray, H. (1981). Normative data on the Rational Behavior Inventory: A further study, *Educational and Psychological Measurement*, 41, 757–760.

Toseland, R. W. and Reid, W. J. (1985). Using rapid assessment instruments in a family service agency, *Social Casework*, 66, 547–555.

Touliatos, J., Perlmutter, B. F., and Straus, M. A. (eds.) (1990). *Handbook of Family Measurement Techniques*. Newbury Park, Calif.: Sage.

van Riezen, H. and Segal, M. (1988). *Comparative Evaluation of Rating Scales for Clinical Psychopharmacology*. New York: Elsevier.

Videcka-Sherman, L. and Reid, W. J. (eds.) (1990). *Advances in Clinical Social Work Research*. Silver Spring, Md.: National Association of Social Workers.

Waskow, I. E. and Parloff, M. B. (eds.) (1975). *Psychotherapy Change Measures*. Rockville, Md.: National Institute of Mental Health.

Webb, E. J., Campbell, D. T., Schwartz, R. D., and Sechrest, L. (1966). *Unobtrusive Measures: Nonreactive Research in the Social Sciences*. Chicago: Rand McNally.

——— Campbell, D. T., Schwartz, R. D., Sechrest, L., and Grove, J. B. (1981). *Nonreactive Measures in the Social Sciences*. 2nd edition. Boston: Houghton Mifflin.

Wetzler, S. (ed.) (1989). *Measuring Mental Illness: Psychometric Assessment for Clinicians*. Washington, D.C.: American Psychiatric Association.

Wicker, A. W. (1981). Nature and assessment of behavior settings: Recent contributions from the ecological perspective. In P. McReynolds (ed.), *Advances in Psychological Assessment*, Vol. V, pp. 22–61. San Francisco: Jossey-Bass.

Wincze, J. P. and Lange, J. D. (1982). Assessment of sexual behavior. In D. H. Barlow (ed.), *Behavioral Assessment of Adult Disorder*, pp. 301–328. New York: Guilford.

Wittenborn, J. R. (1984). Psychological assessment in treatment. In G. Goldstein and M. Hersen (eds.), *Handbook of Psychological Assessment*, pp. 405-420. Elmsford, N.Y.: Pergamon Press.

Woody, R. H. (ed.) (1980). *Encyclopedia of Clinical Assessment*, Vols. I and II. San Francisco: Jossey-Bass.

Zung, W. K. (1965). A self-rating depression scale. *Archives of General Psychiatry*, 12, 63–70.

——— (1974). *The Measurement of Depression*. Milwaukee: Lakeside Laboratories.